Practical Kindergarten

An Essential Guide to Creative Hands-on Teaching

by

Renée Berg

and

Karen Petersen Wirth

CAMBRIA
PRESS

Youngstown, New York

No part of this publication may be reproduced, stored in or introduced into
a retrieval system, or transmitted, in any form, or by any means (electronic,
mechanical, photocopying, recording, or otherwise), without the prior
permission of the publisher. Requests for permission should be directed to
permissions@cambriapress.com, or mailed to Permissions, Cambria Press,
PO Box 350, Youngstown, New York 14174-0350.

This book has been registered with the Library of Congress.

Berg, Renée, 1951-
  Practical kindergarten : an essential guide to creative hands-on teaching / by Renée
Berg and Karen Petersen Wirth.
     p. cm.
  Includes bibliographical references.
  ISBN 978-1-934043-39-4
  1. Kindergarten--Activity programs. 2. Kindergarten--Curricula. I. Wirth, Karen
Petersen. II. Title.

  LB1180.B45 2007
  372.21'8--dc22

                    2007002048

Practical Kindergarten

An Essential Guide to Creative Hands-on Teaching

The authors would like to dedicate their work to
Ellen Rubin and Maria Nini Villasenor
for their excellence in the field of education.

May we all walk in their footsteps.

Table of Contents

Preface . . . . **xv**

Part One: Planning Activities **1**

Chapter One: Introduction to Practical Kindergarten 1
  Overview 1
  Targeted Areas of Learning 4
  Preparation 5
  Lowering the Ratio 7
  Encouraging Classroom Volunteers 8

Chapter Two: Practical Pedagogy 11

Chapter Three: Targeted Areas of Learning 21
  What is a Targeted Area of Learning 21
  Regarding the Learning Environment 23
  General Areas of Learning 24

Chapter Four: Evaluation Rubrics 33

Chapter Five: Descriptions of Learning Diversity 37
  Attention Deficit Disorder 40
  Developmental Delays 41
  Autism and Autism Spectrum Disorders 42
  Visual Impairments 43
  Orthopedic Impairments 43
  Gifted and Talented Education (GATE) 44
  English Language Learners (ELL) 45

Chapter Six: Accommodations for Learning Diversity, Including: General,
      Fine Motor and Gross Motor Accommodations 47
  Attention Deficit Disorder 48
  Developmental Delays 50
  Autism and Autism Spectrum Disorders 53

Visual Impairments 56
Orthopedic Impairments 59
Gifted and Talented Education (GATE). 61
English Language Learners (ELL). 63

Chapter Seven: The Learning Plan. 65
Section One: Creating the Learning Plan. 65
Section Two: Customizing the Learning Plans 73
Sample Learning Plan 77

Chapter Eight: Using Personal Laminators in Classroom 81

Part Two: Activities and Learning Plans 83
Chapter Nine: Language Activities and Learning Plans 83
Writing on Filled Zip-Type Freezer Bags 84
   Activity 84
   Learning Plan 89
Journaling. 92
   Activity 92
   Learning Plan 100
Journal Making 103
   Activity 103
   Laminated Journal Cover Plan. 113
   Tag Board Journal Cover Plan 117
Laminated Letters for Magnetic Play 121
   Activity 121
   Learning Plan 126
Name Tags 129
   Activity 129
   Learning Plan 134
Oil Pan Magnet Center. 137
   Activity 137
   Learning Plan 143
Rainbow Writing 146
   Activity 146
   Learning Plan 151
Story Blocks. 154
   Activity 154
   Learning Plan 160
Word Hunt 163
   Activity 163
   Learning Plan 168

Chapter 10: Math Activities and Learning Plans 171

Candy Math 172
    Activity 172
    Learning Plan 177
Construction Manipulatives 180
    Activity 180
    Learning Plan 187
Graphing 190
    Activity 190
    Learning Plan 198
Patterning 201
    Activity 201
    Learning Plan 208
Sound and Movement Patterns 211
    Activity 211
    Learning Plan 218
Quilting 221
    Activity 221
    Learning Plan 229
Salt "Sand" Art 232
    Activity 232
    Learning Plan 238
Sorting 241
    Activity 241
    Learning Plan 248
Treasure Hunt 251
    Activity 251
    Learning Plan 256

Chapter 11: Science Activities and Learning Plans 259

Animals in the Classroom 260
    1. Naming the Classroom Pet 262
        Activity 262
        Learning Plan 269
    2. Fish 272
        Activity 272
        Learning Plan 280
    3. Hermit Crabs 283
        Activity 283
        Learning Plan 291
Pine Cone Bird Feeders 294
    Activity 294
    Learning Plan 301

Composting 304
    Activity 304
    Learning Plan 312
Germinating (including: Seeds in Plastic Zip-type Bags, Rooting Cuttings
    in Clear Containers, Forcing Bulbs) 315
    Activity 315
    Learning Plan 322
Ocean in a Bottle 326
    Activity 326
    Learning Plan 333
Water Drops on Pennies 336
    Activity 336
    Learning Plan 343
Water Table Measuring 346
    Activity 346
    Learning Plan 354
Oobleck 357
    Activity 357
    Learning Plan 365
Smelly Jelly 368
    Activity 368
    Learning Plan 375

Chapter 12: History and Social Studies Activities and Learning Plans 379
Bread Tasting 380
    Activity 380
    Learning Plan 387
Family Magnets 390
    Activity 390
    Learning Plan 397
Spoon Puppets 400
    Activity 400
    Learning Plan 407
Puppet Theater 410
    Activity 410
    Learning Plan 419
Making Paper Beads 423
    Activity 423
    Learning Plan 431
Doll Making 435
    Activity 435
    Learning Plan 444

Basic Braiding 448
   Activity 448
   Learning Plan 454
Learning Non-English Words and Phrases 457
   Activity 457
   Learning Plan 470
Multicultural Dances 473
   Activity 473
   Learning Plan 480

Chapter 13: Cooking Activities and Learning Plans 483
Basic Cooking Introduction 484
Ice Cream in Zip-Type Bags 486
   Activity 486
   Learning Plan 491
Ants on a Log 494
   Activity 494
   Learning Plan 500
Smoothies 503
   Activity 503
   Learning Plan 510
Making Tortillas 513
   Activity 513
   Learning Plan 520
Flavored Popcorn 523
   Activity 523
   Learning Plan 531
Cookies In A Jar 534
   Activity 534
   Learning Plan 544
   Jar Recipe Tags 548
Veggie Dips 549
   Activity 549
   Learning Plan 558
Classroom Cookbook 562
   Activity 562
   Learning Plan 570

Glossary **573**

References **589**

Appendices and Learning Plans
(see www.cambriapress.com/kindergarten)

Appendix A

A-1 Reproducible Learning Plan Forms
Blank Learning Plan Form
Learning Plans for Language Activities
Learning Plans for Math Activities
Learning Plans for Science Activities
Learning Plans for History and Social Science Activities
Learning Plans for Cooking Activities

A-2 Reproducible Letter-sized Primary Picture/Writing Paper
Picture/Writing Paper - Landscape orientation
Picture/Writing Paper - Portrait orientation

A-3 Adaptive Materials for Children with Learning Diversity
(Available through Discount School Supply)

Online Resources for Large Squared Graph Paper

Appendix B

B-1 Children's Books (Listed by Author)
B-2 Children's Books (Listed by Subject)
B-3 Children's Books (Spanish, and English / Spanish Language Editions)

Appendix C

Cross References - California State Content Standards to Activities
C-1 English Language Arts Content Standards to Activities
C-2 Mathematics Content Standards to Activities
C-3 Science Content Standards to Activities
C-4 History and Social Science Content Standards to Activities
C-5 Visual Arts Content Standards to Activities
C-6 Theatre Content Standards to Activities
C-7 Dance Content Standards to Activities
C-8 Music Content Standards to Activities
C-9 California Department of Education
Kindergarten Content Standards Web Site Information

List of Illustrations

All photographs, unless otherwise noted, attributed to Luther J. Berg

Illustration 1: Children can develop letter recognition by tracing through zipper bags filled with gel.

Illustration 2: A child's emergent skill in writing is more meaningful to the child when writing about his/her own experiences

Illustration 3: A variety of materials may be used when making journals with the duct tape binding method

Illustration 4: Children can decorate their journals

Illustration 5: Journal covers may be laminated. For a more finished product, teachers may have all of the pages of the journal laminated.

Illustration 6: Envelope books are a unique type of journal

Illustration 7: Children can use zipper bag books to collect a wide variety of small items.

Illustration 8: Children can laminate any dry, flat item and make it into a magnet.

Illustration 9: Oil pan trays and cookie sheets can be used as magnetic centers in many curricular areas.

Illustration 10: Children learn letter and number symbols in the process of rainbow writing.

Illustration 11: Salt can be colored with sidewalk chalk, and can be substituted for sand in this patterning activity

Illustration 12: Young children can sort large buttons by quantity or physical attributes

Illustration 13: Ocean in a bottle

Illustration 14: Children often enjoy the inexpensive and easy activity of counting drops of water on a penny.

Illustration 15: Children can start out with white Oobleck and add color to add a broader dimension to the experience

Illustration 16: Oobleck is fun and, oh, so very messy

Illustration 17: Children have the opportunity to use creative problem solving skills when making plastic flatware puppets.

Illustration 18: Wrapping paper around macaroni simplifies making paper beads.

Illustration 19: Yarn dolls can be an interesting introduction to multicultural curriculum

Illustration 20: Making cookies in a jar teaches children measuring and patterning.

Preface

Practical Kindergarten is intended to transform the conversation of education from the domination of test scores (outcomes) to embracing the idea that meaningful learning occurs in the context of a potentially pleasurable process.

While working with pre-service and new elementary teachers and preschool teachers, we see that education is taking a terrible turn toward academic outcome-oriented seatwork. Educators are crying out for more developmentally appropriate, hands on process-based activities, while simultaneously crying about the need to meet mandated academic standards.

This trend for continual assessment, and assessment of assessments brings to mind the individual who has "gone on a diet" and weighs himself at six a.m., ten a.m., 2 p.m., and ten at night. Like weight management, learning is an ongoing process. Both take time. Just as time is required to measure an authentic shift in weight, time is also needed to process information and generate a working body of knowledge.

Another issue with outcome-based learning is that there is only one "right" answer. Mistakes are fatal in that paradigm. Great learning occurs in the context of making mistakes. If learners fear to make a mistake, they will learn to fear taking initiative. Within greatness lies a solid foundation of willingness to take risks. Assessment, particularly over-assessment, kills initiative.

When teachers fear trying interesting activities with children because the children may not, at the end, be able to parrot out a "right" answer, we also take the risk out of the teachers. Our culture is closing the box ever more tightly around teachers, historically a body of people who deeply care about children, learning, and our future. Rather than removing all possibility for teaching as an expression of creativity and individuality, let's empower teachers. Let's tap into this fabulous resource of dedication, commitment, initiative, and creativity. Let teachers do that which they are trained for, teaching!

A wonderful educator, Bev Bos, once said, "If the hands do it, the mind remembers". It seems clear that people learn best by doing, whether it is dance, sewing, learning to use a yardstick, or care for living things. Human beings can develop a working body of knowledge, a body of applicable skill, from working with materials, and from participation in meaningful activities. To make this possible, "someone" needs to associate interactive, fun, interesting learning activities with state standards. The old aphorism says, "When one finger points outward, four point back at you". Hence, ***Practical Kindergarten***.

There is also within ***Practical Kindergarten,*** a concern for the effort of teachers involved not only in gathering materials and preparing for an activity, but for assembling a document that justifies using that activity in a classroom. The writing of learning plans can, in itself, be a monumental task. So the question becomes, if there were a document that included not only preparation and materials, but also targeted learning, assessment, grade level standards met, and suggestions for accommodations for seven areas of special need, would that document be useful for teachers? To think that a teacher could look at an activity and plan the presentation, with the intended learning in mind, is a very attractive idea.

That document should be called a "learning" plan, as the term "lesson" has connotations of not-so-very-much-fun associated with it. Plan for learning, and in that process of working with interesting "stuff", students can, and often will, produce an intended working body of knowledge.

Over the years Renee Berg has developed the learning plan used in *Practical Kindergarten* so that pre-service or new teachers will consider all these possibilities when thinking about an activity for their classes.

Having all the generic information for a wide selection of activities available in reproducible form opens the possibility for teachers to devote more time and energy to working with the children. The specialized information, such as the standards selected, target learning intended, and accommodations for special needs can be entered into the basic learning plan, customizing it for a particular class, and then printed out for administrator perusal. (Go to www.cambriapress.com/kindergarten)

Teachers (as well as people hoping to become teachers) can be variously described as being intelligent, responsible, talented, compassionate, energetic, enthusiastic, idealistic, erudite, dedicated, creative, sharing, caring, and a host of other positive qualities. It rarely is said of teachers that they have too much time and too much money. We choose our vocations based on one of two things: love or money. We do what we do because we passionately love and believe in what we do, or we do it for the money, because we need a job. To be brutally honest, anyone who goes into the teaching profession because they believe it to be an easy and lucrative way to buy a new BMW every year, is seriously out of touch with the economic realities of our world. People suffering from such delusions should not be allowed close contact with the children of the world.

Seriously, we know that teachers are not in this for the money. What we do know is that they want to make a contribution to our society, and to the world of children. Our children are our future. We may remember a time (whether as a sibling, friend or parent) when we first saw the light in a child's eyes when s/he was able to do something for the very first time. There is joy, rapture and sheer delight in the building of a block tower SO high, and watching it as it stays UP. The child squeals with delight and knocks it down, knowing full well that s/he can rebuild it with success, and does so, over and over again. The child realizes that s/he has "got it". And this makes learning fun! Fun! This is the silent "f" that education has lost. We look forward to teaching because it is that joy, that rapture that ensues when the "cup" runs over with success and self-confidence. We want to be a part of that process. And, when the child smiles, we smile. And we laugh. It's contagious. And then, we realize that we want to create more experiences for children that elicit that response. And that's what we feel makes "educa**fun**"!

Practical Kindergarten is intended to spark teacher creativity, to allow the possibility of fun as an important aspect of the process of education. Learning is a profoundly psychological process. When learners feel safe and happy, they learn more. Teachers unconstrained to "teaching to the test" will gain more satisfaction from this essential profession.

Acknowledgements

The authors would like to acknowledge, and thank, the following people, without whom this project may not have become a reality:

Luther Berg, for his meticulous care in shooting photographs, over and over... until we could feel that they "spoke" to us

Élan Berg, for her assistance in research, and for her generosity, when she would drop what she was doing in order to help us out

Gregory Wirth, for his laborious assistance in proofreading and editing

Kristin Wirth, for her invaluable help in proofreading, and for generously choosing to follow her own career in early childhood education

Dr Rie Mitchell, for her support and contagious enthusiasm

Dr Mike Spagna and **The Center For Teaching and Learning**, for their support of our endeavors

Again, **our loving husbands and children**, for giving us the physical and emotional space and support to complete our first book.

And **Marian Pedroarena**, and all parents, who generously instill in their children a life-long love of learning

Chapter One

Introduction To Practical Kindergarten

"Learning is not a race, but a stroll through discovery"...
– Bev Bos
(Good Stuff for Kids workshop, 2005)

Overview

The most effective teaching is well planned. Why? Because, just as a strong bone structure supports a healthy body, a strong structure of planning supports learning. Some may argue that structure can stifle creativity and spontaneity. It can, but if used properly, organization and preparation actually can support and encourage creativity, spontaneity, and learning in the classroom.

When a teacher is clear on the intended learning for the activity, and has all the needed supplies and the area made ready, that teacher has the freedom and leisure to consider possible extensions for that activity. Should the children make suggestions for related activities, known as emergent curriculum extensions, the teacher can reflect upon them in terms of building self-esteem and initiative for the children, time available, relevance to the targeted area of learning and so forth. There is freedom for the teacher in having the ideas in order before presenting an activity to the class.

Some people call the document used for activity planning a "lesson plan." The dictionary can often give insights into simple words and phrases that will empower us when we choose to take the course of action described by those words. Random House's 2000 edition of Webster's Dictionary defines "lesson" as: "n. 1. a section into which a course of study is divided, esp. a single continuous session of instruction … 3. something to be learned or studied;" (page 762). In comparison, the definition of "plan" or "planning" says: "n. 1. a scheme or method of acting or proceeding developed in advance. 2. a design or arrangement 7. a program for specified benefits, 11. to have in mind as an intention;" (page 1011). By the dictionary's definition, lesson planning is a design developed in advance for specified benefits for a single continuous session of instruction. The design developed in advance would be choosing and organizing materials. The specified benefits would be the targeted areas of learning, and the single continuous session of instruction would be the class presentation.

Unfortunately, those are not the sole definitions of the word "lesson". The same volume goes on to elaborate, "6. a reproof or punishment intended to teach one better ways...v.t. 8. to admonish or reprove". Those negative underpinnings somehow insinuate themselves within the concept of "lesson planning". The word "lesson" somehow sends a subliminal message that the process of learning *should not* be pleasurable. Look within. Are not those activities that bring pleasure the very activities we choose to repeat over and over? To paraphrase Steven Tyler from Aerosmith in the film, *Wayne's World*, "If you make learning feel good, the students will stay (in school)."

So, if the intended result is *learning*, why not call the plan a "learning plan"? Random House's Webster's (2000, page 756) defines the word "learn" more positively, encompassed by a general definition of acquiring knowledge through study and/or experience, to become informed or versed in an area of knowledge through experience or instruction. So framing the concept of preparing learning experiences for students as a learning plan draws into it a more positive attitude from the designation of the document to the classroom presentation.

Where would a teacher find activities in the first place? There is a wealth of books, web site information, magazines, and handouts readily available for anyone. The greater challenge is to select activities relevant to the curriculum being presented. The teacher should choose personally satisfying projects that the children will enjoy as well. If the teacher does not like caring for little fuzzy creatures, having rabbits in the class is a bad choice. Find a balance: the teacher should play to personal strengths and interests, as well as to those of the students. To accomplish that, the teacher will need to get to know the students. **Know your students.** Children are not interchangeable parts. Each one of them is unique, and brings something to the character of the class. As a result, every class has a personality of its own. Know **your** students.

It is advisable that all teachers keep activity binders, files, or folders. Binders work very well. The binders are quite portable, and that makes it easy to bring the book to planning meetings. Create a binder for each designated area of learning, such as sorting activities, journaling activities, plant science, animal keeping and so on in clear plastic sleeves. Keep learning plans next to the activities in the teacher folders in plastic sleeves. This allows the teacher to take an activity or learning plan out of the sleeve in the binder to photocopy to share with other teachers.

Consider the interests and academic needs of the children in the class when planning curriculum. If the teacher takes an existing interest of the children and finds activities that will support learning in areas of identified weakness, the group will be more responsive to the activities the teacher chooses to share with them. It is so much more fun and rewarding for a teacher to present projects to the children that the children (and the teacher) actively enjoy.

Be aware of the children's interests and plan the curriculum into them. By doing so, the teacher will create opportunities for teachable moments. A **teachable moment** is a period of time when a child is so fully engaged in an activity that an educator can introduce the next step in a way that the child constructs the new concept by him or herself. Using open-ended questions works well. An open-ended question is a question that has no specific right answer, and guides the child to the learning, but does not merely hand the information to the student. This particular teaching strategy is called **scaffolding** and was articulated by **Lev Vygotsky**, a Russian educational theorist. (Berk & Winsler, 1997)

Look out for spontaneous teachable moments with the students, since these are the best opportunities to maximize academic growth and assimilation. During a teachable moment the child is constructing his or her own learning, and will retain it as his or her own. Make the selection of activities fun. In the author's opinion, people are often most relaxed and uninhibited when they are having fun, and children explore most freely when the activities are fun. Therefore in that context, there may be more engagement and more opportunities for those invaluable teachable moments.

The field of education is, at its best, collaborative. Reinventing education for an individual teacher can be overwhelming and exhausting. Newer teachers can benefit from the experience of seasoned teachers. More experienced teachers gain value from the energy and enthusiasm of teachers new to the field. Network. Work together. Find great resources. Be inspired and share that which inspires with fellow educators. Together, as Bev Bos says, we're better.

There are some people, some companies, and some organizations that stand for creating a positive future for the field of education. Educators work best when they collaborate, share ideas, and are a part of a cooperative network functioning with the intention to offer the most positive learning environments and experiences possible. Teachers, and other people working in learning environments need to constantly be seeking, need to be on an on-going quest for ways to improve learning experiences for all. Five such entities include Bev Bos (turnthepage.com), Dr. Mel Levine (allkindsofminds.org, schoolsattuned.org), Richard Lavoie (ricklavoie.com), Resource and Referral services, located all across the United States and British Columbia, (naccrra.org) and Discount School Supply Company (discountschoolsupply.com).

Bev Bos is an extraordinary educator, author, and lecturer whose home base and preschool is in the Sacramento area of northern California. She has written numerous books including Before the Basics and Together We're Better. There is an inspiring video of her speaking engagement entitled, "Starting At Square One". The ideas Ms. Bos shares regarding working with young children can easily be extrapolated and applied to working with learners of all ages from preschool through university. To find out more about Bev Bos, check out her website at www.turnthepage.com.

Dr. Mel Levine is a pediatrician, author, college professor, and researcher. He has long studied and identified learning styles, strengths, and weaknesses and come up with strategies for working with students with diverse learning styles. Among his many books are A Mind at a Time and Ready or Not Here Life Comes. He is a major designer of the widespread training called "**Schools Attuned**", which prepares teachers to identify a learner's particular strengths and weaknesses, and work with students using a strategy called "teaching by profile". **Teaching by profile** involves looking at a student through the lens of the eight neurodevelopmental constructs, which are broken down into sub strengths within each category. Using this information can assist an educator in designing meaningful learning for a particular individual or group using these tools. Although Dr. Levine's work focuses on children with learning differences, one can see that every student learns uniquely, and that many of these strategies are, in truth, excellent teaching. Information about Mel Levine's work can be found at either www. allkindsofminds.org or www.schoolsattuned.org.

Richard Lavoie became well-known in the learning community when his PBS video, *How Difficult Can This Be? F.A.T. City (Frustration, Anxiety, and Tension)* video was released by PBS in 1989. In this video, Mr. Lavoie leads a group of parents, teachers, and siblings through an excellent simulation of the experience of having a learning disability. Mr. Lavoie continues to speak and produce videos about children with learning disabilities through PBS, including: *Beyond F.A.T. City: A Look Behind, A Look Ahead (2005)* and *Richard Lavoie: Learning Disabilities and Discipline: When the Chips Are Down (2005)*. Although Mr. Lavoie speaks about "our children", meaning children who have specific learning disabilities, his words describe all of us, and all of our children in learning situations and in life. Richard Lavoie's videos are available at www.pbs.org. His website is www.ricklavoie.com.

When putting the academic schedule together, plan for sufficient time for in-depth play. Allow children enough time to explore materials. Sometimes it will take children a half an hour or more to settle in on a project. Have several options available (centers). When possible, offer large time blocks (60 to 70 minutes) for children to explore materials. Children do thrive within the confines of a reliable structure, but planning flexibility into the schedule allows freedom for teachable moments to occur. Be mindful that the structure is there to support learning and the children's community. Be vigilant about avoiding reversing the situation; it is tragic when the structure becomes more important than the children and the learning they acquire. Make decisions that will support the maximum possibility for creating learning, fun, and teachable moments.

A happy teacher is a key element in creating an effective learning environment. When children respond positively to activities the teacher has organized, it will help keep the teacher happy. If the class likes trains, or dinosaurs, or sewing crafts, allow the momentum of their interest to work toward goals designated by the teacher. If the teacher is teaching measuring, does it really matter whether the children are measuring the length of a plastic dinosaur, recreating the length of an actual dinosaur on the play ground, or measuring fabric to make a classroom hand print quilt? This brings us to targeted areas of learning.

A key tool for a teacher is a collection of activities intended for possible classroom use. These can be collected by subject area, by season, or organized in any way that works for the teacher. Placing found activities in plastic sheet protectors (often available in bulk at club stores) and saving them in subject designated three ring binders works very well. Where can these activities be found? Using a search engine, such as Google, type in the kind of activity needed. If there is no specific idea already in mind, just type in the subject area. Two reliable websites include enchantedlearning.com and turnthepage. com. These websites are very worthy of a visit from any educator. In addition, many wonderful, classic children's books are available through their website. When looking for multicultural activities, enchantedlearning.com might be the best place to start. For ages 3 to 8, this website offers many downloadable books and web links to activities in many languages such as: Dutch, French, German, Italian, Japanese, Portugese, Spanish and Swedish. Teachers should also peruse magazines and activity books. Most importantly of all, share with other teachers. Education at its very best is collaborative. When teachers share with each other, a sense of community is built at the school. Ultimately and best of all, the children will benefit the most.

Share! Share! Share!

Targeted Areas of Learning

It is the teacher's responsibility to determine areas of learning needing to be strengthened. Those would be the targeted areas of learning. Identifying the intended areas of learning will determine the presentation of an activity. For example, the teacher may have a group of children who need some support in learning laterality, that is, the difference between left and right. There are many ways to increase the children's awareness of left and right just in the classroom and circle time conversations alone. Simply pointing out that Jonah is sitting to the right of Hayley, and then asking who is sitting to the right of each child as a game during group time would be an effortless exercise in laterality. In the group games of Hokey Pokey or Little Red Wagon, a teacher wanting to teach left and right would present left and right pinkie fingers, ears, eye brows, knees and so on. A teacher wanting to teach body parts might choose to include names of parts of the body the children have difficulty remembering, while someone wanting to teach turn taking, patience, sharing and cooperation might break the group into two parts and let the children sequentially present a part.

Think of the wealth of learning that the Hokey Pokey offers. It encompasses learning about laterality (as mentioned above), but there is also the gross motor activity of body movement, as well as vocabulary development (particularly regarding learning all the different parts of the body in English or other languages) and also the socialization skills needed to play the game, such as cooperation, following directions, and possibly taking turns. That wealth is present in process-based learning activities.

Preparation

Before presenting an activity to any group, gather the materials together. As there is limited space available at most teaching facilities, set an area aside for supplies at home, stored in clear plastic tubs. Storing the tubs on baker's shelves works well.

As much as possible use recycled items in class projects. Save toilet paper rolls (Children like to refer to them as "who-whos"), 1/2 pint plastic water bottles, washed old socks, letter and legal size laminator pouches, all kinds of beads, buttons, ribbon, glitter glue, and so forth. Using recycled items for classroom activities sends the children the message of using our resources fully, by doing so in fact.

Local resource and referral services are great for finding licensed childcare placements. Less well known is that these facilities often have toy and book lending libraries that can include use of die cutting machines, laminators, and are excellent resources for borrowing water tables, manipulatives, puppets, books, and so on for up to a month at a time. It is better to borrow a manipulative toy to see if it works with the curriculum and the class to whom the curriculum is being presented before going to the expense of purchasing the item. And for large, infrequently used items, borrowing may be a better overall strategy than purchase. Then there is no issue of storage. Often resource and referral agencies have books about curricular activities as well as books and information on other aspects of child development. Library lending policies vary from site to site. Head Start programs are often affiliated with the centers. They sometimes offer workshops covering all areas of child care and teaching methods for free or at a low cost. There is at least one resource and referral center in each county in California and in most counties across the country. Los Angeles alone has about eleven centers of the nine hundred across the U.S. To check them out personally, go to their website: http://Childcareaware. org., or call 1-800-424-2246.

One of our very favorite resources is Discount School Supply (1-800-627-2829, www.discountschool supply.com). Discount School Supply offers a wealth of creative, low-cost classroom supplies. It is an incredible and extensive resource for arts and crafts as well as for classroom (child sized) furniture, books, desks, curricular materials, and any item an educator with a large imagination can dream of. Generally shipping takes only two days and sometimes there is no shipping charge. All of their materials are safe for children's use. Their specialty is art materials: paints (liquid watercolors are bright and beautiful), glues, and every type of art paper and supplies a teacher might ever wish for. They also offer many kinds of adaptive implements for writing, drawing and art for children with unique learning needs. The people who take orders are friendly and helpful. (See pages 593–594 for a list of adaptive tools and art media for children with unique learning needs available through Discount School Supply).

Other fabulous sources for supplies are yard sales, thrift stores, and rummage sales. Yarn can be found for a couple of dollars for a box instead of a skein. Old buttons, beads, canning jars, Duplo blocks, plastic dinosaurs, you name it, can be found inexpensively. Mention that these items are intended for classroom use. Sometimes the people running the yard sale will give the teacher a break on the price if they know that their castoffs are destined for classroom use. Some will pull out other treasures, if they know children will be using those materials. Try asking parents to donate old buttons, socks, and other materials for the supply closet. Renée's best find was a large old Minolta copier for twenty-five dollars and a ten dollar little red wagon. She constantly uses that invaluable little wagon to carry supplies to her classes. A little wood-sided wagon can be a fabulous way to carry each day's or week's activities to class. Load it up, learning plan in hand. Once that is done, the teacher is then free to consider the project and how it might be evolved or improved.

Make sure any items that are purchased from yard sales and thrift stores, to be used with children, are scrupulously clean.

- All plastic non-electronic toys (tea sets, Duplos, dinos et cetera) can be placed into mesh bags and run through a dishwasher.
- Run canning jars through the dishwasher. Buy new rings and lids.
- Wipe electronic toys down with a 10% solution of bleach water.
- Wash all dress ups and cloth items in the washing machine, and dry on high heat.
- If the clothes or toys are non-washable, place them into plastic bags, store them in the garage with mothballs for at least a month, then air them out for several days before putting them out for the children's use. Yarn and ribbon should be included in this group, as they will become hopelessly tangled when washed.

Some tubs can be pre-assembled to store materials, such as a "sensory activities" tub and the "kaleidoscope-making" tub. Other items can be stored separately, as the component parts can be used in so many different activities. For example, birdseed can be used to make **"Pinecone Bird Feeders"** (see Science Activities), and to fill socks for sock snow people, gnomes, and other creatures. Birdseed is also useful in the water table. Five-pound bags can be purchased at the 99-cent store. Pinecones can be made into winter trees or bird feeders. Store the multi-use items separately from single project tubs.

Once the teacher has found something the class will enjoy, and from which they would get value, the activity should be tested out **beforehand**. There was an intriguing project on television one day that Renée thought would be great for students. It involved cooking toothbrushes, and bending them into a bracelet. Without trying it out at home, she went to the 99-cent store, bought some toothbrushes, and presented the activity to her class of about 50 college-level child development students. The procedure required simmering toothbrushes (with the bristles pulled out) for about twenty minutes, and then bending the brushes into shape with hot mitts and pliers. There were many well-cooked brushes (some simmered for over two hours!), but every time an attempt was made to bend them, they would snap. Fortunately, everyone got a good laugh from the experience. It was a good lesson learned. Try everything before presenting it to any class, no matter what the age-level.

Lowering the Ratio of Children to Adults in the Class

In any activity such as the one described above there are obvious safety considerations. When planning activities for children considering the ratio of teachers to children is critical. Obviously a lower ratio, that is the fewer children per supervising teacher and/or adult, allows for a higher quality of learning, and a greater selection of activities and materials for the children to use in the classroom.

When the ratio is lowered, a far wider variety of curricula will be possible in the classroom. For example, if the ratio is one teacher to fifteen children (shown as 1:15), or even one to eight (1:8), carpentry with wood, nails, saws, and hammers would not be a recommended activity. To effectively present carpentry, the ratio should be quite low, one to three (1:3), at the outside. To achieve low ratios, the teacher would need to be proficient in enrolling parental participation.

Kindergarten parents can be a wealth of supervision and assistance for the appreciative, resourceful teacher. If the teacher was planning to attempt the toothbrush bracelet activity (which is not actually encouraged as a choice) it would be important to be sure that the teacher had enough parental volunteers scheduled for that day. A good ratio would be one adult to three or four children. Let the volunteers know what their intended task is to be. Be sure to consider where the parents should be placed in terms of their abilities and strengths. There would need to be an adult constantly standing by the simmering toothbrushes, making certain the children were well away from them. It would be necessary to have two parents at the kidney-shaped table, with no more than five children working on bending (breaking) the toothbrushes. One adult would be required for every three children pulling the brush part of the toothbrush out with round-ended pliers.

If a volunteer offers to present an activity to the class with which the teacher is unfamiliar, ask to see the directions for the activity before the volunteer presents it to the class. Better still, the teacher should try it beforehand, to be sure that the activity is safe for the class, and to ascertain that it is developmentally appropriate for the children. Ultimately, the teacher is responsible for the safety and well being of the children, and the content of the curriculum presented in the classroom. The teacher doesn't have to be harsh or rude. Simply say something such as, "I'd like to check it out first." While checking the activity, the teacher may also consider possible extensions to the activity within the curriculum.

Many states have put forth curriculum content frameworks from preschool and up. Should the teacher have some general academic content planned for the children, suggest that the parent present the activity so that it coincides with the academic planning. For example, if a parent volunteer wants to work with silk worms late in the fall, and the schedule has a unit on butterflies set during the spring when mulberry leaves are plentiful, tell the parent that activity would be fantastic during the time planned for the butterfly unit.

Never leave children unattended with volunteers

When choosing activities for the class, the teacher needs to know the students, and understand the nature of the activity being offered to the class. Curriculum planning is a matching game. Plan according to the students' attention span, and ability to focus, and follow directions. Activity choices and placement of them within the classroom's daily schedule will be quite different for a particularly high energy group of children with poor impulse control than for a more easy-going group. Visualize for a moment opening the class day with a mellow circle time, including reading a gentle story, with a high energy group coming into the classroom after a breakfast of cocoa puffs and pop tarts. Sounds like fun, doesn't it? If the school is in an area that has a climate that supports outdoor play for the first quarter to half hour of the school day most of the year, the high energy group will be better able to concentrate on curricula requiring internalized behavior management after expending some of the early morning energy outside. In any event, when the teacher offers exciting but potentially dangerous projects, the teacher must to supervise closely, even with the most cooperative group of children.

Encouraging classroom volunteers

The teacher has a great project requiring a low ratio. Now, how can a teacher get volunteers?

- Hand out a flier on the first day of school telling parents their volunteerism and parent participation is welcomed, appreciated, and embraced.
- At the first day of school orientation, emphasize the value of parent volunteers to the curriculum, the children, and the kinds of enriching activities that can be presented to their children when the child to adult ratio is lowered.
- Greet the volunteers warmly. Remember, they *could* be somewhere else. They are *choosing* to be in this classroom. Volunteerism is not obligatory
- Thank the volunteers as they leave. They have given the class their time. This is a great gift.
- Have the children thank the volunteers as well. It is important for children to understand what a valuable contribution the volunteers are making to them. It teaches the children appropriate social courtesy.
- Use the volunteers well. Find out if they have special abilities, talents, and skills (such as cooking, computers, speaking a language other than English) that they would be willing to share with the class. When a volunteer feels they are making a special contribution, they will want to return.
- If the teacher has parents that would like to help out, but are not comfortable working with children, find contributions they can make from home: washing field trip T-shirts and/or sheets that cover rest time cots; preparatory work for class activities (such as cutting out paper shapes, drawing outlines, pre-assembling activity bags), and so on.
- If the teacher has volunteers who have made a weekly (or more frequent) commitment to volunteer in the class, and the teacher can afford it, a small gift could be given at the winter break. If the teacher cannot afford a small gift, at least give the volunteer a nice holiday card, or thank you card.
- If the school or facility publishes a monthly newsletter or web site, acknowledge the volunteers for that month. Be sure to include the classroom volunteers as well as those who volunteer from home, and parents who make donations of all types.
- At the end of the year, some acknowledgement of volunteers will encourage the continued participation of this valuable resource, such as: a school or facility-wide volunteer appreciation event that offers some kind of light meal, a volunteer certificate signed by the head administrator, and/or perhaps a small gift.

- Encourage the students to be part of the volunteer recognition effort. Gifts or acknowledgment from the children at the end of the year, or after a particularly significant contribution (such as making handmade journals for the class or repairing the class computers), are particularly meaningful to parent volunteers. It is essential that the children appreciate and understand that these people are giving the gift of their time.

- Sometimes it is more challenging for a parent to separate from the child, than for the child to leave the parent. The opportunity of volunteering in their child's classroom may ease the ache of separation for both parent and child, and, in fact, teaches the child that his or her parents value learning enough to participate in the process.

Chapter Two
Practical Pedagogy

*"We don't stop playing because we grow old.
We grow old because we stop playing."*
– George Bernard Shaw

At the very best, teaching is an expression of an educator's creativity. As with any artistic expression, teaching requires passion (or love for the work and for children), plenty of practice, ingenuity and inspiration, not to mention the investment of time, effort, and money. Why money? Sadly, most school districts have few resources for basic, much less supplemental, resources. So, yes, many teachers find themselves paying for enrichment materials for their classes, if not some of the basic materials as well.

Most of the ideas contained here below are painfully obvious. And they bear repeating frequently, because within them are contained the spirit and essence of good teaching. To begin:

Decide who you want to be as an educator. There is no fairy godmother that determines your identity as a teacher or parent or partner. It is a decision made intentionally or by default. Make that decision consciously, and it will allow you to give rise to an entire body of behaviors. Steven Covey, author of *The Seven Habits of Highly Effective People: Powerful Lessons in Personal Change* (1990, page 97), says, "Begin with the end in mind." The theorists at Landmark Education say, "Being gives rise to doing." The point is that a person may have a commitment to be a great educator. Although that person's commitment might be less than great from time to time, it will still be coming from an inner intention to become a quality teacher. That person's behaviors will be entirely different than those of an educator whose primary commitment is to make it through the day and get the paycheck.

So who do you *want* to be?

Vocabulary

pedagogy: "the art, science, or profession of teaching", as defined by Merriam-Webster's Collegiate Dictionary (1996, page 856); and as defined by *Practical Kindergarten*: the art, attitudes, and practices for successful teaching

child-centered teaching: an educator taking the time to see which activities interest the students; looking at subject areas of interest to children; taking their lead; giving them some power in the area of their curriculum (emergent curriculum) builds their ability to make decisions, and self-esteem

developmentally appropriate: having activities and expectations designed for the age/ability of the group of children

emergent curriculum: curriculum that is created from teachable moments, student interest, or events that draw student interest which create unexpected opportunities for learning

structured classroom environment: Children are comfortable with simple, clearly defined boundaries and rules, such as: when you arrive hang up your jacket, put your things in your cubby, put the toy you are using away before you take out another. Wash your hands before you eat, and so on.

teachable moment: a moment in which children are so fully engaged in an activity or project that they unselfconsciously want to explore it further

Vygotsky-scaffolding: the process of finding the child's level of learning: teacher review subject content a bit to build a comfortable learning zone, and encourage the child to climb out of the comfort zone a bit, from there recreate comfort zone including the new content, and begin process once more; (Berk, 2005, Berk & Winsler, 1997)

Practical Practices for Teachers

❖ **When teaching, be practical**. It is not only impractical but impossible to produce perfection. Common sense is practical. Use common sense when planning, preparing, presenting, adjusting and cleaning up activities. Use it when managing classroom behavior. Impracticality by definition is impractical. Reflect upon Maslow's hierarchy of human needs. If a teacher's choices fall outside the hierarchy, they are very likely to be impractical.

❖ **Have fun.** If a teacher is not having any fun, it is unlikely that anyone around the teacher is having fun either. People learn best in an environment characterized by good spiritedness, relaxation, a sense of security, and acceptance. If students are experiencing enjoyment in the activities presented, it will feel great. The teacher will have a sense that what s/he is doing is worthy and successful, and that it is worth the effort. The students will too.

❖ **Be there for the kids.** Teachers should, to the best of their abilities, leave personal issues at home. Give the children the best services possible at any moment. In return, children will carry that teacher's memory in their hearts for a lifetime.

❖ **Be the teacher you always wanted to have.** Be the teacher who is patient and generous-hearted. A generous educator's primary investment is in the student's overall success, rather than in the necessity of being "right" or "looking good". Teachers have a choice. They can be honest, fair, accepting and caring. No doubt, especially with young adolescents, there will very challenging students. Remember that the teacher is the adult, with more education and experience than the child. That may make it possible to dredge up the very best self to handle challenges that will occur in the classroom. Being that memorable, honest, fair human being who chooses to make a difference, will teach the students that they also have a say in who they become as well.

❖ **Forgive yourself.** Don't expect that you will do everything perfectly, ever. Expecting perfection becomes a set up for upset and anxiety. An upset, anxious person will be unavailable to the students, and no one will have any fun.

- ❖ **Forgive your students.** People in the learning process sometimes make mistakes. Young people sometimes misbehave. If a child misbehaves regularly, something may be going on at home, the child may have special needs, or the class work may be too hard or too easy for the child.

- ❖ **When behavior is out of control, address the behavior and not the child.** The child is always okay. The behavior may need some intervention. Be sure to articulate that the issue is with the child's behavior. When a teacher treats a misbehaving child respectfully, while clearly managing the behavior, correct human interaction is being modeled, which is essential. Some of the most important teaching may occur in this context. Bev Bos gives excellent suggestions for dealing with children in her article "Conflict Resolution" stating "All of us lose it occasionally." We as adults may find that we often treat children in ways that we would never think of treating another adult. She maintains that we should never threaten children and that discipline should always be "kind, tender and humane." (http://www.turnthepage.com/articles.php?pid=301)

- ❖ **Know your students.** This is essential for any teacher. Every class has its own personality whether it is an infant-toddler room, or a college classroom. Knowing the audience to whom the material is being presented will give an educator an insight into activities, topics, and style of presentation.

- ❖ **Teach the way your students learn.** If the class is a high energy, highly verbal group, it would be wise to choose presentation styles to "fit" the personality of that class. A quieter, more reflective group may require some drawing out. If a student is really not getting the material presented, and it is being presented in an age appropriate manner, consider two possibilities. One, try another teaching strategy, or two, consider that the student may have special needs that require accommodation. Try making changes in the presentation, the environment, or the curriculum to see if those strategies work. Keep a little notebook of behaviors and academic strengths and weaknesses to see if patterns can be identified. Enlist the help of administrative staff. If learning or behavioral patterns can be found, it is then easier to come up with accommodations to provide a learning environment suitable for that child.

- ❖ **When in doubt, accommodate.** Even if a student has not been identified as having special needs, but there are ways to be supportive toward that student's success, then make those changes. A child who is struggling to survive in an academic environment is heartbreaking to see, can possibly become a distraction for other children, may misbehave, and make the environment less enjoyable for all. As a professional educator, it is a courtesy to provide an environment supportive to the learning of everyone.

- ❖ **Set your students up to "win".** People who feel relaxed, safe, and comfortable are more likely to open up to learning new information. Let them know that they can trust you to be consistent, to be fair. Trying to figure out the "rules du jour" will make the students nervous, and they will not trust a teacher who is inconsistent. Trust is at the core of all successful relationships. When students feel they can succeed, they will be willing to attempt more, to take more risks. Present material in incremental, building steps whenever possible. Success builds self-esteem. Remember the compliment from the 1997 Tristar film "As Good As

It Gets"? Jack Nicholson (playing the male lead) says," You make me want to be a better man." To be a better person. Is that not the result we intend for our students? We want them to *want* to be better people.

❖ **Look for teachable moments.** A teachable moment is a moment wherein the child is engaged, relaxed, and comfortable with the activity such that you can ask open-ended questions and leading comments to lead him to the next level of understanding.

❖ **If an activity is not working, stop doing it.** If the story being read is too easy or too complex, a teacher can tell. The children's behavior will begin to break down. The teacher will find that as much time is spent managing behavior, as reading. The teacher is suffering, and the class is suffering. It's not worth it. Do something else.

❖ **Know when to quit.** This is slightly different from the previous problem. At one point, your class was engaged in the activity. Now they are not. It may be time for a break.

❖ **Have back-up activities.** In case an activity does not work or has to be postponed, be prepared. Have back-up activities planned. This enables a smooth transition to another activity or subject. This eliminates the possibility of being caught "empty-handed" at a crucial "last minute", due to inclement weather, schedule changes, and so on.

❖ **Be trustworthy.** If the class knows they can rely on the teacher to be evenhanded and fair, they will trust that teacher. Most children, especially younger children, want to trust their assigned teacher. Make that inclination toward trust to be a foundation for an enriching learning experience for all. Learning involves building a relationship with the class. If students feel they can relax and trust the teacher, that sense of trust then enables taking the quality of the children's learning to entirely higher levels, than if the class feels they need to remain guarded.

❖ **Be consistent.** When students feel they must figure out the "rules du jour" in the classroom, they will take their attention away from learning. Learning is why the children are in the classroom.

❖ **Mistaking is learning.** Often the greatest value in learning occurs when one makes mistakes. Having a safe environment in which to grapple with educational material often will produce more authentic learning than being able to parrot back rote responses correctly. Daring to attempt is more of what education is about than producing a pretty result. Piaget believed that errors are just a natural part of the learning process. (Labinowicz, 1980).

❖ **Play is children's work.** Frederich Froebel, the distinguished German educator, started the very first kindergarten in 1837. Froebel was also responsible for developing one of the very first curricula for young children. He strongly believed that children learn best through purposeful play. He first used the name *kindergarten*, meaning "garden of children". (http://www.froebelweb.org) The Swiss educator Jean Piaget drew from Froebel's work when developing his own theories on the stages of development of the young child. All people learn best in the context of play. Play involves voluntary engagement with a subject or activity. When one plays, one is self-motivated and unselfconscious, and one is feeling good. Allow the *experience* of learning to *feel like play* whenever possible.

❖ **Self-esteem is crucial to the learning process.** Treat children with the same courtesies as would be accorded adults. The teacher's behavior teaches more than any other strategy.

Richard Lavoie (2005) draws the analogy between self-esteem and poker chips, in "When the Chips are Down." Children will not take academic risks if they don't feel good about themselves, and their abilities to produce academic results. A child with a shaky self-esteem, according to Lavoie, "will not have enough chips to get into the game of life". Children attend school to achieve more in adult life.

- ❖ **"If the hands do it, the mind remembers."** (Bos, B., workshop at Burbank High school, 2005) This is an extension of the idea that play is children's work. Many people learn best when they are learning by doing. If there is some way that you can legitimately contextualize a concept with an activity, do it! Activities do require a little more prep planning and materials, but the learning available from working with animals, planning and growing a garden, making art, journaling is real, and will be enjoyed and retained far longer than pencil, crayons and worksheets.

- ❖ **People tend to repeat activities that are pleasurable**. Present activities that are not only educational, but also fun. When an experience makes someone feel good, they will want to repeat that experience. If the learning process is a source of good feelings, then one will get into the learning habit. If a person learns a bit of information, but leaves the experience hating participation in the learning process, did the teacher really succeed?

- ❖ **Be a role model**. What kind of person do you really want to be? Rigid, inflexible, judgmental, demanding, and not much fun? Or respectful, loving life, accepting, and being excited about the subject matter, and the process of learning in general? What a teacher does as a person speaks far more loudly than anything actually said. Model important values, such as: a certain flexibility, an acceptance of people for who they are and their individual learning styles, a generosity of spirit. No matter what grade level taught, the teacher's behavior will teach volumes in terms of important social and behavioral values, and what type of person students may become. Reflect on who you are and who you want to be. You do have a choice. Your behavior as an educator will have an impact upon your students, and of course, yourself.

- ❖ **Choose your fights:** If a teacher is determined to "be right" and "to win" in every instance, the cost in personal satisfaction of the teaching experience may be forfeit. Every day may become a battle. As the teacher and the adult in the classroom, when reduced to a battle of wills with a child, that battle will be lost. Certainly there are appropriate areas in which to make a stand. Slurs against individuals are unacceptable. Hurting others physically is unacceptable. Do not lose your temper unless it is really worth it. Reserve a meltdown for the equivalent of an emotional nuclear catastrophe. Late homework is just late homework. Cheating is cheating. Figure out a course of action, take it, move on, and never hold grudges. Do not be naive, however. If there is a thief in the midst of your class, take your wallet or purse with you. What you do is what you teach.

- ❖ **Construction is better than instruction.** Children, in the learning process, should be encouraged to find out things for themselves. Dr. Jerome Bruner, (The Process of Education, 1960) the main architect in the 1960s of the innovative early childhood program Head Start, developed the constructivist approach to education. When a person goes through the process of trial and error and discovery, they will "own" whatever results they produce. The results will be meaningful, and relevant to them. A child may be able to parrot back a memorized response, but when the child has solved a problem himself, it becomes contextualized and relevant to the child. Information acquired through the process of investigation is more useable. (For a short overview of Bruner's Constructivist Theory go to: "Theory In Practice (TIP)" @ http://tip.psychology.org/bruner.html)

❖ **Use developmentally appropriate practices**: If classroom structure is presented at a level too difficult or too easy for the cognitive and emotional level of understanding of the students in the class, the teacher will lose them. The same thing holds for behavioral expectations. Make life easier for everyone involved. Consider the students to whom the material is presented. When working with a group of highly gifted second graders, the classroom environment and curricular presentation would be different than working in a SRLDP pre-k (School Readiness Language Development Program Pre-School).

❖ **Make homework meaningful:** Consider this guideline when assigning homework: Try to set up homework in such a way that an average child will still have time to play in the late afternoon when homework is completed. Is it really fair to fill up precious minutes of childhood with worksheet busy work? Homework is mandatory for grades kindergarten and up, at most schools in the LAUSD (Los Angeles Unified School District), and many other districts as well. Try to keep the homework load reasonable. Make it as fun as you can. (Note: Many parents resent cut and paste worksheets.) Figure on 15 minutes or so for primary homework. (Elementary, middle and high school have 30 minutes and more. Teachers at these levels would need to be aware that they may not be the only teacher assigning homework, and moderate accordingly.)

❖ **Grade supportively**: If a student does not really understand material presented in an age appropriate manner, consider two possibilities. One is to try another teaching strategy and another is to make other accommodations. If the teacher sees a child putting forth good effort and making progress, this should be noted to the child, to the parents, and when it is possible, on the report card. As Richard Lavoie says in *When the Chips Are Down* (2005, PBS video), "Reward direction, not perfection". If a student receives reinforcement and acknowledgment in the process of learning, the student will feel more motivated to keep on learning. If a child is floundering, contact the parents and perhaps school support staff, to help the child succeed, before the deadly "1" or "2", or "D" or even worse, "F", is on the report card. There are times when an educator has no choice. But while there is time, make that phone call, work with the child or perhaps both. Sometimes a well placed "A" or "B" can give the child the psychological boost of self-confidence and success. Absolutely do not use grades punitively or as a "power trip". Grading harshly can do immeasurable damage to a child's self-esteem and the desire to continue working academically.

❖ **Catch children "being good":** One word of praise will produce better results than an hour of corrections, or worse yet, reprimands. The teacher may need to be very observant and quick to accomplish this, but the best strategy to produce desired behavior is positive acknowledgment. Writing neatly, sitting straight, sharing, any instance of the appropriate behavior will reward the child with the greatest reward a teacher can give, positive attention. Sometimes children will behave badly just for attention, even negative attention, but as they learn that the teacher acknowledges positive actions, they will be inclined to desire positive attention.

❖ **Teach learning strategies** Higher order thinking is a crucial skill for survival in our culture. Find ways to help students acquire skills to excel in school. After learning the basics of math, reading, and a little bit of history, teach children to think for themselves, to think critically. Do this by encouraging collaboration, and asking the children *open-ended questions*, that is, asking questions without a right or wrong answer. "What do you think this passage means?" "How do you think the science experiment will turn out?" "Can you think of another way to do this?" If there is a breakdown in communication, ask the students to resolve the problem (with supervision) on their own, "How can this be resolved" or "What should we do about this?"

❖ **Think about the bigger picture and the bigger goals for the child**: Don't squabble with a child about small stuff. Keep in mind the final outcomes you really want to produce. For example, feeling comfortable with self-expression versus writing letters and numbers, loving the process of learning, wonder, curiosity, love and respect for life and all that lives. Teachers are often some of the most pivotally influential people in the lives of students. What an awesome opportunity to make a difference!

❖ **Separation anxiety:** If possible, perhaps the parent(s) can remain a little while for the first few days, leaving progressively sooner as the child becomes more comfortable. This can make the transition into school less traumatic for a child. Bev Bos, in "Separation Anxiety" (www.turnthepage.com/articles), discusses some of the fears and concerns that children have at different ages, and gives suggestions for facing and comforting them. In fact she states "Separation anxiety is lifelong." (para. 2) Remember that, even as adults, we may also feel those pangs when we are separated from those we love.

Habits of Highly Effective Teachers

1. **Know Your Children.** The more familiar a teacher is with the people being taught, the easier it will be to present curriculum tailored to the abilities, interests and maturity of that particular group.

2. **It is not how you teach, but how your students learn.** Teaching is about the children, not about you.

3. **Teach because you love it**. The best teachers are teachers because the actual process is fulfilling to them, and is in fact, part of the compensation for the work. All living beings on this earth get a minute of life for just one minute. Choose the way you spend your minutes wisely. If you are enjoying teaching, your students, no matter what their age, will sense it. If you are actively sharing your love and excitement about learning and the material you are sharing, your enthusiasm will touch the learners and inspire them. The reason we learn Piaget's schemas and Erickson's stages is to empower us to recognize where a child is in development. By knowing this we can respond to the child in a way that empowers the child's learning.

4. **Process is more important than product.** It is more important for the children to develop skills, higher order cognition, socialization, and so on, than it is to produce pretty pictures

or identical little crafts. "Young children do art for the experience, the exploration, the experimentation. In the process they discover mystery, creativity, joy, frustration. (Kohl, *Preschool art: it's the process, not the art* 1994, page 11)

5. **Who you are with children is the most important part of a teaching.** If an *educarer* nurtures the spirit of a child, fosters growth in socialization and academic skills, sparks a desire to continue learning, the educarer has succeeded. Acquiring individual bits of information or mastering a skill is secondary to creating an environment wherein children bloom.

6. **Never talk with other people (teachers, parents, administrators, other children) about a child, in the presence of that child, as if the child is not there.** This is disrespectful and potentially damaging to a child's self-esteem. If the child is there, speak to the child directly. If the child is there, the child should be part of the conversation.

7. **Get down to the child's eye level.** Imagine how huge a teacher must seem to a five or six year old child. A teacher will seem so much less intimidating if the adult is at eye level to the child. Maintain eye contact when speaking directly to a child whenever possible. If getting down to the child's level seems odd or uncomfortable, practice doing this with another adult, talking over one another, with one person sitting down and then trade off.

8. **Generally use a soft tone of voice.** Unless there is extreme danger, shouting across a room is disruptive to the class and negatively raises level of energy. Shouting in a classroom models that shouting is acceptable.

9. **Speak supportively.** If a child is not behaving appropriately, observe to the child that the behavior is not okay. The child is okay. It is the behavior that is the issue. Suggest taking a thinking break for a few minutes.

10. **Listen to the child.** Listen carefully. Then repeat to the child, what you believe you heard the child say, particularly if the child is very upset (i.e., **active listening**). Bev Bos, in *Before the Basics: Creating Conversations with Children* (1987) speaks of the importance of taking our cues from the child. "Acting positively on the basis of those cues is the difference between a conversation and a lecture, a conversation and a performance, a conversation and a monologue."

11. **The teacher is the adult.** It is up to the teacher to model appropriate behavior for students.

12. **Foster independence.** Allow children to figure out how to do things for themselves whenever possible: putting on or tying shoes, putting together a puzzle, and so on. If a child becomes very frustrated, suggest (without touching the project) that they might try turning it another way, or trying the shoe on the other foot.

13. **When disagreements arise, get the children to work out solutions between themselves by making their solution the best option.** This will help to foster independence, self-help and negotiation skills as well as problem solving and thinking skills, self-esteem, and socialization, as opposed to a learned helplessness. For example, tell the children, if the problem has to be settled by an adult, then the toy will just be put away. Propose that the kids can invent their own (i.e., better) solution. Children who work out their own problems and challenges are more likely to retain the information they constructed, than if

the teacher does things for them. This allows the children ownership of their learning. (Bev Bos's article on *Conflict Resolution* @ www.turnthepage.com, may be a good reference for further suggestions)

14. **Provide an environment where children organize and put toys away (with help and supervision).** Give definite indications of transitions (clean up songs, good-bye songs, etc.) This allows children to take ownership of their environment and lets them adjust to the next activity with less stress.

15. **Plan ahead for activities (learning plans).** Realize that learning plans are a framework. Be willing to adjust them to children's interests (i.e., **emergent curriculum**). The structure, the plan, is there to support the children's successful learning. This structure facilitates making changes regarding events, children's interest, and so on.

16. **Positive reinforcement.** Catch a child being good. Be specific and use positive comments such as, "I like the way you shared the art materials" or "The colors you used in the collage are very striking". Comments such as, "OOOh you are sooooo pretty" are empty and have no power.

17. **Encourage children to use their words.** Instead of acting out a feeling, children need to learn to identify and verbally express their feelings. Help them by saying, "Oh I see you're angry at Jean. What do you need to say to her?"

18. **"For 13 years, school is a child's job".** In *How Difficult Can This Be? F.A.T City*, Richard Lavoie (1989, United States: PBS Video) says, "Kids go to school for a living. That's their job. And they have the feeling that they are failing at their job everyday." At no other time do individuals need to be "good at everything. By the time an individual reaches adulthood, they need only be good at one thing." The adult world is more designed for specialists than generalists. Be present to what a daunting prospect that must be for children. Look inside to find the generosity of spirit each of us hopes to find in the face of our weaker areas. When that generosity is shared, and modeled, the world becomes a more generous space. The best and most meaningful learning occurs in a context of generosity.

Chapter Three
Targeted Areas of Learning

"It is of the utmost importance that we recognize and nurture all of the varied human intelligences ... If we can mobilize the spectrum of human abilities, not only will people feel better about themselves and more competent; it is even possible that they will also feel more engaged and better able to join the rest of the world community in working for the broader good."

– Dr. Howard Gardner,
Multiple Intelligences: The Theory in Practice. (1993, p. 12)

What is a Targeted Area of Learning?

Knowing the value a child can potentially reap from participating in any given activity answers the question, "Why are you presenting this activity to my child?" Teachers need to be able to respond to this question with some authority. The teacher is, after all, the person who is responsible for the learning going on in the classroom. By knowing the learning associated with activities, a teacher will have confidence when presenting them to the children. Knowing why the activity is being presented will make the experience more meaningful to everyone involved. The "why" associated with an activity will have a measurable impact on the "how" and "when" of the teacher's presentation.

There are five general areas of learning:

1. **Physical**: motor learning dealing with the large and small muscle groups of the body; this area includes gross motor activities, fine motor activities, eye-hand coordination, balance, physical principals, sensory discrimination, and coordination between the use of one aspect of the physical and one or more of the other aspects of physical development.

2. **Cognitive**: or intellectual; Webster (2000, page 258) defines "cognitive" as "2. of or pertaining to the mental processes of perception, memory, judgment, and reasoning as contrasted to the emotional and volitional processes". The term **"curriculum"** describes the courses of study offered by a school. For the purposes of this book, **"cognitive"** will refer to the subject areas of language arts and literacy, math, science, social studies and cooking.

3. **Social**: developing skills related to interacting with others in socially acceptable ways; This area includes: following directions, socialization skills, sharing, taking turns, patience,

being comfortable with delayed gratification, collaboration, working as a member of a team or a group, cooperation, taking responsibility for the classroom environment, and internalized social values: appreciation and respect for self and others

4. **Emotional**: closely related to socialization; this area covers: learning to recognize and identify different emotional states, and manage them in socially acceptable ways ("I am feeling angry now"), building self-esteem, developing a willingness to take appropriate risks, differentiating between appropriate and inappropriate risks, and learning to be nurturing and caring toward others, empathy

5. **Creative**: creativity is often, but not always, related to emotional expression; using materials in individual ways, trying out creative ideas using a variety of materials, learning to risk creatively, experimentation though working with creative media, learning a sense of aesthetics and aesthetic appreciation for music, movement, visual, written, and dramatic arts, but not limited to those areas. Initiative is fostered in process-oriented artistic endeavors wherein there are no wrong outcomes. Independent thinking is an aspect of creativity.

No activity is isolated to a single area of growth. In cooking, the social skills of following directions and cooperation combine with the physical abilities of eye-hand coordination and movement of the small muscles of the hands and fingers (fine motor), as well as the cognitive areas of math (measuring, putting the ingredients together in a particular sequence) and science (understanding that changes occur to foods when they are subjected to heat, cold, or a food processor). When teachers are present to the diversity of learning available in all creative projects, it is possible for teachers to present any activity chosen in such a way that those areas of learning are emphasized.

In learning, the process is more important than the product.

Please consider that in the world of outcome-based learning, developing and honing an effective skill is less relevant than producing a passing grade on a test or a pretty craft, identical to all the other students' crafts from the class. Outcome-based learning is passive in nature. Students are often only marginally involved with any part of such an activity with the exception of producing the "right answer". It is very difficult to perceive engagement in outcome-based learning. The primary determinant of learning in this environment is the test score. Outcome-based learning does not take into consideration learning strengths other than logical / mathematical or verbal / linguistic areas. Dr. Howard Gardner, Harvard professor, author and theorist, believes that our society tends have a bias towards being "Testist". People like to focus on those abilities "that are readily testable. If it can't be tested, it sometimes seems, it is not worth paying attention to. My feeling is that assessment can be much broader, much more humane than it is now..." (*Multiple Intelligences: The Theory in Practice.* 1993, page 12). Dr. Gardner has identified nine learning strengths (multiple intelligences). There are an infinite number of combinations of strengths and weaknesses related to each person's unique intelligence profile. Each individual reflects a unique combination of intelligences and the expression of those intelligences. Of those nine types, the logical / mathematical and linguistic intelligences, are the two most often stressed in education today. The other types of intelligences (bodily / kinesthetic, intrapersonal, interpersonal, musicality, naturalistic, spatial and existential) are almost entirely ignored in outcome-based learning.

Making mistakes in outcome-based learning is to the learner's detriment. Swiss educator and theorist Jean Piaget believed that errors are a part of the learning process. Labinowicz, states in the *Piaget Primer,* "A child's errors are actually the natural steps to understanding." (1980, page 55).

Often the product of a test is not a working body of knowledge but merely anxiety. Anxiety tends to impair retention of information at the neurochemical level. What administrators find attractive about test scores is that they can be neatly placed upon a statistical scale. Outcome-based learning is neat, easy and cheap. There's not a lot of prep time. Unfortunately, outcome-based learning is often neither interesting nor fun for the children.

In process-based learning, children learn how to interpret and give meaning to concrete life experiences. They are actively involved in the process, and are generally having fun. Yes, it is true that it is more difficult to measure and quantify the learning from interactive experiences. Consider that people who learn to enjoy the process of learning tend to become lifelong learners. Making mistakes is a part of process-based learning. Making a mistake in a process is as informative as getting the right answer. Teaching children to be willing to risk investigation and feel comfortable when making a mistake is as important (if not more important) as acquiring a single piece of information.

Mistaking *is* learning. Bev Bos, the American author and educator said, "It has to be in the hand and the body before it can be in the brain." (*How do our children grow*, http://www.turnthepage.com/articles.php). Process-based learning integrates the whole person in learning, making the possibility of producing a meaningful working body knowledge much more likely. Process-based learning is fun. It also requires additional preparation time, expense, and can be really, really messy. For these reasons many administrative types shrink away from it. If one were to look into the long-term outcomes though, process-based learning is worth it, if the children are a higher priority than the numbers.

Regarding the Learning Environment

The general psychological and physical environments, including the strategies used for behavior modification, the acceptance of learners as individuals, the books chosen for the class library, and the use of "free" time, sets a tone for the classroom, which in and of itself teaches. Generating this tone comes forth best from the teacher's commitment to the field of education and from honoring the embodiment of our future, which we call children.

If children are not sure whether they are safe to venture forth into the universe of learning, they will take much more cautious steps into this universe. If the classroom structure or the teacher's commitment to them is unclear, a less than satisfying learning experience will be the result for all, including the teacher.

Remember that people in general learn better when they feel safe. If students feel as though there is a reasonable likelihood that they can "win" in an educational setting, then the learners are much more willing to take a bigger risk. If making a mistake will not produce reprimands and humiliation, children will gleefully jump into the learning process. Pediatrician and author, Dr. Mel Levine emphasizes in numerous contexts that the quality learning environment is characterized by freedom from humiliation. A willingness to risk is essential for authentic functional learning. When creating a learning environment, the teacher must create a nonjudgmental atmosphere. Certainly the teacher needs to teach in such a way that allows for the teacher's personal comfort. Bearing that in mind, an environment that welcomes self-expression and initiative will produce a body of learners willing to seek and leap out into learning opportunities.

Below are the general areas of learning broken down into the smaller, more specific components of each area.

General Areas of Learning

Physical Development
- ❖ **Gross motor skills:** using the large muscles of the arms, legs, and torso: development and coordination of large muscles; balance, rhythm, walking, laterality, jumping, hopping, throwing, tumbling, running, dancing
- ❖ **Fine motor skills:** using the small muscles of the hand and fingers: tactile discrimination (see below), cutting; drawing shapes; holding a pencil/crayon; pouring liquid; throwing a ball accurately; writing
- ❖ **Eye-hand coordination:** coordinating visual acuity with using the small muscles of the hand and fingers: cutting; drawing shapes; holding a pencil/crayon; pouring liquid; throwing a ball accurately; writing; use of mouse (computers)
- ❖ **Physical principals:** learning physical weight; stability; equilibrium; balance; leverage
- ❖ **Articulation:** vocally creating letter and word sounds correctly using mouth, tongue, and lips
- ❖ **Sensory Discrimination**

  - **Tactile discrimination** (touch): identifying and differentiating textures and sensations with touch: soft, hard, rough, smooth, sticky, slippery, and so on
  - **Auditory discrimination** (hearing): identifying sounds: loud / soft; high / low pitch; fast / slow rhythms; comparing sounds using auditory receptors
  - **Visual discrimination** (sight): identifying shapes; colors; sizes; recognizing various objects visually
  - **Oral discrimination** (taste): identifying sweet, salty, sour, and bitter tastes; identifying textures with tongue and mouth; identifying flavors by taste
  - **Olfactory discrimination** (smell): identifying different smells: sweet, spicy; pungent, floral, unpleasant odors

Cognitive Development
- ❖ **Language Arts**

  - **Verbal skills**

    - ○ **Language development**: acquiring and using language appropriately in interactions with others; ability to carry on a conversation
    - ○ **Vocabulary development**: adding to the body of words and phrases understood and the body of words/phrases that can be used in speech

o **Grammatical development**: learning the rules of grammar; conventions of the use of language in various contexts: formal speech, informal speech, private code

- **Emergent literacy**

    o **Symbol recognition**: recognizing that particular marks have meaning apart from other marks, which may or may not have a different meaning
    o **Symbol interpretation**: identifying the particular meaning associated with a specific symbol including environmental print
    o **Letter recognition**: learning the letter symbols of a specific language and correctly identifying the associated phonemes
    o   **Phonemic awareness:** awareness of sounds associated with letters and letter combinations
    o **Word recognition**: understanding that groups of letters create a composite sound which is meaningful; correctly decoding letter groups
    o **Emergent writing**: developing the fine motor skills for the pincer grasp and creating marks to which they attach meaning
    o **Journal writing:** activities associated with committing personal thoughts, ideas, reflections, invented stories, observations related through scribble writing, dictation, or emergent writing and drawings
    o **Spelling skills**: using correct letter symbol combinations to form words
    o **Penmanship:** developing legible handwriting for writing projects: tracing letters, writing name, writing new words in a readable hand
    o **Creative writing**: expressing self in marks and pictures upon which the child has placed meaning
    o **Matching spoken words to written words**: correctly associating the auditory expression with the written symbol grouping
    o **Story recall/sequencing (temporal ordering)**: retelling and relating stories/ events the child has heard/experienced. Within temporal ordering are aspects of language, math, and per state standards, social science as it relates to ordering events as they occur in time.

❖ **Math Skills**

- **Conservation**

    o **Conservation of quantity**: understanding that the number in a group of items remains constant no matter how the items are arranged
    o **Conservation of volume**: equivalent quantities of fluid remain constant no matter what size or shape container of that fluid
    o **Conservation of mass**: equivalent masses are the same, no matter the shape the mass takes

- o **Reversibility**: a mass, fluid, or configuration of items can be changed back to its original form without changing the quantity of mass, fluid, or quantity of items

- **Mathematical literacy**

  - o **1 to 1 correspondence**: counting items in an organized way that shows understanding of the object's placement as a single entity in a group; understanding that each single count is associated with a specific item in a count
  - o **Number recognition**: recognizing that a specific symbol is associated with a specific quantity, and that symbol is constant in association with that symbol
  - o **Associating number symbols with quantity**: understanding that a specific symbol is always associated with a specific quantity of items in a count
  - o **Recognizing number words**: associating the number symbol with the written word for the number with the count of items represented by both the written word and the symbol

- **Mathematical applications**

  - o **Measurement**: using a standard measure to determine the size (height, length, weight, quantity, volume) of an object; comparing some aspect of size of one object to another
  - o **Equivalency**: comparing an object or a number of objects in terms of size or quantity
  - o **Seriation**: ordering objects or events in a graduation of size from smallest to largest or vice versa, or in the context of time from earliest to latest

    - **Calendar**: placing numbers in order to denote the passage of days, weeks, months, seasons, years
    - **Time**: noting the sequential relationship from one event to another as measured by a standard interval such as a minute, an hour; associating specific events with an appointed time in the day and identifying that appointed time on a clock
    - **Temporal ordering**: placing events in a particular predetermined sequence, retelling a story or an event in the sequence in which it happened. Within temporal ordering are aspects of language, math, and per state standards, social science as it relates to ordering events as they occur in time.

  - o **Spatial relationships**: relating the aspects of physical objects to one another, thinking about objects in three dimensions
  - o **Construction**: building or forming by putting together parts to create a three dimensional object
  - o **Charting**: using an outcome to create various preliminary statistical diagrams; to reflect the outcomes of an activity presented in a diagram

o **Common relatedness**: linking items that are not the same, but are associated with each other such as bat and ball, shoes and socks. Common relatedness can be considered in multiple categories. Matching related items is mathematical, however, there are components of language such as vocabulary building.

o **Opposites**: identifying and relating one aspect or property of an item or its condition to another object or condition of another item by virtue of the differences between the objects, e.g. tall/short; soft/loud. Opposites are a subset of common relatedness. Within it are elements of language as well as math.

o **Algebra**: sorting and matching for one or more properties: looking at items and placing them in an invented order for similarities and differences of properties

o **Geometry**: recognizing and naming two and three-dimensional shapes: circle, square, triangle, rectangle, oval, diamond, hexagon, octagon; sphere, cone cylinder, cube, rectangular/hexagonal/ octagonal prism

❖ **Science**

• **Scientific processes**:

o **Inquiry**: an organized search for knowledge regarding a particular scientific question; testing personal theories

o **Prediction**: relating an anticipated outcome-based on logic, experience, or research

o **Observation:** carefully watching attentively and noting what is seen for a scientific purpose

o **Documentation**: writing observations of scientific events which support/disprove claims for a particular prediction or outcomes

o **Review**: comparing predictions and actual outcomes, assessing value of any mistakes that occurred

• **Cause and effect**

o **Relationships between actions and outcomes**: developing curiosity which leads to scientific inquiry: "educated why"

• **Life science**

o **Differentiation:** organisms from inorganic objects or substances
o **Understanding common needs:** all living things have common needs for life
o **Responsibility**: understanding that living things need a certain level of care, in the absence of which that living thing will either become sick or die
o **Recognizing health**: noticing appearance and behavior of healthy living things
o **Death**: if a plant or animal lives, it will sometime die
o **Plant keeping**: germination and nurturing plant life; harvesting flowers/fruits

- o **Animal keeping**: caring for and nurturing animal life
- o **Nurturing**: animals need gentle care to thrive; abused animals react out of fear, may perceive danger when there is none
- o **Hygiene**: maintaining an appropriate level of personal cleanliness

  - Washing hands thoroughly after toileting, before eating, when caring for animals or plants, after coughing or sneezing into hand
  - Covering cough or sneeze to prevent spread of illness
  - Coughing or sneezing into upper arm

- **Chemistry and Physics**

  - o Objects and materials can be described in terms of materials from which they are made (CA. Science Content Standard K-1a.)
  - o Changes in the state of water: liquid, steam, ice, evaporation
  - o Beginning observations related to surface tension of water

- **Earth science**:

  - o Children understand that earth is composed of land, air and water, which includes geological formations of the earth, weather changes, and ecological conservation.
  - o **Ecology**: understanding that the earth's resources need to be used in a way that will create a healthy balance for all living organisms on the planet

❖ **Social Studies**

- **Recognizing diversity**: recognizing what makes people similar *and* different: knowing that superficial differences do not mean *bad*.
- **Accepting human diversity**: types of families, cultures, race, languages, gender, differently-abled, economic status, age; learning to evaluate humankind based upon the impact of their choices and internal values on the rest of humanity rather than superficial differences of race or religious preferences, and so on
- **Democratic process:** building a sense of equality, understanding a system wherein each person has one vote
- **Environmental responsibility**: developing a sense of stewardship for the planet and all that lives upon it
- **Understanding that being a good citizen and member of the school community involves certain behavior:** following rules, sharing, taking turns, individual responsibilities and consequences, recognizing appropriate behavior
- Children understand that history relates to people, events, and places in times past

o Understanding how people lived in earlier times and how their lives were different from life today: using traditional tools

- **Comparing and contrasting locations of people, places, and environments**

  o **Determining relative locations:** near/far, left/right, behind/in front

Social Development

- ❖ **Self-respect:** valuing themselves, recognizing their strengths and weaknesses, loving themselves for who they are, just as they are; recognizing personal strengths and weaknesses
- ❖ **Sharing:** understanding, and behaving in such a way that reflects that understanding, that items intended for use by the community (family, classroom) are available for the use by everyone in that community and may not be available at all times for individual use
- ❖ **Taking turns:** everyone in the classroom deserves opportunities to participate in class activities, allowing others a fair use of materials as a community resource and turns at tasks that might be considered a privilege
- ❖ **Patience:** managing a delay in gratification of a desire; diligence: staying with a project or activity until it is completed
- ❖ **Working cooperatively with others in a group:** good sportsmanship; working well as a member of a team and as a community that supports all members
- ❖ **Collaboration:** planning, creating, and presenting group projects; taking responsibility for tasks associated with group projects including clean up
- ❖ **Negotiation:** learning to represent one's wishes in such a way that others in the group will consider those wishes favorably; learning to be generous to the wishes of others
- ❖ **Following directions:** carrying out directions given by a person in authority
- ❖ **Impulse control:** managing an impulse to behave in a less socially acceptable way and choosing to behave in a socially acceptable way, despite having that impulse
- ❖ **Respecting others as individuals (behaving appropriately with others):** making and maintaining relationships / ongoing friendships; behaving appropriately in social situations; learning the general rules of courtesy (manners) for their family and school; developing the ability to participate in conversation; learning table manners
- ❖ **Leadership:** initiating and managing activities that involve others
- ❖ **Internalizing social values:** learning appropriate behavior in the context of the culture in which the child is living; per Vygotsky's sociocultural theory, believing that culture is socially mediated. For a child to succeed within a particular cultural group, the child must internalize an appreciation for the skills, behaviors, and interactions that are valued by that culture. (Berk, 2005 page 328)
- ❖ **Social boundaries:** understanding that just as others have a right to accept or refuse the attentions of others, so they also have that right
- ❖ **Community building:** creating a sense of belonging in a group, particularly through working cooperatively with others toward common goals

❖ **Taking responsibility**: recognition that each person in the community is responsible for the community as a whole; developing a willingness to take on tasks that support the individual and the group as a whole

❖ **Taking care of classroom environment**: participating in cleanup; caring for classroom as a community environment; taking personal ownership of responsibilities associated with being part of a defined community and the environment in which it exists

❖ **Safety practices and appropriate behavior in emergency situations**: fire, earthquake, natural disasters; dealing with strangers; what behaviors are safe and not safe, e.g.: running in the parking lot, wearing bike helmets, wearing close toed shoes to school, and so on

Emotional Development

❖ **Self-esteem**: feeling good about oneself, just as one is and is not; feeling good about that which one does and does not; building self-confidence by participating in activities wherein there is no "wrong" answer; feeling safe to try out new activities in a nonjudgmental environment, wherein there is no pressure to produce a particular outcome, rather an environment that supports curiosity, investigation; developing a stable sense of self worth

❖ **Self-confidence**: feeling secure within one's self; being able to be present to uncomfortable feelings without having those feelings overcome or dominate the child's ability to be with others, or for the child to stand for internalized values

❖ **Stress relief**: finding acceptable vents for stress and frustration such as manipulating different types of dough, washing toys in warm water, squeezing squishy toys, or manipulating substances such as oobleck or flubber.

❖ **Accomplishment**: developing a sense of achievement and self-worth from participating in and completing various activities

❖ **Identifying and expressing emotions appropriately**

- **Naming human feelings:** sad, happy, angry, hurt, loving, excited, afraid, proud, sorry
- **"Use your words":** expressing feelings of joy, happiness, upset and anger appropriately
- **Generosity**: sharing of one's self and perhaps of one's "things"; listening attentively; experiencing enjoyment in giving/sharing with others; enjoying the success of others; accepting other's generosity graciously
- **Appropriate affection**: showing feelings of affection with respect for the recipient's willingness to accept demonstrative actions
- **Nurturing:** developing and expressing feelings of appropriate care and gentleness for other living things, other people (particularly those younger, smaller, more fragile); stewardship of the planet
- **Empathy**: awareness of and identification with the feelings of others'; behaving appropriately in the context of those feelings
- **Courage**: ability to face one's own fears, and real or perceived threats; a willingness to be true to one's self in the face of disapproval from others
- **Integrity**: keeping one's word; living by internalized values

Creative Expression

❖ **Use of creative media and expression of imagination**:

- **2-dimensional visual arts**: painting/collage/drawing: expressing self using 2 dimensional media
- **3-dimensional visual arts:** play dough / clay / construction expressing self in 3 dimensional sculptural media; gardening; building with construction manipulatives
- **Music**: expressing self through vocal and instrumental sounds
- **Movement/dance**: expressing self through movement
- **Dramatization and story telling**: expressing oneself through acting, puppetry, and theater arts
- **Writing and story telling**: expressing self through written and illustrated media
- **Culinary arts**: expressing self through food preparation and presentation
- **Event presentation**: expressing self through planning and preparing celebrations, events, and other social functions
- **Gardening**: expressing self through nurturing plant life
- **Animal care**: expressing self through care and nurturing of animals

❖ **Aesthetic appreciation:** developing appreciation for arts, books, drama, music, puppetry, theatrical events, movement, and nature; the works of others

❖ **Artistic vocabulary**: learning the names of the art styles and tools

❖ **Creative risk**: being comfortable playing creatively, actively and confidently following through on use of imagination; experimenting freely with creative media without focus on the outcome

❖ **Problem solving**: gathering data, collaborating, delegating responsibility within the small and large group; having small and large group discussion relative to the possible choices available

❖ **Creative thinking**: brainstorming: considering all possible solutions to a problem or challenge posed

❖ **Persuasion**: learning to represent one's ideas in such a way that appeals to others and causes them to consider one's suggestions

When planning, the teacher will want to refine the area of learning specifically targeted. The more specific the desired value that the children are to obtain from an activity, the easier it will be for teacher to develop a presentation that will successfully produce the result sought. Often the children will acquire unexpected learning from an activity presented. This is fine. It should also be fine for the child to learn something else entirely. If the teacher is mindful of what is intended for the children to learn, a good aim will develop, and will have the satisfying effect of hitting the targeted result.

Preparing an environment in advance with certain intended learning in mind helps the teacher produce that specific area of learning. The teacher should select projects that strongly support the acquisition of the desired information. As a presentation strategy, the teacher may want to ask some leading open-ended questions that will direct the children's attention toward the intended learning.

One possibility would be to ask the children to discuss a problem in small groups and report the results to the class. Each collaborative group could select a spokesperson.

It is important for the teacher to be supportive as the students develop the skill of deductive reasoning, or said more simply, how to figure things out and put ideas together.

Acknowledge, praise, and support all the children's attempts to problem solve.

Daring to attempt is more of what education is all about than producing a pretty result. Learning is a process, and it often happens that more value is gained from concerted efforts during an activity than an easily achieved success. The process of discovery, making mistakes, and finding out what doesn't work sometimes offers more value to a learner than producing the "right" answer quickly.

Chapter Four

Evaluation Rubrics

"We judge ourselves by what we feel capable of doing,
while others judge us by what we have already done."
– Henry Wadsworth Longfellow

The word "rubric" can be intimidating for some teachers. A **rubric** is an evaluation chart for any targeted area of learning in an activity. A teacher may choose to evaluate one or several learning areas. For each area chosen to evaluate, a separate rubric must be created.

Contrary to popular misconception, teachers remain human, with all of the associated biases of humanity, even when they are teaching. That means that the evaluation process is entirely *subjective* rather than being *objective*. To produce the most objective assessment possible, create an evaluation rubric prior to presenting an activity to a class. In this way a teacher will look for particular intended learning and processes during an activity.

When creating a rubric, teachers rely upon their background of training and hands-on experience with learners, to determine reasonable developmentally appropriate output from students. To assess learning appropriately, teachers need to be mindful of who they are teaching. Every learner and every group of learners is unique.

Three forms of rubrics commonly used are A, B, C, D, F, and I (incomplete) (five levels of assessment); 4, 3, 2, 1 (four levels of assessment); and E (excellent), S (satisfactory), and U (unsatisfactory) (3 levels of assessment). The authors happen to like the five-step A through F and I (incomplete) method of evaluation, because it has five levels of competency for a teacher to select. This perspective on using fewer levels of skill means more generalized, less specific benchmarks. The "Pass - Not Pass" option with a narrative evaluation, is also very acceptable, since it shows that the instructor actually took time to be aware of the learner and his or her learning as an individual.

Generally, the facility, institution, school, or district determines the method of evaluation. Teachers are not usually, if ever, offered a chance to choose their method of evaluation.

Contrary to popular misconception, evaluation is not objective, particularly with respect to the curriculum for young children. Assessment of competency and evaluation is absolutely subjective. Constructing an evaluation rubric, or chart of benchmarks for success in activity, before presenting the activity, helps to make the process of evaluation more objective.

A rubric can contains within it directions for executing the activity, particularly for children who are reading. For example, a second-grade writing rubric for a sentence could say:

A   Has a subject, predicate, and correct use of capitals, punctuation, and correct spelling
B   Correct use of any four of the above
C   Correct use of any three of the above
D   Correct use of any two of the above
F   Correct use of one or none of the above

Another form that is used in the four-level style of evaluation is used in this text. There are many ways to identify the benchmarks. To begin, the easiest is to use the format for example with the socialization skill of clean up after an activity:

4	(Mastery of Skill) Exceeds Standard	Always participates willingly in clean up after an activity
3	(Skill Developing Age Appropriately) or Meets Standard	Usually participates willingly in clean up after an activity
2	(Emerging Skill) or Emerging skills Moving Toward Standard	Sometimes participates willingly in clean up after an activity
1	(Skill Not Yet Developed) or Standard not yet seen	Rarely participates willingly in clean up after an activity

It is preferable for the "1" evaluation to use the word "rarely" as opposed to "never", which seems to preclude that the desired skills could be developing for the child.

The three-step evaluation form, which is the most general of all, looks something like this for the cognitive skill of measuring milk into a zip-type freeze bag to make the "Ice Cream in Zip-Type Bags" activity:

E	Excellent	Measures milk accurately
S	Satisfactory	Measures milk with acceptable accuracy
U	Unsatisfactory	Does not measure milk with acceptable accuracy

Although many educators are loath to admit the relationship between evaluation systems, they do exist. The "E" in the three-step system is equivalent to the "4" in the four-step system, which is approximately equivalent to the "A" and "B" in the five-step system. Continuing to create correlation between these systems will lead one to the following equivalencies "S" (three-step) is about the same as "3" in the four-step system, which is comparable to a "B" and "C" in the five-step system. A "U" in the three-step system is about equal to a "2" or "1" in the four-step system and "F" in the five-step system. A "2" is about a "C" or "D" in the five-step, and a "1" of the four-step system is approximately an "F".

Whenever the teacher evaluates children's learning, the teacher will want to look carefully for the successes, strengths, and achievements the child has developed. Harsh evaluation can have an impact on the interaction between the parents and child, and/or the interaction between the educational system and the family. Without being dishonest, since an educator's honest evaluation is crucial to support the learning of the child, consider the possibility of evaluating supportively rather than punitively.

The teacher's evaluation of a child can, in fact, help the child to feel capable of taking on tasks, or, alternately, as though no matter how hard s/he tries, feel doomed to failure. Setting a child up in a pattern of success is the optimal outcome for the educational system.

The educator is responsible to support the child in producing the best learning results possible. Fun activities, responsive teaching, accommodating the special needs of a child, even if those needs have not been formally identified, and supportive, responsible evaluation can produce remarkable results for children's learning. A teacher can be "right" about a child's failure, grading strictly and harshly. But consider the possibility that grading standards are more like guidelines. When reflecting upon one's purpose as an educator, and the power and opportunity that role opens up to make a difference in the lives of people evaluating learning from a broader perspective becomes crucial.

An educator needs to be trained to see learning in order to evaluate learning. The process of learning appears different from one child to another. To accurately evaluate a child's growth and success in an activity, a teacher needs to be familiarized with the way a child learns. A highly extroverted, high-energy child will evidence learning quite differently from a more introspective, cautious child. The teachable moments of the first child may look very different from those of the second child.

At the beginning of the school year, observe the children. Watch them, and see how they explore creative materials. As the teacher learns the children's learning styles and ways they interact with educational experiences and materials, the teacher will have the power to set them up for success. It is essential for the educator to teach the way the children learn, so that the educator can also evaluate supportively, and set the children up for a successful academic future.

Chapter Five

Descriptions of General Areas
of Learning Diversity

To know a mind is to know its specific strengths and weaknesses (dysfunctions), preferences, and traits. These salient individual differences, if accurately perceived, can provide crucial direction to a kid's education ultimately helping him to opt for a life of successful pursuits. ... A mind whose assets and deficits are misunderstood and whose strengths are improperly nurtured may be on the way to long-term faulty function and needless failure during the startup years. The phenomenon is alarmingly common. Our culture has to get over its craving for childhood uniformity.

– Mel Levine, M.D., Ph.D.
Ready Or Not Here Life Comes. (2005, page 64).

The definitions of general areas of learning diversity addressed in this book, are adapted from many sources, including: the *Inclusive Early Childhood Classroom* (Gould, P. & Sullivan, J., 1999) and the *California Special Education Programs*: *A Composite of Laws 26* [Hinkle, P. (consultant), 2004]. These definitions are not clinical in nature and are not intended to be used for diagnostic purposes. These are thumbnail sketches to be used as a guide for teachers in the process of creating an environment in which every child is served in the learning process.

Every learner is unique. Every person alive learns in unique ways, with particular strengths and weaknesses, like learning "DNA". Teachers must remember this as they teach. In point of fact, teachers would be well served to reflect upon their own learning strengths and weaknesses in some detail to better empathize with the learning diversity they will surely encounter on a daily basis. Recognition of learning diversity will give power and flexibility to a teacher's presentation, and identity as an educator.

Whether a child has a formal diagnosis or not, is, in the bigger scheme of teaching, irrelevant. Teachers succeed with their classes when they observe the children, know the children, take into account the way each child and the class as a whole learns. Every child in the class helps create a particular classroom dynamic. Each class is also unique. When selecting an accommodation for a child, the teacher may want to take the classroom dynamic into consideration, as well as the child with learning needs.

As a teacher becomes experienced in the process of teaching, s/he will begin to notice patterns, and combinations of learning traits that commonly appear in students. Dr. Mel Levine, pediatrician, researcher, and professor at the University of North Carolina has looked deeply into understanding learning, and how individual students acquire knowledge. His definitions of the eight neurodevelopmental constructs can help teachers understand individual learning diversity. (*A Mind at a Time*, 2002) The eight constructs are: attention, memory, language, spatial ordering, temporal sequential ordering, neuromotor function, higher order cognition, and social cognition (Neurodevelopmental Placemat). Every student is a unique combination of those constructs. Children whose learning challenges are greater than average may need to be "attuned", a phrase used by Dr. Levine's All Kinds of Minds Institute for deeply looking into a student's learning profile, and creating accommodations based on the information from that profile.

The All Kinds of Minds (AKOM) website, **allkindsof minds.org**, is an excellent resource for looking more deeply into neurodevelopment as part of identifying the best ways to teach children. Briefly, as defined by All Kinds of Minds, attention is a student's ability to pay attention to, process, and monitor information to be learned. Memory is gathering, prioritizing, sorting, and recalling information and processes used in life and learning. AKOM describes temporal sequential ordering as how one learns and utilizes information as it occurs in a sequence, such as time. Time management is included here. Spatial ordering includes an ability to be organized, and working with information that has spatial characteristics. Dr. Levine points out in his film on language that our educational system "is intended for linguists". Most academic products and processes involve either receptive, incoming language or expressive, outgoing language. Neuromotor functions relate to a student's body awareness and movement in the gross motor, fine motor, and graphomotor senses. Levine's people give special attention to graphomotor, as specialized skills are needed to produce writing. Social cognition, the skills students must know to survive in various social contexts, is a very important concept. Many educators believe that behavior is learned by proximity. Dr. Levine and Richard Lavoie, both state in a variety of contexts, that appropriate socialization, also known as "social cognition", usually needs to be taught. There are many who do not learn behavior without direct instruction. Higher order cognition involves utilizing all the other constructs, adding creativity and critical thinking to come up with solutions to unique problems. This returns us to the conversation regarding a learner's level of comfort with taking risks and making mistakes. A person who fears making a mistake will be far less likely to attempt to apply current knowledge to solve new problems. To reiterate, welcome mistakes in the learning process!

These constructs can help teachers to identify areas of weakness and strength with some specificity. When working with students it is essential for teachers to point out areas of strength, as self-esteem is crucial to the quality of life for all people. If learners feel as though they are being "picked apart" by educational personnel, eventually those students will give up in resignation. This must not occur.

The accommodations brought up in this book are suggestions only. There are no "cookie cutter" accommodations that are appropriate for all children at all times. Look through the suggested accommodations for each special need to find the best combinations of changes for the child or children in question. Do not expect that, just because a child has a particular diagnosis, that the child will present any specific behaviors. Therapists do their best to diagnose their clients, and it is possible that they do not see a behavior or a need. Sometimes an initial diagnosis may be incorrect. Richard Lavoie discusses differential diagnosis: having the same symptoms for very different reasons. In education, some children will exhibit similar behaviors, but not for the same reason, and will probably not respond to the same intervention in the same or desired manner (Lavoie, 2005b.)

The teacher is not licensed to diagnose, and should not do so. However, the teacher can note behaviors in the classroom and can either report them to the parent or the school administrator. The teacher's input can help the child's parents and doctor to select the best course of treatment for that child. The doctors, parents and school can optimally become a cooperative team in support of the child. Parents are not obligated to have a child evaluated, treated or medicated. If they do not choose to do so, the teacher can still assist the child by making adjustments in the classroom and curriculum. Remember that in the final evaluation, the school and teachers are there to serve the children.

The Individuals with Disabilities Education Act Amendments of 1997 (**IDEA 1997**) "strengthens academic expectations and accountability for the nation's 5.8 million children with disabilities and bridges the gap that has too often existed between what children with disabilities learn and what is required in regular curriculum." (Archived information for the United States Department of Education regarding the IDEA 1997: http://www.ed.gov/offices/OSERS/Policy/IDEA/index.html) This federal law has a provision for "Least Restrictive Environment" (LRE), which actually emphasizes services as opposed to the actual placement of children. Regarding the educational environment, it requires that children with disabilities can and should receive "free and appropriate public education" (FAPE), designed to meet the child's specific needs, in a regular educational setting with peers without disabilities, to the maximum extent that is appropriate.

Although not covered under IDEA 1997, two other categories of accommodation are also included herein. These are areas of learning which educators need to consider when planning activities for a group of students. The first group is English Language Learners (**ELL**) and the second is the gifted, (**GATE** - Gifted And Talented Education) who will need to have enrichments or opportunities for further investigation.

Look through the list of the all the types of accommodations when considering making a change for a child. Just because a child is identified "**ADHD**" does not preclude the possibility that the child may also "have an obsession to maintain sameness". If a modification fits a need and works well, it is not important whether it falls under one label or another. Many accommodations for children with special needs will meet the learning needs of a child whose first language or home language is not English. Remember that the best measure of a compensatory strategy is in its effectiveness.

Teachers must understand that a change that worked famously with a particular child may not work at all with the same child on another day or with a different child with similar learning needs.

If the accommodations are not successful, try something else. Don't beat yourself up if an accommodation for an activity doesn't work. Change strategies during the activity, or try something else the next time. These suggestions are just that, suggestions. Teachers should try to give a child the best shot at having the most fun and getting the most value from an activity. A teacher can use these suggestions as a stepping off point for personal ideas for changes to be used.

By law, special needs must "adversely affects a pupil's academic performance" for the child to have an **IEP** (Individualized Educational Program) or an **IFSP** (Individualized Family Service Plan).) [Hinkle, P. consultant. (2004). *California Special Education Programs: A Composite of Laws 2*]. The teacher can, though, make modifications without either of those legally binding documents in place. If the teacher notices a child presenting some of the behaviors listed below, it seems logical to consider adapting the curriculum for the child. Making changes for children who need them helps create a positive learning environment for all students. A child needing additional direct instruction or some other minor change, like additional time, could become a behavior challenge. With appropriate supports, that child could be learning. Choose: manage behavior or teach... It is the teacher's choice in the final analysis.

Seven Common Areas of Learning Diversity

ADHD / Attention Deficit Hyperactivity Disorder and ADD / Attention Deficit Disorder

This designation includes behavioral and/or impulsivity problems; may be characterized by unusually high energy, restlessness, lack of impulse control, distractibility, inattention, lack of concentration, a tendency towards day-dreaminess and an inability to self-manage behavior which often affects social skills and the ability to relate well with others.

These children have special needs in the areas of concentration, attention, distractibility and impulse control; ADHD is generally not identified until kindergarten or later, however, some children show symptoms earlier. As much as 60% of children identified and treated develop self-management skills in adulthood. (Dr. Arjun Reyes, M.D., adult, adolescent and child psychiatrist in private practice in the Los Angeles area, in a personal communication with Renée Berg, August 2001) Social skills & ability to relate to others, particularly in a structured environment are often impaired due to lack of ability to self-manage behavior. Neurodevelopmentally, children may show strengths in higher order cognition and neuromotor functions. However the high level of energy may impair the learner from evidencing these strengths. Often this child is distractible, verbally impulsive, attending to everything. Richard Lavoie points out in his video, *How Difficult Can This Be: F.A.T. City*, 1989, that this child has difficulty tuning attention. He pays attention to everything. The child who attends to nothing, is most probably cognitively impaired. The person with ADHD attends to everything. This distinction must be recognized to best serve a learner with attentional issues.

ADD: better impulse control than ADHD, tendency towards day-dreaminess and distractibility

ADHD: Lacks impulse control, often has unusually high energy

- ❖ Distractibility by outside stimuli
- ❖ Inability to filter out outside stimuli
- ❖ Extremely high energy
- ❖ Poor impulse control
- ❖ Reckless
- ❖ Takes actions impulsively without regard to possible outcomes
- ❖ Highly impulsively verbal, making verbal outbursts without raising hand
- ❖ Needs constant support to stay on task
- ❖ Difficulty recalling directions, particularly if there are multiple steps involved

❖ Difficulty socializing appropriately: fighting, uninvited hugging and touching
❖ Pushing oneself to the head of the line
❖ Difficulty taking turns
❖ Difficulty remaining in seat for any length of time
❖ Lacks perception of other people's needs, wishes, physical space

Developmental Delays

Identification as developmental delayed includes possible cognitive impairment such as mental retardation and Down syndrome. This condition may be characterized by slowed development in all areas which may include all cognitive areas, emotional maturity, social skills, both fine and gross motor skills and the coordination between physical skills. These impairments may be evidenced by difficulties in learning new skills, short duration of attention, high distractibility, difficulty understanding verbal directions, missing social cues and taking social cues literally.

Developmental delays may result in slowing the overall development of a child (physically, emotionally, socially and cognitively) may be from environmental factors, such as lead poisoning. These may improve significantly with appropriate instruction. On the other hand, regarding developmental delays due to genetic factors, appropriate instruction can afford a child the ability to live more independently and utilize the existing intelligence fully. At this time, however, genetic delays cannot be reversed.

All areas of neurodevelopment may be impacted in a child with developmental delays. The task for the support team in this situation is to find the "islands of competence", (Richard Lavoie, *When the chips are down*, 2005b.), the child's areas of strength, and reinforce them. At no time does impaired cognitive ability imply that the person so defined is condemned to a life without meaning.

Mental Retardation: may include other special needs in involving vision, hearing, attention and also seizures

Down Syndrome: (three of the 21st chromosome, are present, as opposed to the normal two): a genetic disability that causes some level of lowered intelligence. Because it is a genetic defect, children with Down syndrome sometimes resemble each other more than they resemble members of their own families. They may also exhibit other types of special needs such as vision, hearing, and attention as well.

❖ Difficulty understanding verbal directions
❖ Difficulty in understanding nonverbal directions
❖ Delays in all motor skills
❖ Difficulty in picking up social cues
❖ Clumsiness, falling, stumbling
❖ Delays in language skills
❖ Difficulty attending to activities
❖ Highly distractible
❖ Inclined to touch and hug others, sometimes inappropriately
❖ Excessive physical energy

Autism and Autism Spectrum Disorders

The determination of Autism Spectrum Disorders (ASD), including autism, Pervasive Developmental Disorder (PDD), and Ausberger's syndrome (also, Childhood Disintegration Disorder and Rett's Disorder), is characterized by slowed language acquisition and echolalic speech and perseveration (repetitive speech patterns). These children may be very sensitive to sensory input: loud sounds (including music), touch, and unfamiliar tastes may produce upset behaviors. Behaviors may seem appropriate for a younger child (i.e., the chronological age does not match the mental age of the child). Children may be identified with PDD /autism and may have an intelligence range anywhere from low to higher than average.

In addition, special needs involving slowed language acquisition and quality can impair the development of social skills and general social cognition, since most social rules are transmitted through language and verbal interaction. Because of this, the individual may often have the need for the security of a very consistent structure (Obsessive Compulsive Disorder - OCD). Individuals with this anxiety disorder often exhibit continually recurring thoughts, excessive and repetitive mannerisms, a desire for sameness and inflexibility to change (e.g.: repeated and unnecessary washing of hands, an overwhelming desire to line objects, such as shoes, in a perfect row).

Children with autism frequently are resistant to new experiences in general, and sensory experiences in particular. One good aspect of extended projects is that they do happen over a long period of time, so the child will have ample opportunity to become familiar with a project. (Dr. Bruce Perry, *Safe From the Start.* Video of the May 2000 symposium)

Neurodevelopmentally children with autism will focus upon certain sequential and spatial orders, perhaps to excess. However if recognized, that focus may be utilized to the student's learning advantage. If the child has focused on a particular body of information to be acquired, the child will remember that information well. Children may have difficulty diversifying attention, may be slow to acquire language, which would tend to slow production of language. Generally children with autism have lower body awareness, and would do well with inclusion of motor activities to increase body awareness. Since much of socialization occurs within language, both spoken and implied, these children may have social challenges, and may benefit from direct instruction regarding social cognition. These students take verbal communication at face value. Generally children with these challenges do not understand jokes, and subtleties within communication. Children with autism may be able to come up with some very interesting, inspired solutions to creative challenges, since people with these characteristics are often "inside their own head" rather than in the world.

- ❖ Impaired ability to use oral language for appropriate communication
- ❖ Extreme withdrawal
- ❖ Impaired understanding of social cognition
- ❖ Relating to people inappropriately
- ❖ Interpersonal and intrapersonal disconnect relating to socio-cultural habits and behaviors
- ❖ Obsession to maintain sameness
- ❖ Extreme preoccupation with objects
- ❖ Inappropriate use of objects
- ❖ Extreme resistance to controls

❖ Motoric mannerisms and motility patterns
❖ Difficulty making eye contact
❖ Self-stimulating
❖ Ritualistic behavior
❖ Delayed motor development
❖ Difficulty staying on task if task is unappealing to child
❖ Is resistant to participating in new activities

Visual Impairments

Visual impairment includes possible reduced quality of vision and the ability to use visual stimuli and information in the process of learning, ranging from a need for corrective lenses to total blindness. Visual impairments may be also associated with other special needs such as hearing loss, mental retardation or cerebral palsy.

Neurodevelopmentally, an individual with visual impairments only would need to acquire information through media other than that which is in print. However, accommodated visual impairments would not necessarily impact attention, memory, temporal ordering, language, social cognition or higher order cognition. There may be an impact on neuromotor functions. It is important to maintain consistency in the room arrangement and school environment to allow the child to be as independent as possible. It is also important not to walk up from behind as that may startle the person. There may be challenges in social cognition, depending upon the temperament of the child. Projects requiring spatial understanding may need some changes. Adjusting an activity so that it utilizes touch instead of sight, will include this child more fully.

❖ Difficulty seeing under average conditions
❖ Difficulty seeing colors in the red or green range (color blindness)
❖ Difficulty seeing fine print or small images even with corrective lenses
❖ Difficulty seeing in bright or low lighting situations
❖ Difficulty seeing in "back lit" conditions
❖ Difficulty discriminating properties of an item visually
❖ Sees better using peripheral (side) vision
❖ Holds objects in close range
❖ Rubs eyes often
❖ Startles easily
❖ Moves around classroom carefully
❖ Has difficulty finding way around classroom
❖ Is hesitant about participating in new activities

Orthopedic Impairments

Orthopedic impairments are often readily apparent. These special needs are usually identified by the medical and school systems. It is unlikely that the teacher will be the initial person to discover these special needs. Severe burns, arthritis, seizure disorders, cerebral palsy, polio, and severely broken bones are part of this group.

Neurodevelopmentally, as stand alone diagnoses, orthopedic impairments, will have little or no impact upon attention, memory, spatial ordering, temporal sequential ordering, language, or higher order cognition unless the presence of pain, discomfort, or use of medications has a negative impact upon the student's learning. Certainly children with this diagnosis will be challenged in the area of neuromotor function, depending on the specific nature of the orthopedic impairment. This child may feel excluded depending on the classroom culture created by the teacher. Depending upon the duration and manner in which this student's impairment occurred, this child may feel a certain level of anger and/or resentment related to it. The presence of this anger may have an impact upon the child's ability to maintain social healthy interactions.

- ❖ Limited physical mobility whether in the use of small muscles of the hands and fingers or of the large muscles of the arms legs and torso
- ❖ Difficulty staying upright
- ❖ Difficulty changing physical position unassisted
- ❖ Inability to sit
- ❖ Inability to walk
- ❖ Difficulty holding head up
- ❖ Joint pain
- ❖ Physical deformities that impair movement
- ❖ Tires easily
- ❖ Muscle shaking, spasms, tics

Gifted and Talented Education (GATE)

Children who are "Gifted and Talented" (GATE) may be able to complete academic tasks with great ease, and may need further academic stimulation to keep them engaged. On the other hand, these same children may show evidence of **dysemia**, an inability to pick up social cues, or may have other special needs in the area of **social cognition**. Offering these children tasks that require learning to work well with others, to develop skills outside of their academic gifts, will help them to become successful, well-rounded human beings. Some intellectually gifted children are disconnected from their bodies. In this situation, opportunities for movement, music, and feeling comfortable playing for the fun of it may be strategies to consider.

When enriching activities for GATE children, be aware that the rest of the class may misperceive enrichment for the bestowing of privileges. That misperception could have a deleterious impact upon the classroom community and the child's place in the social community. Teachers will want to set up the classroom culture to embrace each learner's unique contribution to the community, by finding areas in which each one has unique talents to offer, rather than just singling out gifted children. Gifted children, indeed all children, need to have a sense of belonging in the classroom and in the school community.

- ❖ Cognitive ability more than 10% above average
- ❖ Completes academic tasks significantly before classmates
- ❖ Requires additional enrichments to sustain interest in academic material
- ❖ May have challenges in socialization; making, maintaining and keeping ongoing friendships

❖ May have challenges in areas of physical fitness

❖ May be sedentary

English Language Learners (ELL)

English language learners are in almost every public classroom in America. In a research forum (March 4, 2005) at California State University, Northridge, Dr. Kenji Hakuta, Dean of Social Sciences, UC Merced, pointed out that language-teaching strategy is not the primary element that has an impact upon an individual's quality of acquisition of English in grades K - 12. Rather, the primary factor impacting the quality of acquisition is the socioeconomic status of the family.

Families with more resources generally reflect a higher level of parental education, which will impact the learning environment in the home. Often non-English speaking parents feel isolated from the general community, and are reluctant to venture into the general population. In this case, the teacher needs to consider that the teacher may be their only liaison for the extended family into the general community. If possible, have used books in a "lending library" for children to "borrow" and take home. If these books are picked up at yard sales and library sales, they will be quite inexpensive, and therefore the return of them is less crucial. Creating a structure for resources and enrichments may be the key to successful acquisition of English.

Neurodevelopmentally, English language learners are much like other average students. People who are learning a new language may not understand the subtleties of that language. Certainly, learning appropriate social cognition will accompany moving from one linguistic community to another as discussed in the theories of Lev Vygotsky. He pointed out that transmission of culture occurs within social and linguistic interaction, in other words that culture is socially mediated (Berk, 2005). These students will need to learn how to function in the school's academic culture, the classroom culture, and the culture of the newly adopted community. In the process of presenting language to these children, direct instruction related to social behaviors and linguistic nuances should be included.

When ELL children begin to venture into using new languages, acknowledge them. A child's willingness to attempt and venture to use language is much more significant than the immediate production of the correct usage. Be sure to set up the environment to support that initiative. Harkening back to embracing mistakes and risk taking, teachers absolutely must set these children up to feel comfortable using English. Progress will be much faster if children feel safe expressing themselves and trying out new words.

❖ English is not the language native to the child

❖ English may/may not spoken in the home

❖ Parents may or may not speak English

❖ Parents may or may not be literate in native language

❖ Child is either immigrant or first generation American born

❖ Parents may have lower income

❖ Parents may have a lower level of education

❖ Culturally family may not be similar to culture of the school system

❖ Parents may be intimidated by the teacher or school system

❖ Children may not be outgoing in class due to home culture and family attitudes toward academic relationships

❖ Children may not understand the nature of the classroom culture

❖ Children may not get academic support in the home environment

Chapter Six

Accommodations for Learning Diversity

Most people believe that fairness means that everyone gets the same treatment, when, in fact, real fairness would imply that everyone would get what he or she really needs. ... In other words, the 'squeaky wheel gets the grease' because, in reality, the other three wheels are just fine and don't need the attention. You can ignore the behavior, but you cannot ignore the need.

– Richard Lavoie, M.A., M.Ed.
Beyond F.A.T. City: A Look Back and a Look Ahead.
(F.A.T.: Frustration, Anxiety and Tension, 2005a)

Below are lists of accommodations for diverse learning styles and abledness. Teachers may want to peruse all the sections for accommodations, as every child's needs, whether identified or not, are unique. It does not matter where an educator finds a strategy if it works to support the child in the process of learning successfully. The role of a teacher is to be the primary support system for children in the process of learning.

Within the breadth of the curriculum, all children will be found to have strengths and weaknesses. Children will understand that, at any time, there will be some kids who may have needs that are greater than those of others.

As Dr. Mel Levine's work has shown, (2002) not all learning needs are the same, even if the children in question have the same diagnosis. Certainly many accommodations are frequently applicable, though not necessarily universally appropriate. Teachers may find that some accommodations will turn out to be great teaching strategies that are useful to all students.

ADHD: Attention Deficit Hyperactivity Disorder (ADD, ADHD and behavioral problems)

Issues related to attention are characterized by distractibility, unusually high energy, poor impulse control, lack of concentration, inattention, day-dreaminess. In a structured environment (i.e., a classroom) social skills and the ability to relate to others are often impaired due to lack of ability to self-manage behavior.

❖ General Accommodations

- "Catch child being good" to reinforce desired behaviors; use positive reinforcement (praise) when child behaves appropriately: staying on task, working well with others, sharing, cooperating, cleaning up, negotiates courteously, treats other's ideas with respect, does not blurt out during group discussion, generally show self-control
- Use positive reinforcement when child works well with a partner
- Check on child often, reward increments of achievement
- Have the child act as your helper, setting up or cleaning up activity
- Present activity after child has had time playing outdoors
- Present activity in a less distracting small group situation to keep energy level in control
- Use direct teaching: go over task step-by-step to be sure child understands
- If necessary, before presenting the instructions to the entire class, go over instructions for task using simplified language, to be sure child understands what to do
- Ask the child to repeat the directions/ instructions for an activity, to insure comprehension
- Ask the child to repeat the guidelines for the activity, to make sure that the rules are understood such as "Raise your hand to speak", "Allow others to speak"
- Explain the activity in short, direct sentences, making sure the child maintains eye contact
- Review and re-teach classroom rules on a regular basis
- Use a "designated centers" time so that child will neither avoid nor dominate magnet center during free play
- The level of supervision may need to be increased with high energy activities
- Set the activity up so the child has maximum opportunities to use physical energy
- Be sure to set out materials in an orderly fashion that invites maintenance of the room organization
- Limit the numbers and types of crafts materials to avoid sensory overload
- Place group in which child is participating away from open doors, windows, busy bulletin boards which may distract child from task at hand
- Keep activities shorter at first so child will feel a quick sense of accomplishment
- For activities that require much clean up, allow a longer clean up/transition time
- Present a messy activity in an environment wherein messes aren't a crisis and are easy to clean up

- Use old tee shirts as smocks over child's clothes for freer play with messy activities (for convenience, disposable children's aprons are available very inexpensively through discountschoolsupply.com)
- Lower the ratio of children to adults when necessary
- Use more supervision when child is using laminator or stapler
- Pair child with another child for opportunities for cooperative play
- Have child work in a group of calmer, less impulsive individuals
- Check on children often, to support and encourage appropriate behavior
- When doing group work, have this child work with only one other child to allow many chances to participate
- Offer a smaller selection of materials
- Allow child to get up, stand, move around when not distracting or disturbing to others
- Allow the activity to go on a little longer if child becomes engaged in it
- Offer more time, when necessary, or break activity up into several smaller sessions to help the child to fully focus on the task at hand
- Offer adapted tools when necessary (see pages 593–594 for resources)
- If child has comments or observations to share, give the child the feeling those comments are worthy, take a few moments, it will build self-esteem, and the time shared is the best reward for an ADHD child
- Consider reducing the number of vocabulary words introduced
- Welcome silliness, when possible, as it will ease sense of pressure or performance anxiety
- If an invitational event is being created, offer child tasks that require a high level of energy
- Place splat mats under tables of ingredients or have activity in an area where accidental spills are easily cleaned up
- Remind and use positive reinforcement when child slows pace in cutting and laminating processes
- Remind child of the manner in which the laminator is to be used, request that child repeat instructions back to teacher or supervisory adult
- Allow child to laminate in a lower ratio, small group supervisory structure

❖ **Fine Motor Activities**

- Offer a carrel to reduce distractions
- Decrease number of vocabulary words to know, to write
- Allow child and partner to work within a carrel to reduce distractions
- Allow more time for child to complete activity
- Allow child to work on a tray to manage materials
- Allow child independent time to write/draw observations in note book
- When painting, fill paint dishes with smaller amounts of paint

- Make sure glitter glue pens are unclogged and have an adequate flow of glue to prevent glue splatter caused by frustrated student
- Explain how to open and close containers and jars for craft materials (i.e. paints, glitter glue pens, glue bottles, etc.)
- For scooping activities, offer a wider mouthed plastic jar, perhaps an automotive oil funnel or a scooper that has a narrowed pouring end
- Offer wired ribbon for easier tying and reduced frustration level, if fine motor skills are still emerging

❖ **Gross Motor Activities**

- Present activity in a small group situation so that child has plenty of room to be self expressed without interfering with other children
- Ask the child to repeat the rules of the game, to make sure that the rules are understood
- Make certain that there are sufficient "best" props to go around
- Select music with a cadence that will not over stimulate child
- Use positive reinforcement when child behaves appropriately with others by allowing others' personal space, not bumping into others intentionally or otherwise, sharing props and space fairly
- Focus on using teaching methods that involve more activity: singing, dancing, dramatizing, playing games

Developmental Delays

This designation includes mental retardation and Down syndrome. It is characterized by slowed development in all developmental areas including cognitive, physical coordination of both fine and gross motor skills, emotional maturity and social skills. These behaviors may be exhibited in difficulties with learning new skills, short duration of attention, high distractibility, difficulty understanding verbal directions and weak social cognition, particularly related to picking up social cues.

❖ **General Accommodations**
- Give direct instruction related to social behaviors, review these instructions regularly to ensure understanding and child's ability to produce those social behaviors (this will help child be accepted in the social community of the class/school)
- Explain the activity using short simple phrases
- Go over task more slowly, step-by-step and check for comprehension
- Ask the child to repeat the directions/ instructions for an activity, to insure comprehension
- Demonstrate activity to class, but in close proximity to child
- If necessary, before presenting the instructions to the entire class, go over instructions for task using simplified language, to be sure child understands what to do

- When working with entire class debriefing an experience, call on the child as one of the first: this child may have only one or two possible responses, Allowing child to contribute will help build confidence and self-esteem
- Offer more time
- Teach and review in a small group setting
- Make sure eye contact is made when teaching and reviewing
- Check in with child frequently to note progress with projects, to assess if additional guidance might be needed
- When reading to child, be sure to read slowly and clearly
- Model the project from start to finish for the whole group, & for the child repeat the modeled instructions as needed
- Model actions to be taken, simplifying the activity whenever possible
- Model activity using photographs or realia
- Use simplified language when giving directions & praise
- Limit the numbers and types of crafts materials to avoid sensory overload
- Give authentic praise frequently for incremental achievements
- Use positive reinforcement as the child succeeds in following instructions, counting, creating patterns
- Allow the child to work with simpler patterns
- Lower the ratio to 1 teacher to 2 or 3 children
- Have child work collaboratively with a gentle peer with higher competency as a partner
- Allow child and "buddy" to play at centers for cooperative play and work
- Check on children often, to support and encourage appropriate behavior
- Allow this child to correct his work first
- Allocate more time for activity, when necessary
- Keep activities shorter at first so child will feel a quick sense of accomplishment
- Simplify vocabulary being introduced
- Introduce fewer words each session
- Allow child to work with selected materials on a tray
- Place activity inside a large baking pan or aluminum roasting pan to contain spills
- Place needed materials where they may be easily viewed and accessed by the child
- For an invitational event: have child help with small tasks that the child will find rewarding and that will build self-esteem
- Place splat mats under tables of ingredients or have activity in an area where accidental spills are easily cleaned up
- Present messy activities in an environment wherein messes aren't a crisis and are easy to clean up
- Use old tee shirt as smock over child's clothes for freer play with messy activities
(for convenience, disposable children's aprons are available very inexpensively through discountschoolsupply.com)
- Give children sufficient time to explore materials

- Have smaller work groups
- Allow child to function as a helper
- Simplify tasks: ask child to sort for less complex types of criterion; break activity down into smaller incremental steps rather than attempting to accomplish too much in one session
- Respond to suggestions from child with developmental delays first, as child may have come up with only one or two ideas
- Lower the ratio: use additional supervision when child is using laminator or stapler
- Use adapted tools; for larger materials to be laminated, use menu size laminator pouches (this may require a larger laminator)

❖ Fine Motor Activities

- Make crafting projects on a larger scale with less detail
- Use adapted tools such as padded scissors and glue dispensers, larger, stubby tools, tools with large hand grips (see pages 593–594 for resources)
- Guide child's hand if cutting is a skill in the early stages of development (**only if necessary**)
- Offer materials in larger sizes and shapes that are easier for the child to manipulate
- Use larger letters to trace
- Simplify words for spelling or vocabulary
- Offer a reference card that has vocabulary words on it so the child can include those words in writing activities
- Use primary picture paper for pages of journal for easier journaling (see Appendix A-2)
- Offer large size graph paper for math and planning activities (see pages 594 for on-line resources)
- Consider having child's journal in a three ring binder so child can write on individual sheets of paper
- When painting, fill paint dishes with smaller amounts of paint
- Use larger printed out letters so child can cut them out easily
- If assembling the project becomes too frustrating for the child, assist child to assemble with hand over hand method (teacher's hand over child's hand)
- Make sure glitter glue pens are unclogged and have an adequate flow of glue to prevent glue splatter caused by frustrated student
- Explain how to open and close containers and jars for craft materials (i.e. paints, glitter glue pens, glue bottles, etc.)
- Provide easy to hold utensils, cleaned plastic quart jar, large size crayons to maximize independence
- For pouring activities, offer a small watering type can for easier dispensing
- For scooping activities, offer a wider mouthed plastic jar, perhaps an automotive oil funnel or a scooper that has a narrowed pouring end
- Offer wired ribbon for easier tying if fine motor skills are still emerging
- Use Nancy bottles instead of eye droppers for dispensing colors for activities

❖ **Gross Motor Activities**

- Using an appropriately adjusted vocabulary level, teach and re-teach any vocabulary words from the activity individually or in small groups including lyrics, music genres, names of props, names for movements and movement patterns such as jumping, spinning, skipping, walking, as well as names for body parts such as arms, legs, head and laterality
- Skipping, walking, as well as names for body parts such as arms, legs, head
- Use modeling to communicate vocabulary: e.g.: when jumping, say the word jump
- When appropriate, have children say the words for their movement as part of the activity
- Present movement activities in a small group

Autism Spectrum Disorders

The phrase "Autism Spectrum Disorders" (ASD), is a reference to several disorders, which are all characterized by delays in language and social skills, and by repetitive behaviors. It includes autism, Pervasive Developmental Disorder (PDD), Ausberger's Syndrome, Childhood Disintegration Disorder and Rett's Disorder. Autism is, by far, the most common disorder in this group and is often characterized by slowed language acquisition, as well as perserverative and echolalic speech (repetitive speech patterns). People with autism have a need for consistent structure in their routines and have a very high sensitivity to sensory input of all kinds. They often show evidence of impairment in social skills as well. Their behavior is quite often more appropriate to that of a younger child. A wide range of intelligence is exhibited from one individual to another.

❖ **General Accommodations**

- Have the magnet center set up in class at the beginning of the school session with photographs of teacher and other staff so that the center and the teachers become familiar
- Give direct instruction related to social behaviors, review these instructions regularly to ensure understanding and child's ability to produce those social behaviors (this will help child be accepted in the social community of the class/school)
- Explain the activity using short simple phrases
- When giving instructions, maintain eye contact with child
- Go over task more slowly, step-by-step and check for comprehension
- Ask the child to repeat the directions/ instructions for an activity, to insure comprehension
- If necessary, before presenting the instructions to the entire class, go over instructions for task using simplified language, to be sure child understands what to do
- Demonstrate the activity in advance steps-by-step using realia, photographs for child
- Present activity more than once; use as part of centers routine; this Allows the child to observe activity, and gives the child time to warm up to activity

- To foster familiarity with materials, offer opportunities to work with various media before presenting this activity
- Allow child to become accustomed to the activity by observing others initially, perhaps even doing task with child a day later when it seems more familiar
- Allow child and "buddy" to play at centers for cooperative play and work
- Limit the numbers and types of crafts materials to avoid sensory overload
- Inform child about activity in advance
- Demonstrate the activity in advance steps-by-step using realia, photographs or videos
- Make sure eye contact is made when teaching and reviewing
- Break activity down into several smaller activities
- Keep activities shorter at first so child will feel a quick sense of accomplishment
- Simplify task: ask child to sort for less complex types of criterion
- Reduce the number of letters, numbers, words so child's selection becomes easier
- Offer a more limited selection of art and craft materials, being sure to include types of materials the child particularly likes
- Use positive reinforcement when child participates; notice child's incremental achievements
- Have activity on the calendar and present the activity later in the week so child can become comfortable with the idea
- If child is sensitive to odors, eliminate using the herbal plant matter from the activities
- If child has tactile sensory issues, have sensory activities available in the water table or in plastic basins daily so that the introduction and play with sensory materials is a part of the daily routine
- Allow child to investigate substances in the child's own time: children with autism make an approach to sensory materials cautiously
- Place small amounts of plain cornstarch and the oobleck in plastic bowls to develop a sense of familiarity with the oobleck
- Have moist towelettes or a damp cloth available in case child becomes overwhelmed by the sensory experience
- Have the materials that will be used in upcoming projects available in the classroom so child has an opportunity to see, touch and become accustomed to them; this creates a familiarity that help to reduce anxiety in the child regarding new activities
- Have activities requiring planning and assembly as part of the regular class routine, allowing child to become accustomed to the type of activity
- Adjust the duration of the activity for each session if it appears the child is more or less engaged with it, and have another activity as back up
- Simplify vocabulary being introduced
- Introduce fewer words each session
- Use larger size fonts with language work
- Lower the ratio of teachers to children
- Teach and review in a small group setting

- Re-teach as necessary, modeling to the class, with particular emphasis on connecting with the child with autism
- Have child work with "buddy" instead of small group
- Have child work with regular "buddy" to create a sense of familiarity with classroom and activities (if possible, use the same peer for the child's buddy throughout the semester or school year for additional familiarity, as autistic children resist change)
- Partner up child with a compatible peer so that there are increased opportunities for building socialization skills and language development
- Check on children often, to support and encourage appropriate behavior
- Place splat mats under tables of ingredients or have activity in an area where accidental spills are easily cleaned up
- Offer more time for clean up when working with messy projects
- Offer more time for transitions from one activity to the next
- If child seems to prefer playing with particular substances, offer those substances more frequently
- Have additional water tables, to allow all children opportunities to play with tables, while concurrently allowing additional play time for child with special needs
- Use old tee shirt as smock over child's clothes for freer play with messy activities
- Offer more time if child becomes engaged by activity
- Allow child to wear some kind of gloves, particularly if child has strong sensory issues

❖ Fine Motor Activities

- Allow child to work with softer materials if planned materials would pose a sensory challenge
- Offer adapted tools such as larger scissors, glue dispensers, chunky writing and drawing implements, if necessary (see page 593–594 for resources)
- Adjust size of crafts materials such that they are easily manipulated by the child
- Simplify words for spelling, vocabulary and writing, if necessary
- If name is long or complicated, shorten for purposes of writing activities
- Use primary picture paper for pages of journal for easier journaling (see Appendix A-2)
- Use pocket chart with words likely to be used in journal near child for easier reference (copying)
- When painting, fill paint dishes with smaller amounts of paint
- Make sure glitter glue pens are unclogged and have an adequate flow of glue to prevent glue splatter caused by frustrated student
- Explain how to open and close containers and jars for craft materials (i.e. paints, glitter glue pens, glue bottles, etc.)
- Provide easy to hold utensils, cleaned plastic quart jar, large size crayons to maximize independence
- Offer wired ribbon for easier tying and reduced frustration level

- For scooping activities, Offer a wider mouthed plastic jar, perhaps an automotive oil funnel or a scooper that has a narrowed pouring end

❖ **Gross Motor Activities**

- Using an appropriately adjusted vocabulary level, teach and re-teach any vocabulary words from the activity individually or in small groups including lyrics, music genres, names of props, names for movements and movement patterns such as jumping, spinning, skipping, walking, as well as names for body parts such as arms, legs, head and laterality
- When appropriate, have children say the words for their movement as part of the activity
- Have playing music and dancing part of the daily routine
- Offer fewer props, but be sure the child's favorites are available
- If the child seems to respond to specific or a specific genre of music, use that music regularly
- Check to make sure volume, cadence is not disturbing to child
- Have child dance in small group settings in proximity to "buddy"

Visually Impaired

One is designated "visually impaired" when a reduced quality of vision and a lowered ability to use visual stimuli and information in the process of learning is present. This may range from a need to use corrective lenses to total blindness. Visual impairments may be associated with other special needs such as hearing loss, mental retardation or cerebral palsy.

❖ **General Accommodations**

- Be cognizant of the possible variations of the lighting conditions in the classroom. These may change during different times of the day, and can adversely affect the child's performance of daily activities (i.e., offer alternate places to sit if glare is a potential problem, classroom lights may be brightened or dimmed as needed).
- Use brightly colored materials
- Make labels for classroom furniture in bright, high contrast letters in a large size
- When writing letters to be traced, use a very wide tipped black marker on white card stock (for highest contrast)
- Allow child with visual impairment to have the first (or early) turn in an activity
- Allow child to function as a helper
- Have child work with a gentle peer with higher competency as a partner
- Allow child and "buddy" to play at centers for cooperative play and work
- Check on children often, to support and encourage appropriate behavior
- Allow child to touch physical items when teaching new vocabulary words

- Offer the child a magnifying glass, hand held or on a stand (similar to the ones used for needlework, found in craft stores)
- If necessary, before presenting the instructions to the entire class, go over instructions for task, to be sure child understands what to do
- For activities that require much clean up, there should be a longer clean up / transition time allowed
- Place splat mats under tables of ingredients or have activity in an area where accidental spills are easily cleaned up
- Use old tee shirt as smock over child's clothes for freer play with messy activities
(for convenience, disposable children's aprons are available very inexpensively through discountschoolsupply.com)
- If child has tactile sensory issues, have sensory activities available in the water table or in plastic basins daily so that the introduction and play with sensory materials is a part of the daily routine
- Place small amounts of plain cornstarch and substances such as oobleck in plastic bowls to develop a sense of familiarity
- Allow child to investigate substances in the child's own time: children with visual impairments may be inclined to approach sensory materials cautiously
- Have moist towelettes or a damp cloth available in case child becomes overwhelmed by sensory experiences
- Adjust lighting to reduce glare
- Journaling can be dictated to teacher, paraprofessional, volunteer
- Break the activity up into several sessions, if necessary to make the activity more manageable for the child
- Demonstrate the activity in advance step-by-step using realia photographs
- When presenting activity to the class, use visual images to demonstrate the process of the activity
- Teach and review in a small group setting
- Lower the ratio: use additional supervision when child is using laminator or stapler
- Use adapted tools; for larger materials to be laminated, use menu size laminator pouches (this may require a larger laminator)
- Allocate more time for their activity if necessary, to allow the child to complete work and feel successful
- Change the point size on the font on the computer such that the child can read the text independently
- Change the background on the computer to provide the appropriate contrast for easier reading
- Use large print encyclopedias and dictionaries
- Place materials in the classroom so that they are easily within the range of view of the child with a visual impairment
- Offer child a task for invitational event that plays to child's strengths and builds self esteem

- If outdoors, move the water table or the activity, etc., to a shady area, if possible
- For pouring activities, offer a small watering type can for easier dispensing

❖ **Fine Motor Activities**

- Adjust lighting so child has optimal vision (reduction of glare)
- Make crafting projects with larger materials involving less detail
- Have child work with a partner for projects requiring very fine hand work
- Offer materials in sizes and colors that are easy for child to see and manipulate
- Provide easy to hold utensils, cleaned plastic quart jar, large size crayons to maximize independence
- Use a standing magnifying glass so child can better see the activity or experiment
- Offer larger sized materials: paper, writing or drawing implements (graph paper can be made larger using a photocopy machine)
- Offer large size graph paper for math and planning activities (see pages 594 for on-line resources)
- Use pocket chart with words likely to be used in journal near child for easier reference (copying)
- Let child's hands follow teacher's hands, while teacher demonstrates an activity
- Guide child's hand if necessary, with the hand over hand method with cutting, writing, etc.
- Allow child to make a simpler designs, using fewer and larger pieces
- For scooping activities, offer a wider mouthed plastic jar, perhaps an automotive oil funnel or a scooper that has a narrowed pouring end
- Offer adapted tools such as easy scissors, padded or finger grip glue dispensers, larger winding cards, larger writing tools, ruler with bolder print numbers, and art media (e.g., larger crayons, dot bottles) (see page 593–594 for resources)
- Offer the child a magnifying glass on a stand (similar to the ones used for needlework, found in craft stores)
- Make sure glitter glue pens are unclogged and have an adequate flow of glue to prevent glue splatter caused by frustrated student
- Explain how to open and close containers and jars for craft materials (i.e. paints, glitter glue pens, glue bottles, etc.)
- Use larger sized, bold print on white, matte card stock for the words to be read or traced
- Journaling can be dictated, or primary picture paper may be used for the child's journal for easier writing and drawing (see Appendix A-2)
- Offer adapted tools (e.g., measuring cups) with larger identifying marks in bold simple script
- Simplify words for spelling, vocabulary and writing, if necessary
- Use larger size fonts
- Offer larger bowls, spoons for their use

- Offer wider mouthed funnels and sand toys
- Offer wired ribbon for easier tying
- Use Nancy bottles instead of eye droppers for dispensing colors for activities

❖ **Gross Motor Activities**

- Adjust lighting so child has optimal vision
- Set up environment so it is free of obstacles
- Present movement activities in a small groups
- Allow sufficient space such that the child is less likely to be startled by movements peripherally, outside of visual range, or from behind
- Have child work with a fully sighted "buddy"
- When activities are outdoors, allow the child to wear sunglasses and/or a wide brimmed hat
- Offer binoculars to observe animals
- When playing games and other physical activities, partner child with teammates who are more skilled; coach teammates to make sure that child with visual impairment has opportunities to play

Orthopedic Impairments

Orthopedic impairments include cerebral palsy, spina bifida, polio, seizure disorders, arthritis, and/or resultant impairments from physical injuries. They may be characterized by limited physical mobility in gross or fine motor coordination or both. This child may exhibit difficulties in writing, sitting, standing, walking, holding head up and may be prone to fatigue.

❖ **General Accommodations**

- Make sure child is positioned comfortably, and check on the child from time to time
- Explain the activity using short simple phrases while making eye contact
- Model activity using photographs or realia
- If necessary, before presenting the instructions to the entire class, go over instructions for task, to be sure child understands what to do
- Keep activities shorter at first so child develops confidence and a feeling of success more quickly
- Allocate more time for activity, when child is engaged in it
- Offer more time to complete task, and for clean up if necessary
- Adjust furniture or position materials to make activity easy accessible to student
- Present activity in a small group setting
- Teach and review in a small group setting
- Request that child's group offer orthopedically impaired child a choice of task
- Give child the task in the classroom which will offer the most success

- Use old tee shirt as smock over child's clothes for freer play with messy activities (for convenience, disposable children's aprons are available very inexpensively through discountschoolsupply.com)
- Place splat mats under tables of ingredients or have activity in an area where accidental spills are easily cleaned up
- Present messy activities in an environment wherein messes aren't a crisis and are easy to clean up
- For an invitational event: have child help with small tasks that play to the child's strength, that the child will find rewarding and that will build self-esteem
- Allow child and "buddy" to play at centers for cooperative play and work
- Check on children often, to support and encourage appropriate behavior
- Place activity on a tray for easier individual access;
- Have moist towelettes or a damp cloth available in case child becomes overwhelmed by sensory experiences
- Use bowls with suction cups on the bottom to stabilize them

❖ Fine Motor Activities

- Allow child to work individually or with a partner
- Allow child to use a tray to contain work materials
- Offer adapted tools such as scissors, padded or finger grip glue dispensers, larger winding cards;
- Offer larger eating utensils, spoons and bowls with suction cups on the bottom for better stability;
- For writing: use a clip board with alligator clips on the bottom to secure journal paper
- Use primary picture paper for pages of journal for easier journaling (see Appendix A-2)
- Offer large size graph paper for math and planning activities (see pages 594 for on-line resources)
- Use pocket chart with words likely to be used in journal near child for easier reference (copying)
- Consider having child's journal in a three ring binder so child can write on individual sheets of paper
- Provide easy to hold utensils, cleaned plastic quart jar, large size crayons to maximize independence
- Simplify words for spelling, vocabulary and writing, if necessary
- Use larger size fonts
- Adjust materials and projects to a size which child can manipulate easily
- If child's hands and fingers lack strength or flexibility, guide the child using the hand-over-hand method
- Guide child's hand if cutting is a skill in the early stages of development (**only if necessary**)
- Make sure glitter glue pens are unclogged and have an adequate flow of glue to prevent glue splatter; give assistance when needed

- Explain how to open and close containers and jars for craft materials (i.e. paints, glitter glue pens, glue bottles, etc.) give assistance when needed
- Use padded or thicker stirring tools for easier grasping
- For scooping activities, offer a wider mouthed plastic jar, perhaps an automotive oil funnel or a scooper that has a narrowed pouring end
- Fill paint dishes with smaller amounts of paint
- Offer wired ribbon for easier tying if fine motor skills are still emerging
- Use Nancy bottles instead of eye droppers for dispensing colors for activities
- For pouring activities, offer a small watering type can for easier dispensing

❖ **Gross Motor Activities**

- Set up environment so it is free of obstacles
- Make sure there is sufficient room so child will not be bumped
- If child lacks mobility or strength to move independently, gently assist child in movement, being sensitive to child's movement cues
- Assist child in holding materials when assistance is needed
- When doing movements activities, adjust tempo of music to accommodate child's movement range

Gifted and Talented Education (GATE)

Characterized by cognitive ability of more than 10% above average, this student completes tasks quickly and often requires additional enrichments to sustain interest in classroom material. Sometimes a gifted child may be socially isolated, and thus may not have a working understanding of social cognition. The gifted student may also have less interest in large motor activities and may be inclined towards a more sedentary lifestyle. To become successful and well rounded, they may need encouragement to work well with others and to develop skills outside of academic gifts. Offer activities that involve social interaction at least as much as solo activities and using electronic media are presented.

❖ **General Accommodations**

- Give direct instruction related to social behaviors, and review these instructions regularly to ensure understanding and child's ability to produce those social behaviors. This may help child be accepted in the social community of the class/school. Be sure to explain to child that pointing out "I am highly gifted" may not draw other children into that child's social circle.
- Introduce greater number of vocabulary words
- Introduce more challenging vocabulary
- Have children chart multiple experiments on a bar graph
- Extrapolate possible outcomes for related activities and materials

- Ask the child to draw analogies / similarities between projects they have created, or aspects of their own lives, and that of other historic times, other cultures, stories and mythology
- Present theatrical activities using selected language being studied
- GATE children may have an aptitude for acquiring and speaking language. Enrichments would be related to the type of activities selected to introduce these languages.
- Introducing languages new to child may be a sufficient enrichment
- Ask child to invent games or songs using selected language
- Ask child to describe the smells experienced from the herbs in writing or drawings
- Make an activity more fun and challenging by using a timer to see how quickly child can correctly complete a puzzle, place words or letters, find something in the classroom, and so on.
- Ask child to predict outcomes prior to finishing activity, to attempt to figure out how the process worked based on own ideas and research
- Allow child additional time or allow projects to be done over several sessions so that more intensive work may be done (i.e. more research, more detail)
- Offer child a task for invitational event that plays to child's strengths and builds self esteem
- Allow child to do an activity, and then experiment by using other materials (i.e. using other liquids instead of water to make oobleck: milk, juice, vinegar, borax or liquid soap dissolved in water and so forth) and observe the results
- Ask child to find out rules of debate and explain them to the class

❖ Fine Motor Activities

- Offer more complex patterning
- Offer the child a timer to use, to see how quickly he/she can do a puzzle, create patterns, place or find words, sort objects, etc., to increase awareness and level of difficulty
- Offer unusual materials that can be integrated into their projects and crafts
- Offer more interesting vocabulary and spelling words for journal writing
- Ask child to document data using a bar chart or venn diagram
- Ask child to write or draw pattern found using letters or geometric shapes to represent movements and patterns

❖ Gross Motor Activities

- When doing movement activities, offer music with more complex tempos and patterns
- Ask child to invent movement patterns to match musical patterns
- Ask child to invent movements that (for the child) fit the music
- Allow the child to invent variations on games and movement activities

English Language Learners (ELL)

Students are designated "ELL" when English is not the native language, and proficiency in English is low. English may or may not be spoken in the home, as the parents may or may not speak English. The child is generally an immigrant or first generation American-born.

❖ **General Accommodations**

- Give direct instruction related to cultural aspects of social behaviors, review these instructions regularly to ensure understanding and child's ability to produce those social behaviors (this will help child be accepted in the social community of the class/school). Explain that academic communities from different places may be different as well.
- Explain the activity using short simple phrases, being sure eye contact is made
- If necessary, before presenting the instructions to the entire class, go over instructions for task using simplified language, to be sure child understands what to do
- Go over task more slowly, step-by-step, and check for comprehension
- Ask the child to repeat the directions/ instructions for an activity, to insure comprehension
- Allow child to function as a helper
- Demonstrate the activity in advance steps-by-step using realia, photographs or videos
- If child is willing to participate in the debriefing of the activity, call on child earlier in the discussion to prevent "Someone else took my answer"; being called on early offers more chance of success
- Debrief after activity is completed, to reinforce vocabulary and to check for understanding
- Offer more time for journaling or note taking of activity
- Teach and re-teach vocabulary associated with doll making including: doll, face, head, arms, body, waist, legs, hair, eyes, nose, mouth, clothing words, raffia, ribbon, buttons, glitter, wet, dry, plant words such as lavender or sage, cut, glue
- Label all items in the classroom that can be easily labeled: furniture, tools, art materials, ingredients used in projects, and so on
- Use positive reinforcement when child attempts to integrate new vocabulary into work, whether oral or written
- Simplify vocabulary being introduced
- Review and re-teach vocabulary
- Introduce fewer words each session
- Teach and review in a small group setting
- Allow child and "buddy" to play at centers for cooperative play and work
- Check on children often, to support and encourage appropriate behavior
- Make sure eye contact is made when teaching
- Teach child same songs in English and language being introduced
- Be sure to teach and allow child to participate in teaching child's home language
- Use positive reinforcement when child shares his or her language with the class

- Give child a small list for reference for any writing activity
- For an invitational event: have child help with small tasks that play to the child's strengths, that the child will find rewarding and that will build self-esteem

❖ Fine Motor Activities

Unless there are symptoms of other kinds of special needs, most English Language Learners will not have specific difficulties with fine motor skills. If needed, check specific activities for suggestions for further accommodations.

❖ Gross Motor Activities

- Teach and re-teach any vocabulary words from the activity individually or in small groups including lyrics, names of props, names for movements and movement patterns such as jumping, spinning, skipping, walking, as well as names for body parts such as arms, legs, head and laterality
- Use modeling to communicate vocabulary: for example, when jumping, say the word "jump"
- When appropriate, have children say the words for their movement as part of the activity
- Model how to play games while explaining the rules

Chapter Seven

The Learning Plan

"Education should consist of a series of enchantments, each raising the individual to a higher level of awareness, understanding, and kinship with all living things."

— Anonymous

Section One

Creating a Learning Plan

There are many "lesson" or "learning" plan styles. The five step and seven step are the most well known. Use a planning system that works for you. A learning plan is a **tool for the teacher** to organize and prepare activities for the classes taught. A written out learning plan is a convenient way to share effective activities with other teachers. The format that helps best present an activity to students is the best plan format for the teacher. Try different types of learning plans to see which works best.

The learning plan in this book has eleven steps. Initially using this form may take more effort than using other activity plans as it considers learning, assessment, California Standards met, and accommodation for diversity. However, when the teacher has all the relevant information in one place at one time, it will be far easier for everyone, including the teacher, to enjoy the activity fully (Appendix C @ www.cambriapress.com/kindergarten references content standards to activities).

Spaces for the teacher to recommend a teacher to child ratio, IV, (shown 1: 3, or 1: 10 et cetera) have been added. The ratio always indicates the teacher as "1" to the number of children for whom that teacher or adult is responsible. Let's say there is a classroom with a teacher, an assistant teacher, and a paraprofessional aide in a class of fifteen children. The ratio would not be three to fifteen but one to five (1: 5). When considering presenting a very low ratio activity, like carpentry that requires a 1: 1 or 1: 2 ratio, and the daily teacher to student ratio is 1: 7, at least three adult volunteers would be needed to present carpentry. Knowing the number of adult volunteers that are needed for an activity before the day of presentation is a very important part of preparing for an activity.

Never leave the children in the unsupervised care of volunteers.

Parts V and VI (targeted areas of learning and evaluation) are added so that an educator may consider which presentation of the activity will best communicate the chosen targeted area of learning and how to evaluate the learning associated with the activity. As a teacher, knowing the desired learning for an activity presented will empower you as an educator. "Why is your class doing this?" is a perfectly legitimate question, deserving a thoughtful response. "Keeping the children busy" is not an acceptable answer for most parents, not to mention one's administrators.

There are five general learning areas, or domains: emotional development, social development, cognitive development, physical development, and creative expression. The activities in this book are primarily aimed at cognitive, or intellectual, learning. Nearly all activities presented in a classroom touch more than one of the domains of learning. For example, a math patterning activity involving the stringing of colored macaroni also involves eye-hand coordination and the fine motor skill of stringing the pasta. The socialization skill of following directions would also be included. When more than one child is working on a project, the socialization skills of sharing and cooperation are added. The teacher does not need to write out every area of learning that an activity could potentially offer to the children. Identify the targeted areas of learning to be emphasized, and which will then be used to evaluate the children's growth.

When writing out a targeted area of learning, break the general learning areas down specifically, such as: cognitive (domain): math (learning area): patterning (specific activity). By identifying the domain (cognitive), the curricular area (math), and the skill (patterning) the teacher will have definitive structure for planning, presentation, and evaluation. Should it become necessary to discuss the activity or evaluation with an administrator or a parent, the teacher will have resources at hand to speak with confidence in that regard.

"Why did you give my child a 'D'?" is another question the teacher should be prepared to address as well. Contrary to popular misconception, evaluation in education is not written in concrete, is not hard and fast, and is not objective. Human educators do the evaluations, complete with opinions, judgments, preconceived ideas, and misconceptions. Evaluation, therefore, has a good degree of subjectivity to it. With training and experience, we hope that the teacher's *subjective* judgment becomes *educated subjective* judgment.

Creating a rubric prior to presenting an activity will allow the teacher to structure subjective assessment so that it can be consistent, and as objective as possible. **A rubric is a step chart describing expectations of the learners for an activity.** Nonetheless, understand as the teacher evaluates, the background of education and growing experience does give the teacher the right to evaluate learning. People evaluate all the time. Teachers get to put their evaluations on a report card that can follow a student for a lifetime. Evaluate responsibly.

Another reason to evaluate young children's learning is to help plan the curriculum to match learning levels and to place children in appropriate academic environments. If all the children whip through the activities presented, the teacher needs to offer more challenging material closer to the students' academic level. If one or two are skating through, perhaps even bored, they might need a more challenging environment or enrichments. On the other hand, if the class is struggling with the materials presented, perhaps the teacher needs to break the curriculum down into more steps, or find curriculum more suitable for the students' level of learning. If most of the class can handle the work, but one child is consistently over his/her head, it may be time to consider putting the child into a class closer to his/her learning level or possibly think about having the child evaluated for possible special needs.

For some parents, discussing the possibility that their child may have special needs is difficult. They may interpret the teacher's concerns for their child as a reflection upon themselves as parents, as genetic material, or they may fear that their child will be stigmatized by being identified as having special needs. The teacher can help parents understand that identifying a child's special learning needs as early as possible will help improve their child's fit into the regular class. A parallel can be drawn between going to a tailor and fitting a garment, to offering a child special services early in their learning career. If one takes a little of the structure of the curriculum in here, and lets it out somewhere else, the educational fit will be better. Their child will be much more likely to get good use and wear from his/her education. A child struggling to keep up may develop self-esteem issues, feel that s/he is "just stupid" or a failure, become disruptive, and/or give up on the educational process entirely. Richard Lavoie, (2005a.) points out in, reference to acting out and inappropriate behavior, that "children will choose to look bad, rather than to look dumb" in front of their peers.

What a tragedy it would be for a child to misperceive learning uniqueness as a lack of inherent ability to succeed in school, and worst of all, perhaps even in life. Self-perception of ability to succeed or not often develops while an individual is in grade school. So, most important of all, when special support is in place, the child will feel better about the process of learning, and therefore, about him / herself as a person as well.

There are so many wonderful support systems, medications, and strategies for children with special needs that often by the middle to late teen years or by early adulthood, behavioral evidence of the special need may be undetectable. Even if not, ongoing support can enable a child with special needs to internalize healthy coping mechanisms to empower him / her to have a meaningful life.

Part IX of the learning plan considers how best to include all children. Accommodating for human diversity is both educational courtesy, and in the case of children with identified special needs, a requirement of federal law. The Internet offers a wealth of knowledge on the subject of accommodation for special needs. Some basic suggestions for changes to academic activities are discussed in the chapter on accommodation, but the best advice is to know your students. Each child in the class is a unique individual. As the teacher prepares curriculum, think of *all* the children in the class. The chances for a successful outcome for the project will increase when it is planned for the students in that specific class. Dr. Mel Levine, author of *A Mind at a Time* (2002), Richard La Voie, presenter, on working with children with specific learning disabilities (available in DVD form; *How Difficult Can This Be? F.A.T. City, 1989,* and *When the Chips are Down*, 2005, are excellent), and learning theorist Dr. Howard Gardner all emphasize learning uniqueness. Teachers who recognize that every human being is unique in all ways, including learning, are far more likely to successfully reach students in their charge. When planning, merely taking into consideration that a child is painfully shy or utterly without fear (neither of which is an identified learning disability on its own), might have a huge impact on the learning either of those students might gain from participating.

When planning, be mindful of the people being taught.

For example, a child with symptoms of unmedicated ADHD (Attention Deficit Hyperactivity Disorder) will need close supervision. The teacher may need to lower the ratio in the class often. ADHD children have very high energy, poor impulse control, are often quite verbal, and need constant support to stay on task. The teacher may need to break down directions into smaller steps and repeat them frequently.

Asking the child to repeat instructions back often works well. Catch the child being good, for often the highly impulsive child doesn't get enough positive reinforcement. People respond to praise better than to criticism or correction. Praise can be a very high motivator. Praise will result in the child's increased efforts. There is a very good chance an ADHD child has often gotten more criticism than praise. Authentic praise could be an opening for a partnership. The child will want to continue to please the teacher, and within that safe partnership the child can learn to internalize behavior management. While planning the curriculum, be mindful of this child's needs. By possibly soliciting parent volunteers, increasing the amount of time allotted for activities, and allowing extra moments to interact with this child individually, there will be a better experience for everyone in the class.

No matter what grade level taught, organizing the activities for the class will also help the teacher to organize thoughts. It also clarifies the objectives planned for that particular activity with that particular group of people. Even a simple activity like the Hokey Pokey, for example, could be presented with an emphasis on creating a community and socialization OR to have a focus on teaching laterality (right from left). Knowing what result is intended will help the teacher to decide on the presentation of any given activity.

Creating a learning plan in advance also helps the teacher to organize materials, and brings it to the front of your thoughts. If the teacher should happen to see a book or another activity that would further enhance the learning from this activity, it can then be incorporated into the plans. A learning plan can also be an outline for a mental rehearsal of an activity. In *Peak Performance* (1984, *16*), Dr. Charles Garfield cited a study that compared four groups of Soviet athletes, one group only doing physical practice, the other three practicing respectively 25 % mental practice, 75 % physical practice; 50 %/50% mental and physical practice, and 75% mental, 25% physical practice. Amazingly, the group that performed the best was the group who did 75% mental rehearsal. As teachers, mentally planning events may impact the quality and results of the activities presented students.

With student teachers, all learning plans need to be presented in writing.

These are basic ideas that should be included in this learning plan:

I. **Name of activity**

II. **Age or grade level for which activity is suitable**

III. **Date of Presentation**

IV. **Teacher to Student Ratio**
     Always shown as 1 (teacher / adult) to number of children assigned to 1 teacher (1: 7 or 1:10), never as 2 (teachers): 20 (children).

V. **Target Areas of Learning / Goals and Objectives**
     On which learning areas do you choose to focus the activity? Not all areas of learning will be covered in every activity. **The goals/learning areas are directly related to evaluation**, which is to say, if you choose a particular target area / skill, how do you assess a child's developing skill in that area? Consider this when choosing

learning areas. There are lists of learning areas in *Chapter Three: Targeted Areas of Learning*. Use that chapter as a reference.

a. **Physical Development**: fine and gross motor skills; sensory experience; eye-hand coordination; balance; auditory and visual discrimination
b. **Cognitive Development**: thinking and reasoning skills; language and literacy; problem solving skills; independent and divergent thinking
c. **Social Development**: creating relationships; developing social skills; cooperative learning; sharing, becoming a community
d. **Emotional Development**: building self-esteem, expressing feelings in an acceptable way; stress relief; personal behavior management skills
e. **Creative Expression**: verbal/nonverbal expression: art, music, dance

VI. **Evaluation Rubric**

This is the measure you use to evaluate a student's progress in any given activity. The **rubric** form is often used if you need to assign a numerical / letter grade to the child's growth in any activity. The best-known rubric form is the A, B, C, D, F, and I (incomplete) (five levels of achievement) format. E (excellent), S (satisfactory), U (unsatisfactory) (three levels) and 4, 3, 2, 1 (four levels) are other forms. If report cards or evaluation forms are sent home, the school district or administrators choose the form in which children are evaluated. The teacher's job is to put the form into use and evaluate the child or student's progress in any learning area as it relates to the standards set by the teacher or the administrator.

A teacher can help identify an area in which a child needs additional support. That identification and additional early support might make a life changing difference for the child relating to his or her future success in school. When support strategies are constructed at an early age, children may better learn to cope with differences in their individual learning styles, and the ever increasing demands upon young people academically.

When children receive needed support in learning at an early age, they feel better about themselves. The self-esteem shattering feelings of being less intelligent, less capable than the peers doesn't come up for children who are getting additional support in certain areas of learning. Used properly, evaluation can be an instrument to support identification of need and in support of learning, and to nurture a positive self-image and healthy self-esteem.

A **rubric** is the measurement instrument, or standards, that the teacher uses to evaluate growth in the learning areas targeted by any given activity. For example, if the teacher brings a rabbit into the class to enhance nurturing behaviors in the children, what behavioral landmarks would one look for to evaluate if having the rabbit is actually producing the desired behavioral goals in the children?

Identify at least three to five levels of growth for each targeted area of learning

For example:

Target area of learning
nurturing behaviors: gentleness with small animals
    4. Spontaneously gentle with rabbit
    3. Needs a few reminders to be gentle with the rabbit
    2. Needs constant reminders to be gentle with the rabbit
    1. Is not gentle with rabbit

A spreadsheet or list rubric format can be used. Microsoft Word and Excel, as well as AppleWorks and iWorks, all have templates for lists and spreadsheets. Try both the list and spreadsheet forms to see what works best as an assessment tool.

VII. Materials and Preparation

This section needs to be easy to read. Presenting it in a list form will make it easier to repeat/share the activity. Include in this section the following information:

   a. Materials needed
   b. Space required
   c. Advance preparation and set up required

VIII. Procedures

A list of steps makes this easier to understand. The procedures list is a plan of actions with the children. Include what the volunteers will be doing, and when. In the case of volunteers, if it is the teacher's activity, the teacher needs to be in charge, including acting as the coordinator of the volunteers, and the activity.

   a. **Description of activity**: steps to actually do the activity in class
   b. **Major ideas to bring up in the activity**
   c. **Closure** (ending the activity): discussion of major relevant learning points
   d. **Clean up**: involving children in the clean up of an activity teaches many concepts as well; responsibility for one's own environment; how to clean up different kinds of mess; a sense of community.

IX. Accommodations (for children with diverse learning needs)

By federal law children with special needs are to be educated in the **least restrictive environment** (LRE). When planning, take into consideration the adaptations that can be made to the activity so that children with diverse learning styles and levels of abledness can participate fully in the activity. Sometimes creating accommodations will take much thought, creativity, and preparation. For a child in a wheelchair, the aisles would have to be wider and height of the tables will need to be adjusted. A child with ADHD would need to be placed near the teacher or paraprofessional; the bulletin boards would need to be non-distracting. An ADHD child should not be placed near a window or a door, as the outside world can be a tempting distraction for a person with that disability. A gifted child would need enrichments, and a child learning English would have to have a focus on developing language skills.

X. Applicable Framework Standards

This book is based upon the framework standards for the state of California. Other state framework standards are similar. The goal of these standards is to determine the competency level expected of a student at the end of the academic year. For example, when a student has completed Kindergarten, it is expected that this student will be able to "Identify & sort common words in basic categories (e.g. colors, shapes, foods)" [California State Board of Education Kindergarten English-Language Arts Content Standards. Vocabulary and Concept Development: 1.17. Adopted December 1997 (http://www.cde.ca.gov/be/st/ss/engkindergarten.asp)]

XI. Evaluation and Comments

    a. How well did the plan work? Great responses?

    b. What aspects are especially effective? Not effective?

    c. What improvements are needed?

    d. Ideas for follow up activities

    e. Other notes

Chapter Seven
part 2

The Learning Plan

"Authentic play, which occurs whenever the playfulness itself gives more pleasure than any goal associated with it, is the means by which adaptability and flexibility are added to the player's existence. Thus play serves as the grounding core of learning."
– Dr. Stuart L. Brown, Founder of the Institute for Play
Play –Evolutionary, Universal & Essential (para. 8)

Section Two

Customizing Learning Plans

The intention of **Practical Kindergarten** is to simplify the process of integrating hands-on, process-based activities for general education teachers. It may seem that there is much to consider using this particular plan, as, initially, none of it may appear simple. For this, we apologize. This plan has been designed to be a comprehensive document in an easily assembled form, that will meet both educational and administrative concerns.

There are the skeletons for the learning plans in the book and on the website (see: www.cambriapress.com/kindergarten) containing the grade level, recommended ratio for the activity, materials and preparation required as well as step-by-step instructions for presenting any given activity.

Step One

Select an activity from the book to present to the class. Go to the website and open the basic learning plan document for the activity. "Journaling" is the sample for this section (see sample plan, pages 77-79).

Step Two

Locate the "Targeted Areas of Learning" section in both the activity plan description (in the book, page 92 for "Journaling") and the corresponding learning plan web document. Choose areas of learning that might be outside of the state standards. This allows a teacher to consider a broader range of diverse learning needs in any given group of children. Not all learning needs are described in the state standards.

Five target areas of learning have been selected for this sample, from pages 94–96. However, a teacher may choose as many or as few areas as seem appropriate.

The sample target learning selections are:
    Physical: fine motor: holding and using implements for writing and drawing
    Cognitive: sequencing: recalling events in temporal order
    Social: following instructions: using tools as directed (writing, and art)
    Emotional: naming human feelings: learning to identify and express emotions
    Creative: expression of self: expressing feelings through the use of art media
        Save the document.

Step Three

After target learning has been selected, a teacher may choose to evaluate those areas. For the purposes of *Practical Kindergarten* a four to one scale has been chosen, but the standard evaluation rubric used in the district may be substituted. The sample plan has selected two areas for evaluation as seen below:

Targeted Area of Learning:
    Cognitive: sequencing: recalling
    order of events
        4. Always recalls order of events
        3. Usually recalls order of events
        2. Sometimes recalls order of events
        1. Rarely recalls order of events

Targeted Area of Learning:
    Emotional: naming feelings:
    identifying emotions
        4. Always able to identify emotions
        3. Usually able to identify emotions
        2. Sometimes able to identify emotions
        1. Rarely able to identify emotions

When evaluating state standards on a four to one scale, a teacher uses the format
    4 - Exceeds standard, **3** - Meets standard, **2** - Standard emerging, and **1** - Standard not yet seen.

Teachers may also want to evaluate learning that is not described in state standards, and feel that measuring the children's progress in those particular areas is important for the children's overall academic growth.
    Save the document.

Step Four

Scroll past **VII. Materials and Preparation Needed:** and **VIII. Procedures** in the learning plan. Both areas have been assembled, and are not likely to change from presentation to presentation.

Step Five

In the learning plan document, scroll down to:
    IX. Accommodations (changes to accommodate learning diversity)
    Name of Accommodated Area

In the book, for the activity plan, locate:
    Possible Accommodations for this Activity (for "Journaling", see pages 96-98)

To complete this section, a teacher will need to be aware of the learning needs of the children in the class. Whether the child has a learning profile, an identified diagnosis or, in the judgment of the teacher, an academic need requiring instructional adjustment, is not as important as selecting the strategies to enable that child to succeed while participating in an activity.

Read through the possible accommodations in the activity plan, and choose as many or as few as seem appropriate for both the students and the activity in the context within which it is being presented.

Step Six

"Enter the name of accommodated area and accommodations for the customized learning plan. "Visually Impaired" has been selected for this sample (see pages 97–98).

IX. Accommodations (changes to accommodate learning diversity)

Name of Accommodated Area: Visually Impaired: including reduced quality of vision and the ability to use visual stimuli and information in the process of learning; may range from a need for corrective lenses to total blindness; may be associated with other special needs such as hearing loss, mental retardation or cerebral palsy.

1. Adjust the lighting to reduce glare
2. Allow child to select a color of paper that makes seeing easier
3. Offer writing and drawing instruments that make larger bolder marks (e.g., larger crayons, dot bottles)
4. Make available the use of a magnifying glass on a stand (similar to ones used for fine needle work found in craft stores)
5. Offer primary writing paper with wider lines if needed
6. Offer bright colors of media for writing and drawing; these allow for better contrast, than paler pastel colors
7. Allow the child to have more time to finish, if necessary, so that the child can complete work and feel successful
8. Check on child frequently, and give positive reinforcement for incremental achievements

Save the document.

Step Seven

In the learning plan form, scroll down to:

X. Applicable Framework Standards: Kindergarten

and in the book, locate **"Content Standards for Kindergarten Met by This Activity"** in the activity plan description (standards for "Journaling" are found on pages 98–99). Consider which content standards need to be emphasized in this activity. Enter the selected standards into the custom learning plan document.

The sample document selected the following:

X. Applicable Framework Standards: Kindergarten

English-Language Arts

Reading (1.0, 1.1, 1.2, 1.3, 1.4, 1.5, 1.6, 1.7, 1.8, 1.9, 1.14, 1.15, 1.16, 1.17, 1.18)

Writing (1.0, 1.1, 1.2, 1.3, 1.4)
Written and Oral English Language (1.0, 1.1, 1.2)
Listening and Speaking (1.0, 1.1, 1.2)
Mathematics
Numbers and Counting (1.0, 1.2)
Algebra and Sorting (1.0, 1.1)
Measurement and Geometry (1.0, 1.2, 1.3, 1.4)
Statistics (1.0, 1.1)
Science
Physical Science (1.a)
Life Science (2.a)
Earth Science (3.a, 3.b)
Investigation and Experimentation (4a, 4b, 4d, 4e)
History and Social Science
Following Rules (K.1, K.1.1)
Visual Arts
Artistic Expression (1.0, 1.1, 1.2, 1.3)
Creative Expression (2.0, 2.1, 2.4, 2.5, 2.6)
Save the document. Print the document.

Step Eight

Finally, after presenting the activity, the teacher may want to reflect on the success of the presentation, and make notations about possible insights about the activity for future reference in the **"Evaluation and Comments"** section of the learning plan.

Save the document.

Learning Plan

   I. Name of Activity: Journaling

  II. Date of Presentation:

 III. Age or Grade Level: Pre-k to Primary

 IV. Ratio of teachers to children needed for this activity: 1:6
      (An excellent kidney-shaped table activity)

  V. Target Areas of Learning / Goals and Objectives (target areas of learning directly relate to "VI. Evaluation Rubric")
      Physical: fine motor: holding and using implements for writing and drawing
      Cognitive: sequencing: recalling events in a temporal order
      Emotional: naming human feelings: learning to identify and express emotions
      Social: following instructions: using tools as directed (writing and art)
      Creative: expression of self: expressing feelings through the use of art media

 VI. Evaluation Rubric: (if more than two learning areas are being evaluated, a spreadsheet form may be preferred)

Targeted Area of Learning	Targeted Area of Learning
Cognitive: sequencing: recalling order of events	**Emotional: naming feelings:** identifying emotions
4. Always recalls order of events	**4.** Always able to identify emotions
3. Usually recalls order of events	**3.** Usually able to identify emotions
2. Sometimes recalls order of events	**2.** Sometimes able to identify emotions
1. Rarely recalls order of events	**1.** Rarely able to identify emotions

VII. Materials and Preparation Needed for Reflection Journals
    1. Writing and drawing implements: crayons, pens, colored markers, colored pencils
    2. Children will use their own journals,
    3. Or children can use plain, line or primary paper

VIII. Procedures
    1. Offer the class a brief period of time each day for personal writing. Initially allow five minutes, if you see that your students are engaged by the activity as time goes on, allow additional time. The first thing in the morning is a wonderful time for journal activities, as it allows the children to settle in, to get into the mood of the school day.
    2. Have a selection of writing and drawing implements (e.g., crayons, markers, colored pencils) available either at the writing center or at each child's desk.
    3. Let the children write about the topic selected, **or** let children decide on a topic

4. Later on in the day, or week, offer children an opportunity share their journal writing with the class, if they choose.

IX. **Accommodations** (changes to accommodate learning diversity)
Name of Accommodated Area: Visually Impaired: including reduced quality of vision and the ability to use visual stimuli and information in the process of learning; may range from a need for corrective lenses to total blindness; may be associated with other special needs such as hearing loss, mental retardation or cerebral palsy.
1. Adjust the lighting to reduce glare
2. Allow child to select a color of paper that makes seeing easier
3. Offer writing and drawing instruments that make larger bolder marks (e.g., larger crayons, dot bottles)
4. Make available the use of a magnifying glass on a stand (similar to ones used for fine needle work found in craft stores)
5. Offer primary writing paper with wider lines if needed
6. Offer bright colors of media for writing and drawing; these allow for better contrast, than paler pastel colors
7. Allow the child to have more time to finish, if necessary, so that the child can complete work and feel successful
8. Check on child frequently, and give positive reinforcement for incremental achievements

X. **Applicable Framework Standards: Kindergarten**
English-Language Arts
> Reading (1.0, 1.1, 1.2, 1.3, 1.4, 1.5, 1.6, 1.7, 1.8, 1.9, 1.14, 1.15, 1.16, 1.17, 1.18)
> Writing (1.0, 1.1, 1.2, 1.3, 1.4)
> Written and Oral English Language (1.0, 1.1, 1.2)
> Listening and Speaking (1.0, 1.1, 1.2)

Mathematics
> Numbers and Counting (1.0, 1.2)
> Algebra and Sorting (1.0, 1.1)
> Measurement and Geometry (1.0, 1.2, 1.3, 1.4)
> Statistics (1.0, 1.1)

Science
> Physical Science (1.a)
> Life Science (2.a)
> Earth Science (3.a, 3.b)
> Investigation and Experimentation (4a, 4b, 4d, 4e)

History and Social Science
> Following Rules (K.1, K.1.1)

Visual Arts
> Artistic Expression (1.0, 1.1, 1.2, 1.3)

Creative Expression (2.0, 2.1, 2.4, 2.5, 2.6)

XI. Evaluation and Comments (i.e.: How well did the plan work? Great responses? What aspects are especially effective? Not effective? What improvements are needed? Ideas for follow up activities and other notes)

_____
_____
_____
_____

Chapter Eight

Using Personal Laminators in the Classroom

"Art is an adventure into an unknown world, which can
be explored only by those willing to take risks."
– Mark Rothko, Abstract Expressionist Painter

It is common knowledge that laminators get too hot for children's use. A teacher cannot let children use professional, full-sized laminators. Even adults occasionally get burned from a laminator. That is very true, for the full-size professional, school style laminators. There are smaller, far less expensive laminators now available at club stores, and K-Mart for as little as $29.99. They are built in such a way that even the most curious little fingers can't get into the laminating rollers, which have a very narrow opening in the insulated plastic casing. One can put a hand on the top of the laminator until one feels bored, and will feel little more than warmth on that hand. Children of all ages love to make art with these fabulous tools.

Renée Berg bought her first personal laminator right after graduate school. Her in-laws gave her $100.00 as a gift. Wanting a personal laminator to save and protect her children's artwork, out she went with her little windfall, and got one. After several days of frantic laminating (three little artists and scholars can accumulate quite a pile of art and awards to save), a peculiar idea sprung forth. "Can tissue paper be laminated?" It worked wonderfully. She went from protecting her children's precious achievements to creating her own art pieces with personal laminators and carrier pouches.

Renée made tissue paper collages and laminated glitter, slightly dried flower petals and thin leaves. Through experimentation she discovered that thicker, juicy leaves and petals are messy and do not laminate well. Tinsel, bits of lace and ribbon were added. Renée brought the new toy to her adult teacher preparation class for students to play with. Sun catchers, journal covers, and mobiles were made. For endless imagination and creativity, what fun it is!!

Laminator art is two-sided, and planning for two-sided art cognitively takes a wholly different level of planning and preparation involving much higher order cognition. This particular tool offers a wide range of creative possibilities for children's creative expression. This is a favorite activity because, aside from a few simple rules, this tool allows for wide, open-ended creativity. There is freedom in setting down an open pouch inside an open carrier and a pile of suitable art materials, and letting the children play. They will delight in their creations, and so will their families.

Smaller personal use type laminators may make bubbles in the pouch during the lamination process. If for some reason tiny bubbles are unacceptable for a particular project, then use the larger professional type machines often available in the supply rooms of certain schools, educational supply stores, and some resource and referral agency's libraries (see the http://www.childcareaware.org website or call 1-800-424-2246 for list of centers nationwide). These agencies are in nearly every county in the United States and offer broad resources for parents, teachers, and others serving the needs of children.

The Laminator Rules

❖ **No matter what the instructions enclosed in the box say, ALWAYS use a carrier**. A carrier is a firm paper pouch closed on one side, into which the plastic laminating pouch is inserted. If not using the carrier, the pouches may become wrapped around the laminating roller. Someone's precious art may be ruined. It is possible for some mechanically inclined computer type to restore it to functionality. But preventatively, it is much easier to run the pouch twice through in a carrier to be sure of satisfactory lamination, than it is to take the machine apart to dislodge the pouch from the roller. Many young artists' tears will be saved.

❖ Use at least **3-millimeter density pouches**, particularly if using pouches without carriers, against strong advice. **The lightweight pouches (1.5 mil) absolutely will wrap around the rollers (see above) if used without a carrier**. The final result is quite flimsy, and is difficult to use for sun catchers, mobiles, journal covers, or family magnets. Discount stationary supply stores carry laminator pouches for about $20.00 for 100 pouches (about 5 cents each).

❖ **NEVER, NEVER, NEVER** use any kind of glue or adhesives with your laminator. The adhesives will actually inhibit the adhesive action of the heat on the plastic and wreck your laminator.

❖ **Try to keep the artwork thin**. Thick artwork wrecks the rollers, can become jammed in the laminator, and will not laminate well (i.e. won't close or seal the pouch well).

❖ **DO NOT LAMINATE THERMAL PAPER**. Laminating documents or photographs on heat sensitive thermal paper (such as Polaroid) will turn your item dark from the heat in the lamination process.

❖ As an educator, it may be helpful to laminate such items as dates for a group time calendar activity (a large size calendar would need to be laminated with a professional size laminator). Try using Velcro tape on the back of the laminate "dates". The soft side of the Velcro is best put onto the numbers, and the rough side onto the calendar (protect those little fingers). In this way, a calendar purchase can last for years.

❖ **Possible uses for laminator art**
  • Sun catchers
  • Mobiles
  • Journal covers
  • Placemats (use the larger legal or menu size pouches) Menu size pouches require a larger laminator.
  • Family magnets
  • Letter and number magnets
  • Displaying and preserving children's artwork

Chapter Nine

Language Activities and Learning Plans

Books and words need to be as familiar to children as the food they eat, the music they hear and the art they do. If we want our children to become literate then we must do everything we can to make them comfortable with books and language.

— Bev Bos
"Children's Books"

Writing on Filled Zipper-Type Freezer Bags

Writing on filled plastic zipper bags is a sensory activity works very well with kinesthetic learners. Part of the fun is the "ooey-gooey-ness" of the foam or gel in the bag. Glitter or flat spangles can be added to the gel or foam in the bag to add another sensory dimension. Children enjoy the kinesthetic feeling of using their fingers to "write" on the filled bags.

Illustration 1: Children can develop letter recognition by tracing through zipper bags filled with gel.

Be sure to use freezer bags, and make certain they can be closed securely before presenting this activity to children. If lighter weight bags are used, they may break with enthusiastic use. If the bags are inappropriately closed, the activity will be more about clean up than literacy!

Materials and Preparation

❖ Letters, words and/or numbers written on card stock in wide-tipped black felt marker; cards prepared in advance by the teacher; (laminating the cards makes them last longer)

❖ 1 quart-size zip-type freezer plastic bag per child

❖ 1/2 cup of child's choice of substance to fill bags: shaving cream, hair gel, etc. **Note:** Colors of unsweetened powdered drink mix can be mixed with shaving cream, or different colors of hair gel can be used

❖ 1/2 cup measuring cup

❖ 1 tablespoon - to scoop unsweetened powdered drink mix into bag or to scoop gel into measuring cup; if using shaving cream it can be squeezed directly into the measuring cup, or into the bag

❖ **Optional**: spangles or plastic glitter

Method

❖ Draw letters, words, or numbers in wide tipped black felt tip marker on card stock (lamination will make the cards last longer)

❖ Fill about 1/4 to 1/2 way quart size zip-type freezer bags with shaving cream and unsweetened powdered drink mix or colored hair gel (zip bags, shaving cream, and hair gel are available at the 99-cent store) Hair gel and shaving cream can be mixed for an interesting effect.

❖ Spangles and glitter

❖ If the children have the dexterity, they can fill the zip bags in a sink or plastic basin.

❖ If using cream, be sure not to over fill zipper bags as it will be difficult to see the words through the colored shaving cream

❖ Place gel or shaving cream filled bags on top of letters or words
❖ Have the children place **a finger** on the bag to trace around the letters (children do not use any kind of writing or drawing implement to "write" on bag)
❖ Ask the children to say the letter, word, or number as they are tracing it
❖ As the children trace through the gel or shaving cream, the unsweetened powdered drink mix will mix and color patterns will appear

Variations
❖ Squirt shaving cream onto a table surface, allow the children to "finger paint" with the shaving cream
❖ Ask children to write their names, if they know how to do so
❖ For older children, they can practice math or spelling in the shaving cream as a fun break from the ubiquitous stacks of worksheets
❖ Teacher bonus: If plain shaving cream is used, the desks will be clean after the shaving cream is wiped off with a paper towel!

Suggested Reading:
Ada, A.F. (1997). *Gathering the Sun: An Alphabet in Spanish and English.* ISBN: 0-688-13903-5. (Winner 1998 Americas Award) (Vibrant paintings illustrate poems of each letter of the alphabet).
Brown, M. (1974). *All Butterflies: An ABC.* ISBN: 0684137712
Pallotta, J. (1996). *The Freshwater Alphabet Book.* ISBN: 0881069000
Wildsmith, B. (1996). *Brian Wildsmith's ABC.* ISBN: 1887734023
> *Note: Brian Wildsmith's beautifully illustrated alphabet books are available in many languages such as Arabic, Chinese, Farsi, French, Korean, Navajo, Spanish, Portugese, Tagalog, and Vietnamese*

Target Areas of Learning

Physical Development
❖ **Fine motor skills**: tracing around letters correctly
❖ **Eye-hand coordination**: coordinating visual acuity with using the small muscles of the hand and fingers; forming letters/words correctly in shaving cream or gel
❖ **Sensory discrimination**:
  • **Tactile discrimination** (touch): experiencing the sensation of touching the gel or shaving cream inside the zip bag
  • **Visual discrimination** (sight): identifying letters/words visually; noting the change in colors as the unsweetened powdered drink mix mixes with the shaving cream
  • **Auditory discrimination** (hearing): correctly associating letter sound with letters and words

Cognitive Development

❖ **Language Arts**
  • **Verbal skills**
    ○ **Language development**: understanding and following simple instructions; recognizing his/her own name, recognizing letters and words;
    ○ **Vocabulary development**: comprehension; using new words;
  • **Emergent literacy**
    ○ **Symbol interpretation**: at the most basic level learning that marks have meaning
  • **Writing skills**
    ○ **Penmanship:** tracing letters, writing name, writing new words;
❖ **Math Skills**
  • **Measurement:** measuring gel or shaving cream into zip bags
❖ **Science**
  • **Cause and effect**
    ○ **Relationships between actions and outcomes**: developing curiosity which leads to scientific inquiry: "educated why"

Social Development

❖ **Working cooperatively with others in a group:** working well as a member of a team and as a community
❖ **Taking turns:** allowing others a fair use of materials as a community resource
❖ **Sharing**: understanding that items intended for use by the community (family, classroom) are available for the use by everyone in that community
❖ **Following directions**: carrying out directions given by a person in authority
❖ **Taking care of the classroom environment:** participating in clean up

Emotional Development

❖ **Self-esteem:** building self-confidence: participating in activities wherein there is no "wrong" answer; feeling safe enough to learn

Creative Expression

❖ **Use of creative media and expression of imagination**
  • **2-dimensional visual arts**: expressing self using 2-dimensional media: creating interesting designs with cream or gel
❖ **Creative risk**: experimenting freely with creative media without focus on the outcome

Possible Accommodations for *Writing on Filled Zip Bags Activity*

ADHD

❖ Use positive reinforcement (praise) when child works well with others and behaves appropriately

❖ Allow the activity to go on a little longer if child becomes engaged in it
❖ Cover zipper opening of bag with duct tape after bag is zipped, in case of enthusiastic play
❖ Be sure to use freezer type bags not sandwich type bags
❖ Pair child with another child for opportunities for cooperative play
❖ Have the child act as your helper, setting up activity
❖ Ask the child to repeat the instructions, to make sure that they are understood

Developmental Delays:
❖ Go over task more slowly to be sure child understands the task
❖ Use gallon size freezer bags and larger letters to trace
❖ Cover zipper opening of bag with duct tape after bag is zipped in case of enthusiastic play
❖ Check in on children frequently
❖ Have child work with a gentle peer
❖ Offer more time to complete task
❖ Use positive reinforcement as the child succeeds in following instructions, measuring ingredients, filling bags and writing
❖ Place materials on a tray or place a splat mat beneath tables to facilitate clean-up
❖ Simplify task: ask child to trace individual letters instead of words

Autism Spectrum Disorders
❖ Explain the activity using short simple phrases
❖ Present the activity as part of the centers' routine, allowing the child to become accustomed to this activity
❖ Use positive reinforcement when child participates, remembering to give praise for incremental achievements
❖ Have child work with a gentle peer who understands the task at hand
❖ Allow child to warm up to the activity, perhaps offering sensory activities inside of zipper bags or balloons: gel, flour, cornstarch, oobleck before presenting activity

Visual Impairments
❖ Adjust the lighting to reduce glare
❖ Have larger letters available to trace
❖ Offer more time to complete task
❖ When writing letters to be traced use a very wide tipped black marker on white card stock (for highest contrast)
❖ Have child work with a gentle peer with higher competency as a partner
❖ Have an adult work with child on any of the tasks that may be challenging for the child, encouraging and supporting the child in the activity, making certain child is working as independently as possible on the task
❖ Offer the child a magnifying glass on a stand (similar to the ones used for needlework, found in craft stores)

Orthopedic Impairments
❖ Lower the adult to child ratio
❖ Be sure the height and angle of the table is adjusted for best access for the child
❖ If child is in a wheel chair, activity can occur on a tray, if that is a more effective presentation
❖ Be sure child is seated in a comfortable position; in the case of cerebral palsy, monitor child to ascertain child is in a comfortable position
❖ If necessary, either place your hand over child's or child's hand over teachers to guide the child's hand through the movement
❖ Allow additional time

Gifted and Talented Education (GATE)
❖ Enrichments should include introducing a greater number of vocabulary words
❖ Introduce more challenging vocabulary
❖ Child can act as an assistant to others in the class

English Language Learners (ELL)
❖ Offer more time
❖ Repeat activity frequently for additional practice, perhaps set it up as a centers activity
❖ Partner child with a peer who understands the task
❖ Explain the activity using short simple phrases
❖ Check in with child frequently to insure comprehension of vocabulary

Content Standards For Kindergarten Met By This Activity

English Language Arts
> Reading (1.0, 1.2, 1.3, 1.5, 1.6, 1.7, 1.14, 1.15, 1.16)
> Writing (1.0, 1.1, 1.2, 1.3, 1.4)
> Written and Oral English Language (1.0, 1.1, 1.2)
> Listening and Speaking Strategies (1.0, 1.1, 2.0, 2.1)

Mathematics
> Measurement and Geometry (1.0, 1.1)

History and Social Science
> Following Rules (K.1, K.1.1)

Science
> Physical Sciences (1.a)

Visual Arts
> Artistic Perception (1.0, 1.1)
> Creative Expression (2.0, 2.1)

Learning Plan

   I. **Name of Activity: Writing on Filled Zipper-Type Freezer Bags**

  II. **Date of Presentation:**

 III. **Age or Grade Level: 3 years and up**

 IV. **Ratio of teachers to children needed for this activity:** 1:6

  V. **Target Areas of Learning / Goals and Objectives** (target areas of learning directly relate to "VI. Evaluation Rubric")
      1. Physical: _____
      2. Cognitive: _____
      3. Social: _____
      4. Emotional: _____
      5. Creative: _____

 VI. **Evaluation Rubric:** (if more than two learning areas are being evaluated, a spreadsheet form may be preferred)

Targeted Area of Learning	**Targeted Area of Learning**
_____	_____
_____	_____
4. Always _____	**4.** Always _____
3. Usually _____	**3.** Usually _____
2. Sometimes _____	**2.** Sometimes _____
1. Rarely _____	**1.** Rarely _____

VII. **Materials and Preparation Needed**
    1. Letters, words and/or numbers written on card stock in wide tipped black felt marker; cards prepared in advance by the teacher; (laminating the cards makes them last longer)
    2. 1 quart-size zip-style freezer plastic bag per child
    3. 1/2 cup of child's choice of substance to fill bags: shaving cream, hair gel; (Note: colors of unsweetened powdered drink mix can be mixed with shaving cream, or different colors of hair gel can be used)
    4. 1/2 cup measuring cup
    5. 1 tablespoon - to scoop unsweetened powdered drink mix into bag or to scoop gel into measuring cup; if using shaving cream, it can be squeezed directly into the measuring cup, or into the bag

VIII. Procedures

1. Draw letters, words, or numbers in wide tipped black felt tip marker on card stock (lamination will make the cards last longer)
2. Have children measure out 1/2 cup of shaving cream and put it into quart size zip-type freezer bags; add 1 tablespoon of unsweetened powdered drink mix (two colors may be added); Or use 1/2 cup of colored hair gel (zip bags, shaving cream, and hair gel are all available at the 99 cent store) Shaving cream may also be squeezed directly into the bag;
3. If the children have the dexterity, they can fill the zip bags in a sink or plastic basin.
4. If using cream, be sure not to over fill zipper bags as it will be difficult to see the words through the colored shaving cream
5. Place filled gel/shaving cream bags on top of letters or words
6. Have the children trace around the letters with their **finger**
7. Ask the children to say the letter, word, or number as they are tracing it
8. As the children trace through the shaving cream, the unsweetened powdered drink mix will mix with it, and color patterns will appear

Variations

- Squirt shaving cream onto a table surface, allow the children to "finger paint" with the shaving cream
- Ask children to write their names, if they know how to do so
- For older children, they can practice math or spelling in the shaving cream as a fun break from worksheets
- **Teacher bonus**: If plain shaving cream is used, the desks will be clean after the shaving cream is wiped off with a paper towel!

IX. Accommodations (changes to accommodate learning diversity)
Name of Accommodated Area:

1. _____
2. _____
3. _____
4. _____
5. _____

X. Applicable Framework Standards: Kindergarten
Standard _____

_____

_____

_____

_____

Standard _____

_____

_____

_____

Standard _____

_____

_____

_____

Standard _____

_____

_____

_____

Standard _____

_____

_____

_____

Comments (i.e.: How well did the plan work? Great responses? What aspects are especially effective? Not effective? What improvements are needed? Ideas for follow up activities and other notes)

_____

_____

_____

_____

Journaling

Journaling is an excellent activity for all levels of learners. Children who have not yet acquired the understanding that marks have meaning have the opportunity to develop that understanding while using prewritten/written media as a method of self expression. Children with more advanced writing skills can enhance them in the process of acquiring careful observation, reflection, introspection, and articulation.

Illustration 2: A child's emergent skill in writing is more meaningful to the child when writing about his/her own experiences.

Using journal making and writing as a whole self-expression activity can inspire interest and excitement for working in written media. This opens up a wide range of interest for learners. Three areas of subject content are addressed: reflection journals, gratitude journals and academic journals. Journaling can be integrated into almost any activity, particularly interactive kinesthetic projects.

Materials

Materials and preparations will vary from project to project. Depending upon the academic use of the journal, such as a science journal, it is important to remember that the use of the journal is contextual. The type of journal made will reflect its intended use. For gratitude and reflection journals, for example, students might make journals comprised of pages of plain or lined primary picture paper (See Appendix A-2 for downloadable primary picture paper @ www.cambriapress.com/kindergarten). A science journal may need envelopes or zip type bags for its "pages", to hold items that the children have collected. Refer to the learning plan for the type of journal that best suits the activity for a complete materials list.

Reflection Journals

The teacher may choose to create personal reflection journals with children of all ages. Whether the children are drawing in the style of the universal paramecium or tadpole figure (human figure consisting of a circle and two lines), and dictating the meaning of the work they're doing, using scribble writing, dictating, and emergent writing, or highly skilled written language, the goal is the same. The child is considering thoughts, feelings, and experiences and committing those reflections onto paper. The teacher determines whether the reflection journal will be interactive (with the teacher) or self-expressive.

Method

❖ Offer the class a brief period of time each day for personal writing. Initially allow five minutes, if you see that your students are engaged by the activity as time goes on, allow additional time. The first thing in the morning is a wonderful time for journal activities, as it allows the children to settle in, to get into the mood of the school day.

❖ Have crayons, markers, and colored pencils either at the writing center or at each child's desk.

❖ Let the children write about a teacher-selected topic, **or** allow the children to decide for themselves.

❖ Later on in the day, or week, you can offer children an opportunity share their writing with the class, if they choose.

Gratitude Journals

This is an area that is of some personal significance to the authors. Oprah Winfrey brought this type of journaling to national attention in the mid 1990's. Oprah asserts that merely experiencing a few moments of gratitude each day can cause anyone's world view to be transformed, and to have improved overall health. In "The Physiological and Psychological Effects of Compassion and Anger", Rein, Atkinson and McCraty reported in 1995, that self-induced positive emotional states created " large increases in S-IgA which were as high as 240% greater in some individuals" (p. 102). (Salivary IgA, is an enzyme present in saliva, which boosts the immune system and helps an individual fight off illness). A child that is not yet writing is still able to become present to areas of life wherein s/he can feel gratitude. This activity, perhaps as a settling in exercise at the beginning of each class day, may instill a lifelong habit of reflection for the children. It may create the potential for a healthier, more fulfilling life. The method for this journal is the same as reflection journals, with the subject area defined as gratitude.

Academic Journals

There are many academic areas wherein journaling activities can be included. Science journals have much value for children.

Method

❖ The teacher and / or the class decides upon a (science) project

❖ The teacher and the children bring in the materials and set up the project

❖ Have the children make the type of journals suitable for the project

❖ Individually, in small groups, or as a class, have the children carefully observe the changes they see in their project and record their observations.

❖ Offer the children time to discuss the findings of their observations in small groups or as a class, or perhaps both.

❖ If the project is a classroom or small group collaborative activity, then all the wonderful aspects of consultation (e.g., comparing what one child sees with that which the others in the group see, group evaluations of outcomes) become available as learning. It is all very exciting. The opportunities for learning available in an activity such as this are endless.

Suggested Reading:

Aliki. (1988). *How a Book Is Made*. (Reading Rainbow book) ISBN: 0064460851. Spanish language edition: 1989). *Como Se Hace un Libro*. ISBN: 8426124003.

Christelow, E. (1997). *What do authors do?* ISBN: 0395866219.

Craven, C. (1999). *What the mailman brought.* ISBN: 0399213074. (Illustrated by Tomie de Paola).

Curtis, J. L. (1995). *When I Was Little: A Four-Year-Old's Memoir of Her Youth.* ISBN: 0064434230.

Curtis, J. L. (1998). *Today I Feel Silly: And Other Moods That Make My Day..* ISBN: 0060245603.

Krauss, R. (1989). *A Hole is to Dig: The First Book of Definitions.* ISBN: 006443205X

Mayer, M. (2001). *One Monster After Another.* (How a little girl's letter finally gets delivered!) ISBN: 1577686888.

Moss, M. (2001). *Rachel's journal: The story of a pioneer girl.* ISBN: 015202168X.

Nixon, J.L. (1995). *If You Were a Writer.* ISBN: 0689719000

Payne. L.M. & Rohling, C. (1994). *Just Because I Am: A Child's Book of Affirmation.* ISBN: 0-915793-60-1.

Silverstein, S. (1974). *Where the Sidewalk Ends.* ISBN: 06-025667-2.

Silverstein, S. (1981). *A Light In the Attic.* ISBN: 0-06-025673-7.

William, V.B (1984). *Three Days On a River in a Red Canoe.* ISBN: 0688040721. (Reading Rainbow book; Child's journal of a canoe trip, what the trip was like; how to plan and take a trip).

Target Areas of Learning

Physical Development
❖ **Fine motor skills:** using the small muscles of the hand and fingers: holding a pencil or crayon; writing or drawing
❖ **Eye-hand coordination:** coordinating visual acuity with using the small muscles of the hand and fingers: drawing shapes; holding a pencil or crayon
❖ **Sensory discrimination**
• **Visual discrimination (sight):** identifying shapes; colors; sizes
Cognitive Development
❖ **Language Arts**
• **Verbal skills**
  o **Vocabulary development:** recognizing new words associated with the subject area of the journal
  o **Language development**: understanding and following simple instructions; describing components of the writing in a journal, letter recognition, name recognition, interacting verbally with others while writing or considering what will be written
• **Emergent literacy**
  o **Symbol interpretation:** recognizing letters and words made from associated letters
  o **Word recognition**: recognizing name, recognizing letters and words; at the most basic level learning that marks have meaning in the process of expressing their own ideas and observations in their own book
  o **Phonemic awareness:** awareness of sounds associated with letters, letter combination as they develop facility with writing

- o **Creative writing**: expressing self in marks and pictures upon which the child has placed meaning in the journal
- o **Penmanship:** tracing letters, writing name, writing new words
- o **Emergent writing:** writing as part of decorating journals
- o **Sequencing** in stories: journal; recalling events of the day or week in order recalling or anticipating events as they occurred in time, writing observable changes in science journals in the order they occurred

❖ **Math Skills**
- **Mathematical literacy**
  - o **1 to 1 correspondence**: counting items in an organized way for science journals
  - o **Recognizing number words**: associating the number symbol with the written word for the number with the count of items represented by both the written word and the symbol particularly in the context of science journal writing
- **Mathematical applications**
  - o **Algebra: categorization/ grouping** (sets): inventing criterion to separate items into groups
    - **Seriation**: ordering objects or events in a graduation of size from smallest to largest or vice versa, or in the context of time from earliest to latest
      - ⊙ **Calendar**: placing numbers in order to denote the passage of days, weeks, months, seasons, years and noting that sequence in a journal
      - ⊙ **Time**: noting the sequential relationship from one event to another as measured by a standard interval such as a minute, an hour; associating specific events with an appointed time in the day and identifying that appointed time on a clock and noting that interval in a journal
      - ⊙ **Temporal ordering**: placing events in a particular predetermined sequence
    - **Common relatedness**: linking items that are not the same, but are associated with each other and writing about those distinctions in a journal
      Note: Mathematical applications are possible in the context of journal writing, depending on the context designated for journal writing

❖ **Science**
- **Scientific processes**: in the context of science journal writing:
  - o **Inquiry**: documenting an organized search for knowledge regarding a particular scientific question
  - o **Prediction**: documenting an anticipated outcome based on logic, experience, or research
  - o **Observation**: carefully watching attentively and noting what is seen for a scientific purpose
  - o **Documentation**: writing observations of scientific events which support claims for a particular prediction or outcomes and making note of what is seen in writing
  - o **Review**: comparing predictions and actual outcomes written in journal, assessing value of any mistakes that occurred as noted in a journal

Social Development
❖ **Self-respect:** developing a sense of self worth through the practice of recording thoughts, ideas, and experiences in a journal writing activity
❖ **Collaboration:** working with others in a group, sharing ideas, techniques relating to the assigned journal writing activity
❖ **Learning patience**: diligence: staying with a writing project until it is completed
❖ **Following directions**: doing the journaling project as directed
❖ **Internalized social values**: through gratitude and reflection journals: appreciation of self and others; reflecting on personal actions and experiences and determining within self whether those behaviors are appropriate in the context of social values
❖ **Taking care of classroom environment**: participating in cleanup

Emotional Development:
❖ **Self-esteem**: feeling a sense of accomplishment by making a book of one's own
❖ **Accomplishment:** developing self worth by participating in and completing class activities
❖ **Appropriate emotions:** learning to identify and express emotions appropriately through writing and drawing**:**
  • **Naming human feelings:** sad, happy, angry, hurt, loving, excited, afraid, proud, sorry
  • **"Use your words":** expressing feelings of upset and anger appropriately

Creative Expression:
❖ **Expressing emotions:** through use of creative media and imagination in the context of journal writing:
  • **2-dimensional visual arts**: painting, collage, and drawing
  • **Writing and storytelling**: expressing self through written and illustrated media
❖ **Developing aesthetic appreciation** for the creative writing and illustrations created by others
❖ **Persuasion**: representing one's observations and ideas in written media which appeals to others sufficiently that those views are taken into consideration
❖ **Creative risk**: willingness to express self creatively in written media

Possible Accommodations for *Journaling Activities*

ADHD
❖ Use positive reinforcement (praise) when child works well: staying on task, completing project, and so forth
❖ Allow the activity to go on a little longer if child becomes engaged
❖ Offer the child a cardboard "carrel" to reduce distractions
❖ Create a vocabulary reference chart as a reminder child of grade level vocabulary words
❖ Lower ratio: use more supervision when child is using laminator or stapler

❖ Offer a smaller selection of materials from which to choose
❖ Ask the child to repeat the instructions, to make sure that the child understands exactly what to do.
❖ Label items around the classroom to help child become familiar with the associated written word

Developmental Delays
❖ Explain the activity using short simple phrases being sure eye contact is made
❖ Demonstrate the activity in advance steps-by-step using realia or photographs
❖ Use positive reinforcement as the child works on her journal
❖ Have child work with a gentle and more competent peer
❖ Offer more time to complete task
❖ Write out words child uses frequently on file cards (with a picture if possible) so child can copy them easily
❖ Use larger writing tools chunky enough for child to grasp them easily, such as large markers, dot bottles, and chunky crayons and pencils
❖ Check in on children frequently to monitor progress, and to gauge any frustration level
❖ Label items around the classroom to help child become familiar with the associated written word

Autism Spectrum Disorders
❖ Explain the activity using short simple phrases being sure eye contact is made
❖ Demonstrate the activity in advance steps-by-step using realia or photographs
❖ Present the activity as part of the class routine, allowing the child to become accustomed to the activity
❖ Write out words child uses frequently on file cards (with a picture if possible) so child can copy them easily
❖ Use positive reinforcement when child participates
❖ Reduce the number of writing/drawing tools so selection is easier
❖ Offer the child a carrell if the child feels uncomfortable working close to others
❖ Label items around the classroom to help child become familiar with the associated written word

Visual Impairments
❖ Adjust the lighting to reduce glare
❖ Allow child to select a color of paper that makes seeing easier
❖ Offer writing and drawing instruments that make larger bolder marks (e.g., larger crayons, dot bottles)
❖ Make available the use of a magnifying glass on a stand (similar to ones used for fine needle work found in craft stores)
❖ Offer primary writing paper with wider lines if needed

❖ Offer bright colors of media for writing and drawing; they allow for better contrast, than paler pastel colors
❖ Allow the child to have more time to finish, if necessary, so that the child can complete work and feel successful
❖ Check on child frequently, and give positive reinforcement for incremental achievements

Orthopedic Impairments

❖ Make sure the child is positioned correctly to make drawing and writing easier
❖ Make sure the furniture is positioned in such a way that the child has best access
❖ Use a tray if that is easier for a child in a wheel chair
❖ Use a hand-over-hand technique to help child form letters
❖ Allow more time
❖ Reduce quantity of writing expected
❖ Offer specialized tools such as larger writing/drawing instruments, adapted scissors, cushioned grip writing tools, etc.

Gifted and Talented Education (GATE)

❖ Increase quantity of assigned writing
❖ If other children in class are dictating their journals, allow gifted child to take other children's dictation for their journals
❖ Encourage gifted children to use broader vocabulary in journal writing
❖ Create a vocabulary reference chart as a reminder child of new or more advanced vocabulary words
❖ Ask children to check for grammatical and spelling errors in their own work

English Language Learners (ELL)

❖ Explain the activity using short simple phrases being sure eye contact is made
❖ Demonstrate the activity in advance steps-by-step using realia, photographs
❖ Write out words child uses frequently on file cards (with a picture if possible) so child can copy them easily
❖ Allow more time for task
❖ Check in on children frequently to monitor progress, and to gauge any frustration level
❖ Label items around the classroom to help child become familiar with the associated written word

Content Standards For Kindergarten Met By This Activity

English-Language Arts
Reading (1.0, 1.1, 1.2, 1.3, 1.4, 1.5, 1.6, 1.7, 1.8, 1.9, 1.14, 1.15, 1.16, 1.17, 1.18)
Writing (1.0, 1.1, 1.2, 1.3, 1.4)
Written and Oral English Language (1.0, 1.1, 1.2)
Listening and Speaking (1.0, 1.1, 1.2)

Mathematics
> Numbers and Counting (1.0, 1.2)
> Algebra and Sorting (1.0, 1.1)
> Measurement and Geometry (1.0, 1.2, 1.3, 1.4)
> Statistics (1.0, 1.1)

Science
> Physical Science (1.a)
> Life Science (2.a)
> Earth Science (3.a, 3.b)
> Investigation and Experimentation (4a, 4b, 4d, 4e)

History and Social Science
> Following Rules (K.1, K.1.1)

Visual Arts
> Artistic Perception (1.0, 1.1, 1.2, 1.3)
> Creative Expression (2.0, 2.1, 2.4, 2.5, 2.6)

Learning Plan

  I. **Name of Activity: Journaling**

  II. **Date of Presentation:**

  III. **Age or Grade Level: Pre-k to Primary**

  IV. **Ratio of teachers to children needed for this activity:** 1:6
     (An excellent kidney-shaped table activity)

  V. **Target Areas of Learning / Goals and Objectives** (target areas of learning directly relate to "VI. Evaluation Rubric")
     1. Physical: _____
     2. Cognitive: _____
     3. Social: _____
     4. Emotional: _____
     5. Creative: _____

  VI. **Evaluation Rubric:** (if more than two learning areas are being evaluated, a spreadsheet form may be preferred)

Targeted Area of Learning	Targeted Area of Learning
_____	_____
_____	_____
4. Always _____	4. Always _____
3. Usually _____	3. Usually _____
2. Sometimes _____	2. Sometimes _____
1. Rarely _____	1. Rarely _____

 VII. **Materials and Preparation Needed**
Materials and preparations will vary from project to project. Depending upon the academic use of the journal, such as a science journal, it is important for the teacher to remember that the use of the journal is contextual. The type of journal that the children make will reflect its intended use. For gratitude and reflection journals, for example, the teacher may have the students make journals comprised of pages of plain or lined primary picture paper. A science journal may need envelopes or zip-type bags for its "pages", to hold items that the children have collected. Refer to the learning plan for the type of journal that best suits the activity for a complete materials list.

VIII. **Procedures**
Reflection Journals
Method
1. Offer the class a brief period of time each day for personal writing. Initially allow

five minutes. If the students are engaged by the activity as time goes on, allow additional time. The first thing in the morning is a wonderful time for journal activities, as it allows the children to settle in, to get into the mood of the school day.
2. Have a selection of writing and drawing implements (e.g., crayons, markers, colored pencils) available either at the writing center or at each child's desk.
3. Let the children write about the topic selected, **or** let children decide on a topic
4. Later on in the day, or week, offer children an opportunity to share their journal writing with the class, if they choose to do so.

Gratitude Journals
The method is the same as reflection journals, with the subject area defined as gratitude.

Academic Journals

Method
1. Teacher, the class, or both, decide upon a (science) project
2. Teacher and the children bring in the materials and set up the project
3. Have the children make the type of journals suitable for the project
4. Individually, in small groups, or as a class, have the children carefully observe the changes they see in their project and record their observations.
5. Offer children time to discuss the findings of their observations in small groups or as a class, or perhaps both.

   Note: If the project is a classroom or small group collaborative activity, then all the wonderful aspects of consultation (e.g., comparing what one child sees with that which the others in the group see, group evaluations of outcomes) become available as learning. It is all very exciting. The learning available in an activity such as this is endless.

IX. Accommodations (changes to accommodate learning diversity)
   Name of Accommodated Area:
   1. _____
   2. _____
   3. _____
   4. _____
   5. _____

X. Applicable Framework Standards: Kindergarten
   Standard _____
   _____
   _____
   _____

Standard _____
_____
_____
_____

Standard _____
_____
_____
_____

Standard _____
_____
_____
_____

Standard _____
_____
_____
_____

Comments (i.e.: How well did the plan work? Great responses? What aspects are especially effective? Not effective? What improvements are needed? Ideas for follow up activities and other notes)

_____
_____
_____
_____

Journal Making Activities

There are many, many ways to make journals. Optimally, the children will do most of the production work for their journals. Four simple types will be described. There are seemingly limitless varieties to select from. If you enjoy using journals and journal making as a classroom activity, there are many wonderful books available.

Journal making and journaling offers opportunities for a wealth of learning. Journaling is a fun way for young children to learn that marks have meaning and that when they make marks, they can communicate with others. This is a very exciting process for children.

There are all types of journals: there are diaries, reflection journals, science journals, gratitude journals and so on. Children can also write individual stories, bind them, and share them with the class in an "author's chair" activity. Any direction into which one chooses to direct a class or a child can be the subject for a journaling activity. Journals encourage children to express themselves in written form.

There are learning plans for making journals, which include: two types of covers, three varieties of "pages"

Illustration 3: A variety of materials may be used when making journals with the duct tape binding method.

(filler), and two methods of binding the books. Any of these various covers, pages, or methods of binding can be combined to make these books special and unique. Choose the method most appropriate for both the class and the subject matter.

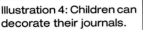

Illustration 4: Children can decorate their journals.

Making Journals

Journal Covers

1. Laminated Covers
Covers made in a personal laminator are quite fun for children to make. As stated in **Chapter Eight: Using Personal Laminators in the Classroom**, tissue paper, small bits of glitter, partially dried flower petals, and all sorts of flat materials laminate beautifully.
Note: ALWAYS use a carrier pouch with a personal laminator and NEVER USE GLUE or other adhesives in a laminator.

Materials

For each set of journal covers

❖ A personal laminator, or laminators depending upon the number of children participating in the activity (the laminating process seems slow to impatient young artists)

❖ 2 laminator pouches

❖ Card stock laminator carrier pouch

❖ Art materials such as bits of tissue paper, plastic glitter, paper lace doilies, bits of iridescent plastic Christmas tree tinsel, dried flower petals, wrapping paper, pretty much anything flat (note that lots of metallic items tend to overheat, so use metallic paper and the like sparingly) clear iridescent ribbon and wrapping paper is quite beautiful laminated

❖ Scissors

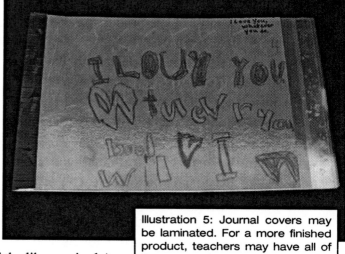

Illustration 5: Journal covers may be laminated. For a more finished product, teachers may have all of the pages of the journal laminated.

Method

❖ Gather items to be laminated as suggested above. Explain to the children that their artwork can be seen from both sides, and to think about that when making their artwork.

❖ Each child needs two laminator pouches for the covers of their journal.

❖ Young children may be more successful if they create their covers with the open laminator pouch inside the open carrier pouch.

❖ Have the child assemble the covers by putting bits of tissue paper, pieces of cut magazines and so forth into the pouch. Make sure the laminator pouch is not too full.

❖ Close the top of the laminator and carrier pouch.

❖ With adult supervision have the child insert the close end of the carrier pouch into the preheated personal laminator.

❖ After it is run through the laminator, check the artwork. Some thicker pieces may need to be run through the laminator twice.

❖ Take covers out of laminator pouches (each cover must be run through the laminator in a separate pouch). Let them cool.

❖ Allow children to continue assembling journal.

❖ Both the duct tape and three-hole punch binding methods work with laminated covers.

2. Tag or Card stock Journal Covers

Materials

- ❖ Card stock or heavier tag board, railroad board or any material into which holes can be punched. With lighter materials, let children punch the holes.
- ❖ Writing and drawing implements: pens, pencils, markers, glitter glue, crayons, brushes and watercolor paints or any other medium that can be imagined.
- ❖ Ruler
- ❖ Scissors
- ❖ "Page" inserts chosen for this activity: paper (stapled lined or picture paper, plain or colored art paper) envelopes, or zip type bags for each child
- ❖ Binding materials: hole punch and materials for tying: any type of material that can be tied, such as yarn, cord, shoelaces, leather strips, ribbons, etc. **or** use the duct tape binding method.

    Note: If the heavier tag board method is chosen for the journal covers, the covers will need to be bound in the duct tape method.

Optional materials if the students will be making collage covers

- • Collage materials: cut paper shapes, torn or cut up art paper, tissue paper, magazine pictures and phrases, glitter, feathers, left over bits of yarn or fabric, any other art materials that might be appropriate, **and** clear or white glue.

Method

- ❖ Card stock or the heavier tag board can be decorated with collage, markers, glitter glue, crayons or any other medium you and your students can imagine.
- ❖ Allow the children to decorate their covers.
- ❖ Allow the covers to dry thoroughly before binding.
- ❖ Remember, if using the heavier tag board for the journal covers, bind them in the duct tape method.

Journal Filler "Pages"

1. Paper

There is a wide variety of different types of paper that can be used for journal pages: from plain and lined papers and newsprint, to many types of plain and colored art papers of different weights and sizes. The choice of paper may reflect the purpose of journals being created (e.g., art paper for drawing, daily writing journals, scientific observations and drawing, etc.). The teacher will need to make enough packets of age appropriate writing or drawing paper for all the journals.

Picture primary paper is very appropriate for most young ages. Generally, it is newsprint with large lined spaces on the bottom, and a place for drawings on the top. Even for pre-writers, the lines can be a structure for their scribble type pre-writing. This paper is also appropriate for upper elementary when creating science and social studies journals, as they can draw pictures of their observations. It may also be appropriate for children with certain varieties of special needs (e.g., dysgraphia, visual processing disorders, developmental delays)

The instructor can staple the packets of paper (some are best folded in half and stapled) depending on the size of the paper, or punch holes in them, depending on the journal style chosen.

2. Envelope Books

Envelope books are good for collecting words, letters, or small samples, such as leaves. They are more unique than the basic "writing" journal, and because of that, quite fun for the children.

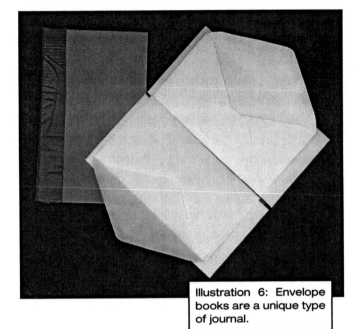

Illustration 6: Envelope books are a unique type of journal.

Materials

❖ Gather together a variety of envelopes. Boxes of envelopes can be found at yard sales. Left over envelopes are sold at card stores and pharmacies that carry cards from time to time at low prices.
❖ Try to find brightly colored or patterned envelopes.
❖ Have the children choose two larger envelopes for the covers and smaller ones in the inside.
❖ Six or seven envelopes is a good quantity for a journal
❖ Cellophane tape
❖ Staples and a stapler
❖ Duct tape
❖ Scissors

Method

❖ Staple the envelopes together with the open end facing out so that the children can insert their letters, words, or items into them easily.
❖ The part of the envelope that usually carries the stamp and address faces out on the covers and can be decorated by the children.
❖ The "page" envelopes can be assembled face to face or in whatever fashion you or the child prefers. Remember that there is much learning in making mistakes. If the child makes a mistake in assembling this book, ask them if they think their method works well, and how they might do it another time to make it function better.
❖ After the book has been put together, staple.
❖ Have children bind over the staples with gaffer's tape on the outside.
❖ For easier use, open the inside covers and bind on the inside with cellophane tape.

3. Zipper Bag Books

Zip-type sandwich bags make great journals. They can be used to collect samples, or they can be used as pages into which the child can insert writing or drawing cards. This type of journal is fairly simple to assemble. Younger children may find the plastic "slippery" and may need additional help keeping their stack (five to seven are good amounts of sandwich bags to use. One can also create a cover for this journal or not as one prefers.

Illustration 7: Children can use zipper bag books to collect a wide variety of small items.

Materials

- ❖ Zipper style bags, appropriately sized for the project at hand
- ❖ Staples
- ❖ Duct tape
- ❖ Scissors

Method

- ❖ Make a stack of zip bags with the opening facing out.
- ❖ The stack may be sandwiched between covers if desired.
- ❖ Staple the closed ends of the zipper bags together.
- ❖ Cover with a strip of gaffer's/duct tape of the appropriate size.
- ❖ The journals are now ready to be used.

Journal Binding Methods

1. Duct Tape Binding

Duct tape makes a wonderful binding material. Duct tape may be purchased at dollar stores, hardware stores, and places like Wal-Mart. It is relatively inexpensive. When used as a book binding, it lasts and lasts.

Materials

- ❖ Duct tape
- ❖ Rulers
- ❖ Scissors
- ❖ Journal to be bound

Method

- ❖ Staple the inside pages together.
- ❖ Make a stack of the materials to be bound.

❖ Have the back cover facing out, place the stapled pages on top of back cover, and top with the front cover, with the cover design facing out.
❖ Measure the length of the cover pages.
❖ Cut a strip of duct tape the length of the covers.
❖ To the best of the child's ability, have the child place the stack to be bound vertically down the center of the duct tape, and smooth the tape over the front and back covers, creating a spine.
❖ Open the book up.
❖ With another piece of duct tape or clear plastic packing tape if you prefer, attach the bound covers to the pages.
❖ Be sure the backs of the staples are covered by tape so that little fingers do not become inadvertently snagged.

2. Hole Punch and Cord Binding

All schools have hole punches, paper, yarn, string and other materials that can be made into journals at no cost to the teacher or the parents. If the teacher or the parents are willing to find or donate other materials, the possibilities are limitless!

Materials

This versatile of binding method can be used with:
❖ Any material into which holes can be punched,
❖ Any number of holes,
❖ Any type of material that can be tied.
> *Note: For convenience in binding, one hole could best be held together with a brad (the little inexpensive metal ones found in any office supply store)*

Method

❖ Using a hole punch, punch holes into the covers and pages making sure the holes line up correctly with each other (three hole, two hole or one hole punches can be used - as long as holes line up correctly)
❖ Stack the covers and pages.
❖ Measure ties to length (predetermined by the teacher)
❖ Cut enough segments of string, cord, ribbon, or yarn for each hole.
❖ Thread one segment through each of the holes in the stack.
❖ Tie with a knot or a bow.

Suggested Reading:

Aliki. (1988). *How a Book Is Made* (Reading Rainbow book). ISBN: 0064460851. Spanish edition. (1989). *Como Se Hace un Libro*. ISBN: 8426124003.
Amery, H. (1994). *Then and Now*. ISBN: 0746007949. (great illustrations: side by side pictures of how things used to be and how they are now)
Christelow, E. (1997). *What Do Authors Do?* ISBN: 0395866219.

Moss, M. (2001). *Rachel's journal: The story of a pioneer girl.* ISBN: 015202168X.

Nixon, J.L. (1995). *If You Were a Writer.* ISBN: 0689719000.

Pallotta, J. (1996). *The Freshwater Alphabet Book.* ISBN: 0881069000.

William, V.B (1984). *Three Days On a River in a Red Canoe.* ISBN: 0688040721. (Reading Rainbow book; Child's journal of a canoe trip, what the trip was like; how to plan and take a trip).

Target Areas of Learning

Physical Development

- ❖ **Fine motor**: using the small muscles of the hand and fingers: cutting, gluing, drawing, placing, threading, holding writing/drawing tools correctly, tying
- ❖ **Eye-hand coordination**: coordinating visual acuity with using the small muscles of the hand and fingers: threading, cutting on lines, lining up holes, assembling pages, placing items in laminator pouches, placing books on duct tape
- ❖ **Sensory discrimination**
  - **Visual discrimination** (sight): identifying and assembling designs with creative materials visually
  - **Tactile discrimination** (touch): identifying and differentiating textures with touch

Cognitive Development

- ❖ **Language Arts**
  - **Verbal skills**
    - o **Vocabulary development**: using and comprehending new words
  - **Language development**: understanding and following simple instructions; describing components of the activity and the processes used to make the journals
  - **Emergent literacy**
    - o **Symbol interpretation**: recognizing name, recognizing letters & words; at the most basic level learning that marks have meaning
    - o **Vocabulary development**: recognizing new words
  - **Writing skills**
    - o **Penmanship**: tracing letters, writing name, writing new words
      - – Using various tools for writing
      - – Writing as part of decorating journals
- ❖ Math Skills
  - **Measurement**: using a standard measure to determine the size (height, length
  - **1:1 correspondence**: counting items in an organized way that shows understanding of the object's placement as a single entity in a group (counting)

Social Development

- ❖ **Working cooperatively with others in a group**: working well as a member of a team and as a community: working well with others
- ❖ **Sharing**: using materials as a class resource

❖ **Taking turns:** allowing others a fair use of materials
❖ **Taking care of classroom environment:** helping with clean up
❖ **Taking responsibility:** developing a willingness to take on tasks that support the individual and the group as a whole, assisting others when needed
❖ **Following instructions:** using the tools as instructed, cleaning up

Emotional Development
❖ **Self-esteem:** feeling a sense of accomplishment by making a book of one's own
❖ **Accomplishment:** developing a sense of self-worth from participating in and completing a personal journal

Creative Expression
❖ **Use of creative media and expression of imagination**
  • **2-dimensional visual arts:** creating journal covers using 2-dimensional media
  • **3-dimensional visual arts:** assembling the journal itself
❖ **Developing aesthetic appreciation** for the other children's journals
❖ **Creative risk:** being comfortable using art materials to create personal journals

Possible Accommodations for *Journal Making Activities*

ADHD
❖ Use positive reinforcement (praise) when child shares
❖ Offer more time or break activity up into several smaller sessions
❖ Place a splat mat beneath tables if wet media are being used
❖ Break activity into smaller steps
❖ Lower ratio: use more supervision when child is using laminator or stapler
❖ Offer a tray to work on to contain activity materials in the child's work space
❖ For activities that require much clean up, allow for a longer clean up / transition time
❖ Put an old tee shirt over child's clothing as a smock for less restricted play

Developmental Delays
❖ Go over task more slowly to be sure child understands the task
❖ Demonstrate the activity in steps for child
❖ Lower ratio: use additional supervision when child is using laminator or stapler
❖ Offer more time or break activity up into several smaller sessions
❖ Have child work with a gentle and more competent peer
❖ Place materials child has chosen on a tray or place a splat mat beneath tables if wet media are being used
❖ Use primary picture paper for pages of journal for easier writing (see Appendix A-2)
❖ Offer positive feedback as the child is working, and as activity is completed

Autism Spectrum Disorders

❖ Explain the activity using short simple phrases
❖ Offer more time or break activity up into several smaller sessions
❖ Present the activity more than once, allowing the child to become accustomed to the activity
❖ Demonstrate the activity in advance
❖ Show child that the activity is on the schedule for this day
❖ Use positive reinforcement when child participates
❖ Pair child with a more competent and patient peer (if possible, use the same peer for the child's buddy as autistic children resist change)
❖ Place a splat mat beneath tables if wet media are being used

Visual Impairments

❖ Use brightly colored materials
❖ Lower the ratio: the child may need assistance using laminator
❖ Offer more time or break activity up into several smaller sessions
❖ Have child work with a gentle and more competent peer
❖ Place materials child has chosen on a tray or place a splat mat beneath tables if wet media are being used
❖ Offer the child a magnifying glass on a stand (similar to the ones used for needlework, found in craft stores)
❖ Offer the child adapted tools for writing, drawing and cutting

Orthopedic Impairments

❖ Offer the child adapted tools for writing, drawing and cutting
❖ Use larger pieces of paper and other collage materials
❖ Make sure that the child is positioned comfortably
❖ Make sure the physical environment makes materials accessible and participation as easy as possible for child
❖ Use a tray if appropriate
❖ If wet media are used, use a smock
❖ Use hand-over-hand method to manipulate materials if child lacks strength or mobility in hands and fingers

Gifted and Talented Education (GATE)

❖ Enrichments could include offering a wider variety of materials
❖ Allow child to work independently
❖ Partner child with children struggling with the task
❖ Use positive reinforcement when child shows patience with non-gifted peers

English Language Learners (ELL)

❖ Explain the activity using short simple phrases
❖ Demonstrate activity step by step as you explain it
❖ Observe child in the process of the activity to check for understanding

❖ Patiently repeat instructions when necessary
❖ Allow more time for activity or break up activity into several sessions totaling a greater amount of time

Content Standards For Kindergarten Met By This Activity

English Language Arts
Reading (1.0, 1.1, 1.2, 1.3, 1.4, 1.5, 1.6)
Writing (1.0, 1.1, 1.2, 1.3, 1.4)
Listening and Speaking (1.0, 1.1, 1.2)

Mathematics
Numbers and Counting (1.0, 1.2, 1.3)
Algebra and Sets (1.0, 1.1)
Measurement and Geometry (1.0, 1.1)

History and Social Science
Following Rules (K.1, K.1.1)

Visual Arts
Artistic Perception (1.0, 1.1, 1.2, 1.3)
Creative Expression (2.0, 2.1, 2.2, 2.3, 2.4, 2.5, 2.6)
Understanding Historical / Cultural Contributions of Visual Arts (3.0, 3.1)

Learning Plan

I. Name of Activity: Journal Making: Laminated Covers, Hole Punch and Cord Binding

II. Date of Presentation:

III. Age or Grade Level: Kindergarten to Primary

IV. Ratio of teachers to children needed for this activity: 1:6
This is an excellent kidney-shaped table activity

V. Target Areas of Learning / Goals and Objectives (target areas of learning directly relate to "VI. Evaluation Rubric")
   1. Physical: _____
   2. Cognitive: _____
   3. Social: _____
   4. Emotional: _____
   5. Creative: _____

VI. Evaluation Rubric: (if more than two learning areas are being evaluated, a spreadsheet form may be preferred)

Targeted Area of Learning	**Targeted Area of Learning**
_____	_____
_____	_____
4. Always _____	**4.** Always _____
3. Usually _____	**3.** Usually _____
2. Sometimes _____	**2.** Sometimes _____
1. Rarely _____	**1.** Rarely _____

VII. Materials and Preparation Needed
   1. One laminator for each group of six children
   2. **At least 2** laminator pouches for **each** child
   3. Laminator carriers, optimally 1 for each child
   4. "Page" inserts chosen for this activity: paper (stapled lined or picture paper, plain or colored art paper) envelopes, or zip type bags for each child
   5. Writing and drawing implements: pens, pencils, markers, crayons, etc.
   6. Decorative & patterned tissue paper, wrapping paper, synthetic winter holiday decorating fibers (note: tear some of the tissue paper into smaller pieces, particularly the sparkly & shiny types that will be in great demand to allow all the children who so choose to have some in their art work
   7. Scissors
   8. Ruler

9. Duct or gaffer's tape
10. Start warming up laminator about 20 minutes before the activity begins

VIII. Procedures

For Making Laminated Journal Covers

1. Set an open laminator carrier at each seat, with an open laminator pouch in it, place the closed end of laminator pouch into the closed end of the laminator carrier
2. Set out a wide selection of tissue papers, magazines to be cut or torn, semi-dried flower petals, small bits of acrylic tinsel etc.
3. Allow children to place the various materials into the pouch, making sure that the artwork does not become too thick
4. Carefully close the pouch and the carrier over it
5. Children insert the closed long end of the carrier pouch into the laminator, holding the sides gently, to assure even movement through the laminator
6. Wait about 30 seconds before opening the pouch to check if the artwork may need to be laminated twice.
7. When the covers have cooled, the children may handle them to begin making their journals. Either of the two following binding methods may be used.

For Making Duct Tape Bindings

1. Children measure the length of the tag board to be bound and cut a length of duct tape to match the length of the tag board
2. Children lay cut strip of duct tape on a flat surface large enough to assemble book
3. Children place the covers along the vertical midpoint of the duct tape, with the stapled paper laying on top of the back cover
4. Children measure the length of the bundle of paper inserted and cut two pieces of either plastic packing tape or duct tape to fit
5. Children carefully lay second piece of tape along the inside of the front cover, and the bundle of inserted papers
6. Children fold the papers over onto the front cover and proceed in the same manner for the back cover
7. If necessary, trim any excess tape

Optional Method For Making Hole and Punch Bindings

1. When slightly cooled, children punch holes in laminated covers with a three-hole punch. Punch holes into the covers making sure the holes line up correctly with each other.
   Note: Three- hole, two-hole or one-hole punches can be used, as long as holes line up correctly; for simplicity, directions here are for three-holes
2. When both covers are laminated and punched, give each child a bundle of three hole punched paper (or other page fillers such as envelopes, zip lock bags, or folded and stapled inserts of wide lined newsprint paper with blank area on the upper half for drawings, "pages" such as these will have to also punched)

3. Stack front cover, bundle of paper (punched), and back cover
4. Children choose cord, ribbon, or string and measure ties to length
   Note: Length of the ties is predetermined by the teacher and the ties may be precut for convenience
5. Cut enough segments of string, cord, ribbon, or yarn for each hole.
6. Stack front cover, bundle of paper, and back cover of the journal
7. Thread one segment through each of the holes in the stack (thru front cover, pages and back cover). Tie with a knot or a bow.
   Note: For convenience in binding, smaller journals with only one hole could best be held together with a brad (the little inexpensive metal ones found in any office supply store)

IX. **Accommodations** (changes to accommodate learning diversity)
Name of Accommodated Area:
1. _____
2. _____
3. _____
4. _____
5. _____

X. **Applicable Framework Standards: Kindergarten**
Standard _____
_____
_____
_____
_____

Standard _____
_____
_____
_____
_____

Standard _____
_____
_____
_____
_____

Standard _____
_____
_____
_____
_____

Standard _____

_____

_____

_____

_____

XI. Evaluation and Comments (i.e.: How well did the plan work? Great responses? What aspects are especially effective? Not effective? What improvements are needed? Ideas for follow up activities and other notes)

_____

_____

_____

_____

Learning Plan

    I.   **Name of Activity: Journal Making: Tag Board Covers**

    II.   **Date of Presentation:**

    III.   **Age or Grade Level: Pre-k to Kindergarten**

    IV.   **Ratio of teachers to children needed for this activity:** 1:4 or 1:6 depending upon the materials chosen

    V.   **Target Areas of Learning / Goals and Objectives** (target areas of learning directly relate to "VI. Evaluation Rubric")

        1. Physical: _____

        2. Cognitive: _____

        3. Social: _____

        4. Emotional: _____

        5. Creative: _____

    VI.   **Evaluation Rubric:** (if more than two learning areas are being evaluated, a spreadsheet form may be preferred)

Targeted Area of Learning   **Targeted Area of Learning**

    _____   _____

    _____   _____

    4. Always _____   **4.** Always _____

    3. Usually _____   **3.** Usually _____

    2. Sometimes _____   **2.** Sometimes _____

    1. Rarely _____   **1.** Rarely _____

    VII.   **Materials and Preparation Needed**

        1. Card stock or heavier tag board, railroad board or any material into which holes can be punched. With lighter materials, let children punch the hole

        2. Writing and drawing implements: pens, pencils, markers, glitter glue, crayons, brushes and watercolor paints or any other medium that can be imagined.

        3. Ruler

        4. Scissors

        5. "Page" inserts chosen for this activity: paper (stapled lined or picture paper, plain or colored art paper) envelopes, or zip type bags for each child

        6. Binding materials: hole punch and materials for tying: any type of material that can be tied, such as yarn, cord, shoelaces, leather strips, ribbons, etc. **or** use the duct or gaffer's tape binding method.

        Note: If the heavier tag board is chosen for the journal covers, the covers will need to be bound in the duct tape method.

Optional materials if making collage covers: collage materials: cut paper shapes, torn or cut up art paper, tissue paper, magazine pictures and phrases, glitter, feathers, left over bits of yarn or fabric, any other art materials that might be appropriate, **and** white glue

VIII. Procedures
For Making Tag Journal Covers
1. Set out two pieces of tag, heavy card stock, or railroad board and the type of pages to be used (e.g., inserts of stapled lined or picture paper, envelopes, or zip-type bags) for each child
2. Make an interesting assortment of materials with which the child might decorate the journal covers: markers, crayons, glitter glue, collage materials: feathers, bits of ribbon, acrylic tinsel, or any other medium the teacher or students can imagine.
3. Children need a sufficient time to create; children design and assemble their own journal covers
4. If wet media are used open the journals face down and allow to dry
5. Allow the covers to dry thoroughly before binding.

For Making Hole and Punch Bindings
1. Using a hole punch, punch holes into the covers and pages making sure the holes line up correctly with each other. Three-hole, two-hole or one-hole punches can be used, as long as holes line up correctly
2. Stack the covers and pages.
3. Measure ties to length (predetermined by the teacher)
4. Cut enough segments of string, cord, ribbon, or yarn for each hole.
5. Thread one segment through each of the holes in the stack.
6. Tie with a knot or a bow.
    Note: For convenience in binding, smaller journals with only one hole could best be held together with a brad (the little inexpensive metal ones found in any office supply store)

Optional Method For Use With Heavier Tag Board (or as preferred)
For Making Hole and Punch Bindings
1. Children measure the length of the tag board to be bound and cut a length of duct tape to match the length of the tag board
2. Children lay cut strip of duct tape on a flat surface large enough to assemble book
3. Children place the covers along the vertical midpoint of the duct tape, with the stapled paper laying on top of the back cover
4. Children measure the length of the bundle of paper inserted and cut two pieces of either plastic packing tape or duct tape to fit
5. Children carefully lay second piece of tape along the inside of the front cover, and the bundle of inserted papers
6. Children fold the papers over onto the front cover and proceed in the same manner

for the back cover

7. If necessary, trim any excess tape

IX. Accommodations (changes to accommodate learning diversity)
Name of Accommodated Area:

1. _____
2. _____
3. _____
4. _____
5. _____

X. Applicable Framework Standards: Kindergarten

Standard _____

_____
_____
_____
_____

Standard _____

_____
_____
_____
_____

Standard _____

_____
_____
_____
_____

Standard _____

_____
_____
_____
_____

Standard _____

_____
_____
_____
_____

XI. Evaluation and Comments (i.e.: How well did the plan work? Great responses? What aspects are especially effective? Not effective? What improvements are needed? Ideas for follow up activities and other notes)

_____

_____

_____

_____

Laminated Letters and Numbers for Magnetic Play

Cutting and laminating is always a source of excitement and fun for learners of all ages. This is a relatively inexpensive way to extend magnet play. It also offers children the opportunity to identify letters, numbers, and/or words that will build a strong sense of success, as well as creating their own personalized set of magnetic letters, numbers, and/or words. The children can keep their letters, numbers, and/or words in their zip lock bag journals or their envelope journals. This activity is best when broken up over a number of days. If the children are in the process of learning the letters and numbers, you may only want to work on one or two letters each week.

Illustration 8: Children can laminate any dry, flat item and make it into a magnet.

Materials

- ❖ Collect old magazines, ads from the newspaper (the ones printed on shiny paper work best), advertisements that contain letters, numbers, and/or words that in a large font size
- ❖ Safety scissors
- ❖ Personal laminator and pouches and carriers for pouches
- ❖ Rolls of narrow magnetic tape; found inexpensively at any craft store; teacher (or adult helper) should cut the rolls into small pieces (i.e., 1/2" to 1") before the activity
- ❖ Oil pan magnet center or cookie trays
- ❖ Magnetic clip to hold word list to oil pan or cookie trays
- ❖ Optional: individualized spelling word lists

Method

- ❖ Collect old magazines, ads from the newspaper (the ones printed on shiny paper work best), advertisements that contain letters, numbers, and/or words that in a large font size
- ❖ Set out the papers to be cut up, along with scissors
- ❖ Ask the children to cut out certain letters, numbers, and/or words each day
- ❖ It is best to ask the children to find both the upper and lower case form of any letter, as they will be learned concurrently
- ❖ When the children have collected enough letters to justify running the laminator (do not wait too long for this), have the children place their letters into the laminator pouch and carrier
- ❖ Laminate
- ❖ Have the children cut out their letters, numbers, and/or words and affix a small piece of magnetic tape on the back of the cut out laminated letters

❖ When the children are at the magnet center they can then take their letters, numbers, and/or words to the center and play with them
❖ Children can take their spelling word list to the magnet center to practice spelling with a partner kinesthetically

Suggested Reading:

Ada, A.F. (1997). *Gathering the Sun: An Alphabet in Spanish and English.* ISBN: 0-688-13903-5. (Winner 1998 Americas Award) (vibrant paintings illustrate poems of each letter of the alphabet).

Fowler, A. (1995). *What Magnets Can Do. (Rookie read-about science).* ISBN: 051646034X.

Knowlton, J. & Barton, H. (1997). *Geography From A to Z: A Picture Glossary.* ISBN: 0064460991.

Pallotta, J. (1996). *The Freshwater Alphabet Book.* ISBN: 0881069000.

Pallotta, J. & Thomson, B. (1992). *The Vegetable Alphabet Book.* ISBN: 0881064688.

Pallotta, J. (1989). *The Ocean Alphabet Book.* ISBN: 0881064580.

Rose, D. L. (2000). *Into the A, B, Sea: An Ocean Alphabet Book.* ISBN: 0439096960.

Target Areas of Learning

Physical Development

❖ **Fine motor skills:** using the small muscles of the hand and fingers: cutting out and assembling magnetic letters
❖ **Eye-hand coordination:** coordinating visual acuity with using the small muscles of the hand and fingers: cutting out letters accurately
❖ **Sensory discrimination**
  • **Visual discrimination** (sight): identifying letters, numbers, words visually
  • **Tactile discrimination** (touch): identifying letters, numbers, words through touch

Cognitive Development

❖ **Language Arts**
  • **Verbal skills**
    o **Language development**: acquiring and using language appropriately: conversation
    o **Vocabulary development**: adding to the body of words and phrases understood and used
  • **Emergent literacy**
    o **Symbol interpretation**: understanding that marks have meaning: identifying letters and numbers; differentiating upper and lower case letters
    o **Letter recognition:** learning upper and lower case letters
    o **Phonemic awareness:** matching sounds to letters
    o **Word recognition**: understanding that groups of letters create many words
    o **Spelling skills**: matching words on word list with magnet letters

o **Matching spoken words to written words**: correctly associating the auditory expression with the written symbol grouping

❖ **Math Skills**
  • **Mathematical literacy**
    o **Number recognition**: recognizing that a specific symbol is associated with a specific quantity; correctly identifying the number symbol by name
  • **Mathematical applications**
    o **Algebra**: sorting and matching for one or more properties: categorization/ grouping: separate and match items into groups
❖ **Social Science**
  • **Recognizing and accepting diversity: cultural/linguistic understanding**: practice finding words in languages other than English

Social Development

❖ **Working collaboratively:** working cooperatively practicing spelling words
❖ **Sharing**: allowing others to use center and materials
❖ **Taking turns:** allowing others to have appropriate turns
❖ **Patience**: being comfortable with delayed gratification
❖ **Following directions**: carrying out directions given by a person in authority
❖ **Negotiation**: persuading classmates to participate in a group magnet activity
❖ **Taking care of classroom environment**: participating in cleanup

Emotional Development

❖ **Self-esteem:** developing a sense of competence in spelling in a low risk environment
❖ **Accomplishment**: developing a sense of self worth from learning to recognize letters and words

Creative Expression
❖ **Use of creative media and expression of imagination**:
  • **2-dimensional visual arts**: making and using magnetic letters, numbers, words in creative ways
❖ **Creative thinking**: inventing games with letters, numbers, words
❖ **Creative writing**: using words to write in individual ways

Possible Accommodations for *Letters for Magnetic Play Activities*

ADHD
❖ Go over task step-by-step to be sure child understands the task
❖ Model activity while explaining activity to children
❖ Use positive reinforcement (praise) when child works well with others and behaves appropriately
❖ Allow the activity go on a little longer if child becomes engaged
❖ Offer the child a carrel to reduce distraction

❖ Offer a smaller selection of print material from which to choose
❖ Allow the child to have an opportunity to act as your helper, to set up the activity
❖ Pair child with another child for opportunities for cooperative play
❖ Offer a tray to work on to contain materials
❖ Go over task more slowly to be sure child understands the task

Developmental Delays
❖ Explain activity using short simple phrases, being sure to make eye contact while doing so
❖ Model the activity while explaining it
❖ Use positive reinforcement as the child succeeds finding and cutting out letters, numbers, words
❖ Check in on child frequently
❖ Have child work with a gentle peer
❖ Offer more time to complete task
❖ Use adapted scissors if necessary
❖ Use larger printed out letters so child can cut them out easily
❖ Lower the ratio: use additional supervision when child is using laminator

Autism Spectrum Disorders
❖ Explain the activity using short simple phrases making sure to maintain eye contact
❖ Model activity while explaining it
❖ Present the activity as part of the regular class routine, allowing the child to become accustomed to the activity
❖ Use positive reinforcement when child participates
❖ Reduce the number of letters, numbers, words so selection is easier
❖ Use larger size fonts
❖ Use adapted scissors
❖ Offer a more limited selection of materials, being sure to include types of materials the child particularly likes
❖ Adjust the duration of the activity for each session if it appears the child is more or less engaged with it, and have another activity as back up

Visual Impairments
❖ Adjust the lighting to reduce glare
❖ Offer brighter, high contrast colors of letters, numbers, words in larger sizes
❖ Use larger size fonts
❖ Use adapted scissors, if necessary
❖ Use positive reinforcement and reward incremental achievements
❖ Allow child to make words, using fewer and larger letters
❖ Check in on children frequently
❖ Offer more time if necessary, for the child to complete the activity and feel successful

Orthopedic Impairments
- ❖ Position child comfortably
- ❖ Adjust furniture or put activity on a tray if it works better for child
- ❖ Use adapted tools such as scissors
- ❖ Use larger font sizes for easier cutting
- ❖ Guide child using hand-over-hand method if child lacks fine motor dexterity
- ❖ Set aside additional time to complete task

Gifted and Talented Education (GATE)
- ❖ Enrichments could include offering a wider selection of materials
- ❖ Offer a broader selection of words to find
- ❖ Pair with a child needing additional support

English Language Learners (ELL)
- ❖ Explain the activity using short simple phrases making sure to maintain eye contact
- ❖ Model activity while explaining it
- ❖ Be sure to praise incremental successes
- ❖ Reduce the quantity of work requested
- ❖ Select less difficult words initially, increasing the challenge as the child becomes skilled at task

Content Standards For Kindergarten Met By This Activity

English Language Arts
> Reading (1.0, 1.3, 1.5, 1.6, 1.7, 1.8, 1.9, 1.10, 1.11, 1.13, 1.14, 1.15, 1.16)
> Writing (1.0, 1.2, 1.3)
> Written and Oral Language (1.2)
> Listening and Speaking (1.0, 1.1)

Mathematics
> Algebra, Sets and Sorting (1.0, 1.1)

History and Social Science
> Following Rules (K.1, K.1.1)

Learning Plan

    I. **Name of Activity: Laminated Letters and Numbers for Magnetic Play**

    II. **Date of Presentation:**

    III. **Age or Grade Level: Pre-k and up**

    IV. **Ratio of teachers to children needed for this activity:** 1:6

    V. **Target Areas of Learning / Goals and Objectives** (target areas of learning directly relate to "VI. Evaluation Rubric")

        1. Physical: _____

        2. Cognitive: _____

        3. Social: _____

        4. Emotional: _____

        5. Creative: _____

    VI. **Evaluation Rubric:** (if more than two learning areas are being evaluated, a spreadsheet form may be preferred)

Targeted Area of Learning	**Targeted Area of Learning**
_____	_____
_____	_____
4. Always _____	**4.** Always _____
3. Usually _____	**3.** Usually _____
2. Sometimes _____	**2.** Sometimes _____
1. Rarely _____	**1.** Rarely _____

    VII. **Materials and Preparation Needed**

       1. Collect old magazines, ads from the newspaper (the ones printed on shiny paper work best), advertisements that contain letters, numbers, and/or words that in a large font size

       2. Safety scissors

       3. Personal laminator and pouches

       4. Laminator pouches and carriers

       5. Rolls of narrow magnetic tape; found inexpensively at any craft store;

       6. Teacher (or adult helper) should cut the rolls into small pieces (i.e. 1/2" to 1") before the activity

    VIII. **Procedures**

       1. Set out the newspapers, ads, and magazines to be cut up, along with scissors

       2. Ask the children to cut out **certain** letters, numbers or words each day

3. It is best to ask the children to find both the upper and lower case form of any letter, as they will be learned concurrently
4. When the children have collected enough letters to justify running the laminator (I would not wait too long for this), have the children place their letters into the laminator pouch and carrier
5. Laminate the letters (numbers or words)
6. Have the children cut out their letters, numbers, and/or words; when children are ready, show them how to remove the protective paper to reveal the sticky back of the magnet; affix a small piece of magnetic tape on the back of the cut out laminated letters
7. When the children are at the magnet center they can then take their letters, numbers, and/or words to the center and play with them

IX. Accommodations (changes to accommodate learning diversity)
Name of Accommodated Area:
   1. _____
   2. _____
   3. _____
   4. _____
   5. _____

X. Applicable Framework Standards: Kindergarten
Standard _____
   _____
   _____
   _____
   _____

Standard _____
   _____
   _____
   _____
   _____

Standard _____
   _____
   _____
   _____
   _____

Standard _____
   _____
   _____
   _____
   _____

Standard _____

_____

_____

_____

_____

XI. **Evaluation and Comments** (i.e.: How well did the plan work? Great responses? What aspects are especially effective? Not effective? What improvements are needed? Ideas for follow up activities and other notes)

_____

_____

_____

_____

Name Tag Activity

The *Name Tag* activity is a spin away from *Rainbow Writing*. It is a wonderful "beginning of the year" activity, which may be used to help the teacher and any paraprofessionals to learn the children's names. In this activity, direct children to write their names decoratively on card stock word strips cut to the appropriate size with holes on either end. There is learning for the children in creating these name tags, as well as in learning to identify their own name and the names of their classmates. As children learn to visually identify their names, the teacher may, in the form of a game, ask one child to retrieve another child's name tag. Be reasonably certain that the child can identify the other child's name, as it is essential to avoid humiliating children at school. Humiliation will undermine the entire learning process. The name tag could be done in *Rainbow Writing* or this could be a separate activity. These name tags can be affixed to pencil boxes later on.

Materials
* ❖ Card stock writing strips (with or without guidelines)
* ❖ Hole punch
* ❖ Yarn or string, or light weight cord
* ❖ Various writing tools: pencils, crayons, markers, glitter glue pens, Nancy bottles filled with paint

Method
* ❖ Prepare card stock strips. Cut to the appropriate length. Punch holes on both ends
* ❖ Cut strips of soft yarn (the non-itchy type) to fit comfortably around the neck of a young child.
* ❖ Offer a variety of writing and drawing tools for the children to use for this activity.
* ❖ Offer enough time for the children to complete the activity to their satisfaction.
* ❖ Allow the nametags to dry. Hang on hooks or a small coat tree.
* ❖ Initially ask children to find their own name tags, later children can read and distribute name tags to their class mates

Suggested Reading:
Carle, E. (1987). *Do You Want To Be My Friend?* ISBN: 0064431274. (Ages 3-6)

Carlson, M.L. (1990). *I Like Me*. ISBN: 0140508198. (Ages 3-6)

Mitchell, L. (2001). *Different Just Like Me*. Inc. ISBN: 1570914907.

Mosel, A. (1968). *Tikki Tikki Tembo*. ISBN: 0805006621.

Orie, S.D. (1996). *Did You Hear the Wind Sing Your Name? An Oneida Song of Spring*. ISBN: 0802774857.

Recorvits, H. & Swiatkowski, G.S. (2003). *My Name Is Yoon* (Ezra Jack Keats New Illustrator Award, 2004). ISBN: 0374351147. (young Korean girl struggles to learn English and adapt to her new country).

Steptoe, J. (1987). *Mufaro's Beautiful Daughters*. (Reading Rainbow Book). ISBN: 0688040454 (African legend, also available in Spanish edition).

Sweeney, J. (1998). *Me On the Map.* ISBN: 0517885573.
Suggested CD:
Greg & Steve. (1987). *We All Live Together. Vol.2.* (includes: English / Spanish months of the year song, **World is a Rainbow,** Popcorn, The Freeze) CD Available from: amazon.com

Target Areas of Learning

Physical Development
❖ **Fine motor skills**: using the small muscles of the hand and fingers: holding writing tools correctly;
❖ **Eye-hand coordination**: coordinating visual acuity with using the small muscles of the hand and fingers: forming letters and words correctly on paper;
❖ **Sensory discrimination**
  • **Visual discrimination** (sight)**:** identifying letters and words visually;
  • **Auditory discrimination** (hearing)**:** correctly associating letter sound with letters;
❖ **Articulation**: creating letter and word sounds correctly

Cognitive Development
❖ Language Arts
  • **Verbal skills**
    o **Vocabulary development**: using and comprehending new words
    o **Language development**: understanding and following simple instructions using new words or phrases
  • **Emergent literacy**
    o **Symbol interpretation**: recognizing name, recognizing letters and words; at the most basic level learning that marks have meaning
    o **Word recognition**: understanding that groups of letters create a composite sound which is meaningful; correctly decoding letter groups as specific words which have meaning: recognizing their names in writing
  • **Writing skills:** developing the fine motor skills for the pincer grasp and creating marks to which they attach meaning
    o **Penmanship:** tracing letters, writing name, writing new words;
    o Using various tools for writing,
❖ **Social Science**
  • **Recognizing and accepting human diversity:** learning words in languages other than English or student's first language

Social Development
❖ **Cooperation:** working well in a group setting
❖ **Sharing**: using community resources fairly
❖ **Taking turns**: allowing others a fair use of materials

- ❖ **Following directions**: completing project as directed
- ❖ **Responsibility:** developing a willingness to take on tasks that support the individual and the group as a whole
- ❖ **Taking care of classroom environment: building** a sense of responsibility for classroom environment; taking care of the classroom environment; participating in clean up

Emotional Development
- ❖ **Self esteem**: participating in an activity wherein there is no "wrong" answer
- ❖ **Building self-confidence:** learning new letters and words in a low risk situation
- ❖ **Risk**: being willing to make mistakes in an environment that encourages inventiveness and invites cognitive risk taking
- ❖ **Accomplishment**: writing and decorating name tag creatively

Creative Expression
- ❖ **Use of creative media and expression of imagination**:
  - • **2-dimensional visual arts**: using art materials to create a decorative name tag
- ❖ **Creative risk**: using artistic materials in creative ways
- ❖ **Developing aesthetic appreciation**: appreciating the creative work of classmates

Possible Accommodations for *Name Tag Activity*

ADHD
- ❖ Use positive reinforcement (praise) when child works well with others and behaves appropriately; "catch" children being good; praise staying on task, working well with others, sharing, cooperating
- ❖ Give praise for incremental achievements
- ❖ Allow the activity to go on a little longer if child becomes engaged in it
- ❖ Pair child with another child for opportunities for cooperative play
- ❖ Have the child act as your helper, setting activity up
- ❖ Explain the activity in short, direct sentences, making sure the child maintains eye contact; have the child repeat the instructions to be certain that the child understands what to do

Developmental Delays
- ❖ Use simplified language when giving directions and praise, and go over task more slowly to be sure child understands the task
- ❖ Model activity while explaining it
- ❖ Demonstrate activity to class, but in close proximity to child
- ❖ Use larger letters to trace
- ❖ Offer larger tag cards, use larger writing tools, and art media (e.g., larger crayons, dot bottles) so child can grasp them easily
- ❖ Check in on child frequently
- ❖ Have child work with a gentle peer

- ❖ Offer more time to complete task
- ❖ Use a clip board or tape card strip down if necessary

Autism Spectrum Disorders

- ❖ Explain the activity using short simple phrases being sure to make eye contact when doing so
- ❖ Model activity while explaining it
- ❖ Have child work with a single partner, perhaps the same class partner throughout the semester or school year for additional familiarity
- ❖ Present the activity as part of the centers routine, allowing the child to become accustomed to the activity
- ❖ Use positive reinforcement when child participates
- ❖ Allow child to warm up to the activity, perhaps offering opportunities to work with various media before presenting this activity
- ❖ Offer a more limited selection of materials, being sure to include types of materials the child particularly likes

Visual Impairments

- ❖ Adjust the lighting to reduce glare
- ❖ When writing letters to be traced use a very wide tipped black marker on white card stock (for highest contrast)
- ❖ Offer larger tag cards, and larger writing tools, and art media (e.g., larger crayons, dot bottles) if needed
- ❖ Use larger letters to trace
- ❖ Guide child's hand if necessary
- ❖ Have child work with a gentle and more competent peer
- ❖ Place materials child has chosen on a tray or place a splat mat beneath tables if wet media are being used

Orthopedic Impairments

- ❖ Make sure child is seated comfortably
- ❖ Adjust furniture for maximum accessibility
- ❖ Use a clip board or tape card strip down if necessary
- ❖ Consider using a tray
- ❖ Use adapted tools such as chunky crayons and markers, or wrap bingo bottles or Nancy bottles with bubble wrap cut to fit so child can grip tools more easily
- ❖ Use the hand-over-hand method to guide the child's hand

Gifted and Talented Education (GATE)

- ❖ Child may write out full name
- ❖ Partner child with a child who may need additional support
- ❖ Enrichments could include offering a variety of artistic tools

❖ Initially, and occasionally thereafter ask the child to read out the names of classmates (be careful that the child does not seem to be getting preferential treatment as it will make socializing more challenging for the child.

English Language Learners (ELL)

❖ Explain the activity using short simple phrases being sure to make eye contact when doing so
❖ Model activity while explaining it
❖ Give praise for incremental achievements
❖ If name is long or complicated, shorten for purposes of activity

Content Standards For Kindergarten Met By This Activity

English Language Arts

Reading (1.0, 1.3, 1.5, 1.6, 1.7, 1.9, 1.13, 1.14, 1.15, 1.16)
Writing (1.0, 1.1, 1.2, 1.2, 1.4)
Written and Oral Language (1.0, 1.1, 1.2)
Listening and Speaking (1.0, 1.1)

History and Social Science

Following Rules (K.1, K.1.1)

Visual Arts

Artistic Perception (1.0, 1.1)
Creative Expression (2.0, 2.1)

Learning Plan

   I. **Name of Activity: Name Tag Activity**

  II. **Date of Presentation:**

 III. **Age or Grade Level: Pre-K, Kindergarten**

 IV. **Ratio of teachers to children needed for this activity:** 1:10

  V. **Target Areas of Learning / Goals and Objectives** (target areas of learning directly relate to "VI. Evaluation Rubric")

      1. Physical: _____

      2. Cognitive: _____

      3. Social: _____

      4. Emotional: _____

      5. Creative: _____

 VI. **Evaluation Rubric:** (if more than two learning areas are being evaluated, a spreadsheet form may be preferred)

Targeted Area of Learning	**Targeted Area of Learning**
_____	_____
_____	_____
4. Always _____	4. Always _____
3. Usually _____	3. Usually _____
2. Sometimes _____	2. Sometimes _____
1. Rarely _____	1. Rarely _____

 VII. **Materials and Preparation Needed**
1. Card stock writing strips (with or without guidelines)
2. Hole punch
3. Yarn or string, or light weight cord
4. Various writing tools: pencils, crayons markers, glitter glue pens, Nancy bottles filled with paint

 VIII. **Procedures**
1. Cut card stock word strips into lengths appropriate for children to decoratively write their name and punch holes for yarn at either end
2. For children unfamiliar with writing their name, print name out in block letters
3. Children more familiar with writing their name can either write the name out independently or copy from a sample
4. Set out writing tools for children to use. Be sure to have more than one of each item to encourage easy sharing.

5. Allow children to decorate their name tag. Let dry.
6. Take a strand of yarn, and tie an end of the yarn in either hole.
7. Hang name tags on several hooks.
8. At the beginning of each day have children get their name tags & wear them during morning meeting or circle time
9. Initially ask children to find their own name tags, later children can read and distribute name tags to their class mates

IX. **Accommodations** (changes to accommodate learning diversity)
   Name of Accommodated Area:
   1. _____
   2. _____
   3. _____
   4. _____
   5. _____

X. **Applicable Framework Standards: Kindergarten**
   Standard _____
   _____
   _____
   _____
   _____

   Standard _____
   _____
   _____
   _____
   _____

   Standard _____
   _____
   _____
   _____
   _____

   Standard _____
   _____
   _____
   _____
   _____

   Standard _____
   _____
   _____
   _____
   _____

XI. Evaluation and Comments (i.e.: How well did the plan work? Great responses? What aspects are especially effective? Not effective? What improvements are needed? Ideas for follow up activities and other notes)

_____

_____

_____

_____

Oil Pan Magnet Center

A metal oil pan, inexpensively available at stores such as Wal-Mart and Home Depot, can become an instant learning center. If you are not allowed to attach items to the walls of your classroom, individual cookie trays work as well for this project. The beauty of the oil pan is that it is concurrently kinesthetic, interactive, and cooperative in nature. Children will sit and play singly and in groups, working with the letters, looking at them, touching them, moving them around, creating alphabet art and patterns for hours. It is an excellent way to reinforce alphabet concepts in a noncompetitive, non-stressed context.

Illustration 9: Oil pan trays and cookie sheets can be used as magnetic centers in many curricular areas.

Materials

❖ A metallic oil pan (for individual use, cookie trays)
❖ A drill with a bit that will go through metal
❖ 4 screws long enough to affix oil pan to walls
❖ (Possibly) molly bolts if wall studs cannot be located
❖ Commercially or home made magnetic letters, numbers, shapes (in a variety of sizes and colors such as tanagram shapes), photographs
❖ Magnetic clips to affix word lists to magnet center
❖ For home made magnets: scissors, magnetic tape, personal laminator, laminator pouches

Method

❖ Assuming that you may affix the oil pan to the wall, you will need to (or have someone else) drill holes in each of the four corners of the oil pan
❖ Find two wall studs into which you can bolt the oil pan
❖ Drill four holes into wall studs that will line up with holes in your oil pan
❖ Attach the pan to the wall with very sturdy screws
❖ All of this, of course, should be done when children are **NOT** present.
❖ Purchase a number of sets of inexpensive magnetic letters and numbers from the dollar store
❖ Have the children make letters, laminate them, and affix magnetic tape to the backs of the homemade letters (if you choose this option, you may want to store the children's letters in "zip-style bag" journals
❖ Or purchase commercially prepared letters and numbers; laminate them; then, the teacher (and / or the children) may cut them out and affix magnetic tape to the back of them

❖ The desired result is to have a large selection of upper and lower case letters, with lots of vowels and numbers

❖ Once assembled, allow children to work in small groups at the magnet center

Spelling activity: words can be written on word strips, which are then laminated and magnetic tape placed on back; children can practice spelling by writing words below with magnetic letters

- A word list can be placed next to the center so children can copy from the word list
- Individual word lists can be created for work groups or individual children which can be clipped to the magnet center by using magnetic clips available at dollar stores, usually in sets of six for a dollar

Suggested Reading:

Brown, M. (1974). *All Butterflies: An ABC*. ISBN: 0684137712.

Fowler, A. (1995). *What Magnets Can Do (Rookie read-about science)*. ISBN: 051646034X.

Knowlton, J. & Barton, H. (1997). *Geography From A to Z: A Picture Glossary*. ISBN: 0064460991.

Pallotta, J. (1996). *The Freshwater Alphabet Book*. ISBN: 0881069000.

Wildsmith, B. (1996). *Brian Wildsmith's ABC*. ISBN: 1887734023.

> *Note: Brian Wildsmith's beautifully illustrated alphabet books are available in many languages such as Arabic, Chinese, Farsi, French, Korean, Navajo, Spanish, Portugese, Tagalog, and Vietnamese*

Target Areas of Learning

Physical Development

❖ **Fine motor skills:** using the small muscles of the hand and fingers: picking up magnetic letters and moving them around the oil pan center

❖ **Eye-hand coordination:** coordinating visual acuity with using the small muscles of the hand and fingers: placing the magnets accurately where intended

❖ **Sensory discrimination**: using senses to identify and differentiate items

- **Visual discrimination** (sight): identifying letters visually
- **Auditory discrimination** (hearing): correctly associating letter sound with letters/ words
- **Tactile discrimination**: differentiating items such as purchased plastic letters through the sense of touch

Cognitive Development

❖ **Language Arts**

- **Verbal skills**
  - ○ **Language development**: conversation
  - ○ **Vocabulary development**: learning and comprehending new words

- **Emergent literacy**
  - **Symbol interpretation**: understanding that marks have meaning by working with magnetic letters to form words, phrases and sentences
  - **Letter recognition: learning** the letter symbols of a specific language and correctly identifying the associated phonemes
  - **Differentiating upper and lower case letters:** correctly identifying upper and lower case letters and associating both with the appropriate phoneme
  - **Word recognition:** correctly decoding letter combinations which form words
  - **Spelling skills:** using correct letter symbols to form words
  - **Matching spoken words to printed words**: correctly matching the phonemic sounds to the visual letter combinations
- ❖ Math Skills
  - **Algebra**: sorting and matching for one or more properties: categorization/ grouping: separate and match items into groups
  - **Recognizing number words**: associating the number symbol with the written word for the number with the count of items represented by both the written word and the symbol
- ❖ Social Science
  - **Recognizing and accepting diversity**: practice writing words in languages other than English

Social Development

- ❖ **Sharing:** understanding that materials and space are community resources
- ❖ **Taking turns:** allowing others a fair use of materials, opportunities to participate in class activities
- ❖ **Learning patience**: being comfortable with delayed gratification
- ❖ **Working cooperatively with others in a group:** assembling words and/or sentences as a group/team activity
- ❖ **Collaboration**: working as a group, inventing strategies for group play
- ❖ **Following directions**: carrying out directions for use of magnet center
- ❖ **Taking care of classroom environment**: leaving magnet center clean and ready for the next person's use

Emotional Development

- ❖ **Self-esteem:** feeling good about oneself, the work one does, one's accomplishments and growth in language skills
- ❖ **Self-confidence**: learning to be comfortable taking academic risks related to spelling/ math/grammar
- ❖ **Accomplishment**: developing a sense of self-worth related to increasing language skills in a low risk environment

Creative Expression
- ❖ **Use of creative media and expression of imagination**
  - • **2-dimensional visual arts**: using magnetic pieces in creative ways such as in artistic patterns or assembling words in colorful creative ways
- ❖ **Creative thinking**: inventing games, patterns, phrases with magnet pieces

Possible Accommodations For *Oil Pan Magnets Activity*

ADHD
- ❖ When explaining the activity, request that child repeats instructions back to you to check for understanding
- ❖ Use positive reinforcement (praise) when child works well with others and behaves appropriately; "catch" children being good; praise child for staying on task, sharing, cooperating
- ❖ Allow the activity to go on a little longer if child becomes engaged
- ❖ Have this child work with only one other child to allow many chances to participate
- ❖ Offer a smaller selection of materials from which to choose
- ❖ Offer the child a cardboard "carrel" to reduce distractions, either while working with the materials at a desk on a metal tray, or by setting up the carrel around the oil pan center

Developmental Delays
- ❖ Go over task more slowly to be sure child understands the task keeping eye contact
- ❖ Model activity while explaining the activity
- ❖ Use positive reinforcement as the child succeeds creating words
- ❖ Check in on child frequently for participation and understanding
- ❖ Have child work with a gentle peer
- ❖ Offer more time to complete task, if necessary
- ❖ For spelling: simplify words to be spelled
- ❖ Decrease number of words on personal word list
- ❖ Decrease number of words on word list
- ❖ Use larger magnetic letters so child can grasp them easily

Autism Spectrum Disorders
- ❖ Explain the activity using short simple phrases maintaining eye contact
- ❖ Model activity while explaining the activity
- ❖ Present the activity as part of the centers routine, allowing the child to become accustomed to the activity
- ❖ Use positive reinforcement when child participates
- ❖ Reduce the number of magnets so selection is easier
- ❖ For spelling: simplify words to be spelled
- ❖ Decrease number of words on word list

❖ Pair the child with a gentle, more competent peer for opportunities for cooperative play; pairing with the same class partner throughout the semester or school year builds familiarity

Visual Impairments
❖ Adjust the lighting to reduce glare
❖ Offer brighter colors of magnets in larger sizes
❖ Write words of word list with a larger, wide tipped marker on white paper in a larger size for easier visibility
❖ Lower the ratio: the child may need assistance with the task; adults encourage and support the child in the activity, making certain child is working as independently as possible on the task
❖ Offer more time to complete task
❖ Offer the child a magnifying glass on a stand (similar to the ones used for needlework, found in craft stores)
❖ Have child work with a gentle and more competent peer

Orthopedic Impairments
❖ Adjust the height of the oil pan so the child can reach it easily
❖ Use a large cookie tray for accessibility instead of working on the oil pan
❖ Make sure the child is positioned comfortably
❖ Use larger magnetic pieces
❖ If child has difficulty manipulating magnets, use hand-over-hand method to assist building fine motor dexterity
❖ Set magnetic pieces made of laminated paper up in such a way that the pieces are easier to grasp

Gifted and Talents Education (GATE)
❖ Offer a broader selection of words for the child to write out
❖ Allow child to self select words for personal word list
❖ Partner gifted child with another child needing additional help

English Language Learners (ELL)
❖ Explain the activity using short simple phrases maintaining eye contact
❖ Model activity while explaining the activity
❖ Praise incremental successes to build self esteem and willingness to risk
❖ Reduce the number of magnets so selection is easier
❖ For spelling: simplify words to be spelled
❖ Decrease number of words on word list

Content Standards For Kindergarten Met By This Activity

English Language Arts

Reading (1.0, 1.2, 1.3, 1.4, 1.5, 1.6, 1.7, 1.8, 1.9, 1.10, 1.11, 1.12, 1.13, 1.14, 1.15, 1.16, 1.17)

Writing (1.0, 1.2, 1.3)

Written and Oral Language (1.0, 1.1, 1.2)

Listening and Speaking Strategies (1.0, 1.1)

Mathematics

Algebra, Sets and Sorting (1.0, 1.1)

History and Social Science

Following Rules (K.1, K.1.1)

Learning Plan

    I. Name of Activity: Oil Pan Magnet Center

   II. Date of Presentation:

  III. Age or Grade Level: Pre-K and up

  IV. Ratio of teachers to children needed for this activity: 1:5

   V. Target Areas of Learning / Goals and Objectives (target areas of learning directly relate to "VI. Evaluation Rubric")
      1. Physical: _____
      2. Cognitive: _____
      3. Social: _____
      4. Emotional: _____
      5. Creative: _____

  VI. Evaluation Rubric: (if more than two learning areas are being evaluated, a spreadsheet form may be preferred)

Targeted Area of Learning	**Targeted Area of Learning**
_____	_____
_____	_____
4. Always _____	**4.** Always _____
3. Usually _____	**3.** Usually _____
2. Sometimes _____	**2.** Sometimes _____
1. Rarely _____	**1.** Rarely _____

 VII. Materials and Preparation Needed
    1. Lots of inexpensive magnetic letters and numbers, purchased from the dollar store. (In lieu of this, use commercial or homemade letters and numbers, affixing magnetic tape to the backs)
    2. Large oil pan, screws and drill to attach oil pan to studs in the wall.
    3. Several cookie sheets for individual desk work
    4. Lined word strips; with markers, write sight words and children's names. Laminate.

VIII. Procedures
    1. When children are not present, drill holes in the corners of an oil pan. Use screws to attach it to the studs in the wall of the classroom, at about desk height for ease of student use.
    2. Have an adequate supply of magnetic letters and numbers (whether commercial or homemade) available for the students' use.

3. Have cookie sheets also available for individual students to use at desks.
4. Children assemble in small groups at the oil pan magnet center to engage in learning activities. These activities can be quite diverse: number recognition, letter, or word recognition, spelling, or physical tracing of the letters and numbers, depending on the ability level of the group. The alphabet and numbers 1 to 20 can be displayed above the Magnet Center for the children to reference.
5. Write the children's names individually on word strips, laminate the names, and keep them in a basket. They will be useful for the children to use at the Magnet Center, as well as for tracing and other language activities. A second basket can hold sight words to read and match.

IX. **Accommodations** (changes to accommodate learning diversity)
Name of Accommodated Area:
1. _____
2. _____
3. _____
4. _____
5. _____

X. **Applicable Framework Standards: Kindergarten**
Standard _____
_____
_____
_____
_____

Standard _____
_____
_____
_____
_____

Standard _____
_____
_____
_____
_____

Standard _____
_____
_____
_____
_____

Standard _____

_____

_____

_____

_____

XI. **Evaluation and Comments** (i.e.: How well did the plan work? Great responses? What aspects are especially effective? Not effective? What improvements are needed? Ideas for follow up activities and other notes)

_____

_____

_____

_____

Rainbow Writing

Rainbow writing is a colorful and fun way to introduce young children to writing basic words, such as the child's own name. Even after the child has learned to writ e his own name and identify it, for rainbow writing can be utilized for "Earth Day" by having children rainbow write "Hello" or other words in languages other than English and decorate the room with them. Often these results are quite beautiful, particularly when laminated. As an open-ended activity, it is very effective. There is no "wrong" way to rainbow write.

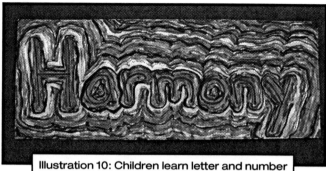
Illustration 10: Children learn letter and number symbols in the process of rainbow writing.

Materials
- ❖ Word strips made of card stock or other firm, but light weight paper
- ❖ Wide tipped marking pen (for teacher to write children's names)
- ❖ Crayons, colored pencils and / or markers, other writing instruments including bingo bottles, fine-tipped bottles of glitter glue and Nancy paint bottles
- ❖ **Optional:** Personal laminator, laminator carriers, and pouches

Method
- ❖ Write the children's names on sturdy white paper in wide-tipped felt pen or sharpie markers. Allow sufficient space between the letters so that the children can trace around their names with colored pencils, crayons, marker, or other art materials including bingo dot bottles and Nancy bottles. If you are considering laminating, crayons, bright markers, bright paints produce an attractive result.
- ❖ Set out crayons, markers, pencils, pens, dot bottles, and any other art materials desired, as tracing materials for the children in your classroom.
- ❖ Give a brief description of the method. "I'd like you to trace around your names using these brightly colored crayons. You may fill up the whole paper if you want to do so."
- ❖ Allow children to work with this activity so long as their interest holds. They do not necessarily need to complete this project in one session. You may offer them the option of setting this project aside for completion later on.
- ❖ If using wet media such as tempera or biocolor in bingo or Nancy bottles, allow the artwork to dry overnight before laminating.
- ❖ If using a personal laminator and laminator pouches, you can allow children to place their artwork inside of the pouches and run it through the laminator when completed. This can be a separate activity, done later in the day or on a subsequent day.

Suggested Reading:

Ada, A.F. (1997). *Gathering the Sun: An Alphabet in Spanish and English.* ISBN: 0-688-13903-5. (Winner 1998 Americas Award) (vibrant paintings illustrate poems of each letter of the alphabet).

Brown, M. (1974). *All Butterflies: An ABC.* ISBN: 0684137712

Cole, J. & Degan, B. (1997). *The Magic School Bus Makes a Rainbow: A Book About Color.* ISBN: 0590922513

Couch, T. (2000). *Tiffany's Guide To Making Brighter Rainbows.* ISBN: 1885473435.

Madrigal, A.H. (De Paola, T. illustrator). (1997*). Eagle and the Rainbow: Timeless Tales From Mexico.* ISBN: 155591-317-2.

Pallotta, J. (1996). *The Freshwater Alphabet Book.* ISBN: 0881069000

Wildsmith, B. (1996). *Brian Wildsmith's ABC.* ISBN: 1887734023

> *Note: Brian Wildsmith's beautifully illustrated alphabet books are available in many languages such as Arabic, Chinese, Farsi, French, Korean, Navajo, Spanish, Portugese, Tagalog, and Vietnamese*

Suggested CD:

Greg & Steve. (1987). *We All Live Together. Vol.2.* (includes: English / Spanish months of the year song, **World is a Rainbow**, Popcorn, The Freeze) CD Available from: amazon.com

Target Areas of Learning

Physical Development

❖ **Fine motor skills**: holding and using writing tools
❖ **Eye-hand coordination**: tracing around letters correctly
❖ **Sensory discrimination:**
  • **Tactile discrimination** (touch): experiencing the physical sensation of placing meaningful marks on paper
  • **Visual discrimination** (sight): identifying letters and colors
  • **Auditory discrimination** (hearing): correctly associating letter sound with letters
❖ **Articulation**: vocally creating letter and word sounds correctly

Cognitive Development

❖ **Language Arts**
  • **Verbal skills**
    o **Language development**: recognizing and adding name, recognizing letters and words to working language; understanding and following simple instructions
    o **Vocabulary development**: learning new words; learning colors
  • **Emergent literacy**
    o **Symbol interpretation**: at the most basic level learning that marks have meaning
    o **Letter recognition**: learning the letter symbols of names and other selected words
    o **Spelling skills**: using correct letter symbol combinations to form words

- **Writing skills**
    - ○ **Emergent writing**: developing the fine motor skills to produce writing
    - ○ **Penmanship**: tracing letters, writing name, writing new words
- ❖ Social Science
    - **Recognizing and accepting diversity**: learning words in languages other than English or the child's first language

Social Development

- ❖ **Sharing**: understanding, and behaving in such a way that reflects that understanding, that the classroom materials are for everyone's use
- ❖ **Taking turns:** everyone in the classroom deserves opportunities to participate in class activities
- ❖ **Patience**: waiting for materials; completing project, delayed gratification; diligence: staying with a project or activity until it is completed
- ❖ **Following directions**: doing the project as instructed
- ❖ **Community building**: learning to read the names of classmates, learning words in languages other than English
- ❖ **Working cooperatively with others in a group**: sharing ideas, materials while creating rainbow writing
- ❖ **Collaboration**: planning, creating artwork with others

Emotional Development

- ❖ **Self-esteem**: feeling good about oneself as one participates in an activity wherein there is no "wrong" answer
- ❖ **Self-confidence**: learning new letters and new words in a safe environment for trying new experiences
- ❖ **Accomplishment**: developing a sense of self-worth from creating decorative work
- ❖ **Risk**: willingness to try something new

Creative Expression

- ❖ **Use of creative media and expression of imagination**
    - **2-dimensional visual arts**: creating interesting patterns with rainbow writing
- ❖ **Working with art tools**: learning to use a variety of creative media
- ❖ **Artistic vocabulary**: learning the names of the art styles and tools
- ❖ **Creative risk**: experimenting with 2 dimensional media

Possible Accommodations for *Rainbow Writing Activity*

ADHD

- ❖ Use positive reinforcement (praise) when child works well with others and behaves appropriately "catch" children being good; praise the child for staying on task, sharing, cooperating
- ❖ Give praise for incremental achievements

❖ Allow the activity to go on a little longer if child becomes engaged in it
❖ Pair child with another child for opportunities for cooperative play
❖ Have the child act as your helper, setting activity up
❖ Explain the activity in short, direct sentences, making sure the child maintains eye contact; have the child repeat the instructions to be certain that the child understands what to do

Developmental Delays
❖ Go over task more slowly to be sure child understands the task maintain eye contact while explaining activity
❖ Model activity as you explain it
❖ Use larger letters to trace
❖ Offer larger tag cards, use larger writing tools, and art media (e.g., larger crayons, dot bottles) so child can grasp them easily
❖ Check in on children frequently
❖ Have child work with a gentle peer
❖ Offer more time to complete task
❖ Tape card strip down or place paper on a clip board to hold it in place using alligator clips on the other side if necessary
❖ Lower the ratio, if necessary
❖ If name is long or complicated, shorten for purposes of activity

Autism Spectrum Disorders
❖ Explain the activity using short simple phrases being certain to maintain eye contact while doing so
❖ Model activity as you explain it
❖ Present the activity as part of the centers routine, allowing the child to become accustomed to the activity
❖ Use positive reinforcement when child participates
❖ Allow child to warm up to the activity, perhaps offering opportunities to work with various media before presenting this activity
❖ Lower the ratio of children to teacher or pair the child up with a more competent peer.
❖ Offer larger writing instruments.
❖ If name is long or complicated, shorten for purposes of activity

Visual Impairments
❖ Adjust the lighting to reduce glare
❖ When writing letters to be traced use a very wide tipped black marker on white card stock (for highest contrast)
❖ Offer larger tag cards, and larger writing tools, and art media (e.g., larger crayons, dot bottles) if needed
❖ Offer media in bright, rather than pastel colors
❖ Use larger letters to trace
❖ Guide child's hand in the hand-over-hand style if necessary

Orthopedic Impairments

❖ Make sure that the furniture is adjusted for maximum accessibility for child
❖ Consider using a tray
❖ Use adapted tools such as chunky crayons and markers, or wrap bingo bottles or Nancy bottles with bubble wrap cut to fit so child can grip tools more easily
❖ Tape card strip down or place paper on a clip board to hold it in place using alligator clips on the other side if necessary
❖ Use the hand-over-hand method to guide the child's hand

Gifted and Talented Education (GATE)

❖ Have the child write out their full name, first and last
❖ Show child the work of famous artists such as Picasso or Van Gough and ask them to create something "in the style of"
❖ Ask child to work with children who might need additional support
❖ If working on other languages, have the child write "hello" in other languages

English Language Learners (ELL)

❖ Explain the activity in short, direct sentences, making sure the child maintains eye contact; have the child repeat the instructions to be certain that the child understands what to do
❖ Model activity as you explain it
❖ Give praise for incremental achievements
❖ If name is long or complicated, shorten for purposes of activity
❖ Re-teach and review word with child in a small group or individually

Content Standards For Kindergarten Met By This Activity

English Language Arts

Reading (1.0, 1.2, 1.3, 1.5, 1.6, 1.7, 1.9, 1.13, 1.14, 1.15, 1.16)
Writing (1.0, 1.1, 1.1, 1.3, 1.4)
Listening and Speaking (1.0, 1.1)

History and Social Science

Following Rules (K.1, K.1.1)

Visual Arts

Artistic Expression (1.0, 1.1, 1.2)
Creative Expression (2.0, 2.1)

Learning Plan

    I. **Name of Activity: Rainbow Writing**

   II. **Date of Presentation:**

  III. **Age or Grade Level: Pre-K, Kindergarten**

  IV. **Ratio of teachers to children needed for this activity:** 1:7

   V. **Target Areas of Learning / Goals and Objectives** (target areas of learning directly relate to "VI. Evaluation Rubric")

      1. Physical: _____

      2. Cognitive: _____

      3. Social: _____

      4. Emotional: _____

      5. Creative: _____

  VI. **Evaluation Rubric:** (if more than two learning areas are being evaluated, a spreadsheet form may be preferred)

Targeted Area of Learning   **Targeted Area of Learning**

_____   _____

_____   _____

    4. Always _____   **4.** Always _____

    3. Usually _____   **3.** Usually _____

    2. Sometimes _____   **2.** Sometimes _____

    1. Rarely _____   **1.** Rarely _____

 VII. **Materials and Preparation Needed**

     1. Word strips made card stock or other firm, but light weight paper

     2. Crayons, colored pencils and / or markers, other writing instruments

     3. Optional: personal laminator, laminator carriers, and pouches

VIII. **Procedures**

     1. On a plain sheet of paper, write out each child's name in marker.

     2. Be sure to space the letters far enough apart so that the child can trace around his or her name many times.

     3. Place a variety of drawing and writing materials for children to write around their names.

     4. Model one or two possible ways for the children to trace around words or their own names.

5. Remember, praise, praise, praise **all** attempts; Remember this is an open-ended activity. The process is **more important** than the product.

6. **Optional:** Laminate completed rainbow writing for display or use as place mats

IX. **Accommodations** (changes to accommodate learning diversity)
Name of Accommodated Area:

1. _____
2. _____
3. _____
4. _____
5. _____

X. **Applicable Framework Standards: Kindergarten**

Standard _____
_____
_____
_____
_____

Standard _____
_____
_____
_____
_____

Standard _____
_____
_____
_____
_____

Standard _____
_____
_____
_____
_____

Standard _____
_____
_____
_____
_____

XI. **Evaluation and Comments** (i.e.: How well did the plan work? Great responses? What aspects are especially effective? Not effective? What improvements are needed? Ideas for follow up activities and other notes)

_____

_____

_____

_____

Story Blocks

Story blocks are a great activity. Story blocks can pique children's imaginations in the area of story invention and telling. Using story blocks gives children the incentive to begin to be silly with word ideas. If the instructor so chooses, story blocks can be used in combination with journals. This activity can be presented to the children as a paired or as an individual activity. Pairing the children adds the learning dimension of developing the ability to work in cooperative and collaborative pair groups.

Sets of story blocks can be purchased at educational supplies stores in the range of $25 to $50, depending on the size of the set to be purchased. On two sides of each block there is a silly picture with a sentence fragment, which can be linked to other sentence fragments in the collection of blocks. The possibilities are endless. The commercial sets are quite beautiful, but comparatively costly.

Materials and Preparation
To make a set of homemade story blocks:
1. Find finished blocks of wood of approximately the same size and shape (sanded so there are smooth surfaces and no splintery ends) Unpainted and unshellaced surfaces are best, so your images can adhere to the plain block.
2. Find and cut out silly images. Look through magazines, wallpaper samples, pictures downloaded from the Internet, wrapping paper, gift cards, etc.
3. After cutting out silly images, print out silly words or sentence fragments on your computer. Use a font style and size easily legible to young children. For very young children, sentence fragments may not be necessary.
4. Apply images and sentence fragments to blocks with Mod Podge or other decoupaging compound according to package directions.
5. Let dry thoroughly.
6. If desired, cover blocks with a coat of clear shellac. This is recommended, as it enhances durability and facilitates cleanability.
7. Dry thoroughly again.
8. Allow block to dry outside for several days so that the odor of the shellac can dissipate completely.

Method
Using Story Blocks:
❖ Set story blocks out on a table or other flat surface.
❖ Be sure that there are sufficient blocks available so that the children can be creative with their ideas and not squabble over individual blocks.
❖ If children are writing, pair them up, and allow them to collaborate on their stories, if they choose to do so. Have them write and draw their stories in their journals or on individual pieces of paper.
❖ With younger children, allow them to assemble their stories, scribble write and draw their stories in their journals. Adult volunteers and instructors can work with children, taking down the stories that the children dictate verbatim.

❖ It is essential in all journal writing involving dictation that the person taking the dictation should be careful to write down the children's words exactly as spoken by the child (Jones, 1998, *Reading, Writing and Talking with Four, Five and Six Year Olds.*).

Suggested Reading:

(Note: Read stories to the class that have an obvious or memorable sequence of events)

Aardema, V. (1981). *Bringing the Rain to Kapiti Plain.* ISBN: 0-803-70809-2 (Reading Rainbow book).

Allard, H. & Marshall. J. (1985). *Miss Nelson Is Missing!* ISBN: 0395401461

Brown, M.W. (1956). *A Home For a Bunny.* ISBN: 0-307-10546-6

Carle, E. (1969). *The Very Hungry Caterpillar.* ISBN: 0-399-22690-7

Freeman, D. 1968). *Corduroy.* ISBN: 0-670-24133-4.

Galdone, P. (2006). *The Little Red Hen.* ISBN: 0618752501. (Also in Spanish)

Hoban, J. (1988). *Amy Loves the Sun.* ISBN:0-590-22225-2.

Hogrogian, N. (1972). *Always Room For one More.* ISBN: 0805003304.

Keats, E. J. (1981). *The Snowy Day.* ISBN: 014050182.

Keats, E. J. (1998). *A Whistle For Willie.* ISBN: 0-670-88046-9.

Krauss, R. (1989). *The Happy Day.* ISBN: 0064431916.

Pluckrose (1995). *Time (Math Counts).* ISBN: 0516454595.

Rowe, J.A, (1998). *The Gingerbread Man.* ISBN: 1-55858-906-6.

Sendak, M. (1964). *Where the Wild Things Are.* ISBN: 0-06025492-0. (Caldecott Medal).

Sendak, M. (1991). *Chicken Soup With Rice: A Book of Months.* ISBN: 006443253X.

Silverstein, S. (1986). *The Giving Tree.* ISBN: 0060256656.

Suess, Dr. (1989). *And to think that I saw it on Mulberry Street.* ISBN: 0394844947.

Vaughn, M.K. & Lofts, P. (2001). *Wombat Stew.* ISBN: 1865044482.

Williams, L. (1988). *The Little Old Lady Who Was Not Afraid of Anything.* ISBN: 0064431835.

Target Areas of Learning

Physical Development

   ❖ **Fine motor:** picking up blocks and holding writing/coloring tools
   ❖ **Eye-hand coordination:** drawing and writing within the designated spaces, setting up blocks
   ❖ **Articulation:** vocally creating letter and word sounds correctly in the silly sentences
   ❖ **Physical principals:** learning physical weight of the blocks while moving the blocks, standing them upright to see if they balance, etc.
   ❖ **Sensory discrimination:**
     • **Tactile discrimination** (touch): identifying and differentiating textures with touch: picking up and assembling silly sentences by moving blocks around
     • **Visual discrimination** (sight): visually identifying pictures and/or words on the blocks

Cognitive Development

❖ **Language Arts**
  • **Verbal skills**
    ○ **Language development**: story telling, story writing: copying the story onto paper or into a journal, reading the silly stories aloud
  • **Grammatical development**: learning rules of grammar; learning correct usage of language by reading and playing with the blocks
  • **Vocabulary development**: adding to the body of words and phrases used; adding words on story blocks to personal vocabulary, increasing vocabulary in usage
  • **Emergent literacy**
    ○ **Symbol recognition:** learning and correctly decoding the letters, letter combinations and word combinations on the blocks
    ○ **Sequencing:** creating a story in a particular order and recalling that order
    ○ **Temporal ordering**: retelling the invented story
    ○ **Phonemic awareness:** awareness of sounds associated with letters, letter combinations
    ○ **Creative writing:** expressing self by creating silly sentences
❖ **Math Skills**
  • **Mathematical applications**
    ○ **Spatial relationships:** seeing the physical blocks in relationship to one another in space
    ○ **Common relatedness:** opposites, similars, congruent relationships of words, phrases, sentence fragments to create sill ideas
    ○ **Construction**: building or forming by putting together parts to create a 3-dimensional object with the story blocks
❖ **Social Science**
  • **Recognizing and accepting diversity**: depending on the nature of the blocks, cultural and social relationships depicting human diversity can be used on the blocks to teach acceptance of human diversity; blocks can be made with words, phrases, sentences fragments from other languages

Social Development

❖ **Working cooperatively with others in a group:** working with others: (if paired) taking turns in assembling blocks
❖ **Collaboration:** planning, creating and inventing stories with partners
❖ **Sharing:** accepting the input of others while creating stories
❖ **Taking turns:** everyone in the classroom deserves opportunities to participate: allowing other children a turn with the story blocks
❖ **Taking care of classroom environment:** when activity is completed, putting blocks away in such a way that they will be ready for another child's use; playing with the blocks in such a way that they will remain in good condition

Emotional Development
❖ **Self-esteem:** feeling good about oneself; valuing oneself and feeling good about the silly sentences/stories created
❖ **Accomplishment:** developing a sense of self-worth from building skills with writing through creative work with silly sentences

Creative Expression
❖ **Use of creative media and expression of imagination:**
  • **3-dimensional visual arts**: constructing with blocks
  • **Writing/story telling: expressing emotions and self through use written words and imagination:** writing, story telling: learning to create with words
❖ **Creative thinking:** developing the imagination and critical thinking by creating and retelling stories
❖ **Aesthetic appreciation:** appreciation for the silly sentences created by other children
❖ **Creative risk:** trying out a variety of combinations of words to see the effect

Possible Accommodations for *Story Blocks Activity*

ADHD
❖ Use positive reinforcement (praise) when child shares blocks
❖ Offer more time or break activity up into several smaller sessions
❖ Place a splat mat beneath tables if wet media are being used for journal writing/drawing
❖ Offer a carrell to help child maintain focus on task at hand
❖ Have the child work on a tray to contain materials
❖ Check on child often, reward increments of achievement
❖ Allow the activity to go on a little longer if child becomes engaged in it

Developmental Delays
❖ Go over task more slowly using simple phrases be sure to make eye contact to ascertain child understands the task
❖ Demonstrate the activity in steps for child
❖ Lower ratio: have child work one to one with an adult
❖ If teacher is making own story blocks: simplify language and pictures on story blocks
❖ Offer more time or break activity up into several smaller sessions
❖ Have child work with a gentle and more competent peer
❖ Place materials child has chosen on a tray or place a splat mat beneath tables if wet media are being used

Autism Spectrum Disorders
❖ Explain the activity using short simple phrases being sure eye contact is made
❖ Model activity while explaining it
❖ Offer more time or break activity up into several smaller sessions

❖ Present the activity more than once, allowing the child to become accustomed to the activity
❖ Demonstrate the activity in advance
❖ Show child that the activity is on the schedule for this day
❖ Use positive reinforcement when child participates
❖ Pair child with a more competent and patient peer (if possible, use the same peer for the child's buddy as children with autism resist change)
❖ Place a splat mat beneath tables if wet media are being used

Visual Impairments
❖ Use brightly colored materials
❖ Lower the ratio
❖ If teacher is making own story blocks: use contrasting colors, low gloss shellac, use a larger size letters in a simple font in a dark color
❖ Adjust the light in the classroom to reduce glare (ask child what is most comfortable for child)
❖ Allow child to stop if you notice signs of tiredness, such as eye rubbing
❖ Offer more time or break activity up into several smaller sessions

Orthopedic Impairments
❖ Make sure child is seated comfortably
❖ Arrange furniture so child can easily reach and manipulate blocks
❖ If placing blocks on a tray facilitates the activity for the child, use this option
❖ Make the blocks of a large enough size so that child can easily grasp the blocks
❖ Use the hand-over-hand method with children who may lack fine motor dexterity
❖ Clip writing materials to a clip board (with an alligator clip on the far side) if child is writing invented story
❖ Offer chunky or adapted writing materials
❖ Allow more time for activity

Gifted and Talented Education (GATE)
❖ Suggest child identify and create a theme about which a silly story can be created
❖ Ask child to write several sentences for the silly story
❖ Have child work with children needing additional assistance

English Language Learners (ELL)
❖ Explain the activity using short simple phrases being sure eye contact is made
❖ Model activity while explaining it
❖ Start the child out making smaller combinations of sentence fragments
❖ Use positive reinforcement for incremental successes

Content Standards For Kindergarten Met By This Activity

English Language Arts

Reading (1.0, 1.2, 1.3, 1.4, 1.5, 1.6, 1.7, 1.9, 1.12, 1.13, 1.14, 1.15, 1.16)

Listening and Speaking Strategies (1.0, 1.1, 1.2, 2.0, 2.1, 2.3)

Mathematics

Numbers and Counting (1.0, 1.2)

Algebra, Sets and Sorting (1.0, 1.1)

Measurement and Geometry (1.0, 1.2, 1.3, 1.4)

History and Social Science

Following Rules (K.1, K.1.1)

Using a calendar to sequence events (K.5)

Understanding that history relates to people and places in the past (K.6)

Visual Arts

Creative Expression (2.0, 2.1)

Learning Plan

I. **Name of Activity: Story Blocks**

II. **Date of Presentation:**

III. **Age or Grade Level: Pre-K and up**

IV. **Ratio of teachers to children needed for this activity:** 1:8

V. **Target Areas of Learning / Goals and Objectives** (target areas of learning directly relate to "VI. Evaluation Rubric")
1. **Physical:** _____
2. **Cognitive:** _____
3. **Social:** _____
4. **Emotional:** _____
5. **Creative:** _____

VI. **Evaluation Rubric:** (if more than two learning areas are being evaluated, a spreadsheet form may be preferred)

Targeted Area of Learning	Targeted Area of Learning
_____	_____
_____	_____
4. Always _____	**4.** Always _____
3. Usually _____	**3.** Usually _____
2. Sometimes _____	**2.** Sometimes _____
1. Rarely _____	**1.** Rarely _____

VII. **Materials and Preparation Needed**
For making set of homemade story blocks
1. Find finished blocks of wood of approximately the same size and shape (sanded so there are smooth surfaces and no splintery ends) Unpainted and unshellaced surfaces are best, so your images can adhere to the plain block.
2. Find and cut out silly images. Look through magazines, wallpaper samples, pictures downloaded from the Internet, wrapping paper, gift cards, etc.
3. After cutting out silly images, print out silly words or sentence fragments on your computer. Use a font style and size easily legible to young children. For very young children, you might choose not to add sentence fragments as they may not be necessary.
4. Apply images and sentence fragments to blocks with mod podge or other decoupaging compound according to package directions.
5. Let dry thoroughly.

6. If desired, cover blocks with a coat of clear shellac. This is recommended, as it enhances durability and facilitates cleanability.
7. Dry thoroughly again.
8. Allow block to dry outside for several days so that the odor of the shellac can dissipate completely.

VIII. Procedures

Using Story Blocks

1. Set story blocks out on a table or other flat surface.
2. Be sure that there are sufficient blocks available so that the children can be creative with their ideas and not squabble over individual blocks.
3. If children are writing, pair them up, and allow them to collaborate on their stories, if they choose to do so. Have them write and draw their stories in their journals or on individual pieces of paper.
4. With younger children, allow them to assemble their stories, scribble write and draw their stories in their journals. Adult volunteers and instructors can work with children, taking down the stories that the children dictate verbatim.
5. It is essential in all journal writing involving dictation that the person taking the dictation should be careful to write down the children's words exactly as spoken by the child (Jones, 1998, *Reading Writing and Talking with Four, Five and Six Year Olds.*).

IX. Accommodations (changes to accommodate learning diversity)
Name of Accommodated Area:

1. _____
2. _____
3. _____
4. _____
5. _____

X. Applicable Framework Standards: Kindergarten

Standard _____

_____

_____

_____

_____

Standard _____

_____

_____

_____

_____

Standard _____

_____

_____

_____

_____

Standard _____

_____

_____

_____

_____

Standard _____

_____

_____

_____

_____

XI. Evaluation and Comments (i.e.: How well did the plan work? Great responses? What aspects are especially effective? Not effective? What improvements are needed? Ideas for follow up activities and other notes)

_____

_____

_____

_____

Word Hunt

Word hunting is a good rainy, snowy, too hot, too smoggy day
who are in the latter part of kindergarten into first or second gra
labeled much of the furniture, the cabinets, and so forth with nam
The second is that your children have acquired the concept "wor

Remember that your classroom is a teaching tool. The teac
there are many wide-open spaces, which are an invitation for run
movements. Or, the teacher can create smaller spaces, by using bo
learning areas for specific activities. This activity is best played in
furniture to break up the room and slow the movement across it.

Suggested Rea

Brown, M. (1974)
Hoban, T. (19
McMillan

Peel

Materials

- ❖ Card stock or word strips cut to size for words selected
- ❖ Words written on card stock and prepared beforehand to correspond with familiar objects
  in the classroom, or the school environment (i.e.: desk, bookcase, rug, window, tree, slide,
  chair, etc.)
- ❖ Should class be learning words and phrases from another language, the labels can be written
  in languages other than English

Method

- ❖ Either before school (if the teacher knows beforehand that the children will be having
  lunch and recess inside) or while the children are actively engaged in another task, move
  the labels around to "wrong objects".
- ❖ Have the children sit in "on the rug".
- ❖ Ask children to repeat the "rules of the game back to you"
- Only walking in the classroom
- Use an "inside voice" in the classroom
- Everyone has a turn before second turns are taken
- ❖ Let each child have a turn a putting the nametags onto the correct objects. Be sure to let the
  children who have a weaker command of written vocabulary go first, so that they can find
  a word with which they are familiar.
- ❖ Make sure every child gets a turn before allowing children to have a second turn.

Variations

- Ask the children to hunt for their word hopping or walking backward (etc.).
- Ask each child to say the word s/he is relocating.
- If preferred, the children can work in pairs. If so, be sure that the tags are also paired up (i.e.,
  "file cabinet" becomes "refrigerator", and "refrigerator" becomes "file cabinet") so that the
  children can swap out the tags.

...ding:

). *All Butterflies: An ABC*. ISBN: 0684137712.

7). *Over, under and through and other spatial concepts*. ISBN: 0689711115.

, B. (1994). *Mouse Views: What the Class Pet Saw*. ISBN: 082341132X. (Reading Rainbow. The school from the mouse's point of view, with a map of his jaunt through the school).

, M. (1998). *Mary Wore Her Red Dress and Henry Wore His Green Sneakers*. ISBN: 0395900220.

Piper, W. (1990). *The Little Engine That Could*. New York: Penguin Young Readers Group. ISBN: 448400413 (Ages 3-8) (also available in Spanish).

Wildsmith, B. (1996). *Brian Wildsmith's ABC*. Long Island, NY: Star Bright Books, Incorporated. ISBN: 1887734023

Note: Brian Wildsmith's beautifully illustrated alphabet, counting and animal books of are available in many languages such as Arabic, Chinese, Farsi, French, Korean, Navajo, Spanish, Portugese, Tagalog, and Vietnamese

Target Areas of Learning

Physical Development
- ❖ **Gross Motor Skills:** using the large muscles of the body: moving around the room (hopping, skipping, crawling, jumping); reaching to move labels
- ❖ **Fine motor:** using the small muscles of the hand and fingers; grasping and picking up name tags; placing labels on correct items
- ❖ **Eye-hand coordination**: seeing and accurately retrieving name tags
- ❖ **Sensory discrimination**
- • **Visual discrimination (sight)**: visually identifying words

Cognitive Development
- ❖ **Language Arts**
  - • **Verbal skills**
    - o **Vocabulary development**: acquiring, using, and comprehending new words
    - o **Language development**: understanding and following simple instructions;
  - • **Emergent literacy**
    - o **Symbol interpretation**: recognizing letters and that combinations of letters form words
    - o **Word recognition:** recognizing new words and identifying words correctly
      - – **Matching spoken words to written words**: correctly associating the auditory expression with the written symbol grouping
- ❖ **Social Science**
  - • **Recognizing and accepting diversity**: using words that reflect human diversity
  - • **Linguistic diversity**: learning words in other languages

Social Development

- ❖ **Working cooperatively**: working as teams to find words and place them correctly
- ❖ **Taking turns**: allowing others to participate
- ❖ **Patience**: waiting to participate; behaving well when gratification is delayed
- ❖ **Working cooperatively with others in a group**: good sportsmanship: working well as a team and as a community that supports all members
- ❖ **Following instructions**: following the rules of the game, following directions, repeating the rules of the game, so that everyone understands

Emotional Development

- ❖ **Self-esteem**: feeling good when demonstrating an increased knowledge of words
- ❖ **Risk taking**: willing to attempt an answer when not certain whether the answer is correct
- ❖ **Self-confidence**: developing movement skills, word recognition skills, feeling like an authentic member of the community

Creative Expression

- ❖ **Creative thinking**: inventing new variations of the game (e.g., new categories for words, or new movements that can be used)
- ❖ **Use of creative media and expression of imagination**: playing the game in new, fun ways
- ❖ **Problem solving**: figuring out the correct placement of word symbols

Possible Accommodations for *Word Hunt Activity*

ADHD

- ❖ Use positive reinforcement (praise) when child works well with others and behaves appropriately, taking turns, and working cooperatively
- ❖ Allow the activity to go on a little longer if child becomes engaged in it
- ❖ Have all the children repeat the rules of the game, having child with ADHD repeat the "walking only in class" and/or "inside voice" rules in particular
- ❖ Have the child paired with a calmer, less impulsive partner

Developmental Delays

- ❖ In explaining how the game works, speak more slowly and use simple and direct sentences to be sure child understand how to play the game being sure to make eye contact
- ❖ Model how the game is to be played
- ❖ Allow this child to correct his word first
- ❖ Partner this child with a gentle peer
- ❖ Offer more time to complete task
- ❖ Offer positive feedback while child is putting his word in the correct place and when s/he succeeds

Autism Spectrum Disorders

❖ Explain the activity using short simple phrases, and go over the task step-by-step to be sure the child understands the task making sure eye contact is made

❖ Model how the game is to be played

❖ Present the activity more than once, allowing the child to become accustomed to the activity

❖ Use positive reinforcement when child participates

❖ Pair child with a more competent and patient peer (if possible, use the same peer for the child's buddy as children with autism resist change)

❖ Have child work with their usual buddy for the game so that it makes the game seem more familiar

❖ Be sure to have the activity on the class schedule, so the child can anticipate what is to happen during the day

Visual Impairments

❖ Adjust the lighting to reduce glare

❖ Use larger sized, bold print on white, matte card stock for the words to be found

❖ Allow child with visual impairment to go first

❖ Have the child pair up with a gentle and more competent peer

❖ Offer more time to complete task

❖ Offer the child a magnifying glass, as both a visual aid for the child, and a "prop" for the game, searching for the hidden words

Orthopedic Impairments

❖ Place many of the items in places accessible to the child

❖ Allow child more time to collect items

❖ Allow the child to "go first" to avoid unnecessary bumping into others

❖ Make sure labels are of a size and thickness that makes grasping them easy

❖ Affix labels with Velcro dots (available @ 99 Cent Stores) for ease in relocating them

Gifted and Talented Education (GATE)

❖ Add words challenging for the gifted children

❖ Time child to see how quickly child can correctly place words

❖ Have child make, and place new words around classroom

English Language Learners (ELL)

❖ Simplify words for child to place and locate

❖ Use short simple phases when explaining the game

❖ Model how to play the game while explaining it

❖ Offer positive feedback while child is putting his word in the correct place and when s/he succeeds

Content Standards For Kindergarten Met By This Activity

English Language Arts

> Reading (1.0,1.3, 1.5, 1.6, 1.7, 1.8, 1.9, 1.14, 1.15)
> Listening and Speaking (1.0, 1.1)

History and Social Science

> Following Rules (K.1, K.1.1)
> Compare and describe people and places (K.4, K4.1)

Theatre

> Creative Expression (2.0, 2.1)

Dance

> Artistic Perception (1.0, 1.1, 1.2)

Learning Plan

    I. Name of Activity: Word Hunt

    II. Date of Presentation:

   III. Age or Grade Level: Pre-K through primary

   IV. Ratio of teachers to children needed for this activity: up to 1:10 (a lower ratio is better)

    V. Target Areas of Learning / Goals and Objectives (target areas of learning directly relate to "VI. Evaluation Rubric")
       1. **Physical:** _____
       2. **Cognitive:** _____
       3. **Social:** _____
       4. **Emotional:** _____
       5. **Creative:** _____

   VI. Evaluation Rubric: (if more than two learning areas are being evaluated, a spreadsheet form may be preferred)

Targeted Area of Learning	**Targeted Area of Learning**
_____	_____
_____	_____
4. Always _____	4. Always _____
3. Usually _____	3. Usually _____
2. Sometimes _____	2. Sometimes _____
1. Rarely _____	1. Rarely _____

  VII. Materials and Preparation Needed
     1. Card stock cut to size for words
     2. Sharpie or broad tipped marking pen
     3. Words written on card stock and prepared beforehand to correspond with familiar objects in the classroom, or the school environment (i.e.: desk, bookcase, rug, window, tree, slide, chair, etc.)
     4. Optional: velcro "dots" to affix labels to furniture, if labeling is used as part of vocabulary development

 VIII. Procedures
     1. Either before school (if the teacher knows beforehand that the children will be having lunch and recess inside) or while the children are actively engaged in another task, move the labels around to "wrong objects"

2. Have the children sit "on the rug"
3. Ask children to repeat the "rules of the game back to you"
   a. Only walking in the classroom
   b. Use an "inside voice" in the classroom
   c. Everyone has a turn before second turns are taken
      4. Let each child have a turn a putting the name tags onto the correct object. Be sure to let the children who have a weaker command of written vocabulary go first, so that they can find a word with which they are familiar.
      5. Make sure every child gets a turn before allowing children to have a second turn.

IX. **Accommodations** (changes to accommodate learning diversity)
Name of Accommodated Area:
   1. _____
   2. _____
   3. _____
   4. _____
   5. _____

X. **Applicable Framework Standards: Kindergarten**
Standard _____
_____
_____
_____
_____

Standard _____
_____
_____
_____
_____

Standard _____
_____
_____
_____
_____

Standard _____
_____
_____
_____
_____

Standard _____

_____

_____

_____

_____

XI. Evaluation and Comments (i.e.: How well did the plan work? Great responses? What aspects are especially effective? Not effective? What improvements are needed? Ideas for follow up activities and other notes)

_____

_____

_____

_____

Chapter Ten

Mathematics Activities and Learning Plans

One element that contributed to (Frank Lloyd) Wright's feeling for space and volume was the set of Froebel's 'gift blocks' he received as a child. They were designed by Frederich Froebel, the German pioneer of early childhood education, during the 1830s to teach children about geometric form. The wooden blocks were of many shapes; not only cubes, but triangles, rectangles, spheres, cylinders. They could be recombined endlessly into houses, barns, bridges and other imaginative creations. In his autobiography, Wright spoke of his debt to Froebel when he wrote 'The maple-wood blocks ... all are in my fingers to this day.'"

– Spencer Hart
(regarding the American architect, Frank Lloyd Wright)
Wright Rooms, "Vista, Breadth, Depth: Spatial Freedom"
(1998, pp. 19-20)

Candy Math

For many of us, mathematics has not been the most fun or pleasant experience. Math is often presented in painful, unhappy, strict, not playful ways. A person's attitude regarding math, or anything else, is directly related to the experience associated with the experience. Many of us recall learning basic addition, subtraction, multiplication, and division tables as an experience of hours and hours of rote memorization.

Candy Math can add a spoonful of sugar to the bitterness of mathematical tedium as it is presented in our overly assessment based educational environment of today. *Candy Math* does not replace necessary memorization, but it can give young children something to enjoy, and hopefully create a positive association with this subject. Of course, with *Candy Math*, subtraction is the most fun.

There are many variations of *Candy Math*. Two easily presented activities are found in Barbara McGrath's two M & M's counting books (1994, 1998; See the **Suggested Reading** section below). The math activities are presented in a pleasant rhyming style. All the teacher will need for these activities is to have a copy of the chosen book, a large bag of colorful candies, and graph paper. Larger size squares (1/2" or bigger) are easier for children to use. Online, http://www.Incomptech.com offers free, downloadable large-squared graph paper. The teacher should copy as many sheets as are needed for presenting the activity. There are also many variations of "candy math " that can be found on the Internet. M & M Math will be discussed here. If there is a preference to not use sugared candy, the teacher may, instead prefer to substitute colorful sugar-free candies, cereal or crackers (see the **Suggested Reading** section below for other similar books that may be used instead).

Materials
❖ One of the M & M counting books, or other similar math activities book that will be read to the children (check **Suggested Reading** below for other references)
❖ A large bag of colorful candies, inexpensively available at club stores; (colorful sugarless candies, cereal or crackers may be substituted)
❖ Graph paper for each child; larger squares (1/2" or bigger) are easier for children to use (http://www.Incomptech.com offers free, downloadable large-squared graph paper)
❖ 1/3 cup for measuring
❖ Large bowl to hold candies, cereal or crackers (for ease of child's measuring)
❖ Paper plate or paper towel for each child
❖ Zipper snack bags (labeled with the children's names) in which candies (cereal, etc.) may be saved for later on in the week
❖ A sharpie marker to label snack bags with children's names

Method
❖ Choose the book that will be read, depending on the developmental age and cognitive ability of your students.
❖ Give each child a paper towel or plate
❖ Let each child measure 1/3 (+/-) cup of candies onto plate or paper towel
❖ Allow the children to eat a piece of the candy (or cereal, crackers), if they would like to do so

❖ If *More M & M Brand Chocolate Candies Math* is chosen, give each child some large sized graph paper

❖ Read the book slowly, making sure that the children are able to complete the instructions before moving on to the next page

❖ As children are working, walk around the classroom, being sure to acknowledge their good work or their restraint from eating the candies (cereal, crackers, etc.).

❖ If a child cannot resist the temptation to munch, don't make a huge issue about it. Do let them know it is more fun to do the whole activity before eating the candy.

❖ When the activity is complete, pass out the labeled plastic zipper type bags into which the children can put the candies, etc. they don't choose to eat at this time

❖ Be sure to let the children have some candy though, so that they associate the activity with good feelings

Suggested Reading:

Anno, M. (1986) *Anno's Counting Book.* ISBN: 0064431231.

Emberley, R. (2000). *My Numbers/ Mis Numeros.* ISBN: 0316233501.

McGrath, B. (1994). *The M & M's Brand Counting Book.* ISBN 1570913676.

McGrath, B. (1998). *More M & M's Brand Chocolate Candies Math.* ISBN: 0439276160.

McGrath, B.B. (1999). *Pepperidge Farm Goldfish Counting Book.* ISBN: 1893017516. (Goldfish crackers now come in colors, too).

McGrath, W. & McGrath, B.B. (1998). *The Cheerios Counting Book.* ISBN: 0590683578. (1 to 1 correspondence; counting from 1 to 20) Spanish edition: McGrath, B.B. (2000). *A Contar Cheerios / The Cheerios Counting Book.* ISBN: 0439149797.

Schwartz, D. (Steven Kellogg illustrator) (2004). *How Much Is a Million?* ISBN: 0688099335. (a humorous book to help children conceptualize large numbers).

Yeatts, K. L. (2000). *Cereal Math.* ISBN: 0-590-51208-0.

Target Areas of Learning

Physical Development

❖ **Fine motor skills:** using the small muscles of the hand and fingers: picking up candies and moving them

❖ **Eye-hand coordination:** coordinating visual acuity with using the small muscles of the hand and fingers: placing the candies accurately where child intends candies to be

❖ **Sensory discrimination:**

• **Visual (sight):** identifying candies colors, shapes, sizes, and patterns visually

Cognitive Development

❖ **Language Arts**

• **Verbal skills**

  o **Language development**: following the instructions as read, conversations

  o **Vocabulary development**: color names, number words, pattern names

❖ Math Skills
  • **Conservation of length**: comparing length of rows of colorful candies
  • **Geometry**: naming and identifying two dimensional geometric shapes Categorization/ **grouping**: separate and match items into groups according to color
  • **Patterning**: creating patterns of colors
  • **Spatial relationships**: understanding the organization of objects in a physical space
  • **1 to 1 correspondence**: counting items in an organized way that shows understanding of the object's placement as a single entity in a group
  • **Sets**: creating sets of various colors of candies
  • **Graphing and equivalency**: more / less; single / plural; longer/ shorter; comparisons.
  • **Measurement**: comparing length weight, height of one object to another
  • **Basic mathematics operations**: addition, subtraction, multiplication, and division

Social Development

❖ Working cooperatively with others in a group:
  • **Sharing materials**
  • **Taking turns**: learning patience / learning to be comfortable with delayed gratification (waiting to eat candies)
❖ **Working collaboratively with others in a group:** planning and generating creative play with other children

Emotional Development

❖ **Self-esteem:** feeling good about oneself, the work one does, one's accomplishments and growth

Creative Expression

❖ **Use of creative media and imagination**: playing with candies in creative ways
❖ **Creative thinking**: inventing games with candies

Possible Accommodations for *Candy Math Activity*

ADHD

❖ Use positive reinforcement (praise) when child works well with others and behaves appropriately, especially if child is able to resist impulse to eat candies
❖ Consider offering fewer candies
❖ Have the child work on a tray to contain materials
❖ Offer positive reinforcement: "catch" children being good; praise staying on task and incremental achievements, working well with others, sharing, cooperating, impulse control, following directions

Developmental Delays

❖ Go over task more slowly being sure to make eye contact to ascertain that the child understands the task
❖ Use positive reinforcement as the child succeeds in following instructions, counting, creating patterns
❖ Check in on child frequently
❖ Have child work collaboratively with a gentle peer
❖ Read book slowly and clearly, asking if certain passages should be repeated
❖ Use large-squared graph paper (graph paper can be made larger using a photocopy machine)

Autism Spectrum Disorders

❖ Explain the activity using short simple phrases be sure to make eye contact
❖ Have the activity on the class schedule, so the child can anticipate what is to happen during the day
❖ Use positive reinforcement when child participates, resists eating the candy
❖ Reduce the number of candies so child is not overwhelmed
❖ Offer activity more than once, to build familiarity with it

Visual Impairments

❖ Adjust the lighting to reduce glare
❖ Offer high contrast, larger sized graph paper (graph paper can be made larger using a photocopy machine)
❖ Use very brightly colored candies not the pastel colored ones, if larger candies can be found, even better!
❖ Offer more time if it is needed to complete the task at hand
❖ Allow the child the opportunity to have more time to clean up, if needed

Orthopedic Impairments

❖ Make sure child is seated comfortably
❖ Adjust table, furniture or place activity on a tray to make candy accessible
❖ Use larger sized graph paper and (if possible) candies
❖ Allow child to move candies with a thick handled wooden spoon for easier grasping
❖ If necessary assist child in moving candies in the hand-over-hand method
❖ Lower the ratio

Gifted and Talented Education (GATE)

❖ Use positive reinforcement when child show patience for children who grasp concepts less quickly
❖ Ask open ended questions about patterns child sees in the activity
❖ Ask child if s/he sees ways the activity could be expanded, and try the suggestions out

English Language Learners (ELL)

- ❖ Explain the activity using short simple phrases
- ❖ Demonstrate activity while explaining it
- ❖ Review significant vocabulary words: colors, numbers, shapes before presenting the activity
- ❖ Allow children to work in cooperative pairs
- ❖ Read book slowly and clearly, asking if certain passages should be repeated

Content Standards For Kindergarten Met By This Activity

English Language Arts

Written and Oral Language (1.0, 1.1)
Listening and Speaking (1.0, 1.1, 1.2, 2.0, 2.1)

Mathematics

Numbers and Counting (1.0, 1.1, 1.2, 1.3, 2.0, 2.1)
Algebra, Sets and Sorting(1.0, 1.1)
Measurement and Geometry (1.0, 1.1, 2.0, 2.1, 2.2)
Statistics (1.0, 1.1, 1.2)

History and Social Science

Following the Rules (K.1, K.1.1)

Visual Arts

Artistic Perception (1.0, 1.1)
Creative Expression (2.0, 2.1)

Online Sources for Downloadable Large Squared Graph Paper

With http://www.Incompetech.com's free "Lite Graph Paper PDF Generator," choose document size, orientation, square size, grid lines and color. *The Sourcebook for Teaching Science* (Norman Herr, Ph.D. of California State University, Northridge) @ http://www.csun.edu/science/ref/measurement/data/graph_paper.html offers free, downloadable graph paper and measurement tools. http://www.Enchantedlearning.com allows members to download graph paper in six sizes.

Learning Plan

   I. **Name of Activity: Candy Math**

  II. **Date of Presentation:**

 III. **Age or Grade Level: Pre-K, Kindergarten**

 IV. **Ratio of teachers to children needed for this activity:** up to 1:10

  V. **Target Areas of Learning / Goals and Objectives** (target areas of learning directly relate to "VI. Evaluation Rubric")

    1. Physical: _____

    2. Cognitive: _____

    3. Social: _____

    4. Emotional: _____

    5. Creative: _____

 VI. **Evaluation Rubric:** (if more than two learning areas are being evaluated, a spreadsheet form may be preferred)

Targeted Area of Learning	**Targeted Area of Learning**
_____	_____
_____	_____
4. Always _____	**4.** Always _____
3. Usually _____	**3.** Usually _____
2. Sometimes _____	**2.** Sometimes _____
1. Rarely _____	**1.** Rarely _____

VII. **Materials and Preparation Needed**

1. One of the M & M counting books or other similar math activities book that will be read to the children (check **Suggested Reading** below for other references)
2. A large bag of colorful candies, inexpensively available at club stores; (colorful sugarless candies, cereal or crackers may be substituted)
3. Graph paper for each child; larger squares (1/2" or bigger) are easier for children to use (http://www.Incomptech.com offers free, downloadable large-squared graph paper)
4. 1/3 cup for measuring
5. Large bowl to hold candies, cereal or crackers (for ease of child's measuring)
6. Paper plate or paper towel for each child
7. Zipper snack bags (labeled with the children's names) in which candies may be saved for later on in the week
8. A sharpie marker to label snack bags with children's names

VIII. Procedures

1. Choose the book that will be read, depending on the developmental age and cognitive ability of the students.
2. Give each child a paper towel or plate
3. Let each child measure 1/3 (+/-) cup of candies onto plate or paper towel
4. Allow the children to eat a piece of the candy (or cereal, crackers), if they would like to do so
5. If *More M & M brand chocolate candies math* is being used, give each child some large sized graph paper
6. Read the book slowly, making sure that the children are able to complete the instructions before moving on to the next page
7. As children are working, walk around the classroom, being sure to acknowledge their good work or their restraint from eating the candies (cereal, crackers, etc.).
8. If a child cannot resist the temptation to munch, don't make a huge issue about it. Do let them know it is more fun to do the whole activity before eating the candy.
9. When the activity is complete, pass out the labeled plastic zipper type bags into which the children can put the candies, etc. they don't choose to eat at that time
   Note: Be sure to let the children have some candy though, so that they associate the activity with good feelings

IX. Accommodations (changes to accommodate learning diversity)
Name of Accommodated Area:

1. _____
2. _____
3. _____
4. _____
5. _____

X. Applicable Framework Standards: Kindergarten
Standard _____

_____
_____
_____
_____

Standard _____

_____
_____
_____
_____

Standard _____

_____

_____

_____

_____

Standard _____

_____

_____

_____

_____

Standard _____

_____

_____

_____

_____

XI. **Evaluation and Comments** (i.e.: How well did the plan work? Great responses? What aspects are especially effective? Not effective? What improvements are needed? Ideas for follow up activities and other notes)

_____

_____

_____

_____

Construction Manipulatives (e.g.: blocks of all sizes and materials, Legos, Duplos, Tinker toys, K'Nex, wooden trains, Lincoln Logs)

Building with construction manipulatives offers children opportunities to develop planning skills, spatial orientation, fine motor and eye-hand coordination skills, number sense, patterning, design and the socialization skills of collaboration, sharing, taking turns, and clean up. The learning associated with using construction manipulatives can possibly include language development and sociodramatic skills.

The National Association for the Education of Young Children - Promoting excellence in early childhood education, discusses the importance of block play in the development of young children in Early Years are Learning Years: Block Play, April, 1997 (www.naeyc.org/ece/1997/04.asp). The article suggests that teachers should have, in the classroom, an area for blocks and manipulatives that is large enough so that several children can work together at the same time. If possible, this area should also be enough out of the way that, if need be, structures that are created can be left standing undisturbed, to be completed or modified at a later time. They stress that using manipulatives to create and to build can enhance children's development in several significant areas: social, physical, cognitive and creative.

The article goes on to state:

> Unit blocks ... are ideal for learning because they involve the child as a whole ... the way she moves her muscles, the way she discovers how different objects feel in her hands, the way she thinks about spaces and shapes, and the way she develops thoughts and interests of her own. ... Block play is open-ended, and its possibilities are limitless. Even as children grow and develop new interests and abilities, blocks remain an active, creative learning tool.

In many cases teachers may need to purchase their own manipulatives, as well as books for the class library, dress ups, and so forth. Many larger communities have toy lending facilities, or resource centers. In the San Fernando and Antelope Valleys in California, the facility is called the Child Care Resource Center; in Ventura, California the facility is named the Child Development Resource Center. If there is a Resource Center facility in the community, the lending libraries offer opportunities to borrow toys and manipulatives (usually for a month). This enables teachers to see if the purchase of a particular material for the classroom would be worth the investment.

An excellent resource for purchasing classic as well as distinctive manipulatives is Discount School Supply (discountschoolsupply.com). They carry a myriad of different sizes and types, for construction and building, for design and patterning, as well as creative storage possibilities. Sometimes it's hard to find just the right materials to suit specific activities or those that are appropriate for a wide range of fine and gross motor skills. It's nice to have choices that are affordable.

Another way to acquire manipulative toys is at yard sales and thrift stores. Before putting used toys in the classroom, make sure the materials are in good repair and are thoroughly clean. If the toys are made of plastic, place them in a mesh bag, and run them through the dishwasher. The bag will need to be hung outside to dry thoroughly. If the toys are wood, wipe them down with a 10% bleach solution. The large card board blocks should also be wiped down, and just make sure that the cloth used to wipe the blocks is not saturated with the bleach solution.

Offer children toys that are appropriate for their developmental age. Children who are still "mouthing" toys should not be offered Legos, K'nex, or small blocks upon which a child could choke. School age children will soon be bored with Duplo blocks. (The jumbo version of Lego blocks)

It is important to make sure that ALL the children work with construction manipulatives since there is such an array of potential learning associated with them. Typically construction manipulatives are considered a "boys" toy, which is untrue. Culturally, males tend to be encouraged to use construction type toys, however all children garner value from their use. Similarly, girls are encouraged to play in the "house corner". Boys get value from playing in the house corner as well. Well-rounded play experience builds a more well-rounded working body of knowledge.

There are a number of ways to encourage girls to play with construction manipulatives.

- Many brands of these manipulatives are now manufactured in pastel colors, various shades of pink, purple and lavender, come with more typical feminine themed accessories.
- The teacher can structure the presentation of centers in by having pre-designated groups move through the different centers as small groups in some predetermined order.
- At other times the students can be offered centers during free play, so that children with a particular interest in a toy or activity will have additional opportunities to use it.
- There are also many accessories available that can be used in conjunction with construction manipulatives to extend the creative play, such as: multicultural "people", animals of all kinds, cars, and other vehicles, mats that have roads or maps and signs, even dollhouse accessories may be appropriate. These items could be hand-made, purchased, or donations from parents.

Materials

❖ Have a designated area for construction toys; Allow children to move the manipulatives around the classroom to integrate those objects into a variety of play;

❖ Collect a variety of toys and objects of all sizes: large cardboard blocks, wooden blocks, Legos, Duplos, K'nex, waffle blocks, Tinker toys, Lincoln Logs, castle blocks, gears, marble race, Matchbox cars and vehicles of all types and wooden toy trains. Adding an assortment of plastic and wooden figures of people and animals will introduce and encourage an element of sociodramatic play (i.e., include figures of people of different ages, cultural backgrounds and occupations, such as the figures available for both Lego and Duplo toys, and figures representing dinosaurs, pets, farm, ocean and zoo animals and so on)

❖ The teacher will find it helpful to have these diverse objects sorted into well-labeled containers

Variation: Having manipulatives designated for outdoor play is recommended. These should be labeled according to type and stored in plastic containers that can be easily carried outside at appropriate times. An extension would be to allow certain manipulatives to be used in conjunction with the water / sand table (i.e., plastic blocks, Legos, cars, figures, farm and zoo animals, and so on, that may be easily cleaned and will also hold up to the water / sand play). In this way, sociodramatic play can be integrated into all kinds of learning experiences.

Method

❖ Have a designated area for construction toys (this area may be indoors, or outdoors, or it may be possible to have both)

❖ Offer children a sufficient amount of time to work with construction manipulatives, at least 45 minutes

❖ Wooden blocks maybe out for every day use, but offer specialized blocks such as waffle blocks for a few days at a time (this way a teacher can offer a variety of manipulative toys to continue to pique the children's interest in the toys)

❖ Collect additional toys which can be added a day or two into the activity to extend the children's play: vehicles: cars, trucks, buses; plastic and wooden animals; plastic and wooden human figures

❖ Set out toys to be played with

❖ Adults can stand by, asking open-ended questions which may lead a child toward creating working solutions

❖ Encourage children to try all possibilities, which will enhance critical thinking and the understanding of cause and effect

❖ Encourage children to work cooperatively and collaboratively

❖ If children are still actively engaged in using the construction manipulatives, the teacher may either offer the children more time, or allow them to leave their work up for continued play later on in the day or on the next day

❖ It may be very useful to keep a camera nearby, so that photographs of the children's structures could be displayed for the parents to see on the class bulletin board.

Suggested Reading:

Burns, M. (1995) *The Greedy Triangle.* (Brainy Day Books). ISBN: 0590489917.

Myller, R. (1991) *How Big Is a Foot?* ISBN: 0440404959

Pallotta, J. (2006). The Construction Counting Book. ISBN: 1570914389.

Pluckrose, H.A. (1995). *Length (Math Counts).* ISBN: 0516454536.

Pluckrose, H. A. (1995). *Pattern (Math Counts).* ISBN: 0516454552.

Tarsky, S. (2001). *The Busy Building Book.* ISBN: 0698118200 (All about building and construction sites; simple explanations of building terminology for budding engineers)

Zelver, P. (2005). *The Wonderful Towers of Watts.* (Reading Rainbow) ISBN: 1590782550. (How one man built his beautiful towers from cast-off materials).

Target Areas of Learning

Physical Development

❖ **Fine motor skills:** using the small muscles of the hand and fingers: picking up blocks and moving them, balancing stacks of blocks

❖ **Eye-hand coordination:** coordinating visual acuity with using the small muscles of the hand and fingers: placing the blocks accurately where child intended blocks to be

❖ **Sensory Discrimination**
  • **Visual discrimination** (sight): identifying block colors, shapes, sizes, and patterns visually
  • **Tactile discrimination** (touch): identifying shapes, materials, and textures of materials through touch

Cognitive Development
  ❖ **Language Arts**
    • **Verbal skills**
      o **Language development**: conversation, names for structures and using associated toys for extended socio-dramatic play, developing language in the planning process
      o **Vocabulary development**: learning and comprehending new words
      o **Spatial vocabulary**: in front, behind, before, after, above, below, between, on top of, inside, outside et cetera
  ❖ Math Skills
    • **Conservation of length**: comparing sizes of blocks during construction
    • **Geometry**: naming and identifying three dimensional geometric shapes
    • **Categorization / grouping**: separate and match items into groups
    • **Patterning**: creating patterns of colors, shapes, sizes, and relatedness
    • **Spatial relationships**: understanding the organization of objects in a physical space
    • **1 to 1 correspondence**: counting items in an organized way that shows understanding of the object's placement as a single entity in a group
    • **Seriation**: graduated ordering
    • **Equivalency:** more / less; single / plural; longer/ shorter; comparisons.
    • **Measurement**: comparing length weight, height of one object to another
  ❖ **Social Science**
    • **Acceptance of human diversity:** add toys for a variety of cultures to extend the activity: horses and carts, different types of vehicles, animals typical of places other than urban/ suburban USA, human figures dressed in a variety clothing, male and female figures dressed in clothing outside of stereotypical roles; human figures of varying abledness;

Social Development
  ❖ **Cooperation:** working cooperatively with others in a group: planning and building structure cooperatively
  ❖ **Sharing materials:** being open to others using materials, others contributing to construction projects
  ❖ **Taking turns:** being comfortable with delayed gratification: allowing other children to have turns at participating in block play
  ❖ **Patience**: being able to stay on task with activity
  ❖ **Leadership**: planning and generating creative play with other children

Emotional Development

❖ **Self-esteem:** feeling good about constructing with manipulatives
❖ **Self-confidence**: developing a willingness to attempt new things, to see "what will happen" without fear of "failure"
❖ **Empathy**: enjoying, identifying with, and being happy for the accomplishments of others in block play

Creative Expression

❖ **Use of creative media and imagination**: using blocks in creative ways
❖ **Creative thinking**: inventing games with blocks; creating patterns; inventing socio-dramatically
❖ **Creativity: sculpture**: making three dimensional works of art with construction manipulatives

Possible Accommodations for *Construction Manipulatives Activities*

ADHD

❖ Go over task step-by-step to be sure child understands the task
❖ Use positive reinforcement (praise) when child works well with others and behaves appropriately
❖ Praise and encourage incremental achievements such as impulse control, sharing, and patience
❖ Allow the activity go on a little longer if child becomes engaged
❖ Have this child work with only one other child to allow many chances to participate
❖ Offer a smaller selection of blocks and other construction manipulatives material from which to choose

Developmental Delays

❖ Go over task slowly making eye contact to be sure child understands the task
❖ Use positive reinforcement as the child succeeds in building structures and creating patterns
❖ Check in on children frequently
❖ Offer more time to complete task
❖ Use larger blocks so child can grasp them easily
❖ Pair child with a gentle and competent peer for opportunities for cooperative play

Autism Spectrum Disorders

❖ Explain the activity using short simple phrases while making eye contact
❖ Present the activity as part of the centers routine, allowing the child to become accustomed to the activity
❖ Use positive reinforcement when child participates

❖ Reduce the number of blocks/types of toys for extended play so selection is not overwhelming, being sure to include types of materials the child particularly likes
❖ Adjust the duration of the activity for each session if it appears the child is more or less engaged with it, and have another activity as back up

Visual Impairments
❖ Adjust the lighting to reduce glare
❖ Offer brighter colors of blocks in larger sizes
❖ Pair child with a gentle and competent peer for opportunities for cooperative play
❖ Have an adult work with child on any of the tasks that may be challenging for the child, encouraging and supporting the child in the activity, making certain child is working as independently as possible on the task
❖ Offer more time if necessary, for the child to complete work and feel successful
❖ Allow the child more time for cleaning up

Orthopedic Impairments
❖ Make sure child is positioned comfortably in a chair, in her wheel chair, or on the floor depending on the nature of the impairment
❖ Place manipulative toys on the floor, table, or tray to make it easy for child to access them and play with them
❖ Offer light to medium weight blocks in a size appropriate for the child to grasp
❖ Let child work as independently as possible to build strength, dexterity, and construction skills: when necessary use the hand-over-hand method to assist the child
❖ If above skills are very weak, use stuffed cloth blocks with Velcro dots attached

Gifted and Talented Education (GATE)
❖ Offer more elaborate construction manipulatives such as K'Nex and Tinker Toys
❖ Ask child to build from patterns that come with more elaborate construction manipulatives
❖ Ask child to sort more elaborate construction manipulatives into clear plastic boxes or zipper bags of similar pieces for easier construction in the future
❖ Ask the child to write out a description of that which was built in a journal

English Language Learners (ELL)
❖ Explain the activity using short simple phrases while making eye contact
❖ Model activity while explaining it
❖ Hold up various sizes, colors and shapes, saying their names slowly and clearly; have child repeat the names after you (this should be brief)
❖ Praise and encourage incremental achievements such as learning words or phrases the child has learned
❖ Have child work with others in groups, encourage children to talk about what they are doing with the blocks

Content Standards For Kindergarten Met By This Activity

English Language Arts

Writing (1.0, 1.1)

Listening and Speaking (1.0, 1.1, 1.2, 2.0, 2.1)

Mathematics

Numbers and Counting (1.0, 1.1)

Measurement and Geometry (1.0, 1.1, 2.0, 2.1, 2.2)

Statistics (1.0, 1.2)

History and Social Science

Following Rules (K.1, K.1.1)

Compare and describe people and places (K.4, K.4.1, K.4.4)

Using a calendar to sequence events (K.5)

Visual Arts

Artistic Perception (1.0, 1.1)

Creative Expression (2.0, 2.1)

Theatre

Artistic Perception (1.0, 1.1, 1.2)

Creative Expression (2.0, 2.1, 2.2, 2.3)

Learning Plan

I. **Name of Activity: Construction Manipulatives**

II. **Date of Presentation:**

III. **Age or Grade Level: Pre-K, Kindergarten**

IV. **Ratio of teachers to children needed for this activity:** up to 1:6

V. **Target Areas of Learning / Goals and Objectives** (target areas of learning directly relate to "VI. Evaluation Rubric")
   1. **Physical:** _____
   2. **Cognitive:** _____
   3. **Social:** _____
   4. **Emotional:** _____
   5. **Creative:** _____

VI. **Evaluation Rubric:** (if more than two learning areas are being evaluated, a spreadsheet form may be preferred)

Targeted Area of Learning	**Targeted Area of Learning**
_____	_____
_____	_____
4. Always _____	**4.** Always _____
3. Usually _____	**3.** Usually _____
2. Sometimes _____	**2.** Sometimes _____
1. Rarely _____	**1.** Rarely _____

VII. **Materials and Preparation Needed**
   1. Have a designated area for construction toys
   2. Collect a variety of toys and objects of all sizes: large cardboard blocks, wooden blocks, Legos, Duplos, K'nex, waffle blocks, Tinker toys, Lincoln Logs, castle blocks, gears, marble race, Matchbox cars and vehicles of all types and wooden toy trains. Adding an assortment of plastic and wooden figures of people and animals will introduce and encourage an element of sociodramatic play (i.e., include figures of people of different ages, cultural backgrounds and occupations, such as the figures available for both Lego and Duplo toys, and figures representing dinosaurs, pets, farm, ocean and zoo animals and so on)
   3. The teacher will find it helpful to have these diverse objects sorted into well-labeled containers
      Variation: Having manipulatives designated for outdoor play is recommended. These should be labeled according to type and stored in plastic containers that can be easily carried outside at appropriate times. An extension would be to allow certain

manipulatives to be used in conjunction with the water / sand table (i.e., plastic blocks, Legos, cars, figures, farm and zoo animals, and so on, that may be easily cleaned and will also hold up to the water / sand play). In this way, sociodramatic play can be integrated into all kinds of learning experiences.

VIII. Procedures

1. Have a designated area for construction toys (this area may be indoors, or outdoors, or it may be possible to have both)
2. Offer children a sufficient amount of time to work with construction manipulatives, at least 45 minutes
3. Wooden blocks may be out for every day use, but offer specialized blocks such as waffle blocks for a few days at a time (this way a teacher can offer a variety of manipulative toys to continue to pique the children's interest in the toys)
4. Collect additional toys which can be added a day or two into the activity to extend the children's play: vehicles: cars, trucks, buses; plastic and wooden animals; plastic and wooden human figures
5. Set out toys to be played with in the designated area
6. Adults can stand by, asking open-ended questions which may lead a child toward creating working solutions
7. Encourage children to try all possibilities, which will enhance critical thinking and the understanding of cause and effect
8. Encourage children to work cooperatively and collaboratively
9. If children are still actively engaged in using the construction manipulatives, the teacher may either offer the children more time, or allow them to leave their work up for continued play later on in the day or on the next day
10. It may be very useful to keep a camera nearby, so that photographs of the children's structures could be displayed for the parents to see on the class bulletin board.

IX. Accommodations (changes to accommodate learning diversity)
Name of Accommodated Area:

1. _____
2. _____
3. _____
4. _____
5. _____

X. Applicable Framework Standards: Kindergarten
Standard _____

_____
_____
_____
_____

Standard _____

_____

_____

_____

Standard _____

_____

_____

_____

Standard _____

_____

_____

_____

Standard _____

_____

_____

_____

XI. Evaluation and Comments (i.e.: How well did the plan work? Great responses? What aspects are especially effective? Not effective? What improvements are needed? Ideas for follow up activities and other notes)

_____

_____

_____

_____

Graphing Activities

Graphing is a way to present various numerical comparisons visually. "Graphing is a basic computational procedural skill. Student should become proficient in interpreting graphs encountered in daily life" (California Math Framework, 1997, ch.1 pg.9). Graphs can teach fractions, and are sometimes used in statistics. Children enjoy simple graphing activities. There are several types of graphs such as Venn diagrams, bar charts, pie charts, and line charts.

Venn diagrams are used for showing the relationship of intersecting groups or sets of data. Bar charts can be presented horizontally or vertically, illustrating comparisons between individual items. Pie charts show the proportional percentages of a whole, which can introduce the concept of fractions. Line charts can be used to reveal trends over time.

Charting information teaches children comparative thinking. In some graphing activities, children can learn to make a hypothesis regarding an outcome for an event and then keep records of information over time on a chart, finally comparing the results of the experiment with the original supposition.

Line Chart (for Germinating Beans in Plastic Cups activity; see chapter on Science activities)
Materials
- ❖ Choose an appropriate germinating activity (i.e., *Germinating Beans*)
- ❖ Chart paper or graph paper
- ❖ Centimeter rulers
- ❖ Pencils

Method
- ❖ Have children begin a germinating activity (i.e., seeds or beans in plastic cups)
- ❖ Give each child a sheet of large sized graph paper (graph paper for *Candy Math* can be used)
- ❖ Either teacher or children (depending on writing ability) write in dates (three per week) on the bottom of the chart; five weeks is a good amount of time for this activity
- ❖ Children measure plant growth on specified days.
- ❖ Children write in length of plant growth in centimeters on the left vertical axis of the chart
- ❖ Each measuring day, work with children to find out where the growth point should be plotted on the chart: by measuring the plant, and then finding the correct date (on the horizontal axis), and finding the closest approximation of the measurement (on the vertical axis) of the chart, then following those two points to their juncture to find the current growth point
- ❖ At the close of the activity, have children write or dictate the pattern of information they discovered by making the chart

Venn Diagrams (for Food Favorites)
Materials
- ❖ Three kinds of fruit, (orange, apple, banana), breads, foods of some sort; candy usually does not work very well, as children like most candy

❖ Large size presentation paper
❖ Easel
❖ Marking pens (three colors)

Method

❖ Have children taste each kind of food sample
❖ Explain that they must decide which fruit they liked and that they can only vote (raise their hand) once
❖ Draw a circle; ask which children liked **apples only**; have a child write the number inside the first circle
❖ Draw an intersecting circle; ask which children liked **bananas only**; have a child write the number inside the second circle, but **not** within the intersecting area
❖ Draw a third circle which intersects the first two circles in such a way that seven distinct areas are created ("apples", "bananas", "oranges", "apples and bananas", "apples and oranges ", "bananas and oranges", **and** "apples, bananas, and oranges")
Note: In this case, the children who prefer the combination of "oranges and apples" are the same as those who prefer "apples and oranges", as it is the same set.
❖ Ask children liking **oranges only** to raise their hands; have a child mark the number inside the appropriate area of the third circle of the diagram, but **not** within the intersecting areas.
❖ Ask children who liked the **apples and bananas** to raise their hands; have a child mark the number inside the appropriate intersecting area of the first two circles of the diagram.
❖ Ask children who liked the **bananas and orange**s to raise their hands; have a child mark the number inside the appropriate intersecting area of the second and third circles of the diagram.
❖ Ask children who liked the **oranges and apples** to raise their hands; have a child mark the number inside the appropriate intersecting area of the first and third circles of the diagram.
❖ Ask children who liked **apples, bananas and oranges** to raise their hands; have a child mark the number inside the appropriate area of the diagram (the center of the three intersecting circles)
❖ Conclude activity with a conversation with the children about the relationship between the numbers they found
❖ Ask the children about other ways they might use a Venn diagram

Bar Charts (for comparing height of children in class)
Materials
This can be presented as an individual, small group, or full class activity
❖ One or more carpenter's tape measures (at least six feet)
❖ Graphed chart paper or sheets of graph paper (http://www.Incomptech.com offers free, downloadable large-squared graph paper)
❖ Pencils, markers, crayons

Method

❖ (For individual or small group - four or more children) pass out sheets of graph paper (see **Candy Math** activity)

❖ If children are working in a small group, have the children choose someone to write the names and numbers on the graph paper, a child to measure the children in the group, another to plot the heights, and another to fill in the bars of the chart

❖ If presented as a whole class activity, select a variety of children to measure, write in names, fill in bars of the chart

❖ Depending on the size of group, children or teacher write the names of the class along the bottom edge of graph paper, evenly spaced

❖ Starting at zero, write measurements along left (0, 4", 8", 1', 1'4", 1'8", 2', 2'4", 2'8", 3', 3'4", 3'8" etc.)

❖ Children measure each other, with adult assistance if necessary, writing down their heights on a separate piece of paper, then plotting the height on the chart

❖ When chart is completed, ask children what patterns they see from the bars and other ways they might use a chart such as this one

Suggested Reading:

Aker, S. (1992). *What Comes In 2's, 3's & 4's?* ISBN: 0671792474.

Anno, M. (1986) *Anno's Counting Book.* ISBN: 0064431231.

Carle, E. (1996). *1, 2, 3 to the Zoo.* ISBN: 0399230130.

Feelings, M. (1992). *Moja Means One: A Swahili Counting Book.* ISBN: 014054662.

Martin, Jr., B. & Archambault, J. (1997). *Knots On a Counting Rope.* ISBN: 0805054790. (Reading Rainbow book).

Onyefulu, I. (1999). *Emeka's Gift: An African Counting Book.* ISBN: 0140565000.

Pluckrose (1995). *Time (Math Counts).* ISBN: 0516454595.

Wallwork, A. (1993). *No dodos. A Counting Book of Endangered Animals.* ISBN: 0590467697.

Target Areas of Learning

Physical Development

❖ **Gross motor skills:** standing, reaching, drawing on large charts, measuring heights of classmates

❖ **Fine motor skills:** using the small muscles of the hand and fingers: cutting writing, measuring, filling in charts

❖ **Eye-hand coordination:** coordinating visual acuity with using the small muscles of the hand and fingers: filling out charts accurately and carefully

❖ **Sensory discrimination**
  • **Visual discrimination** (sight): identifying letters, numbers, words on chart visually; noticing changes/patterns for various experiments and representing them graphically

Cognitive Development

- ❖ **Language Arts**
  - • **Verbal skills**
    - o **Language development**: conversation, class discussions, group problem solving
    - o **Vocabulary development**: identifying types of charts, numbers, words used in measurement
  - • **Emergent literacy**
    - o **Symbol recognition and interpretation**: recognizing and utilizing the relevant meaning conveyed in the use of charts
    - o **Emergent writing**: utilizing charts to convey information
  - • **Temporal ordering**
    - o **Recalling / anticipating events as they occur in time**: documenting progress of plant growth
    - o **Planning/charting:** class projects and activities step-by-step
- ❖ **Math Skills**
  - • **Conservation of quantity, length, weight**
  - • **1 to 1 correspondence**: noting and recording relevant data in chart form through counting measuring and comparing
  - • **Seriation** (graduated ordering): what comes next in terms of graduated weight and size
  - • **Equivalency:** more / less; single / plural; longer/ shorter; comparisons
  - • **Mathematical applications**
    - o **Measurement**: comparing length weight, height of one object to another
    - o **Calendar**: numbers used in a practical and sequential order
    - o **Time**: noting the sequential relationship from one event to another as measured by a standard interval such as a minute, an hour; associating specific events with an appointed time in the day and identifying that appointed time on a clock
  - • **Categorization/ grouping** (sets): sorting activities, inventing criterion to separate items into groups beginning with a single property and adding multiple criterion as the child begins to master the skill
    - o Give children opportunities to develop the skill of articulating properties for categorization: let the children select the categories into which they are sorting objects.
  - • **Spatial relationships**: relating the aspects of physical objects to one another, thinking about objects in three dimensions
  - • **Algebra**: sorting and matching for one or more properties: looking at items and placing them in an invented order for similarities and differences of properties
- ❖ **History and Social Science**
  - • **Diversity:** kinds of food presented, perhaps comparisons in height, skin color, hair texture may relate to human diversity

❖ **Science**
- **Scientific processes**: using charts in the contexts of:
  - **Inquiry**: an organized search for knowledge regarding a particular scientific question; testing personal theories
  - **Prediction**: relating an anticipated outcome based on logic, experience, or research
  - **Observation:** carefully watching attentively and noting what is seen for a scientific purpose
  - **Documentation**: writing observations of scientific events which support claims for a particular prediction or outcomes
  - **Review**: comparing predictions and actual outcomes, assessing value of any mistakes that occurred
- **Cause and effect: relationships between actions and outcomes**: prediction: What do you think will happen if we..." or "What do you think made that happen?" and recording predictions/outcomes on charts:
- **Life science**
  - All forms of observation of and caring for (with predictions/outcomes on charts)
  - **Plant life**: rooting plant cuttings in clear plastic cups, germinating seeds in a plastic bag / clear plastic cup, composting; growing a garden; counting seeds in fruits
  - **Animal life**: keeping animals in the classroom: fish, hermit crabs, reptiles, birds, rodents; observing wild birds feeding at class-made winter bird feeders or nesting in class-made bird houses. Some children can be allergic to various kinds of animal life. When planning activities involving proximity to animals, those special needs would **have** be taken into consideration.
- **Physics**
  - The science of matter and motion, including understanding of surface tension of water, movement of light, movement of sound; the action of force on an moving or stationary object. The results of these studies can be put in a graph format, to represent the results pictorially.
  - **Other possible activities for graphing**: counting water drops on pennies, light moving through crystals, how far will a pumpkin roll on dry concrete, wet concrete / plastic; making kaleidoscopes; which items float, which items sink & why?
- **Chemistry**
  - Children have the opportunity to learn some of the **properties of substance**s in their environment and "what happens when" different substances are combined or subjected to different environments, and representing the results in a chart or graph format.

Social Development
❖ **Working collaboratively**
- Planning and preparing project and charts with others

- Determining possible outcomes collaboratively
- Working cooperatively with others in a group
❖ **Community building**: creating a sense of belonging in a group, particularly through working cooperatively on group projects and by treating others in group with fairness and respect
❖ **Sharing:** utilizing tools fairly with others
❖ **Taking turns**: sharing jobs and assigned tasks appropriately
❖ **Good sportsmanship**: learning to be okay with assigned task
❖ **Following directions**: carrying out directions for assigned task

Emotional Development
❖ **Self-esteem:** feeling good about oneself by participating in group activities/feeling part of a larger community
❖ **Self-confidence**: developing a sense of confidence via community participation

Creative Expression
❖ **Use of creative media and expression of imagination**:
  - **2-dimensional visual arts**: creating colorful and decoratively interesting charts
❖ **Creative thinking**: predicting possible outcomes
❖ **Problem solving**: gathering data, collaborating, delegating responsibility to document data on a chart

Possible Accommodations for *Graphing Activity*

ADHD
❖ Have the child repeat the instructions to be certain that the child understands what to do
❖ Use positive reinforcement (praise) when child works well with others and behaves appropriately
❖ Give child a task requiring a modicum of responsibility and acknowledge as the child succeeds at the task
❖ Offer the child a carrel to reduce distraction, if working individually

Developmental Delays
❖ Go over task more slowly while making eye contact to be sure child understands the directions for the task
❖ Model activity while explaining it
❖ Simplify charting: round the numbers up or down to be plotted and/or reduce the number items to be plotted
❖ Use positive reinforcement as the child succeeds identifying and plotting appropriate coordinates
❖ Check in on child for understanding frequently
❖ Have child work with a gentle peer

- ❖ Offer more time to complete task
- ❖ Use paper with larger graph squares so child can plot them more easily

Autism Spectrum Disorders

- ❖ Explain the activity using short simple phrases being certain eye contact is made
- ❖ Model activity while explaining it
- ❖ Check in with child frequently for understanding
- ❖ Lower the ratio
- ❖ Offer more time to complete task
- ❖ Present the activity as part of the regular class routine, allowing the child to become accustomed to the activity
- ❖ Use positive reinforcement when child participates
- ❖ Simplify task: round the numbers up or down to be plotted and/or reduce the number items to be plotted
- ❖ Use paper with larger graph squares so child can plot them more easily

Visual Impairments

- ❖ Adjust the lighting in the classroom to reduce glare
- ❖ Offer brighter, high contrast graph paper in larger sizes
- ❖ Place child at the front of the activity, so child can better see what is to be charted
- ❖ Use adapted tools: i.e.: easier scissors, ruler with bolder print numbers
- ❖ If measuring in centimeters, have child collaborate with a non-visually impaired child; check on children frequently
- ❖ Use brightly colored writing and drawing materials
- ❖ Offer more time if necessary, for the child to complete work and feel successful

Orthopedic Impairments

- ❖ Make certain child is positioned comfortably
- ❖ Adjust furniture (tables, chart boards, et cetera) for maximum accessibility
- ❖ Use adapted tools such as chunkier or padded writing tools
- ❖ If child tires easily break activity down into smaller time blocks
- ❖ Make sure child works as independently as possible to build a sense of capability
- ❖ If necessary use hand-over-hand method to assist child in completing data on charts

Gifted and Talented Education (GATE)

- ❖ Ask child to make more detailed charts
- ❖ Ask child to observe (as in grass guy) and note observations more frequently
- ❖ Ask child to make comparative charts noting predictions and outcomes

English Language Learners (ELL)

- ❖ Explain the activity using short simple phrases being certain eye contact is made

❖ Model activity while explaining it
❖ Check in with child frequently for understanding

Content Standards For Kindergarten Met By This Activity

English Language Arts

Reading (1.0, 1.3, 1.17, 1.18)
Listening and Speaking (1.0, 1.1, 1.2, 2.0, 2.1, 2.3)

Mathematics

Numbers and Counting (1.0, 1.1, 1.2, 1.3)
Algebra, Sets and Sorting (1.0, 1.1)
Measurement and Geometry (1.0, 1.1, 1.2, 1.3, 1.4, 2.0, 2.1, 2.2)
Statistics (1.0, 1.1, 1.2, 2.0, 2.1, 2.2)

Science

Physical Sciences (1.a)
Life Sciences (2.a)
Earth Sciences (3.b)
Investigation and Experimentation (4a, 4b, 4d, 4e).

History and Social Science

Following Rules (K.1, K.1.1)

Learning Plan

   I. **Name of Activity: Graphing**

  II. **Date of Presentation:**

 III. **Age or Grade Level: Pre-K, Kindergarten**

 IV. **Ratio of teachers to children needed for this activity:** up to 1:6

  V. **Target Areas of Learning / Goals and Objectives** (target areas of learning directly relate to "VI. Evaluation Rubric")
     1. Physical: _____
     2. Cognitive: _____
     3. Social: _____
     4. Emotional: _____
     5. Creative: _____

 VI. **Evaluation Rubric:** (if more than two learning areas are being evaluated, a spreadsheet form may be preferred)

Targeted Area of Learning	**Targeted Area of Learning**
_____	_____
_____	_____
4. Always _____	**4.** Always _____
3. Usually _____	**3.** Usually _____
2. Sometimes _____	**2.** Sometimes _____
1. Rarely _____	**1.** Rarely _____

 VII. **Materials and Preparation Needed**
     For Making Bar Charts **(for comparing height of children in class)**
     Note: This can be presented as an individual, small group, or full class activity
    1. One or more carpenter's tape measures (at least six feet)
    2. Graphed chart paper or sheets of graph paper (http://www.Incomptech.com offers free, downloadable large-squared graph paper)
    3. Pencils, markers, crayons

VIII. **Procedures**
    1. (For individual or small group - four or more children) pass out sheets of graph paper (see *"Candy Math"* activity)
    2. If children are working in a small group, have the children choose someone to write the names and numbers on the graph paper, a child to measure the children in the group, another to plot the heights, another to fill in the bars of the chart

3. If presented as a whole class activity, select a variety of children to measure, write in names, fill in bars of the chart

4. Depending on the size of group, children or teacher write the names of the class along the bottom edge of graph paper, evenly spaced

5. Starting at zero, write measurements along left (0, 4", 8", 1', 1'4", 1'8", 2', 2'4", 2'8", 3', 3'4", 3'8" etc.)

6. Children measure each other, with adult assistance if necessary, writing down their heights on a separate piece of paper, then plotting the height on the chart

7. When chart is completed, ask children what patterns they see from the bars and other ways they might use a chart such as this one

Variation
Line Chart (for Germinating beans in plastic cups activity)
Materials
1. Choose an appropriate germinating activity (i.e., *Germinating beans*)
2. Chart paper or graph paper
3. Centimeter rulers
4. Pencils

Method
1. Have children begin a germinating activity (i.e., seeds or beans in plastic cups)
2. Give each child a sheet of large sized graph paper (graph paper for *Candy Math* can be used)
3. Either teacher or children (depending on writing ability) write in dates (three per week) on the bottom of the chart; five weeks is a good amount of time for this activity
4. Children measure plant growth on specified days.
5. Children write in length of plant growth in centimeters on the left vertical axis of the chart
6. Each measuring day, work with children to find out where the growth point should be plotted on the chart: by measuring the plant, and then finding the correct date (on the horizontal axis), and finding the closest approximation of the measurement (on the vertical axis) of the chart, then following those two points to their juncture to find the current growth point
7. At the close of the activity, have children write or dictate the pattern of information they discovered by making the chart
   NOTE: For further information on Venn Diagrams and other types of graphs, please refer to **Graphing** activities

IX. **Accommodations** (changes to accommodate learning diversity)
Name of Accommodated Area:
1. _____
2. _____
3. _____
4. _____
5. _____

X. **Applicable Framework Standards: Kindergarten**
Standard _____
_____
_____
_____
_____

Standard _____
_____
_____
_____
_____

Standard _____
_____
_____
_____
_____

Standard _____
_____
_____
_____
_____

Standard _____
_____
_____
_____
_____

XI. **Evaluation and Comments** (i.e.: How well did the plan work? Great responses? What aspects are especially effective? Not effective? What improvements are needed? Ideas for follow up activities and other notes)
_____
_____
_____
_____

Patterning Activities

When children begin to recognize patterns, they are beginning to grasp algebraic concepts, as well as a basic scientific grasp that our world is filled with recognizable patterns. The essential phrase for children learning patterns is "a pattern repeats". Teachers can introduce patterns in a wide variety of ways. Patterns occur in music, movement, in block play, tinker toy play, with Lego blocks, and Unifix cubes to mention a few. Even clapping or tossing a beanbag around a circle during group time can introduce concepts of patterning to young children. For a comprehensive list of manipulative and original math activities, *Mathematics Their Way* and *Mathematics... A way of thinking*, (Barratta-Lorton, 1976, 1977) are excellent resources.

Teaching children to name the patterns using mathematical symbols is an essential part of the teacher's role. An "a-b" pattern, would appear as "a-b, a-b, a-b", and so on. Similarly an "a-b-b-c" pattern would look like this "a-b-b-c, a-b-b-c", a-b-b-c" and so forth. The same would hold true for any pattern, not matter how complex, the key being consistent recognizable repetition.

Pattern Discovery Walk

This is a middle of the unit activity that is done as part of a patterning unit. Break the class into small groups of perhaps four or five. If the teacher has sufficient co-teacher or adult volunteer help, each group would walk around the yard or campus looking for patterns. This is a great activity on beautiful spring days when everyone wants to get out or on the first day or two after inclement weather when the class has begun to suffer from cabin fever. Let parents know you are planning a walk with the children. Advise them to put sun block on their children before going to school that day.

Materials
For each child or group / team
* Writing and drawing implements
* Paper for writing observations or drawing patterns during the walk; paper can be plain, lined or primary paper
* Clipboard: can be made from a piece of sturdy cardboard and an alligator clip; inexpensive clip boards can also be found at 99 cent stores

Preparation and Procedure
* In the days prior to this activity, introduce the idea of patterns to the children using construction manipulatives.
* Be sure to identify the patterns by the color or shape, such as "red, red, blue" and transition to representative letter patterns, which in this case would be "a-a-b"
* Give each child or group/team a clipboard
* Have the children walk around the yard, school campus, or in a short neighborhood walk looking for patterns.
* When the children get back to class, have the groups meet, discuss the patterns they found, and share with the class.

❖ This could then be linked to a graphing activity using Venn diagrams to show which groups found the same patterns and which groups did not find the same patterns.
NOTE: During the Pattern Discovery Walk, it will serve teachers well to remember that ALL children may be more productive if allowed to stop and sit when possible, to better document their findings.

Variations

- Rhythmic movement games such as *Simon Says, Freeze, Statues, Mirrors* encourage gross motor development and the concept of recognizing patterns in movement
- Simple clapping games (i.e.: clapping fast, slow, loud, soft, varying the number of claps, inserting pauses into the clapping pattern, etc.)
- Call and response games can involve the recall of vocal patterns, as well as patterns of movement

Suggested Reading:

De Paola, T. (1985). *The Cloud Book.* ISBN: 0823405311.

Glaser, L. (2000). *Our Big Home: An Earth Poem.* ISBN: 0439397529.

Pluckrose, H. A. (1995). *Pattern (Math Counts).* ISBN: 0516454552.

Shaw, C. G. (1988). *It Looked Like Spilt Milk.* ISBN: 0064431592. (Finding patterns and images in the shapes of clouds)

Showers, P. (1993). *The Listening Walk (Let's-Read-and-Find-out Science Book). ISBN:* 0064433226.

Williams, S. (1990). *I Went Walking.* ISBN: 0-15-238011-6. Spanish language edition: Vivas, J., Translator. (2000). *Salí de Paseo.* ISBN: 015200288X. Both available from: www.turnthepage. com.

Suggested CD:

Greg & Steve. (1987). *We All Live Together. Vol.2.* (includes: English / Spanish months of the year song, World is a Rainbow, Popcorn, **The Freeze**) CD Available from: amazon.com.

Target Areas of Learning

Physical Development

- ❖ **Gross motor skills:** using the large muscles of the body: walking, running while on discovery walk
- ❖ **Fine motor skills:** using the small muscles of the hand and fingers: writing and drawing for their "pattern notes"
- ❖ **Eye-hand coordination:** coordinating visual acuity with using the small muscles of the hand and fingers: writing and drawing
- ❖ **Physical Principals:** learning physical weight; stability; equilibrium while moving through space

❖ **Sensory discrimination**
  • **Visual discrimination** (sight): identifying patterns visually
  • **Tactile discrimination** (touch): identifying textural patterns by feeling the texture with hands and fingers
  • **Auditory discrimination** (hearing): identifying patterns with hearing

Cognitive Development
❖ **Language Arts**
  • **Verbal skills**
    ○ **Language development**: conversation, discussion regarding criteria of selected patterns
    ○ **Vocabulary development**: naming types of patterns seen
  • **Emergent literacy**
    ○ **Note taking:** allowing children to write or draw about the patterns they find using their clip boards with scribble writing, drawings, and invented spelling
    ○ **Spelling skills:** using correct letter symbol combinations to form words
    ○ **Penmanship:** developing legible handwriting for note taking
    ○ **Temporal ordering:** observing, noting observations as occurring in time
    ○ **Matching spoken words to written words:** corresponding notes taken with discussions held
❖ **Math Skills**
  • **Mathematical literacy**
    ○ **1 to 1 correspondence:** counting items in an organized way that shows understanding of the object's placement as a single entity in a group to examine the single object's relatedness to the other objects in the process of determining if a pattern exists
  • **Mathematical applications**
    ○ **Pattern recognition:** developing the ability to transition the theoretical idea of pattern to actual recognition of patterns in the world
      – **Finding jumping and /or movement patterns** (e.g.: Simon Says / Punchinello), finding patterns in chalk shapes on the concrete; swinging when on the playground, or the size of holes dug in the sand
  • **Geometry:** shape names: two dimensional: triangle, square, circle, rectangle; three dimensional: cone, cube, sphere, cylinder, pyramid if these shapes occur in the context of a pattern
  • **Algebra:** group/classification: if a child invents his own criterion and has opportunities to explain the properties for which he is classifying, there is an opportunity for more advanced thinking; equivalency: more / less; single / plural; longer/ shorter; comparisons
  • **Measurement:** comparing length, weight, height of one quantity to another to identify relatedness and patterns that occur within the context of measurement
  • **Common relatedness:** linking items that are not the same, but are associated with each other in the context of determining a pattern

❖ **Science**
  • **Identifying patterns occurring in nature**: prediction: shapes of puddles after rain, the way flowers bloom, behaviors of ants or other animals living in groups
  • **Scientific processes**
    o **Prediction**: identifying a pattern is a skill which will empower children to develop skills relating to predicting outcomes
    o **Observation:** carefully watching attentively and noting what is seen for a scientific purpose
    o **Documentation:** writing observations of scientific events which support/disprove claims for a particular prediction or outcomes
    o **Review:** comparing predictions and actual outcomes, assessing value of any mistakes that occurred
❖ **Social Science**
  • **Diversity:** culturally specific types of patterns found in the manner walls or fences are constructed, gardens are laid out, laundry lines, graffiti

Social Development

❖   **Collaboration:** planning, creating, and presenting group projects; working as a team to find and record, then report patterns found
❖   **Sharing:** sharing information such as patterns located in the environment or tools for documentation
❖   **Taking turns:** learning patience while others report their findings
❖   **Following directions**: behaving as directed when on walk
❖   **Negotiation**: convincing members of the team to include or not include a pattern observed

Emotional Development

❖ **Self-esteem:** feeling good about going for a discovery walk and succeeding in identifying patterns
❖ **Self-esteem:** the pleasant feeling of successfully interacting with others
❖ **Accomplishment:** feeling good about finding patterns in the environment

Creative Expression

❖ **Creative thinking**: inventing types of patterns in the process of discovery
❖ **Use of creative media and expression of imagination:**
  • **Writing:** drawing and noting patterns discovered in journal
❖ **Creative risk:** having a willingness to suggest possible patterns without fear of disapproval
❖ **Aesthetic appreciation:** developing appreciation for nature

Possible Accommodations for *Pattern Discovery Walk Activity*

Note: All children may be more productive if allowed to stop and sit when possible, to better document their findings.

ADHD
- Use positive reinforcement (praise) when child works well with others and behaves appropriately
- Lower the ratio/increase level of adult supervision
- Stay close to child, particularly if the walk is off campus
- Have child work in a group of calmer, less impulsive individuals
- Repeat modeled instructions as needed, making sure eye contact is made when giving child directions
- Ask the child to repeat the instructions, to make sure that the child understands what to do

Developmental Delays
- Explain task using simplified language and making eye contact to be sure child understands what to do
- Model activity when explaining it
- Have child work in a smaller group, with gentle peer
- Use positive reinforcement as the child succeeds identifying patterns
- Lower ratio/increase adult supervision: check in on child frequently
- Offer more time if child is enjoying activity
- Simplify task: ask child to identify less complicated types of patterns

Autism Spectrum Disorders
- Explain task using simplified language and making eye contact to be sure child understands what to do
- Model activity when explaining it
- Have the activity on the class calendar, so child is aware in the change of routine
- Have treasure hunt/discovery walk type activities as part of regular class routine, allowing the child to become accustomed to the type of activity
- Have discovery walks in the same areas, changing them only very slightly to increase familiarity with the area to be visited
- Have child work with a single partner, perhaps the same walking partner for additional familiarity
- Make the walk of a shorter duration
- Have child work with a gentle peer who understands the task at hand
- Offer more time if child becomes engaged by activity
- Use positive reinforcement when child participates
- Simplify task: ask child to identify less complicated types of patterns

Visual Impairments

❖ Find out if child needs sunglasses or a hat to see better
❖ Lower the ratio
❖ Have child work with a single partner, perhaps the same walking partner for all discovery walks
❖ Ask child to identify larger sized objects, sounds, or textures in patterns
❖ Give child tinted paper with large, dark writing tools so the child can more easily write what is observed.

Orthopedic Impairments

❖ Plan the route for the walk to ascertain the child will be able to participate easily: check for hazards or places which may be inaccessible to that child
❖ Accommodate the pace of the group to include the child
❖ Have an adult assigned to child to provide assistance in case the unforeseen occurs
❖ Shorten the length of the walk or take frequent rest breaks
❖ Have another child act as a "scribe" to take notes, if the child so desires

Gifted and Talented Education (GATE)

❖ Ask child to look for more elaborate patterns
❖ Ask child to describe patterns in mathematically correct language
❖ Ask child to make a chart of the patterns observed

English Language Learners (ELL)

❖ Explain task using simplified language and eye contact, to be sure the child understands task
❖ Model activity when explaining it
❖ Introduce vocabulary one-on-one prior to walk
❖ Review vocabulary after walk to check for increased understanding
❖ Praise child for willingness to use new vocabulary

Content Standards For Kindergarten Met By This Activity

English Language Arts

> Listening and Speaking (1.0, 1.1, 1.2, 2.0, 2.1)
> Writing (1.0, 1.1, 1.2, 1.3, 1.4)

Mathematics

> Numbers and Counting (1.0, 1.1, 1.2, 1.3, 2.0, 2.1)
> Algebra, Sets and Sorting (1.0, 1.1)
> Measurement and Geometry (1.0, 1.1, 2.0, 2.1, 2.2
> Statistics (1.0, 1.1, 1.2)

History and Social Science

     Following Rules (K.1, K.1.1)

Visual Arts

     Artistic Perception (1.0, 1.1)

     Creative Expression (2.0, 2.1)

Theater

     Artistic Perception (1.0, 1.2)

     Creative Expression (2.0, 2.1)

Learning Plan

    I. **Name of Activity: Patterning Activities**

  II. **Date of Presentation:**

 III. **Age or Grade Level: Pre-K, Kindergarten**

 IV. **Ratio of teachers to children needed for this activity:** up to 1:10

  V. **Target Areas of Learning / Goals and Objectives** (target areas of learning directly relate to "VI. Evaluation Rubric")

      1. Physical: _____

      2. Cognitive: _____

      3. Social: _____

      4. Emotional: _____

      5. Creative: _____

 VI. **Evaluation Rubric:** (if more than two learning areas are being evaluated, a spreadsheet form may be preferred)

Targeted Area of Learning	**Targeted Area of Learning**
_____	_____
_____	_____
4. Always _____	**4.** Always _____
3. Usually _____	**3.** Usually _____
2. Sometimes _____	**2.** Sometimes _____
1. Rarely _____	**1.** Rarely _____

 VII. **Materials and Preparation Needed For Pattern Discovery Walk**

     1. Writing and drawing implements for making observations of examples of patterning in the environment: pencils, pens, crayons,

     2. Paper for writing observations or drawing patterns during the walk; paper can be plain, lined or primary paper

     3. Clipboard: can be made from a piece of sturdy cardboard and an alligator clip inexpensive clip boards can also be found at 99 cent stores

VIII. **Procedures**

     1. Prior to this activity, introduce the idea of patterns to the children using construction manipulatives.

     2. Always identify the patterns by the color or shape, such as "red, red, blue"; Transition to representative letter patterns, which in this case would be "a-a-b"

     3. Give each child (or group) a clip board

4. Children will walk around the yard, school campus, or go on a short supervised walk in the neighborhood looking for patterns.
5. When the children get back to class, have the groups meet, discuss the patterns they found, and share with the class.
6. This could then be linked to a graphing activity using Venn diagrams to show which groups found the same patterns and which groups did not find the same patterns. *NOTE: During the **Pattern Discovery Walk**, it will serve teachers well to remember that ALL children may be more productive if allowed to stop and sit when possible, to better document their findings.*

Variations

-   Rhythmic movement games such as Simon Says, Freeze, Statues, Mirrors encourage gross motor development and the concept of recognizing patterns in movement
-   Simple clapping games (i.e. clapping fast, slow, loud, soft, varying the number of claps, inserting pauses into the clapping pattern, etc.)
-   Call and response games can involve the recall of vocal patterns, as well as patterns of movement

IX. **Accommodations** (changes to accommodate learning diversity)
Name of Accommodated Area:
1. _____
2. _____
3. _____
4. _____
5. _____

X. **Applicable Framework Standards: Kindergarten**
Standard _____
_____
_____
_____
_____

Standard _____
_____
_____
_____
_____

Standard _____
_____
_____
_____
_____

Standard _____

_____

_____

_____

_____

Standard _____

_____

_____

_____

_____

XI. **Evaluation and Comments** (i.e.: How well did the plan work? Great responses? What aspects are especially effective? Not effective? What improvements are needed? Ideas for follow up activities and other notes)

_____

_____

_____

_____

Sound and Movement Patterns

Music and movement easily lend themselves to pattern discovery. Young children often enjoy singing songs that contain within them recognizable patterns such as the Wheels on the Bus, Bingo, Five Little Monkeys, and Down by the Bay. In fact all music contains patterns within it by definition. Music is "the science or art of ordering tones or sounds in succession, in combination, and in temporal relationships to produce a composition having unity and continuity" (Merriam-Webster, 1996, p.767). Webster similarly defines dance as, "a series of rhythmic and patterned bodily movements usually performed to music" (1996, pg 292). Young children are often willing to dance and move unselfconsciously and will often do so freely and happily. Integrating these theoretical concepts with kinesthetic activity helps the child learn at a very basic physical level.

Begin working with simple musical/rhythmic/vocal or movement patterns, after having introduced the basic concept of patterns to your students. Once the children have grasped the idea of musical/rhythmic/vocal or movement patterns, the teacher and the children can invent more elaborate and complex patterns. "Recycled Symphony", wherein children make instruments from junk that is destined for the trash can be adapted to this activity.

Procedure
Note: This activity requires an open, uncluttered area of the classroom or, if the weather permits, it could be done outside

- ❖ Have the children sit on the rug or stand in a circle
- ❖ Initiate a simple musical or movement pattern
- ❖ Ask the children to repeat the pattern
- ❖ Ask the children to name the pattern (a-b, a-b, a-b) or (a-b-b-c, a-b-b-c)
- ❖ Go around the circle, ask individual children to demonstrate a pattern
- ❖ With each child have the children repeat the pattern, and ask them to name the pattern
- ❖ Be certain that all children get a turn before giving a child a second turn

Especially now, when physical education has been generally de-emphasized in public schools, using movement within the context of the curriculum will reinforce the concept that physical activity is healthy for all people, and especially for young children. Weight-bearing exercise is known to help people maintain healthy bone density all throughout their lives, as well as contributing to heart health, keeping the body at a healthy weight, and for psychological well being.

These are good inside (too wet, snowy, hot, smoggy) day activities to burn off pent-up energies.

Movement Patterns (Rhythm Sticks)
A teacher needs nothing more than an open, uncluttered area of the classroom to initiate movement patterns. There are many options available for movement activities: ball or bean bag tossing, dancing to structured pieces of music (of which there is an infinite variety available at educational supply stores), parachute activities, and a particular favorite, rhythm or lummi sticks. Rhythm sticks can be purchased. However, a 1/4" to 1/2 " dowel from the hardware store, cut in half, sanded at the ends

(a grinder makes that go faster, but the children can make them themselves using sand paper), and occasionally wiped down with cooking oil produces an inexpensive facsimile that works just as well.

Materials
- ❖ A pair of rhythm sticks for each child
- ❖ A CD with music designed for rhythm stick activities (see below for list of suggested CDs)
- ❖ A playful spirit and a willingness to laugh

Method
- ❖ Pass out rhythm sticks
- ❖ Turn on CD
- ❖ Sing and dance
- ❖ Laugh
- ❖ Go around the circle asking children if they recognized any patterns
- ❖ Play another song
- ❖ Dance and laugh some more
- ❖ Ask for patterns again

Variations
For Simple Musical / Rhythmic / Vocal Patterns:
- Have the children sit on the rug or stand in a circle
- Initiate a simple musical or movement pattern
- Ask the children to repeat the pattern
- Ask the children to name the pattern (a-b, a-b, a-b) or (a-b-b-c, a-b-b-c)
- Go around the circle, ask individual children to demonstrate a pattern
- With each child, have the children repeat the child's pattern, and ask them to name the pattern
- Be certain that all children get a turn before giving a child a second turn

Suggested Reading:
Ackerman, K. (1992). *Song and Dance Man.* ISBN: 0679819959.
Aliki. (2003). *Ah, Music!* ISBN: 0060287195.
Kovalski, M. (1990). *The Wheels On the Bus.* ISBN: 0921103921.
Wood, A. (1992). *Silly Sally.* ISBN: 0152744282.
Wood, A. & Wood D. (1990). *Quick As a Cricket.* ISBN: 0859533069.
Suggested CDs:
Jenkins, E., (1992). *Adventures in Rhythm* (multicultural songs and activities with rhythm sticks). Ella
        Jenkins' CDs available from amazon.com.
Jenkins, E. (1993). *Play Your Instruments (And make a pretty sound).*
Jenkins, E. (1994). *This Is Rhythm.* (Songs and rhythms for simple instruments).
Johnson, L.T. (1976). *Simplified Rhythm Stick Activities: Fun With Rhythm Sticks CD*
Laura Johnson's CDs available from fitnessbeginnings.com.

Johnson, L.T. (1984). *Lummi Sticks For Kids CD*.

Palmer, H. (1972). *Getting to Know Myself.* (songs about rhythms, laterality, feelings, and body awareness). Hap Palmer pioneered concept of movement and music in early childhood education to teach language development, reading readiness, math concepts and self-awareness. His CDs are available from amazon.com.

Stewart, G.L. (1992). *Multicultural Rhythm Stick fun.*

Stewart, G.L. & Buck D. (1997). *A World of Parachute Play.* Georgiana Stewart's CDs are available from fitnessbeginnings.com.

Target Areas of Learning

Physical Development

- ❖ **Gross motor skills**: dancing: using large muscles of body: arms, shoulders, legs, et cetera in movement pattern activities
- ❖ **Fine motor skills:** using the small muscles of the hand and fingers in movement pattern activities
- ❖ **Eye-hand coordination:** coordinating visual acuity with using the small muscles of the hand and fingers: movement pattern activities
- ❖ **Physical Principals:** learning physical weight; stability; equilibrium; balance; leverage; **dance:** finding physical stability movement pattern activities
- ❖ **Articulation:** learning to speak various sounds clearly
- ❖ **Sensory Discrimination**
  - **Visual discrimination** (sight): identifying movement patterns visually by watching others move
  - **Auditory discrimination:** identifying musical patterns with hearing

Cognitive Development

- ❖ **Language Arts**
  - **Verbal skills**
    - o **Language development**: conversation, singing songs
    - o **Vocabulary development**: identifying types of patterns verbally
- ❖ **Math Skills**
  - **Mathematical literacy**
    - o **1 to 1 Correspondence**: counting movements in an organized way that shows understanding of the movement's placement as a single entity of a group of movements in the process of determining if a pattern exists
  - **Mathematical applications**
    - o **Algebra**: sorting and matching for pattern properties: considering the order of movements and placing them in an invented order
      - – **Pattern recognition**: developing the ability to transition the theoretical idea of pattern to actual recognition of patterns in the world

– **Group/classification**: if a child **invents his own criterion for a pattern** and has opportunities to explain the properties for which he is classifying, there is an opportunity for **more advanced critical thinking.**

  o **Equivalency of individual entities within a pattern:** more / less; single / plural; longer/ shorter; comparison

  o **Temporal ordering**: placing events in a particular predetermined sequence or pattern

  o **Spatial relationships**: relating the aspects of the movement patterns, and of children to one another in the process of creating a pattern

❖ **Science**
  • **Identifying patterns occurring in nature**: prediction: kinds of sounds/movements occurring in the environment
  • **Scientific processes**
    o **Prediction**: identifying a pattern is a skill which will empower children to develop skills relating to predicting outcomes
    o **Observation:** carefully watching attentively and noting what is seen for a scientific purpose
    o **Documentation**: writing observations of scientific events which support/disprove claims for a particular prediction or outcomes
    o **Review**: comparing predictions and actual outcomes, assessing value of any mistakes that occurred
  • **Cause and effect**
    o **Relationships between actions and outcomes**: developing curiosity which leads to scientific inquiry: "educated why"

❖ **Social Science**
  • **Diversity:** culturally specific types of patterns found in types of music and movement selected for the activity

Social Development

❖ **Collaboration**: working as a team to create and identify movement, reporting patterns found; making music/dance together
❖ **Working cooperatively with others in a group**: working well while dancing
❖ **Respecting others as individuals (behaving appropriately with others):** behaving appropriately in social dancing situations
❖ **Taking turns:** learning patience while others report their patterns
❖ **Following directions:** following the instructions for patterns from the CD
❖ **Impulse control:** movement activities stimulate impulsive behavior; the child chooses to behave in a socially acceptable way, despite having that impulse
❖ **Community building:** creating a sense of belonging in a group through group dancing

Emotional Development

- ❖ **Self-esteem:** good feeling about group dancing, interacting well with others, feeling good about finding patterns they create
- ❖ **Self-confidence**: being willing to participate in group movement activities
- ❖ **Accomplishment**: developing a sense of achievement through improving motor skills
- ❖ **Stress relief**: releasing stress through movement

Creative Expression

- ❖ **Use of creative media and expression of imagination**:
  - • **Movement/dance**: expressing self through movement
- ❖ **Creative risk**: being comfortable trying out new movement patterns

Possible Accommodations for *Sound and Movement Patterns Activity*

ADHD

- ❖ Use positive reinforcement (smile and otherwise send messages of approval) when child works well with others and behaves appropriately
- ❖ Lower the ratio/increase level of adult supervision
- ❖ Place child near an adult
- ❖ Have children work in small groups to reduce the energy level while children are finding their patterns

Developmental Delays

- ❖ Explain task to be sure child understands what to do using simplified language; be sure eye contact is made
- ❖ Model activity while explaining it
- ❖ Have child work in a smaller group, with gentle peers
- ❖ Use positive reinforcement as the child succeeds in creating and identifying patterns
- ❖ Lower ratio/increase adult supervision: check in on child frequently
- ❖ Offer more time if child is enjoying activity
- ❖ Simplify task: ask child to identify less complicated types of patterns

Autism Spectrum Disorders

- ❖ Explain task to be sure child understands what to do using simplified language; be sure eye contact is made
- ❖ Model activity while Explaining it
- ❖ Have the activity on the class calendar, so child is aware in the change of routine
- ❖ Have patterning type activities as part of the regular class routine, allowing the child to become accustomed to the type of activity
- ❖ Have child work with a single partner, perhaps the same class partner for additional familiarity
- ❖ Make the activity of a shorter duration, or have another activity as back up if more than one or two children seem to lose interest

❖ Have child work with a gentle peer who understands the task at hand
❖ Offer more time if child becomes engaged by activity
❖ Use positive reinforcement when child participates
❖ Simplify task: ask child to identify less complicated types of patterns

Visual Impairments

❖ Adjust lighting to reduce glare
❖ Make sure child is looking away from the windows to reduce "back lighting" that children the visually impaired child is watching
❖ Have child work with the same partners so the children learn to work well with the visually impaired child

Orthopedic Impairments

❖ Select a song with directed movements in which the child is physically able to participate
❖ Use larger sized or padded rhythm sticks
❖ If child lacks strength either place child's hands and arms over yours or yours over the child's to assist the child in movement
❖ Observe child carefully to notice signs of tiring
❖ Praise incremental growth, willingness to participate

Gifted and Talented Education (GATE)

❖ Choose music with more complex patterns
❖ Ask child to write or draw pattern found using letters or geometric shapes to represent the individual movements in the pattern

English Language Learners (ELL)

❖ Explain task to be sure child understands what to do using simplified language; be sure eye contact is made
❖ Model activity while Explaining it
❖ Teach vocabulary of song individually or in a small group prior to activity
❖ Review vocabulary after dancing

Content Standards For Kindergarten Met By This Activity

English-Language Arts

    Reading (1.0, 1.17, 1.18)
    Written and Oral Language (1.0, 1.1)
    Listening and Speaking (1.0, 1.1, 1.2, 2.0, 2.1, 2.2, 2.3)

Mathematics

    Algebra, Sets and Sorting (1.0, 1.1)
    Measurement and Geometry (2.0, 2.2)

Statistics (1.0, 1.2)
Mathematical Reasoning (1.0,1.1, 1.2, 2.0, 2.1)

History and Social Science
Following the Rules (K.1, K.1.1)
Compare and describe people and places (K.4, K.4.1)

Science
Investigation and Experimentation (4.a, 4.c, 4.e)

Dance
Artistic Perception (1.0, 1.1, 1.2, 1.3, 1.4)
Creative Expression (2.0, 2.1, 2.2)
Valuing Aesthetics (4.0, 4.1)
Applications (5.0, 5.1)

Music
Artistic Perception (1.0, 1.2)
Creative Expression (2.0, 2.1, 2.3)
Understanding Historical /Cultural Contributions of Music (3.0, 3.2)
Valuing Aesthetics (4.0, 4.1, 4.2)

Theatre
Creative Expression (2.0, 2.1)

Visual Arts
Artistic Perception (1.0, 1.1)
Applications and Relationships (5.0, 5.1)

Learning Plan

    I. **Name of Activity: Sound and Movement Patterns**

   II. **Date of Presentation:**

  III. **Age or Grade Level: Pre-K, Kindergarten**

  IV. **Ratio of teachers to children needed for this activity:** up to 1:10

   V. **Target Areas of Learning / Goals and Objectives** (target areas of learning directly relate to "VI. Evaluation Rubric")

      1. Physical: _____

      2. Cognitive: _____

      3. Social: _____

      4. Emotional: _____

      5. Creative: _____

  VI. **Evaluation Rubric:** (if more than two learning areas are being evaluated, a spreadsheet form may be preferred)

Targeted Area of Learning

    _____

    _____

    4. Always _____

    3. Usually _____

    2. Sometimes _____

    1. Rarely _____

Targeted Area of Learning

    _____

    _____

    4. Always _____

    3. Usually _____

    2. Sometimes _____

    1. Rarely _____

  VII. **Materials and Preparation Needed**

For Rhythm Sticks:

1. Open, uncluttered area of the classroom (or could be done outside)
2. A pair of rhythm sticks for each child
3. A CD with music designed for rhythm stick activities (*Simplified Rhythm Stick Activities*, and *Lummi Sticks for Kids CD*, both by Laura Johnson are quite good) There are others that emphasize cultural diversity through musical forms, such as *Multicultural Rhythm Stick Fun* by Georgiana Stewart, 1992. (Refer to the **Suggested Reading** section in *Sound and Movement Pattern Activities for* a more complete list)
4. A playful spirit and a willingness to laugh

  VIII. **Procedures**

1. Pass out rhythm sticks
2. Turn on CD

3. Sing and dance
4. Laugh
5. Go around the circle asking children if they recognized any patterns
6. Play another song
7. Dance and laugh some more
8. Ask for patterns again
9. Be certain that all children get a turn before giving a child a second turn

Variations
For Simple Musical / Rhythmic / Vocal Patterns:
1. Have the children sit on the rug or stand in a circle
2. Initiate a simple musical or movement pattern
3. Ask the children to repeat the pattern
4. Ask the children to name the pattern (a-b, a-b, a-b) or (a-b-b-c, a-b-b-c)
5. Go around the circle, ask individual children to demonstrate a pattern
6. With each child, have the children repeat the child's pattern, and ask them to name the pattern
7. Be certain that all children get a turn before giving a child a second turn

IX. **Accommodations** (changes to accommodate learning diversity)
Name of Accommodated Area:
1. _____
2. _____
3. _____
4. _____
5. _____

X. **Applicable Framework Standards: Kindergarten**
Standard _____
_____
_____
_____
_____

Standard _____
_____
_____
_____
_____

Standard _____
_____
_____
_____
_____

Standard _____

_____

_____

_____

Standard _____

_____

_____

_____

_____

XI. **Evaluation and Comments** (i.e.: How well did the plan work? Great responses? What aspects are especially effective? Not effective? What improvements are needed? Ideas for follow up activities and other notes)

_____

_____

_____

_____

Quilting Activities

Quilting-type activities provide children with opportunities for learning in a broad span of subject areas. For this reason, a quilting project could easily be translated into a thematic unit, if a teacher chooses to do so. Of course, all areas of math are represented in quilting: matching, measuring, patterning, and planning. Making a quilt as a class or school activity will include the social skills of collaboration, cooperation, group planning, and negotiation. Physically, the process of quilting involves fine motor skills and eye-hand coordination. Depending on the materials used, quilting can be a sensory experience as well. When the final project is completed, the children will also feel proud of their part in the group project.

Many cultures produce some kind of quilt-type blanket artwork. There are numerous books suitable to read while a class is making a quilt. *The Keeping Quilt* and *Tar Beach* are two favorites. Teaching children that, although the cultural styles and fabrics used may vary widely, the process of creating quilts is common to many cultures. This will help children to embrace human diversity. We are all unique, and yet within each of us, we are the same.

For children, quilting does not need to be a fabric, needle and thread activity. Older children may want to make sewn quilts. Younger children can begin by making "collage quilts" of recycled wrapping paper and glue or they can make fabric quilts by cutting and gluing pieces together. A jigsaw puzzle type of quilt can be assembled by cutting up pieces of butcher paper. This can be a center or table activity, or even a school wide project. Have the different groups decorate their piece on a theme, and finally, reassemble by gluing the pieces onto another piece of butcher paper.

Quilting type activities can be presented briefly, over the passage of a few days, or can be extended for several weeks. If the instructor intends to extend the duration of a quilting activity, a schedule of the unit would facilitate a smooth presentation. The schedule should include books to be read, and actual quilts to be shown. Perhaps a family member or an employee of a local sewing shop could visit the class and discuss quilts. Should the teacher want to really "get thematic", cookie, cake or sandwich quilts could be prepared for snack.

Depending upon the method used and the age of the children, teachers should plan that quilt making activities may not be completed in one or two days, but can become an ongoing project over a number of days or perhaps even weeks.

Collage Quilts Made of Paper or Fabric
This can be done on a theme or as independent art. Hand print quilts are quite charming. This type of quilt does not necessarily require sewing. For this reason this project can be presented to younger children at the kidney shaped table. The ratio should probably be no more than 1: 5 or 6.

Materials
- ❖ Pieces of fabric, decorative craft or wrapping paper
- ❖ Rulers
- ❖ Fabric glue (for fabric) or glitter glue (for paper)
- ❖ Stickers, stampers, markers, paint (test different art materials to see if they adhere well to the fabric or paper)

❖ Water-based acrylic fabric paint (larger size bottles) for "hand print" quilt
❖ Larger piece of fabric or paper upon which decorated pieces can be glued

Method

❖ Collect larger pieces of fabric, wrapping and decorative craft paper
❖ Have children sort materials by shape and perhaps size
❖ Children discuss size of pieces to be used, then measure and cut out their fabric/paper pieces
❖ Children select the materials with which they want to work
❖ Write child's name on the back or bottom of their "piece"
❖ Children decorate their "quilt piece" by drawing and cutting their own pieces and/or cutting other pieces of fabric or paper; the pieces of the quilt are then arranged and glued in place; if desired, other materials such as feathers, light weight buttons can be used or added;
❖ If quilt is in the hand print theme:
  • Each child dips his or her hand into an appropriately sized shallow tray of water-based fabric paint in a color contrasting to the color of the fabric s/he chose (tempera is fine for paper hand print quilts)
  • Child places hand as carefully as possible onto the square
  • Let dry
❖ Child can then continue decorating the square with fabric paint, glitter glue and so forth, as the child chooses
❖ Allow pieces to dry thoroughly (at least overnight)
❖ Instructor can pre-draw squares onto the larger piece of fabric or paper or not
❖ Lay base material out onto clean floor or large table
❖ Allow children to glue their piece onto the base
❖ Let dry
❖ To display, hang on the wall

Sewn Quilts Using Large Weave Fabrics

This activity can be presented as part of centers or at the kidney-shaped table, so that the teacher can supervise the children as they work. This particular activity is best for children four and above, as they will have more mature eye- hand coordination and fine motor skills.

Materials

❖ Large pieces of any large weave type of fabric such as burlap or hopsacking, in a variety of colors
❖ Pieces of paper roughly the same indented size as the piece of fabric child will work with
❖ Rulers
❖ Embroidery hoops (see large eye needles for inexpensive sources, Wal-Mart Stores often have good crafts departments, and from time to time offer a discount if one happens to have a teacher ID)
❖ Sharpie markers

❖ Plastic large eye needles (available at educational supply stores or through discount warehouses such as Discount School Supply or Oriental Trading Company)
❖ Yarn, embroidery thread, or other thread type material that will fit through the eye of the plastic needle
❖ **Optional:** glittery fabric paints (in applicator tubes), buttons, beads for added embellishments

Method
❖ Give each child a piece of paper
❖ Children draw their design on paper with pencil or crayon
❖ Children discuss size of pieces to be used, then measure and cut out their fabric pieces
❖ Children select their fabric piece
❖ Write child's name on the back of fabric with sharpie marker
❖ Place fabric piece inside embroidery hoop
❖ Children draw their design on fabric piece with sharpie or water based art markers
❖ Tighten fabric inside hoop if necessary
❖ Teacher demonstrates threading needle to children
❖ Teacher demonstrates stitching on the drawn lines
❖ Children select threads they will use
❖ Children begin to stitch in their design with the threads they have selected
❖ Children may also stitch in feathers, beads, buttons on their piece
❖ When design is completed to child's satisfaction, child may further decorate with fabric paints (in applicator tubes)
❖ Allow children's pieces to dry
❖ Teacher or adult volunteer can either machine or hand sew squares together

Suggested Reading:
Burns, M. (1995) *The Greedy Triangle.* (Brainy Day Books). ISBN: 0590489917.
Johnson, T. (De Paola, T. illustrator). (1996). *The quilt story.* ISBN: 0-399-21009-1. (a quilt is passed down through generations).
Jonas, C. (1994). *The Quilt.* ISBN: 0140553088. (a quilt is made from a child's favorite things).
Polacco, P. (2001). *The Keeping Quilt.* ISBN: 0689844476. (a story of four generations of quiltmakers)
Ringgold, F. (1991). *Tar Beach.* ISBN: 0517885441. (the making of a quilt).
Willard, N. (De Paola, T. illustrator). (1987). *Mountains of Quilt.* ISBN: 0-15-256010-6.

Target Areas of Learning

Physical Development
❖ **Fine motor skills:** using the small muscles of the hand and fingers in movement pattern activities
  • Cutting, gluing, decorating, sewing, drawing quilts

❖ **Eye-hand coordination:** coordinating visual acuity with using the small muscles of the hand and fingers: movement pattern activities
❖ Cutting, gluing, decorating, sewing, drawing quilts
❖ **Physical Principals:** comparing weight of various materials
❖ **Sensory discrimination**
  • **Visual discrimination** (sight): identifying fabric and decorative patterns visually
  • **Tactile discrimination** (touch): identifying fabric and decorative patterns through touch; determining flexibility of materials

Cognitive Development
❖ **Language Arts**
  • **Verbal skills**
    o **Language development:** conversation, planning discussion for creation and assembly of quilt
    o **Vocabulary development:** teach names for parts of the quilt, fabrics, styles of quilts, types of embellishments colors, shapes, actions
  • **Emergent literacy**
    o **Symbol recognition:** recognizing that particular marks have meaning as in pictures of, directions for assembly of quilt whether written or drawn
    o **Sequencing (temporal ordering):** planning and assembling quilt in a particular order verbally or in writing
❖ **Math Skills**
  • **Mathematical literacy**
    o **1 to 1 correspondence:** counting quilt pieces in an organized way that shows understanding of the quilt piece's placement as a single entity in a group
  • **Mathematical applications**
    o **Measuring:** comparing length of one piece of fabric to another; measuring fabric pieces and measuring areas where final pieces will be placed
    o **Temporal ordering**
  • **Planning (anticipating) events as they occur in time:** planning class quilt in advance step-by-step
    o **Algebra:** sorting and matching for one or more properties
      – **Pattern recognition:** developing the ability to transition the theoretical idea of pattern to actual recognition of patterns in a craft
      – **Common relatedness:** examining a single object's relatedness to the other objects in a process of determining if a pattern exists
      – **Categorization/ grouping** (sets):
  • Sorting the fabric pieces and materials used for decorating pieces
  • Inventing criterion to separate items into groups beginning with a single property, such as shape, and adding multiple criterion, like color and size, as the child begins to master a skill

- o **Equivalency of individual entities within a pattern:** bigger/smaller, bright/less bright, complex/simple
- o **Spatial relationships:** how does one quilt piece relate to the other quilt pieces?
- o **Time:** time needed to make quilt
- o **Geometry**
  - – **Shape names:** two dimensional: triangle, square, circle, rectangle
- ❖ **Science**
  - • **Chemistry:** discussing whether the glue will adhere to the type of fabric/materials
  - • **Scientific processes**
    - o **Inquiry:** an organized search for knowledge regarding a particular scientific question; testing personal theories
    - o **Prediction:** relating an anticipated outcome based on logic, experience, or research
    - o **Review:** comparing predictions and actual outcomes

Social Science

- ❖ **Diversity:** culturally specific types of patterns found in types quilts from around the country/world
  - • Developing different kinds of textile skills: braiding, weaving, paper making, hand spinning yarn
  - • **Not all people (cultures, traditions, spiritual expressions) are the same. These differences make people unique, not** *bad*.

Social Development

- ❖ **Collaboration:** group problem solving to create a quilt
- ❖ **Working cooperatively with others in a group:** working as a team to create quilt pieces and assembling the pieces into a single community created art piece
- ❖ **Negotiation:** working out differing ideas for a project
- ❖ **Sharing:** using materials and tools with others in the group in a friendly manner
- ❖ **Taking turns:** waiting while others add their pieces to the quilt
- ❖ **Patience:** moving through the activity methodically so project is completed as intended
- ❖ **Following directions:** following teacher or collaborative group instructions
- ❖ **Community building:** creating a sense of belonging in a group by working with others toward a common goal
- ❖ **Taking care of classroom environment:** participating in clean up, set up, managing the space so everyone can be productive

Emotional Development

- ❖ **Self-esteem:** relationships: feeling good about interacting well with others; creating a group project
- ❖ **Accomplishment:** developing a sense of self worth from participation creating the quilt

Creative Expression

- ❖ **Use of creative media and expression of imagination**
  - **3-dimensional art:** inventing quilt for the classroom project inventing ways to decorate the quilt piece
- ❖ **Creative risk:** being comfortable trying out original patterns for quilt
- ❖ **Aesthetic appreciation:** developing appreciation for art of quilting
- ❖ **Artistic vocabulary:** learning quilt making vocabulary
- ❖ **Problem solving:** considering possibilities for quilt to be made, selecting and executing the plan
- ❖ **Creative thinking:** brainstorming: considering all possible solutions to a creating a quilt

Possible Accommodations for *Quilting Activity*

ADHD

- ❖ Use positive reinforcement (praise) when child works well with others and behaves appropriately
- ❖ Lower the ratio/increase level of adult supervision
- ❖ Have children work in small groups to reduce the energy level while children are working on the quilt pieces
- ❖ Have child work in a group of calmer, less impulsive individuals
- ❖ Offer child a carrell to reduce external distractions while working on the quilt piece

Developmental Delays

- ❖ Explain the activity using short simple phrases while making eye contact
- ❖ Model activity using photographs or realia
- ❖ Have child work in a smaller group, with gentle peers
- ❖ Use positive reinforcement as the child succeeds in creating the quilt piece
- ❖ Lower ratio/increase adult supervision: check in on child frequently
- ❖ Offer more time if child is enjoying activity
- ❖ Simplify task: break the activity down into smaller incremental steps rather than attempting to accomplish a number of steps in one or two sessions

Autism Spectrum Disorders

- ❖ Explain the activity using short simple phrases while making eye contact
- ❖ Model activity using photographs or realia
- ❖ Have the activity on the class calendar, so child is aware in the change of routine
- ❖ Have activities requiring planning and assembly as part of the regular class routine, allowing the child to become accustomed to the type of activity
- ❖ Have child work with a single partner, perhaps the same class partner throughout the semester or school year for additional familiarity
- ❖ Adjust the duration of the activity for each session if it appears the child is more or less engaged with it, and have another activity as back up

- ❖ Have child work with a gentle peer who understands the task at hand
- ❖ Use positive reinforcement when child participates
- ❖ Simplify task: ask child to create a less complicated quilt piece
- ❖ Offer a more limited selection of materials, being sure to include types of materials the child particularly likes

Visual Impairments
- ❖ Adjust lighting to reduce glare
- ❖ Use brightly colored high contrast materials
- ❖ Have child work with the same partners so the children learn to work well with the visually impaired child
- ❖ Use adapted tools: i.e.: easier scissors, ruler with bolder print numbers
- ❖ Allow child to make a simpler design, using fewer and larger pieces for the quilt piece

Orthopedic Impairment
- ❖ Make sure child is positioned comfortably
- ❖ Adjust furniture so child can access activity easily
- ❖ Offer a tray for easy access
- ❖ Offer adapted tools such as scissors, glitter glue bottles with hand grips
- ❖ Clip paper or fabric down to steady it while child is cutting
- ❖ Use hand-over-hand method to guide child if hands lack strength or dexterity

Gifted and Talented Education (GATE)
- ❖ Offer more challenging quilt patterns
- ❖ Ask child to invent a quilt pattern using tanagram squares, and attempt to replicate it using paper or fabric
- ❖ Ask child to design a quilt using designated geometric shapes

English Language Learners (ELL)
- ❖ Explain the activity using short simple phrases while making eye contact
- ❖ Model activity using photographs or realia
- ❖ In a small group situation, assign a paraprofessional to review vocabulary words using photographs or realia
- ❖ Use positive reinforcement (smiles, praise, a sticker, et cetera) when child begins to use new vocabulary

Content Standards For Kindergarten Met By This Activity
English Language Arts
> Listening and Speaking (1.0, 1.1, 1.2, 2.0, 2.1)

Mathematics

Numbers and Counting (1.0, 1.1, 1.2, 1.3)
Algebra, Sets and Sorting (1.0, 1.1)
Measurement and Geometry (1.0, 1.1, 1.2, 1.3, 1.4, 2.0, 2.1, 2.2)
Statistics (1.0, 1.1, 1.2
Mathematical Reasoning (1.0, 1.1, 1.2)

History and Social Science

Following Rules (K.1, K.1.1)
Understanding that history relates to people and places in the past (K.6, K.6.3))

Visual Arts

Artistic Perception (1.0, 1.1, 1.2, 1.3)
Creative Expression (2.0, 2.1, 2.2, 2.3, 2.6
Understanding Historical / Cultural Contributions of Visual Arts (3.0, 3.1)

Learning Plan

I. **Name of Activity:** Quilting Activities

II. **Date of Presentation:**

III. **Age or Grade Level: Pre-K to Kindergarten**

IV. **Ratio of teachers to children needed for this activity:** up to 1:5 (or 6)

V. **Target Areas of Learning / Goals and Objectives** (target areas of learning directly relate to "VI. Evaluation Rubric")
   1. **Physical:** _____
   2. **Cognitive:** _____
   3. **Social:** _____
   4. **Emotional:** _____
   5. **Creative:** _____

VI. **Evaluation Rubric:** (if more than two learning areas are being evaluated, a spreadsheet form may be preferred)

Targeted Area of Learning	Targeted Area of Learning
_____	_____
_____	_____
4. Always _____	**4.** Always _____
3. Usually _____	**3.** Usually _____
2. Sometimes _____	**2.** Sometimes _____
1. Rarely _____	**1.** Rarely _____

VII. **Materials and Preparation Needed**
   1. Pieces of fabric, decorative craft or wrapping paper
   2. Rulers
   3. Fabric glue (for fabric) or glitter glue (for paper)
   4. Stickers, stampers, markers, paint (test different art materials to see how well they adhere to the fabric or paper)
   5. Water-based acrylic fabric paint (larger size bottles) for "hand print" quilt
   6. Larger piece of fabric or paper upon which decorated pieces can be glued

VIII. **Procedures**
   1. Collect larger pieces of fabric, wrapping and decorative craft paper
   2. Have children sort materials by shape and perhaps size
   3. Children discuss size of pieces to be used, then measure and cut out their fabric/ paper pieces
   4. Children select the materials with which they want to work

5. Write child's name on the back or bottom of the "piece"
6. Children decorate their "quilt piece" by drawing and cutting their own pieces and/ or cutting other pieces of fabric or paper; the pieces of the quilt are then arranged and glued in place; if desired, other materials such as feathers, light weight buttons can be used or added;
7. If quilt is in the hand print theme:
8. Each child dips his or her hand into an appropriately sized shallow tray of water-based fabric paint in a color contrasting to the color of the fabric chosen (tempera is fine for paper hand print quilts)
9. Child places hand as carefully as possible onto the square
10. Let dry
11. Child can then continue decorating the square with fabric paint, glitter glue and so forth, as the child chooses
12. Allow pieces to dry thoroughly (at least overnight)
13. Instructor can pre-draw squares onto the larger piece of fabric or paper or not
14. Lay base material out onto clean floor or large table
15. Allow children to glue their piece onto the base
16. Let dry
17. To display, hang on the wall

Variation: *Sewn Quilts Using Large Weave Fabrics*
*Note: For further information regarding this activity, please refer to **Quilting Activities***

IX. **Accommodations** (changes to accommodate learning diversity)
Name of Accommodated Area:
1. _____
2. _____
3. _____
4. _____
5. _____

X. **Applicable Framework Standards: Kindergarten**
Standard _____
_____
_____
_____
_____

Standard _____
_____
_____
_____
_____

Standard _____

_____

_____

_____

Standard _____

_____

_____

_____

Standard _____

_____

_____

_____

XI. **Evaluation and Comments** (i.e.: How well did the plan work? Great responses? What aspects are especially effective? Not effective? What improvements are needed? Ideas for follow up activities and other notes)

_____

_____

_____

_____

Salt "Sand" Art

Salt "Sand" Art is a method to teach the mathematical skills of measuring and patterning. Children enjoy the creative aspect of making layers while tilting the jar this way and that. The end product is uniquely theirs, which helps build self-esteem. The children also learn about how friction creates the colored salt by the rubbing action of the chalk upon the sand. As this project can be potentially messy, the teacher may wish set it up in an area of the classroom easily swept up (i.e.: linoleum floor) or it could even be set up on tables outside.

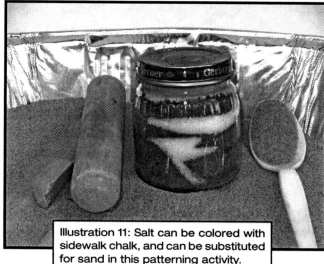

Illustration 11: Salt can be colored with sidewalk chalk, and can be substituted for sand in this patterning activity.

This is an excellent activity to include when presenting a unit on Native American people, especially tribes of the Southwest, such as the Navajo. The unit could include the presentation of different foods, clothing, dance, and music as well as Native American art and customs.

Materials

- ❖ 1 clean baby food ajr or any other small clear glass or plastic container for each child
- ❖ 25 pounds of salt, inexpensive - available from restaurant supply and any club store
- ❖ Several pieces of "sidewalk" chalk in bright colors (at least one for each tray of salt)
- ❖ Plastic or metal roasting type trays at least 3 inches deep
- ❖ White glue
- ❖ Spoons, small laundry scoops, small craft funnels, tongue depressor sticks
- ❖ Quart-size zipper-type freezer bags

Method

- ❖ Set out several foil or plastic roasting size pans
- ❖ Fill each about 1"-2" deep with regular table salt.
- ❖ Give each child a clean baby food jar or other small glass or plastic container.
- ❖ Choose a brightly colored piece of sidewalk chalk (to accommodate smaller hands, break the chalk in half, if necessary). Place a different color in each pan of salt (i.e.: separate trays by color).
- ❖ In small groups (3 to 5 at a time) have the children first rub the chalk into the salt. Ask open-ended questions: such as, why the children think the salt is changing color
  Note: Make small batches of colored salt to allow as many children to participate as possible.
- ❖ Once the salt is colored to the desired shade, put spoons, funnels or laundry scoops into each tray of salt; allow small groups of children to create their *Salt "Sand" Art Jars*, by filling their jars with layers of different colored salts; jars may be filled up to within 1/4 inch of the top

❖ Children can make more interesting patterns by tilting jars to one side or the other, using small craft funnels (inserted in large straws), or sliding colored salt down the side of a tongue depressor

❖ When jars are completed, allow children to fill last 1/4" or so with white glue to cover top layer of colored salt. (This prevents spills or loss of pattern)

❖ Have children put the lids on their jars.

❖ Allow jars to dry for 1 to 2 days.

❖ Any leftover colored salt may be placed in zipper-type freezer bags by color, for possible future use.

Variation:

• Before beginning the activity, allow the children to have the opportunity to plan the pattern of their jars
  Note: This could be done on the same day, or the day before the activity is planned)

• After explain the activity and reminding them that " a pattern repeats", give children a piece of paper (perhaps a copy of a simple outline of a jar), and crayons (or colored pencils) to draw the pattern they choose (planning activity)

• When the pattern is drawn, have child wash hands, & dry thoroughly, to be ready to begin creating the *Salt "Sand" Art Jar*

Suggested Reading:

Martin, Jr., B. & Archambault, J. (1997). *Knots on a Counting Rope.* ISBN: 0805054790. (Reading Rainbow)

Chanin, M. (1998). *The Chief's Blanket.* ISBN: 0915811782.

De Paola, T. (1996). *Legend of the Indian Paintbrush.* ISBN: 0698113608.

Flood, N.B. (2006). *The Navajo Year Walk Through Many Seasons.* ISBN: 189335406.

Orie, S.D. (1996). *Did You Hear the Wind Sing Your Name? An Oneida Song of Spring.* ISBN: 0802774857.

Pluckrose, H. A. (1995). *Pattern. (Math Counts).* ISBN: 0516454552.

Pluckrose, H.A. (1995). *Weight. (Math counts).* ISBN: 0516454609.

Pluckrose, H.A. & Choos, R.G. (1995). *Capacity (Math Counts).* ISBN: 051645451X.

Target Areas of Learning

Physical Development

❖ **Gross motor**: rubbing chalk vigorously into salt

❖ **Eye-hand coordination**
  • Pouring, scooping
  • Creating layers by manipulating sand in jars

❖ **Fine motor**
  • Rubbing chalk into salt
  • Digging, holding tools

❖ **Physical principals:** experiencing the change in weight while filling jar
❖ **Sensory discrimination**
  • **Tactile discrimination** (touch): texture: feeling and identifying texture of salt; identifying sensory experience of rubbing the chalk into the salt
  • **Visual discrimination** (sight): identifying the change in the appearance of the salt

Cognitive Development
❖ **Language Arts**
  •   **Verbal skills**
    o **Language development**: describing sensations of rubbing chalk into salt, talking about friction as it relates to coloring salt, layering salt, discussing and comparing the jars the class members created
    o **Vocabulary development**: learning names of colors and substances, quantities of substances
  • **Emergent literacy**
    o **Sequencing (temporal ordering)**: recalling the activity as it occurred in time
❖ **Math Skills**
  • **Conservation**
    o **Conservation of volume:** understanding quantities of salt do not change, regardless of appearance
  • **Mathematical applications**
    o **Measurement:** measuring out salt into pans
    o **Equivalency:** comparing an salt in terms of quantity
    o **Spatial relationships:** relating the aspects layers of salt in the jar to one another, thinking about salt art jar three dimensionally
    o **Construction:** forming salt jar by putting together layers to create a three dimensional object
    o **Algebra:** placing items in an invented order for similarities and differences of properties
    o **Patterning:** placing layers into jar in a recognizable pattern "a pattern repeats"
❖ **Science**
  • **Physical science:** noticing properties of substances, seeing how the properties of salt change when chalk is rubbed into it; seeing how the glue affects the salt
  • **Scientific processes**
    o **Prediction:** relating an anticipated outcome-based on logic, experience, or research
    o **Observation:** carefully watching and noting what is seen for a scientific purpose: rubbing the chalk into the salt, possibly by shaking the jar, watching the appearance of the glue and how it changes over time
  • **Cause and effect**
    o **Relationships between actions and outcomes**: noticing the action of the salt on the chalk, the glue on the colored salt

Social Development

- ❖ **Following directions**: participating in the activity as instructed
- ❖ **Working cooperatively with others in a group**: participating in the salt art activity being mindful and considerate of others
- ❖ **Sharing**: allowing everyone in the group to have a fair turn creating colored salt and to have access to all the colors when assembling the jars
- ❖ **Taking care of classroom environment**: participating in cleanup

Emotional Development

- ❖ **Self-esteem:** feeling good about oneself, the work one does; participating in activities wherein there are no "wrong" answers, feeling comfortable with creative self expression
- ❖ **Accomplishment**: satisfaction in having produced salt jar

Creative Expression

- ❖ **Use of creative media and expression of imagination**
  - • **3-dimensional visual arts:** creating the salt jar as an art piece
- ❖ **Creative risk**: experimenting freely with a goal of investigating the outcome, without fear of "failure"

Possible Accommodations for *Salt Sand Art Activity*

ADHD

- ❖ Use positive reinforcement (praise) when child works well with others and behaves appropriately; "catch" children being good; praise staying on task, working well with others, sharing, cooperating
- ❖ Lower the ratio; fewer children filling jars equals more supervision
- ❖ Simplify: break the activity up into two activities (making colored salt and putting the salt into the jars), to allow children to focus fully on the task at hand
- ❖ Place splat mats under tables of ingredients or have activity in an area where accidental spills are easily cleaned up
- ❖ Allow the child to have an opportunity to act as your helper, to set up the activity
- ❖ Decrease quantity of salt in trays, being prepared to refill more frequently, to prevent spills from enthusiastic chalk rubbing

Developmental Delays

- ❖ Go over task step-by-step using short simple phases maintaining eye contact to be sure child understands the task
- ❖ Demonstrate activity while explaining it using real salt art jars or photos
- ❖ Use positive reinforcement as the child succeeds and completes the various tasks related to sand art project (be sure praise is authentic)
- ❖ Check in on children frequently

❖ Have an adult work with child on any of the tasks that may be challenging for the child, encouraging and supporting the child in the activity, making certain child is working as independently as possible on the task
❖ Offer more time to complete task
❖ Use larger jars (plastic?), larger spoons and scoops for easier grasping
❖ Place splat mats under tables of ingredients or have activity in an area where accidental spills are easily cleaned up
❖ Break the activity up into two sessions: coloring the salt, filling the jars

Autism Spectrum Disorders

❖ Go over task step-by-step using short simple phases maintaining eye contact to be sure child understands the task
❖ Demonstrate activity while explaining it using real salt art jars or photos
❖ Present activity later on in the week; have it on the weekly schedule so that child will have time to become used to the idea of the activity
❖ Show sample "sand salt art jars" early on in the week, so child will become used to the idea of this activity
❖ Use positive reinforcement when child participates
❖ Place splat mats under tables of ingredients or have activity in an area where accidental spills are easily cleaned up
❖ Break the activity up into several sessions: coloring the salt, filling the jars

Visual Impairments

❖ Adjust the lighting to reduce glare
❖ Place splat mats under tables of ingredients or have activity in an area where accidental spills are easily cleaned up
❖ Have an adult work with child on any of the tasks that may be challenging for the child, encouraging and supporting the child in the activity, making certain child is working as independently as possible on the task
❖ Offer more time to complete task
❖ Have larger plastic jars available with wider mouths, if necessary

Orthopedic Impairment

❖ Make sure child is positioned comfortably
❖ Adjust furniture for easy access for child
❖ Offer child a tray
❖ Use smaller pans (such as cleaned tofu tubs) so child can create individual amounts of colored salt)
❖ Use bowls with suction cups on the bottom so child can scoop out colored chalk with less concern regarding spilling
❖ Offer larger (plastic) jars with wider mouths for easier filling
❖ If child lacks hand and finger strength and/or dexterity, use hand-over-hand method to assist in creating colored chalk and filling jars

Gifted And Talented Education (GATE)

❖ Ask child to plan pattern in advance using letters to designate the pattern in advance
❖ Ask child to predict outcome if jars are tilted or moved when being filled
❖ Ask child to create jar based on predictions made
❖ Offer child unusually shaped jars to investigate outcome
❖ Ask child to predict outcome of rubbing chalk in flour, sugar, white cornmeal, cornstarch and offer child the opportunity to use journal

English Language Learners (ELL)

❖ Go over task step-by-step using short simple phases maintaining eye contact to be sure child understands the task
❖ Demonstrate activity while explaining it using real salt art jars or photos
❖ Pre-teach and review vocabulary words such as salt, chalk, jar, glue, color words individually or a in small group setting
❖ Use positive reinforcement when child attempts to use vocabulary words

Content Standards For Kindergarten Met By This Activity

English Language Arts

Reading (1.0, 1.17, 1.18)
Listening and Speaking 1.0, 1.1, 1.2, 2.1)

Mathematics

Numbers and Counting (1.0,1.1)
Measurement and Geometry (1.0, 1.1)
Statistics, Data Analysis and Probability (1.0, 1.2)

Science

Physical Science (1.a)
Investigation and Experimentation (4a, 4b, 4d, 4e)

History and Social Science

Following Rules (K.1, K.1.1)

Visual Arts

Artistic Perception (1.0, 1.1)
Creative Expression (2.0, 2.1)

Learning Plan

    I. **Name of Activity: Salt "Sand" Art**

   II. **Date of Presentation:**

  III. **Age or Grade Level: Pre-K to Kindergarten**

  IV. **Ratio of teachers to children needed for this activity:** up to 1:5

   V. **Target Areas of Learning / Goals and Objectives** (target areas of learning directly relate to "VI. Evaluation Rubric")
      1. Physical: _____
      2. Cognitive: _____
      3. Social: _____
      4. Emotional: _____
      5. Creative: _____

  VI. **Evaluation Rubric:** (if more than two learning areas are being evaluated, a spreadsheet form may be preferred)

Targeted Area of Learning	**Targeted Area of Learning**
_____	_____
_____	_____
4. Always _____	**4. Always** _____
3. Usually _____	**3. Usually** _____
2. Sometimes _____	**2. Sometimes** _____
1. Rarely _____	**1. Rarely** _____

VII. **Materials and Preparation Needed**
    1. 1 clean baby food or other small clear glass or plastic container per child
    2. 25 pounds of salt, inexpensive - available from restaurant supply and club stores
    3. Several pieces of "sidewalk" chalk in bright colors (at least one for each tray of salt)
    4. Plastic or metal roasting type trays at least 3 inches deep
    5. White glue
    6. Spoons, small laundry scoops, small craft funnels, tongue depressor sticks
    7. Quart-size zipper-type freezer bags

VIII. **Procedures**
    1. Set out several foil or plastic roasting size pans
    2. Fill each about 1"-2" deep with regular table salt.
    3. Give each child a clean baby food jar or other small glass or plastic container.

4. Choose a brightly colored piece of sidewalk chalk (to accommodate smaller hands, break the chalk in half, if necessary). Place a different color in each pan of salt (i.e.: separate trays by color).

5. In small groups (3 to 5 at a time) have the children first rub the chalk into the salt. Ask open-ended questions: such as, ask the children why they think the salt is changing color (Make small batches of colored salt to allow as many children to participate as possible).

6. Once the salt is colored to the desired shade, put spoons, funnels or laundry scoops into each tray of salt; allow small groups of children to create their their *Salt "Sand" Art Jars*, by filling their jars with layers of different colored salts; jars may be filled up to within 1/4" of the top

7. Children can make more interesting patterns by tilting jars to one side or the other, using small craft funnels (inserted in large straws), or sliding colored salt down the side of a tongue depressor

8. When jars are completed, allow children to fill last 1/4" or so with white glue to cover top layer of colored salt. (This prevents spills or loss of pattern)

9. Have children put the lids on their jars.

10. Allow jars to dry for 1 to 2 days.

11. Any leftover colored salt may be placed in zipper-type freezer bags by color, for possible future use.

Variation:

- Before beginning the activity, allow the children to have the opportunity to plan the pattern of their jars (This could be done on the same day or the day before the activity is planned)

- After explaining the activity and reminding them that " a pattern repeats", give children a piece of paper (perhaps a copy of a simple outline of a jar), and crayons (or colored pencils) to draw the pattern they choose (planning activity)

- When the pattern is drawn, have child wash hands, & dry thoroughly, to be ready to begin creating the *Salt "Sand" Art Jar*

IX. Accommodations (changes to accommodate learning diversity)
Name of Accommodated Area:

1. _____
2. _____
3. _____
4. _____
5. _____

X. Applicable Framework Standards: Kindergarten

Standard _____

_____
_____
_____

Standard _____

_____
_____
_____

Standard _____

_____
_____
_____

Standard _____

_____
_____
_____

Standard _____

_____
_____
_____

XI. Evaluation and Comments (i.e.: How well did the plan work? Great responses? What aspects are especially effective? Not effective? What improvements are needed? Ideas for follow up activities and other notes)

_____
_____
_____
_____

Sorting Activities

Sorting for one or more properties is the making of sets. Making sets is an algebraic activity. When introducing sorting, have the children sort items for a single property. As the children become skilled at the less complicated levels of sorting, introduce sorting for two, three, or more criterion.

Sorting is wonderful as a "centers" activity. Sorting can be presented as an individual or small group activity. Sorting is most fun when one is sorting items that are of interest to the children. The teacher needs to take into consideration choking hazards when selecting items to

Illustration 12: Young children can sort large buttons by quantity or physical attributes.

be sorted. Should you have children who for whatever reason are still "mouthing" toys and manipulatives, Offer that child larger items to sort, such as bigger plastic dinosaurs.

The button box is a classic sorting activity, particularly if the buttons you offer are brightly colored and there is a wonderful variety of them. Paper clips, brads, rubber bands all tossed together can be fun to sort, as well as sea shells, rocks, leaves, the different types of K'Nex manipulatives, plastic colored Teddy bears, crayons. Almost anything can be sorted. The primary limitation is your imagination.

If there are several different types of sorting activities going on (for example: buttons, small office supplies, and K'Nex pieces), it is better to conduct the activities sufficiently far apart so that the three types of materials to be sorted remain a sorting activity and not a sorting nightmare.

Sorting

Materials
- ❖ Stuff to be sorted
- ❖ Writing paper **or**
- ❖ A (laminated) sorting board
    - To make the sorting board, the teacher needs to draw lines across a 12" x 18" (or larger) piece of poster board with a sharpie marker
    - Either write the name or glue pictures of the criterion for sorting in each square
    - Laminate - Because of the large size, it will require the use of a professional type laminator. Laminating will maintain the integrity of the board. With any use at all, an unlaminated board will become worn out, and will need to be replaced frequently
    Variation: Teacher just draws in lines and laminates; children can draw or write in properties for sorting using a dry erase marker

Method

- ❖ Set out the box of items to be sorted next to the "sorting board"
- ❖ Children sort items by whatever criterion is on the "sorting board"
- ❖ Children can count and compare numbers of items within different criterion groups
- ❖ Children can make notes or drawings about the sorting activity in their journals or in their math notebooks

Jigsaw Puzzles

Working a jigsaw puzzle involves many cognitive skills including sorting and matching. Visual discrimination is key for the completion of a jigsaw puzzle. If the puzzle is left out so that children can work on it after their other tasks are completed, during centers or free time, then an added dimension of learning to work cooperatively will be added.

Jigsaw puzzles vary widely in difficulty. There are wooden puzzles with pegs, which are the simplest variety. Then there are twenty, fifty, one hundred, five hundred, and one thousand piece puzzles, which span a broad range of difficulty in as broad a range of subjects and interests. When a puzzle is selected for the class, the teacher must be sure the puzzles are neither impossibly difficult nor too easy for the children. Subject matter is also important. If the class has a particular interest in dinosaurs, the teacher should choose dinosaur puzzles. If the teacher is presenting a thematic unit, select puzzles that follow the theme being presented during that period of time. Cultural puzzles, puzzles showing human diversity are great for classroom use as well.

Materials

- ❖ A jigsaw puzzle with a number of pieces that is challenging but not impossible for the developmental maturity of the children in the class
- ❖ A table placed in an area that can be undisturbed while the puzzle is being completed
- ❖ One or two low trays into which the puzzle pieces can be placed
- ❖ Good lighting

Method

- ❖ Set out jigsaw puzzle
- ❖ Children turn all puzzle pieces face up onto the low trays
- ❖ Children find the "border" pieces (pieces with a flat side which defines the outside edge of the puzzle)
- ❖ Children can, if they choose to do so, sort the puzzle pieces by color and design
- ❖ Children can work on puzzle as time allows during the day
- ❖ The picture on the box top can help children match pieces to the design of the puzzle
- ❖ After puzzle is completed, leave puzzle out for all to admire for a day or two
- ❖ Children assembling puzzle have first opportunity to disassemble puzzle and return to the box

Suggested Reading:

Aber, L.W. (2002). *Grandma's Button Box (Math Matters)*. ISBN: 1575651106.
Aker, S. (1992). *What Comes In 2's, 3's & 4's?* ISBN: 0671792474.

Pluckrose, H.A., (1995). *Sorting (Math Counts)*. ISBN: 0516454587.

Reid, M.S. (1995). *The Button Box*. ISBN: 0140554955.

Wallwork, A. (1993). *No Dodos. A Counting Book of Endangered Animals*. ISBN: 0590467697. (counting animals in sets, one whale, two tigers, and zero - no dodos, they are extinct; also gives information about each animal).

Target Areas of Learning

Physical Development
- ❖ **Fine motor skills:** using the small muscles of the hand and fingers
  - Manipulating objects to be sorted including holding, examining and placing in designated places/containers
  - Assembling jigsaw puzzles
- ❖ **Eye-hand coordination:** coordinating visual acuity with using the small muscles of the hand and fingers
  - Manipulating objects to be sorted including holding, examining and placing in designated places/containers
  - Assembling puzzle pieces
- ❖ **Sensory discrimination**
  - **Visual discrimination** (sight): identifying patterns visually; identifying puzzle pieces by colors and shapes
  - **Tactile discrimination** (touch): identifying items being sorted through feeling and touch

Cognitive Development
- ❖ **Language Arts**
  - **Verbal skills**
    - o **Language development**: conversation, identifying types of properties for sorting, for puzzles: describing the image to be completed
    - o **Vocabulary development**: using number, color, shape, size, descriptive words for pieces correctly
  - **Emergent literacy**
    - o **Sequencing (temporal ordering)**: describing the process of sorting in the order it occurred
- ❖ **Math Skills**
  - **Conservation math**
    - o **Conservation of quantity**: recognizing that the number of items being sorted remains constant regardless of the configuration of the pieces
    - o **Reversibility**: a configuration can be returned to the original form without impact on the quantity of items

- **Mathematical literacy**
  - ○ **1 to 1 Correspondence**: counting items to be sorted in an organized way that shows understanding of the object's placement as a single entity in a group to examine the single object's relatedness to the other objects
- **Mathematical applications**
  - ○ **Measurement:** comparing some aspect of size of one object to another
  - ○ **Equivalency of individual entities within the sorting activity:** more / less; single / plural; longer/ shorter; comparing an object or a number of objects in terms of size or other properties while sorting
  - ○ **Seriation:** ordering objects in a graduation of size from smallest to largest or vice versa while sorting
  - ○ **Spatial relationships:** relating the aspects of physical objects to one another, thinking about objects in three dimensions, organizing objects in sequence
  - ○ **Common relatedness:** ordering and sorting objects that are not the same but are related to one another including **opposites:** dark/light, narrow/wide; front/back; big/small, edge piece/not edge piece
  - **Algebra:** sorting and matching for one or more properties
  - ○ **Group/classification:** if a child **invents his own criterion for a property** and has opportunities to explain the properties for which he is classifying, there is an opportunity for **more advanced critical thinking**
  - ○ **Pattern Recognition:** developing the ability to identify patterns in puzzles
- ❖ **Science**
  - **Identifying sorting criterion for items occurring in nature**: observing the various properties of plants, stones, sea shells, types of soil or sand, and animals as they are in nature
  - **Scientific processes**
    - ○ **Inquiry:** an organized search for finding relatedness of objects
    - ○ **Observation:** identifying properties of items within the natural environment and laboratory situations carefully
- ❖ **Social Science**
  - **Recognizing diversity: including** culturally specific types of materials to be sorted/ puzzles to be completed; puzzles reflecting different races, ages, abledness, occupations, socioeconomic statuses

Social Development

- ❖ **Collaboration:** working as a team to create and identify criterion for sorting, then report results found; assembling puzzles as a group project
- ❖ **Working cooperatively with others in a group**: allowing everyone working on the project opportunities to participate and contribute
- ❖ **Negotiation:** learning to represent one's suggestions for sorting criterion in such a way that others in the group will consider them favorably
- ❖ **Sharing:** letting all children who choose to do so, work on the puzzle
- ❖ **Taking turns:** learning patience while others share their findings, while others work on a specific part of the puzzle or sorting activity

❖ **Following directions:** sorting as teacher instructs, completing puzzle per instructions
❖ **Caring for the classroom as a community environment**: helping to clean up

Emotional Development

❖ **Self-esteem:** having positive feelings while successfully sorting items
❖ **Empathy**: being kind to others as they work or struggle with sorting objects or assembling puzzles
❖ **Accomplishment**: developing a sense of achievement while sorting or assembling a puzzle

Creative Expression

❖ **Use of creative imagination**: inventing types of criterion in the process of sorting
❖ **Use of creative media and expression of imagination**:
  • **2-dimensional visual arts**: creating decorative arrangements in the process of sorting objects
❖ **Creative risk**: defining sorting criterion without concern for approval/disapproval, but for inquiry
❖ **Aesthetic appreciation: developing appreciation** for art
❖ **Problem solving**: gathering data, collaborating to sort or assemble a puzzle

Possible Accommodations for *Sorting Activity*

ADHD

❖ Use positive reinforcement (praise) when child works well with others and behaves appropriately
❖ Ask child to repeat instructions back to you to check for understanding
❖ Offer child a carrell to reduce level of distraction
❖ Reduce the number of items to be sorted
❖ Offer the child more time to complete the task
❖ Lower the ratio/increase level of adult supervision
❖ Have children work in small groups to reduce the energy level while children are inventing their criterion
❖ Have child work in a group of less high energy, impulsive individuals

Developmental Delays

❖ Go over task step-by-step using short simple phases maintaining eye contact to be sure child understands the task
❖ Demonstrate activity while explaining it using real objects or photographs
❖ Have child work in a smaller group, with gentle peers
❖ Use positive reinforcement as the child succeeds in creating and sorting for properties created
❖ Lower ratio/increase adult supervision: Check in on child frequently
❖ Offer more time if child is enjoying activity

❖ Simplify task: ask child to sort for less complex types of criterion
❖ For activities that require much clean up, there should be a longer clean up or transition time allowed.

Autism Spectrum Disorders

❖ Go over task step-by-step using short simple phases maintaining eye contact to be sure child understands the task
❖ Demonstrate activity while explaining it using real objects or photographs
❖ Have sorting type activities as part of the regular class routine, allowing the child to become accustomed to the type of activity
❖ Have child work with a single partner, perhaps the same class partner for additional familiarity
❖ Adjust the amount of time child participates in the activity to match child's involvement (have another activity as back up in case child loses interest)
❖ Have child work with a gentle peer who understands the task at hand
❖ Use positive reinforcement when child participates
❖ Simplify task: ask child to sort for less complicated types of criterion

Visual Impairments

❖ Adjust lighting to reduce glare
❖ Offer larger items with high contrast detail to be sorted
❖ Use puzzles with large size, high contrast pieces; brighter colors work very well
❖ Make a laminated board that has larger spaces or have big trays available that have sections large enough hold the larger items that the child will be sorting
❖ Have the child work with the same gentle partners so the children learn to work well with the visually impaired child
❖ Check on children frequently, or lower the ratio, to allow supervising adults the opportunity to Offer help if it is needed
❖ Offer more time to complete the task at hand and for cleaning up if necessary

Orthopedic Impairment

❖ Make sure child is seated comfortably
❖ Adjust furniture to make activity accessible for child
❖ Place activity on tray
❖ Use adapted puzzles and puzzle pieces (with pegs, larger and thicker pieces)
❖ Use larger objects to be sorted and larger containers (with lower sides) into which the child can sort the pieces
❖ If hands and fingers lack strength or dexterity, assist child using hand-over-hand method, when necessary

Gifted and Talented Education (GATE)
❖ Offer more complex puzzles
❖ Request that child sort for multiple criterion such as color, shape and size

English Language Learners (ELL)
❖ Go over task step-by-step using short simple phases maintaining eye contact to be sure child understands the task
❖ Demonstrate activity while explaining it using real objects or photographs
❖ Pre-teach and review vocabulary words individually: color words, shape names, relative size (big, bigger, smaller, et cetera) names, image names (for puzzles), object names (for sorting), action words (pick up, sort, put), spatial words (above, below, inside, under, before, after)
❖ Use positive reinforcement when child integrates words into vocabulary

Content Standards For Kindergarten Met By This Activity

English Language Arts
Listening and Speaking (1.0, 1.1, 1.2, 2.0, 2.1)

Mathematics
Numbers and Counting (1.0, 1.1, 1.2, 1.3)
Algebra, Sets and Sorting (1.0, 1.1)
Measurement and Geometry (1.0, 1.1, 2.0, 2.1, 2.2)
Statistics (1.0, 1.1, 1.2)

Science
Physical Science (1.a)
Life Science (2.a)
Investigation and Experimentation (4a, 4b, 4d, 4e)

History and Social Science
Following Rules (K.1, K.1.1)
Matching work descriptions to related jobs in history and community (K.3)
Compare and describe people and places (K.4).

Learning Plan

   I. **Name of Activity: Sorting**

  II. **Date of Presentation:**

 III. **Age or Grade Level: Pre-K to Kindergarten**

 IV. **Ratio of teachers to children needed for this activity:** up to 1:3 teams

  V. **Target Areas of Learning / Goals and Objectives** (target areas of learning directly relate to "VI. Evaluation Rubric")

     1. Physical: _____

     2. Cognitive: _____

     3. Social: _____

     4. Emotional: _____

     5. Creative: _____

 VI. **Evaluation Rubric:** (if more than two learning areas are being evaluated, a spreadsheet form may be preferred)

Targeted Area of Learning

Targeted Area of Learning

_____

_____

    4. Always _____

    3. Usually _____

    2. Sometimes _____

    1. Rarely _____

    4. Always _____

    3. Usually _____

    2. Sometimes _____

    1. Rarely _____

VII. **Materials and Preparation Needed**

   1. Items to be sorted

   2. Writing paper or

   3. A sorting board (laminated)

- To make the sorting board, the teacher needs to draw lines across a 12" x 18" (or larger) piece of poster board with a sharpie marker
- Either write or glue pictures of the criterion for sorting in each square
- Laminate: because of the large size, it will require the use of a professional type laminator. Laminating will maintain the integrity of the board. With any use at all, an unlaminated board will become worn out, and will need to be replaced frequently

Variation: Teacher just draws in lines and laminates; children can draw or write in properties for sorting using a dry erase marker

VIII. Procedures
1. Set out the box of items to be sorted next to the "sorting board"
2. Children sort items by whatever criterion is on the "sorting board"
3. Children can count and compare numbers of items within different criterion groups
4.   Children can make notes or drawings about the sorting activity in their journals or in their math notebooks

Variation: *Jigsaw Puzzles*
Materials
1. A jigsaw puzzle with a number of pieces that is challenging but not impossible for the developmental maturity of the children in the class
2.   A table placed in an area that can be undisturbed while the puzzle is being completed
3. One or two low trays into which the puzzle pieces can be placed
4. Good lighting

Procedure
1.   Set out jigsaw puzzle
2. Children turn all puzzle pieces face up onto the low trays
3. Children find the "border" pieces (pieces with a flat side which defines the outside edge of the puzzle)
4. Children can, if they choose to do so, sort the puzzle pieces by color and design
5. Children can work on puzzle as time allows during the day
6. The picture on the box top can help children match pieces to the design of the puzzle
7. After puzzle is completed, leave puzzle out for all to admire for a day or two
8. Children assembling puzzle have first opportunity to disassemble puzzle and return to the box

IX. Accommodations (changes to accommodate learning diversity)
Name of Accommodated Area:
1. _____
2. _____
3. _____
4. _____
5. _____

X. **Applicable Framework Standards: Kindergarten**

Standard _____

_____

_____

_____

Standard _____

_____

_____

_____

Standard _____

_____

_____

_____

Standard _____

_____

_____

_____

Standard _____

_____

_____

_____

XI. **Evaluation and Comments** (i.e.: How well did the plan work? Great responses? What aspects are especially effective? Not effective? What improvements are needed? Ideas for follow up activities and other notes)

_____

_____

_____

_____

Treasure Hunts

Treasure hunting is an active and playful way to help children develop the skill of recognizing, differentiating, and correctly identifying any one of many discrete areas of information. This activity also reinforces the "classroom as a cooperative community" feeling. If children can be coached to support the success of one another instead of competing, they will develop a profound sense of generating success as a group. The teacher as the instructor of the class sets the tone for this. Working cooperatively promotes a successful society.

Place numbers and number words around the classroom, or on the yard, for children to find. If your class is studying an area such as leaves or bugs, the children can either collect or draw what they see in their science journal. To reinforce one-to-one correspondence, the children can count trees in the play yard, piles of leaves, or the number of pencil boxes in the classroom.

This is a great activity for high energy children and for children that learn kinesthetically. Treasure hunting can be used inside on "bad" weather days (too rainy, snowy, hot, or smoggy). The excitement level is likely to increase, due to the children moving about the classroom during this activity. It may be helpful to inquire if the teacher in the next classroom is presenting a test or some other activity that requires quiet and a minimum of distraction!

Variation: Use letters of the alphabet. Make the sets in both upper and lower case. When children have assimilated the alphabet and alphabetical order, they can "draw list" or list the names of things they see that begin with the letters of the alphabet.

Materials

❖ One or more sets of numbers or number words (or alphabet letters) made from card stock; the use of brighter colors and larger sizes are appropriate for younger or children with special needs

❖ Large, gallon-size zip-type freezer bags (one for each group of children)

❖ A small treat for everyone in the class to be shared at the end of the activity (pretzels, goldfish crackers, etc.)

Method

❖ Make the numbers or number words (or alphabet letters) from brightly colored card stock. Make more than a single set, perhaps three or four sets

❖ Place numbers (or letters) around the playground or classroom while children are otherwise occupied.

❖ Break children up into cooperative groups of two or three.

❖ Give each group a large zipper bag into which they will put the numbers (letters) they find.

❖ Ask children to read the numbers, number words or letters they have found (if there are children in the class for whom this is an emerging skill, do this as a small group activity rather than a whole class activity)

❖ Meet all efforts with welcome and enthusiasm; make children feel safe enough to make attempts

❖ When the children's interest seems to wane or all the numbers (words, letters) appear to be found, tally up the scores by counting the number of items found
❖ Make sure everyone wins; offer a treat of pretzels or another healthy snack

Suggested Reading:

Anno, M. (1986) *Anno's Counting Book.* ISBN: 0064431231.

Emberley, R. (2000). *My Numbers/ Mis Numeros.* ISBN: 0316233501.

Cheng, A. & Zhang, A. (2003). *Grandfather Counts.* (Reading Rainbow Book; An inter-generational story: Grandfather Gong Gong teaches granddaughter how to count in Chinese). ISBN: 1584301589.

Hoban, T. (1987). *Over, under and through and other spatial concepts.* ISBN: 0689711115.

Jenness, A. (1993). *Come Home With Me: A Multicultural Treasure Hunt.* (A look at four different families and their homes and customs - Africa, Ireland, Cambodia, and Puerto Rico). ISBN: 156584064X.

McGrath, B.B. (1999). Pepperidge Farm Goldfish Counting Book. ISBN: 1893017516.

McMillan, B. (1994). *Mouse views: What the Class Pet Saw.* ISBN: 082341132X. (Reading Rainbow; The school from the mouse's point of view, with a map of his jaunt through the school).

Onyefulu, I. (1999). *Emeka's gift: An African Counting Book.* ISBN: 0140565000.

Wallwork, A. (1993). *No dodos. A Counting Book of Endangered Animals.* ISBN: 0590467697.

Target Areas of Learning

Physical Development

❖ **Gross motor**: using and coordinating the large muscles of the body: running, walking, reaching, bending
❖ **Physical Principals:** developing stability; equilibrium and balance
❖ **Fine motor:** using the small muscles of the hand and fingers: grasping and picking up items to be discovered, placing items in the bags
❖ **Eye-hand coordination**: seeing and accurately retrieving letters, numbers, or words
❖ **Sensory discrimination**
   • **Visual discrimination** (sight): identify sought after item visually
   • **Tactile Discrimination** (touch): identifying and differentiating textures and sensations of sought after items with touch

Cognitive Development

❖ **Language Arts**
   • **Verbal skills**
      o **Vocabulary development**: recognizing, using, and comprehending new words; finding and naming the letters, words, numbers, number words
      o **Language development**: discussions with team in the process of having the treasure hunt; understanding and following simple instructions
   • **Emergent literacy**
      o **Word recognition:** recognizing new words and identifying words correctly

- o **Matching spoken words to written words**: correctly associating the auditory expression with the written symbol grouping
- o **Sequencing (temporal ordering)**: retelling treasure hunt event in the order it occurred

❖ **Math Skills**
- • **Mathematical literacy**
  - o **1 to 1 correspondence**: counting items in an organized way that shows understanding of the object's placement as a single entity in a group
  - o **Number recognition**: recognizing that a specific symbol is associated with a specific quantity, and that symbol is constant in association with that symbol
  - o **Recognizing number words**: associating the number symbol with the written word for the number with the count of items re-presented by both the written word and the symbol
- • **Mathematical applications**
  - o **Spatial relationships**: relating the aspects of sought after objects to one another, thinking about objects in three dimensions

❖ **Social Studies**
- • **Diversity of languages**: looking for words or number symbols from other languages

Social Development

❖ **Community membership**: developing a sense of belonging in a community through working cooperatively with others

❖ **Working cooperatively with others in a group**: working well as a team, working well with others, being a good sport no matter whose team "won"

❖ **Collaboration**: creating a team strategy for the activity

❖ **Following instructions**: playing game as directed

❖ **Taking responsibility**: making sure everyone gets to take part in activity

❖ **Taking care of classroom/school environment**: helping in any clean up

Emotional Development

❖ **Self-esteem**: feeling a sense of accomplishment by finding and identifying letters and numbers

❖ **Accomplishment**: developing a sense of self worth from participating in and completing treasure hunt

❖ **Generosity**: experiencing enjoyment in the success of others

Creative Expression

❖ **Team building**: developing strategies to find sought after items cooperatively

❖ **Problem solving**: gathering data, collaborating as a group effort

Possible Accommodations for *Treasure Hunt Activity*

ADHD
❖ Use positive reinforcement (praise); "Catch" children being good; praise for staying on task, working well with others and behaving appropriately
❖ Allow the activity to go on a little longer to give the child an opportunity to expend some energy
❖ Allow the activity to go on a little longer if child becomes engaged in it
❖ Ask the child to repeat rules of the game; make sure rules are understood

Developmental Delays
❖ Go over task step-by-step using short simple phases maintaining eye contact to be sure child understands the task
❖ Demonstrate activity while explaining it using the numbers words, letters to be found before activity begins to reinforce task visually
❖ Have child work with a gentle and more competent peer
❖ Place number and number words in places easily in child's view
❖ Make pieces big and thick enough for child to grasp them easily
❖ Allow child to "practice" finding objects independently before presenting activity to class

Autism Spectrum Disorders
❖ Go over task step-by-step using short simple phases maintaining eye contact to be sure child understands the task
❖ Demonstrate activity while explaining it using numbers, number words, letters to be found before activity begins to reinforce task visually
❖ Present the activity more than once, allowing the child to become accustomed to the activity
❖ Show the child the numbers, number words or letters before the activity begins
❖ Use positive reinforcement when child participates
❖ Pair child with a more competent and patient peer (if possible, use the same peer for the child's buddy as autistic children resist change)

Visual Impairments
❖ Make the items to be found very large and brightly colored
❖ Place items in places easily within the range of the child's view
❖ Partner child with teammates who are more skilled: coach teammates to make sure that visually impaired child has opportunities to find items
❖ Offer more time to complete task, if necessary
❖ Check on child frequently, give positive reinforcement for incremental achievements

Orthopedic Impairments
❖ Make sure child is positioned comfortably
❖ Use larger pieces for easier grasping
❖ Place pieces in areas accessible to child
❖ Adapt bag for pieces so that child can put them into the bag easily
❖ If child lacks strength, mobility, or dexterity to manipulate pieces, assist child in the hand-over-hand method

Gifted and Talented Education (GATE)
❖ Use multiple digit numbers or more complex words
❖ Reduce amount of allotted search time
❖ Increase number of items to be located

English Language Learners (ELL)
❖ Go over task step-by-step using short simple phases maintaining eye contact to be sure child understands the task
❖ Demonstrate activity while explaining it using actual numbers, number words, or letters before activity begins to reinforce task visually
❖ Practice words, and number names in a small group setting/individually prior activity; review vocabulary in same setting afterward
❖ Use positive reinforcement for all attempts to use new vocabulary

Content Standards For Kindergarten Met By This Activity

English Language Arts
> Reading (1.3, 1.5, 1.6, 1.14, 1.15)
> Listening and Speaking (1.0, 1.1)

Mathematics
> Numbers and Counting (1.0, 1.1, 1.2, 1.3)

Science
> Investigation and Experimentation (4a, 4.c)

History and Social Science
> Following Rules (K.1, K.1.1)
> Compare and describe people and places (K.4, K.4.1, K.4.5)

Dance
> Artistic Perception (1.0, 1.1, 1.2)

Learning Plan

   I. **Name of Activity: Treasure Hunts**

  II. **Date of Presentation:**

 III. **Age or Grade Level: Pre-K through Primary**

 IV. **Ratio of teachers to children needed for this activity:** up to 1:10

  V. **Target Areas of Learning / Goals and Objectives** (target areas of learning directly relate to "VI. Evaluation Rubric")

      1. Physical: _____

      2. Cognitive: _____

      3. Social: _____

      4. Emotional: _____

      5. Creative: _____

 VI. **Evaluation Rubric:** (if more than two learning areas are being evaluated, a spreadsheet form may be preferred)

Targeted Area of Learning   **Targeted Area of Learning**

_____   _____

_____   _____

    4. Always _____   **4.** Always _____

    3. Usually _____   **3.** Usually _____

    2. Sometimes _____   **2.** Sometimes _____

    1. Rarely _____   **1.** Rarely _____

 VII. **Materials and Preparation Needed**

     1. One or more sets of numbers or number words made from card stock; the use of brighter colors and larger sizes are appropriate for younger or children with special needs

     2. Large, gallon-size zip-type freezer bags (one for each group of children)

     3. A small treat for everyone in the class to be shared at the end of the activity (pretzels, goldfish crackers, etc.)

     Variation: Use letters of the alphabet. Make the sets in both upper and lower case. When children have assimilated the alphabet and alphabetical order, they can "draw list" or list the names of things they see that begin with the letters of the alphabet.

VIII. **Procedures**

     1. Make the numbers or number words (or alphabet letters) from brightly colored card stock. Make more than a single set, perhaps three or four sets

2. Place numbers (or letters) around the playground or classroom while children are otherwise occupied.
3. Break children up into cooperative groups of two or three.
4. Give each group a large zipper bag into which they will put the numbers (letters) they find.
5. Ask children to read the numbers, number words or letters they have found (if there are children in the class for whom this is an emerging skill, do this as a small group activity rather than a whole class activity)
6. Meet all efforts with welcome and enthusiasm; make children feel safe enough to make attempts
7. When the children's interest seems to wane or all the numbers (words, letters) appear to be found, tally up the scores by counting the number of items found
8. Make sure everyone wins; offer a treat of pretzels or another healthy snack

IX. to accommodate learning diversity)
Name of Accommodated Area:
1. _____
2. _____
3. _____
4. _____
5. _____

X. **Applicable Framework Standards: Kindergarten**
Standard _____
_____
_____
_____
_____

Standard _____
_____
_____
_____
_____

Standard _____
_____
_____
_____
_____

Standard _____
_____
_____
_____
_____

Standard _____

_____

_____

_____

_____

XI. Evaluation and Comments (i.e.: How well did the plan work? Great responses? What aspects are especially effective? Not effective? What improvements are needed? Ideas for follow up activities and other notes)

_____

_____

_____

_____

Chapter Eleven

Science Activities and Learning Plans

I am among those who think that science has great beauty. A scientist in his laboratory is not only a technician: he is also a child placed before natural phenomena, which impress him like a fairy tale.

– Marie Curie (1867 - 1934)
First woman professor of Physics at Sorbonne University
Winner of two Nobel prizes for Chemistry and Physics for her ground-breaking work in the field of radioactivity

Animals in the Classroom

Allowing children to interact with animals offers a broad span of learning. As with all interactive classroom ventures, the quality of learning children acquire from caring for and observing animals is far better than pencil-and-paper worksheet tasks.

It is important for the teacher to reflect about having animals in the classroom. If the teacher does not enjoy having animals in the environment, then it is important for the teacher not to bring animals into the classroom. Much of the learning associated with animals in the classroom comes from the concern, interest, and nurturing behavior that the teacher models. The teacher needs to find a type of classroom pet that will fit into the teacher's own life. The animal will need to be cared for on weekends, holidays, and during summer and winter breaks. When school is not in session, the pet belongs to the teacher. Choose only an animal that will fit not only into the classroom life, but into the teacher's personal life as well.

Having animals in the classroom increases the level of liability for the school. If a child is injured or becomes sick because of the animal in the class, there is a chance that the child's parents might sue the school for damages. It is sad to bear this in mind, but our litigious society makes it important to bring this up to teachers who are considering bringing animals into the classroom.

Part of animal care involves teaching hygiene to children. After a child touches any animal, the child needs to wash his or her hands. Reptiles in particular carry salmonella, a potentially deadly bacteria, so in that case specifically and in all cases generally, hand washing is a very necessary aspect of having animals in the classroom.

If the teacher allows children to handle classroom pets, the children must be supervised when handling animals.

Animals are living creatures. The children need to learn to touch gently and respectfully. For some children being gentle may not come naturally. Ultimately the teacher is responsible for the well being of both the animal and the children in the classroom. Be advised that animals have a variety of temperaments. An animal may behave defensively if it perceives, for whatever reason, that it is being mishandled by a child. This could happen even if the mishandling is unintentional. So, in the best interests of both the child and the animal, an adult must supervise all interactions.

To extend the learning in the kindergarten classroom, label the tank or living environment with the animal's name, its species, the type of living environment, the container of food, and so forth. In this way, the children will begin to associate the spoken words for these items with the physical object, and the words in print.

Become knowledgeable about the selected animal. Having an animal can be a learning experience for everyone. It is up to the teacher to find and set up the learning experience for all. Remember, the animal is a living creature that now is depending upon the adults in the environment for its survival. In the final analysis, the life of the animal is the responsibility of the teacher who has accepted into the classroom, regardless of what the circumstances were that brought it there.

The information presented here is not meant to be sufficient for a teacher to bring an animal and keep it in the classroom. No matter which animal the teacher decides to include into the classroom community, it is crucial that the teacher be knowledgeable about the care and maintenance of the animal in the classroom. This will give the teacher the best skills to care for this living creature and to best teach about the care of the animal to the children. **DO YOUR HOMEWORK!** Teachers can find appropriate grade level books about the classroom pet and make them available in the classroom library for the children to use to learn more about this particular animal.

If a school site has the inclination, space, and resources, the facility may want to consider the possibility of setting up a small "farm" on campus. There is a wealth of opportunities for learning which are associated with interacting with farm animals, particularly in an urban setting. Do consider that this is a long-term commitment for the school, a commitment not to be taken lightly. If a school chooses to have a farm, there would need to be a commitment for financial resources not only for food, shelter, and appropriate space for the animals, but also supervisory personnel who would need to attend the animals even on non-school days. There are schools with farms on site in the Los Angeles area. They effectively teach children about animals, and the responsibilities as well as the pleasures associated with working with those animals. One such public school has a pig, several goats, a couple of sheep, some caged rabbits, pigeons, free-range chickens, some ducks and geese. The children collect the eggs, incubate eggs, feed and clean up after the animals, compost the animal waste, work in the garden, and generally maintain the site, with adult supervision. Consider the opportunity for these suburban children. Most urban and suburban children have very little opportunity to interact with farm type animals. Just think about all the practical knowledge these children can acquire from having regular access to "the farm". Be aware that having this incredible learning opportunity for the children on the site also creates an expenditure for competent, appropriately skilled supervisory personnel.

Naming the Class Pet

Giving a new member of the classroom community a name can be a fun and exciting way to integrate a number of different disciplines into the curriculum. This should be considered a collaborative brainstorming activity wherein there are no wrong answers. This is a very important concept. Consider all possibilities first without regard to preconceived ideas of "correctness". This is an opportunity for the children to build self-esteem, initiative, and cognitive courage. Academic excellence occurs best in an environment that encourages safe risk taking. If there are shy children, or even children who are merely uncomfortable speaking out their ideas publicly, they can write or dictate their suggestions down to be read in the classroom forum. Children can be allowed time on the computer and in the library to look up names and meanings of possible names for the classroom pet. Allow the children to entertain the ridiculous. A friend's young daughter once suggested the name "Silverware" for their new gray kitten. It was named something else, but "Silverware" always seemed such a brilliant idea.

Naming the animal involves the whole classroom working together. This will build upon the classroom's sense of community and identity. Within this, there is also the opportunity to teach about socialization, including appropriate classroom interactions, community decision-making, classroom democracy, and dealing appropriately with the outcome (being a good winner as well as a good loser).

Academically speaking, children can research their choice of names and practice defending their choices in the classroom forum. What does the name mean? Why was that particular moniker chosen? What makes that name better for this pet than the others?

Materials
- ❖ Writing and drawing materials
- ❖ Chalk board, white board, large sized lined chart paper to write children's suggestions, possibly large graph paper to create comparative bar charts
- ❖ Access to class or school library, dictionaries, encyclopedias, and/or a computer with an encyclopedia or appropriate access to the internet
- ❖ File cards or pieces of card stock onto which children can write, dictate, or draw their suggestion, placed in a container, and read in classroom forum

Method
- ❖ Discuss bringing pet into classroom prior to actually bringing it to class (in this way the teacher can find out about children's responses, fears, excitement, phobias, allergies, experiences with animals
- ❖ Teach the children about the appropriate care for this animal; explain that all living things must be treated gently, place particular emphasis upon the unique needs of this particular species of animal, how being unique make the animal special and interesting
- ❖ If appropriate, allow children to help in setting up the animal's living environment
- ❖ Bring animal into the classroom, introduce it to the children
- ❖ Ask children to begin to think of names for the new class member, perhaps even as a "homework assignment"
- ❖ Explain to the children that a name should be found for the animal, so not all suggestions will be chosen

- ❖ At some point allow children to form groups so they can brainstorm possible names for this creature; be sure to encourage children to consider all suggestions put forward, even if they seem silly
- ❖ Allow groups to go to the class library, go on the computer, research in encyclopedias and dictionaries for their suggestions
- ❖ Have the children write, draw or dictate their suggestions onto their file card or piece of card stock (more than one suggestion per group can be acceptable)
- ❖ Gather the children into a whole class group
- ❖ Have a spokesperson from each group read aloud their suggestion for the animal's name and why they think it would be a good name for the animal or (if there are very shy children in the group) ask the children to place their suggestions into a basket or container
- ❖ Someone can read aloud the different suggestions for the name presented by the groups
- ❖ Teacher writes the suggestions on the lined chart paper using letter or number designation by each name (a-b-c.../1-2-3...)
- ❖ Offer class an opportunity to debate the various suggestions in a positive manner, reminding them that all names are "good names" and that everyone in the classroom must be respectful of everyone else in the class as well as their contributions to the conversation
- ❖ Have children return to their seats, pass out pieces of paper for children to "cast their vote", and allow the children to vote for the name they like best by letter or number designation; remind children that they must vote for one name only
- ❖ Assure children that all the suggestions were "good names" and whatever the outcome is the outcome
- ❖ Count the votes as a class counting activity, if using graph chart paper, a student score keeper can place a mark in boxes adjacent to the suggested names, thus creating a graphing activity (bar chart)

Variation:

Children can place their mark next to the name on the chart paper and vote in that way, and similarly create a bar chart

Suggested Reading:

Kellogg, S. (1992). *Can I Keep Him?* ISBN: 014054867X. (A little boy is searching for a pet; written and illustrated by Steven Kellogg).

McMillan, B. (1994). *Mouse Views: What the Class Pet Saw.* New York: Holiday House. ISBN: 082341132X. (Reading Rainbow. The school from the mouse's point of view, with a map of his jaunt through the school).

Nadler, B. (1995). *The Magic School Bus Inside Ralphie: A book about germs.* ISBN: 0590400258. (The importance of hand washing; hands should always be washed before and after handling any animals).

Numeroff, L. (2002). *If You Take a Mouse to School.* ISBN:0060283289 (Ages 5-7)

Noble, T.H. (Steven Kellogg illustrator) (1992). *The day Jimmy's Boa Ate the Wash.* ISBN: 0140546235. (Reading Rainbow book; great book to read for fun about problems with pets on a class trip to a farm!)

Varley, S. (1984). *Badger's Parting Gifts*. New York: Lothrop, Lee & Shepard Books. ISBN: 0-688-02699-0. (Winner Britain's Mother Goose award for illustration). Available from: www. turnthepage.com/ (Each friend gets a special gift, and Badger lives on in the memory of his friends)

Target Areas of Learning

Physical Development
❖ **Fine motor skills:** using the small muscles of the hand and fingers: drawing shapes; holding a pencil/crayon, writing
❖ **Eye-hand coordination:** coordinating visual acuity with using the small muscles of the hand and fingers: drawing; holding a pencil/crayon; writing; use of mouse (computers)
❖ **Sensory: visual discrimination** (sight): identifying properties of animal, recognizing various letters, words, and images visually

Cognitive Development
❖ **Language Arts**
  • **Verbal skills**
    o **Language development: conversation, sharing during circle time, class discussions, group problem solving, discussion, debate**
    o **Vocabulary development: finding words that describe pet**
  • **Emergent literacy:** doing research to find possible names, finding out what those names mean, discussing why those names were selected
    o **Symbol interpretation:** understanding that marks have meaning in the process of writing names down, creating charts, casting votes
    o **Letter recognition/word recognition/matching spoken words to printed words:** children associating the sound of the names proposed with the written words, copying words to cast their vote
    o **Journal "writing":** allowing children to write their argument for the name they prefer
❖ **Math Skills**
  • **Mathematical literacy**
    o **1 to 1 Correspondence:** counting votes in an organized way
    o **Associating number symbols with quantity:** understanding that a specific symbol is always associated with a specific quantity of votes in a count
  • **Mathematical applications**
    o **Algebra:** categorization/ grouping (sets): sorting activities, inventing criterion to separate reasons to choose various names into groups beginning with a single property and adding other qualities that might contribute to a particular selection
    o **Algebra:** group/classification: if a child invents his own criterion and has opportunities to explain the properties for which he is classifying, there is an opportunity for more advanced thinking. Have children choose ideas which have

properties that are similar but not identical including: common relatedness (items that are not the same and are associated with one another), opposites, congruent relationships

- o **Ordering:** what comes next in terms of graduated quantity (comparing votes)
- o **Charting:** using the outcome to create various preliminary statistical diagrams to reflect the outcome of the activity presented

❖ **Social Science**
- • **Developing an understanding of, and respect for, human society and cultures, human relationships, and human diversity;** respect for all life in general
- • **Basic, low stakes introduction to the democratic process**
  - o **Respecting the right of other's to have and promote their own ideas in society:** people in a democratic society do not have to agree
  - o **Practicing appropriate persuasion and argument**
  - o **Being a good "winner" or "loser" and maintaining the sense of community**
  - o **Creating the classroom as cooperative and collaborative as opposed to competitive**
  - o **Building the sense of greater community partnership in the classroom:** "Our class got a new pet. We voted and decided to name our pet "Silverware.""

Social Development

- ❖ **Taking turns:** listening, behaving appropriate while others present reasoning for their suggestions before and after child's own group presents
- ❖ **Patience:** learning patience as others present and argue their point of view
- ❖ **Working cooperatively with others in a group**: taking a leadership role or not, delegating and completing responsibilities within the group, contributing and accepting other's contributions within the group
- ❖ **Following directions:** participating in discussions and votes as instructed
- ❖ **Good sportsmanship:** graciously accepting the outcome of the naming process whether one's suggestion was chosen or not
- ❖ **Respecting others as individuals (behaving appropriately with others)**: making and maintaining relationships / ongoing friendships, behaving appropriately in social situations, learning the general rules of courtesy (manners) for the classroom within the democratic process, developing the ability to participate in conversation, learning discussion manners
- ❖ **Self-respect:** learning to value themselves, recognizing their strengths and weaknesses, loving themselves for who they are as they are, knowing they have a right to their own point of view even if it is not the popular idea within the group
- ❖ **Social boundaries:** behaving appropriately in a discussion/debate situation
- ❖ **Negotiation:** learning to represent one's ideas in such a way that others in the group will consider those ideas favorably
- ❖ **Leadership**: initiating and managing discussions, ideas, and interactions related to naming a pet that involves others
- ❖ **Community building:** creating a sense of belonging in a group even if not everyone agrees with the outcome of the naming process

Emotional Development

❖ **Self-esteem:** feeling good about oneself, and one's participation in the classroom debate regarding name selection, no matter what the outcome

❖ **Self-confidence:** developing a willingness to risk sharing ideas with the class

❖ **Generosity:** graciously listening and being kind to those whose suggestions might seem amusing, peculiar, inappropriate

❖ **Learning to identify and express emotions appropriately**

- **Learning to name human feelings:** sad, happy, angry, hurt, loving, excited, afraid, proud, sorry
- **"Use your words":** expressing feelings of upset and anger appropriately

Creative Expression

❖ Problem solving: gathering data, collaborating, delegating responsibility within the small and large group, having small and large group discussion relative to the possible choices available

❖ Creative thinking: brainstorming: considering all possible names and solutions to a choosing a good name

❖ Writing: using words creatively to come up with a name acceptable to all

❖ Persuasion: learning to represent one's ideas in such a way that appeals to others and causes them to consider one's suggestions

Possible Accommodations for *Naming Class Pet Activity*

ADHD

❖ Use positive reinforcement (praise) when child negotiates courteously, treats other's ideas with respect, does not blurt out during group discussion, and generally show self control

❖ Ask the child to repeat the guidelines for the activity, to make sure that the rules are understood such as "raise your hand to speak", "allow others to speak"

❖ Use direct teaching: go over activity step-by-step to be sure child understands the task

❖ Place group in which child is participating away from open doors, windows, busy bulletin boards which may distract child from task at hand

Developmental Delays

❖ Use direct teaching: use simplified language when giving directions and praise making sure eye contact is made

❖ Model the project from start to finish for the whole group using photographs, videotape, and realia, and again for the child

❖ Repeat modeled instructions as needed, making sure eye contact is made when giving child directions

❖ Respond to suggestions from child with developmental delays first as child may have come up with only one or two ideas

❖ Remind class to treat all possible name suggestions respectfully

❖ Allow child to dictate his ideas for name and/or reason for his choice to an adult or peer in the class, if necessary
❖ Offer larger or adapted writing and drawing instruments

Autism Spectrum Disorders

❖ Use direct teaching: use simplified language when giving directions and praise making sure eye contact is made
❖ Go over task step-by-step to be sure child understands the task
❖ Model the project from start to finish for the whole group using photographs, videotape, and realia, perhaps again for the child
❖ Re-teach as necessary, modeling to the class, with particular emphasis on connecting with the child with autism
❖ If the child presents an idea, be sure to respond immediately to encourage child's participation
❖ Remind class to treat all possible name suggestions respectfully
❖ Use positive reinforcement when child participates, notice child's incremental achievements throughout the task
❖ Inform class and child about activity in advance

Visual Impairments

❖ Adjust lighting to reduce glare
❖ Change the point size on the font on the computer such that the child can read the text independently
❖ Change the background on the computer to provide the appropriate contrast for easier reading
❖ Use large print encyclopedias and dictionaries
❖ Offer larger sized materials - paper, adapted writing or drawing implements (perhaps using a very wide tipped black marker)
❖ Offer brighter colors, materials with more contrast
❖ Offer more time if it is needed

Orthopedic Impairments

❖ Make sure the child is positioned comfortably in seat
❖ Adjust furniture or use a tray to make writing easier
❖ Use a clip board and an alligator clip at the bottom to steady any writing paper
❖ Offer adapted writing and drawing tools
❖ If child needs assistance writing use hand-over-hand method

Gifted and Talented Education (GATE)

❖ Ask child to do research on the type of animal on line, in the library or in the encyclopedia
❖ Ask child to do research on choosing names on line, in the library or in the encyclopedia
❖ Ask child to do background research about proposed names on line, in the library or in the encyclopedia
❖ Ask child to find out rules of debate and explain them to the class

English Language Learners (ELL)
- ❖ Use direct teaching: use simplified language when giving directions and praise making sure eye contact is made
- ❖ Go over task step-by-step to be sure child understands the task
- ❖ Model the project from start to finish for the whole group using photographs, videotape, and realia, perhaps again for the child

Content Standards For Kindergarten Met By This Activity

English Language Arts

Reading (1.0, 1.3, 1.5, 1.17, 1.18)

Reading Comprehension (2.0, 2.3)

Literary Analysis (3.0, 3.1, 3.2)

Writing (1.0, 1.1, 1.3, 1.4)

Written and Oral language (1.0, 1.1, 1.2)

Listening and Speaking (1.0, 1.2, 2.0, 2.1, 2.3)

Mathematics

Statistics (1.0, 1.1)

Mathematical reasoning (1.0, 1.1, 2.0, 2.1)

Science

Life sciences (2.a, 2.b, 2.c)

Investigation and Experimentation (4.e)

History and Social Science

Following rules (K.1, K.1.1)

Using a calendar to sequence events (K.5)

Visual Arts

Artistic Perception (1.0, 1.2)

Creative Expression (2.0, 2.4, 2.5)

Understanding Historical / Cultural Contributions of Visual Arts (3.0, 3.1)

Valuing Aesthetics (4.0, 4.3)

Theatre

Artistic Perception (1.0, 1.2)

Applications (5.0, 5.1)

Learning Plan

I. **Name of Activity:** Naming the Classroom Pet

II. **Date of Presentation:**

III. **Age or Grade Level:** Pre-K, Kindergarten

IV. **Ratio of teachers to children needed for this activity:** 1:10

V. **Target Areas of Learning / Goals and Objectives** (target areas of learning directly relate to "VI. Evaluation Rubric")

    1. Physical: _____

    2. Cognitive: _____

    3. Social: _____

    4. Emotional: _____

    5. Creative: _____

VI. **Evaluation Rubric:** (if more than two learning areas are being evaluated, a spreadsheet form may be preferred)

Targeted Area of Learning   **Targeted Area of Learning**

_____   _____

_____   _____

    4. Always _____   **4.** Always _____

    3. Usually _____   **3.** Usually _____

    2. Sometimes _____   **2.** Sometimes _____

    1. Rarely _____   **1.** Rarely _____

VII. **Materials and Preparation Needed**

1. Writing and drawing materials
2. Chalk board, white board, large sized lined chart paper to write children's suggestions, possibly large graph paper to create comparative bar charts
3. Access to class or school library, dictionaries, encyclopedias, and/or a computer with an encyclopedia or appropriate access to the internet
4. File cards or pieces of card stock onto which children can write, dictate, or draw their suggestion, placed in a container, and read in classroom forum

VIII. **Procedures**

1. Discuss bringing pet into classroom prior to actually bringing it to class; in this way the teacher can find out about children's responses, fears, excitement, phobias, allergies, experiences with animals
2. Teach the children about the appropriate care for this animal; explain that all living things must be treated gently, place particular emphasis upon the unique needs of

this particular species of animal, how being unique make the animal special and interesting

3. If appropriate, allow children to help in setting up the animal's living environment
4. Bring animal into the classroom, introduce it to the children
5. Ask children to begin to think of names for the new class member, perhaps even as a "homework assignment"
6. Explain to the children that a name should be found for the animal, so not all suggestions will be chosen
7. At some point allow children to form groups so they can brainstorm possible names for this creature; be sure to encourage children to consider all suggestions put forward, even if they seem silly
8. Allow groups to go to the class library, go on the computer, research in encyclopedias and dictionaries for their suggestions
9. Have the children write, draw or dictate their suggestions onto their file card or piece of card stock (more than one suggestion per group can be acceptable)
10. Gather the children into a whole class group
11. Have a spokesperson from each group read aloud their suggestion for the animal's name and why they think it would be a good name for the animal or (if there are very shy children in the group) ask the children to place their suggestions into a basket or container
12. Someone can read aloud the different suggestions for the name presented by the groups
13. Teacher writes the suggestions on the lined chart paper using letter or number designation by each name (a-b-c.../1-2-3...)
14. Offer class an opportunity to debate the various suggestions in a positive manner, reminding them that all names are "good names" and that everyone in the classroom must be respectful of everyone else in the class as well as their contributions to the conversation
15. Have children return to their seats, pass out pieces of paper for children to "cast their vote", and allow the children to vote for the name they like best by letter or number designation; remind children that they must vote for one name only
16. Assure children that all the suggestions were "good names" and whatever the outcome is the outcome
17. Count the votes as a class counting activity, if using graph chart paper, a student score keeper can place a mark in boxes adjacent to the suggested names, thus creating a graphing activity (bar chart)
    Variation: Children can place their mark next to the name on the chart paper and vote in that way, and similarly create a bar char

IX. Accommodations (changes to accommodate learning diversity)
   Name of Accommodated Area:
   1. _____
   2. _____
   3. _____
   4. _____
   5. _____

X. Applicable Framework Standards: Kindergarten
   Standard _____
   _____
   _____
   _____
   _____

   Standard _____
   _____
   _____
   _____
   _____

   Standard _____
   _____
   _____
   _____
   _____

   Standard _____
   _____
   _____
   _____
   _____

   Standard _____
   _____
   _____
   _____
   _____

XI. Evaluation and Comments (i.e.: How well did the plan work? Great responses? What aspects are especially effective? Not effective? What improvements are needed? Ideas for follow up activities and other notes)

   _____
   _____
   _____
   _____

Fish In The Classroom

If the teacher decides to have a fish in the classroom, it is the teacher's responsibility to research the needs of that particular type of fish before bringing it into the classroom. This book contains but the thinnest of suggestions regarding the care of any variety of animal.

Fish can be the easiest animal for the classroom. Varieties of fresh water fish in a thirty-gallon tank with a good filter bring animal life into the classroom with a minimum of care, maintenance, and effort for the teacher or the students. "Feeder fish" (small gold fish used to feed fish eating larger fish and reptiles) are very inexpensive and remarkably live for years and years. One excellent quality about these fish is that if the fish does happen to die, although sad, it is not the loss of a significant investment. Being a kindergarten fish can be a dangerous existence. If fish demise is too traumatic for the children for one reason or another, a substitute can be slipped in with none the wiser. However, part of learning about life is learning about death. So long as the room temperature remains relatively constant, neither below freezing or over 100 degrees Fahrenheit for extended time periods, fish can go a three or four day weekend without being fed.

Filters generally need to be changed about once a month or as needed, and water needs to be added to the tank about once a week, depending on the air temperature and humidity. Some filters can be rinsed out once a week, and changed monthly, which will keep the water looking cleaner. Filtered water is good, but tap water left in a wide-mouthed open container for several days (to allow the chlorine and other chemicals to evaporate) works just fine as well. Each time the jar of "stale" water is added to the tank, it needs to be refilled again. This is an on-going process, and could be a rotating classroom job, along with feeding fish, or brushing the inside of the tank. Dechlorinating chemicals can also be purchased, but it is up to the teacher to find out which chemicals are used in the purification process of the local tap water to find out if using them is necessary or not. If the local water district uses chloramines, it may be necessary to use chemicals to neutralize the water.

An inexpensive dish scrubber with plastic bristles, or long-handled brush, can be picked up at the local 99-cent store, and be used to clean the interior of the aquarium. It would need to be dedicated to the task of cleaning the tank and never be used for any other purpose (as any type of soap or cleaner residue could easily be to toxic to the fish). Would anyone want to eat from plates that were cleaned with the same scrubber that is used to clean the fish tank? The scrubber will help to keep the tank clean, and prevent the growth of algae. It is more aesthetically pleasing as well as being healthier for the fish to have a clean aquarium tank and water.

Put fish food out of sight and reach. Young children often perceive time as longer than it actually is, and may have the overwhelming urge to feed the fishy more than the recommended once a day. Multiply this situation by twenty! If there is a bit of plant life in the tank to nibble, it is far better to let the fish go without for a week or so than to overfeed them. So for spring break, and Thanksgiving weekend, the fish can go without food with a strong probability that they will be okay. Overfeeding will kill fish. On the other hand, if winter break is longer than two weeks, it may be a good idea to stop by the school once or twice to sprinkle in some fish food. During summer break the fish should go home with the teacher or a willing parent.

Materials

❖ A fish tank, select a size suitable for the number of fish the teacher intends to have and the space available in the classroom

❖ Fresh water fish, goldfish are the hardiest (and least expensive, ask about "feeder fish")

❖ Stale water (water left to air for several days, possibly treated with dechlorinating chemicals, if necessary)

❖ Optional: water plants, stones, decorative figurines for tank

❖ Labels for tank, species of fish, et cetera for vocabulary building and associating written word with the specific object

❖ Fish food appropriate for the type of fish you select

❖ Observation journals, crayons, markers, colored pencils

Method

❖ Place tank in area of classroom selected for the tank

❖ Set up tank and filter per instructions on the package.

  • If the teacher has acquired a tank and filter without instructions, the teacher should first rinse out the tank with clear water, to be rid of any dust or debris that has collected in it.

  • **DO NOT USE SOAP OR CLEANING AGENTS OF ANY SORT ON A FISH TANK.**

  • In an area outside that will not be damaged by water leaks, fill the tank with water to see if the water seal is still good. Find out what kind of filter is used and purchase a new one. Then proceed from the top.

❖ Place marbles, decorative stones, or any other tank decor the children/teacher selects for tank.

❖ Fill tank with water and let "air" for a couple of days. Use de-chlorinating chemicals if necessary.

❖ Add plants as desired.

❖ Add fish.

❖ Water will evaporate, so keeping a quart-sized plastic container airing water to add to the tank is a good idea.

❖ There are chemicals (keep out of reach of the children) such as "Stress-zyme" which will keep the water from becoming cloudy.

❖ The tank walls sometimes may develop a filminess, which can be cleaned with a plastic squeegee designed for aquariums.

❖ One of the "class jobs" can be "fish monitor". That child can feed the fish once a day and record observations regarding the fish in the class "fish journal".

❖ Or - the children can write about their personal observations in their personal fish journals.

❖ If the filter is changed regularly, many manufacturers recommend once a month, tank cleaning will be necessary only two or possibly three times each year. Remember, never use soap or other cleaning agents on a fish tank.

Suggested Reading:

Aliki. (1993). *My Visit to the Aquarium.* ISBN: 0060214589.

Cheng, A. (2003). *Goldfish and Chrysanthemums.* ISBN: 1584300574. (Granddaughter builds a pond in the backyard to remind her grandmother of her home faraway).

Lionni, L. (1974). *Fish is Fish.* ISBN: 0394827996.

Lionni, L. (1992). *Swimmy.* ISBN: 0394826205.

Macaulay, K. & Kalman, B. (2004). *Goldfish.* ISBN: 0778717917.

Pallotta, J. (1996). *The Freshwater Alphabet Book.* ISBN: 0881069000.

Pfeffer, W. (1996). *What's It Like To Be a Fish?* ISBN: 0064451518.

Pfister, M. & James, J.A. (1996). *The Rainbow Fish.* ISBN: 1558585362. Spanish language edition: (1996). El pez arco iris. New York: North South Books, ISBN: 1558585591.

Rose, D. L. (2000). *Into the A, B, Sea: An Ocean Alphabet Book.* ISBN: 0439096960.

Varley, S. (1984). *Badger's Parting Gifts.* ISBN: 0-688-02699-0. (Winner Britain's Mother Goose award for illustration). Available from: www.turnthepage.com. (Each friend gets a special gift and Badger lives on in the memory of his friends).

Wildsmith, B. (1968). *Fishes.* ISBN: 0531015289.

Target Areas of Learning

Physical Development

❖ **Fine motor skills:** using the small muscles of the hand and fingers: drawing shapes; holding a pencil/crayon; pouring liquid; writing: sprinkling fish food

❖ **Eye-hand coordination:** coordinating visual acuity with using the small muscles of the hand and fingers: drawing shapes; holding a pencil/crayon; pouring liquid; writing; using pincer grasp to sprinkle fish food

❖ **Sensory discrimination including:**
  • **Tactile discrimination (touch):** identifying and differentiating textures with touch: wet, dry, soft, slippery, cool
  • **Visual discrimination (sight):** identifying shapes; colors; sizes; recognizing various fish and parts of the aquarium visually
  • **Olfactory discrimination** (smell): identifying different smells: fishy

Cognitive Development

❖ **Language Arts**
  • **Verbal skills**
    o **Language development:** conversation, sharing during circle time, class discussions, group problem solving through discussion
    o **Vocabulary development:** names of species of fish, foods, plants, fish behavior
  • **Emergent literacy**
    o **Symbol interpretation, letter recognition, word recognition:** identifying the type of animal, the species of fish and other information from familiarity with labels on items associated with fish

- o **Journal "writing":** allowing children to write stories using scribble writing, drawings, and invented spelling about the fish and what the children observe
- o **Matching spoken words to printed words:** relating dictated words or written thoughts in journal writing activities
- o **Creative writing:** using the medium of writing to creatively express ideas related to the fish

❖ **Math Skills**
- **Conservation**
  - o **Conservation of quantity:** seeing that (absent of mortality or new fish) the number of fish in the tank remains constant no matter where the fish are in the tank
- **Mathematical literacy**
  - o **1 to 1 correspondence:** counting items in an organized way that shows understanding of the fish's placement as a single entity in a group of fish
  - o **Equivalency:** more / less; single / plural; longer/ shorter; comparisons: if there are more than one type of fish in the tank, numbers can be compared
  - o **Associating number symbols with quantity:** understanding that a specific symbol is always associated with a specific quantity of fish in a count
- **Mathematical applications**
  - o **Measurement:** comparing some aspect of size of one object to another
  - o **Categorization/ grouping (sets):** sorting activities, inventing criterion to separate items into groups beginning with a single property and, as the children become more skilled, adding multiple criterion
  - o **Spatial relationships:** relating aspects of physical placement of fish to one another
- **Common relatedness:** linking items that are not the same, but are associated with each other such as fish and tank
- **Temporal ordering**
  - o **Calendar:** numbers used in a practical and sequential order; passage of time
  - o **Recalling / anticipating events** as they occur in time: recall events of the day
  - o **Planning class projects** related to the fish in advance step-by-step

❖ **Science**
- **Scientific processes**
  - o **Observation:** carefully watching attentively and noting fish behavior
  - o **Documentation:** writing observations of fish behavior in journal
- **Cause and effect**
  - o **Relationships between actions and outcomes:** "What do you think will happen if we..." or "Why do you think the fish did that?"
- **Life Science**
  - o **Differentiating:** organisms from inorganic objects
  - o **Understanding:** all living things have common needs of for life
  - o **Responsibility:** understanding that living things need a certain level of care absent of which that living thing will either become sick or die

- o **Recognizing health:** noticing appearance and behavior of healthy fish
- o **Death:** if a fish lives it will sometime die
- o **All forms of observation of and caring for:**
  - Animal life: keeping animals in the classroom: fish
  - Nurturing: animals need gentle, consistent care to thrive
  - Hygiene / health practices: cleanliness after interacting with animals/fish food/fish tank
- ❖ **Social Science**
  - **Diversity of life:** social studies is developing an understanding of, and respect for, human society and cultures, human relationships, and human diversity; respect for all life in general and responsibly caring for our planet (this can be called science as well).
  - **Not all people, or other living beings, are the same.** Each fish, each bird, each life is unique. All living things deserve to be treated with respect. Differences make living things unique, not "bad".

Social Development

- ❖ **Sharing:** using class materials in a cooperative way for journaling and so forth
- ❖ **Taking turns:** allowing others to have a turn at caring for the fish
- ❖ **Patience:** waiting until the appropriate time to "feed the fish"
- ❖ **Working cooperatively with others in a group:** caring for the aquarium as a class project
- ❖ **Following directions:** taking care of fish and observing as directed
- ❖ **Self respect:** learning to value themselves, recognizing their strengths and weaknesses by being responsible for the fish
- ❖ **Taking responsibility:** doing assigned task related to the fish regardless of how child is "feeling" about the task at that moment
- ❖ **Taking care of classroom environment:** participating in cleanup; caring for classroom as a community environment, taking personal ownership of responsibilities associated with being part of a defined community and the environment in which it exists

Emotional Development

- ❖ **Self-esteem:** feeling good about oneself as the steward of another life form
- ❖ **Nurturing:** developing and expressing feelings of appropriate care and gentleness toward fish

Creative Expression

- ❖ **Expressing emotions and self through use of creative media and imagination:** painting, drawing, writing, story telling about the fish in journal writing activities

Possible Accommodations for *Fish in the Classroom Activity*

ADHD

❖ Give direct instructions for caring for fish

❖ Use positive reinforcement (praise) when child works well with others and behaves appropriately

❖ Allow child independent time to write/draw observations of the fish in note book

❖ Offer a carrel for independent journal writing/drawing

❖ Review/re-teach rules regarding having fish in the classroom (feeding once a day, no tapping on the glass, keeping tank free of debris/inappropriate objects)

Developmental Delays

❖ Use simplified language when giving directions and praise, being sure teacher is making eye contact while talking to child

❖ Model instructions for caring for the fish including photos and realia

❖ Use primary picture paper for pages of journal for easier journaling (see Appendix A-2)

❖ Offer chunkier or cushioned writing tools for easier grasping

❖ Review/re-teach rules regarding having fish in the classroom (feeding once a day, no tapping on the glass, keeping tank free of debris/inappropriate objects)

❖ Give authentic praise frequently for incremental achievements such as feeding fish on time only once a day

❖ Allow the child sufficient time to draw or write in journal as measured by child's ability to maintain sustained interest in task

❖ Use pocket chart with words likely to be used in journal near child for easier reference (copying)

Autism Spectrum Disorders

❖ Go over task step-by-step using simplified language when giving directions and praise, being sure teacher is making eye contact while talking to child

❖ Model instructions for caring for the fish including photos and realia

❖ Review/re-teach rules regarding having fish in the classroom (feeding once a day, no tapping on the glass, keeping tank free of debris/inappropriate objects)

❖ Be sure to have the activity on the class schedule, so the child can anticipate what is to happen during the day

❖ Use positive reinforcement when child participates; notice child's incremental achievements in terms of appropriate behavior with fish

❖ Adjust the duration of the activity for each session if it appears the child is more or less engaged with it, and have another activity as back up

❖ Use a pocket chart with words likely to be used in journal near child for easier reference (copying)

❖ Simplify words to be spelled, if necessary

❖ Show child that the activity is on the schedule for this day, include journal writing on the daily schedule

Visual Impairments

- ❖ Offer brighter colored, high-contrast (possibly larger) paper and art/writing materials
- ❖ Offer the child a magnifying glass on a stand (similar to the ones used for needlework, found in craft stores) for viewing fish and/or working on journal
- ❖ Adjust lighting to reduce glare
- ❖ Use specialized fish tank lights for best visibility (there are reflective, pink, green, blue tank lights available at pet supply shops
- ❖ Place poster board in a color that contrasts with the color of the fish for more visibility
- ❖ Have big fish
- ❖ Offer more time if necessary, for the child to complete work and feel successful

Orthopedic Impairments

- ❖ Make sure tank is positioned so that child can easily see the tank
- ❖ Adjust table or offer a tray for journaling
- ❖ Use a clip board with additional alligator clips to steady journal
- ❖ Consider having child's journal in a three ring binder so child can write on individual sheets of paper
- ❖ Offer adapted writing and drawing tools (chunkier pencils and crayons, padded soft grip style markers, or add large soft grips)
- ❖ If hands and fingers lack strength or dexterity assist child in writing using the hand-over-hand method of writing

Gifted and Talented Education (GATE)

- ❖ Ask child to find more information about the species of the class fish on the internet, in the library, or in the encyclopedia
- ❖ Ask the child to relate the behavior of the class fish to fish in stories such as "Swimmy", "Finding Nemo", "Rainbow Fish", and "Rainbow Fish to the Rescue" and indicate whether the stories seem real or not
- ❖ Ask child to write a fictional story or a poem about the fish
- ❖ Ask child to respond to silly questions like how would a fish make a painting? or what does fish music sound like?
- ❖ Expand vocabulary list

English Language Learners (ELL)

- ❖ Go over task step-by-step using simplified language when giving directions and praise, being sure teacher is making eye contact while talking to child
- ❖ Model instructions for caring for the fish including photos and realia
- ❖ Review/re-teach rules regarding having fish in the classroom (feeding once a day, no tapping on the glass, keeping tank free of debris/inappropriate objects)
- ❖ Practice vocabulary words as whole class activity and in small groups
- ❖ Use positive reinforcement when child attempts to use new vocabulary words

Content Standards For Kindergarten Met By This Activity

English Language Arts

      Reading (1.0, 1.2, 1.3, 1.4, 1.5, 1.17, 1.18)

      Writing (1.0, 1.1, 1.2, 1.3)

      Written and Oral Language (1.0, 1.1)

      Listening and Speaking (1.0, 1.1, 1.2, 2.0, 2.1)

Mathematics

      Numbers and Counting (1.0, 1.2)

      Algebra, Sets and Sorting (1.0, 1.1)

      Measurement and Geometry (1.0, 1.1)

      Statistics (1.0, 1.1)

      Mathematical Reasoning (1.0, 1.1, 1.2, 2.0, 2.1, 2.2)

Science

      Physical Science (1.a, 1.c)

      Life Science (2.a, 2.b, 2.c)

      Investigation and Experimentation (4a, 4b, 4.c, 4d, 4e)

History and Social Science

      Following Rules (K.1, K.1.1)

      Compare and describe people and places (K.4, K.4.1)

      Using a calendar to sequence events (K.5)

Visual Arts

      Artistic Perception (1.0, 1.1, 1.3)

      Creative Expression (2.0, 2.1, 2.4, 2.5)

      Valuing Aesthetics (4.0, 4.1, 4.2, 4.3, 4.4)

      Applications (5.0, 5.4)

Learning Plan

I.   **Name of Activity: Fish in the Classroom Activity**

II. **Date of Presentation:**

III. **Age or Grade Level: Pre-K, Kindergarten**

IV. **Ratio of teachers to children needed for this activity:** 1:10

V.   **Target Areas of Learning / Goals and Objectives** (target areas of learning directly relate to "VI. Evaluation Rubric")
     1. **Physical**: _____
     2. **Cognitive:** _____
     3. **Social**: _____
     4. **Emotional**: _____
     5. **Creative:** _____

VI. **Evaluation Rubric:** (if more than two learning areas are being evaluated, a spreadsheet form may be preferred)

Targeted Area of Learning	Targeted Area of Learning
_____	_____
_____	_____
4. Always _____	**4.** Always _____
3. Usually _____	**3.** Usually _____
2. Sometimes _____	**2.** Sometimes _____
1. Rarely _____	**1.** Rarely _____

VII. **Materials and Preparation Needed**
     1. A fish tank, select a size suitable for the number of fish the teacher intends to have and the space available in the classroom
     2. Fresh water fish, goldfish are the hardiest (and least expensive, ask about "feeder fish")
     3. Stale water (water left to air for several days, possibly treated with dechlorinating chemicals, if necessary)
     4. Optional: water plants, stones, decorative figurines for tank
     5. Labels for tank, species of fish, et cetera for vocabulary building and associating written word with the specific object
     6. Fish food appropriate for the type of fish you select
     7. Observation journals, crayons, markers, colored pencils

VIII. **Procedures**
     1. Place tank in area of classroom selected for the tank

2. Set up tank and filter per instructions on the package.

    a) If the teacher has acquired a tank and filter without instructions, the teacher should first rinse out the tank with clear water, to be rid of any dust or debris that has collected in it.

    b) **DO NOT USE SOAP OR CLEANING AGENTS OF ANY SORT ON A FISH TANK.**

    c) In an area outside that will not be damaged by water leaks, fill the tank with water to see if the water seal is still good. Find out what kind of filter is used and purchase a new one. Then proceed from the top.

3. Place marbles, decorative stones, or any other tank decor the children/teacher selects for tank.
4. Fill tank with water and let "air" for a couple of days. Use de-chlorinating chemicals if necessary.
5. Add plants as desired.
6. Add fish.
7. Water will evaporate, so keeping a quart-sized plastic container airing water to add to the tank is a good idea.
8. There are chemicals (keep out of reach of the children) such as "Stress-zyme" which will keep the water from becoming cloudy.
9. The tank walls sometimes may develop a filminess, which can be cleaned with a plastic squeegee designed for aquariums.
10. One of the "class jobs" can be "fish monitor". That child can feed the fish once a day and record observations regarding the fish in the class "fish journal".
11. **Or**: the children can write about their personal observations in their personal fish journals.
12. If the filter is changed regularly (many manufacturers recommend once a month) tank cleaning will be necessary only two or possibly three times each year. Remember to never use soap or other cleaning agents on a fish tank.

IX. Accommodations (changes to accommodate learning diversity)
Name of Accommodated Area:

1. _____
2. _____
3. _____
4. _____
5. _____

X. Applicable Framework Standards: Kindergarten

Standard _____

_____

_____

_____

_____

Standard _____

_____

_____

_____

_____

Standard _____

_____

_____

_____

_____

Standard _____

_____

_____

_____

_____

Standard _____

_____

_____

_____

_____

XI. Evaluation and Comments (i.e.: How well did the plan work? Great responses? What aspects are especially effective? Not effective? What improvements are needed? Ideas for follow up activities and other notes)

_____

_____

_____

_____

Hermit Crabs In The Classroom

If the teacher decides to have a hermit crab in the classroom, it is the teacher's responsibility to research the needs of hermit crabs before bringing it into the classroom. This book contains but the thinnest of suggestions regarding the care of any variety of animal.

Hermit crabs are excellent classroom pets. Hermit crabs can live for years and require a minimum of care. Teacher should emphasize the importance of hygiene (hand washing) after touching the crab or the things inside the crab's living environment.

They need fresh water and a certain amount of humidity. Hermit crabs like to eat frozen "crab cakes" which can be purchased at pet food stores, as well as bits of fruit or veggies or even bits of meat. If your hermit crab is happily growing, you will need to offer your crab a variety of shells. Often a crab will decide to change shells in the middle of the night. The teacher may want to boil the found shells and let them cool entirely before offering the new shells to the crab.

One hermit crab is enough for the classroom. Hermit crabs molt from time to time (by burying themselves into wet sand for a week or more). If a roommate crab happens to be molting, the other crab may likely find and eat the molting crab, which would be sad for everyone, particularly the molting crab.

If a young crab has been selected, it, like many other types of young animals, can be raised to be "hand-friendly". "Hand-friendly" animals in the classroom enrich the experience for everyone. Gentle, regular handling of the animal increases the likelihood of its becoming a "hand-friendly" creature.

It is important to admonish children that not all animals are friendly. The children must find out from the animal's owner and their teacher or parent if it is all right to touch any animal not known to the child, the teacher, and/or parents.

Materials
- ❖ A clear covered container with suitable ventilation for the crab
- ❖ Sand deep enough that the crab can bury itself in it
- ❖ Bits of a branch, a rock or other items upon which the crab can crawl
- ❖ A container or two for water (small lids for jars are suitable)
- ❖ A hermit crab
- ❖ A few extra shells slightly larger than the hermit crab's existing shell
- ❖ Hermit crab food
- ❖ Observation journals, crayons, markers, colored pencils

Method
- ❖ Make sure container for crab's house has been thoroughly rinsed off with clear water (Do not use soap or other cleaning agents, as those substances are toxic to hermit crabs)
- ❖ Place sand, water containers, bits of wood branches, rocks, shells intended for the crab to crawl upon in the container
- ❖ Fill water containers. The crab must have access to water at all times. On Fridays be certain those containers have sufficient water for the weekend.
- ❖ Do not flood the tank. Hermit crabs that are generally kept as pets are NOT aquatic animals. This type of hermit crab lives in proximity to the sea not directly in the ocean.

❖ Add the crab and a little bit of crab food.
❖ A weekly "crab monitor" can be chosen, whose duties are to feed and record by drawing and writing the crab's activities in the "class journal". Included in some of these observations could be changes in the relative position of the crab (moving forward or backward, up or down, the day and time in which behaviors are noted an so forth), the amounts of food consumed, the size, shape and length of time the crab decides to stay in one shell or another.

OR

❖ All children can write their observations (see above) in personal journals.
Note: To make the crab "hand friendly", it is important to hold and touch it regularly and with great gentleness.

Suggested Classroom Reading:
Bornstein, R.B. (1990). *A beautiful Seashell.* ISBN: 0060205946.
McCloskey, R. (1989). *Time of wonder.* ISBN: 0140502017. (Written and illustrated by McCloskey; beautiful descriptions of life on the seashore).
McDonald, M. (1993). *Is This a House For a Hermit Crab?* ISBN: 0531070417.
Nadler, B. (1995). *The Magic School Bus Inside Ralphie: A Book About Germs.*
ISBN: 0590400258. (The importance of hand washing; hands should always be washed before and after handling any animals).
Varley, S. (1984). *Badger's Parting Gifts.* New York: Lothrop, Lee & Shepard Books. ISBN: 0-688-02699-0. (Winner Britain's Mother Goose award for illustration). Available from: www.turnthepage.com/ (Each friend gets a special gift, and Badger lives on in the memory of his friends).
Zoehfeld, K.W. (1994). *What Lives in a Shell?* ISBN: 0064451240.

Target Areas of Learning

Physical Development
❖ **Fine motor skills:** using the small muscles of the hand and fingers: drawing shapes; holding a pencil/crayon; placing crab food in crab's living environment; writing
❖ **Eye-hand coordination:** coordinating visual acuity with using the small muscles of the hand and fingers: picking up hermit crab, holding hermit crab carefully, transferring crab from hand to hand or other surfaces, drawing shapes; holding a pencil/crayon; writing
❖ **Physical principals:** learning physical weight: feeling the weight of the crab in the hand
❖ **Sensory discrimination**
  • **Tactile discrimination** (touch): identifying and differentiating textures with touch: wet, dry, soft, hard, rough, smooth, the experience of having the crab crawl across the hand

- **Visual discrimination** (sight): identifying shapes various objects visually related to the crab, its behavior, and its living environment
- **Olfactory discrimination** (smell): identifying different smells: learning the odors associated with the crab and the fishy smell of its food

Cognitive Development:
- ❖ **Language Arts**
  - **Verbal skills**
    - o **Language development**: group discussion and conversations between students regarding the hermit crab
    - o **Vocabulary development**: learning and using words to describe the hermit crab, its behavior and environment
  - **Emergent literacy**
    - o **Symbol interpretation**: journal writing: understanding that marks have meaning by making notations related to their observations of the hermit crab in its environment
    - o **Letter recognition/word recognition**: practicing vocabulary and learning vocabulary words from labels
    - o **Journal "writing"**: allowing children to write their observations in their "crab" or science journals using scribble writing, drawings, and invented spelling about the crab
    - o **Matching spoken words to printed words**: making a connection between the actual labeled items, the word on the label, and the spoken word
- ❖ **Math Skills**
  - **Mathematical literacy**
    - o **1 to 1 correspondence**: counting items in an organized way that shows understanding of the object's placement as a single entity in a group such as the placement of rocks or other objects in the hermit crab's living environment
  - **Mathematical applications**
    - o **Equivalency:** more / less; single / plural; longer/ shorter; comparisons including documenting the passing of time/duration of hermit crab behaviors
    - o **Measurement**: making note of the changes in the size of the hermit crab and the relative size shells it selects over time
    - o **Algebra: categorization/ grouping** (sets): sorting activities: sorting the types of shells the crab selects, the various types of behavior seen from the crab over time from the children's documentation
    - o **Calendar**: noting the crab's behavior relative to the passage of time.
  - **Temporal ordering**
    - o **Recalling / anticipating events as they occur in time**: recall daily crab behavior
- ❖ **Science**
  - **Scientific processes**

- o **Inquiry**: an organized search for knowledge regarding hermit crab
- o **Observation:** carefully watching attentively and noting what is seen for a scientific purpose
- o **Documentation:** writing observations of scientific events which support claims for a particular prediction or outcomes
- o **Review:** comparing predictions and actual outcomes, assessing value of any mistakes that occurred
- **Cause and effect**
  - o **Relationships between actions and outcomes:** "What do you think will happen if we..." or "What do you think made that happen?" as related to the observed crab behavior
- **Life science**:
  - o **Differentiating:** organisms from inorganic objects
  - o **Observation of and caring for all forms of:**
    - – **Animal life**: keeping animals in the classroom: hermit crabs
    - – **Hygiene / health practices:** cleanliness after interacting with hermit crab, crab living environment, crab food
    - – **Responsibility**: understanding that hermit crabs need a certain level of care absent of which that living thing will either become sick or die
    - – **Recognizing health**: noticing appearance and behavior of healthy hermit crabs
    - – **Death**: if a hermit crab lives it will sometime die
- ❖ **Social Science**
  - • Social studies is developing an understanding of, and respect for, human society and cultures, human relationships, and human diversity; respect for all life in general and responsibly caring for our planet (this can be called science as well).
  - • **Not all people, or other living beings, are the same. Each hermit crab, each bird, each life is unique. All living things deserve to be treated with respect. Differences make living things unique, not "*bad*".**

Social Development

- ❖ **Working cooperatively with others in a group**: interacting with the crab as a *class pet* as opposed to a *personal pet*
- ❖ **Taking turns:** being comfortable with allowing others to play with the hermit crab
- ❖ **Taking responsibility**: making sure that child's assigned task is completed, helping out if another child is absent and cannot help care for the crab
- ❖ **Learning patience:** hermit crabs take their own time to move, change shells; children learn to let the animal be, and wait
- ❖ **Following directions**: interacting with crab as instructed
- ❖ **Behaving appropriately with the hermit crab:** touching and handling living things with gentleness and respect
- ❖ **Taking care of classroom environment**: participating in maintenance and cleanup related to caring for the hermit crab

Emotional Development

- ❖ **Self-esteem:** feeling good regarding taking care of another creature
- ❖ **Nurturing:** developing and expressing feelings of appropriate care and gentleness for a more delicate life form
- ❖ **Courage:** becoming comfortable interacting with the hermit crab; hermit crab appearance may be frightening to some children

Creative Expression

- ❖ **Expressing emotions and self through use of creative media and imagination**: painting, drawing, writing in journal regarding the child's imaginative and real impressions of the hermit crab

Possible Accommodations for *Hermit Crab Activity*

ADHD

- ❖ Give direct instructions for care of hermit crab; re-teach regularly
- ❖ Use positive reinforcement (praise) when child works well with others and is gentle with hermit crab, allows others to interact with the crab
- ❖ Allow child independent time to write/draw observations in note book
- ❖ Offer a carrel for independent journal writing/drawing
- ❖ Review/re-teach rules regarding having hermit crabs in the classroom (feeding only when there is no food in the living environment (about 3 times each week), making sure there is enough water for crab, spraying crab cage once a day, no tapping on the glass, keeping tank free of debris/inappropriate objects, handling the crab gently and not trying to pull crab out of it's shell)
- ❖ Remind children that the hermit crab is a living creature that needs to be treated gently and with respect

Developmental Delays

- ❖ Give direct instructions for care of hermit crab; re-teach regularly
- ❖ Use primary picture paper for pages of journal for easier journaling (see Appendix A-2)
- ❖ Review/re-teach rules regarding having hermit crabs in the classroom (feeding only when there is no food in the living environment (about 3 times each week), making sure there is enough water for crab, spraying crab cage once a day, no tapping on the glass, keeping tank free of debris/ inappropriate objects, handling the crab gently and not trying to pull crab out of it's shell)
- ❖ Remind children that the hermit crab is a living creature that needs to be treated gently and with respect
- ❖ Use simplified language when giving directions and praise, being sure teacher is making eye contact while talking to child
- ❖ Give authentic praise frequently for incremental achievements
- ❖ Allow the child sufficient time to draw or write in journal as measured by child's ability to maintain sustained interest in task

❖ Use pocket chart with words likely to be used in journal near child for easier reference (copying)

Autism Spectrum Disorders

❖ Give direct instructions for care of hermit crab; re-teach regularly: explain the activity using short simple phrases being sure to make eye contact while teaching

❖ Go over task step-by-step to be sure child understands about caring for the hermit crab

❖ Review/re-teach rules regarding having hermit crabs in the classroom (feeding only when there is no food in the living environment (about 3 times each week), making sure there is enough water for crab, spraying crab cage once a day, no tapping on the glass, keeping tank free of debris/inappropriate objects, handling the crab gently and not trying to pull crab out of it's shell)

❖ Be sure to have watching the hermit crab on the class schedule, so the child can anticipate what is to happen during the day

❖ Use positive reinforcement when child participates; notice child's incremental achievements

❖ Adjust the duration of the activity for each session if it appears the child is more or less engaged with it, and have another activity as back up

❖ Use pocket chart with words likely to be used in journal near child for easier reference (copying)

❖ Simplify words to be spelled, if necessary

❖ Show child that the activity is on the schedule for this day, include journal writing on the daily schedule

Visual Impairments

❖ Offer brighter colored, high-contrast (possibly larger) paper and art/writing materials

❖ Buy a larger crab

❖ Purchase a smaller hand carrier type terrarium in which the crab can be placed so child can hold it up close for better viewing

❖ Offer the child a magnifying glass on a stand (similar to the ones used for needlework, found in craft stores) for observing crab and/or working on journal

❖ Adjust lighting to reduce glare

❖ Put paper (dark colored?) behind crab's living environment for better viewing

❖ Select and offer only brightly colored shells for so crab is more easily seen

❖ Offer child a flash light to use briefly while looking for crab in tank

❖ Offer more time if necessary, for the child to complete observe crab and feel successful

❖ If child is nervous about touching crab, teacher may hold the crab and allow child to touch shell, or teacher can place crab on another surface (where crab is safe from falling or crawling into inaccessible places) so that the child can touch the crabs shell

Orthopedic Impairments

❖ Position crab tank so it is easily viewable for child

❖ Purchase a smaller hand carrier type terrarium in which the crab can be placed to bring to child

❖ Teacher may gently hold crab and let child touch shell, or guide child's hand to touching shell

❖ For journal activity, use a 3 ring binder so child can work on single sheets of paper affixed to a clip board

❖ Use adapted writing tool

Gifted and Talented Education (GATE)

❖ Ask child to research hermit crabs on the internet, in the library, and encyclopedia

❖ Print a photo from the internet labeled with the parts of the crab's body, teach to child as part of their vocabulary

❖ Ask child to write a fictional story or a poem about the hermit crab

❖ Ask child to respond to silly questions like how would a hermit crab paint? Or what does hermit crab dancing look like?

English Language Learners (ELL)

❖ Give direct instructions for care of hermit crab; explain the activity using short simple phrases being sure to make eye contact while teaching

❖ Model instructions while speaking slowly and clearly, making sure to articulate words clearly using photos and realia

❖ Label the terrarium and other items associated with the hermit crab so child associates the written word with the object

❖ Go over vocabulary individually or in small group settings to reinforce

❖ Review/re-teach rules regarding having hermit crabs in the classroom (feeding only when there is no food in the living environment (about 3 times each week), making sure there is enough water for crab, spraying crab cage once a day, no tapping on the glass, keeping tank free of debris/inappropriate objects, handling the crab gently and not trying to pull crab out of its shell)

Content Standards For Kindergarten Met By This Activity

English Language Arts

Reading (1.0, 1.2, 1.3, 1.4, 1.5, 1.12, 1.17, 1.18)
Writing (1.0, 1.1, 1.2, 1.3)
Written and Oral Language (1.0, 1.1)
Listening and Speaking (1.0, 1.1, 1.2, 2.0, 2.1, 2.3)

Mathematics

Measurement and Geometry (1.0, 1.1, 1.2, 2.0, 2.2)
Statistics (1.0, 1.1)
Mathematical Reasoning (1.0, 1.2, 2.0, 2.1)

Science

    Physical Science (1.a)

    Life Science (2.a, 2.c)

    Investigation and Experimentation (4a, 4b, 4.c, 4d, 4e)

History and Social Science

    Following Rules (K.1, K.1.1)

    Compare and describe people and places (K.4, K.4.1)

    Using a calendar to sequence events (K.5)

Visual Arts

    Artistic Perception (1.0, 1.1, 1.3)

    Creative Expression (2.0, 2.1)

Learning Plan

I. **Name of Activity: Hermit Crab in the Classroom**

II. **Date of Presentation:**

III. **Age or Grade Level: Pre-K, Kindergarten**

IV. **Ratio of teachers to children needed for this activity:** 1:10

V. **Target Areas of Learning / Goals and Objectives** (target areas of learning directly relate to "VI. Evaluation Rubric")

    1. Physical: _____
    2. Cognitive: _____
    3. Social: _____
    4. Emotional: _____
    5. Creative: _____

VI. **Evaluation Rubric:** (if more than two learning areas are being evaluated, a spreadsheet form may be preferred)

Targeted Area of Learning	**Targeted Area of Learning**
_____	_____
_____	_____
4. Always _____	**4.** Always _____
3. Usually _____	**3.** Usually _____
2. Sometimes _____	**2.** Sometimes _____
1. Rarely _____	**1.** Rarely _____

VII. **Materials and Preparation Needed**

1. A clear covered container with suitable ventilation for the crab
2. Sand deep enough that the crab can bury itself in it
3. Bits of a branch, a rock or other items upon which the crab can crawl
4. A container or two for water (small lids for jars are suitable)
5. A hermit crab
6. A few extra shells slightly larger than the hermit crab's existing shell
7. Hermit crab food
8. Observation journals, crayons, markers, colored pencils

VIII. **Procedures**

1. Make sure container for crab's house has been thoroughly rinsed off with clear water (do not use soap or other cleaning agents, as those substances are toxic to hermit crabs)

2. Place sand, water containers, bits of wood branches, rocks, shells intended for the crab to crawl upon in the container

3. Fill water containers. The crab must have access to water at all times. On Fridays be certain those containers have sufficient water for the weekend.

4. Do not flood the tank. Hermit crabs live in proximity to the sea not directly in the ocean. They are NOT aquatic animals.

5. Add the crab and a little bit of crab food.

6. A weekly "crab monitor" can be chosen, whose duties are to feed and record by drawing and writing the crab's activities in the "class journal". Included in some of these observations could be changes in the relative position of the crab (moving forward or backward, up or down, the day and time in which behaviors are noted an so forth), the amounts of food consumed, the size, shape and length of time the crab decides to stay in one shell or another. **OR**

7. All children can write their observations (see above) in personal journals.
   NOTE: To make the crab hand friendly, it is important to hold and touch it regularly and with great gentleness

IX. **Accommodations** (changes to accommodate learning diversity)
   Name of Accommodated Area:
   1. _____
   2. _____
   3. _____
   4. _____
   5. _____

X. **Applicable Framework Standards: Kindergarten**
   Standard _____
   _____
   _____
   _____
   _____

   Standard _____
   _____
   _____
   _____
   _____

   Standard _____
   _____
   _____
   _____
   _____

Standard _____

_____

_____

_____

_____

Standard _____

_____

_____

_____

_____

XI. **Evaluation and Comments** (i.e.: How well did the plan work? Great responses? What aspects are especially effective? Not effective? What improvements are needed? Ideas for follow up activities and other notes)

_____

_____

_____

_____

Pinecone Bird Feeder Activity

This is a great activity for areas of the country that become snowy and frigid during the winter months. This activity can be fun even in areas that have mild winters. But for those areas with severe weather, these bird feeders will attract quite a community of over wintering birds and squirrels. Children can watch the animals coming to eat from their feeders. This can be an exciting and gratifying experience for children. In some small way the children will learn the satisfaction of caring and contributing to the well being of other creatures. Bear in mind that if there are rats around, they too will be drawn to the pinecones.

Children learn to notice the world around them and the changes happening within it through observation oriented activities. Through practice in observation, children can learn to predict the outcome of different events more accurately. In our culture today, prediction, careful observation and critical interpretation of unbiased observations are powerful skills for success in life.

It is important to admonish the children not to approach the wild animals visiting their bird feeders as wild animals can behave defensively and may even injure the children. So long as the children leave the animals in peace, this should not be a problem. Place the feeders on a fence or tree away from the play areas of the children than can be viewed from a classroom window or from a respectful distance. In this way both the children and the animals are protected.

Unless the teacher is fortunate enough to live in a place filled with pine trees, the teacher will need to collect and request pinecones in advance of the activity. Use the less perfect pinecones for this activity, as the beautifully shaped ones can be used for art projects.

If there is a child with allergies to nuts in the class, substitute suet, or rendered beef fat (found in the meat departments of many grocery stores) instead. Check with the child's parents to find out if the child is sensitive to seeds such as sunflower seeds as well. If so, this activity may not be suitable for this class. A child with allergies to nuts can have intense, life threatening reactions. Contact with even the smallest trace can be dangerous. The teacher must take this into consideration when making plans for activities.

Materials
- ❖ Pinecones
- ❖ String
- ❖ Peanut butter or suet (suet must be refrigerated until a couple hours before the activity is presented)
- ❖ Birdseed (available at the dollar store)
- ❖ Foil pans (the type used as disposable roasting pans)
- ❖ Spoons, plastic knives, or wide craft sticks for spreading peanut butter
- ❖ Journals and journal writing supplies
- ❖ Binoculars (optional)

Method
- ❖ Plan to have this activity in an area that can be easily swept
- ❖ Set out a basket or box of pinecones, foil roasting trays about one quarter filled with birdseed, containers of suet or peanut butter, and tools for spreading buffet style

❖ In small groups children move through the "buffet" first selecting their pinecones, tying a string around the top of the cone for tying to a fence or tree, and spreading them with peanut butter or suet

❖ When the first small group is completed with the first two steps, have group two start (this prevents "traffic jams" and "pile ups" at the buffet line)

❖ The children then roll their pinecones in the trays of seed until the cone is well covered with birdseed

❖ Select a place where the children can hang the pinecones up that can be easily seen from the classroom window

❖ Children will be quite excited to use binoculars. If binoculars are included in the activity, either set up a structure for using them, such that everyone can use them, or better yet, try to obtain several sets for this purpose

❖ Admonish the children that the animals eating from the pinecones are wild and should not be approached. Usually wild animals will be frightened away, but if a wild animal allows itself to be handled, it may bite or scratch or otherwise injure the child,

Variation

The children could document this project on digital video as a media arts extension of this activity. Unless the teacher has skill in that media, parental or staff assistance might need to be requested in support of the media arts aspect of the project.

Suggested Reading:

Ginsberg, M. (1994). *The Old Man and His Birds.* ISBN: 0688046037

Holub, J. (2004). *Why Do Birds Sing?* New York: Puffin (2004) ISBN: 0142401064. (Great book for learning about birds and bird-watching, discusses feathers, diet, and nesting)

McCloskey, R. (1941). *Make Way For Ducklings.* ISBN: 0670451495

Pallotta, J. (1987). *The Bird Alphabet Book.* ISBN: 0881064513.

Wildsmith, B. (1981). *Birds.* ISBN: 0192721178.

Wood, A. J. (1993). *Egg!* ISBN: 0-316-8161607. (Twelve different eggs, twelve different creatures to guess!)

Target Areas of Learning

Physical Development

❖ **Gross motor:** using the large muscles of the arms, legs, and torso: reaching up and tying pinecone to trees or fences in view of classroom window, perhaps ladder climbing

❖ **Fine motor:** using the small muscles of the hands and fingers: cutting, tying string around top of cone, spreading cone with nut butter, rolling cone in seed hanging cone on tree or fence, writing, drawing, holding writing/drawing tools correctly

❖ **Eye-hand coordination:** coordinating visual acuity with using the small muscles of the hand and fingers: tying string, spreading nut butter, hanging cone, writing, drawing

❖ **Sensory discrimination**
  • **Visual discrimination (sight):** visually identifying and assembling feeder cone, visually identifying the different animals visiting the feeder cone
  • **Tactile discrimination (touch):** differentiating physical properties of materials through touch: touching nut butter, pinecone, seeds et cetera
  • **Olfactory discrimination (smell):** differentiating physical properties through the sense of smell: smelling the nut butter, suet, and seeds
  • **Auditory discrimination (hearing):** listening to and identifying the bird songs and sounds of animals visiting the bird feeder

Cognitive Development
❖ **Language Arts**
  • **Verbal skills**
    ○ **Language development:** acquiring and using language appropriately in interactions with others, discussing observations with team or classmates
    ○ **Vocabulary development:** acquiring vocabulary to describe components of the activity and the processes used to create feeder cones, describing visiting animals by species, behaviors, number of visits, number words by counting
  • **Emergent literacy**
    ○ **Emergent writing:** journal writing including scribble writing, picture drawing to communicate observations of animal behavior
    ○ **Sequencing (temporal ordering):** documenting observations as they occurred in time
❖ **Math Skills**
  • **Mathematical literacy**
    ○ **1 to 1 correspondence:** counting visiting animals in an organized way that reflects understanding that each single count is associated with a specific item in a count
    ○ **Associating number symbols with quantity:** understanding that a specific symbol is always associated with a specific quantity of animal visitors to the bird feeders
  • **Mathematical applications**
    ○ **Measurement:** using a standard measure to determine length of the string to hang the bird feeder
    ○ **Algebra:** sorting, matching, and grouping types of birds/animals visiting feeder
❖ **Science**
  • **Scientific processes**
    ○ **Inquiry:** an organized search for knowledge regarding how many of which species of animals will visit the bird feeder
    ○ **Prediction:** relating an anticipated number of which species of animals will visit the bird feeder
    ○ **Observation:** carefully watching attentively and noting number of which species of animals visiting the bird feeder and their associated behavior

  o **Documentation:** writing observations of numbers of which species of animals will visit the bird feeder
  o **Review:** comparing predictions and actual outcomes, assessing value of any mistakes that occurred
- **Life Science**
  o **Differentiating:** organisms from inorganic objects
  o **Understanding:** all living things have common needs of for life
  o **Responsibility:** understanding that living things need to be fed all year round absent of which that living thing will either become sick or die
  o **Recognizing health:** noticing appearance and behavior of healthy living things by observing the animal visitors feeding
- **Cause and effect**: relationships between actions and outcomes: what happens when feeder cone is placed outside, amount of time between placing cones outside and visitation of animals
- **Environmental awareness:** noting the seasonal availability of food for wild animals

Social Development

- ❖ **Cooperative learning:** working well as a member of a community creating a project for nurturing the local animal life
- ❖ **Sharing:** considering the feeder materials and journaling materials as classroom resources available to all
- ❖ **Taking turns:** moving graciously through assembling the project materials
- ❖ **Patience:** waiting to observe animals natural behavior without giving into restlessness
- ❖ **Collaboration:** planning, creating, and participating in an animal feeding project as a class member
- ❖ **Maintaining classroom environment:** helping with set up and clean up
- ❖ **Following instructions:** using the tools and participating in the project as instructed
- ❖ **Nurturing behaviors:** taking care of other living things

Emotional Development

- ❖ **Self-esteem**: feeling a sense of self worth by caring for living creatures by feeding
- ❖ **Generosity:** sharing resources with other creatures
- ❖ **Empathy:** understanding wild creatures may become hungry, especially in winter when food supplies are less
- ❖ **Nurturing behaviors:** learning a sense of responsibility in caring for creatures in the environment

Creative Expression

- ❖ **Writing:** expression of observations of animal behavior by writing and drawing in notebook
- ❖ **Expression of self:** feeding animals

❖ **Problem solving:** gathering information and considering various ideas regarding the types of seeds to be used for the local animals life to be fed and appropriate placement of the feeder

Possible Accommodations for *Pinecone Bird Feeders Activity*

ADHD
❖ Use positive reinforcement (praise) when child follows directions, works well with others
❖ Offer more time or break activity up into several smaller sessions (e.g.: covering cones in suet and rolling the cones in seeds for first session, and hanging feeder cone second session)
❖ Allow child to function as a helper in setting up or cleaning up
❖ Allow child independent time to write/draw observations in note book
❖ Offer a carrel for independent note taking
❖ Lower the ratio

Developmental Delays
❖ Go over task more slowly using simplified language while making eye contact to be sure child understands the task
❖ Demonstrate the activity using realia, photos or perhaps video of the activity in steps for child
❖ Offer a larger pinecone and adapted tools, such as large spoons to spread nut
❖ Use butter on pinecone
❖ Lower the ratio
❖ Offer more time or break activity up into several smaller sessions
❖ Have child work with a gentle and more competent partner
❖ Use primary picture paper for pages of journal for easier note taking (see Appendix A-2)

Autism Spectrum Disorders
❖ Go over task more slowly using simplified language while making eye contact to be sure child understands the task
❖ Demonstrate the activity using realia, photos or perhaps video of the activity in steps for child
❖ Offer more time or break activity up into several smaller sessions
❖ Hang a sample outside so child will begin to see the purpose in the activity
❖ Allow child to become accustomed to the activity by observing others initially, perhaps even doing task a day later when task seems more familiar
❖ If child has tactile sensory issues, allow child to use surgical gloves to avoid getting sticky nut butter on fingers
❖ Clip any sharp points off pinecones before letting child cover their pinecone feeder with nut butter
❖ Show child that the activity is on the schedule for this day

❖ Use positive reinforcement when child participates
❖ Pair child with the child's designated buddy (autistic children prefer familiarity)

Visual Impairments
❖ Lower the ratio
❖ Offer binoculars to observe animals
❖ If possible do observation activity when cone feeders are not backlit by sun
❖ Journaling can be dictated
❖ Offer more time if needed
❖ Use primary picture paper for pages of journal for easier note taking (see Appendix A-2)

Orthopedic Impairments
❖ Pay attention to how the child is positioned in chair
❖ Set up a viewing station that accommodates child's mobility challenges
❖ Hold binoculars for child if child lacks strength or mobility to do so for self
❖ Adjust furniture or use a tray for easy access for putting together pinecone and writing activities
❖ Clip any sharp points off pinecones before letting child cover their pinecone feeder with nut butter
❖ If child's hands lack strength or mobility, assist child by placing their hands over yours or your hands over theirs to assemble pinecone and write
❖ Use a clipboard and alligator clips to secure writing paper

Gifted and Talented Education(GATE)
❖ Ask child to research the backgrounds of the various species visiting the feeders on line, in the library and encyclopedia
❖ Ask child to observe the feeders in a measured period of time (five minutes is good) and note which animals were viewed during that time and their behaviors (a timer is helpful for this)
❖ If child finds one particular species interesting, challenge child to find out as much as possible about that species
❖ Ask child to write a story about the animals visiting the bird feeder

English Language Learners (ELL)
❖ Go over task more slowly using simplified language while making eye contact to be sure child understands the task
❖ Demonstrate the activity using realia, photos or perhaps video of the activity in steps for child
❖ Teach and review vocabulary in small groups or individually
❖ Use positive reinforcement when child uses vocabulary words

Content Standards For Kindergarten Met By This Activity

English Language Arts

Reading (1.0, 1.18)

Writing (1.0, 1.1)

Written and Oral Language (1.0, 1.1)

Listening and Speaking (1.0, 1.1, 1.2, 2.0, 2.1)

Mathematics

Numbers and Counting (1.0, 1.1, 1.2, 1.3)

Algebra, Sets and Sorting (1.0, 1.1)

Measurement and Geometry (1.0, 1.2, 1.3, 1.4)

Statistics (1.0, 1.1)

Science

Life Science (2.a)

Investigation and Experimentation (4.c, 4.d, 4.e)

History And Social Science

Following Rules (K.1, K.1.1)

Using a calendar to sequence events (K.5)

Learning Plan

   I. **Name of Activity: Pinecone Bird Feeder**

  II. **Date of Presentation:**

 III. **Age or Grade Level: Pre-K to Kindergarten**

  IV. **Ratio of teachers to children needed for this activity:** 1:6

   V. **Target Areas of Learning / Goals and Objectives** (target areas of learning directly relate to "VI. Evaluation Rubric")

   1. Physical: _____

   2. Cognitive: _____

   3. Social: _____

   4. Emotional: _____

   5. Creative: _____

  VI. **Evaluation Rubric:** (if more than two learning areas are being evaluated, a spreadsheet form may be preferred)

Targeted Area of Learning   **Targeted Area of Learning**

_____   _____

_____   _____

   4. Always _____   **4.** Always _____

   3. Usually _____   **3.** Usually _____

   2. Sometimes _____   **2.** Sometimes _____

   1. Rarely _____   **1.** Rarely _____

 VII. **Materials and Preparation Needed**
   1. Pinecones
   2. String
   3. Peanut butter or suet (this must be refrigerated until a couple hours before the activity is presented)
   4. Birdseed (available at the dollar store)
   5. Foil pans (the type used as disposable roasting pans)
   6. Spoons, plastic knives, or wide craft sticks for spreading peanut butter
   7. Journals and journal writing supplies

VIII. **Procedures**
   1. Plan to have this activity in an area that can be easily swept
   2. Set out a basket or box of pinecones, foil roasting trays about one quarter filled with birdseed, containers of suet or peanut butter, and tools for spreading buffet style

3. In small groups children move through the "buffet" first selecting their pine cones, tying a string around the top of the cone for tying to a fence or tree, and spreading them with peanut butter or suet

4. When the first small group is completed with the first two steps, have group two start (this prevents "traffic jams" and "pile ups" at the buffet line)

5. The children then roll their pinecones in the trays of seed until the cone is well covered with birdseed

6. Select a place where the children can hang the pinecones up that can be easily seen from the classroom window

7. Admonish the children that the animals eating from the pinecones are wild and should not be approached. Usually wild animals will be frightened away, but if a wild animal allows itself to be handled, it may bite or scratch or otherwise injure the child

IX. **Accommodations** (changes to accommodate learning diversity)
Name of Accommodated Area:
1. _____
2. _____
3. _____
4. _____
5. _____

X. **Applicable Framework Standards: Kindergarten**
Standard _____
_____
_____
_____
_____

Standard _____
_____
_____
_____
_____

Standard _____
_____
_____
_____
_____

Standard _____
_____
_____
_____
_____

Standard _____

_____

_____

_____

_____

XI. **Evaluation and Comments** (i.e.: How well did the plan work? Great responses? What aspects are especially effective? Not effective? What improvements are needed? Ideas for follow up activities and other notes)

_____

_____

_____

_____

Composting

If the school site has an area suitable for composting and gardening, the teacher should feel quite lucky, particularly if the school is in an urban setting. Children living within the city often have little opportunity to watch the cycle of life in this manner.

Many community waste disposal programs also have composting programs. The teacher may choose to ask for a speaker from that program or may personally attend one of the composting programs. The description herein is meant not to be complete directions for a composting project in your geographical area, but does provide a starting off point and learning plans for the project.

Composting is an outdoor activity. Encourage parents to give children a hat to wear while working outside that can be kept at school, and to apply sun block to their child's skin. Try to plan to work on the compost pile at a time of the day when the temperature is neither too hot nor cold. If the weather is warm, be sure the children drink sufficient water.

This is a long-term project, which could actually cover more than a year's worth of learning. If teachers choose to work cooperatively, the project has within it the possibility to be a source of continuous learning for all grade levels participating within the school.

If the class includes children struggling with vocabulary development, the teacher can write the vocabulary words associated with composting on file cards or word strips, laminate them, and affix the labels to the bins, shovels, and wheel barrel. If that is unworkable, create a bulletin board that shows the different tools, appropriate items for composting including easily read labels, photos of the children at work, and some of the children's writing relating to the composting project.

Composting is the ultimate recycling. Composting can be done on a pile in a dirt corner of the schoolyard, in plastic "official" recycling containers, or in a three-sided defined wooden "area". Children may add to the compost heap, but the compost heap is not a suitable area for play.

Children should wear sunscreen when working outside on a gardening type project.

Teachers must emphasize hygiene. The earth is filled with bacteria and fungi, all of which have a good purpose in the soil. Compost, and manure in particular, is filled with bacteria. This is good, as the bacteria break down the different types of matter to be composted. However, after people handle soil, compost, or manure, it is essential that hands and fingernails be thoroughly cleaned to stay healthy. The teacher could purchase plastic fingernail brushes at the Dollar Store. Each child could keep his or her nailbrush in their garden cubby or box. The teacher will have to demonstrate the proper use of a fingernail brush to the class a few times.

Most vegetable matter such as grass or leaves, fruit scraps, and certain kinds of animal fecal matter can be composted. Rabbit and chicken droppings are considered excellent for the garden or compost heap. Do not put too many foodstuffs into the compost as it may attract rats. If the school does not have rabbits or chickens, add an occasional five or ten pound bag of weed free steer manure. The fecal matter will cause the compost to "heat up", thus encouraging the helpful bacteria to do their work decomposing that which is in the compost pile. Compost piles need to be watered from time to time to keep the bacteria alive. Worms are an excellent addition to the compost pile for as the worms eat the matter to be broken down, a wonderful rich soil is created.

DO NOT COMPOST MEAT OR MEAT BY PRODUCTS AS THOSE ITEMS WILL DEFINITELY ATTRACT UNWANTED VERMIN.

Materials

- ❖ An area suitable for composting, out of the main traffic flow of the student population, preferably near the area to be gardened and optimally close to a source of water
- ❖ A container into which recyclable plant materials can be left
- ❖ Recyclable plant materials, appropriate animal fecal matter (which "heats up" compost pile, encouraging bacterial growth)
- ❖ Shovels
- ❖ Rakes
- ❖ Child-sized work gloves
- ❖ Sun hats
- ❖ A source of water, preferably a spigot to which a hose can be attached or watering cans and buckets to carry water to the compost pile
- ❖ Wheel barrows or buckets suitable for children to use to carry finished compost to garden
- ❖ Child-sized garden gloves (available at Dollar Stores or Target for a dollar a pair, less at the end of summer)
- ❖ A camera or video recorder (optional)

Variation:

The children could document this project on digital video as a media arts extension of this activity. Unless the teacher has skill in that media, parental or staff assistance might need to be requested in support of the media arts aspect of the project.

Method

- ❖ Class sets up area for composting in a container in layers like a lasagna: starter materials for composting: leaves, manure, worms (optional)
- ❖ After every few layers, the children water down the pile (the bacteria need water to survive and to begin the process of decomposition)
- ❖ Children gather leaves, weeds pulled from garden areas, vegetable and fruit waste (without fat or grease) each day or week to add to the compost pile
- ❖ Children water compost pile each week
- ❖ If the school or class has access to rabbit or chicken droppings, those can be added to the compost pile
- ❖ Every three to four weeks, the children can "turn" the compost. Turning compost means shoveling the material from the top of the pile to the middle or bottom.
- ❖ After "turning" the compost, the pile should be watered.
- ❖ Depending on the weather, the compost should be ready to be put into the garden within six to eight weeks. Children can shovel finished compost into a wheelbarrow or buckets and put compost into garden.

Suggested Reading:

Cole, J., & Beech, L.W. (1995). *The Magic School Bus Meets the Rot Squad: A Book About Decomposition.* ISBN: 0590400231.

Cole, J., & Beech, L.W. (1996). *The Magic School Bus Gets Ants in its Pants: A Book About Ants.* ISBN: 059040024X.

Fredericks, A.D. (2001). *Under One Rock: Bugs, Slugs and Other Ughs. (Sharing nature with children).* ISBN: 1584690275. (2003 Learning Magazine Teacher's Choice Award).

Glaser, L. (2000). *Our Big Home: An Earth Poem.* ISBN: 0439397529.

Himmelman, J. (2001). *An Earthworm's Life.* ISBN: 0-516-26535-0. Available from: www.turnthepage. com

Kalman, B. & Schaub, J. (1992). *Squirmy Wormy Composters.* ISBN: 0865055815. (Everything about composting and the life cycle of earthworms).

Lionni, L. (1995). *Inch by inch.* ISBN: 0688132839.

Pallotta, J. & Masiello, R. (1992). *The icky bug counting book.* ISBN: 0881064963.

Pfeffer, W. (2003). *Wiggling worms at work.* ISBN: 0064451992.

Silverstein, A. & Silverstein, V. (2000). *Life in a Bucket of Soil.* ISBN: 0486410579.

White, N. (2002). *The Magic School Bus Explores the World of Bugs.* ISBN: 0439225175.

Wright, J. (1988). *Bugs.* ISBN: 0688082963. (Reading Rainbow book).

Target Areas of Learning

Physical Development

❖ **Fine motor skills:** using the small muscles of the hands and fingers: using hand shovels, holding hose for watering compost

❖ **Gross motor skills:** using the large muscles of the body (e.g., arms and legs) to lift and handle gardening tools (e.g., shovels, rake, wheelbarrow) to turn over the layers of compost material

❖ **Eye-hand coordination:** coordinating visual acuity with using the small muscles of the hand and fingers: pouring water, putting hands full of leaves into the compost pile, shoveling compost to turn and putting finished compost into wheel barrows/buckets

❖ **Sensory discrimination**
  • **Visual discrimination (sight):** visually identifying materials for compost pile, noticing the appearance of the materials change from leaves and scraps into friable soil
  • **Tactile discrimination (touch):** differentiating physical properties of materials through touch: touching leaves, soil, tools, water et cetera
  • **Olfactory discrimination (smell):** learning to differentiate the odors related to that which is in the compost pile, and to determine which of those odors are appropriate for "healthy" compost

Cognitive Development

❖ **Language Arts**
  • **Verbal Skills**

- o **Vocabulary development**: learning the appropriate words to describe the materials processes involved with composting
- o **Language development**: acquiring and using language appropriately in interactions with others while working in the garden
- **Emergent literacy**
  - o **Word recognition**: correctly associating the written words for tools, et cetera, with the actual tools
  - o **Emergent writing**: documenting observations and experiences related to creating compost
  - o **Creative writing**: expressing self in marks and pictures about working in the garden
  - o **Sequencing (temporal ordering)**: relating what the child has observed regarding the process of creating compost
- ❖ **Math Skills**
  - **Mathematical applications**
    - o **Measuring** ingredients for composting/quantities of water/amounts of compost created
    - o **Seriation**:
      - **Calendar:** counting days and weeks involved in the process of making compost
    - o **Construction**: building compost area by putting together parts
- ❖ **Science**
  - **Scientific processes**
    - o **Inquiry:** an organized search for knowledge regarding the process of composting
    - o **Prediction:** relating an anticipated outcome of composting activity
    - o **Observation:** carefully watching attentively and noting what is seen in the composting project
    - o **Documentation**: writing observations of composting project
    - o **Review**: comparing predictions and actual outcomes of composting project
  - **Life Science**
    - o **Ecology:** developing an understanding of and a sense of responsibility for the environment by experiencing the process of taking leaves, manure, and various vegetable materials to create a rich soil
  - **Cause and effect: relationships between actions and outcomes:** what happens when compost is watered, what happens if compost is not watered; what happens if worms are added; what happens when different ingredients are added to the pile, et cetera
  - **Hygiene:** maintaining an appropriate level of personal cleanliness after interacting with bacteria filled compost materials

Social Development

- ❖ **Cooperative learning**: work well as a team on community composting project, working well with others

❖ **Sharing**: allowing others to have a turn at using yard tools

❖ **Taking turns**: alternating tasks associated with making compost

❖ **Collaboration:** planning and creating composting project, considering alternatives for placement and items to be included in the project

❖ **Maintaining yard environment**: helping with clean up; picking up leaves, adding them to compost; putting tools away

❖ **Following instructions**: using the tools as instructed, cleaning up, only placing appropriate matter into compost pile

❖ **Safety**: putting tools away so others will not be injured by tools left out

Emotional Development

❖ **Self-esteem**: feeling a sense of accomplishment by participating in planning and creating a compost project

❖ **Nurturing behaviors**: learning a sense of responsibility for care for the environment by composting

❖ **Accomplishment**: developing a sense of self worth from participating in and completing compost activity

Creative Expression

❖ **Expression of self through garden keeping**: creating good soil, gardening

❖ **Writing:** using words and drawings creatively to describe impressions of compost activity

❖ **Developing aesthetic appreciation:** enjoying the beauty of healthy soil and gardens

❖ **Problem solving**: gathering data, collaborating, delegating responsibility within the small and large group to create the compost

Possible Accommodations for *Composting Activity*

ADHD

Because this activity utilizes physical energy, this project may be excellent for high-energy children. If the children are highly impulsive, the level of supervision may need to be increased.

❖ Use positive reinforcement (praise) when child follows directions, works well with others

❖ Set the activity up so the child has maximum opportunities to use physical energy

❖ Offer more time or break activity up into several smaller sessions

❖ Allow child to function as a helper

❖ Allow child independent time to write/draw observations in note book

❖ Decrease number of vocabulary words

❖ Lower ratio

Developmental Delays

❖ Explain slowly the activity using short simple phrases being sure eye contact is made

❖ Demonstrate the activity in advance steps-by-step using realia, photographs or videos

❖ Demonstrate the activity for child or show child pictures of the steps of the activity

❖ Lower ratio
❖ Offer more time or break activity up into several smaller sessions
❖ Have child work with a gentle and more competent partner
❖ Use primary picture paper for pages of journal for easier note taking (see Appendix A-2)
❖ Simplify vocabulary words
❖ Offer a reference card that has vocabulary words on it so child can include those word in writing activities

Autism Spectrum Disorders:

Autistic children frequently are resistant to new experiences in general, and sensory experiences in particular. One good aspect of this project is that it is long term, so the child will have ample opportunity to become familiar with the project.

❖ Explain the activity using short simple phrases being sure eye contact is made
❖ Demonstrate the activity in advance steps-by-step using realia, photographs or videos
❖ Offer more time or break activity up into several smaller sessions
❖ Allow child to become accustomed to the activity by observing others initially, perhaps even doing task a day later when task seems more familiar
❖ Allow child to use small gardening gloves
❖ Use positive reinforcement when child participates
❖ Bring in a small amount of compost to class before the project, to allow child to become familiar with the smell and texture of compost
❖ Show child that the activity is on the schedule for this day
❖ Simplify vocabulary words
❖ Offer a reference card that has vocabulary words on it so child can include those word in writing activities
❖ Have child work with a regular "buddy"

Visual Impairments

❖ Allow the child to wear sunglasses and/or a large brimmed hat to help cut the glare from sunlight
❖ Lower the ratio
❖ Offer a large, standing or hand held magnifying glass to observe changes
❖ Journaling can be dictated, or primary picture paper may be used for the child's journal
❖ Extend time
❖ Have the child work with a buddy

Orthopedic Impairments

❖ Set up a smaller compost environment inside a (clear) plastic bucket
❖ Turn compost in bucket using hand shovels or wooden spoons
❖ Make sure that garden and access areas are free of debris or clutter on the ground so child can safely move into and around garden area
❖ Offer adapted tools: shovels with padded handles, writing and drawing tools

❖ If child lacks strength or flexibility to use tools, assist child by placing your hands over the child's (or vice versa) (hand-over-hand method)

❖ Use positive reinforcement for child's attempts

Gifted and Talented Education (GATE)

❖ Increase number and challenge of vocabulary words

❖ Ask child to research information regarding the process of composting or information about worms

❖ Allow child to work on the planning and preparation of documenting the project with a camera/video recorder

❖ Set up an observational site of one foot by one foot near the compost site; have the child observe changes, insect life seen therein on a daily basis (perhaps for ten minutes each day) for a week using drawings, photographs and journal notes for documentation

❖ Ask child to write a fictional story about working in the garden

English Language Learners (ELL)

❖ Explain the activity using short simple phrases being sure eye contact is made

❖ Demonstrate the activity in advance steps-by-step using realia, photographs or videos

❖ Simplify vocabulary words

❖ Offer a reference card that has vocabulary words on it so child can include those word in writing activities

❖ Teach and review vocabulary words in small groups or individually

Content Standards For Kindergarten Met By This Activity

English Language Arts
  Writing (1.0, 1.1)
  Listening and Speaking (1.0, 1.1, 1.2, 2.0, 2.1)

Mathematics
  Numbers and Counting (1.0)
  Measurement and Geometry (1.0, 1.1, 1.2, 1.3)
  Statistics (1.0, 1.1)

Science
  Physical Science (1.a)
  Earth Science (3.c)
  Investigation and Experimentation (4.a, 4.e)

History and Social Science
Following Rules (K.1, K.1.1)
Using a calendar to sequence events (K.5)

Learning Plan

I. **Name of Activity: Composting Activity**

II. **Date of Presentation:**

III. **Age or Grade Level: Pre-K to Kindergarten**

IV. **Ratio of teachers to children needed for this activity:** 1:6

V. **Target Areas of Learning / Goals and Objectives** (target areas of learning directly relate to "VI. Evaluation Rubric")

   1. **Physical**: _____
   2. **Cognitive:** _____
   3. **Social:** _____
   4. **Emotional**: _____
   5. **Creative:** _____

VI. **Evaluation Rubric:** (if more than two learning areas are being evaluated, a spreadsheet form may be preferred)

Targeted Area of Learning	Targeted Area of Learning
_____	_____
_____	_____
4. Always _____	**4.** Always _____
3. Usually _____	**3.** Usually _____
2. Sometimes _____	**2.** Sometimes _____
1. Rarely _____	**1.** Rarely _____

VII. **Materials and Preparation Needed**

   1. Choose an area suitable for composting, out of the main traffic flow of the student population, preferably near garden area and optimally close to a source of water
   2. A source of water, preferably a spigot to which a hose can be attached, or watering cans and buckets to carry water to the compost pile
   3. A container into which recyclable plant materials can be left
   4. Recyclable plant materials, appropriate animal fecal matter (which "heats up" compost pile, encouraging bacterial growth)
   5. Shovels
   6. Rakes
   7. Child-sized work gloves
   8. Sun hats
   9. Wheel barrows or buckets suitable for children to use to carry finished compost to garden

Optional: Worms can be added to the compost to help speed up the process of breaking down the plant matter into compost.

VIII. Procedures

1. Class sets up area for composting in a container in layers like a lasagna: starter materials for composting: leaves, manure, worms (optional)
2. After every few layers, the children water down the pile (the bacteria need water to survive and to begin the process of decomposition)
3. Children gather leaves, weeds pulled from garden areas, vegetable and fruit waste (without fat or grease) each day or week to add to the compost pile
4. Children water compost pile each week
5. If the school or class has access to rabbit or chicken droppings, those can be added to the compost pile
6. Every three to four weeks, the children can "turn" the compost. Turning compost means shoveling the material from the top of the pile into the middle or bottom.
7. After "turning" the compost, the pile should be watered
8. Depending on the weather, the compost should be ready to be put into the garden within six to eight weeks. Children can shovel finished compost into wheelbarrow or buckets and put into garden.

IX. Accommodations (changes to accommodate learning diversity)
Name of Accommodated Area:

1. _____
2. _____
3. _____
4. _____
5. _____

X. Applicable Framework Standards: Kindergarten
Standard _____

_____
_____
_____
_____

Standard _____

_____
_____
_____
_____

Standard _____

_____

_____

_____

_____

Standard _____

_____

_____

_____

_____

Standard _____

_____

_____

_____

_____

XI. **Evaluation and Comments** (i.e.: How well did the plan work? Great responses? What aspects are especially effective? Not effective? What improvements are needed? Ideas for follow up activities and other notes)

_____

_____

_____

_____

Germinating Activities

Watching a seed or bulb transform into a plant almost occurs as a miracle that can teach children about nurturing plant life. Seeds and bulbs can be purchased inexpensively, some even from the 99-cent store. Alternatively creating a class garden with vegetables and flowers in a raised or window box can be a great project if there is room in the teaching environment.

1. Germinating Seeds in Zip Sandwich Bags or Clear Plastic Cups

This is a time honored springtime activity. Every time this activity is presented the children will become excited when their seeds begin to sprout.

Materials

- ❖ Zipper-style sandwich bags
- ❖ Seeds or unsprayed, undamaged white beans
- ❖ Paper towels
- ❖ Spray bottle
- ❖ Water
- ❖ Flat tray or pan for soaking seeds/beans (a few inches deep)
- ❖ Small pots
- ❖ Potting soil

Method

- ❖ Children and teacher soak beans or seeds overnight (soak a few extra in the event that one of the seeds doesn't germinate, there will be a few extras so everyone can continue to participate in the activity) in a flat pan, a few inches deep
- ❖ Give each child a zip-type sandwich bag
- ❖ Teacher writes child's name on bottom of zip bag using a sharpie marker
- ❖ Children snip a few (three to four) small holes on "top" of zip bag so seed can breathe
- ❖ Give each child a paper towel
- ❖ Children moisten their paper towel
- ❖ Children select bean (s) or seeds they choose to grow (again, allowing children to germinate more than one bean or seed will increase the chances they will have of actually growing a plant)
- ❖ Children place damp paper towel into zipper bag
- ❖ Children place seed into zipper bag (hole side up) on top of damp towel on tray in area with indirect light
- ❖ Children spray inside of bag lightly every other day (unless weather is quite hot and dry, in which case, spray daily)
- ❖ Children can document their observations about their seed in science journals
- ❖ When seeds have sprouted strongly, transplant into small clay or peat pots
- ❖ Children can decorate pots before planting if plants are intended for gift giving

Variation:
Germinate seeds between two plastic cups nested inside one another

2. Rooting Cuttings in Clear Containers
Many types of plants can be rooted from cuttings. Rosemary, some tomato plants (although I have never heard of a rooted tomato plant bearing fruit), African basil, wandering jew, and coleus root quite easily. Watching the roots sprout is very exciting. Somehow creating an environment wherein a plant can be brought to life gives children a true sense of accomplishment.

Materials
- ❖ Plant cuttings
- ❖ Clear containers (plastic is better)
- ❖ Water
- ❖ Window sill or an area with indirect lighting

Method
- ❖ Children select plant cuttings they want to root
- ❖ Children fill container with water and place cuttings in the container
- ❖ Children place containers in an area with sunlight
- ❖ Children observe plant and make sure container has sufficient water
- ❖ Children document their observations in their science journal
- ❖ When cuttings have rooted strongly, transplant into small clay or peat pots
- ❖ Children can decorate pots before planting if plants are intended for gift giving

3. Forcing Bulbs
This project requires advance planning. Bulbs are best forced after being chilled for several weeks in a refrigerator. Forcing bulbs is most successful in late December through March. Bulbs can be purchased inexpensively at garden supply stores, stores such as Wal-Mart, and sometimes even 99-cent stores. Some bulbs can be quite toxic. If you have children inclined to mouth materials, do not present this activity to them.

Materials
- ❖ Bulbs, chilled for several weeks
- ❖ Gravel, small pebbles, marbles
- ❖ Measuring cups or scoops (for measuring pebbles)
- ❖ Containers (clear is good as roots can sometimes be seen)
- ❖ Water
- ❖ A shelf (or other appropriate location which receives adequate light) onto which containers can be placed for several weeks

Method
- ❖ Write children's name with an indelible marking pen on the bottom of containers they select for bulb forcing

❖ Children can decorate container before planting if plants are intended for gift giving

❖ Children fill containers with small pebbles or other similar material

❖ Children select bulb they choose to force

❖ Children place bulbs in their containers

❖ Children add water

❖ Place bulbs in area with sunlight

❖ Children observe and document changes they see in their science journals

❖ Children make sure bulbs have sufficient water

Suggested Reading:

Carle, E. (1991). *The Tiny Seed.* ISBN: 088708155X (Ages 5-8)

Cole, J., Degan, B., & Relf, P (1995). *The Magic School Bus Plants Seeds: A Book About How Living Things Grow.* ISBN: 0590222961

Ehlert, L. (1990). *Growing Vegetable Soup.* ISBN: 0152325808

Ehlert, L. (1992). *Planting a Rainbow.* ISBN: 0152626107

Ehlert, L. (1993). *Eating the Alphabet: Fruits & Vegetables From A to Z.* ISBN: 0152244360.

Flood, N.B. (2006). *The Navajo Year Walk Through Many Seasons.* ISBN: 189335406. (April is the time to plant corn, beans and squash).

Galdone, P. (2006). *The Little Red Hen.* ISBN: 0618752501. (Bread: from planting the seeds to harvest, grinding flour, to baking and enjoying).

Jordan, H.J. (1992). *How a Seed Grows.* (Let's-Read-and-Find-Out Science 1) ISBN:0064451070.

Krauss, R. (1989). *The Carrot Seed.* ISBN: 0064432106.

Orie, S.D. (1996). *Did You Hear the Wind Sing Your Name? An Oneida Song of Spring.* ISBN: 0802774857. (Spring is the time for planting).

Pallotta, J. & Thomson, B. (1992). *The Vegetable Alphabet Book.* ISBN: 0881064688.

Pluckrose, H.A. (1995). *Time. (Math Counts).* ISBN: 0516454595.

Target Areas of Learning

Physical Development

❖ **Fine motor skills:** using the small muscles of the hands and fingers: cutting, gluing, writing, drawing, placing plants into containers, holding writing/drawing tools correctly, filling containers with stones, zipping bags

❖ **Eye-hand coordination:** coordinating visual acuity with using the small muscles of the hand and fingers: pouring water, writing, drawing picking up stones (etc.), placing plants and cuttings into containers

❖ **Sensory discrimination:**

• **Visual discrimination** (sight): visually identifying materials and assembling plant containers

• **Tactile discrimination** (touch): differentiating physical properties of materials through touch: touching plants, gravel, pebbles et cetera

Cognitive Development

- ❖ **Language Arts**
  - • **Verbal skills**
    - ○ **Language development**: carrying on conversations relating to the growth and development of plants
    - ○ **Vocabulary development**: adding words relating to plants in general and germinating plants into the working vocabulary
  - • **Emergent literacy**
    - ○ **Word recognition**: connecting word symbols with labeled physical object
    - ○ **Emergent writing**: writing in science journals, describing components of the activity and the processes used to write in the journals
    - ○ **Sequencing (temporal ordering)**: relating the process of germinating a plant in the order it occurred
- ❖ **Math Skills**
  - • **Mathematical literacy**
    - ○ **1 to 1 Correspondence**: counting plants that germinate, counting numbers of rocks
  - • **Mathematical applications**
    - ○ **Measuring**: stones, quantities of water, amounts of change in growth of plants
    - ○ **Seriation**
      - – **Time**: noting the sequential relationship from one event to another as measured by a standard interval such as a minute, an hour; associating specific events with an appointed time in the day and identifying that appointed time on a clock
      - – **Calendar**: placing numbers in order to denote the passage of days, weeks, months, seasons while plants are growing and when plants die
    - ○ **Common relatedness**: linking items that are not the same but are related such as plant and pot, plant and soil, and so on
- ❖ **Science**
  - • **Scientific processes**
    - ○ **Inquiry**: an organized search for knowledge regarding plant germination
    - ○ **Prediction**: relating an anticipated outcome regarding plant growth and development
    - ○ **Observation:** carefully watching attentively and noting plant growth and development
    - ○ **Documentation**: writing and drawing observations of plant growth and development
    - ○ **Review**: comparing predictions and actual outcomes of plant growth, assessing value of any mistakes that occurred
  - • **Life science**
    - ○ Differentiating organisms from inorganic objects
    - ○ Understanding all living things have common needs of for life

- o **Responsibility**: understanding that plants need a certain level of care absent of which that plant will either become sick or die
- o **Recognizing health**: noticing appearance of plants
- o **Death**: if a plant lives it will sometime die
- **Cause and effect: relationships between actions and outcomes:** what happens when plant is watered, what happens if plant is not watered
- **Hygiene:** maintaining an appropriate level of personal cleanliness by washing hands thoroughly afterward when working in the garden

Social Development

- ❖ **Cooperative learning**: working well with others
- ❖ **Sharing**: understanding that classroom materials for project are intended to be shared by all students in the class and behaving accordingly
- ❖ **Taking turns:** allowing others a fair use of materials as a community resource and turns at tasks that might be considered a privilege
- ❖ **Collaboration**: planning, creating, and caring for plants as a group project
- ❖ **Patience**: diligence: ongoing care of the plant
- ❖ **Maintaining classroom environment**: helping with clean up
- ❖ **Following instructions**: using the tools as instructed, cleaning up

Emotional Development

- ❖ **Self-esteem**: feeling a sense of accomplishment by successfully growing a plant of one's own
- ❖ **Nurturing**: learning a sense of responsibility and concern in the process of caring for plants

Creative Expression

- ❖ **Expression of self**: 3-dimensional arts: garden keeping and growing plants
- ❖ **Expression of self**: 2-dimensional arts: decorating containers
- ❖ **Writing and illustration:** drawing pictures of the plant growth sequence in science journals
- ❖ **Creative risk**: attempting to grow plants and document experience in a journal
- ❖ **Developing aesthetic appreciation**: appreciating the beauty of plant life

Possible Accommodations for *Germinating Activities*

ADHD

- ❖ Use positive reinforcement (praise) when child follows directions, works well with others
- ❖ Offer more time or break activity up into several smaller sessions
- ❖ Allow child to function as a helper
- ❖ Allow child independent time to write/draw observations in note book
- ❖ Lower the ratio to allow for more supervision

❖ For activities that require much clean up, allow for a longer clean up/ transition time

❖ Put an old tee shirt over child's clothing for freer play

❖ Offer a tray to contain activity materials in the child's workspace, and a splat mat underneath the desk if needed.

Developmental Delays

❖ Explain the activity using short simple phrases being sure eye contact is made

❖ Demonstrate activity in advance step-by-step using realia, photographs or videos

❖ Lower the ratio to allow for more supervision

❖ Offer more time or break activity up into several smaller sessions

❖ Have child work with a buddy

❖ Use primary picture paper for pages of journal for easier note taking (see Appendix A-2)

❖ Place materials child has chosen on a tray or place a splat mat beneath tables if wet media are being used

❖ Offer positive feedback as the child is working, and when activity is being completed

Autism Spectrum Disorders

❖ Explain the activity using short simple phrases being sure eye contact is made

❖ Demonstrate the activity in advance steps-by-step using realia, photographs or videos

❖ Offer more time or break activity up into several smaller sessions

❖ Allow child to become accustomed to the activity by observing others initially, perhaps even doing task a day later when task seems more familiar

❖ Demonstrate the activity in advance

❖ Show child that the activity is on the schedule for this day

❖ Use positive reinforcement when child participates

❖ Pair child with a more competent and patient partner (if possible, use the same partner for the child's buddy as autistic children prefer familiarity)

❖ Reduce quantity of choices

Visual Impairments

❖ Use larger bulbs, cuttings, beans, stones, containers

❖ Lower the ratio

❖ Offer a desk top size magnifying glass to observe changes (similar to the ones used for needlework, found in craft stores)

❖ Journaling can be dictated

❖ Offer more time, if needed, to complete activity, or for cleanup

❖ Have child work with a buddy

❖ Offer the child adaptive tools for planting, writing, drawing, cutting, and so on.

Orthopedic Impairments

❖ Check child's positioning

❖ Adjust furniture and situate activity in such a way that activity is accessible to the child

❖ Place activity on an individual tray for easier accessibility

❖ Use hand-over-hand method of guiding child's hands if hands or fingers lack strength or dexterity for working with plants or journal writing
❖ Use large clear plastic containers for rooting plants
❖ Use larger containers, rocks, bulbs for *Forcing Bulbs* (for easier grasping)

Gifted and Talented Education (GATE)
❖ Increase the number of vocabulary words
❖ Add more challenging words to the vocabulary list
❖ Set up activity such that child observes plant at regular intervals (every two hours for example) to note changes
❖ Ask child to find stories about plants and gardening in the class or school library and share with the class
❖ Ask child to change growing conditions for plants (e.g. remove light, water with juice instead of water) and compare to plant grown in regular conditions

English Language Learners (ELL)
❖ Explain activity using short simple phrases being sure eye contact is made
❖ Demonstrate the activity in advance steps-by-step using realia, photographs or videos
❖ Simplify vocabulary words
❖ Place vocabulary words on cards for reference when journal writing
❖ Teach and review vocabulary words in small groups or individually
❖ Use positive reinforcement when child uses or attempts to us vocabulary words

Content Standards For Kindergarten Met By This Activity

English Language Arts
> Reading (1.0, 1.1, 1.2, 1.3, 1.5, 1.6, 1.17, 1.18)
> Writing (1.0, 1.1, 1.2, 1.3, 1.4)
> Written and Oral Language (1.0, 1.1, 1.2)

Mathematics
> Algebra, Sets and Sorting (1.0, 1.1)
> Measurement and Geometry (1.0, 1.1, 1.2, 1.3)
> Statistics (1.0, 1.1)

Science
> Physical Science (1.a)
> Life Science (2.a, 2.c)
> Investigation and Experimentation (4.a, 4.b, 4.c, 4.d, 4.e)

History and Social Science
> Following Rules (K.1, K.1.1)
> Using a calendar to sequence events (K.5)

Learning Plan

    I. **Name of Activity:** Germinating Activities

   II. **Date of Presentation:**

  III. **Age or Grade Level: Pre-K to Kindergarten**

  IV. **Ratio of teachers to children needed for this activity:** 1:10

   V. **Target Areas of Learning / Goals and Objectives** (target areas of learning directly relate to "VI. Evaluation Rubric")

      1. Physical: _____

      2. Cognitive: _____

      3. Social: _____

      4. Emotional: _____

      5. Creative: _____

  VI. **Evaluation Rubric:** (if more than two learning areas are being evaluated, a spreadsheet form may be preferred)

Targeted Area of Learning	Targeted Area of Learning
_____	_____
_____	_____
4. Always _____	**4.** Always _____
3. Usually _____	**3.** Usually _____
2. Sometimes _____	**2.** Sometimes _____
1. Rarely _____	**1.** Rarely _____

Germinating Seeds in Zip Sandwich Bags or Clear Plastic Cups

 VII. **Materials and Preparation Needed**

    1. Zipper style sandwich bags
    2. Seeds or unsprayed, undamaged white beans
    3. Paper towels
    4. Spray bottle
    5. Water
    6. Flat tray or pan for soaking seeds/beans (a few inches deep)
    7. Small pots
    8. Potting soil

VIII. **Procedures**

    1. Children and teacher soak beans or seeds overnight in a flat pan, a few inches deep (**Note:** Soak a few extra in the event that some of them don't germinate)
    2. Give each child a zip-type sandwich bag

3. Teacher writes child's name on bottom of zip bag using a sharpie marker
4. Children snip a few (three to four) small holes on "top" of zip bag so seed can breathe
5. Give each child a paper towel
6. Children moisten their paper towel
7. Children select bean (s) or seeds they choose to grow (again, allowing children to germinate more than one bean or seed will increase the chances they will have of actually growing a plant)
8. Children place damp paper towel into zipper bag
9. Children place seed into zipper bag (hole side up) on top of damp towel on tray in area with indirect light
10. Children spray inside of bag lightly every other day (unless weather is quite hot and dry, in which case, spray daily)
11. Children can document their observations about their seed in science journals
12. When seeds have sprouted strongly, transplant into small clay or peat pots
13. Children can decorate pots before planting if plants are intended for gift giving
   Optional method: Seeds can be germinated between two plastic cups nested inside one another

Variations

1. Rooting Cuttings in Clear Containers

Materials and Preparation
1. Plant cuttings
2. Clear containers (plastic is better)
3. Water
4. Window sill or an area with indirect lighting

Procedures
1. Children select plant cuttings they want to root
2. Children fill container with water and place cuttings in the container
3. Children place containers in an area with sunlight
4. Children observe plant and make sure container has sufficient water
5. Children document their observations in their science journal
6. When cuttings have rooted strongly, transplant into small clay or peat pots
7. Children can decorate pots before planting if plants are intended for gift giving

2. Forcing Bulbs
Materials and Preparation
1. Bulbs, chilled for several weeks
2. Gravel, small pebbles, marbles

3. Measuring cups or scoops (for measuring pebbles)
4. Containers (clear is good as roots can sometimes be seen)
5. Water
6. A shelf (or other appropriate location which receives adequate light) onto which containers can be placed for several weeks

Procedures
1. Write children's name with an indelible marking pen on the bottom of containers they select for bulb forcing
2. Children can decorate container before planting if plants are intended for gift giving
3. Children fill containers with small pebbles or other similar material
4. Children select bulb they choose to force
5. Children place bulbs in their containers
6. Children add water
7. Place bulbs in area with sunlight
8. Children observe and document changes they see in their science journals
9. Children make sure bulbs have sufficient water

IX. **Accommodations** (changes to accommodate learning diversity)
   Name of Accommodated Area:
   1. _____
   2. _____
   3. _____
   4. _____
   5. _____

X. **Applicable Framework Standards: Kindergarten**
   Standard _____
   _____
   _____
   _____
   _____

   Standard _____
   _____
   _____
   _____
   _____

   Standard _____
   _____
   _____
   _____
   _____

Standard _____

_____

_____

_____

_____

Standard _____

_____

_____

_____

_____

XI. Evaluation and Comments (i.e.: How well did the plan work? Great responses? What aspects are especially effective? Not effective? What improvements are needed? Ideas for follow up activities and other notes)

_____

_____

_____

_____

Ocean in a Bottle

This has the potential to be an exceptionally messy activity. It is best presented in an area wherein spills of liquid water color (or food coloring) and oil will not create an environmental or decorating tragedy. Outside is best.

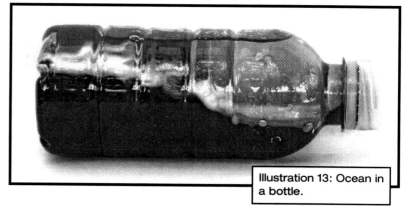

Illustration 13: Ocean in a bottle.

Ocean in a Bottle teaches that water is lighter than oil and will not mix with it. This activity uses recycled materials, which is in and of itself an excellent lesson. There are brands of drinking water that sell the half pint size of drinking water in longer and thinner bottles, which are preferable to the shorter fat ones. The teacher will need to start collecting the water bottles in advance. Each child will need an empty bottle with the label taken off.

If there is some residue of adhesive, a little bit of baby oil rubbed on the bottle may be helpful in removal. Buff the area with a paper towel. If the teacher is fanatical, the adhesive can be completely removed with a product called "Oops". This product must be used away from children, and in a well-ventilated environment. The fumes are quite strong. Another alternative is to just leave a bit of the label on the spot where the adhesive is used, and call it "The Bottom".

Ask the children to make predictions about possible outcomes of this activity. Have the children write down these predictions. After the activity is completed (complete with allowing the glued caps to dry prior to playing with their oceans), ask them to check their predictions and determine how accurate they were.

Blue and green liquid water colors look nice with baby oil, if the teacher is using the yellower vegetable oils, red and yellow liquid water colors look better. Liquid watercolor comes in a spectrum of colors. It may be fun to select unusual combinations to see what the outcome will be. Liquid watercolors are available from Discount School Supply (www.discountschoolsupply.com or 1-800-627-2829). They are much less expensive than food color and the company ordinarily gets orders to customers within a week. Large bottles of food coloring are available at restaurant supply stores such as Smart and Final. If a teacher buys the larger sizes of coloring, strongly consider decanting it into smaller containers such as a Nancy bottle or bottles that have eyedroppers. This is recommended for two reasons. The first is that spills will be of a smaller quantity, and the second is that the large quantities seem to encourage the use larger amounts of coloring. Larger quantities of color do not necessarily create a more attractive result. Also be advised that food coloring tends to stain fingers, tables, clothing, and so on.

The teacher may want to add funnels to the water table and sand box a few weeks before this activity so children get some experience using them prior to this activity.

Particularly if there are a number of children in the class who are emergent readers, take the time to label the items used in this, and all, activities as much as is practical. This way the children will begin to associate the written word with the actual objects being used for the activity.

Assembling *Ocean in a Bottle* might best be done in a sink, plastic basins or pans that are not too deep to control the inevitable splatters and spills. This is a smock activity, as the children's fingers and everything that comes in contact with the coloring medium with become that color. Discount

School Supply also has disposable children's aprons and well as plastic gloves, both of which are very inexpensive. Many brands of baby oil (available at Dollar Stores) have a pull out spout, which will also reduce the level of mess generated. Using droppers (one pipette dropper filled with color should be sufficient to color a half or one pint water bottle) will also control some mess and add the possibility of counting squirts or drops, and the sensory experience of touching the soft plastic.

Materials

- ❖ Plastic pans, basins or trays
- ❖ One label free, clean, empty half pint water bottle for each person participating in this activity
- ❖ Plastic dish basins, in which pouring can occur (available at Dollar Stores)
- ❖ Mineral or baby oil (available at Dollar Stores)
- ❖ Liquid water color, preferably decanted into eye dropper type containers or Nancy bottles
  Note: When choosing coloring agents, consider using a couple of tablespoons of Colorations brand liquid water color (available from Discount School Supply 1-800-627-2829) rather than food coloring, the colors are brighter and liquid watercolors are significantly less expensive. They stain less as well.
- ❖ Pipette eye droppers
- ❖ Water
- ❖ Funnels
- ❖ White glue
- ❖ Smocks, or disposable children's aprons (available through Discount School supply as well, at time of press about $5 for 100)
- ❖ **Optional:** plastic glitz, or other little items that can be added to "float on the ocean"

Method

- ❖ Set out materials "buffet style" along a table or work surface on plastic pans
- ❖ Teacher demonstrates activity to the class.
- ❖ Using funnels, children first fill bottle a bit more than half full with water; add several drops of food coloring to mixture and whichever glitz children select.
- ❖ Fill the rest of the way (up into the bottle neck) with baby oil. Doing this portion of the activity in a sink may avert a clean up disaster.
- ❖ Finally, put white glue very lightly around the threads of the water cap, and screw cap onto bottle (this keeps this delightful mixture inside the bottle rather than in other less welcome areas). Using too much glue on cap will cloud the ocean.
- ❖ Allow bottles to sit upright without playing with them for at least overnight, and better yet, over a weekend. This will allow the glue in the cap to dry thoroughly and prevent messes.

Suggested Reading:

Bix, C.O., & Rauzon, M. (1994). *Water, Water Everywhere.* ISBN: 0—87156-598-6. (Reading Rainbow book. Discusses the importance of this resource: the water cycle, the ocean, recreation, transportation, and commerce).

Branley, F.M. (1967). *Floating and Sinking*. ISBN: 3-3341-00078-9114.

Cole, J. & Degan, B. (1994). *The Magic School Bus on the Ocean Floor*. ISBN: 0590414313.

Cole. J., Mason, J. B. & Degan, B. (1997). *The Magic School Bus Ups and Downs: A Book About Floating and Sinking*. ISBN: 0590921584 (Ages 4-8)

Cole, J., & Relf, P. *The Magic School Bus Wet All Over: A Book About Water Cycles*. ISBN: 0590508334.

McCloskey, R. (1989). *Time of Wonder*. ISBN: 0140502017. (Written and illustrated by McCloskey; beautiful descriptions of life on the seashore).

Pallotta, J. (1989). *The Ocean Alphabet Book*. ISBN: 0881064580.

Rose, D. L. (2000). *Into the A, B, sea: An Ocean Alphabet Book*. ISBN: 0439096960.

Target Areas of Learning

Physical Development

❖ **Fine motor**: using the small muscles of the hands and fingers: twisting bottle cap from water bottle on and off, holding water bottle steady, holding and squeezing eye droppers or Nancy bottles

❖ **Eye-hand coordination**: coordinating visual acuity with using the small muscles of the hand and fingers: pouring baby oil and water into bottle, dropping color into bottle

❖ **Sensory discrimination**
  • **Visual discrimination** (sight)
    o Visually identifying materials
    o Visually identifying how the oil and water do not mix
    o Visually determining the shade or tint of colors created by the amount of colors added to bottle (or the colors created if teacher chooses to allow children to mix colors- recommended)
  • **Tactile discrimination** (touch): differentiating physical properties of materials through touch: touching the baby oil and the water, comparing the sensations
  • **Olfactory discrimination** (smell): differentiating physical properties through the sense of smell: smelling baby oil
  • **Auditory discrimination** (hearing): listening and recognizing the sound pouring liquid, liquid moving inside the bottle

Cognitive Development

❖ **Language Arts**
  • **Verbal skills**
    o **Language development**: describing components of the activity and the processes used to create ocean in a bottle, describing the interaction between oil and water
    o **Vocabulary development**: adding words relating to *Ocean in a Bottle* activity to working vocabulary
  • **Emergent literacy**
    o **Word recognition**: relating objects and spoken words to written words

- o **Emergent language**: writing and drawing about *Ocean in a Bottle* in science observation journals
- o **Sequencing (temporal ordering)**: relating the experience of making and playing with ocean in a bottle

❖ **Math Skills**
- **Mathematical literacy**
  - o **Associating number symbols with quantity**: understanding that a specific symbol is always associated with a specific quantity
- **Mathematical applications**:
  - o **Measuring**: measuring out oil, water, and color using standard measures
  - o **Spatial relationships**: relating the oil and water to each other

❖ **Science**
- **Science processes**
  - o **Inquiry**: an organized search for knowledge regarding ocean in a bottle
  - o **Prediction**: relating an anticipated outcome based on logic, experience, or research
  - o **Observation**: carefully watching and noting what is seen
  - o **Documentation**: writing observations of *Ocean in a Bottle* which support/ disprove claims for a particular prediction or outcomes
  - o **Review**: comparing predictions and actual outcomes, assessing value of any mistakes that occurred
- **Cause and effect**
  - o **Relationships between actions and outcomes:** "What prevents oil and water from mixing permanently in the ocean bottle?" "What colors result from combinations of food colors?"
- **Differentiating:** organisms from inorganic objects/substances
- **Chemistry and physics**
  - o Objects and materials can be described in terms of the materials from which they are made (CA. Science Content Standard K-1a.)

❖ **Social Studies**
- **Environmental responsibility**: using recycled materials in activities

Social Development
- ❖ **Cooperative learning**: working well with others
- ❖ **Sharing**: all members of the class community have a right to utilize classroom resources during a project
- ❖ **Taking turns**: allowing other a fair turn with classroom resources
- ❖ **Collaboration**: consulting with one another to compare ideas of execution of activity and interpreting outcomes
- ❖ **Maintaining classroom environment**: helping with set up and clean up of activity
- ❖ **Impulse control**: resisting the urge to play with ocean in the bottle before the glue has dried
- ❖ **Following instructions**: using the supplies as instructed, following instructions for activity, cleaning up

Emotional Development
* **Self-esteem**: feeling a sense of self worth by creating ocean in a bottle, all attempts are successful, not matter the physical appearance
* **Accomplishment**: developing a sense of self worth from participating in and completing ocean in a bottle

Creative Expression
* **Use of creative media and expression of imagination**:
  * **3-dimensional visual arts:** creating a three dimensional decorative object
* **Creative risk**: being comfortable playing with colors and adding stuff to ocean in a bottle
* **Problem solving**: gathering data to see why oil and water do not mix

Possible Accommodations for *Ocean in a Bottle Activity*

ADHD
* Use positive reinforcement (praise) when child follows directions, works well with others
* Offer more time for activity
* Pour oil and water out of doors or in a room with linoleum floors, perhaps inside plastic basins or on trays
* Use Nancy bottles instead of eye droppers for dispensing colors
* Pour oil into a small watering type can for easier dispensing
* Allow child to function as a helper in setting up or cleaning up
* Allow child independent time to write/draw observations in note book
* Offer a carrel for independent journal writing/drawing
* Lower ratio

Developmental Delays
* Go over instructions for task more slowly being sure eye contact is made to be sure child understands the task using simplified language before presenting the instructions to the entire class
* Demonstrate the activity in advance steps-by-step using realia, photographs for child
* Pour oil into a small watering type can for easier dispensing
* Use Nancy bottles instead of eye droppers for dispensing colors
* Have ocean bottles made in teams, one child holding bottle, one child pour or adding color and switch
* Offer more time
* Use primary picture paper for pages of journal for easier journaling (see Appendix A-2)

Autism Spectrum Disorders
* Go over instructions for task more slowly being sure eye contact is made to be sure child understands the task using simplified language before presenting the instructions to the entire class

❖ Demonstrate the activity in advance steps-by-step using realia, photographs for child

❖ Pour oil into a small watering type can for easier dispensing

❖ Use Nancy bottles instead of eye droppers for dispensing colors

❖ Have ocean bottles made in teams, one child holding bottle, one child pour or adding color and switch

❖ Offer more time

❖ Allow child to become accustomed to the activity by observing others initially, perhaps even doing task with child having autism a day later when it seems more familiar

❖ If child has tactile sensory issues, bring baby oil into class so child can touch and smell it before the activity

❖ Show child that the activity is on the schedule for this day, include journal writing on the daily schedule

❖ Use positive reinforcement when child participates

❖ Pair child with a regular buddy

Visual Impairments

❖ Lower the ratio

❖ Use a bottle with a larger mouth

❖ Pour oil into a small watering type can for easier dispensing

❖ Use Nancy bottles instead of eye droppers for dispensing colors

❖ Use a funnel for pouring

❖ Have ocean bottles made in teams, one child holding bottle, one child pour or adding color and switch

❖ Adjust lighting to reduce glare

❖ Journaling can be dictated to teacher, paraprofessional, volunteer

❖ Offer more time if needed

Orthopedic Impairments

❖ Make activity accessible by adjusting the furniture or allowing child to work individually or with a buddy on a tray

❖ Check from time to time that child is positioned comfortably

❖ Have moist towelettes or a damp cloth available in case child becomes overwhelmed by the sensory experience

❖ Use a larger bottle

❖ If child lacks strength or mobility in hands or fingers use the hand over hand method to assist child in pouring or using dropper

❖ Pour oil into a small watering type can for easier dispensing

❖ Use Nancy bottles instead of eye droppers for dispensing colors

Gifted and Talented Education (GATE)

❖ Ask child predict possible out comes of and to try out mixing liquids other than water in bottle such as vinegar, milk (which will begin to smell after a while), liquid soap

❖ Ask child to respond creatively to the statement, "Mixing oil and water is like..." in writing

❖ Ask child to predict the out come of . . ., and then allow child to experiment with mixing colors

❖ Allow child to invent names for colors created

English Language Learners (ELL)

❖ Go over instructions for task more slowly being sure eye contact is made to be sure child understands the task using simplified language before presenting the instructions to the entire class

❖ Demonstrate the activity in advance steps-by-step using realia, photographs for child

❖ Be sure to label ingredients and tools

❖ Go over vocabulary associated with this activity: cornstarch, water, bowls, spoons, slimy, hard, soft, runny, evaporation, power, wet dry beforehand individually or in small groups

❖ Review and re-teach vocabulary

❖ Use positive reinforcement when child uses or attempts to use new words in speaking

Content Standards For Kindergarten Met By This Activity

English Language Arts

Written and Oral Language (1.0, 1.1)

Listening and Speaking (1.0, 1.1, 1.2, 2.0, 2.1, 2.3)

Mathematics

Measurement and Geometry (1.0, 1.1)

Statistics (1.0, 1.1)

Science

Physical Science (1.b, 1.c)

Earth Science (3.c)

Investigation and Experimentation (4.a, 4.b, 4.c, 4.d, 4.e)

History and Social Science

Following Rules (K.1, K.1.1)

Visual Arts

Artistic Perception (1.0, 1.2)

Creative Expression (2.0, 2.2)

Valuing Aesthetics (4.0, 4.1)

Learning Plan

   I. **Name of Activity:** Ocean in a Bottle Activity

  II. **Date of Presentation:**

 III. **Age or Grade Level:** Pre-K, Kindergarten

 IV. **Ratio of teachers to children needed for this activity:** 1:10

  V. **Target Areas of Learning / Goals and Objectives** (target areas of learning directly relate to "VI. Evaluation Rubric")

     1. Physical: _____

     2. Cognitive: _____

     3. Social: _____

     4. Emotional: _____

     5. Creative: _____

 VI. **Evaluation Rubric:** (if more than two learning areas are being evaluated, a spreadsheet form may be preferred)

Targeted Area of Learning   **Targeted Area of Learning**

_____   _____

_____   _____

   4. Always _____   **4.** Always _____

   3. Usually _____   **3.** Usually _____

   2. Sometimes _____   **2.** Sometimes _____

   1. Rarely _____   **1.** Rarely _____

Germinating Seeds in Zip Sandwich Bags or Clear Plastic Cups

 VII. **Materials and Preparation Needed**

    1. Plastic pans, basins or trays

    2. One label free, clean, empty half-pint water bottle for each person participating in this activity

    3. Plastic dish basins, in which pouring can occur (available at Dollar Stores)

    4. Mineral or baby oil (available at Dollar Stores)

    5. Liquid water color, preferably decanted into eye dropper type containers or Nancy bottles

      Note: When choosing coloring agents, consider using a couple of tablespoons of Colorations brand liquid water color {available from Discount School Supply 1-800-627-2829} rather than food coloring, the colors are brighter and liquid water colors are significantly less expensive. They stain less as well.

    6. Pipette eye droppers

    7. Water

8. Funnels
9. White glue
10. Smocks or disposable plastic children's aprons (also available from Discount School Supply; at time of press about $5 for 100)

    Optional: plastic glitz, or other little items that can be added to "float on the ocean"

VIII. Procedures

1. Set out materials "buffet style" along a table or work surface on plastic pans
2. Teacher demonstrates activity to the class.
3. Using funnels, children will first fill bottle a bit more than half full with water; then add several drops of liquid water color to the mixture and whichever glitz the children select.
4. Fill the rest of the way (up into the bottle neck) with baby oil. Doing this portion of the activity in a sink may avert a clean up disaster.
5. Finally, put white glue very lightly around the threads of the water cap, and screw cap onto bottle (this keeps this delightful mixture inside the bottle rather than in other less welcome areas). Using too much glue on cap will cloud the ocean.
6. Allow bottles to sit upright without playing with them for at least overnight, and better yet, over a weekend. This will allow the glue in the cap to dry thoroughly and prevent messes.

IX. Accommodations (changes to accommodate learning diversity)
Name of Accommodated Area:

1. _____
2. _____
3. _____
4. _____
5. _____

X. Applicable Framework Standards: Kindergarten
Standard _____

_____
_____
_____
_____

Standard _____

_____
_____
_____
_____

Standard _____

_____

_____

_____

Standard _____

_____

_____

_____

Standard _____

_____

_____

_____

XI. **Evaluation and Comments** (i.e.: How well did the plan work? Great responses? What aspects are especially effective? Not effective? What improvements are needed? Ideas for follow up activities and other notes)

_____

_____

_____

_____

Water Drops on Pennies Activity

This is a beautifully simple activity. Certainly it can be part of "a curriculum" or it can be a fun enrichment. The number of water droplets that a careful individual can get onto a single dry penny amazes people. One diligent community college group was able to get one hundred eight droplets of water onto the surface of their penny! The type of eyedropper used was the "pipette" type. The individual acting in the role of "dropper" happened to be both GATE (gifted and talented) and ADHD. Who knows which of those factors had an impact upon that accomplishment!

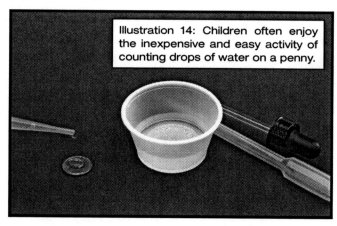

Illustration 14: Children often enjoy the inexpensive and easy activity of counting drops of water on a penny.

The teacher will want to have children work in groups. Three is a great number of children to be a designated as a group. In that way each child will have a job for the activity: one as the "dropper", one as a "counter", and a third as the "recorder".

Materials

❖ Paper towel pieces (one for each experiment)
❖ Pennies (one for each experiment)
❖ Eye droppers; either medicine bottle or pipette type (one for each experiment) the pipette type seems to allow children to get smaller, therefore more droplets onto the pennies
❖ Small, clean plastic containers (i.e.: lunch fruit containers) for holding water
❖ Pieces of paper and pens
❖ Chart paper
❖ Markers

Method

❖ Ask children to estimate how many drops of water they think a penny can hold
❖ Have children write down their estimate on a piece of paper
❖ Ask several children to share their estimate with the class and explain the reasoning behind it
❖ Write some estimates on the board
❖ Break students up into groups of three for each experiment
❖ Distribute paper towels, pennies, plastic containers, eye droppers to children
❖ Tell children to place penny on the paper towel
❖ With a small watering can or pitcher, pour water into each of the plastic containers
❖ Ask children to decide which person is the dropper, counter, and "recorder"
❖ Have droppers begin to place droplets of water onto their pennies
❖ The counter counts each drop, the recorder makes a tally mark for each drop counted
❖ Teacher may want to challenge the groups to determine which group can get "the most" drops on their penny

❖ When activity is complete, ask children about their results:
  • What happened?
  • Why did the outcome turn out the way it did?
  • Was it what they predicted?
  • Would dropping water onto the other side of the penny make a difference to the outcome?
  • Would the outcome be different if the penny were wet?
❖ The teacher can use chart paper or draw diagrams on the board of the children's predictions and outcomes
❖ Ask the children the differences between the two charts.

Suggested Reading:

Bix, C.O., & Rauzon, M. (1994). *Water, Water Everywhere*. ISBN: 0—87156-598-6. (Reading Rainbow book. Discusses the importance of this resource: the water cycle, the ocean, recreation, transportation, and commerce).

Cole, J., & Relf, P. (1996). *The Magic School Bus Wet All Over: A Book About Water cycles*. ISBN: 0590508334 (Ages 4-8; Discusses evaporation, condensation, precipitation)

McKinney, B. (1998). *A Drop Around the World*. ISBN: 1883220726.

Wick, W. (1997). *A Drop of Water*. ISBN: 0590221973. (Beautiful photographs of what can happen with a drop of water, also vapor steam and ice; discusses surface tension of water, evaporation, condensation)

Target Areas of Learning

Physical Development

❖ **Fine motor skills**: using the small muscles of the hands and fingers: squeezing bulb of eye dropper in such a way as to release very small drops of water onto penny, writing, drawing, holding writing/drawing/painting tools correctly if documenting the activity
❖ **Eye-hand coordination**: coordinating visual acuity with using the small muscles of the hand and fingers: dropping water onto penny with accuracy, writing, drawing in journal
❖ **Sensory discrimination**
  • **Visual discrimination** (sight): seeing the drops go onto the penny visually and counting them
  • **Tactile discrimination** (touch): differentiating physical properties of materials through touch: feeling the drops of water come out of the eye dropper

Cognitive Development

❖ **Language Arts**
  • **Verbal Skills**
    o **Language development**: describing components of the activity and the processes used to predict and produce the event of dropping water onto pennies with team mates and reporting results of their experiment to class

- o **Vocabulary development**: adding to the body of words and phrases understood and used in speech relating to the experiment such as the phrases "surface tension" and "pipette droppers"
- **Emergent literacy**
  - o **Symbol and word recognition, and interpretation:** recognizing that particular marks have meaning and understanding that groups of letters create a word
  - o **Emergent writing**: noting results of the experiment; writing predictions and reasons for prediction, writing outcomes and possible reasons for outcomes; comparing the two events
  - o **Sequencing (temporal ordering)**: describing the experiment as it occurred in time
- ❖ **Math Skills**
  - **Mathematical literacy**
    - o **1 to 1 correspondence**: counting items in an organized way that shows understanding of the object's placement as a single entity in a group: counting water drops onto penny
    - o **Counting**: enumerating the drops as tally marks to quantify the number of droplets that fit onto the penny
  - **Mathematical applications**
    - o **Equivalency**: comparing the quantity of drops from the different groups of children's experiments
    - o **Seriation**: ordering the outcomes of the experiments in a graduation of quantity from smallest to largest or vice versa
- ❖ **Science**
  - **Scientific processes**
    - o **Inquiry**: inquiry: how many drops of water fit onto a penny
    - o **Prediction**: relating the anticipated number of drops based on logic, experience, or research
    - o **Observation:** carefully watching attentively and counting water drops for a scientific purpose
    - o **Documentation**: writing observations of dropping water onto pennies
    - o **Review**: comparing predictions and actual number of water drops their penny held, assessing value of any mistakes that occurred
  - **Cause and effect**
    - o **Relationships between actions and outcomes:** "What causes water to behave in the manner it does when being placed on the penny in small droplets?
  - **Physics**: the science of matter and motion, including understanding of surface tension of water which causes droplets of water to cling together until overcome by the force of gravity

Social Development
* **Cooperative learning**: working well with others as team members
* **Taking turns**: allowing other children to have a turn as whichever part of the activity the child perceives as fun
* **Collaboration**: consulting with one another to compare ideas of execution of activity and interpreting outcomes; working out which child will be responsible for which activity in an appropriate way
* **Maintaining classroom environment**: helping with set up and clean up of activity
* **Following instructions**: cleaning up, doing the experiments as instructed

Emotional Development
* **Self-esteem**: feeling a sense of self worth by successfully getting drops of water onto a penny
* **Accomplishment**: developing a sense of self worth from participating in a enjoyable group activity
* **Generosity**: allowing others to have the "cool jobs"

Creative Expression
* **Expression of self**: creating experiments in the appropriate manner and environment
* **Using creative materials**: trying out other kinds of liquids on the penny: does milk, juice, cooking oil produce a different result than the water?
* **2-dimensional visual arts and writing**: documenting experiment in journal writing and drawings
* **Problem solving**: gathering data, collaborating, delegating responsibility within the small group, having small and large group discussion relative to the possible and actual outcomes that occurred
* **Creative thinking**: brainstorming: considering all possible solutions to the water dropping experiment

Possible Accommodations for *Water Drops on Pennies Activity*

ADHD
* Use positive reinforcement (praise) when child follows directions, works well with others
* Offer more time
* Have the child work on a tray to contain materials
* Allow child to function as a helper in setting up or cleaning up
* Allow child independent time to write/draw observations in note book
* Offer a carrel for this child's group, if child finds the level of energy in class distracting
* Lower the ratio

Developmental Delays

- ❖ If necessary, before presenting the instructions to the entire class, go over instructions for task using simplified language, making sure the child maintains eye contact, to be sure child understands what to do
- ❖ Ask the child to repeat the directions/ instructions for an activity, to insure comprehension
- ❖ Demonstrate the activity in advance steps-by-step using realia, photographs for child
- ❖ When presenting the activity to the class, use visual images to demonstrate the process of the activity
- ❖ Check for understanding
- ❖ Use larger coins and droppers
- ❖ Have the child work on a tray to contain materials
- ❖ When working with entire class debriefing the experience, call on this child as one of the first: this child may have only one or two possible responses, allowing child to contribute will help build confidence and self esteem
- ❖ Offer more time
- ❖ Use primary picture paper for pages of journal for easier journaling (see Appendix A-2)

Autism Spectrum Disorders

- ❖ Go over instructions for task more slowly using short simple phrases being sure eye contact is made to be sure child understands the task using simplified language before presenting the instructions to the entire class
- ❖ Demonstrate the activity in advance step-by-step using realia, photographs for child
- ❖ When presenting the activity to the class, use visual images to demonstrate the process of the activity
- ❖ Put activity on daily class schedule, perhaps having a regular "science time" on the schedule
- ❖ Offer more time for the activity
- ❖ Give child the task which will afford him the most success (dropping, counting, recording)
- ❖ Allow child to repeat experiment after the initial presentation, so child has multiple opportunities to experience the concepts
- ❖ Make sure the activity is on the schedule for this day, and include journal writing on the daily schedule
- ❖ Use positive reinforcement when child participates
- ❖ Have the child work on a tray to contain materials
- ❖ Group child with her regular partners (autistic children prefer familiarity)

Visual Impairments

- ❖ Lower the ratio
- ❖ Use a standing magnifying glass so child can better see the experiment
- ❖ Place coin on dark paper for better visibility
- ❖ Adjust lighting to reduce glare

❖ Journaling can be dictated to teacher, paraprofessional, volunteer
❖ Offer more time if needed

Orthopedic Impairments
❖ Set the activity up so it is accessible to the child which may involve adjusting furniture or allowing that child's group to work on a tray
❖ Request that child's group offer orthopedically impaired child a choice of task
❖ Use hand-over-hand method to assist child on chosen task if hands and fingers lack strength or flexibility
❖ Use adapted tools: larger eye dropper, pens with cushions
❖ For writing: use a clip board with alligator clips on the bottom to secure journal paper

Gifted and Talented Education (GATE)
❖ Allow children to extend the experiment by predicting whether one side of the coin will hold more drops than the other, whether a clean or dirty coin has an impact on the number of drops, damp or dry
❖ Trying out other kinds of liquids on the penny: does milk, juice, cooking oil produce a different result than the water?
❖ Allow children to repeat the experiment several time to figure out the average number of drops: the mean, the median, and the mode
❖ Have children chart their multiple experiments on a bar graph
❖ Extrapolate possible outcomes for larger coins
❖ Have gifted children work with other children special needs children
❖ Have children discuss "What determines 'a drop" for the purposes of this activity"

English Language Learners (ELL)
❖ Go over instructions for task more slowly using short simple phrases being sure eye contact is made to be sure child understands the task using simplified language before presenting the instructions to the entire class: include going over the primary words children will learn from the activity: water, penny, dropper, surface tension, as well as number words
❖ Demonstrate the activity in advance steps-by-step using realia or photographs for child
❖ Demonstrate the activity in steps for child
❖ When presenting the activity to the class, use visual images to demonstrate the process of the activity
❖ Check for understanding
❖ If child is willing to participate in the debriefing of the activity, call on child earlier in the discussion to prevent "someone else took my answer"
❖ Debrief after activity is complete to reinforce vocabulary and to check for understanding
❖ Offer more time for journaling or note taking of activity

Content Standards For Kindergarten Met By This Activity

English Language Arts

      Reading (1.0, 1.3, 1.17, 1.18)

      Written and Oral Language (1.0, 1.1)

      Listening and Speaking (1.0, 1.1, 1.2, 2.0, 2.1, 2.3)

Mathematics

      Numbers and Counting (1.0, 1.2, 1.3, 2.0, 2.1, 3.0, 3.1)

      Measurement and Geometry (1.0, 1.1, 1.2, 1.4)

      Statistics (1.0, 1.1)

      Mathematical Reasoning (1.0, 1.1, 1.2, 2.0, 2.1, 2.2)

Science

      Physical Science (1.a, 1.b, 1.c)

      Investigation and Experimentation (4.a, 4.b, 4.c, 4.d, 4.e)

History and Social Science

      Following Rules (K.1, K.1.1)

Learning Plan

    I. **Name of Activity: Ocean in a Bottle Activity**

   II. **Date of Presentation:**

 III. **Age or Grade Level: Pre-K, Kindergarten**

 IV. **Ratio of teachers to children needed for this activity:** 1:10

  V. **Target Areas of Learning / Goals and Objectives** (target areas of learning directly relate to "VI. Evaluation Rubric")
      1. Physical: _____
      2. Cognitive: _____
      3. Social: _____
      4. Emotional: _____
      5. Creative: _____

 VI. **Evaluation Rubric:** (if more than two learning areas are being evaluated, a spreadsheet form may be preferred)

Targeted Area of Learning	**Targeted Area of Learning**
_____	_____
_____	_____
4. Always _____	**4.** Always _____
3. Usually _____	**3.** Usually _____
2. Sometimes _____	**2.** Sometimes _____
1. Rarely _____	**1.** Rarely _____

 VII. **Materials and Preparation Needed**
     1. Paper towel pieces (one for each experiment)
     2. Pennies (one for each experiment)
     3. Eye droppers; either medicine bottle or pipette type (one for each experiment) the pipette type seems to allow children to get smaller, therefore more droplets onto the pennies
     4. Small, clean plastic containers (i.e.: lunch fruit containers) for holding water
     5. Pieces of paper and pens
     6. Chart paper
     7. Markers

 VIII. **Procedures**
     1. Ask children to estimate how many drops of water they think a penny can hold
     2. Have children write down their estimate on a piece of paper
     3. Ask several children to share their estimate with the class and explain the reasoning behind it

4. Write some estimates on the board
5. Break students up into groups of three for each experiment
6. Distribute paper towels, pennies, plastic containers, eye droppers to children
7. Tell children to place penny on the paper towel
8. With a small watering can or pitcher, pour water into each of the plastic containers
9. Ask children to decide which person is the dropper, counter, and "recorder"
10. Have droppers begin to place droplets of water onto their pennies
11. The counter counts each drop, the recorder makes a tally mark for each drop counted
12. Teacher may want to challenge the groups to determine which group can get "the most" drops on their penny
13. When activity is complete, ask children about their results:
    a. What happened?
    b. Why did the outcome turn out the way it did?
    c. Was it what they predicted?
    d. Would dropping water onto the other side of the penny make a difference to the outcome?
    e. Would the outcome be different if the penny were wet?
14. The teacher can use chart paper or draw diagrams on the board of the children's predictions and outcomes
15. Ask the children the differences between the two charts.

IX. **Accommodations** (changes to accommodate learning diversity)
Name of Accommodated Area:
1. _____
2. _____
3. _____
4. _____
5. _____

X. **Applicable Framework Standards: Kindergarten**
Standard _____
_____
_____
_____
_____

Standard _____
_____
_____
_____
_____

Standard _____
_____
_____
_____
_____

Standard _____
_____
_____
_____
_____

Standard _____
_____
_____
_____
_____

XI. Evaluation and Comments (i.e.: How well did the plan work? Great responses? What aspects are especially effective? Not effective? What improvements are needed? Ideas for follow up activities and other notes)

_____
_____
_____
_____

Water Table Measuring Activities

Water tables are most frequently employed at the preschool level, which is excellent. Since many kindergartners, particularly children from lower socioeconomic levels, are still at the preoperational level per Jean Piaget, it is appropriate to continue using the water table in kindergarten.

If no water tables are available at the school site, check to see if there are any local resource and referral centers. These centers often have toy lending libraries from which an educator can take a water table on loan for a month. If that is not a possibility, teachers may wish to go to the Dollar Store and pick up plastic washing basins, which, though less elaborate, work quite well.

The water table can be the source of myriad opportunities to learn to dump, pour, measure, compare, quantify and thereby conserve the concepts of quantity for a wide variety of substances. And although the water table is not just for water any more, , water play remains an excellent activity for children. On a hot summer day, the water table can be filled with cool water and ice cubes. If the class, or an individual in the class, is experiencing high levels of stress, a water table that is filled with warm water and a very small amount of liquid tear free soap, may be used for washing trucks or dollies or house corner kitchen utensils. This can be quite a soothing activity.

Children with sensory issues may need time to warm up to this type of activity. If it is possible, have the water table out all the time. Keep it filled with whatever substance has been selected for a week, or even longer, should the children show serious interest in playing with that particular substance. If a child shows some reluctance to play at the water table, the teacher may consider placing small quantities in plastic bowls to allow the child to become familiar with the substances.

However, the water table can also be filled with a myriad of different substances: cornstarch, shaving cream, wet and dry flax seed, oobleck, cooked pasta, cooked or uncooked grains, white glue and shaving cream (equal parts) mixed with a small amount of unsweetened powdered drink mix, dirt or mud with or without straw or a combination of any of them. Wet paper shreds are very interesting, especially when mixed with shaving cream and a small amount of unsweetened powdered drink mix. Some educators or school sites object to foodstuff being used for school activities because people could eat that food. This is a value, which needs to be considered individually. If it is site policy, use other materials instead. Consider that, from time to time, foodstuffs can also feed the mind as well as the body.

Children begin to conserve when offered multiple opportunities to play with quantifiable and comparable substances. The water table can be an ongoing activity. What is put into the water table can be changed, either weekly, or more or less frequently, depending upon the interest exhibited by the children. Because children who are working at the table may have tendency to become messy, this activity is best offered in an area that easily swept and mopped up: outside in a shaded area or on a linoleum area indoors is recommended.

Water Table Measuring Activities
Materials
❖ One or more water tables, or plastic wash basins
❖ Fill the water table half to three-quarters full. Choose one or more substances, such as: water, water and ice, soapy water (use a few drops of no-tears type baby shampoo), cornstarch, wet or dry flax seed, wet paper shreds, shaving cream and small amount of unsweetened powdered

drink mix, dry bulgur wheat, cooked bulgur wheat, cooked pasta, mud or dirt, with and without straw (which will make an "adobe" like material), Oobleck (mixing cornstarch and water – see *Oobleck Activity* in the Science Activities chapter), or anything else that strikes a creative fancy. (Just be sure to test any new substances or ideas at home, before presenting to the classroom!)

❖ Measuring cups, bowls, spoons, funnels
❖ Sand toys
❖ If a potentially messy substance is chosen, the use of aprons or old t-shirts may be desired to protect children's clothing

Method

❖ Make sure water table is empty and clean of any substance used in it prior to presenting activity
❖ Fill water table about half to three quarters filled with the substance of the teacher's choice
❖ Add cups, bowls, spoons, and sand toys (shovels, pails, funnels, even waterwheels, sieves, etc.)
❖ Depending on size of water table, allow two to three children at a time to play with substance in each water table
❖ If children seem engaged, allow additional time for activity, and perhaps consider offering activity again during the next free play/centers time
❖ Ask children open-ended questions to encourage children to reflect upon the relative quantities in each measure of the substances
❖ Activity is best offered in an area that easily swept and mopped up: outside in a shaded area or on a linoleum area indoors; water table can be an ongoing activity.

Variations:

• A possible extension of this activity is to offer children opportunities to draw or journal about the water table play
• Having manipulatives designated for outdoor play is recommended. These should be labeled according to type and stored in plastic containers that can be easily carried outside at appropriate times. Allow certain manipulatives to be used in conjunction with the water / sand table (i.e., plastic blocks, Legos, cars, figures, farm and zoo animals, and so on, that may be easily cleaned and that will also hold up to the water / sand play). In this way, sociodramatic play can be integrated into all kinds of learning experiences.

Suggested Reading:

Allen, P. (1996) *Who Sank the Boat?* ISBN: 069811373.

Arnold, T. (1998). *No More Water in the Tub.* ISBN: 014056430.

Bix, C.O., & Rauzon, M. (1994). *Water, Water Everywhere.* ISBN: 0—87156-598-6. (Reading Rainbow book. Discusses the importance of this resource: the water cycle, the ocean, recreation, transportation, and commerce).

Branley, F.M. (1967). *Floating and Sinking.* ISBN: 3-3341-00078-911.

Buchanan, K. (2004). *Esta Casa Esta Hecha de Lodo / This House is Made of Mud.* Bilingual edition English / Spanish. ISBN: 0873585801 (World view through the eyes of a Native American child)

Cole. J., Mason, J. B. & Degan, B. (1997). *The Magic School Bus Ups and Downs: A Book About Floating and Sinking.* ISBN: 0590921584 (Ages 4-8)

McKinney, B. (1998). *A Drop Around the World.* ISBN: 1883220726.

Pluckrose, H.A. (1995). *Weight. (Math Counts).* ISBN: 0516454609.

Pluckrose, H.A. & Choos, R.G. (1995). *Capacity. (Math Counts).* 051645451X.

Wick, W. (1997). *A Drop of Water.* ISBN: 0590221973. (Beautiful photographs of what can happen with a drop of water, vapor, steam and ice, and simple experiments).

Zion, E. (1956). *Harry, the dirty dog.* ISBN: 0-06-026865-4.

Target Areas of Learning

Physical Development

❖ **Gross motor skills:** using the large muscles of the body: standing, bending, leaning, lifting up containers of substances with large muscles of upper torso, arms, shoulders

❖ **Fine motor skills:** using the small muscles of the hand and fingers: scooping, pouring, dumping, measuring, perhaps writing

❖ **Eye-hand coordination:** coordinating visual acuity with using the small muscles of the hand and fingers: filling cups and containers, pouring from one container to another, scooping, shaping manually, spreading, grasping squeezing

❖ **Physical principals:** learning physical weight of a variety of substances

❖ **Sensory discrimination:**
  • **Visual discrimination** (sight): identifying substances and their properties visually (by sight)
  • **Tactile discrimination:** feeling the texture and sensory experiences of touching a variety of substances

Cognitive Development

❖ **Language Arts**
  • **Verbal skills**
    o **Language development:** conversations with other children in the context of the activity
    o **Vocabulary development:** identifying types of measuring tools, numbers, words used in measuring quantities, words describing the sensory qualities of substances to be measured to body of working language
  • **Emergent literacy**
    o **Journal "writing":** allowing children to write about water table activities using scribble writing, drawings, and invented spelling
    o **Sequencing (temporal ordering):** relating activities that occurred in water table in order

❖ **Math Skills**
  • **Conservation**
    o **Conservation of quantity**: understanding that the number in a group of items remains constant no matter how the items are arranged in the water table
    o **Conservation of volume**: equivalent quantities of fluid remain constant no matter what size or shape container of that fluid in the water table
    o **Conservation of mass**: equivalent masses are the same, no matter the shape the mass takes in the water table
    o **Reversibility**: a mass, fluid, or configuration of items cab be changed back to its original form without changing the quantity of mass, fluid, or quantity of items in the water table
  • **Mathematical literacy**
    o **1 to 1 correspondence**: counting items in an organized way that shows understanding of the object's placement as a single entity in a group
    o **Associating number symbols with quantity**: if children are writing about water table activities in any context, add number symbols to the writing list for children to use
  • **Mathematical applications**
    o **Equivalency:** more / less; single / plural; longer/ shorter; comparisons of materials scooped, poured, and manipulated at the water table
    o **Measurement**: comparing length weight, height, volume of substances used in water table
  • **Spatial relationships**: relating the aspects of physical objects to one another in the water table
❖ **Science**
  • **Scientific processes**
    o **Inquiry**: (informally) wondering how different materials behave when mixed, when poured, when wet, and so on
    o **Prediction**: articulating an expectation of the manner in which materials will behave; "What do you think will happen if we..." or "What do you think made that happen?" as the children play with the substances in the water table
    o **Observation**: playing with and noting (mentally) the manner in which materials behave in various circumstances
  • **Cause and effect**: hands on experiences relating to "what happens if...?" or "What happens when...?"
    o **Properties of water:** melting/evaporation: noticing that ice melts, water left in water table evaporate if left out long enough
  • **Physics:** the science of matter and motion, including understanding of surface tension of water, movement of light, movement of sound; the action of force on an moving or stationary object; including inquires related to: which items float, which items sink and why?
  • **Chemistry**
    o Noting (mentally) some of the properties of substances in their environment

    o Noting (mentally) "what happens when" different substances are combined or subjected to different environments as the child plays with the various substances in the water table

❖ **Social Science**
- **Diversity:** culturally specific types of substances presented (bulgur, cornmeal, flour, flax seed, dirt or mud with or without straw)
- **Diversity:** culturally specific types of tools used in water table play

Social Development

❖ **Working collaboratively**: inventing socio-dramatic scenarios at the water table, inventing water table games collaboratively

❖ **Sharing**: common use of water table scoops, spoons, toys

❖ **Taking turns**: allowing all children a fair turn at playing at the water table

❖ **Working cooperatively:** playing with other children at the water table in a group game

❖ **Taking care of classroom environment**: participating in cleanup

Emotional Development

❖ **Self-esteem:** developing a sense of self-worth while exploring materials, taking perceived risks while mixing substances

❖ **Self-confidence:** feeling secure being with others, experimenting with materials wherein there are no wrong answers

Creative Expression

❖ **Creative use of substances**: mixing a variety of substances as an investigation and as part of play

❖ **Creative thinking**: predicting possible outcomes of mixtures

❖ **Creative risk**: experimenting freely with substances without focus on the outcome

Possible Accommodations for *Water Table Measuring Activities*

ADHD

❖ Use positive reinforcement (praise) when child works well with others and behaves appropriately

❖ Lower the ratio/increase level of adult supervision

❖ Put a slightly smaller quantity of substances into water table to reduce mess

❖ Put an old tee shirt over child's clothing for less restricted play

❖ Place splat mats under tables of ingredients or have activity in an area where accidental spills are easily cleaned up

❖ Pair child with another child for opportunities for cooperative play

❖ Check on children often, to support and encourage appropriate behavior

Developmental Delays

❖ Go over instructions for activity more slowly using short simple phrases being sure eye contact is made to be sure child understands the activity using simplified language before presenting the instructions to the entire class

❖ Demonstrate the activity in advance steps-by-step using realia, photographs for child

❖ Put a slightly smaller quantity of substances into water table to reduce mess

❖ Place splat mats under tables of ingredients or have activity in an area where accidental spills are easily cleaned up

❖ Use positive reinforcement as the child succeeds identifying quantities

❖ Lower ratio/increase adult supervision: check in on child frequently

❖ Offer more time if child is enjoying activity

❖ Put an old tee shirt over child's clothing for less restricted play

Autism Spectrum Disorders

❖ Go over instructions for activity more slowly using short simple phrases being sure eye contact is made to be sure child understands the activity using simplified language before presenting the instructions to the entire class

❖ Demonstrate the activity in advance steps-by-step using realia, photographs for child

❖ Allow child to start out by touching very small amounts of sensory materials in a bowl and work up to large quantities incrementally

❖ Present the activity as part of the regular class routine, allowing the child to become accustomed to the activity

❖ If child seems to prefer playing with particular substances, offer those substances more frequently

❖ Keep a towel or moist wipes around to quickly wipe off hands if child seems to be going into sensory overload

❖ Have additional water tables, to allow all children opportunities to play with tables, while concurrently allowing additional play time for child with special needs

❖ Offer more time if child becomes engaged by activity

❖ Reduce the number of children playing at the water table to avoid overwhelming child

❖ Use positive reinforcement when child participates

❖ Simplify task: offer fewer bowls and cups: note which ones child particularly likes, and make those available for child's play

Visual Impairments

❖ Adjust the lighting to reduce glare, if used indoors, and move the table to the shade outdoors, if necessary

❖ If presenting the water table outside, offer the child the use of a shady hat or sunglasses

❖ Offer more time for child to become accustomed to tactile experiences at water tables

❖ Offer adapted tools (e.g., measuring cups) with larger identifying marks in bold simple script

❖ Offer larger bowls, spoons for their use

- ❖ Offer wider mouthed funnels and sand toys
- ❖ Put an old tee shirt over child's clothing for less restricted play
- ❖ Place splat mats under tables of ingredients or have activity in an area where accidental spills are easily cleaned up

Orthopedic Impairments
- ❖ Make sure child is comfortably positioned
- ❖ Place water table in a position that makes it accessible to the child
- ❖ Use a smaller plastic basin or bowl on a tray
- ❖ Put suction cups on the bottom of basins or bowls child is using to stabilize
- ❖ If child lacks strength or mobility, guide the child's hand into the material
- ❖ Place splat mats under tables of ingredients or have activity in an area where accidental spills are easily cleaned up
- ❖ Have moist towelettes or a damp wash cloth nearby to wipe hands off, if child becomes overwhelmed by the experience

Gifted and Talented Education (GATE)
- ❖ Ask child to predict possible outcomes from combining a variety of materials
- ❖ Ask child to measure out specific amounts of materials and place in another container
- ❖ Ask child to measure out 1/4 cup measures until a 1 cup measure is filled, 1/3 cup measures until 1 cup measure is filled, tablespoon measures until 1/4 cup is filled and so forth
- ❖ Ask child to write or dictate a story that includes descriptions of some of the sensory experiences child had at the water table

English Language Learners (ELL)
- ❖ Go over instructions for activity more slowly using short simple phrases being sure eye contact is made to be sure child understands the activity using simplified language before presenting the instructions to the entire class
- ❖ Demonstrate the activity in advance steps-by-step using realia, photographs for child
- ❖ Label the materials, and review the words on the labels individually or in small groups
- ❖ Include in list of words being taught the sensory words of cold, hard, soft, smooth, rough, sticky, slimy, dry, wet et cetera
- ❖ Use positive reinforcement when child includes or attempts to include new words in speaking

Content Standards For Kindergarten Met By This Activity
English Language Arts
Reading (1.117, 1.18)
Listening and Speaking (1.0, 1.1, 1.2, 2.0, 2.1)

Mathematics
> Numbers and Counting (1.0, 1.1, 1.3)
> Algebra, Sets and Sorting (1.0, 1.1)
> Measurement and Geometry (1.0, 1.1)

Science
> Physical Science (1.a, 1.b, 1.c)
> Investigation and Experimentation (4.a, 4.b, 4.c, 4.d)

History and Social Science
> Following Rules (K.1, K.1.1)

Learning Plan

    I. **Name of Activity: Water Table Measuring Activities**

   II. **Date of Presentation:**

 III. **Age or Grade Level: Pre-K to Kindergarten**

 IV. **Ratio of teachers to children needed for this activity:** 1:4

  V. **Target Areas of Learning / Goals and Objectives** (target areas of learning directly relate to "VI. Evaluation Rubric")
      1. Physical: _____
      2. Cognitive: _____
      3. Social: _____
      4. Emotional: _____
      5. Creative: _____

 VI. **Evaluation Rubric:** (if more than two learning areas are being evaluated, a spreadsheet form may be preferred)

Targeted Area of Learning	**Targeted Area of Learning**
_____	_____
_____	_____
4. Always _____	**4.** Always _____
3. Usually _____	**3.** Usually _____
2. Sometimes _____	**2.** Sometimes _____
1. Rarely _____	**1.** Rarely _____

VII. **Materials and Preparation Needed**
    1. One or more water tables, or plastic wash basins
    2. Fill the water table half to three-quarters full. Choose one or more substances, such as: water, water and ice, soapy water (use a few drops of no-tears type baby shampoo), cornstarch, wet or dry flax seed, wet paper shreds, shaving cream and small amount of unsweetened powdered drink mix, dry bulgur wheat, cooked bulgur wheat, cooked pasta, mud or dirt, with and without straw (which will make an "adobe" like material), Oobleck (mixing cornstarch and water – see *Oobleck Activity* in the Science Activities chapter), or anything else that strikes a creative fancy. (Just be sure to test any new substances or ideas at home, before presenting to the classroom!)
    3. Measuring cups, bowls, spoons, funnels
    4. Sand toys
    5. If a potentially messy substance is chosen, the use of aprons or old t-shirts may be desired to protect children's clothing (or disposable plastic aprons)

VIII. Procedures
1. Make sure water table is empty and clean of any substance used in it prior to presenting activity
2. Fill water table about half to three quarters filled with substance of your choice
3. Add cups, bowls, spoons, and sand toys
4. Depending on size of water table, allow two to three children at a time to play with substance in each water table
5. If children seem engaged, allow additional time for activity, and perhaps consider offering activity again during the next free play/centers time
6. Ask children open-ended questions to encourage children to reflect upon the relative quantities in each measure of the substances
7. Activity is best offered in an area that easily swept and mopped up: outside in a shaded area or on a linoleum area indoors; water table can be an ongoing activity.

Variations:

A possible extension of this activity is to offer children opportunities to draw or journal about the water table play

Having manipulatives designated for outdoor play is recommended. These should be labeled according to type and stored in plastic containers that can be easily carried outside at appropriate times. Allow certain manipulatives to be used in conjunction with the water / sand table (i.e., plastic blocks, Legos, cars, figures, farm and zoo animals, and so on, that may be easily cleaned and that will also hold up to the water / sand play). In this way, sociodramatic play can be integrated into all kinds of learning experiences.

IX. Accommodations (changes to accommodate learning diversity)

Name of Accommodated Area:

1. _____
2. _____
3. _____
4. _____
5. _____

X. Applicable Framework Standards: Kindergarten

Standard _____

_____

_____

_____

_____

Standard _____

_____

_____

_____

_____

Standard _____
_____
_____
_____
_____

Standard _____
_____
_____
_____
_____

Standard _____
_____
_____
_____
_____

XI. Evaluation and Comments (i.e.: How well did the plan work? Great responses? What aspects are especially effective? Not effective? What improvements are needed? Ideas for follow up activities and other notes)

_____
_____
_____
_____

Oobleck

Oobleck is a source of amusement for children of all ages. Working with this sensory material builds strength and flexibility in the small muscles of the hands and fingers, can soothe an angry spirit, and presents myriad opportunities for creativity and imagination.

Illustration 15: Children can start out with white Oobleck and add color to add a broader dimension to the experience.

Oobleck has the wonderful quality of being liquid and solid simultaneously. It can be grabbed as a solid, and when grabbed the *Oobleck* becomes slithery slimy and oozy, which may not be a word, but *Oobleck* deserves words of its own. It has been said that *Oobleck* got its name when children would play with it and respond, "Ooo-blech!"

All sorts of materials can be added to the basic recipe to augment or change the experience of working with this material. *Oobleck* can also be put into zipper bags for both storage, and for play. The true sensory experience requires that one just sticks one's hands into it, and plays freely.

In a college level advanced placement class presented at a high school just outside Los Angeles, the curriculum on one day included recreating some of Piaget's conservation experiments. It was getting toward Halloween, so a batch of *Oobleck* was added, just for fun. A young man attended who was probably in his junior year of high school. We could not get him to put his hand into the bowl of *Oobleck*. And once we succeed in doing so, we could not get him to give the bowl of *Oobleck* back, or let others touch it. *Oobleck* has that impact on people. It is wonderful, and creepy.

There is a delightful book by Dr. Seuss entitled, *Bartholomew Cubbins and the Oobleck*. If the teacher decides to read this book to the class, it may take more than one reading session. Plan according to the class' attention span. Another book suitable for reading before this activity is *Horrible Harry and the Green Slime* by Suzy Kline. This book is good for younger children whose attention spans are limited. The teacher may not want to bring up making *Oobleck* until the class has become involved with either of the books. Green is the formal color of *Oobleck*. Another great time (as if there are any poor times to make *Oobleck*) is Halloween. Green, red and red orange are good colors for Halloween *Oobleck*.

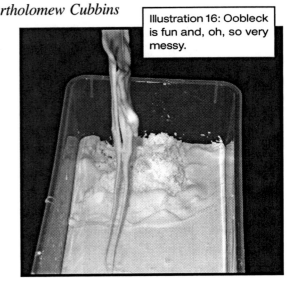

Illustration 16: Oobleck is fun and, oh, so very messy.

For children beginning to recognize word, labeling the box of cornstarch and other materials and tools used for making *Oobleck* will enhance the process of connecting the written and the actual items.

Materials

For each batch of Oobleck

❖ One box of cornstarch (available at the dollar store) for each batch of Oobleck to be made

❖ Two packages of powdered colored unsweetened beverage mix per batch of *Oobleck* (If choosing to use other coloring agents, consider using a couple of tablespoons of Colorations brand liquid water color {available from Discount School Supply 1-800-627-2829} rather than food coloring, the colors are brighter and liquid water colors are significantly less expensive. They stain less as well)

❖ A large bowl for each batch of *Oobleck*

❖ Large metal, plastic or wooden spoons

❖ Water in a container suitable for slow pouring, such as a small watering can

Method

❖ Children open and pour cornstarch into bowls

❖ Children add dry unsweetened powdered beverage mix

❖ Supervise children as they slowly add water and mix into the beverage mix-cornstarch combination. *Oobleck* is the "right texture" when it is at the same time hard to the touch, and melts over the fingers.

To dispose of *Oobleck*: set the bowl of *Oobleck* open to the air and the water will evaporate, leaving colored cornstarch. This could be a science activity wherein the children could predict how much time will be required for the water to evaporate from the concoction. Wet or dried *Oobleck* may best be disposed of in the wastebasket. It is not a good idea to put *Oobleck* in any form down a sink or a sink with a garbage disposal, as it may clog the drain.

Suggested Reading:

Kline, S. (1998). *Horrible Harry and the Green Slime.* ISBN: 0140389709.

Pascone, E. (1998). *Slime, mold and fungi: Nature close-up.* ISBN: 1567111823. (Great photographs of nature and simple experiments such as gray mold on white bread, bluish-green penicillium on a lemon wedge).

Suess, Dr. (1949). *Bartholomew Cubbins and the Oobleck.* ISBN: 0394900758. (Caldecott Honor Book).

Target Areas of Learning

Physical Development

❖ **Fine motor:** using the small muscles of the hands and fingers: stirring *Oobleck*, squeezing *Oobleck*, scooping, pouring, rubbing between fingers

❖ **Eye-hand coordination:** coordinating visual acuity with using the small muscles of the hand and fingers: pouring, measuring out ingredients, stirring ingredients

❖ **Sensory discrimination**

  • **Visual discrimination** (sight): visually identifying materials:

o Visually identifying colors, shapes, sizes of mixtures in use
o Visually identifying the process by which the substances are made
o Visually observing "the *Oobleck* effect"

❖ **Tactile discrimination** (touch): differentiating physical properties of materials through touch:
  • Touching the ingredients: corn starch,
  • Touching mixtures and differentiating the experiences through touch: *Oobleck* as hard or soft

❖ **Olfactory discrimination** (smell): differentiating physical properties through the sense of smell: smelling various "flavors" of beverage powder

❖ **Auditory discrimination** (hearing):
  • Listening and recognizing the sound of pouring liquid
  • Hearing and recognizing the sounds of mixtures being mixed

Cognitive Development

❖ **Language Arts**
  • **Verbal skills**
    o **Language development**
      – Discussing and describing the play involving the substances
      – Describing the sensory experience while playing with the substances
    o **Vocabulary development**
      – Naming ingredients and components of the activity and the processes used to create the various substances
      – Names of games invented, color words
  • **Emergent literacy**
    o **Matching spoken words, physical objects to written words**: correctly associating the auditory expression with the written symbol grouping
    o **Emergent writing**: writing and drawing in observation journals
    o **Sequencing (temporal ordering)**: recalling process of *Oobleck* making, play, and disposal in order

❖ **Math Skills**
  • **Conservation:** (leading, open-ended questions can scaffold the child into constructing these concepts)
    o **Conservation of volume**: equivalent quantities of *Oobleck* remain constant no matter what size or shape container of the *Oobleck*
    o **Conservation of mass**: equivalent masses of *Oobleck* (if difficult to hold) are the same, no matter the shape the mass takes
    o **Reversibility**: *Oobleck* can be changed back to its original form without changing the quantity of *Oobleck*
  • **Mathematical applications**
    o **Measuring**
      – Measuring out ingredients
      – Comparing one mass of *Oobleck* to another

- o **Equivalency**: comparing an *Oobleck* in terms of size or quantity
- o **Seriation**
  - **Time**: recalling how the substances were put together in correct order, recalling personal experience of the activity in order of occurrence, length of time required for evaporation
- o **Spatial understanding:** thinking about Oobleck three dimensionally

❖ **Science**
- **Scientific processes**
  - o **Inquiry**: an organized search for knowledge questions relating to how and why *Oobleck* behaves as it does; testing personal theories
  - o **Prediction**: relating an anticipated outcome based on logic, experience, or research
  - o **Observation:** carefully watching and playing with *Oobleck* and noting what is seen for a scientific purpose
  - o **Documentation**: writing observations of *Oobleck* which support claims for a particular prediction or outcomes
  - o **Review**: comparing predictions and actual outcomes, assessing value of any mistakes that occurred
- **Cause and effect**
  - o **Relationships between actions and outcomes**
    - "What happened when we...?" in the process of making the *Oobleck*
    - "What can we do with the *Oobleck*?"
    - "Why does Oobleck behave in the way it does?"
    - "How long will evaporation take?"
  - o **Problem Solving**: creating solutions to self-designed problems:
    - How the materials work
    - What can be done/constructed with the substances
    - Invented measuring tools
    - Creating variations with the different substances
  - o **Differentiating:** organisms from inorganic materials and substances
  - o **Chemistry/Physics**
    - Describing the objects in terms of the materials from which they are made
    - Changes in the state of water: liquid, steam, ice, evaporation

❖ **Social Studies**
- **Environmental responsibility**: developing a sense of stewardship for the planet and all that lives upon it: disposing of the *Oobleck* responsibly

Social Development

❖ **Cooperative learning**: working well with others
❖ **Sharing**: behaving according to the policy that community resources are for the entire community; making sure that each person has a fair opportunity to use those resources
❖ **Taking turns**: allowing others to play with the *Oobleck*

❖ **Collaboration**: inventing and consulting as a group to compare ideas of execution of activity and interpreting outcomes

❖ **Maintaining classroom environment**: helping with set up and clean up of activity

❖ **Following instructions**: using the supplies as instructed, following instructions for activity, cleaning up

Emotional Development

❖ **Self-esteem**: feeling a sense of self-worth through play with materials wherein there is no wrong answer or outcome

❖ **Self-confidence**: feeling secure within one's self through working in a "mistake free" and mistake embracing environment

❖ **Stress relief**: releasing stress and frustration through manipulating the *Oobleck*

Creative Expression

❖ **Use of creative media and expression of imagination**
  • **Dramatization**: inventing socio-dramatically in the context of playing with *Oobleck*

❖ **Using creative materials**
  • **Designing and creating the *Oobleck***: perhaps mixing different colors of powdered drink mix or liquid water colors
  • **Using tools creatively** with *Oobleck*
  • **Creative risk**: being comfortable playing creatively, actively and confidently following through on use of imagination, experimenting freely with *Oobleck* without focus on the outcome

Possible Accommodations for *Oobleck Activity*

ADHD

❖ Use positive reinforcement (praise) when child follows directions, works well with others

❖ Offer more time for activity if child seems engaged in play

❖ Make several batches of the substance so child will have more opportunities to play with it

❖ Measure out ingredients from inside plastic basins on floors that are easily cleaned

❖ Allow child to function as a helper in setting up or cleaning up

❖ Allow child independent time to write/draw observations in note book

❖ Offer a carrel for independent journal writing/drawing/substance play

❖ Lower the ratio of adults to children

Developmental Delays

❖ Go over instructions for task more slowly being sure eye contact is made to be sure child understands the task using simplified language before presenting the instructions to the entire class

❖ Demonstrate the activity in advance steps-by-step using realia, photographs for child

❖ Make several batches of the substance so child will have more opportunities to play with it

❖ Offer more time

❖ Use primary picture paper for pages of journal for easier journaling (see Appendix A-2)

Autism Spectrum Disorders

❖ Go over instructions for task more slowly being sure eye contact is made to be sure child understands the task using simplified language before presenting the instructions to the entire class

❖ Demonstrate the activity in advance steps-by-step using realia, photographs for child

❖ Offer more time

❖ Allow child to become accustomed to the activity by observing others initially, perhaps even doing task with child a day later when it seems more familiar

❖ If child has tactile sensory issues, have sensory activities available in the water table or in plastic basins daily so that the introduction and play with sensory materials is a part of the daily routine

❖ Place small amounts of plain cornstarch and the *Oobleck* in plastic bowls to develop a sense of familiarity with the *Oobleck*

❖ Have moist towelettes or a damp cloth available in case child becomes overwhelmed by the sensory experience

❖ Show child that the activity is on the schedule for this day, include journal writing on the daily schedule

❖ Use positive reinforcement when child participates

❖ Have the child work with a regular buddy

Visual Impairments

❖ Lower the ratio

❖ Offer larger quantities of substances for use

❖ Color brightly

❖ Use larger tools

❖ If child has tactile sensory issues, have sensory activities available in the water table or in plastic basins daily so that the introduction and play with sensory materials is a part of the daily routine

❖ Place small amounts of plain cornstarch and the *Oobleck* in plastic bowls to develop a sense of familiarity with the *Oobleck*

❖ Allow child to investigate substances in the child's own time: children with visual impairments make approach sensory materials cautiously

❖ Adjust lighting to reduce glare

❖ Journaling can be dictated to teacher, paraprofessional, volunteer

❖ Extend available time

Orthopedic Impairments

- ❖ Make activity accessible by adjusting the furniture or allowing child to work individually or with a buddy on a tray
- ❖ Check from time to time that child is positioned comfortably
- ❖ Have moist towelettes or a damp cloth available in case child becomes overwhelmed by the sensory experience
- ❖ Guide child's hand into bowl if child lacks strength or mobility using the hand over hand method
- ❖ Place a small amount of *Oobleck* into the child's hands
- ❖ Use padded or thicker stirring tools for easier grasping
- ❖ Use bowls with suction cups on the bottom to stabilize them

Gifted and Talented Education (GATE)

- ❖ Ask child to write and illustrate a story that has *Oobleck* in it
- ❖ Ask child to respond creatively to the statement, *"Oobleck* is like..." in writing; the child may wish to use a journal
- ❖ Ask child predict how long it will take for the water to evaporate from the *Oobleck* and to observe the evaporation process and record what is seen at regular intervals (1 time a day)
- ❖ Ask child to reconstitute evaporated *Oobleck* to see what will happen
- ❖ Allow child to make Oobleck using other liquids: milk, juice, vinegar, borax or liquid soap dissolved in water and so forth

English Language Learners (ELL)

- ❖ Go over instructions for task more slowly being sure eye contact is made to be sure child understands the task using simplified language before presenting the instructions to the entire class
- ❖ Demonstrate the activity in advance steps-by-step using realia, photographs for child
- ❖ Be sure to label ingredients and tools
- ❖ Go over vocabulary associated with this activity: cornstarch, water, bowls, spoons, slimy, hard, soft, runny, evaporation, power, wet dry beforehand individually or in small groups
- ❖ Review and re-teach vocabulary
- ❖ Use positive reinforcement when child uses or attempts to use new words in speaking

Content Standards For Kindergarten Met By This Activity

English Language Arts

      Writing (1.0, 1.1, 1.3)
      Written and Oral Language (1.0, 1.1)
      Listening and Speaking (1.0, 1.1, 1.2, 2.0, 2.1, 2.3)

Mathematics

      Numbers and Counting (1.0, 1.1, 1.2)
      Measurement and Geometry (1.0, 1.1, 2.0, 2.1, 2.2)
      Statistics (1.0, 1.1, 1.2)

Science

    Physical Science (1.a, 1.b, 1.c)

    Investigation and Experimentation (4.a, 4.b, 4.c, 4.d, 4.e)

History and Social Science

    Following Rules (K.1, K.1.1)

Dance

    Creative Expression (2.0, 2.1)

Visual Arts

    Artistic Perception (1.0, 1.2, 1.3)

    Creative Expression (2.0, 2.1, 2.2, 2.6, 2.7)

    Valuing Aesthetics (4.0, 4.1, 4.2, 4.3, 4.4)

Learning Plan

    I. **Name of Activity: Oobleck**

    II. **Date of Presentation:**

    III. **Age or Grade Level: Pre-K to Kindergarten**

    IV. **Ratio of teachers to children needed for this activity:** 1:6

    V. **Target Areas of Learning / Goals and Objectives** (target areas of learning directly relate to "VI. Evaluation Rubric")

        1. Physical: _____

        2. Cognitive: _____

        3. Social: _____

        4. Emotional: _____

        5. Creative: _____

    VI. **Evaluation Rubric:** (if more than two learning areas are being evaluated, a spreadsheet form may be preferred)

Targeted Area of Learning	**Targeted Area of Learning**
_____	_____
_____	_____
4. Always _____	**4.** Always _____
3. Usually _____	**3.** Usually _____
2. Sometimes _____	**2.** Sometimes _____
1. Rarely _____	**1.** Rarely _____

    VII. **Materials and Preparation Needed**

        For each batch

        1. One box of cornstarch (available at the dollar store) for each batch of oobleck to be made

        2. Two packages of powdered, colored unsweetened beverage mix per batch of oobleck (If choosing to use other coloring agents, consider using a couple of tablespoons of Colorations brand liquid water color {available from Discount School Supply 1-800-627-2829} rather than food coloring, the colors are brighter and liquid water colors are significantly less expensive. They stain less as well)

        3. A large bowl for each batch of oobleck

        4. Large metal, plastic or wooden spoons

        5. Water in a container suitable for slow pouring, such as a small watering can

    VIII. **Procedures**

        1. Children open and pour cornstarch into bowls

2. Children add dry unsweetened powdered beverage mix
3. Supervise children as they slowly add water and mix into the beverage mix - cornstarch combination. Oobleck is the "right texture" when it is at the same time hard to the touch, and melts over the fingers.

Variation
The bowl of Oobleck can be left open to the air. The water will evaporate, leaving colored cornstarch. This could be a science activity wherein the children could predict how much time will be required for the water to evaporate from the concoction. Oobleck can then be easily disposed of in the wastebasket.
*Note: It is important to dispose of Oobleck appropriately. Although, as wet oobleck, it can be flushed down the toilet, it **should not** be poured down the sink or garbage disposal, wet or dried, as it could potentially clog the drain.*

IX. Accommodations (changes to accommodate learning diversity)
Name of Accommodated Area:
1. _____
2. _____
3. _____
4. _____
5. _____

X. Applicable Framework Standards: Kindergarten
Standard _____
_____
_____
_____
_____

Standard _____
_____
_____
_____
_____

Standard _____
_____
_____
_____
_____

Standard _____
_____
_____
_____
_____

Standard _____

_____

_____

_____

_____

XI. Evaluation and Comments (i.e.: How well did the plan work? Great responses? What aspects are especially effective? Not effective? What improvements are needed? Ideas for follow up activities and other notes)

_____

_____

_____

_____

Smelly Jelly Air Freshener

Smelly Jelly is a fun kindergarten activity that can beautifully demonstrate absorption and evaporation. *Smelly Jelly* makes a wonderful gift if the teacher enjoys recognizing the various gift giving holidays.

Smelly Jelly involves the use of **water absorbing polymer crystals**: available as "Soil Moist" @ independent gardening stores. These are used to conserve water in agriculture. This material is pricey, however 1/3 cup will expand hundreds of times its size when a gallon of water is added. One container will go a long way. If the school or center purchases these crystals from the manufacturer, a much better price can be obtained. Food color or liquid watercolor can also be added, which, of course will make this a very, very, messy activity.

The polymer crystals absorb water very quickly. In the passing of a few months, depending on the width of the mouth of the jar, the quantity of jelly in the jar, and the warmth of the environment, the water will evaporate from the jar, leaving a very small amount peculiarly dried colored matter. Ask the children what they think happened, and the possibilities of what would happen, if some water were added to the jar. When asking those questions, one might want to include, "If the crystals absorb the water, how long will it take?" The estimates can be noted on a chart and compared to the actual time period required for the absorption of the colored water.

When using this activity for scientific investigation, it is advisable to use small jars like baby food jars, and the same scent for all of them. Combining a variety of scents in a single classroom may be overwhelming for the olfactorily-sensitive. If the intention of this activity is to be more of a science presentation, a single fragrance oil can be added to the mix with a very light hand. If the intention is for the project to become gifts that are quickly sent home, (a Mother's Day gift, for example) a wider selection of oils and a more liberal amount of fragrance oils can be added to the *Smelly Jelly* mix.

Materials

❖ 1/4 to 1/2 cup (depending on the number of jelly jars to be made) polymer water absorbing crystals (these are available @ garden supply stores such as Orchard Supply Hardware; they are not cheap but go a long way)

❖ A small jar for each child (a baby food jar, or a small jelly jar works; if using jelly jars, purchase also the rings and lids)

❖ Food coloring or liquid water colors
Note: When choosing coloring agents, consider using a couple of tablespoons of Colorations brand liquid water color {available from Discount School Supply 1-800-627-2829} rather than food coloring, the colors are brighter and liquid water colors are significantly less expensive. They stain less as well.

❖ Long handled wooden spoons

❖ Tablespoon measuring spoons

❖ Scented essential oils (available at craft stores)

❖ Water

❖ A large bucket (big enough to hold up to a gallon of water) or bowl for each scent

❖ A scooper or ladle for filling jars

❖ An oil funnel (available in the auto supply area of K-Mart or Target)

❖ Pieces of ribbon
❖ Pieces of open weave fabric such as lace (cut into squares large enough to cover mouth of jar)
❖ Heavy duty rubber bands
❖ Cellophane wrap (colored is cute) (cut into squares large enough to cover mouth of jar) or if using jelly jars, lids and rings

Method

❖ Mix 1/4 cup polymer crystals in each bucket or bowl
❖ Allow children to touch the dried crystals, ask them to describe what the crystals feel like to them
❖ Mix liquid water colors or food coloring into a gallon of water (use a different color for each bucket)
❖ Pour colored water into buckets
❖ Stir with long handled spoons
❖ Allow to set for 10 minutes, if all the water is not absorbed, stir and wait
❖ When crystals have absorbed all the water, children add a tablespoon or two of scent to each bucket (it is more fun to put different scents into different colors)
❖ Stir in scent
❖ Children use scooper or ladle to scoop crystals into jar (if mouth of jar is narrow, use funnel) until full within 1/4 inch of jar top
❖ Wipe jars off of any excess moisture
❖ Have children place colored cellophane over mouth of jar and affix in place with a rubber band; for jelly jars, place lid over the top of the jar and affix with ring (this is to prevent leakage on the trip home
❖ Place lace square on top of jar, tie with a ribbon piece

To Use

❖ Remove cellophane wrap or lid
❖ Replace lace and ribbon
❖ As crystals "dry out", more warm water can be added to freshen crystals
❖ These crystals last for up to a year, even if allowed to completely dry out, just add more water and essential oil, when necessary

For science experiment only:

Place a plastic ruler or a stick into jars with marks at regular intervals so children can accurately determine amount of evaporation over time; this information may be charted, or included in journals

Suggested Reading:

Cole, J., & Relf, P. (1996). *The Magic School Bus Wet All Over: A Book About Water cycles.* ISBN: 0590508334 (Ages 4-8; discusses evaporation, condensation, precipitation)
McKinney, B. (1998). *A Drop Around the World.* ISBN: 1883220726

Wick, W. (1997). *A Drop of Water.* ISBN: 0590221973. (Beautiful photographs of what can happen with a drop of water, also vapor, steam and ice; discusses evaporation, capillary action, condensation)

Target Areas of Learning

Physical Development
- ❖ **Eye-hand coordination**: pouring, scooping, cutting, tying, drawing, decorating jar
- ❖ **Fine motor skills**: cutting, holding, tying, writing, gluing
- ❖ **Physical principals:** experiencing the change in the physical weight of the polymer crystals
- ❖ **Sensory discrimination**
  - • **Tactile discrimination** (touch): identifying and differentiating textures with touch: soft, hard, rough, smooth, squishy, slippery
  - • **Visual discrimination** (sight): identifying colors; sizes; recognizing the change in the polymer crystals visually
  - • **Olfactory discrimination** (smell): identifying different smells: sweet, spicy; pungent, floral, odors pleasing and not pleasing to child

Cognitive Development
- ❖ **Language Arts**
  - • **Verbal skills**
    - o **Language development**: expressing responses to making smelly jelly verbally, having conversations while assembling smelly jelly jars
    - o **Vocabulary development**: learning names of substances, quantities of substances; describing sensations of touching substances; vocabulary explaining the process of absorption
  - • **Emergent literacy**
    - o **Letter and word recognition**: recognizing and reading letter combinations that create words from "Smelly Jelly" activity
    - o **Emergent writing**: describing in writing and with drawings predictions and observations of what was seen during activity in science journal
    - o **Sequencing (temporal ordering)**: relating the process of creating smelly jelly in the order it occurred
- ❖ **Math Skills**
  - • **Mathematical literacy**
    - o **Utilizing number symbols**: reading designated measurements on measuring cups and spoons
  - • **Mathematical applications**
    - o **Measurement**: using a standard measure to determine the appropriate volume of ingredients for "Smelly Jelly"
    - o **Equivalency**: comparing quantities of "Smelly Jelly" various jars

❖ **Science**
  • **Scientific processes**
    o **Inquiry:** "What will happen when we add a gallon of water to 1/2 cup of crystals?" "How long will the "Smelly Jelly" last?" "What will happen when all the water evaporates?" "What will happen if we add more water, will the crystals still work, once they have been used?"
    o **Prediction:** relating an anticipated outcome based on logic, experience, or research
    o **Observation:** carefully watching the process in the polymer crystals and noting what is seen for a scientific purpose
    o **Documentation:** writing observations of smelly jelly which support/do not support claims for a particular prediction or outcomes
    o **Review:** comparing predictions and actual outcomes, assessing value of any mistakes that occurred
  • **Cause and effect**
    o **Relationships between actions and outcomes:** developing curiosity which leads to scientific inquiry: "educated why"
  • **Differentiating:** organisms from inorganic materials
  • **Chemistry:** changes in the state of water: evaporation

Social Development

❖ **Cooperative play:** working well as a member of a team
❖ **Sharing:** items intended for use by the community are available for the use of everyone and may not be available at all times for individual use
❖ **Taking turns:** allowing others a fair use of materials as a community resource and turns at tasks that might be considered a privilege
❖ **Following directions:** making smelly jelly as directed
❖ **Collaboration:** planning, and creating "Smelly Jelly" in a group, sharing ideas
❖ **Negotiation:** learning to represent one's wishes for a particular color or fragrance in such a way that others in the group will consider those wishes favorably
❖ **Taking care of classroom environment:** helping with set up and clean up

Emotional Development

❖ **Developing a willingness to take a risk:** trying out and experimenting with polymer crystals, fragrance oils, and liquid water colors
❖ **Self-esteem:** as children feel confident when playing freely, they increase a sense of personal value, a stable sense of self-worth

Creative Expression

❖ **Use of creative media and expression of imagination:**
  • **2-dimensional visual arts:** decorating the tag and jar with 2 dimensional media
  • **3-dimensional visual arts:** decorating jar with ribbons, buttons and 3 dimensional media

❖ **Creative risk**: using decorative materials inventively: design/creativity trying out interesting combinations of colors and scents for "Smelly Jelly"

❖ **Problem solving**: gathering data in a group setting regarding polymer crystals to consider possible outcomes of how "Smelly Jelly" will work

❖ **Creative thinking**: brainstorming: considering all possible solutions to making smelly jelly

Possible accommodations for *Smelly Jelly Activity*

ADHD

❖ Ask child to repeat directions back to you

❖ Take out a small quantity of polymer crystals and place in a bowl to reduce quantity of any accidental spills

❖ Plan the activity on a linoleum floor, outside, or place splat mats underneath for easier clean up

❖ Present activity in a small group setting to keep energy level in control

❖ Use old tee shirts as smocks for freer play

❖ Use positive reinforcement frequently when child is producing desired behavior

❖ Offer a wider mouthed plastic jar, perhaps an automotive oil funnel or a scooper that has a narrowed pouring end

Developmental Delays

❖ Go over instructions for task more slowly being sure eye contact is made to be sure child understands the task using simplified language before presenting the instructions to the entire class

❖ Demonstrate the activity in advance steps-by-step using realia photographs for child

❖ When presenting the activity to the class, use visual images to demonstrate the process of the activity

❖ Ask the child to repeat the directions/ instructions for an activity, to insure comprehension

❖ Use old tee shirts as smocks for freer play

❖ Present activity in an environment wherein messes aren't a crisis and are easy to clean up

❖ Offer a wider mouthed plastic jar, perhaps an automotive oil funnel or a scooper that has a narrowed pouring end

❖ Offer wired ribbon for easier tying if fine motor skills are still emerging

Autism Spectrum Disorders

❖ Go over instructions for task being sure eye contact is made to be sure child understands the task using simplified language before presenting the instructions to the entire class

❖ Demonstrate the activity in advance steps-by-step using realia photographs for child

❖ When presenting the activity to the class, use visual images to demonstrate the process of the activity

❖ Have some "Smelly Jelly" around for a while to let the child become accustomed to it

❖ Have child work in a small group and/or with regular buddy
❖ Allow child to wear surgical gloves
❖ Present activity later in the week and place it on the posted weekly schedule (created with words and pictures)
❖ Allow more time
❖ Offer wired ribbon for easier tying if fine motor skills are still emerging

Visual Impairments
❖ Adjust lighting to reduce glare
❖ Offer a larger, wide mouthed jar, a scooper with a narrowed pouring end
❖ Present activity in a small group setting
❖ Choose a bright color for "Smelly Jelly"
❖ Allow child to select a scent that is not overpowering
❖ Offer wired ribbon for easier tying

Orthopedic Impairments
❖ Set the activity up so it is accessible to the child which may involve adjusting furniture or allowing that child' to work on an individual tray
❖ Offer a larger, wide mouthed jar, a scooper with a narrowed pouring end
❖ Present activity in a small group setting
❖ If hands or fingers lack strength assist child using the hand over hand method
❖ Pad scoopers and wooden stirring spoons with foam and tape or use professionally adapted tools for easier grasping
❖ Offer wired ribbon for easier tying

Gifted and Talented Education (GATE)
❖ Ask child to measure out using measuring cups and spoons that are not exact for example smaller are larger measures than are required so that child must calculate appropriate measures before mixing ingredients
❖ Ask child to create a chart or graph documenting class predictions
❖ Utilize "science experiment only" option
❖ Ask child to find out more information about water absorbing polymer crystals and the uses of them on the internet

English Language Learners (ELL)
❖ Go over instructions for task more slowly being sure eye contact is made to be sure child understands the task using simplified language before presenting the instructions to the entire class
❖ Demonstrate the activity in advance steps-by-step using realia, photographs for child
❖ Label items used in activity and review words associated with the activity: crystals, jars, water colors, fragrance oils, absorption, evaporation, color words individually or in small groups

❖ Check for understanding
❖ Give child a small list for reference for any writing activity
❖ Use positive reinforcement when child includes or attempts to include new words in speaking

Content Standards For Kindergarten Met By This Activity

English Language Arts

Reading (1.0, 1.2, 1.3, 1.4, 1.5, 1.17, 1.18)
Reading Comprehension (2.0, 2.3)
Literary Response & Analysis (3.0, 3.1, 3.2)
Writing (1.0, 1.1, 1.3)
Written and Oral Language (1.0, 1.1)
Listening and Speaking (1.0, 1.1, 1.2, 2.0, 2.1, 2.3)

Mathematics

Numbers and Counting (1.0, 1.1, 1.2, 1.3, 3.0, 3.1)
Measurement and Geometry (1.0, 1.1, 1.2, 1.4, 2.0, 2.1, 2.2)
Statistics (1.0, 1.1)
Mathematical Reasoning (1.0, 1.1, 1.2, 2.0, 2.1, 2.2)

Science

Physical Science (1.a, 1.b, 1.c)
Investigation and Experimentation (4.a, 4.b, 4.c, 4.d, 4.e)

History and Social Science

Following Rules (K.1, K.1.1)
Using a calendar to sequence events (K.5)

Visual Arts

Artistic Perception (1.0, 1.2)
Creative Expression (2.0, 2.1, 2.2)

Learning Plan

   I. **Name of Activity: Smelly Jelly Activity**

  II. **Date of Presentation:**

 III. **Age or Grade Level: Pre-K, Kindergarten**

 IV. **Ratio of teachers to children needed for this activity:** 1:4

  V. **Target Areas of Learning / Goals and Objectives** (target areas of learning directly relate to "VI. Evaluation Rubric")

     1. Physical: _____

     2. Cognitive: _____

     3. Social: _____

     4. Emotional: _____

     5. Creative: _____

 VI. **Evaluation Rubric:** (if more than two learning areas are being evaluated, a spreadsheet form may be preferred)

Targeted Area of Learning   **Targeted Area of Learning**

_____   _____

_____   _____

     4. Always _____   **4.** Always _____

     3. Usually _____   **3.** Usually _____

     2. Sometimes _____   **2.** Sometimes _____

     1. Rarely _____   **1.** Rarely _____

 VII. **Materials and Preparation Needed**

    1. 1/4 to 1/2 cup (depending on the number of jelly jars to be made) polymer water absorbing crystals (these are available @ garden supply stores such as Orchard Supply Hardware; they are not cheap but go a long way)

    2. A small jar for each child (a baby food jar, or a small jelly jar works; if using jelly jars, purchase also the rings and lids)

    3. Food coloring or liquid water colors

      Note: When choosing coloring agents, consider using a couple of tablespoons of Colorations brand liquid water color {available from Discount School Supply 1-800-627-2829} rather than food coloring, the colors are brighter and liquid water colors are significantly less expensive. They stain less as well.

    4. Long handled wooden spoons

    5. Tablespoon measuring spoons

    6. Scented essential oils (available at craft stores)

    7. Water

8. A large bucket (big enough to hold up to a gallon of water) or bowl for each scent
9. A scooper or ladle for filling jars
10. An oil funnel (available in the auto supply area of K-Mart or Target)
11. Pieces of ribbon
12. Pieces of open weave fabric such as lace (cut into squares large enough to cover mouth of jar)
13. Heavy duty rubber bands
14. Cellophane wrap (colored is cute) (cut into squares large enough to cover mouth of jar) or if using jelly jars, lid

VIII. Procedures
1. Mix 1/4 cup polymer crystals in each bucket or bowl
2. Allow children to touch the dried crystals, ask them to describe what the crystals feel like to them
3. Mix liquid water colors or food coloring into a gallon of water (use a different color for each bucket)
4. Pour colored water into buckets
5. Stir with long handled spoons
6. Allow to set for 10 minutes, if all the water is not absorbed, stir and wait
7. When crystals have absorbed all the water, children add a tablespoon or two of scent to each bucket (it is more fun to put different scents into different colors)
8. Stir in scent
9. Children use scooper or ladle to scoop crystals into jar (if mouth of jar is narrow, use funnel) until full within 1/4 inch of jar top
10. Wipe jars off of any excess moisture
11. Have children place colored cellophane over mouth of jar and affix in place with a rubber band; for jelly jars, place lid over the top of the jar and affix with ring (this is to prevent leakage on the trip home
12. Place lace square on top of jar, tie with a ribbon piece

To use
1. Remove cellophane wrap or lid
2. Replace lace and ribbon
3. As crystals "dry out", more warm water can be added to freshen crystals
4. These crystals last for up to a year, even if allowed to completely dry out, just add more water and essential oil, when necessary

For science experiment only
Place a plastic ruler or a stick into jars with marks at regular intervals so children can accurately determine amount of evaporation over time; this information may be charted, or included in journals

IX. Accommodations (changes to accommodate learning diversity)
Name of Accommodated Area:

1. _____
2. _____
3. _____
4. _____
5. _____

X. Applicable Framework Standards: Kindergarten

Standard _____
_____
_____
_____
_____

Standard _____
_____
_____
_____
_____

Standard _____
_____
_____
_____
_____

Standard _____
_____
_____
_____
_____

Standard _____
_____
_____
_____
_____

XI. Evaluation and Comments (i.e.: How well did the plan work? Great responses? What aspects are especially effective? Not effective? What improvements are needed? Ideas for follow up activities and other notes)

_____
_____
_____
_____

Chapter Twelve

History and Social Studies Activities and Learning Plans

A common thread in Vygotsky-based educational practices ... is the planning of activities that teach culturally meaningful cognitive concepts and skills. At the same time, activities are sensitively tuned to each child's capacity to learn, and they nourish children's natural curiosity, drive to discover, and desire to become competent members of their community.

– Laura E. Berk and A. Winsler
(regarding the Russian theorist, Lev Semonich Vygotsky)
Scaffolding Children's Learning 1997, page 147

Bread Tasting Activity

Teachers who enjoy cooking and exploring a broad palate of culinary experiences will very much relish presenting this genre of activities. It cannot be emphasized enough that teachers need to present activities that are satisfying to the teacher personally. A teacher sharing personal preferences will present the material with increased enthusiasm.

Food is always an excellent introduction to human diversity. *Bread Tasting* can be presented as an elegant, "grown-up" type activity, wherein the children are offered samples of a wide selection of different kinds of breads in a very grown up fashion. The children can be offered sips of apple juice to "clear the palate" as they try various different kinds of breads.

As a point in fact there can be all kinds of "tasting" activities: sandwich tastings, cake tastings, juice tastings, vegetable tastings, soup tastings and so on. The importance in this is that the children begin to be exposed to cultural diversity in the context of foods.

The sampling can be of raised or flat breads, or both depending on the diversity of breadstuff available. If there is access to many types of flat breads, then do a "flat bread tasting" and a "raised bread tasting". If not, consolidate to a "bread tasting".

Ask parents to recommend or bring in representative breads from their country of origin. Some may respond that they are "All-American", however people other than Native Americans came to the American continent from somewhere. If there are such parents in the class, it is recommended that you allow them to participate at the level they feel most comfortable. A teacher will win nothing in the educational arena by forcing unwilling parents to participate in any activity. It is possible to make the classroom environment and the curriculum presented so enticing that a good turn out will be predictable. One way to get better participation is to give parents advance warning. Let them know that their participation in an activity will greatly enhance the nature of the activity. Breads that can be prepared in advance, and frozen, are one alternative. Another suggestion is to give parents a chance to purchase traditional breads beforehand.

Extension 1: *Tasting Activities* can be connected to "charting" activities (see *Graphing* in the Math Activities section) so that the children can see how the information about their responses can be charted statistically.

Extension 2: Have the children create a "**Tasting Journal**". The children can write responses to the different food types presented. If this option is included, be sure to write unfamiliar words on the board or on individual journal vocabulary cards.

Extension 3: If children choose to present this as an "event", other classes or parents could be invited to participate in the "event". Invitations could be made. Children could create the event with teacher acting as a facilitator.

Materials

❖ A clean presentation surface such as a work table

❖ A table cloth for each table
❖ Trays or plates covered with a paper towel or a paper napkin (one for each type of sample)
❖ Napkins for the children (be sure there are extras)
❖ A selection of different types of breads cut into child bite size pieces, presenting in the manner traditional to the originating culture (for example, corn tortillas are more palatable when warm)
❖ A name tag for each bread type and country of origin printed neatly on word cards or pieces of sentence strip
❖ Small cups and small plates (one for each child, with extras)
❖ Water or juice

Method
❖ Cover tables with table cloths
❖ Set out breads on individual trays on table with identifying labels in front of serving trays
❖ Teacher teaches and reviews the vocabulary words with the class such as, "lefse, Norway; matzohs, Israel; chapati, India" while showing the various foods to the class
❖ The teacher or person bringing the foods can talk about the method of preparation of the foods
❖ Teacher asks children to predict which foods children will like most and least
❖ Teacher may chart predictions on chart paper
❖ Teacher and adult helpers offer children samples of the various types of bread presented - if a child is unwilling to try any (or all) variety of bread sample, let it go, forcing a child to participate is an ineffective strategy
❖ As children try different foods, ask them to describe the foods using words like creamy, sweet, soft, crunchy, crisp, soggy, and any flavors with which they might be familiar such as chocolaty, vanilla, fruity, sour, spicy in the same way one would describe flavors at a wine tasting
❖ Encourage children to discuss the flavors with one another in small groups using as many descriptive words as possible
❖ Teacher asks children their preferences, noting the preferences on chart paper
❖ Teacher asks children to compare their predictions with the results predicted
❖ Children may document predictions, experiences, opinions, and/or outcomes in a journal or other writing exercise

Suggested Reading:
De Paola, T. (1989). *Tony's Bread: An Italian Folktale.* ISBN: 0-399-21693-6.
Friedman, I. R. (1987). *How My Parents Learned to Eat.* ISBN: 039544235.
Galdone, P. (2006). *The Little Red Hen.* ISBN: 0618752501. (Bread: from planting the seeds to harvest, to grinding flour, to baking and enjoying)
Gershator, D. & Gershator, P. (1998). *Bread is for Eating.* ISBN: 0805057986. (Bilingual English / Spanish. Vibrant illustrations and song about the Mexican culture and the journey of bread from seed to flour to store to baking)

Harbison, E.M. (1999). *Loaves of Fun: A History of Bread with Activities and Recipes From Around the World.* ISBN: 1556523114. (A lively history of bread from ancient times to present, with glossary and recipes).

Hoban, R. (1993). *Bread and Jam for Frances.* ISBN: 0064430960. (Ages 5-8)

Jenness, A. (1993). *Come Home With Me: A Multicultural Treasure Hunt.* (a look at four different families and their homes and customs - Africa, Ireland, Cambodia, and Puerto Rico). ISBN: 156584064X.

Target Areas Of Learning

Physical Development
- ❖ **Fine Motor Skills:** using the small muscles of the hand and fingers: picking up pieces of bread, possibly cutting (with a butter knife) pieces of bread, writing
- ❖ **Eye-Hand Coordination:** coordinating visual acuity with using the small muscles of the hand and fingers: cutting bread, pouring beverages, writing, moving food from plate to mouth
- ❖ **Sensory Discrimination**
  - **Tactile Discrimination** (touch): identifying and differentiating textures of bread stuff with touch
  - **Visual Discrimination** (sight): identifying bread stuff visually (color, shape, texture)
  - **Oral Discrimination** (taste): identifying sweet, salty, sour, and bitter tastes; identifying textures with tongue and mouth; identifying flavors by taste
  - **Olfactory Discrimination** (smell): identifying different smells: sweet, spicy, pungent, whether the odor is pleasing or unpleasant

Cognitive Development
- ❖ **Language Arts**
  - **Verbal Skills**
    - o **Language development**: acquiring and using language appropriately as related to participating in the tasting activity
    - o **Vocabulary development**: adding to the body of words and phrases related to the types of breads presented, the way the breads are made, and the cultures from which they come
  - **Emergent literacy**
    - o **Word recognition**: learning and identifying words identifying the food and the country or culture of origin
    - o **Creative writing**: expressing self in marks and pictures related to experience of trying breads from a variety of cultures
    - o **Matching spoken words to written words**: correctly associating the written words for the breads with the spoken words
- ❖ **Math Skills**
  - **Mathematical literacy**

- o **Associating number symbols with quantity**: when creating a bar chart, the number of tally marks, or indicator of children preferring one type of food to another with the number symbol
  - **Mathematical applications**
    - o **Equivalency**: comparing an number of children preferring one type of food to the preferences for others
    - o **Common Relatedness**: linking foods and the country or culture of origin
    - o **Algebra**: sorting and matching for one or more properties: noting food preferences
- ❖ **Science**
  - **Scientific processes**
    - o **Inquiry**: an organized search for knowledge regarding food preferences in the class
    - o **Prediction**: relating an anticipated outcome based on logic, experience, or research in relationship to food preferences
    - o **Observation:** carefully watching attentively and noting what is seen
    - o **Documentation**: writing observations of food tasting which support/disprove claims for a particular prediction or outcomes
    - o **Review**: comparing predictions and actual outcomes, assessing value of any mistakes that occurred
- ❖ **Social Studies**
  - **Understanding what it means to be a good citizen and member of the school and classroom community:** behaving appropriately during food tasting; sharing, taking turns, following instructions
  - **Recognizing diversity**: recognizing what makes people similar *and* different through traditional foods
  - **Accepting human diversity**: people from various regions of the world have different food resources and styles of preparation which may be new or unusual to an individual, but not "*bad*"

Social Development

- ❖ **Self-respect:** valuing themselves in the process of sharing an aspect of their home culture, and as children learn to appreciate each person's individuality from that point of view
- ❖ **Sharing**: sharing foods from personal culture, understanding food samples are available for all
- ❖ **Taking turns:** after child has taken a sample, allowing the next to do so as well
- ❖ **Working cooperatively with others in a group**: working well with others
- ❖ **Collaboration**: planning, creating, and presenting "bread tasting"
- ❖ **Following directions**: participating in the "bread tasting" as directed
- ❖ **Impulse Control**: curtailing desire to make inappropriate responses to foods presented, or to grab extra samples from tray
- ❖ **Taking responsibility**: in preparation for "bread tasting" developing a willingness to take on tasks that support the individual and the group as a whole

❖ **Taking care of classroom environment**: participating in cleanup

Emotional Development

❖ **Self-esteem**: feeling good about oneself through presenting foods traditional to home culture and in recognizing that every person in the class has a valuable culture or tradition to share
❖ **Self-confidence**: feeling secure within one's self by presenting something of value from home culture
❖ **Accomplishment**: developing a sense of self worth from sharing traditional foods from home culture
❖ **Generosity**: freely sharing favorite foods

Creative Expression

❖ **Food or cooking**: expressing creativity through the preparation or presentation of food
❖ **Presenting an event**: expressing creativity by planning and presenting an event
❖ **Writing**: expressing opinions and experiences in writing
❖ **Developing aesthetic appreciation for foods and food preparation from other cultures**
❖ **Creative risk**: trying out foods with which one is unfamiliar or from other cultures
❖ **Problem solving**: how to put together an event that includes others

Possible Accommodations for *Bread Tasting Activity*

ADHD

❖ Use positive reinforcement when child waits, shares, shows patience, resists making outbursts
❖ If some foods presented have strong odors or flavors, offer small portions, and "baby bites"
❖ Allow child to refuse any food without confrontation
❖ Make sure (as much as possible) that food anticipated to be popular with children have enough for second helpings
❖ If an invitational event is being created, offer child tasks that require a high level of energy

Developmentally Delayed

❖ Explain the activity using short simple phrases being sure eye contact is made
❖ Demonstrate the activity in advance steps-by-step using realia, photographs or videos
❖ Unless child is familiar with strong flavors, encourage parents to bring mild flavored foods
❖ Have samples cut into smaller portions
❖ Ask child for descriptive words first, so child has the opportunity to share
❖ For an invitational event: have child pass out "bread list" or other tasks that child will find rewarding and that will build self esteem

Autism Spectrum Disorder

❖ Explain the activity using short simple phrases being sure eye contact is made
❖ Demonstrate the activity in advance steps-by-step using realia, photographs or videos
❖ Unless child is familiar with strong flavors, encourage parents to bring mild flavored foods
❖ Have samples cut into smaller portions
❖ Before event, offer a variety of breads for snacks so child can build familiarity with them
❖ Place event on the class calendar including any activities on prior days in preparation for the "bread tasting"
❖ Allow the child the right to refuse any food the child chooses not to eat.

Visually Impairments:

❖ Allow child to approach new experiences cautiously, as senses of smell and taste may be quite sensitive
❖ Adjust lighting so child can best see foods
❖ Offer larger sized pieces of food, but do not demand child finish portions
❖ Offer writing paper that has larger spaces and use high contrast writing instruments
❖ Offer child a task for invitational event that plays to child's strengths and builds self esteem

Orthopedic Impairments

❖ Ascertain child is positioned comfortably
❖ Adjust furniture or placement of foods for maximum access
❖ Cut foods into smaller pieces
❖ If child has difficulty feeding self or writing, guide child's hand using the hand-over-hand method
❖ Offer child a task for invitational event that plays to child's strengths and builds self-esteem

Gifted and Talented Education (GATE)

❖ Ask child to count responses using tally marks
❖ Ask child to document responses using a bar chart or venn diagram
❖ Ask child to find out more about the foods or cultures from which they came on-line or in the library
❖ Offer child a task for invitational event that plays to child's strengths and builds self esteem

English Language Learner (ELL)

❖ Explain the activity using short simple phrases being sure eye contact is made
❖ Demonstrate the activity in advance steps-by-step using realia, photographs or videos
❖ Teach and review vocabulary in small groups or individually including words for types, flavors, tastes, and textures of foods
❖ Be sure child has a card or piece of paper listing the new vocabulary words for reference when writing

❖ Praise and reward child when child begins or tries to use new words in working vocabulary

❖ Offer child a task for invitational event that plays to child's strengths and builds self esteem

Content Standards For Kindergarten Met By This Activity

English Language Arts

Reading (1.0, 1.16, 1.17, 1.18)

Writing (1.0, 1.1, 1.2, 1.3)

Written and Oral Language (1.0, 1.1)

Listening and Speaking (1.0, 1.1, 1.2, 2.0, 2.1, 2.3)

Mathematics

Numbers and Counting (1.0, 1.1, 1.2, 1.3)

Algebra, Sets and Sorting (1.0, 1.1)

Statistics (1.0, 1.1)

Mathematical Reasoning (1.0, 1.1, 1.2, 2.0, 2.1)

Science

Physical Sciences (1.a)

Investigation and Experimentation (4.a, 4.b, 4.d, 4.e)

History and Social Science

Following Rules (K.1, K.1.1)

Compare and describe people and places (K.4, K.4.1)

Understanding that history relates to people and places in the past (K.6, K.6.3)

Theatre

Creative Expression (2.0, 2.3)

History of Theatre (3.0, 3.2)

Learning Plan

  I. **Name of Activity:** Bread Tasting Activity

 II. **Date of Presentation:**

III. **Age or Grade Level:** Pre-K, Kindergarten

IV. **Ratio of teachers to children needed for this activity:** 1:6

 V. **Target Areas of Learning / Goals and Objectives** (target areas of learning directly relate to "VI. Evaluation Rubric")

    1. Physical: _____

    2. Cognitive: _____

    3. Social: _____

    4. Emotional: _____

    5. Creative: _____

VI. **Evaluation Rubric:** (if more than two learning areas are being evaluated, a spreadsheet form may be preferred)

Targeted Area of Learning	**Targeted Area of Learning**
_____	_____
_____	_____
4. Always _____	**4.** Always _____
3. Usually _____	**3.** Usually _____
2. Sometimes _____	**2.** Sometimes _____
1. Rarely _____	**1.** Rarely _____

VII. **Materials and Preparation Needed**

1. A clean presentation surface such as a work table
2. A table cloth for each table
3. Trays or plates covered with a paper towel or a paper napkin (one for each type of sample)
4. Napkins for the children (be sure there are extras)
5. A selection of different types of breads cut into child bite size pieces, presenting in the manner traditional to the originating culture (for example, corn tortillas are more palatable when warm)
6. A name tag for each bread type and country of origin printed neatly on word cards or pieces of sentence strip
7. Small cups and small plates (one for each child, with extras)
8. Water or juice

VIII. Procedures

1. Cover tables with table cloths
2. Set out breads on individual trays on table with identifying labels in front of serving trays
3. Teacher teaches and reviews the vocabulary words with the class such as, "lefse, Norway; matzohs, Israel; chapati, India" while showing the various foods to the class
4. The teacher or person bringing the foods can talk about the method of preparation of the foods
5. Teacher asks children to predict which foods children will like most and least
6. Teacher may chart predictions on chart paper
7. Teacher and adult helpers offer children samples of the various types of bread presented - if a child is unwilling to try any (or all) variety of bread sample, let it go, forcing a child to participate is an ineffective strategy
8. As children try different foods, ask them to describe the foods using words like creamy, sweet, soft, crunchy, crisp, soggy, and any flavors with which they might be familiar such as chocolaty, vanilla, fruity, sour, spicy in the same way one would describe flavors at a wine tasting
9. Encourage children to discuss the flavors with one another in small groups using as many descriptive words as possible
10. Teacher asks children their preferences, noting the preferences on chart paper
11. Teacher asks children to compare their predictions with the results predicted
12. Children may document predictions, experiences, opinions, and/or outcomes in a journal or other writing exercise

IX. Accommodations (changes to accommodate learning diversity)
Name of Accommodated Area:

1. _____
2. _____
3. _____
4. _____
5. _____

X. Applicable Framework Standards: Kindergarten
Standard _____
_____
_____
_____
_____

Standard _____
_____
_____
_____
_____

Standard _____

_____

_____

_____

_____

Standard _____

_____

_____

_____

_____

Standard _____

_____

_____

_____

_____

XI. Evaluation and Comments (i.e.: How well did the plan work? Great responses? What aspects are especially effective? Not effective? What improvements are needed? Ideas for follow up activities and other notes)

_____

_____

_____

_____

Family Magnets

Socio-dramatic play empowers a child to work out family relationships, interpersonal experiences, how society works in the specific area of human roles in society. These magnetic images of family, friends, and classmates add a dimension of reality to imaginary play.

When making the family magnets, it is important to use non-polaroid or heat-processed photographs, as the heat will turn polaroid-type photos black. The best photos to use are those, which are full body images separate from other people, furniture, pets, or complex backgrounds. Images of socio-dramatic accoutrements cut from magazines such as houses, furniture, desks, and CD players can be added to stimulate or enhance imaginary play. These magnets can be used at the oil pan magnet center or on individual cookie trays.

When not in use, this center can become a display of the students and their families. This will make the room become more personal. Displays that are inclusive and reflect the community served will produce a sense of the classroom as a community, the existence of which produces a powerful learning environment.

Variation 1: Laminate a diagram of the school, a map of the local neighborhood (available through the auto club), affix to magnetic center with larger magnets. Ask children to place magnetic photographs of school employees, grocers, names of neighborhood landmarks onto map to familiarize children with the school and surrounding neighborhood.

Variation 2: Ask children to draw pictures of their family members, laminate and allow children to use for magnet center play.

Materials
- ❖ Non-polaroid (heat-developed) photographs of children, possibly their family members. Ask parents to give you photographs that can be cut up or the teacher may take some personally. Photographs need to be of separate people, in order to be made into individual magnets.
- ❖ Personal laminator
- ❖ Laminator pouches and carriers
- ❖ Adhesive-type magnetic tape
- ❖ Cookie trays or a large oil pan tray which can be bolted into the wall
- ❖ Zipper-style freezer style bags to store family magnets

Method
- ❖ Have children cut out the pictures of their family members. Encourage the children to work slowly, so as not to cut off heads or arms, etc. (this alone can be a one or several days' activity if you are breaking up the activity).
- ❖ The teacher or children can also cut out photographic images from magazines and laminate for extended play.
- ❖ Place opened laminator pouches, closed end to closed end, into laminator carriers (It

reduces the chance of the images shifting when filled pouch is moved into carrier)

❖ Have children put their cut images into opened carrier, taking care to leave a margin of 1/2 inch or so around the edge of the image being prepared. Depending on the size of images, a carrier will hold about six or eight cut out images. Encourage children to share pouches if there is room to add other children's images. Close pouch, and close carrier on top of pouch.

❖ With supervision, allow children to laminate photos. Place closed end of carrier into the mouth of the personal laminator, holding carrier gently on both the right and left sides of the bottom end of the carrier pouch, making sure that the rollers "catch" the carrier evenly. This is important as it insures a decent quality of lamination.

❖ When carrier emerges from personal laminator, wait 10-15 seconds. Open carrier, take out laminated pouch. Sometimes pouches (in carriers) need to be run through the laminator more than once. Air bubbles in laminated pouches are normal. If you are breaking this activity up into segments, this is another good point to take a break.

❖ If more than one child has photos in the laminator pouch, the instructor should separate each child's images without actually cutting the images out for them.

❖ Have children cut out laminated photos of their family members. Cut small pieces of magnetic tape (one for each image) and let the children attach one piece to each photo. Place family pieces in zipper style freezer bags or use the center as a display for the classroom.

❖ Word magnets may be added to use the activity as a "matching game".

❖ **To play**: Give each child a small steel cookie sheet, and allow children to "play with their family". Alternatively, if you choose to make a "magnet center" using an oil pan tray bolted to studs in the wall, you may allow more than one child to play with their family pieces cooperatively.

Suggested Reading:

Amery, H. (1994). *Then and Now*. ISBN: 0746007949. (Great illustrations: side by side pictures of how things used to be and how they are now)

Curtis, J.L. (2002). *I'm gonna like me: Letting off a little self-esteem*. ISBN: 0060287616

De Regniers, B. S. (1974). *May I Bring a Friend?* ISBN: 0689713533. (Ages 5-8)

Hamanaka, S. (1999). *All the Colors of the Earth*. ISBN: 0688170625.

Hoban, R. (1976). *Baby Sister For Frances*. ISBN: 0064430065.

Jenness, A. (1993). *Come Home With Me: A Multicultural Treasure Hunt*. (A look at four different families and their homes and customs - Africa, Ireland, Cambodia, and Puerto Rico). ISBN: 156584064X.

Katz, K. (2002). *The Colors of Us*. ISBN: 0805071636.

Mayer, M. (2001). *Just Me and My Dad*. ISBN: 0307118398.

Mayer, M. (2001). *Just Me and My Mom*. ISBN: 030712584X.

Mitchell, L. (2001). *Different Just Like Me*. ISBN: 1570914907.

Reiser, L. (Rebecca Hart translator)(1998). *Tortillas and Lullabies / Tortillas y Cancioncitas*. ISBN: 0-688-14628-7. (Three generations make tortillas, sing songs, wash clothes and gather flowers; words and music for lullaby provided).

Sendak, M. (1964). *Where the Wild Things Are.* ISBN: 0-06-025492-0. (1964 Caldecott Medal)

Viorst, J. (1987). *Alexander and the Terrible, Horrible, No Good, Very Bad Day.* ISBN: 0-689-71173-5. (Also available in Spanish)

Williams. V. (1984). *A Chair For My Mother.* ISBN: 068804074. (Reading Rainbow; also available in Spanish).

Wood, A. (1984). *The Napping House.* ISBN: 0152567089. (also in Spanish)

Zemach, M. (1990). *It Could Always Be Worse.* ISBN: 0374436363.

Zolotow, C. (Illustrated by Arthur Lobel) (1982). *The Quarreling Book.* ISBN: 0064430340.

Note: Appendix B3 lists children's books in Spanish @ www.cambriapress.com/kindergarten

Targeted Areas Of Learning

Physical Development

❖ **Fine motor skills:** using the small muscles of the hand and fingers: cutting with scissors, holding carrier pouch, during play moving and manipulating magnetic pieces

❖ **Eye-hand coordination:** coordinating visual acuity with using the small muscles of the hand and fingers: cutting; holding magnet pieces, manipulating magnetic pieces around center during play

❖ **Sensory Discrimination**
  • **Tactile discrimination** (touch): feeling the smoothness of the laminated images; experiencing the pull of the magnet toward the tray in the hands and fingers
  • **Visual discrimination** (sight): correctly identifying the images, and possibly matching the correct word symbol to the photographic image

Cognitive Development

❖ **Language Arts**
  • **Verbal skills**
    o **Language development**: acquiring and using language appropriately within the context of socio-dramatic play whether at individually or within social interactions
    o **Vocabulary development**: adding socio-dramatic role play vocabulary to the working body of words and phrases
  • **Emergent literacy**
    o **Emergent writing**: developing the fine motor skills for the pincer grasp and creating marks to which they attach meaning as related to magnet play
    o **Creative writing**: expressing self in marks and pictures related to socio-dramatic magnet play
  • **Matching spoken words and images of physical objects to written words**: correctly associating the auditory expression with the written symbol grouping if word magnet pieces are used as a matching game
  • **Story recall/sequencing (temporal ordering)**: retelling stories/events the child has heard through the use of magnet play

- ❖ **Math Skills**
  - **Mathematical literacy**
    - o **One-to-one correspondence**: counting magnetic images
  - **Mathematical applications**
    - o **Measurement**: comparing the size of magnetic pieces to each other
    - o **Spatial relationships**: relating the aspects of magnetic images to one another per placement on the tray
    - o **Common relatedness**: linking items that are not the same, but are associated with each other in the context of socio-dramatic play
- ❖ **Science**
  - **Cause and Effect**
    - o **Relationships between actions and outcomes**: working with magnets
  - **Physical sciences**
    - o Awareness of the physical attraction of magnets to some metals
    - o Physical objects can be described in terms of the materials from which they are made
- ❖ **Social Studies**
  - **Recognizing diversity**: recognizing what makes people similar *and* different: comparing various observable differences between photographic images of people
  - **Accepting human diversity**: types of families, cultures and how they show up in socio-dramatic play
  - **Compare and describe the locations of people, places, and environments:**
    - o Determine relative locations: near/far, left/right, behind/in front
    - o Being familiar with the layout of the school
    - o Understanding the jobs of people who work at the school and in the local community.

Social Development

- ❖ **Self-respect:** valuing themselves in a context of relatedness to others in their family and social groupings
- ❖ **Sharing:** understanding that the magnet center is intended for use by the community is available for the use by everyone and may not be available at all times for individual use
- ❖ **Working cooperatively with others in a group:** interacting socio-dramatically with others through magnet center play
- ❖ **Collaboration:** planning, creating, and participating in socio-dramatic magnetic play
- ❖ **Following directions:** carrying out the directions relating to the magnet center play
- ❖ **Respecting others as individuals:** playing courteously, developing skill at culturally acceptable behaviors in socio-dramatic interactions
- ❖ **Social boundaries:** developing the skill to recognize and behave within social boundaries
- ❖ **Community building**
  - Creating a sense of belonging in a group through socio-dramatic play
  - Using the magnet center as a display tool

❖ **Taking responsibility**: recognition that each person in the community is responsible for the community as a whole, through socio-dramatic role playing

Emotional Development
❖ **Self-esteem**
  • Feeling good about oneself just as one is and is not, by dramatically playing out relationships at the magnet center
  • Building self-confidence by participating in socio-dramatic role play wherein there is no "wrong" answer
❖ **Identifying and expressing emotions appropriately**
  • **Naming human feelings:** sad, happy, angry, hurt, loving, excited, afraid, proud, sorry in the context of socio-dramatic interactions
❖ **Generosity**: sharing of one's self and magnet pieces, roles played in invented games

Creative Expression
❖ **Use of creative media and expression of imagination**:
  • **2-dimensional visual arts**: using magnetic pieces in creative, visually pleasing ways
  • **Dramatization/story telling**: expressing self through socio-dramatic interactions
❖ **Creative risk**: being comfortable playing creatively, actively and confidently during invented interactive socio-dramatic play
❖ **Problem solving**: collaborating in the process of inventing socio-dramatic game
❖ **Creative Thinking**: considering a variety of different possible directions for game play

Possible Accommodations for *Family Magnets Activity*

ADHD
❖ Use positive reinforcement (praise) when child follows directions, works well with others
❖ Offer more time or break up the magnet making activity into several smaller sessions
❖ Magnet play: use a "designated centers" time so that child will neither avoid nor dominate magnet center during free play
❖ Remind and use positive reinforcement when child slows pace in cutting and laminating processes
❖ Remind child of the manner in which the laminator is to be used, request that child repeat instructions back to teacher or supervisory adult
❖ Allow child to laminate in a lower ratio, small group supervisory structure

Developmental Delays
❖ Explain the activity using short simple phrases being sure eye contact is made
❖ Demonstrate the activity in advance steps-by-step using realia, photographs or videos
❖ Offer more time or break activity up into several smaller sessions
❖ Offer adapted scissors
❖ Guide child's hand (only if necessary) if cutting is a skill in the early stages of development

❖ Select larger photographs with less detail for child to cut out
❖ Use positive reinforcement when child plays appropriately at the magnet center

Autism Spectrum Disorders
❖ Explain the activity using short simple phrases being sure eye contact is made
❖ Demonstrate the activity in advance steps-by-step using realia, photographs or videos
❖ Offer more time or break activity up into several smaller sessions
❖ Have magnet center set up in class at the beginning of the school session with photographs of teacher and other staff already on it so that the idea becomes familiar often
❖ Have magnet play be part of daily class routine
❖ Reduce number of pieces in play
❖ Drawn or purchased "emoticons" (smiles, frowns, sad faces) for working with child learning to identify feelings
❖ Allow child and "buddy" to play at magnet center
❖ If verbal skills are developing, work with child individually or with one other, going over vocabulary, giving positive reinforcement for participation, correct identification, and speech

Visual Impairments
❖ Adjust lighting to reduce glare and reflection from oil pan
❖ Use larger photographs for cutting
❖ Use adapted scissors
❖ Use a magnifying glass on a stand for seeing finer detail
❖ Guide child's hand to assist cutting

Orthopedic Impairments
❖ Check child's positioning
❖ Adjust furniture and situate activity in such a way that activity is accessible to the child
❖ Place activity on an individual tray for easier accessibility
❖ Use padded or otherwise adapted scissors
❖ Offer larger images for child to cut out
❖ Guide child's hand using the hand-over-hand method

Gifted and Talented Education (GATE)
❖ Play "matching game" with child
❖ Ask child to locate different areas of the school on a diagram magnetically affixed to magnet center, placing magnetic photos of various school personnel and words that describe different areas on the diagram
❖ Using a laminated local area map affixed to magnet center, have child place words that identify local landmarks such as "my school", "my house", "grocery store", "gas station"
❖ Ask child to draw their own school diagram or map of local area
❖ Ask child to designate the compass point directions of own diagram/map

English Language Learners (ELL)
- ❖ Explain the activity using short simple phrases being sure eye contact is made
- ❖ Demonstrate the activity in advance steps-by-step using realia, videos or photographs
- ❖ Teach and review vocabulary with child at magnet center in a small group or individually
- ❖ Affix vocabulary words to magnetic images
- ❖ Use positive reinforcement when child uses or attempts to use new vocabulary words

Content Standards For Kindergarten Met By This Activity

English Language Arts
Listening and Speaking (1.0, 1.2, 2.0, 2.1, 2.3)

Mathematics
Numbers and Counting (1.0, 1.1, 1.2)
Algebra, Sets and Sorting (1.0, 1.1)
Measurement and Geometry (1.0, 1.2, 2.0, 2.1, 2.2)

History and Social Science
Compare and describe people and places (K.4)
Using a calendar to sequence events (K.5)

Visual Arts
Artistic Perception (1.0, 1.1, 1.2)
Creative Expression 2.0, 2.4)
Applications (5.0, 5.3)

Theatre
Artistic Perception (1.0, 1.2, 2.2, m2.3
History (3.0, 3.1, 3.2)

Learning Plan

I. Name of Activity: Family Magnets

II. Date of Presentation:

III. Age or Grade Level: Pre-K to Kindergarten

IV. Ratio of teachers to children needed for this activity: 1:5. This activity is good for the kidney-shaped table, especially with younger children and particularly when they are using the laminator.

V. Target Areas of Learning / Goals and Objectives (target areas of learning directly relate to "VI. Evaluation Rubric")

   1. Physical: _____
   2. Cognitive: _____
   3. Social: _____
   4. Emotional: _____
   5. Creative: _____

VI. Evaluation Rubric: (if more than two learning areas are being evaluated, a spreadsheet form may be preferred)

Targeted Area of Learning	**Targeted Area of Learning**
_____	_____
_____	_____
4. Always _____	**4.** Always _____
3. Usually _____	**3.** Usually _____
2. Sometimes _____	**2.** Sometimes _____
1. Rarely _____	**1.** Rarely _____

VII. Materials and Preparation Needed

   1. Non-polaroid (heat developed) photographs of children, possibly their family members. Ask parents to give you photographs that can be cut up.
   2. Photographs need to be of separate people, in order to be made into individual magnets.
   3. Personal laminator
   4. Laminator pouches and carriers
   5. Scissors
   6. Adhesive type magnetic tape
   7. Cookie trays or a large oil pan tray which can be bolted into the wall
   8. Zip-style freezer bags to store family magnets

VIII. Procedures

1. Have children cut out the pictures of their family members. Encourage them to work slowly, so as not to cut off heads or arms, etc. (this can be one day's activity if you are breaking up the activity).

2. Place opened laminator pouches, closed end to closed end, into laminator carriers (It reduces the chance of the images shifting when filled pouch is moved into carrier)

3. Have children put their cut images into opened carrier. Depending on the size of images, a carrier will hold about six or eight cut out images. Encourage children to share pouches if there is room to add other children's images. Close pouch, and close carrier on top of pouch.

4. With supervision, allow children to laminate photos. Place closed end of carrier into the mouth of the personal laminator, holding carrier gently on both the right and left sides of the carrier, making sure that the rollers "catch" the carrier evenly.

5. When carrier emerges from personal laminator, wait 10-15 seconds. Open carrier, and take out laminated pouch. Sometimes pouches (in carriers) need to be run through the laminator more than once. Air bubbles in laminated pouches are normal. If you are breaking this activity up into segments, this is another good point to take a break.

6. If more than one child has photos in the laminator pouch, the instructor should separate each child's images without actually cutting the images out for them.

7. Have children cut out laminated photos of their family members.

8. Cut small pieces of magnetic tape (one for each image) and let the children attach one piece to each photo. Place family pieces in zipper style freezer bags or use the center as a display for the classroom.

9. **To play**: Give each child a small steel cookie sheet, and allow children to "play with their family". Alternatively, if you choose to make a "magnet center" using an oil pan tray bolted to studs in the wall, you may allow more than one child to play with their family pieces cooperatively.

Variations:

- Children may draw pictures of their families if they do not have or cannot afford to take family pictures. In this case, it would be best if all the children in the class had "drawn families" so that other children will not point out the differences in the magnet families.

- You may take photos of the children while in class. Especially with the convenience of digital photography, it would not be a disaster if the child were to inadvertently cut off an arm or head of the doll he is cutting out.

- Images from magazines can be cut out and laminated to perfect cutting techniques before cutting family photos

IX. Accommodations (changes to accommodate learning diversity)
Name of Accommodated Area:

1. _____
2. _____
3. _____
4. _____
5. _____

X. Applicable Framework Standards: Kindergarten

Standard _____
_____
_____
_____

Standard _____
_____
_____
_____

Standard _____
_____
_____
_____

Standard _____
_____
_____
_____

Standard _____
_____
_____
_____

XI. Evaluation and Comments (i.e.: How well did the plan work? Great responses? What aspects are especially effective? Not effective? What improvements are needed? Ideas for follow up activities and other notes)

_____
_____
_____
_____

Multicultural Family Spoon Puppets

Spoon puppets are inexpensive, adaptable to a variety of purposes, available to productive silliness, and unlimited creativity. Using multicolored plastic ware, a plastic spoon (or fork for an obvious male with a crew cut) can become any creature the child designates.

Plastic utensils are small enough that scraps of felt or other creative materials can actually be used as part of the project. If the teacher is emphasizing human diversity, the best place to purchase multi-colored plastic utensils is the party store. Should brown utensils be found, purchase a good quantity of them, as they are less common than other colors of plastic spoons.

Any puppet opens an avenue for socio-dramatic play. Like family magnets, the children can invent

Illustration 17: Children have the opportunity to use creative problem solving skills when making plastic flatware puppets.

these to be family members if they choose. Just as easily the spoon puppet can become a rabbit, dog, or mythical creature merely by declaring it to be so and adding a few well-placed scraps of felt.

Select adhesives that dry quickly. Glue sticks do not work on this project and hot glue, even the low melt variety, is inappropriate and dangerous for young children. Use glitter glue pens, which are smaller and release finer lines of decorative glue, to manage the flow of the glue onto the spoon. The caps of glitter pens pull off. Teach the children how to use the pens, as twisting off the cap will take off the pen tip. This creates the possibility that the contents may not produce the intended result, but instead, a mess. Spoon puppets need a minimum of twenty-four hours to dry. With less drying time the young artisans' masterpieces will suffer relocated eyes and dripping glue conditions. Even so, occasionally eyes will fall off and the teacher will get to preside as the puppet doctor.

When assembling a project box or preparing for a puppet making event, bear in mind that practically any little bit of creative paraphernalia can be used. Such little bits may be lying around or can be found at a craft store, Discount School Supply, the Oriental Trading Company, or at yard sales where a crafter is purging long unused supplies. When asked, parents are often too willing to Part Company with "little bits of this and that" for classroom use. It helps to give generalized guidelines for desirable "this and that" or soon the classroom will resemble an unkempt thrift store. Clear plastic boxes and tubs with labels are excellent for storing, keeping, and organizing these treasures.

The teacher needs to decide whether the children are to create their puppets at their desks or at an area other than their desks. If working in a small group setting is planned, then the activity should be away from the children's desks. If the activity will include the entire group, then situating the children at their cleared desks is preferable.

Materials

- ❖ Plastic spoons, in as many colors as possible, skin tones if teacher is emphasizing racial diversity
- ❖ Tacky or other nontoxic quick drying glue
- ❖ Many colors of yarn, primarily for hair
- ❖ Pieces of card board to use for wrapping yarn (for hair)
- ❖ Glitter glue
- ❖ Wiggle eyes
- ❖ Bric-a-brac: feathers, ribbon pieces, faux fur, bits of felt and other fabric, spangles, chenille stems (for arms and legs), all sizes of pom-poms, spangles, sequins, etc.
- ❖ Scissors, punches, and decorative scissors (last two items are optional)
- ❖ Multicolored Sharpie type markers (washable markers wipe off a plastic spoon)
- ❖ Trays on to which children to place selected items
- ❖ An area set aside for drying the spoons covered with an inexpensive plastic table cloth
- ❖ Slips of paper with children's names to identify puppets

Method

- ❖ Set out spoons, glues, and craft materials onto a table or work surface buffet style
- ❖ Set up drying area in advance
- ❖ Explain intention of activity to children:
  - Emphasis racial diversity particularly related to physical characteristics of racial groups
  - Puppet making purely for socio-dramatic play
  - Creating characters for stories
  - Creating real and imaginary animals
- ❖ Allow children to select the materials they plan to use (remind them that taking all of a given material is inappropriate) for creating their puppet onto their tray and return to designated work area
- ❖ Allow children to create their puppets: remember that when children enter into the creative process, they may stray from the predetermined task. Straying is part of the process; allow the process to occur.
- ❖ When puppets are complete, carefully transport puppet to the drying area and place slip of paper with the child's name on it next to the puppet the child made.

Suggested Reading:

Carle, E. (1987). *Do You Want To Be My Friend?* ISBN: 0064431274 (Ages 3-6)

Curtis, J.L. (2002). *I'm Gonna Like Me: Letting Off a Little Self-Esteem.* ISBN: 0060287616

De Regniers, B. S. (1974). *May I Bring a Friend?* ISBN: 0689713533 (Ages 5-8)

Hamanaka, S. (1999). *All the Colors of the Earth.* ISBN: 0688170625

Hoban, R. (1976). *Baby Sister For Frances.* ISBN: 0064430065

Hoban, R. (1976). *Best Friends For Frances.* ISBN: 0064430081

Katz, K. (2002). *The Colors of Us.* ISBN: 0805071636.

Mitchell, L. (2001). *Different Just Like Me.* ISBN: 1570914907

Spier, P, (1988) *People.* ISBN: 038524469X. Caldecott Medalist. (Wonderful introduction to cultural diversity about people on four continents)

Suggested CD:
Greg & Steve. (1987). *We All Live Together. Vol.2.* **(includes: English / Spanish months of the year song, World is a Rainbow,** Popcorn, The Freeze) CD Available from: amazon.com

Jenkins, E. (1995) *Multi-Cultural Children's Songs.* (Greetings, thank yous, ABCs, counting, songs and dances in many languages).

Jenkins, E. (2003) *Sharing Cultures.* (28 songs from around the world). Available from: amazon.com

Target Areas of Learning

Physical Development
- ❖ **Fine motor skills:** using the small muscles of the hand and fingers: to cut, paste, glue, tie, wrap, spread, sprinkle, or twist materials
- ❖ **Eye-hand coordination:** coordinating visual acuity with using the small muscles of the hand and fingers: cutting, placing glue in designated spots on utensil, controlling the flow of glue from the glue pen, placing wiggle eyes, placing yarn or material selected for hair, clothing et cetera
- ❖ **Sensory discrimination**
  - **Visual discrimination** (sight): identifying materials and assembly of puppet visually
  - **Tactile discrimination** (touch): identifying and differentiating textures of craft materials with touch

Cognitive Development
- ❖ **Language Arts**
  - **Verbal skills**
    - ○ **Language development**: acquiring and using language related to the creation and use of the puppet and any diversity curriculum associated with the puppets being made
    - ○ **Vocabulary development**: adding to the body of words and phrases related to puppet making and human diversity related to the presentation of the activity
  - **Emergent literacy**
    - ○ **Sequencing (temporal ordering)**: retelling puppet-making event the child has recalls in the order the child recalls it occurred.
- ❖ **Math Skills**
  - **Mathematical literacy**
    - ○ **1 to 1 correspondence**: counting materials in preparation for puppet making
  - **Mathematical applications**
    - ○ **Spatial relationships**: relating the aspects of physical objects to one another: placement of decorations and features on puppet
    - ○ **Common relatedness**: linking items that are not the same, but are associated, such as the parts of the puppet eyes, nose, and mouth
    - ○ **Geometry**: recognizing and naming two and three dimensional shapes of items used to make puppets such as pom-poms and wiggle eyes

❖ **Social Studies**
  - **Understanding that being a good citizen and member of the school community involves certain behavior:** following rules, sharing, taking turns, individual responsibilities and consequences, recognizing appropriate behavior
  - **Recognizing diversity**: recognizing what makes people similar *and* different through constructing puppets: knowing that superficial differences do not mean *bad*.
  - **Accepting human diversity**: types of families, cultures, race in making and playing with puppets

Social Development

❖ **Self-respect:** valuing themselves, loving themselves for who they are just as they are and as they are not, particularly as related to superficial racial appearance

❖ **Sharing:** understanding that items intended for puppet making are for everyone's use

❖ **Patience:** diligence: staying with a project or activity until it is completed

❖ **Working cooperatively with others in a group**: working well as a class member and small group member

❖ **Collaboration**: planning and creating puppets, sharing ideas about puppet making with other class members

❖ **Following directions**: carrying out directions for puppet making including staying on task

❖ **Respecting others as individuals:** behaving appropriately in social situations particularly as related to racial and cultural diversity, learning the general rules of courtesy (manners) for their family and school

❖ **Internalizing social values**: learning appropriate behavior in the context of the culture in which the child is living: acceptance of human diversity even when it is unfamiliar to the child

❖ **Community building**: creating a sense of belonging in a group by accepting all members within it

❖ **Taking care of classroom environment**: participating in cleanup, making sure all drying projects are treated carefully

Emotional Development

❖ **Self-esteem**: feeling good about oneself just as one is and is not as related to racial and cultural identity

❖ **Self-confidence**: feeling secure within one's self and one's position within the community

❖ **Accomplishment**: developing a sense of self worth from participating in and completing puppet making

❖ **Empathy**: awareness of/ identification with the feelings of others, particularly in relationship to cultural identity and racial characteristics

Creative Expression

❖ **Use of creative media and expression of imagination**:
  - **3-Dimensional visual arts**: making puppets
  - **Dramatization/story telling**: expressing self through acting, puppetry, and theater arts

❖ **Developing aesthetic appreciation** for puppets and puppetry
❖ **Creative risk**: being comfortable playing and experimenting with puppet making materials and creating puppet representations of family members

Possible Accommodations for *Spoon Puppets Activity*

ADHD
❖ Present activity in a less distracting small group situation
❖ Limit the numbers and types of crafts materials to avoid sensory overload
❖ Offer child a carrel to reduce distractions
❖ Use emphasis and make eye contact when teaching student to pull cap off rather than twisting as that detaches pen top from glitter glue, producing less desired results
❖ Make sure glitter glue pens are unclogged and have an adequate flow of glue to prevent glue splatter caused by frustrated student over squeezing
❖ Offer a second session for creating puppets, if necessary, to reduce possibility of frustration with time constraints
❖ Use positive reinforcement when child works well with others and produces improvements in behavior patterns (this means the teacher must be observing for positive choices, rather than waiting for less desired ones)

Developmental Delays
❖ Explain the activity using short simple phrases being sure eye contact is made
❖ Demonstrate the activity in advance steps-by-step using realia, photographs or videos
❖ Offer adapted tools and materials such as scissors, adapted glue dispensers, self adhesive large size wiggle eyes, larger pieces of ribbon et cetera
❖ Offer larger (serving type) plastic ware
❖ Set aside a larger time block for completion of activity
❖ Reduce selection of crafts materials or make the selection process an initial activity
❖ Present as a small group activity

Autism Spectrum Disorders
❖ Explain the activity using short simple phrases being sure eye contact is made
❖ Demonstrate the activity in advance steps-by-step using realia, photographs or videos
❖ Offer adapted tools and materials such as scissors, adapted glue dispensers, self adhesive large size wiggle eyes, larger pieces of ribbon et cetera
❖ Set aside a larger time block for completion of activity
❖ Reduce selection of crafts materials or make the selection process an initial activity
❖ Present as a small group activity; keeping child's group membership as consistent as possible, or with child's regular partner
❖ Put activity on the calendar (later in the week, so child has time to become familiar with the idea)
❖ Go over the week's schedule on a daily basis, perhaps showing the class the spoons and materials in the days before to increase familiarity

Visual Impairments

- ❖ Adjust lighting
- ❖ Offer adapted tools and materials such as scissors, adapted glue dispensers, self adhesive large size wiggle eyes, larger pieces of ribbon et cetera
- ❖ Use serving size plastic ware
- ❖ Offer brightly colored, high contrast pieces of craft materials
- ❖ Use larger wrapping cards for yarn
- ❖ Use a lighted magnifying glass on a stand
- ❖ Set aside a larger time block for completion of activity
- ❖ Present in small group or partnered format

Orthopedic Impairments

- ❖ Adjust furniture and placement of activity for maximum accessibility
- ❖ Set up a second tray for puppet assembly
- ❖ Offer adapted tools and materials such as scissors, adapted glue dispensers, self adhesive large size wiggle eyes, larger pieces of ribbon et cetera
- ❖ Use serving size plastic ware
- ❖ Use larger size wrapping cards
- ❖ If child's hands or fingers lack strength or flexibility use hand over hand method to strengthen or guide child's hands
- ❖ Allow more time, or break activity up into a few sessions

Gifted and Talented Education (GATE)

- ❖ Encourage children dramatize a particular cultural story (of their own choosing?) using their own puppets
- ❖ Allow children to create "character" puppets from stories being read in class
- ❖ Take class to a culturally oriented puppet presentation and allow gifted children to extrapolate their own work from that experience
- ❖ Have children draw and write cultural scenarios in story board fashion

English Language Learners (ELL)

- ❖ Explain the activity using short simple phrases being sure eye contact is made
- ❖ Demonstrate activity in advance step-by-step using realia, photographs or videos
- ❖ Teach and review vocabulary associated with puppet making activity in small groups or individually including: puppet, spoon, fork, glue, yarn, color names, scissors, material names, wiggle eyes, ribbon, gender designation (boy or girl), textural words, family members, occupations, animals depending on focus of activity
- ❖ Use positive reinforcement when child attempts to use or uses new vocabulary

Content Standards For Kindergarten Met By This Activity

English Language Arts

  Reading (1.0, 1.17, 1.18)
  Written and Oral Language (1.0, 1.1)
  Listening and Speaking (1.0, 1.1, 1.2, 2.0, 2.1)

Mathematics

  Algebra, Sets and Sorting (1.0, 1.1)
  Measurement and Geometry (2.0, 2.1, 2.2)
  Science
  Physical Sciences (1.a)
  Investigation and Experimentation (4.a, 4.b, 4.c, 4.d, 4.e)

History and Social Science

  Following Rules (K.1, K.1.1)
  Matching work descriptions to related jobs in history and community (K.3)
  Compare and describe people and places (K.4, K4.1)
  Using a calendar to sequence events (K.5)
  Understanding that history relates to people and places in the past (K.6, K.6.3)

Visual Arts

  Artistic Perception (1.0, 1.1, 1.2)
  Creative Expression (2.0, 2.2, 2.4, 2.6, 2.7)
  Valuing Aesthetics (4.0, 4.1)

Theatre

  Creative Expression (2.0)
  History of Theatre (3.0, 3.1, 3.2)
  Applications (5.0, 5.1, 5.2)

Learning Plan

   I. **Name of Activity: Multicultural Family Spoon Puppets Activity**

  II. **Date of Presentation:**

 III. **Age or Grade Level: Pre-K, Kindergarten**

  IV. **Ratio of teachers to children needed for this activity:** 1:6

   V. **Target Areas of Learning / Goals and Objectives** (target areas of learning directly relate to "VI. Evaluation Rubric")
       1. **Physical:** _____
       2. **Cognitive:** _____
       3. **Social:** _____
       4. **Emotional:** _____
       5. **Creative:** _____

  VI. **Evaluation Rubric:** (if more than two learning areas are being evaluated, a spreadsheet form may be preferred)

Targeted Area of Learning	**Targeted Area of Learning**
_____ _____	_____ _____
4. Always _____	**4.** Always _____
3. Usually _____	**3.** Usually _____
2. Sometimes _____	**2.** Sometimes _____
1. Rarely _____	**1.** Rarely _____

 VII. **Materials and Preparation**
       1. Plastic spoons, in as many colors as possible, skin tones if teacher is emphasizing racial diversity
       2. Tacky or other nontoxic quick drying glue
       3. Many colors of yarn, primarily for hair
       4. Pieces of card board to use for wrapping yarn (for hair)
       5. Glitter glue
       6. Wiggle eyes
       7. Bric-a-brac: feathers, ribbon pieces, faux fur, bits of felt and other fabric, spangles, chenille stems (for arms and legs), all sizes of pom-poms, spangles, sequins, etc.
       8. Scissors, punches, and decorative scissors (last two, optional)
       9. Multicolored Sharpie-type markers (washable markers wipe off a plastic spoon)
      10. Trays on to which children to place selected items
      11. An area set aside for drying the spoons covered with an inexpensive plastic table cloth
      12. Slips of paper with children's names to identify puppets

VIII. Procedure

1. Set out spoons, glues, and craft materials onto a table or work surface buffet style
2. Set up drying area in advance
3. Explain intention of activity to children:

   a. Emphasis racial diversity particularly related to physical characteristics of racial groups
   b. Puppet making purely for socio-dramatic play
   c. Creating characters for stories
   d. Creating real and imaginary animals

4. Allow children to select the materials they plan to use (remind them that taking all of a given material is inappropriate) for creating their puppet onto their tray and return to designated work area
5. Allow children to create their puppets: remember that when children enter into the creative process, they may stray from the predetermined task. Straying is part of the process. Allow the process to occur.
6. When puppets are complete, carefully transport puppet to the drying area and place slip of paper with the child's name on it next to the puppet the child made.

IX. Accommodations (changes to accommodate learning diversity)
Name of Accommodated Area:

1. _____
2. _____
3. _____
4. _____
5. _____

X. Applicable Framework Standards: Kindergarten
Standard _____

_____
_____
_____
_____

Standard _____

_____
_____
_____
_____

Standard _____

_____

_____

_____

Standard _____

_____

_____

_____

Standard _____

_____

_____

_____

_____

XI. Evaluation and Comments (i.e.: How well did the plan work? Great responses? What aspects are especially effective? Not effective? What improvements are needed? Ideas for follow up activities and other notes)

_____

_____

_____

_____

Puppet Theater Making

Making puppet theaters can be such an enjoyable activity in which to participate, and honestly, to watch unfolding. In this messy, creative, collaborative project, people often lose awareness that they are learning. They become so involved in the process that there is not a line of demarcation between learner and learning. The potential for that very elevated state of learning is entirely possible when children construct puppet theaters.

Puppet theaters can be constructed from a variety of materials. It is recommended that each class make a few puppet theaters, depending on the number of children in the class. Large sheets of cardboard work great. It is often possible to get large cardboard at club store cardboard recycling bins for no charge. Get to know one or two of the store managers of club stores, who often will be more than pleased to set aside a few choice pieces of cardboard destined to become a classroom theater.

Puppet theater making can be part of a larger unit. Attending a puppet play (Children's Fairyland in Oakland California presents on-going puppet productions), and seeing photographs of puppet theaters or video productions of puppet productions will all help children to integrate the distinction of a puppet theater into their working body of knowledge. Making a puppet theater will involve more than a single day's work. Attempting to complete this in one day would diminish the value of this activity.

The teacher may want to ask children to form collaborative planning groups of three to five individuals to discuss and draw possible options for the project in advance before handing out the sheets of cardboard. Ask open-ended but leading questions, such as, "What kind of opening do you want for your theater?" "Will someone be able to hide behind the space beneath that opening?" "Will the puppet theater be able to stand up well if it is made that way?" "What shape should the window be? "Should the window be open, or should it be cut in such a way that there are doors to close on it?" Asking these questions will introduce planning and problem solving into the activity, crucial skills in our collaborative, technological society.

Much of the materials needed to make puppet theaters are available inexpensively. The local 99-cent store sells house painting sized brushes, felt tipped marking pens, tubes of glitter glue for 99 cents each. Stay away from stencils and stampers as the children's original art is much more expressive and offers a wider scope of learning for the children.

After children have created and settled in on their "blue print" for their theater (which by the way will change as it is being made), distribute the sheets of cardboard and ask the children to draw some of the more significant parts of the theater onto the cardboard. Be sure to ask the children to designate the window as THEY want it to be. It is THEIR project, so let them have it according to THEIR plan. This is important. Children need to see what happens, even if, and especially if, it doesn't work. IF IT DOESN'T WORK, DON'T MAKE THEM WRONG FOR THEIR INQUIRY. Remember, "Mistaking is learning". Experience is an awesome teacher. Be generous, laugh and say "Oops". Edison made 10,000 light bulbs before he made one that worked.

Cutting the window: The best tool for cutting the window is a box cutter. **CHILDREN NEVER SHOULD TOUCH BOX CUTTERS,** as they are razor blades in a metal casing. It is best to have the children talk through how they have decided to do the window to the person cutting the box. They should then go to recess, lunch or elsewhere, in order to be entirely away from where the window cutting will occur, and not even within sight of the cutting. If children know where the box cutters are, they may want to try them out. Don't even **allow** that to be a possibility. Window cutting is an adult only activity, entirely XXX rated. A box cutter could take off a tiny finger in a heartbeat or that of a teacher's, or adult volunteer's, if they don't know how to use the box cutter properly. As best as the teacher can, cut the window as directed by the children. If the opening is inconsolably incorrect, have back up cardboard pieces. Often the children will be so eager to get on with creating the puppet theater that teacher mistakes are quickly forgiven.

CHILDREN ARE NOT ALLOWED TO RETURN TO THE CLASS UNTIL ALL ADULT BOX CUTTING ACTIVITIES ARE COMPLETED

Tell parents to send their children to school in old clothing on painting days. Painting the theater is wonderfully messy and the mess is unavoidable. Set it up so children do not feel suppressed because they feel they must protect their clothing. How sad would that be??

It is best if painting can be done outside in the yard if it can be done without enticing children from other classrooms to the project. If for any reason painting must be done inside, choose an area that is easily cleaned. Carpet does not survive tempera or any kind of paint very well. Linoleum floors do much better for this type of activity.

A suitable area for drying the theaters lying flat to avoid drips going down the art work must be set aside. Theaters require a minimum of twelve better yet twenty-four or more hours to dry undisturbed. Admonish janitorial staff and any other people who may have reason to be near these works of art to leave them undisturbed. Painting the theaters may take more than a single painting session. Try to set it up so this outcome is okay.

Collect larger size containers such as one-pound tofu tubs into which paint can be dispensed. Add just a little (no more than a teaspoonful squirt per tofu tub) of clear dishwashing liquid to make clean up a little easier. Set out pain brushes in a variety of sizes, plastic buckets filled 1/3 full for rinsing brushes (one for each group). And the cut the children loose. The teacher may want to video-tape children doing this project as parents will be touched as they watch this process unfold on back-to-school night.

Materials
Step One (Planning)
- ❖ Pencils
- ❖ Paper (graph paper is good)
- ❖ Rulers

Step Two (Constructing)
- ❖ Clean sheets of cardboard used for packing items sold in large stores
- ❖ Pencils
- ❖ Yard sticks
- ❖ Tofu tubs
- ❖ Clear dishwashing liquid
- ❖ A variety of colors of tempera paint

❖ Paint brushes of all shapes and sizes
❖ Glitter glue
❖ Multicolored felt tipped markers of all shapes and sizes
❖ **Box cutters:** *NOTE: FOR TEACHER/ADULT USE ONLY*

Clean up

❖ Brooms
❖ Dust pans
❖ Mops
❖ Sponges
❖ Liquid soap
❖ Rags or paper towels

Method

Step One

❖ Expose children to puppet theater oriented experiences before Allowing them to make a puppet theater
❖ Ask children to form collaborative groups of three to five (if there are children often left out of activities, teacher should select; otherwise children self select)
❖ Ask open ended questions to the class, write them out on the board, write them out and give photocopies of the questions to each group
❖ Ask children to discuss their thoughts about the puppet theater, this could take as much as an hour
❖ After having serious discussion, distribute pencils, paper, rulers, and yard sticks; children can also have their cardboard to look at (but not draw on) in the planning process
❖ Children create their drawing or "blue print" for their theater
❖ Teacher may want to get together with groups individually to discuss the effectiveness of their plans, reiterating the open ended questions
❖ Children sketch plan onto their box while working out details particularly designating window

CHILDREN LEAVE FOR WINDOW CUTTING CEREMONY

Step Two

❖ Children select paints, brushes et cetera
❖ Children select an appropriate place to lay out theater for painting
❖ Children paint and decorate the theater cooperatively
❖ Set completed, or theaters to be completed later, in an area suitable for flat drying where they will be left undisturbed

Clean up

❖ When done properly, theater making creates huge messes: do this when the teacher can be generous about that inevitability

❖ Clean up can be fun
❖ Play clean up CD's {Whistle While You Work (Snow White), Barney Clean Up Song, A Spoon Full of Sugar (Mary Poppins), CSUN clean up song (put your toys a-way, don't de-lay, then when you want them you can find them right a-way)} during clean up
❖ Empty buckets used for cleaning brushes, collect all brushes into a single bucket to avoid dripping paint
❖ Refill buckets: some with a little soap, some with clear water, pass out rags and sponges
❖ Some children can clean brushes: make sure the clean brushes are dried brush side up handles down in a container
❖ Other children can wipe up spills, dribs and drabs or paint on floors, tables, and cabinets with mildly soapy water
❖ Others can take a rag and clear water to wipe off soap residue
❖ Teacher can use mop if necessary
❖ Be happy

Suggested Reading:

Butterfield, M. (1998). *The Tortoise and the Hare.* ISBN: 1575727218.
Butterfield, M. (1998). *The Three Little Pigs.* ISBN: 1575727196.

    (See **Story Blocks Suggested Reading** section, in the Language Arts chapter, for more stories to read to the class, that have an obvious or memorable sequence of events, for further ideas for puppet shows)

Targeted Areas of Learning

Physical Development

❖ **Gross motor skills:** using the large muscles of the arms, legs, and torso: painting (house painting style, crawling on the floor, making large movements to draw and paint on cardboard, carrying cardboard
❖ **Fine motor skills:** using the small muscles of the hand and fingers: cutting; drawing shapes; holding a pencil/crayon/marking pens, gluing, sketching
❖ **Eye-hand coordination:** coordinating visual acuity with using the small muscles of the hand and fingers: cutting; drawing shapes; holding a pencil/crayon/marking pen/paint brush
❖ **Physical principals:** learning physical weight; stability; equilibrium; balance; leverage as related to stabilizing a puppet theater behind which children will be Presenting shows
❖ **Sensory discrimination**
 • **Tactile discrimination** (touch): identifying and differentiating textures with touch: soft, hard, rough, smooth, sticky, wet, dry, heavy, light
 • **Visual discrimination** (sight): identifying shapes; colors; sizes; recognizing various aspects of puppet theater making visually

Cognitive Development

- ❖ **Language Arts**
  - **Verbal skills**
    - o **Vocabulary development**: adding to the body of words and phrases understood as relating to the construction of the puppet theater
    - o **Language development**: using acquired language appropriately in interactions with others; ability to carry on a conversation and negotiation for planning and creating a puppet theater
  - **Emergent literacy**
    - o **Sequencing (temporal ordering)**: relating the process of planning and making the puppet theater in the order the child remembers it occurring
- ❖ **Math Skills**
  - **Mathematical literacy**
    - o **Associating number symbols with quantity**: understanding the quantitative meaning of number symbols on a measuring stick in constructing the puppet theater
  - **Mathematical applications**
    - o **Measurement**: using a standard measure to determine the size (height, length) of an puppet theater, puppet theater opening; comparing some aspect of size of one object to another part of the theater
    - o **Spatial relationships**: relating the aspects of the theater to one another, thinking about the theater in three dimensions
    - o **Construction**: building or forming by putting together parts to create a puppet theater
- ❖ **Science**
  - **Scientific processes**
    - o **Inquiry**: an organized search for knowledge regarding puppet theater making
    - o **Prediction**: relating an anticipated outcome of ideas about plan for puppet theater based on logic, experience, or research
    - o **Observation**: watching attentively and noting what happens when puppet theater is made
    - o **Documentation**: writing observations of scientific events which support/disprove claims for predictions or outcomes of puppet theater plans
    - o **Review**: comparing predictions and actual outcomes of puppet theater, assessing value of any mistakes that occurred
  - **Cause and effect**
    - o **Relationships between actions and outcomes**: developing curiosity which leads to scientific inquiry: "educated why" regarding aspects of puppet theater construction
- ❖ **Social Studies**
  - **Understanding that being a good citizen involves certain behavior**: following rules, sharing, taking turns, individual responsibilities and consequences in process of assembling puppet theater

- **Recognizing diversity**: recognizing what makes people similar *and* different: knowing that superficial differences do not mean *bad* in the context of creative expression
- **Accepting human diversity**: types of families, cultures, race, languages, gender, differently-abled, economic status, age represented by the theater design
- **Environmental responsibility**: developing a sense of stewardship for the planet and all that lives upon it: participating with the rest of the class in clean up, using recycled materials in the manufacture of puppet theater
- **Comparing and contrasting locations of people, places, and environments**
  o **Determining relative locations:** near/far, left/right, behind/in front

Social Development

❖ **Self-respect:** valuing themselves while working as part of a team designing and producing a work of art
❖ **Sharing**: understanding that paints, brushes, and art materials intended for use by the community for theater making are available for the use by everyone in that community and may not be available at all times for individual use
❖ **Patience**: diligence: staying with theater making project until it is completed
❖ **Working cooperatively with others in a group**: working well as a member of a team making a puppet theater
❖ **Collaboration**: planning, creating, and Presenting puppet theater in a collaborative situation
❖ **Negotiation**: learning to represent one's ideas about the puppet theater in such a way that others in the group will consider those ideas favorably
❖ **Following directions**: carrying out directions for puppet theater construction
❖ **Leadership**: initiating and managing theater making project (this may show up for some students, but clearly not all)
❖ **Community building**: creating a sense of belonging in a group by working together on puppet theaters
❖ **Taking care of classroom environment**: participating in cleanup of theater making mess

Emotional Development

❖ **Self-esteem**: feeling good about oneself just as one is and is not, participating in making a puppet theater, wherein there is no "wrong" answer
❖ **Self-confidence**: feeling secure within one's self through collaborative interactions on creative group projects
❖ **Accomplishment**: developing a sense of self worth from participating in and completing a puppet theater

Creative Expression

❖ **Use of creative media and expression of imagination**:
  - **2-dimensional visual arts**: painting/drawing: expressing self using 2 dimensional media on puppet theater

- **3-dimensional visual arts:** construction expressing self in three dimensional sculptural media, construction of puppet theater
- ❖ **Developing aesthetic appreciation** for arts as used in puppet theaters
- ❖ **Creative risk**: being comfortable playing creatively, actively and confidently following through on use of imagination, experimenting freely with creative media without focus on the outcome for the puppet theaters
- ❖ **Problem solving**: gathering data, collaborating, delegating responsibility within the small and large group, having small and large group discussion relative to the possible choices available for making a puppet theater the children find pleasing
- ❖ **Creative Thinking**: brainstorming: considering all possible solutions to a problem or challenge posed of creating a usable puppet theater
- ❖ **Persuasion**: learning to represent one's ideas about the creation of a puppet theater in such a way that appeals to others and causes them to consider one's suggestions

Possible Accommodations for *Puppet Theater Activities*

ADHD
- ❖ Place containers with paint, buckets with water for rinsing paint brushes, and paint brushes on a splat mat whose edge is slightly under the puppet theater under construction
- ❖ Fill tofu containers with smaller quantities of paint
- ❖ Present activity after child has had time playing outdoors
- ❖ Allow for longer clean up and transition times
- ❖ Be sure ADHD child is wearing old clothes
- ❖ Give positive reinforcement when child is seen behaving cooperatively
- ❖ Make a point of seeing child behaving appropriately

Developmental Delays
- ❖ Explain puppet theater making using short simple phrases being sure eye contact is made
- ❖ Simplify instructions, speaking slowly
- ❖ Check for comprehension
- ❖ Demonstrate puppet theater making in advance steps-by-step using realia, videos or photographs
- ❖ Review instructions as needed
- ❖ Fill paint dishes with smaller amounts of paint
- ❖ Give children sufficient time to explore and select materials to use
- ❖ Have smaller work groups

Autism Spectrum Disorders
- ❖ Explain puppet theater making using short simple phrases; be sure of eye contact
- ❖ Demonstrate puppet theater making in advance steps-by-step using realia, videos or photographs
- ❖ Present this activity as part of a larger unit so child has the opportunity to process the ideas and become willing to participate

- ❖ Be sure child is working with a familiar "buddy"
- ❖ Offer large easel painting activities often and prior to theater making activities to develop familiarity with the process

Visual Impairments

- ❖ Adjust lighting for best visibility
- ❖ Offer bright high contrast colors of paint
- ❖ Make sure child is in old clothes
- ❖ Larger paint brushes
- ❖ If painting outdoors Offer sunglasses or a wide brimmed hat
- ❖ Place child's group in an area in which the child will not be approached from behind
- ❖ Dispense smaller quantities of paint

Orthopedic Impairments

- ❖ Make sure child is positioned comfortably
- ❖ Adjust furniture and placement of activity such that the child has maximum accessibility to the puppet theater
- ❖ Offer adapted tools such as long handled paint brushes, very large markers, chunky drawing materials
- ❖ Use hand over hand method to guide child's hand if there is a lack of strength or flexibility in the hands or fingers

Gifted and Talented Education (GATE)

- ❖ Show child books (and websites) about famous theaters, architecture, and interior design; ask child to create a theater based on a self-selected theme from information found in those books (historical, fantasy, contemporary)
- ❖ Ask child to write puppet scene or vignette based on the style of his or her theater
- ❖ Ask child to create puppets suitable for his or her theater
- ❖ Allow child to make theater in several session (to give additional drying time) so more detail can be added

English Language Learners (ELL)

- ❖ Explain puppet theater making using short simple phrases being sure eye contact is made
- ❖ Demonstrate puppet theater making in advance steps-by-step using realia, videos or photographs
- ❖ Label items that can be labeled
- ❖ Teach and Review vocabulary associated with puppet theater making in small groups or individually: puppet, theater, stage, doors, windows, color names, paint brush, wet, dry, top, bottom, inside, outside, over, under, between, up, down, markers, pencil, crayon, picture, clean, clean up, rags, water, soap, sponge, mop
- ❖ Use positive reinforcement when child attempts to use or uses puppet theater making vocabulary in conversation or other speech

Content Standards For Kindergarten Met By This Activity

English Language Arts

Reading (1.0, 1.17, 1.18)

Written and Oral Language (1.0, 1.1)

Listening and Speaking (1.0, 1.1, 1.2, 2.0, 2.3)

Mathematics

Numbers and Counting (1.0, 1.2, 3.0, 3.1)

Measurement and Geometry (1.0, 1.1, 2.0. 2.1, 2.2)

Statistics, (1.0, 1.1)

Mathematical Reasoning (1.0, 1.1)

Science

Physical Sciences (1.a)

Investigation and Experimentation (4.a, 4.b, 4.c, 4.d, 4.e)

History and Social Science

Following the Rules (K.1, K.1.1)

Compare and describe people and places (K.4, K.4.1)

Visual Arts

Artistic Perception (1.0, 1.1, 1.2, 1.3)

Creative Expression (2.0, 2.1, 2.2, 2.4, 2.5, 2.6, 2.7)

Understanding Historical / Cultural Contributions of Visual Arts (3.0, 3.1)

Valuing Aesthetics (4.0, 4.1, 4.2, 4.3, 4.4)

Theatre

Artistic Perception (1.0, 1.1)

Learning Plan

    I. **Name of Activity: Puppet Theater Making Activity**

   II. **Date of Presentation:**

  III. **Age or Grade Level: Pre-K, Kindergarten**

  IV. **Ratio of teachers to children needed for this activity:** 1:10

   V. **Target Areas of Learning / Goals and Objectives** (target areas of learning directly relate to "VI. Evaluation Rubric")

      1. Physical: _____

      2. Cognitive: _____

      3. Social: _____

      4. Emotional: _____

      5. Creative: _____

  VI. **Evaluation Rubric:** (if more than two learning areas are being evaluated, a spreadsheet form may be preferred)

Targeted Area of Learning	**Targeted Area of Learning**
_____	_____
_____	_____
4. Always _____	**4.** Always _____
3. Usually _____	**3.** Usually _____
2. Sometimes _____	**2.** Sometimes _____
1. Rarely _____	**1.** Rarely _____

 VII. **Materials and Preparation**

      Step One (Planning)

    1. Pencils

    2. Paper (graph paper is good)

    3. Rulers

      Step Two (Constructing)

    1. Clean sheets of cardboard used for packing items sold in large stores

    2. Pencils

    3. Yard sticks

    4. Tofu tubs

    5. Clear dishwashing liquid

    6. A variety of colors of tempera paint

    7. Paint brushes of all shapes and sizes

    8. Glitter glue

9. Multicolored felt tipped markers of all shapes and sizes
10. Box cutters: **FOR TEACHER/ADULT USE ONLY**

Clean up
1. Brooms
2. Dust pans
3. Mops
4. Sponges
5. Liquid soap
6. Rags or paper towels

VIII. Procedure
Step One
1. Expose children to puppet theater oriented experiences before allowing them to make a puppet theater
2. Ask children to form collaborative groups of three to five (if there are children often left out of activities, teacher should select; otherwise children self select)
3. Ask open ended questions to the class, write them out on the board, write them out and give photocopies of the questions to each group
4. Ask children to discuss their thoughts about the puppet theater, this could take as much as an hour
5. After having serious discussion, distribute pencils, paper, rulers, and yard sticks; children can also have their cardboard to look at (but not draw on) in the planning process
6. Children create their drawing or "blue print" for their theater
7. Teacher may want to get together with groups individually to discuss the effectiveness of their plans, reiterating the open ended questions
8. Children sketch plan onto their box while working out details particularly designating window
9. **CHILDREN LEAVE FOR WINDOW CUTTING CEREMONY**

Step Two
1. Children select paints, brushes et cetera
2. Children select an appropriate place to lay out theater for painting
3. Children paint and decorate the theater cooperatively
4. Set completed, or theaters to be completed later, in an area suitable for flat drying where they will be left undisturbed

Clean up
1. When done properly, theater making creates huge messes: do this when the teacher can be generous about that inevitability
2. Clean up can be fun

3. Play clean up CD's , such as: Whistle While You Work (Snow White), Barney Clean Up Song, A Spoon Full of Sugar (Mary Poppins), CSUN clean up song (Put your toys a-way, don't de-lay, then when you want them you can find them right a-way) during clean up

4. Empty buckets used for cleaning brushes, collect all brushes into a single bucket to avoid dripping paint

5. Refill buckets: some with a little soap, some with clear water, pass out rags and sponges

6. Some children can clean brushes: make sure the clean brushes are dried brush side up handles down in a container

7. Other children can wipe up spills, dribs and drabs or paint on floors, tables, and cabinets with mildly soapy water

8. Others can take a rag and clear water to wipe off soap residue

9. Teacher can use mop if necessary

10. Be happy

IX. **Accommodations** (changes to accommodate learning diversity)
Name of Accommodated Area:

1. _____
2. _____
3. _____
4. _____
5. _____

X. **Applicable Framework Standards: Kindergarten**

Standard _____
_____
_____
_____
_____

Standard _____
_____
_____
_____
_____

Standard _____
_____
_____
_____
_____

Standard _____

_____

_____

_____

Standard _____

_____

_____

_____

_____

XI. Evaluation and Comments (i.e.: How well did the plan work? Great responses? What aspects are especially effective? Not effective? What improvements are needed? Ideas for follow up activities and other notes)

_____

_____

_____

_____

Making Paper Beads

Children love to play with beads. Contrary to stereotypical notions, boys and girls both enjoy this activity. Consider what beads are: colorful bits of plastic, wood, glass, bone, that were once used as money. There is nothing gender specific about beadwork, making beads or wearing of beaded items.

Illustration 18: Wrapping paper around macaroni simplifies making paper beads.

This low-cost activity requires perseverance and a willingness to get a little sticky. Perseverance is necessary, because it takes making more than one bead to make an aesthetically satisfying result. Bead making may take several days for this reason; to make the beads, and then string them another day when they are dry. The nice part is that perfection is not required for this activity, and in fact beads can be different colors, different shapes and different sizes for the same project. Children will tend to get sticky, though, because glue is used to turn strips of torn magazine pages into beads.

When torn, paper has a "grain". Test the paper to see in which direction the "grain" runs. Inform the children about this by demonstrating the tearing process. This will help children avoid a certain level of frustration. If finding the "grain" is part of a scientific inquiry, the teacher should pose a question such as, "What can you find out about tearing paper?" or "Which way does the paper tear best?" But leaving the children to their own devices in this area will produce naught but children calling for assistance from the teacher.

There are wide options for variations on this activity that could be used as part of a unit on aboriginal native peoples of the Americas, Africa, South Seas, and Australia. Included among these variations are types of paper used, types of glue used, addition of color or use of glitter glue, rolling damp beads in dried plant material or other light weight matter, and the manner and pattern of stringing the beads. If desired, matter or spices can be ground with an old coffee grinder, in a suribachi, or with a mortar and pestle.

Diluted glue is often one of the materials used in activities for children. It is easy enough to have in a closed container. Non-dairy creamer or squirt type containers are quite good. It is easy for children to dispense controlled amounts of pre-diluted glue from them. Any type of glue can be diluted. Discount School Supply, located in Salinas California, manufactures School Brand Glue as well as a wide variety of cost effective paints and so forth. Their brand of clear glue is excellent.

This is a fabulous activity for the kidney-shaped table. It is also possible to present it at the children's desks in a large group. If this activity will be presented to the whole class, make sure the children have a tray or some other protection for the desktops.

Sociodramatic use of these beads could include the use of beads in monetary interactions. Use of traditional grinding tools such the Japanese suribachi or mortar and pestle can bring an historical connection to this activity. Only teachers should use the coffee grinder. Make sure children in the class are not sensitive to any materials used for this project.

Variation 1:   Dilute glue with a variety of colors of liquid watercolors into the glue instead of water

Variation 2:   For a wider selection of shapes and sizes, use pasta pieces with holes instead of straws for bead forms (rigatoni, penne, mini penne, elbow macaroni, mostacioli, and so on). The size and shape of the pasta used can vary depending upon the fine motor skills of the children, and also the interest of the children. When done making the beads, leave the cut straw or pasta inside the beads to dry.

Variation 3:   Mix ground spices, dried plant matter or both into the glue

Variation 4:   Use diluted Biopaint® instead of glue

Materials

❖ Old magazines with lots of ads, glossy ads from newspapers, or cut or torn strips of paper about 4" to 6" long, width may vary according to the type and size of cut up plastic drinking straws or pasta that is chosen as the base materials of the bead. Glossy magazine ads are commonly used as they are quite colorful and easy to handle.

❖ Diluted glue dispensed into small clean tofu tubs or Styrofoam meat trays (school glue, clear glue, glitter glue, colored glue are all acceptable)

❖ Plastic drinking straws cut into 1" pieces, (lengths could vary from 1/2" to 1 1/2" depending upon the fine motor skills of the children, and do not need to be all the same size) to be used as forms for wrapping the paper strips

❖ Paintbrushes (optional)

❖ Scissors are optional, as cording, string or yarn may be pre-cut; children may cut the plastic straws themselves or use pre-cut pieces depending on fine motor development.

❖ Plastic glitter, plant matter (such as finely ground lavender, cinnamon, or other finely ground spices) also spread out onto clean Styrofoam meat trays

❖ Mortar and pestle, suribachi, or coffee grinder (optional)

❖ Small Styrofoam meat trays, or paper plates for the diluted glue

❖ Trays upon which beads are dried. Small individual trays should be labeled with children's names to help avoid confusion of beads, and could be Styrofoam meat trays or paper plates with child's name

❖ Beading cord or string; if children are using larger-sized pasta, yarn could also be used

Method

❖ Have children grind plant material or spices used in advance as a separate activity

❖ Place a variety of paper on a table for children to choose from. This may be on a different table than the area where the children will be doing the tearing and gluing

❖ On the table where the children will be working, place trays of diluted glue

❖ If children will be cutting straws themselves, place children's scissors and a tray with plastic straws on the table. Otherwise offer small bowls of pre-cut straws or bowls of pasta with holes, or both. Straws cut by the children do not have to be all the same length, varying from 1/2" to 1 1/2", and children may wish to use more than one type of form for wrapping; Emphasize to the children that uniformity and perfection are not necessarily needed, and they may find, in fact, that a combination of colors, shapes and sizes may indeed be more pleasing

❖ Give each child a paper plate or Styrofoam meat tray and have child write name on it.

❖ Children select paper and if there is more than one kind of glue, a tray of glue

❖ At the kidney-shaped table, several trays of glue and dried materials can be made and shared between the four to six children seated

❖ Seating two children opposite each other for whole class activity, encourages sharing and collaboration; desks permitting, this is preferable

❖ Children tear (or cut) strips of paper (4" to 6" is optimal), dip one end of the torn strip of paper lightly in glue and gently drawing through the glue

❖ Roll moistened paper strip over a straw (or section of pasta)

❖ Roll damp beads over ground spices, plant material, and so on, if desired

❖ Repeat for as many beads as desired

❖ Allow the beads to dry. The length of time needed to reach that point is determined by how wet the paper strip became, the heaviness of the spice coating, and even the humidity of the day. Allow the beads to dry until the next day for ease of stringing

❖ When beads are completely dried, string them onto a piece of cord or firm string

Suggested Multicultural Reading:

Amery, H. (1994). *Then and Now.* (Great side by side illustrations of how things used to be and how they are now).

Chanin, M. (1998). *The chief's blanket.* New York: H.J. Kramer. ISBN: 0915811782.

De Paola, T. (1996). *Legend of the Indian paintbrush..* ISBN: 0698113608.

Flood, N. B. (2006). *The Navajo year walk through many seasons.* ISBN: 189335406.

Jenness, A. (1993). *Come home with me: A multicultural Treasure Hunt.* (A look at four different families and their homes and customs - Africa, Ireland, Cambodia, and Puerto Rico). ISBN: 156584064X.

Knowlton, J. & Barton, H. (1986). *Maps and globes.* ISBN: 0064460495. (Reading Rainbow)

Knowlton, J. & Barton, H. (1997). *Geography from A to Z: A picture glossary.* ISBN: 0064460991.

Longfellow. H.W. (Ilustrated by Susan Jeffers). (1996). *Hiawatha.* ISBN: 0140558829. (Ages 3-8)

Martin, Jr., B. & Archambault, J. (1997). *Knots on a counting rope.* New York: Henry Holt & Company, Inc. ISBN: 0805054790 (A Reading Rainbow Book)

Smith, C., L, (2000). *Jingle Dancer.* ISBN: 068816241X. (About the Ojibway origins of jingle dancing, and the passing down of traditions through generations).

Spier, P. (1988). *People.* Caldecott Medalist. ISBN: 038524469X (Wonderful introduction to cultural diversity about people on four continents)

Steptoe, J. (1987). *Mufaro's Beautiful Daughters.* ISBN: 0688040454.

Las bellas hijas de Mufaro. (Reading Rainbow Book). ISBN: 0688154816 (African legend; Received the Coretta Scott King award for illustration)

Targeted Areas of Learning

Physical Development
- ❖ **Fine motor skills:** using the small muscles of the hand and fingers: cutting, tearing, dipping, rolling paper around straws, dipping formed beads into dried materials, massaging partially dried beads free of straws
- ❖ **Eye-hand coordination:** coordinating visual acuity with using the small muscles of the hand and fingers: cutting, tearing, dipping, rolling paper around straws, dipping formed beads into dried materials, stringing beads
- ❖ **Sensory discrimination**
  - **Tactile discrimination** (touch): feeling sensation of paper dipped into glue, rolling paper into bead form
  - **Visual discrimination** (sight): identifying and recognizing qualities visually
  - **Olfactory discrimination** (smell): smelling the ground plant materials (if used)

Cognitive Development
- ❖ **Language Skill**
  - **Verbal skills**
    - ○ **Language development**: using newly acquired vocabulary in verbal interactions/ conversations
    - ○ **Vocabulary development**: adding words relating to bead making to the working body of words and phrases
  - **Emergent literacy**
    - ○ **Creative writing**: expressing self in marks and pictures related to bead making activities
- ❖ **Math Skills**
  - **Mathematical literacy**
    - ○ **1 to 1 correspondence**: counting beads in an organized way
  - **Seriation:**
    - ○ **Time**: noting the sequential relationship from one event to another as measured by a standard interval of time: drying the beads
  - **Spatial relationships**: relating beads to one another as placed on cord or string
- ❖ **Science**
  - **Scientific processes**
    - ○ **Inquiry**: an organized search for knowledge regarding making paper beads
    - ○ **Prediction**: posing an anticipated outcome based on logic, experience, or research about the beads
    - ○ **Observation**: carefully watching and noting what is seen in the bead making process
    - ○ **Review**: comparing predictions and actual outcomes of bead making, assessing value of any mistakes that occurred

- **Cause and effect**
  - **Relationships between actions and outcomes**: inquiry associated with how paper bead making works
- ❖ **Social Studies**
  - **Understanding that being a good citizen and member of the school community involves certain behavior:** following rules, sharing, taking turns, individual responsibilities and consequences, recognizing appropriate behavior
  - **Recognizing diversity**: learning that cultural groups create unique wearable art such as jewelry
  - **Accepting human diversity**: learning to be comfortable with diverse cultural expressions in terms of dress, wearable art, and so on
  - **Environmental responsibility**: creating art using recycled materials
  - **Understanding that history relates to people, events, and places in times past**
    - Understanding how people lived in earlier times and how their lives were different from life today: using traditional grinding tools

Social Development

- ❖ **Self-respect:** valuing oneself as a creative person and as part of a community
- ❖ **Sharing:** utilizing materials fairly, as community resources
- ❖ **Taking turns:** allowing others to select materials in fair turns
- ❖ **Patience:** staying with bead making until it is completed
- ❖ **Working cooperatively with others in a group:** working well as a member of a community centered team
- ❖ **Collaboration:** sharing ideas and insights about creating paper beads
- ❖ **Following directions:** making beads as directed
- ❖ **Taking care of classroom environment:** participating in cleanup

Emotional Development

- ❖ **Self-esteem:** feeling good about oneself from creating beads from paper
- ❖ **Accomplishment:** developing a sense of self worth from participating in and completing paper beads

Creative Expression

- ❖ **Use of creative media and expression of imagination:**
  - **3-dimensional visual arts**: bead making
- ❖ **Developing aesthetic appreciation** for bead work
- ❖ **Creative risk:** playing with ideas related to making beads

Possible Accommodations for *Paper Bead Making Activity*

ADHD

❖ Have child work on a tray to contain possible spills and assured drips

❖ If trays are unavailable be sure to cover work surfaces (99-cent plastic table cloths are a good option) affix with masking tape

❖ Be sure to model paper tearing or the classroom might appear to have snowed magazines

❖ Use larger size dipping trays (Styrofoam meat trays are quite good) with smaller amounts of diluted glue, refilling occasionally (rather than spilling)

❖ Offer smocks

❖ If trays are unavailable be sure to cover work surfaces (99-cent plastic table cloths are a good option) affix with masking tape

❖ When child behaves appropriately acknowledge the desired behavior, the acknowledgment encourages the child to continue behaving in that way

Developmental Delays

❖ Explain the activity using short simple phrases being sure eye contact is made

❖ Demonstrate the activity in advance steps-by-step slowly, repeating as necessary

❖ Offer larger size "Boba" type straws (available at Filipino or other Asian grocery stores) or large rigatoni type pasta for wrapping to simplify wrapping paper strip (pasta would stay inside the bead)

❖ Allow children to cut the straw and leave it inside the bead instead, if fine motor skills are such that gently massaging bead from straw breaks the bead

❖ Use plastic needles to help thread the beads onto cord or wrap end of cord with a piece of cellophane tape to act as a needle

Autism Spectrum Disorders

❖ Explain the activity using short simple phrases being sure eye contact is made

❖ Model the activity slowly and repeat as necessary

❖ Allow child to "paint" the glue onto paper with a brush or offer latex gloves

❖ Offer larger size "Boba" type straws (available at Filipino or other Asian grocery stores) or large rigatoni type pasta for wrapping to simplify wrapping paper strip (pasta would stay inside the bead)

❖ If child has olfactory sensory sensitivity, use less strong smelling spices or plant materials, or eliminate that aspect of the activity entirely

❖ Allow children to cut the straw and leave it inside the bead instead if fine motor skills are such that gently massaging bead from straw breaks the bead

❖ Use plastic needles to help thread the beads onto cord or wrap end of cord with a piece of cellophane tape to act as a needle

❖ Before making beads, present other activities that utilize beading to build familiarity

❖ Place activity on the schedule, later on in the week so child has time to become accustomed to the idea

❖ Present this as an ongoing activity for a week or two, or as fits in the class schedule so child has time to observe others and become relaxed about participating

Visual Impairments
❖ Adjust lighting for best visibility
❖ Offer larger size "Boba" type straws (available at Filipino or other Asian grocery stores) or large rigatoni type pasta for wrapping to simplify wrapping paper strip (pasta would stay inside the bead)
❖ Allow children to cut the straw and leave it inside the bead instead if fine motor skills are such that gently massaging bead from straw breaks the bead
❖ Use a lighted magnifying glass on a stand
❖ Use plastic needles to help thread the beads onto cord or wrap end of cord with a piece of cellophane tape to act as a needle
❖ Offer heavier cord

Orthopedic Impairments
❖ Make sure child is seated in a comfortable position
❖ Adjust furniture and situate activity for best accessibility
❖ Allow child to work individually or with a single partner
❖ Offer larger size "Boba" type straws (available at Filipino or other Asian grocery stores) or large rigatoni type pasta for wrapping to simplify wrapping paper strip (pasta would stay inside the bead)
❖ Allow children to cut the straw and leave it inside the bead instead if fine motor skills are such that gently massaging bead from straw breaks the bead
❖ Use plastic needles to help thread the beads onto cord or wrap end of cord with a piece of cellophane tape to act as a needle
❖ Offer heavier cord in colors that are easiest for child to see

Gifted and Talented Education (GATE)
❖ Allow children to experiment with sizes, shapes and techniques to see which produces the most pleasing result
❖ Use Biopaint™ option 3
❖ Include advanced beading vocabulary and techniques including using spacers, clasps, and beading trays
❖ Allow children to play with paper strips in other ways such as wrapping strips around an inflated balloon or bottle as papier maché, or making other sculptural pieces
❖ Ask children to research beads from a particular cultural group and attempt to make similar style beads
❖ Offer a broader selection of papers and materials such as brown paper bags, tissue paper, cloth, wax paper and ask children to predict anticipated outcomes of any variations selected

English Language Learners (ELL)

❖ Explain the activity using short simple phrases, being sure eye contact is made with the child

❖ Demonstrate the activity in advance steps-by-step emphasizing vocabulary words

❖ Teach and re-teach vocabulary to children in small groups or individually: paper, glue, wet, dry, hard, soft, words describing smells, color words, shape words, pattern words

❖ Use labels to identify materials; review written words verbally

❖ Acknowledge child's attempts to use new vocabulary in speaking or writing

Content Standards For Kindergarten Met By This Activity

English Language Arts

Reading (1.0, 1.17, 1.18)
Literary Analysis (3.0, 3.2)
Written and Oral Language (1.0, 1.1)
Listening and Speaking (1.0, 1.1, 1.2, 2.0, 2.1, 2.3)

Mathematics

Numbers and Counting (1.0, 1.2)
Algebra, Sets and Sorting (1.0, 1.1)
Measurement and Geometry (1.0, 1.2)

Science

Physical Science (1.a, 1.c)
Investigation and Experimentation (4.a, 4.b, 4.c, 4.d, 4.e)

History and Social Science

Following the rules (K.1, K.1.1)
Using a calendar to sequence events (K.5)
Understanding that history relates to people and places in the past (K.6, K.6.3)

Visual Arts

Artistic Perception (1.0, 1.1, 1.2, 1.3)
Creative Expression (2.0, 2.1, 2.2)
Understanding Historical / Cultural Contributions of Visual Arts (3.0, 3.1)
Valuing Aesthetics (4.0, 4.1, 4.3, 4.4)

Learning Plan

    I. **Name of Activity:** Paper Bead Making Activity

    II. **Date of Presentation:**

    III. **Age or Grade Level:** Pre-K, Kindergarten

    IV. **Ratio of teachers to children needed for this activity:** 1:6

    V. **Target Areas of Learning / Goals and Objectives** (target areas of learning directly relate to "VI. Evaluation Rubric")
        1. Physical: _____
        2. Cognitive: _____
        3. Social: _____
        4. Emotional: _____
        5. Creative: _____

    VI. **Evaluation Rubric:** (if more than two learning areas are being evaluated, a spreadsheet form may be preferred)

Targeted Area of Learning	**Targeted Area of Learning**
_____	_____
_____	_____
4. Always _____	**4.** Always _____
3. Usually _____	**3.** Usually _____
2. Sometimes _____	**2.** Sometimes _____
1. Rarely _____	**1.** Rarely _____

    VII. **Materials and Preparation**
        1. Old magazines with lots of ads, glossy ads from newspapers, or cut or torn strips of paper about 4" to 6" long, width may vary according to the type and size of cut up plastic drinking straws or pasta that is chosen as the base materials of the bead. Glossy magazine ads are commonly used as they are quite colorful and easy to handle.
        2. Diluted glue dispensed into small clean tofu tubs or Styrofoam meat trays (school glue, clear glue, glitter glue, colored glue are all acceptable)
        3. Plastic drinking straws cut into 1" pieces, (lengths could vary from 1/2" to 1 1/2" depending upon the fine motor skills of the children, and do not need to be all the same size) to be used as forms for wrapping the paper strips
        4. Paintbrushes (optional)
        5. Scissors are optional, as cording, string or yarn may be pre-cut
        6. Plastic glitter, plant matter (such as finely ground lavender, cinnamon, or other finely ground spices) also spread out onto clean Styrofoam meat trays

7. Mortar and pestle, suribachi, or coffee grinder (optional)
8. Small Styrofoam meat trays, or paper plates for the diluted glue
9. Trays upon which beads are dried. Small individual trays should be labeled with children's names to help avoid confusion of beads, and could be Styrofoam meat trays or paper plates with child's name
10. Beading cord or string; if children are using larger-sized pasta, yarn could also be used

Variation 1: Dilute glue with a variety of colors of liquid watercolors into the glue instead of water

Variation 2: For a wider selection of shapes and sizes, use pasta pieces with holes instead of straws for bead forms (rigatoni, penne, mini penne, elbow macaroni, mostacioli, and so on). The size and shape of the pasta used can vary depending upon the fine motor skills of the children, and also the interest of the children. When done making the beads, leave the cut straw or pasta inside the beads to dry.

Variation 3: Mix ground spices, dried plant matter or both into the glue

Variation 4:Use diluted Biopaint® instead of glue

VIII. Procedure
1. Have children grind plant material or spices used in advance as a separate activity
2. Place a variety of paper on a table for children to choose from. This may be on a different table than the area where the children will be doing the tearing and gluing
3. On the table where the children will be working, place trays of diluted glue
4. If children will be cutting straws themselves, place children's scissors and a tray with plastic straws on the table. Otherwise offer small bowls of pre-cut straws or bowls of pasta with holes, or both. Straws cut by the children do not have to be all the same length, varying from 1/2" to 1 1/2", and children may wish to use more than one type of form for wrapping; Emphasize to the children that uniformity and perfection are not necessarily needed, and they may find, in fact, that a combination of colors, shapes and sizes may indeed be more pleasing
5. Give each child a paper plate or Styrofoam meat tray and have child write name on it.
6. Children select paper and place them on their paper plate and if there is more than one kind of glue, a tray of glue
7. At the kidney-shaped table, several trays of glue and dried materials can be made and shared between the four to six children seated
8. Seating two children opposite each other for whole class activity, encourages sharing and collaboration, desks permitting, this is preferable

9. Children tear (or cut) strips of paper, dip one end of the torn strip of paper lightly in glue and gently drawing through the glue
10. Roll moistened paper strip over a straw (or section of pasta)
11. Roll damp beads over ground spices (and so on) if desired
12. Repeat for as many beads as are desired
13. Allow the beads to dry. The length of time needed to reach that point is determined by how wet the paper strip became, the heaviness of the spice coating, and even the humidity of the day. Allow the beads to dry until the next day for ease of stringing
14. When beads are completely dried, string onto a piece of cord or firm string

IX. **Accommodations** (changes to accommodate learning diversity)
    Name of Accommodated Area:
    1. _____
    2. _____
    3. _____
    4. _____
    5. _____

X. **Applicable Framework Standards: Kindergarten**
   Standard _____
   _____
   _____
   _____
   _____

   Standard _____
   _____
   _____
   _____
   _____

   Standard _____
   _____
   _____
   _____
   _____

   Standard _____
   _____
   _____
   _____
   _____

Standard _____

_____

_____

_____

_____

XI. **Evaluation and Comments** (i.e.: How well did the plan work? Great responses? What aspects are especially effective? Not effective? What improvements are needed? Ideas for follow up activities and other notes)

_____

_____

_____

_____

Doll Making

Dolls have been utilized in socio-dramatic play throughout human history. The exquisite imagination of children for all of time transforms a stick into a baby or a gun depending on the need.

Doll making can be as simple as wrapping yarn or raffia, or as complex as pouring porcelain slip into a mold and painting delicate features upon the doll faces.

The wrapped raffia dolls described in this activity are similar to dolls made in pioneer United States. The technique is simple and the materials inexpensive, which was important at that time in history when manufactured goods were outrageously expensive and almost impossible to acquire.

Illustration 19: Yarn dolls can be an interesting introduction to multicultural curriculum.

This can be done as a two-step activity. One day, assemble the dolls. Another day, embellish with paints, fabric and so forth. This will keep the level of energy generated under control, the mess manageable, and the process and value more distinct. If all the stuff for assembly and decoration is out at the same time, the possibility of overwhelming chaos opens.

Model the process of this activity. Take care not to do the best possible work, or worse yet, to make a "sample". When samples are provided, some children will try very hard to make the same item as the teacher's, and may even compare their product to the teacher's work. If a sample must be made, make it as simple and rough as possible. Without "samples" the child has a chance to create freely without the constraint of preconceived ideas.

Raffia is dried palm leaves that are processed into flexible straw colored ribbons. Packages with enough raffia to make several school years' worth of dolls can be picked up at craft supply stores for just a few dollars.

Raffia can be dyed. Dying raffia is a very messy project that the teacher may choose to do in advance. Create loosely wrapped skeins of material to be dyed so material dyes as evenly as possible (which, in point of fact is not particularly even at all). Use packaged dyes as directed; add raffia or other undyed string, cord or similar materials. When desired color is achieved, rinse out excess dye, and take dyed material outside to hang dry in an area that will not be damaged by the dripping dye. When dried, raffia is ready to use.

When laying out raffia, have all the strips set out in a single direction. A tangled mass of raffia invites a less controlled level of energy. The value is better accessed when there is less chaos. Chaos distracts from the process.

Forms for the dolls are pieces of cardboard or railroad board (often found in the paper room of public schools). From there the teacher can offer as many or as few embellishments as the teacher feels will work for that particular class.

Recommended embellishments include, but are not limited to, yarn for hair, wiggle eyes, glitter glue pens for adding faces, fabric paint, Nancy bottles filled with Biocolor™ for making faces, bits of ribbon, buttons, beads, bits of fabric or leather, feathers, dried flowers and other plant material, silk flowers ... the possibilities are endless.

If adding plant material to dolls, consider using fresh or dried sprigs of lavender (the lovely purple flowers could become hair or raiment), fresh rosemary (it does ooze just a little), fresh sage, fennel, sea grass (if school is near the ocean), or other pleasant smelling plant material the grows on long flexible stems. If part of the activity is for the class to go out into the surrounding area to find plant embellishments, the teacher should recon the walk prior to the class taking the walk. Be aware that not all plant materials are appropriate or safe for children to select. It is recommended that there be a very low ratio for such an excursion. If the teacher is unfamiliar with local flora, it is better to pick up the embellishments at a craft store. Honey suckle is a bit sticky and draws ants, poison oak, sumac, and ivy cause very uncomfortable rashes, oleanders are phenomenally poisonous, nettles and many berry bushes have little stinging hairs that could irritate the hands of young explorers. Supervision is paramount.

This is an excellent activity to include when presenting a unit on the everyday people of early United States. The unit could include presenting foods, clothing, and music from that era. Doll making could be placed in the middle of the unit, which could be wrapped up by a pioneer style meal.

The Doll Hospital (any one of the books in the series) could be read aloud to the class as part of this unit. (See **Suggested Reading** section below)

Variation 1:   Yarn can be substituted for raffia: it is softer and easier to wind and manipulate

Variation 2:   Cloth cut into strips can be substituted for raffia

Variation 3:   Use completed dolls, particularly ones that have pleasantly scented herbs in them for a lovely gift for a mom

Variation 4:   If garlic is grown locally, dried garlic stalks make great decorative dolls as well

Materials

❖ Raffia: the quantity of the raffia used determines whether the doll is "fat" or "skinny"
❖ Cardboard or railroad winding forms cut to a size appropriate for the children from class to hold easily: the size of the cardboard form determines the height of the doll
❖ Smaller pieces of cardboard for winding yarn "hair"
❖ Quick drying glue such as Tacky™ glue
❖ Scissors
❖ String for tying top of raffia bundle, articulating head, torso, arms, and legs, possibly hands, and feet
❖ Embellishments

Method

Part One (Making the Doll)

- ❖ Set out materials for making doll's body which could include raffia, dried plant matter, string, cardboard and material used for hair wrapping forms buffet style - present materials in an organized way to encourage focus
- ❖ Model the wrapping and tying method for the raffia without creating a "sample".
- ❖ Children select raffia and board
- ❖ Children can work in pairs or at the kidney shaped table to create their dolls by winding raffia and additional plant materials, ribbon, or yarn into the body of the doll, if desired
- ❖ Children wind yarn around smaller piece of cardboard for hair, if desired
- ❖ Remove "hair from cardboard, tie top of "hair" loop tightly, cut open bottom of yarn loop
- ❖ Children remove raffia wound around cardboard, holding the top of the head another child can take a strip of raffia, yarn to tie top of raffia loop and yarn hair together tightly
- ❖ At the minimum, children will need to fashion a head and arms to make a doll; children create a head by tying a piece of string around loop of raffia approximately where child wants the neck to be
- ❖ Cut the raffia loop at the bottom of the doll
- ❖ Separate out "arms" from sides of the "body", and, if desired, tie a piece of string around the center of the body of the doll to create a "waist"
- ❖ "Arms" and "legs" can be braided if children know or are developing that skill
- ❖ Arms may need to be trimmed slightly for a more human appearance
- ❖ For arms: tie bottom ends with string to increase appearance as "arms" and "hands"
- ❖ Separate bottom into two sections and tie to create "legs" if desired; tie each section at the bottom to create appearance of "legs" and "feet";
- ❖ Alternately the area below may be left unarticulated for a "skirt"; for an even more complex option select two smaller quantities to be articulated as "legs" and leave the rest free to be a skirt or a dress

Part Two (Decorating the Doll)

- ❖ Set out paints and other materials buffet style: present the materials in an organized way, for example, buttons, wiggle eyes, silk flowers et cetera are best presented in individual (clear) plastic containers with the tops taken off rather than placing scattered piles of materials out which encourages the children to treat creative materials disrespectfully
- ❖ Children select creative materials they are considering
- ❖ Children may return to supply table at any time after all children have had a turn in order to return or exchange creative decorating materials, with the provision that there should be only a specified number of children at the supply table at any given time (in the creative process changing the plan is acceptable/crucial)
- ❖ Bits of fabric can be cut and tied to create clothing, faces can be created with paint and wiggle eyes, yarn hair can be styled, jewelry can be added, the options are limited to imagination, which hopefully will not be constrained
- ❖ If glue or paint is used the dolls will need to be set in a safe place aside for drying, label drying dolls

❖ Embellishment may require more than one session, if possible make that option available to children
❖ Children can write in their journals about anything they do, however asking them if they have gained insight about the cultural differences between pioneer United States and the United States as it is today may be quite a valuable reflection for young kindergartners

Suggested Reading:

Amery, H. (1994). *Then and Now*. ISBN: 0746007949. (Great illustrations; side by side pictures of how things used to be and how they are now).

Holub, J. (2002). *Tatiana Comes to America: An Ellis Island Story*. (Doll Hospital, Book 1, 112 pages). ISBN: 043940178X. (Story of immigrants coming to America)

Holub, J. (2003). *Glory's Freedom: A Story of the Underground Railroad*. (Doll Hospital, Book 3, 112 pages). ISBN: 0439401801.

Moss, M. (2001). *Rachel's Journal: The Story of a Pioneer Girl*. ISBN: 015202168X.

Ringgold, F. (1995). *Aunt Harriet's underground railroad in the sky*. ISBN: 0517885433.

Spier, P, (1988) *People*. ISBN: 038524469X. Caldecott Medalist. (Wonderful introduction to cultural diversity about people on four continents)

Wright, D. (1998). *The Lonely Doll*. ISBN: 0395899265.

Zolotow, C. (2985). *Willliam's Doll*. ISBN: 0064430677.

Targeted Areas of Learning

Physical Development

❖ **Fine Motor Skills:** using the small muscles of the hand and fingers: cutting, winding, tying, painting, gluing and assembling dolls
❖ **Eye-Hand Coordination:** coordinating visual acuity with using the small muscles of the hand and fingers: cutting, winding, tying, creating a face with paint, making doll clothes, jewelry, styling or braiding "hair", "arms", or "legs"
❖ **Sensory Discrimination including:**
  • **Tactile Discrimination** (touch): identifying and differentiating textures with touch: feeling the different materials used, feeling the sensation of winding, tying, braiding
  • **Visual Discrimination** (sight): identifying materials and the various body part created visually
  • **Olfactory Discrimination** (smell): identifying different smells: sweet, spicy, pungent, floral particularly if dried plant/herbal matter is used as part of the doll's body

Cognitive Development:

❖ **Language Skills**
  • **Verbal skills**
    o **Vocabulary development**: adding doll making distinctions to the body of words and phrases understood
    o **Language development**: using doll making distinctions appropriately in verbal interactions with others

- **Emergent literacy**
  - o **Creative writing**: expressing, in writing, the experience of doll making and how play is similar and different between now and pioneer United States
- **Sequencing (temporal ordering)**: telling how the doll was constructed in the order the doll was made
- ❖ **Math Skills**
  - **Mathematical applications**
    - o **Measurement**: using a standard measure to determine the size (height, length, thickness) of a doll being made
    - o **Spatial relationships**: relating the relative size of the dolls arms, head, torso, legs to each other; selecting body proportions for doll
    - o **Construction**: building or forming by putting together parts to create a doll
    - o **Common Relatedness**: linking items used for doll that may not be the same but are related
- ❖ **Science**
  - **Scientific processes**
    - o **Inquiry**: an organized question about how dolls were made and what different processes will produce
    - o **Prediction**: relating an anticipated outcome of doll making
    - o **Observation**: watching attentively and noting the process of doll making
    - o **Documentation**: writing observations in personal journal
    - o **Review**: comparing predictions and actual outcomes, assessing value of any mistakes that occurred
  - **Cause and effect**
    - o **Relationships between actions and outcomes**: Why did the raffia fall apart when it wasn't tied securely? Why did the painted face drip when held upright before drying was complete? Why did the wiggle eyes fall off?
- ❖ **Social Studies**
  - **Students understand that being a good citizen involves acting in certain ways** (CA. Social Science Content Standards K.1): following rules, sharing, taking turns, individual responsibilities and consequences
  - **Recognizing diversity**: recognizing what makes people similar *and* different: noting the differences in toys from earlier times and today
  - **Accepting human diversity**: types of families, cultures, race particularly as it relates to the types of toys children use in other places
  - **Temporal ordering**: children put events in order using a calendar placing days, weeks, and months in proper order (CA. Social Science Content Standards K-5): relating historical toys to current toys, recalling the event of doll making in the ordering which it occurred
  - **Understanding that history relates to people, events, and places of other times** (CA. Social Science Content Standards K-6)

o Understand how people lived in earlier times and how their lives were different from life today (K-6.3)

Social Development

❖ **Self-respect:** valuing themselves as creative individuals through working with materials and in activities wherein the outcome is less important than active participation the doll making process

❖ **Sharing:** using doll making materials as a community resource rather than an individual resource; if not using a selected material, allowing another to use it

❖ **Taking turns:** after selecting materials, waiting for rest of class to have a first opportunity before returning to the supply table

❖ **Patience:** diligence: staying with doll making until doll is completed, not giving up in frustration

❖ **Working cooperatively with others in a group:** working well as a member of a team with a desire for everyone's success

❖ **Collaboration:** planning and creating in partnership, sharing ideas

❖ **Following directions:** carrying out directions for doll making, use, and care for materials

❖ **Respecting others as individuals (behaving appropriately with others):** being courteous with table mates

❖ **Community building:** working cooperatively with others toward common goal of making dolls

❖ **Taking care of classroom environment:** participating in cleanup, maintaining orderly presentation of materials, treating materials respectfully

Emotional Development

❖ **Self-esteem:** feeling good about that which one does and does not; building self confidence by participating in activities wherein there is no "wrong" answer; feeling safe to try out new activities in a nonjudgmental environment

❖ **Self-confidence:** feeling secure within one's self as one works in a group with creative materials

❖ **Accomplishment:** developing a sense of self worth from participating in and completing doll making

❖ **Generosity:** sharing of one's art materials and one's ideas about doll making

Creative Expression

❖ **Use of creative media and expression of imagination:**
  • **3-Dimensional visual arts:** expressing self in the 3 dimensional media of doll crafting
  • **Dramatization/story telling:** expressing self through playing with the hand crafted doll
  • **Writing/story telling:** expressing self in journal as related to doll crafting and contrasting child play from earlier times to current child play

❖ **Developing aesthetic appreciation** for hand made dolls, the work of classmates, and for own work
❖ **Creative risk**: being comfortable trying something new just to see how/if it will work
❖ **Problem Solving**: checking out techniques for making this type of doll

Possible Accommodations for *Doll Making Activity*

ADHD
❖ Offer a smaller selection of materials
❖ Offer a carrel to reduce distractions
❖ Allow more time for child to complete activity
❖ Allow child to work on a tray to manage doll crafting materials
❖ "Catch child being good" to reinforce desired behaviors
❖ If child has comments or observations to share, give the child the feeling those comments are worthy, take a few moments, it will build self esteem, and the time shared is the best reward for an ADHD child

Developmental Delays
❖ Explain the activity using short simple phrases being sure eye contact is made
❖ Model actions to be taken, simplifying the activity whenever possible
❖ Offer larger winding cards
❖ Use yarn or fabric strips for easier manipulation instead of raffia
❖ Make bigger dolls with less detail
❖ Use adapted tools such as scissors and glue dispensers
❖ Offer materials in sizes and shapes easy for child to manipulate

Autism Spectrum Disorders
❖ Explain the activity using short simple phrases being sure eye contact is made
❖ Demonstrate the activity in advance steps-by-step using realia, photographs or videos
❖ Allow child to work with softer materials such as yarn or fabric strips if raffia poses a sensory challenge
❖ Have raffia in the classroom so child has an opportunity to touch it and become accustomed to it
❖ Offer adapted tools such as scissors, glue dispensers
❖ Adjust size of crafts materials such that they are easily manipulated by the child
❖ Have activity on the calendar and present the activity later in the week so child can become comfortable with the idea
❖ If child is sensitive to odors, eliminate using the herbal plant matter from the activity

Visual Impairments
❖ Adjust lighting
❖ Use larger winding cards

❖ Make larger dolls involving less detail
❖ Have child work with a partner for wrapping and tying
❖ Offer adapted tools: larger scissors, materials in sizes and colors that are easy for child to see and manipulate

Orthopedic Impairments
❖ Make sure child is positioned comfortably
❖ Adjust furniture or position materials to make activity easy accessible to student
❖ Allow child to work individually or with a partner on a tray
❖ Offer adapted tools such as scissors, padded or finger grip glue dispensers, larger winding cards
❖ Have child create a doll in a size which child can manipulate easily
❖ Adjust materials to a size which child can manipulate easily
❖ If hands and fingers lack strength or flexibility work with child using the hand-over-hand method
❖ Allocate more time for activity

Gifted and Talented Education (GATE)
❖ Ask child to find similarities between playing with toys today and the ways toys were played with in pioneer days, and explain which they think is better and why
❖ Ask child to write a creative story about the doll as if it were from an earlier time
❖ Ask child to draw stories or ideas about what life was like when such toys were really in use
❖ Ask child to describe the smells experienced from the herbs in writing or drawings

English Language Learners (ELL)
❖ Explain the activity using short simple phrases being sure eye contact is made
❖ Demonstrate the activity in advance steps-by-step using realia, photographs or videos
❖ Teach and re-teach vocabulary associated with doll making including: doll, face, head, arms, body, waist, legs, hair, eyes, nose, mouth, clothing words, raffia, ribbon, buttons, glitter, wet, dry, plant words such as lavender or sage, cut, glue
❖ Use positive reinforcement when child attempts to integrate new vocabulary into work body of language.

Content Standards For Kindergarten Met By This Activity
English Language Arts
Reading (1.0, .1.7, 1.18)
Writing (1.0, 1.3, 1.4)
Written and Oral Language (1.0, 1.1, 1.2)
Listening and Speaking (1.0, 1.1, 1.2, 2.0, 2.1)

Mathematics

Algebra, Sets and Sorting (1.0, 1.1)

Measurement and Geometry (1.0, 1.1, 2.0, 2.2)

Science

Physical Sciences (1.a)

Investigation and Experimentation (4.a, 4.b, 4.c, 4.d, 4.e)

History and Social Science

Following the rules (K.1, K.1.1)

Compare and describe people and places (K.4)

Understanding that history relates to people and places in the past (K.6, K.6.3)

Visual Arts

Artistic Perception (1.0, 1.2)

Creative Expression (2.0, 2.2, 2.7)

Understanding Historical / Cultural Contributions of Visual Arts (3.0, 3.1, 3.3)

Valuing Aesthetics (4.0, 4.1, 4.3, 4.4)

Learning Plan

    I. Name of Activity: Doll Making

    II. Date of Presentation:

    III. Age or Grade Level: Pre-K, Kindergarten

    IV. Ratio of teachers to children needed for this activity: 1:10

    V. Target Areas of Learning / Goals and Objectives (target areas of learning directly relate to "VI. Evaluation Rubric")
        1. Physical: _____
        2. Cognitive: _____
        3. Social: _____
        4. Emotional: _____
        5. Creative: _____

    VI. Evaluation Rubric: (if more than two learning areas are being evaluated, a spreadsheet form may be preferred)

Targeted Area of Learning   **Targeted Area of Learning**

_____   _____
_____   _____

    4. Always _____   **4.** Always _____
    3. Usually _____   **3.** Usually _____
    2. Sometimes _____   **2.** Sometimes _____
    1. Rarely _____   **1.** Rarely _____

    VII. Materials and Preparation
        1. Raffia: the quantity of the raffia used determines whether the doll is "fat" or "skinny"
        2. Cardboard or railroad winding forms cut to a size appropriate for the children from class to hold easily: the size of the cardboard form determines the height of the doll
        3. Smaller pieces of cardboard for winding yarn "hair"
        4. Quick drying glue such as Tacky™ glue
        5. Scissors
        6. String for tying top of raffia bundle, articulating head, torso, arms, and legs, possibly hands, and feet
        7. Embellishments

VIII. Procedure

Part One (Making the Doll)

1. Set out materials for making doll's body which could include raffia, dried plant matter, string, cardboard and material used for hair wrapping forms buffet style - present materials in an organized way to encourage focus

2. Model the wrapping and tying method for the raffia without creating a "sample".

3. Children select raffia and board

4. Children can work in pairs or at the kidney shaped table to create their dolls by winding raffia and additional plant materials, ribbon, or yarn into the body of the doll, if desired

5. Children wind yarn around smaller piece of cardboard for hair, if desired

6. Remove "hair from card board, tie top of "hair" loop tightly, cut open bottom of yarn loop

7. Children remove raffia wound around cardboard, holding the top of the head another child can take a strip of raffia, yarn to tie top of raffia loop and yarn hair together tightly

8. At the minimum, children will need to fashion a head and arms to make a doll; children create a head by tying a piece of string around loop of raffia approximately where child wants the neck to be

9. Cut the raffia loop at the bottom of the doll

10. Separate out "arms" from sides of the "body", and, if desired, tie a piece of string around the center of the body of the doll to create a "waist"

11. "Arms" and "legs" can be braided if children know or are developing that skill

12. Arms may need to be trimmed slightly for a more human appearance

13. For arms: tie bottom ends with string to increase appearance as "arms" and "hands"

14. Separate bottom into two sections and tie to create "legs" if desired - tie each section at the bottom to create appearance of "legs" and "feet";

15. Alternately the area below " may be left unarticulated for a "skirt" ; for an even more complex option select two smaller quantities to be articulated as "legs" and leave the rest free to be a skirt or a dress

Part Two (Decorating the Doll)

1. Set out paints and other materials buffet style: present the materials in an organized way, for example, buttons, wiggle eyes, silk flowers et cetera are best presented in individual (clear) plastic containers with the tops taken off rather than placing scattered piles of materials out which encourages the children to treat creative materials disrespectfully

2. Children select creative materials they are considering

3. Children may return to supply table at any time after all children have had a turn in order to return or exchange creative decorating materials, with the provision that

there should be only a specified number of children at the supply table at any given time (in the creative process changing the plan is acceptable/crucial)

4. Bits of fabric can be cut and tied to create clothing, faces can be created with paint and wiggle eyes, yarn hair can be styled, jewelry can be added, the options are limited to imagination, which hopefully will not be constrained

5. If glue or paint is used the dolls will need to be set in a safe place aside for drying, label drying dolls

6. Embellishment may require more than one session, if possible make that option available to children

7. Children can write in their journals about anything they do, however asking them if they have gained insight about the cultural differences between pioneer United States and the United States as it is today may be quite a valuable reflection for young kindergartners

IX. **Accommodations** (changes to accommodate learning diversity)
   Name of Accommodated Area:
   1. _____
   2. _____
   3. _____
   4. _____
   5. _____

X. **Applicable Framework Standards: Kindergarten**
   Standard _____
   _____
   _____
   _____
   _____
   _____

   Standard _____
   _____
   _____
   _____
   _____
   _____

   Standard _____
   _____
   _____
   _____
   _____

   Standard _____
   _____
   _____
   _____
   _____

Standard _____

_____

_____

_____

_____

XI. **Evaluation and Comments** (i.e.: How well did the plan work? Great responses? What aspects are especially effective? Not effective? What improvements are needed? Ideas for follow up activities and other notes)

_____

_____

_____

_____

Basic Braiding

Braiding is an ancient skill used in hunting, agricultural, and ranching cultures. Communities that worked on, by or near the sea and those that husbanded horses particularly valued the skill of interweaving cords and knotting rope for adding strength. In many human communities, the interweaving strands of hair for decorative purposes was also considered a highly valued skill.

Braiding involves fine motor and eye-hand coordination, as well as an ability to visually retain the position of the current strand and mentally maintain a pattern for weaving the materials in the process of seeking a particular result.

There are wonderful resources available in libraries, bookstores, and on-line for suggestions for beautiful, intricate braid work. The basic overhand three-strand braid is an excellent place to start. The easiest way to learn braiding is to have a partner holding (with moderate tension) the end that has three pieces tied together.

Any material that can be cut, torn or somehow manipulated to resemble a strand or divided into sections of appropriate length can be braided. Strips of torn sheets, scrap fabric, ribbon, strands of yarn or raffia are good places to start. For a three-part braid, each child will need three strands or groups of strands for braiding.

Braiding can be used as part of a unit on pioneer United States, as it was a skill used in many areas of life. Samuel Clemens' book, *Tom Sawyer*, spoke of dipping Becky Thatcher's braids into an inkwell (Clemens - better known by his pen name "Mark Twain"). It might be appropriate to read Tom Sawyer in a unit looking at pioneer life in early United States history.

If children show interest and become proficient at three-part braiding, the teacher can consider introducing more complicated braiding patterns such as four to six strand flat braids (which is similar to weaving), fishtail braids, French braids, or a four strand round braids.

Variation: braid, right to left pattern going under instead of over the middle section

Materials
* ❖ Cord, string, yarn, rope, ribbon, lanyard or raffia separated into three strands (making a strand con involve on piece or several of material being braided so long as the total number of sections being braided equals three
* ❖ Yardstick or other measuring tools
* ❖ Scissors
* ❖ Two pieces of cord, yarn, or other to tie sections together at top and bottom which will prevent the braid from coming undone; these pieces of cord can be the same or contrasting as desired

Method
* ❖ Children select material to be braided
* ❖ Children measure out three pieces of designated length of braiding material, checks measurement with partner, and cuts designated length
* ❖ Tie three sections to be braided together at top tightly

- ❖ Have partner (braid holder) hold tied end, or make a loop from the cord holding the ends together and loop it over a drawer pull or door handle
- ❖ The braider holds the three pieces of cord to be braided evenly lifting the section on the right over the piece in the middle
- ❖ Lift the section on the left over the middle, check for tension and evenness
- ❖ Lift the section now on the far right over the middle section, and the left over the middle section checking for evenness of the braid
- ❖ Again, lift the section on the right over the middle, and then the left over the middle, again checking for evenness
- ❖ Continue with this pattern until there is no more cord or one is bored
- ❖ Tie off braid with second smaller piece of cord

Suggested reading and references:

To encourage further classroom discussions regarding other types of braiding, and the importance of braiding and knotwork down through history, the following books are recommended. *The Ultimate Encyclopedia of Knots and Ropework* (2002) is a beautifully illustrated book that explains the "history, origins and uses" (pp. 8-13) of knots and braiding. It also shows many different types of both knots and braids, with simple directions and photographs (simple three strand braiding page 246, four strand braiding page 247).

Also:

Johnson, A.A. (1992). *Braids and Bows. Klutz Books.* ISBN: 187825717X. (simple instructions and illustrations of several different types of braiding)

Johnson, A.A. (1995). *Hair: A Book of Braiding and Styles.* ISBN: 1570540187

Madrigal, A., (1989). Erandi's Braids. ISBN: 0-39923212-5. (The book is illustrated by Tomie de Paola).

Targeted Areas of Learning

Physical Development

- ❖ **Gross Motor Skills:** using the large muscles of the arms and hands: using hand over hand movements for braiding
- ❖ **Fine Motor Skills:** using the small muscles of the hand and fingers: holding, measuring, cutting materials to be braided, maintaining tension in the braiding process
- ❖ **Eye-Hand Coordination:** coordinating visual acuity with using the small muscles of the hand and fingers: cutting materials to be braided, maintaining continuity of braiding (right over middle, left over middle, right over middle, left over middle et cetera)
- ❖ **Sensory Discrimination**
  - • **Tactile Discrimination** (touch): identifying and differentiating textures with touch: soft, hard, rough, smooth tactile sensation of materials being braided, having the physical sensation of the braiding process and the feeling of braided materials

- **Visual Discrimination** (sight): identifying the pattern of the braid, the appearance of braided materials

Cognitive Development
❖ **Language Arts**
- **Verbal skills**
  - ○ **Vocabulary development**: adding language related to braiding to the body of words and phrases understood and used
  - ○ **Language development**: using language associated with braiding appropriately in interactions with others
- **Emergent literacy**
  - ○ **Creative writing**: expressing experience of braiding in a journaling exercise
  - ○ **Story recall/sequencing (temporal ordering)**: retelling *Tom Sawyer* story the child heard or the braiding experience in the order it occurred.
❖ **Math Skills**
- **Conservation**
  - ○ **Conservation of quantity**: understanding that the number in a group of items remains constant no matter how the items are arranged
  - ○ **Reversibility**: a configuration of items can be changed back to its original form without changing the quantity of quantity of items
- **Mathematical literacy**
  - ○ **One-to-one correspondence**: counting items in an organized way
- **Mathematical applications**
  - ○ **Measurement**: using a standard measure to determine the length of materials to be braided
  - ○ **Spatial relationships**: relating the aspects of physical objects to one another in braiding
❖ **Social Studies**
- **Students understand that being a good citizen involves acting in certain ways** (CA. Social Science Content Standards K.1): following rules, sharing, taking turns, individual responsibilities and consequences
- **Compare and contrast locations of people, places, and environments** (CA. Social Science Content Standards K-4):
  - ○ Determine relative locations: near/far, left/right, behind/in front (K-4.1)
- **Understanding that history relates to people, events, and places of other times** (CA. Social Science Content Standards K-6)
  - ○ Understand how people lived in earlier times and how their lives were different from life today (K-6.3)

Social Development
❖ **Self-respect:** valuing themselves and developing skills
❖ **Sharing:** sharing materials for braiding as community resources

- ❖ **Taking turns:** holding partner's braiding cords in a way that supports a successful outcome, then having a turn at braiding
- ❖ **Patience**: diligence: staying with braiding project until it is completed
- ❖ **Working cooperatively with others in a group**: working well as a member of a team to empower the making of braids
- ❖ **Following directions**: carrying out directions making a braid as directed
- ❖ **Taking responsibility**: helping others out in the process of making braids, being supportive of others if they acquire the skill less quickly
- ❖ **Taking care of classroom environment**: participating in cleanup of braiding activity

Emotional Development
- ❖ **Self-esteem**: feeling good about oneself by participating in activities wherein there is no "wrong" answer; feeling safe to try out new activities in a nonjudgmental environment, wherein there is no pressure to produce a particular outcome
- ❖ **Accomplishment**: developing a sense of self-worth from participating in, development of, and completing braiding skills

Creative Expression
- ❖ **Use of creative media and expression of imagination**

  - • **3-dimensional visual arts:** expressing self in 3 dimensional media

- ❖ **Aesthetic appreciation:** developing appreciation for skill in braiding

Possible Accommodations for *Braiding Activities*

ADHD
- ❖ Be sure to set out materials in an orderly fashion that invites maintenance of the room organization
- ❖ Use positive reinforcement when child works well with braiding partner
- ❖ Keep sections of materials shorter at first so child will feel a quick sense of accomplishment
- ❖ Use three colors for easy identification of pattern
- ❖ Allow child and partner to work within a carrel to reduce distractions

Developmental Delay
- ❖ Explain the activity using short simple phrases while making eye contact
- ❖ Model activity using photographs or realia
- ❖ Keep sections of materials shorter at first so child will feel a quick sense of accomplishment
- ❖ Use adapted scissors
- ❖ Select soft, thick, medium weight round shaped cords in three colors (to be able to identify the pattern more easily) for easiest braiding

Autism Spectrum Disorders
❖ Explain the activity using short simple phrases while making eye contact
❖ Model activity using photographs or realia
❖ Keep sections of materials shorter at first so child will feel a quick sense of accomplishment
❖ Use adapted scissors
❖ Select soft, thick, medium weight round shaped cords in three colors (to be able to identify the pattern more easily) for easiest braiding
❖ Select materials that child enjoys touching
❖ Have materials around the classroom for a week or so before the activity so they seem familiar
❖ Practice braiding regularly
❖ Have child work with regular "buddy"

Visual Impairments
❖ Adjust lighting so child has maximum vision
❖ Offer thicker, round braiding materials
❖ Use three bright, high contrast colors for easiest visibility
❖ Allow child to feel a completed braid
❖ Let child follow teacher's hands with their hands while teacher is braiding

Orthopedic Impairments
❖ Explain the activity using short simple phrases while making eye contact
❖ Model activity using photographs or realia
❖ Keep sections of materials shorter at first so child develops confidence and a feeling of success at braid making
❖ Select soft, thick, medium weight round shaped cords in three colors (to be able to identify the pattern more easily) for easiest braiding
❖ Use adapted scissors
❖ If hands lack strength or flexibility use hand over hand method to guide child while braiding

Gifted and Talented Education (GATE)
❖ Offer more complex braiding patterns
❖ Offer unusual materials to be braided such as raffia, sea grass, lavender, sections of clean panty hose, decorative paper ribbon, interesting brightly colored wire
❖ Ask child to draw an analogy between the braiding process and some part of being in school or other aspect of their lives in writing
❖ Ask child to think of as many ways that braids have been or could be used as possible
❖ Ask child to turn a braid into a basket, pot holder or trivet

English Language Learners (ELL)

❖ Explain the activity using short simple phrases while making eye contact
❖ Model activity using photographs or realia
❖ Teach and review vocabulary related to braid making: rope, cord, yarn, cloth, over, under, right, left, middle, tie, color words
❖ Ask child about braiding in the country of origin, encourage child to respond to questions in English allowing gestures and pointing
❖ Use positive reinforcement when child attempts to use or uses vocabulary related to braiding when speaking

Content Standards For Kindergarten Met By This Activity

English Language Arts

Reading (1.0, 1.17, 1.18)
Written and Oral Language (1.0, 1.1)
Listening and Speaking (1.0, 1.1, 1.2, 2.0, 2.1)

Mathematics

Numbers and Counting (1.0, 1.2)
Algebra, Sets and Sorting (1.0, 1.1)
Measurement and Geometry (1.0, 1.1)

Science

Physical Sciences (1.a)
Investigation and Experimentation (4.a, 4.b, 4.c, 4.d., 4.e)

History and Social Science

Following the rules (K.1, K.1.1)
Matching work descriptions to related jobs in history and community (K.3)
Compare and describe people and places (K.4, K.4.1)
Understanding that history relates to people and places in the past (K.6, K.6.3)

Visual Arts

Artistic Perception (1.0, 1.2, 1.3)
Creative Expression (2.0, 2.1, 2.2, 2.7)
Understanding Historical / Cultural Contributions of Visual Arts (3.0, 3.1, 3.3)
Valuing Aesthetics (4.0, 4.1)

Learning Plan

I. **Name of Activity: Basic Braiding**

II. **Date of Presentation:**

III. **Age or Grade Level: Pre-K, Kindergarten**

IV. **Ratio of teachers to children needed for this activity:** 1:10

V. **Target Areas of Learning / Goals and Objectives** (target areas of learning directly relate to "VI. Evaluation Rubric")
1. **Physical**: _____
2. **Cognitive**: _____
3. **Social**: _____
4. **Emotional**: _____
5. **Creative**: _____

VI. **Evaluation Rubric:** (if more than two learning areas are being evaluated, a spreadsheet form may be preferred)

Targeted Area of Learning	**Targeted Area of Learning**
_____	_____
_____	_____
4. Always _____	**4.** Always _____
3. Usually _____	**3.** Usually _____
2. Sometimes _____	**2.** Sometimes _____
1. Rarely _____	**1.** Rarely _____

VII. **Materials and Preparation**
1. Cord, string, yarn, rope, ribbon, lanyard or raffia separated into three strands (making a strand con involve on piece or several of material being braided so long as the total number of sections being braided equals three
2. Yardstick or other measuring tools
3. Scissors
4. Two pieces of cord, yarn, or other to tie sections together at top and bottom which will prevent the braid from coming undone; these pieces of cord can be the same or contrasting as desired

VIII. **Procedure**
1. Children select material to be braided
2. Children measure out three pieces of designated length of braiding material, checks measurement with partner, and cuts designated length
3. Tie three sections to be braided together at top tightly

4. Have partner (braid holder) hold tied end, or make a loop from the cord holding the ends together and loop it over a drawer pull or door handle
5. The braider holds the three pieces of cord to be braided evenly lifting the section on the right over the piece in the middle
6. Lift the section on the left over the middle, check for tension and evenness
7. Lift the section now on the far right over the middle section, and the left over the middle section checking for evenness of the braid
8. Again, lift the section on the right over the middle, and then the left over the middle, again checking for evenness
9. Continue with this pattern until there is no more cord or one is bored
10. Tie off braid with second smaller piece of cord

Variation: braid, right to left pattern going under instead of over the middle section

IX. **Accommodations** (changes to accommodate learning diversity)
   Name of Accommodated Area:
   1. _____
   2. _____
   3. _____
   4. _____
   5. _____

X. **Applicable Framework Standards: Kindergarten**
   Standard _____
   _____
   _____
   _____
   _____

   Standard _____
   _____
   _____
   _____
   _____

   Standard _____
   _____
   _____
   _____
   _____

   Standard _____
   _____
   _____
   _____
   _____

Standard _____

_____

_____

_____

_____

XI. **Evaluation and Comments** (i.e.: How well did the plan work? Great responses? What aspects are especially effective? Not effective? What improvements are needed? Ideas for follow up activities and other notes)

_____

_____

_____

_____

Learning Non-English Words and Phrases

The best time in human life to acquire language skills is between birth and the age of six. This is when the brain is laying down the hardwiring for language. In point of fact, six is somewhat on the late side for introducing new languages at that level. But in general, it will be far easier for a six-year old to learn new languages other than English (or whatever the native language may be) than for a sixteen year old or worse yet a sixty year old.

Language occurs in the Broca's area of the brain. At birth the human brain is set up to acquire and speak any language. The languages to which the child is exposed at this very early age predispose that child to understand and produce those sounds in particular. The ability for this acquisition diminishes over time. If one were to reflect on and extrapolate from this point of view, the appropriate time for expose children to multiple languages would be in day care and preschool. In that light, all childcare providers should be multilingual. It seems so strange that Florida is the only officially bilingual state in the Union, and that the American educational system does not introduce "foreign" languages until high school!

How can a teacher accomplish introducing multilingualism into the curriculum? It is very helpful if the teacher is familiar with other languages. Other possibilities for incorporating the use of other languages into the classroom include the following:

Does the classroom have labels on the furniture, computers, and other materials found around the classroom? Add the words from other languages to the cards as well. Adding vocabulary to music (i.e., creating and singing simple songs) acts as a mnemonic device which has proved to be effective for teaching language since the beginning of time. How many people have struggled with the letter "LMNOP" from the alphabet song? Joking aside, teaching vocabulary through music is an excellent strategy. Are there parents who speak languages other than English in the classroom community? How about your paraprofessional? Ask them to share their language with the class. Consider how powerful it would be for an English language learner to share his or her native language with the class. That child would go from feeling like an outsider to being a person who has a significant contribution to give to the class.

Often when people hear others speaking and do not understand what is being said, a wall goes up. Being exposed to a variety of other languages at an early age creates a structure for something much more powerful than that separating wall. It can create an opening for understanding that people are people no matter what language is being spoken by them. Language is not an indicator of good or bad. Having that powerful basis for human interaction at an early age will have a huge impact on the kind of culture we are producing. The world, in all of its beautiful diversity, has become accessible to much of humanity because of the advances in technology. Through understanding, and through language, children can be taught to appreciate diversity rather than fear it.

This activity includes sample words from a number of languages, and many others can be found via the internet and local cultural centers. One useful website is enchantedlearning.com. It offers wonderful downloadable information about many cultures and languages for children Pre-K through primary. Languages include: Dutch, French, German, Italian, Japanese (Romanji), Portugese, Spanish and Swedish. Some activities and printable books are downloadable for free and much more is available for a nominal fee with their subscription service.

Using language can be integrated in all areas of the curriculum: dancing, singing, drama, language, math, art, and so on. Teaching children the structure of language in general enhances the usage and comprehension of English. Many conventions of language are similar and common to most languages. All of life occurs in language, no matter which language is being spoken.

Rather than presenting language in isolation, or emphasizing the teaching of language as an ordeal, if the teacher can adopt an attitude of "This is just what we're doing. It's no big deal", the charge, the stigma that language learning is difficult, will not be transmitted. Strangely, when people *think* something is difficult, it *becomes* difficult. If one *says* an activity is fun, it *becomes* fun. Life occurs in our speaking. Choose your words wisely. That being said, teachers should adopt the attitude that "Teaching and learning language is fun, easy, and normal".

Materials

❖ Vocabulary list of words to be introduced to the children
❖ File cards or word strips for classroom labels
❖ Permanent marker
❖ Choose music to share with children in group settings to enhance the acquisition of other non-English languages, such as: De Colores, Mi Cuerpo, Sur le Pont D'Avignon, Savez-Vous Plantez les Choux?
❖ Children's books, comic books with stories in English and selected languages
❖ Multi-lingual books for class library
❖ Audio tapes / CD's with music and stories in the selected language(s)
❖ Children's games from other countries
❖ Photographs from countries where selected language(s) are spoken
❖ Video from countries where languages are spoken

Method

❖ Talk about the places where people speak the language(s) you are introducing
❖ Using word lists or other sources of vocabulary words to be introduced, make multi-lingual labels for items around the class
❖ Play *Word Hunt* language activity in many languages
❖ Sing songs in selected language(s) during group time
❖ Play children's games/dances from selected countries during group or physical education time
❖ Play CD's with music from those countries softly in the background any time
❖ Teach children basic commands in other languages such as "allons-y" (French), "vamos" (Spanish), "andiamo" (Italian) or "wir gehen" (German) all of which are roughly translated to "We're going" or "Let's go."
❖ Invite visitors who speak and who may be from countries that speak the languages selected for the class
❖ Present foods from selected countries for snacks or for a "feast"
❖ Very occasionally (on too snowy, wet, windy, hot, smoggy days) play a short video (cartoon or child-oriented) from other countries, that is in or includes some words from the language being introduced

❖ Dramatize known folklore stories (such as *The Three Little Pigs*) in both English and the language being introduced
❖ Create vocabulary journals for each selected language
❖ Utilize English activities indicated in **Practical Kindergarten** and any other source chosen for introducing selected language(s)
❖ Introduce children to work and artistic techniques used by prominent artists and from various cultures
❖ Have children work in pairs to play with the language being introduced, encourage pairs to invent games, tell jokes using selected language

Suggested Reading:

Geography and Maps
Knowlton, J. & Barton, H. (1986). *Maps and Globes.* ISBN: 0064460495. (Reading Rainbow book)
Rabe, T. (2002). *There's a Map on My Lap! All About Maps* (Cat in the Hat's Learning Library) ISBN: 0375810994.
Sweeney, J. (1998). *Me On the Map.* ISBN: 0517885573.

People and Cultures
Aardema, V. (1981). *Bringing the Rain to Kapiti Plain.* ISBN: 0-803-70809-2. (Reading Rainbow book)
Aardema, V. (1975). *Why Mosquitoes Buzz in People's Ears: A West African Tale.* ISBN: 0-14-054905-6.
Altman, L.J. (1995). *Amelia's Road.* ISBN: 188000027X. . (Illustrated by Enrico Sanchez, the story of a community of farm workers; Ages 4-10)
Amery, H. (1994). *Then and Now.* ISBN: 0746007949. (Great illustrations: side-by-side pictures of how things used to be and how they are now)
Bruchac, J. & Vojtech, A. (1998). *First Strawberries: A Cherokee Story.* ISBN: 0140564098.
Carlstrom, N. W. (1992). *Northern Lullaby.* New York: Philomel Books. ISBN:0-399-21806-8. (Bidding good night to all the people and animals of Alaska on a snowy winter night; illustrated by Caldecott Medal / Coretta Scott King award winners, Leo and Diane Dillon).
Chanin, M. (1998). *The chief's blanket.* ISBN: 0915811782.
Cheng, A. & Zhang, A. (2003). *Grandfather Counts.* (Reading Rainbow book). (intergenerational story: Grandfather Gong Gong teaches granddaughter how to count in Chinese) ISBN: 1584301589.
Friedman, I. R. (1987). *How My Parents Learned To Eat.* ISBN: 039544235.
Holub, J. (2004). *My First Book of Sign Language.* ISBN: 0439635829.
Longfellow. H.W. (Jeffers, S., illustrator). (1996). *Hiawatha.* ISBN: 0140558829 (Ages 3-8)
Madrigal, A., (De Paola, T. illustrator). (1997). *Eagle and the Rainbow: Timeless Tales From Mexico.* ISBN: 155591-317-2.
Peterson, D. K. & Ray, D (1984). *I have a sister. My sister is deaf.* ISBN: 0064430596. (Reading Rainbow book).

Recorvits, H. & Swiatkowski, G.S. (2003). *My Name Is Yoon* (Ezra Jack Keats New Illustrator Award, 2004). ISBN: 0374351147 (Young Korean girl struggles to learn English and adapt to her new country).

Spier, P. (1988). *People.* ISBN: 038524469X (Wonderful introduction to cultural diversity about people on four continents; Caldecott Medalist.)

Books in Spanish

(See Appendix B3 for more complete list @ www.cambriapress.com/kindergarten)

Ada, A.F. (1997). *Gathering the Sun: An Alphabet in Spanish and English.* ISBN: 0-688-13903-5. (Winner 1998 Americas Award; Vibrant paintings illustrate poems of each letter of the alphabet).

Buchanan, K. (2004). *Esta Casa Esta Hecha de Lodo / This House Is Made Of Mud.* Bilingual edition: English / Spanish. ISBN: 0873585801 (Worldview through the eyes of a Native American child).

Emberley, R. (2000). *My Numbers/ Mis Numeros.* ISBN: 0316233501.

Fox, M. Staub, L. & Compoy, F.I. (2002). *Quienquiera Que Seas / Whoever You Are.* ISBN: 0613832248. (Reading Rainbow book).

Lowell, S., & Harris, J. (2004). *The Three Little Javelinas / Los tres pequeños jabalíes* (Humorous Southwestern re-telling of the three little pigs) Bilingual edition. English / Spanish. ISBN: 0873586611.

Martin, B. (Carle, E., illustrator). (1998). *¿Oso pardo, oso pardo, que ves ahi?* (Brown Bear, Brown Bear What Do You See?). New York: Henry Holt and Co. ISBN: 0805059679.

Numeroff, L. (1995). *Si le Das una Galletita a un Raton. (If You Give a Mouse a Cookie)* New York: Rayo: HarperCollins. ISBN: 0060254386.

Piper, W. (1992). *La Pequena Locomotora Que si Pudo. (The Little Engine That Could).* ISBN: 0448410966

Reiser, L. (Hart. R., translator). (1998). *Tortillas and Lullabies / Tortillas y Cancioncitas.* ISBN: 0-688-14628-7. (Three generations make tortillas, sing songs, wash clothes and gather flowers; words and music for lullaby provided).

Rey, H.A. (Fernandez, P.V., Translator). (1976). *Jorge el Curioso (Curious George)* ISBN: 0395249090.

Slobodkina, E. (1995). *Caps for Sale: Se Venden Gorras.* ISBN: 006443401X.

Steptoe, J. (1987). *Mufaro's Beautiful Daughters.* New York: Amistad Publishing Company. ISBN: 0688040454. Spanish Edition: (1987). *Las Bellas Hijas de Mufaro.* ISBN: 0688154816. (Reading Rainbow book; African legend; Received the Coretta Scott King Award for illustration)

Suess, Dr. aka Geisel, T. (Marcuse, A. E., translator). (1992). *Huevos verdes con jamón.* (Green Eggs and Ham) ISBN: 1880507013.

Willliams, V.B. (Marcuse, A. E., translator). (1984). *Un Sillon Para Mi Mama. (A Chair for my Mother)* New York: HarperCollins Publishers. ISBN: 0688132006. (Reading Rainbow book; Caldecott Honor Book)

Books in Other Languages

Bemelmans, L. (1958). *Madeline.* (French language edition). ISBN: 082881113X. English language edition: (1958). ISBN: 0-670-44580-0. (The beloved children's classic)

Brown, M. W. (2002). Bonsoir Lune (Goodnight Moon, French language edition). ISBN: 2211072933.

Brown, M. W. (). Bon Nuit Lune.

Cheng, A. & Zhang, A. (2003). *Grandfather Counts.* ISBN: 1584301589. (Reading Rainbow book; Intergenerational story: Grandfather Gong Gong teaches granddaughter how to count in Chinese).

Fedor, J. (1995). *Table, Chair, Bear: A Book in Many Languages.* ISBN: 0-395-65938-8. (A simple naming scheme of everyday objects in twelve languages plus English: Korean, French, Arabic, Vietnamese, Japanese, Portugese, Lao, Spanish, Chinese, Tagalog, Cambodian, and Navajo, with pronunciation phonetics)

Feelings, M. (1992). *Jambo Means Hello: A Swahili Alphabet Book.* ISBN: 0140546529.

Feelings, M. (1992). *Moja Means One: A Swahili Counting Book.* ISBN: 014054662

Onyefulu, I. (1999). *Emeka's Gift: An African Counting Book.* ISBN: 0140565000

Wildsmith, B. (1996). *Brian Wildsmith's ABC.* ISBN: 1887734023.

Wildsmith, B. (2005). *Les Animaux de la Ferme/Farm Animals* (Bilingual Edition: French / English). ISBN: 1595720324.

Note: Brian Wildsmith's beautifully illustrated alphabet, counting and animal books are available in many languages including: Arabic, Chinese, French, Farsi, Korean, Mandarin, Navajo, Spanish, Portugese, Tagalog, and Vietnamese

Suggested CDs

Greg & Steve. (1987). *We All Live Together. Vol.2.* **(Includes: English / Spanish months of the year song, World is a Rainbow,** Popcorn, The Freeze) CD Available from: amazon.com

Jenkins, E. (1992) *Adventures in Rhythm.* (Multicultural songs and activities with rhythm sticks). Ella Jenkins' CDs available from: amazon.com

Jenkins, E. (1995) *Multicultural Children's Songs.* (Greetings, thank yous, ABCs, counting, songs and dances in many languages).

Jenkins, E. (2003) *Sharing Cultures.* (28 songs from around the world). Available from: amazon.com

Suggested Software:

KidSpeak: Spanish, Franch, German, Italian, Japanese, Hebrew From Transparent Language; Available for Macintosh / Windows computers @ www.transparent.com/store

Targeted Areas of Learning

Physical Development

❖ **Gross Motor Skills:** using the large muscles of the arms, legs, and torso: balance, rhythm, walking, laterality; jumping; hopping; throwing; tumbling; running, dancing: development and coordination of large muscles while participating in movement activities from selected cultures

❖ **Physical Principals:** learning physical weight; stability; equilibrium; balance; leverage in movement activities from selected cultures
❖ **Sensory Discrimination**
- **Auditory Discrimination** (hearing): identifying sounds: loud/soft; high/ low pitch; fast/slow rhythms; comparing sounds using auditory receptors for selected languages
- **Visual Discrimination** (sight): identifying words and various objects visually using selected language
- **Oral Discrimination** (taste): identifying sweet, salty, sour, and bitter tastes; identifying textures with tongue and mouth; identifying flavors by taste in selected languages

Cognitive Development
❖ **Language Arts**
- **Verbal skills**
  o **Vocabulary development**: adding to the body of words and phrases understood in multiple languages
  o **Language development**: acquiring and using language appropriately in interactions with others in multiple languages
  o **Grammatical development**: learning rules of grammar, conventions of the use of language in multiple languages
- **Emergent literacy**
  o **Symbol recognition**: recognizing that particular marks have meaning in multiple languages
  o **Symbol interpretation**: identifying the particular meaning associated with a specific symbol in various ways depending upon the language in which it is being used
  o **Phonemic awareness:** awareness of sounds associated with letters, letter combinations in multiple languages
  o **Word recognition**: understanding that groups of letters create a composite sound which is meaningful in multiple languages
  o **Matching spoken words to written words**: correctly associating the auditory expression with the written symbol grouping in multiple languages
❖ **Math Skills**
- **Mathematical literacy**
  o **1 to 1 correspondence**: counting items in an organized way that shows understanding of the object's placement as a single entity in a group in a variety of languages
  o **Associating number symbols with quantity**: understanding that a specific symbol is always associated with a specific quantity of items in a count in a number of languages
  o **Recognizing number words**: associating the number symbol with the written word for that number, with the count of items in selected languages
- **Mathematical applications**

- **Seriation**: ordering objects or events in the context of time in multiple languages
  - o **Calendar**: placing numbers in order to denote the passage of days, weeks, months, seasons, years in multiple languages
- **Common relatedness**: linking items that are not the same or similar, but have an association with each other, such as knowing the words for "bat and ball" in selected language
- ❖ **Social Studies**
  - **Understanding that being a good citizen involves certain expected behavior:** following rules, sharing, taking turns, individual responsibilities and consequences, honesty, courage, determination, and patriotism in all countries and cultures
  - **Recognizing diversity**: recognizing what makes people similar *and* different: knowing that superficial differences do not mean *bad*, particularly as applied to language.
  - **Accepting human diversity**: all languages are used to express human experience; learning to evaluate humankind based upon the impact of their choices and internal values on the rest of humanity rather than superficial differences of language
  - **Comparing and contrasting the locations of people, places, and environments:**
    - o Determining relative locations: near/far, left/right, behind/in front using multiple languages
  - **Temporal ordering**: children use a calendar to put events in order; placing days, weeks, and months in proper order in multiple languages
  - **Understanding that the context of history relates to people, events, and places of other times;** as related to multiple cultures and languages, and different people

Social Development

- ❖ **Self-respect:** valuing themselves from their cultural origins, and from any languages spoken in the home
- ❖ **Patience**: diligence: persisting in the process of learning language as an important skill
- ❖ **Working cooperatively with others in a group**: working well as a member of a team and as a community that supports all members while embracing linguistic diversity
- ❖ **Collaboration**: working with others in the language learning process
- ❖ **Following directions**: carrying out directions for language learning tasks
- ❖ **Respecting others as individuals (behaving appropriately with others):** behaving appropriately in social situations, learning the general rules of courtesy (manners) for their family and school, developing the ability to participate in conversation as it relates to various cultures associated with linguistic diversity
- ❖ **Internalizing social values**: learning appropriate behavior in the context of the culture in which the child is living and the cultures about which the child is learning; internalizing an appreciation for the skills, behaviors, and interactions valued by various cultures
- ❖ **Community building**: creating a sense of belonging in a group, particularly through working cooperatively with others toward common goals of embracing human diversity

Emotional Development

❖ **Self-esteem**: feeling good about oneself just as one is and is not, feeling good about that which one does and does not; building self-confidence by participating in activities wherein there is no "wrong" answer; feeling safe to try out new activities in a nonjudgmental environment, wherein there is no pressure to produce a particular outcome, rather an environment that supports curiosity, investigation; developing a stable sense of self-worth as related to learning language

❖ **Self-confidence**: being able to be present to uncomfortable feelings without having those feelings overcome or dominate the child's ability to be with others, or for the child to stand for internalized values as the child works through the process of acquiring language

❖ **Accomplishment**: developing a sense of self-worth from participating in language learning

❖ **Generosity**: experiencing enjoyment in using words with someone who does not speak English well, reaching across linguistic barriers to find a common ground

❖ **Empathy**: identification with the feelings of others' and behaving appropriately in the context of those feelings in the shared experience of language learning

❖ **Courage**: willingness to try out speaking words from languages with which the child has not grown up using

Creative Expression

❖ **Use of creative media and expression of imagination**:
  • **Music**: expressing self through vocal music in selected languages
  • **Movement/dance**: expressing self through movement games using selected languages
  • **Dramatization/story telling**: expressing self through acting, puppetry, and theater arts using selected languages
  • **Writing/story telling**: expressing self through written and illustrated media about learning or using selected languages

❖ **Developing aesthetic appreciation** for arts, books, drama, music, puppetry, theatrical events, movement representing cultures speaking selected languages

❖ **Creative risk**: being comfortable playing creatively in the process of learning selected languages

❖ **Creative Thinking**: inventing new ways to play with and learn selected languages

Possible Accommodations for *Non-English Activities*

ADHD

❖ Allow child to work in a carrel when writing in designated language journal
❖ Focus on using teaching methods that involve more activity: singing, dancing, dramatizing, playing games
❖ Consider reducing the number of vocabulary words introduced
❖ Allow child to get up, stand, move around when not distracting or disturbing to others
❖ Welcome silliness as it will ease sense of pressure/performance anxiety

Developmental Delays

❖ Simplify vocabulary being introduced
❖ Introduce fewer words each session
❖ Teach and review in a small group setting
❖ Make sure eye contact is made when teaching and reviewing
❖ Teach child same songs in English and language being introduced
❖ Play children's games from culture of selected language

Autism Spectrum Disorders

❖ Simplify vocabulary being introduced
❖ Introduce fewer words each session
❖ Teach and review in a small group setting
❖ Have child work with "buddy" instead of small group
❖ Make sure eye contact is made when teaching vocabulary from the selected language
❖ Teach child same songs in English and language being introduced
❖ Use multiple languages from the first day so that it quickly becomes familiar rather than starting one way and introducing another element as the educational structure of the class

Visual Impairments

❖ Make labels for classroom furniture in bright, high contrast letters in a large size
❖ Allow child to touch physical items when teaching the word in the selected language
❖ Accommodate per the activities selected, as, in general, those who solely are visually impaired are generally not challenged in the process of acquiring and using language

Orthopedic Impairments

❖ Orthopedic impairments, of themselves, do not impair an individual in the process of acquiring and speaking multiple languages
❖ For the purely orthopedically impaired, accommodations would need to be related to the nature of the activity (such as journal writing or dance) used to present vocabulary from the selected language; e.g. if the child's hands lack strength or flexibility, one may need to guide the child's hand using the hand-over-hand method for journal writing

Gifted and Talented Education (GATE)

❖ Ask child to invent games or songs using selected language
❖ Allow child to work with language-oriented computer programs such as *Kid Speak* (ISBN 1-930550-77-4)
❖ Introduce more vocabulary
❖ Introduce more challenging vocabulary
❖ Present theatrical activities using selected language
❖ GATE children may have an aptitude for acquiring and speaking language. Enrichments would be related to the type of activities selected to introduce these languages.
❖ Introducing languages new to child may be a sufficient enrichment

English Language Learners (ELL)

- ❖ Simplify vocabulary being introduced
- ❖ Introduce fewer words each session
- ❖ Teach and review in a small group setting
- ❖ Make sure eye contact is made when teaching
- ❖ Teach child same songs in English and language being introduced
- ❖ Be sure to teach and allow the child to participate in teaching the child's home language
- ❖ Use positive reinforcement when child shares his or her language with the class
- ❖ Use positive reinforcement when child attempts to use or uses new vocabulary

Content Standards For Kindergarten Met By This Activity

English Language Arts

The content standards presented here are for English, however they often generalize to other languages. When children begin to acquire conventions in multiple languages, the possibility arises for a broader understanding of the child's native language, which, in this case, is assumed to be English.

Reading (1.0, 1.1, 1.2, 1.3, 1.4, 1.5, 1.7, 1.8, 1.9, 1.10, 1.11, 1.12, 1.13, 1.14, 1.15, 1.16, 1.17, 1.18, 2.0, 2.2, 2.3, 2.4, 2.5, 3.0, 3.2, 3.3)

Writing (1.0, 1.1, 1.2, 1.3)

Written and Oral Language (1.0, 1.1, 1.2)

Listening and Speaking (1.0, 1.1, 1.2, 2.0, 2.1, 2.2, 2.3)

Mathematics

Numbers and Counting (1.0, 1.2)

Algebra, Sets and Sorting (1.0, 1.1)

Measurement and Geometry (1.0, 1.1, 1.2, 1.3, 1.4, 2.0, 2.1, 2.2)

History and Social Science

Following Rules (K.1, K.1.1, K.1.2, K.1.3)

Matching work descriptions to related jobs in history and community (K.3)

Compare and describe people and places (K.4, K.4.1, K.4.2, K.4.3)

Understanding that history relates to people and places in the past (K.6, K.6.3)

Visual Arts

Artistic Perception (1.0, 1.1, 1.2)

Understanding Historical /Cultural Contributions of Visual Arts (3.0, 3.1, 3.2, 3.3)

Applications (5.0, 5.3)

Theatre

Understanding Historical /Cultural Contributions of Theatre (3.0, 3.1, 3.2)

Applications (5.0, 5.1, 5.2)

Dance

Artistic Perception (1.0, 1.1, 1.3, 1.4)
Creative Expression (2.0, 2.2)
Understanding Historical /Cultural Contributions of Dance (3.0, 3.1)

Music

Creative Expression (2.0, 2.1, 2.2, 2.3, 2.4)
Understanding Historical /Cultural Contributions of Music (3.0, 3.1, 3.2, 3.3, 3.4)
Valuing Aesthetics (4.0, 4.1, 4.2)
Applications (5.0, 5.1, 5.2)

Days of the Week

English	Espanol	Francaise	Deutsch	Italiano
Monday	lunes	lundi	Montag	lunedi
Tuesday	martes	mardi	Dienstag	martedi
Wednesday	miércoles	mecredi	Mittwoch	mercoledi
Thursday	jueves	jeudi	Donnerstag	giovedi
Friday	viernes	vendredi	Freitag	venerdi
Saturday	sabado	samedi	Samstag	sabato
Sunday	domingo	dimanche	Sonntag	dimenica

Months of the Year

English	Espanol	Francaise	Deutsch	Italiano
January	enero	janvier	Januar	gennaio
February	febrero	février	Februar	febbraio
March	marzo	mars	Marz	marzo
April	abril	avril	April	aprile
May	mayo	mai	Mai	maggio
June	junio	juin	Juni	giugno
July	julio	juillet	Juli	luglio
August	agosto	août	August	agosto
September	septiembre	septembre	September	settembre
October	octubre	octobre	Oktober	ottobre
November	noviembre	novembre	November	novembre
December	diciembre	decembre	Dezember	dicembre

Numbers

English	Espanol	Francaise	Deutsch	Italiano
zero	zero	zero	null	zero
one	uno	un, une	ein	uno, una
two	dos	deux	zwei	due
three	tres	trois	drei	tre
four	cuatro	quatre	vier	quattro

five	cinco	cinq	fünf	cinque
six	seis	six	sechs	sei
seven	siete	sept	sieben	sette
eight	ocho	huit	acht	otto
nine	nueve	neuf	neun	nove
ten	diez	dix	zehn	dieci
eleven	once	onze	elf	undici
twelve	doce	douze	zwölf	dodici
thirteen	trece	treize	dreizehn	tredici
fourteen	catorce	quatorze	veirzehn	quattordici
fifteen	quince	quinze	fünfzehn	quindici
sixteen	dieciseis	seize	sechzehn	sedici
seventeen	diecisiete	dix-sept	siebzehn	dicisette
eighteen	dieciocho	dix-huit	achtzehn	diciotto
nineteen	diecinueve	dix-neuf	neunzehn	dicinove
twenty	veinte	vingt	zwanzig	venti
thirty	treinta	trente	dreissig	trenta
forty	cuarenta	quarante	vierzig	quaranta
fifty	cincuenta	cinquante	fünfzig	cinquanta
hundred	cien	cent(e)	hundert	cento
thousand	mil	mille	tausend	mille

Colors

English	Espanol	Francaise	Deutsch	Italiano
red	rossa	rouge	rot	rosso
orange	anaranjado	orange	orange	arancione
yellow	amarillo	jaune	gelb	giallo
green	verde	verte	grün	verde
blue	azul	bleu	blau	azzurro
purple	morado	pourpre	purpur	porpora
pink	rosa	rose	rosa	rosa
brown	marrón	brun	braun	marrone
white	blanco	blanc	weiss	bianco
black	negro	noir	schwarz	nero
grey	gris	gris	grau	grigio

Other Vocabulary

English	Espanol	Francaise	Deutsch	Italiano
please	por favor	s'il vous plaît	bitte	per favore
thank you	gracias	merci	danke	grazie
hello	buenos dias	bonjour	guten tag	ciao
good bye	adios	au revoir	auf Wiedersehen	ciao (arrivederci)
love	amor	amour	liebe	amore

we're going	vamos	allons-y	wir gehen	andiamo
come here	venga aqui	venez ici	kommen siehier	venni a qui
sit down	sientate	assoyez vous	sitzen	sedersi
toilet	banos	toilette	toilette	toletta
mother	madre	mama	Mutter	mama (madre)
father	padre	papa	Vater	papa (padre)
school	escuela	ecole	schüle	scuola
my house	mi casa	ma maison	mein haus	mia casa
friend	amigo	ami/ amie	freund	amico / amica
teacher	maestre(a)	professeur	Lehrer	maestro

Learning Plan

    I. **Name of Activity: Introducing Non-English Words**

    II. **Date of Presentation:**

    III. **Age or Grade Level: Pre-K, Kindergarten**

    IV. **Ratio of teachers to children needed for this activity:** 1:10

    V. **Target Areas of Learning / Goals and Objectives** (target areas of learning directly relate to "VI. Evaluation Rubric")

        1. Physical: _____

        2. Cognitive: _____

        3. Social: _____

        4. Emotional: _____

        5. Creative: _____

    VI. **Evaluation Rubric:** (if more than two learning areas are being evaluated, a spreadsheet form may be preferred)

Targeted Area of Learning	**Targeted Area of Learning**
_____	_____
_____	_____
4. Always _____	**4.** Always _____
3. Usually _____	**3.** Usually _____
2. Sometimes _____	**2.** Sometimes _____
1. Rarely _____	**1.** Rarely _____

    VII. **Materials and Preparation**

      1. Vocabulary list of words to be introduced to the children
      2. File cards or word strips for classroom labels
      3. Permanent marker
      4. Choose music to share with children in group settings to enhance the acquisition of other non-English languages, such as: De Colores, Mi Cuerpo, Sur le Pont D'Avignon, Savez-Vous Plantez les Choux?
      5. Children's books, comic books with stories in English and selected languages
      6. Multi-lingual books for class library
      7. Audio tapes/CD's with music and stories in other language(s)
      8. Children's games from other countries
      9. Photographs from countries where selected language(s) are spoken
      10. Video from countries where languages are spoken

VIII. Procedure

1. Talk about the places where people speak the language(s) you are introducing
2. Using word lists or other sources of vocabulary words to be introduced, make multi-lingual labels for items around the class
3. Play "Word Hunt" in many languages
4. Sing songs in selected language(s) during group time
5. Play children's games/dances from selected countries during group or physical education time
6. Play CD's with music from those countries softly in the background any time
7. Teach children basic commands in other languages such as "allons-y" (French), vamos (Spanish), "andiamo" (Italian) or "wir gehen" (German) all of which are roughly translated to "We're going" or "Let's go."
8. Invite visitors who speak and who may be from countries that speak the languages selected for the class
9. Present foods from selected countries for snacks or for a "feast"
10. Very occasionally (on too snowy, wet, windy, hot, smoggy days) play a short video (cartoon or child-oriented) from other countries, that is in or includes some words from the language being introduced
11. Dramatize known folklore stories (such as *The Three Little Pigs*) in both English and the language being introduced
12. Create vocabulary journals for each selected language
13. Utilize English activities indicated in ***Practical Kindergarten Language Activities*** *section* and any other source chosen for introducing selected languages
14. Introduce children to work and artistic techniques used by prominent artists and from various cultures
15. Have children work in pairs to play with the language being introduced, encourage pairs to invent games, tell jokes using selected language

IX. Accommodations (changes to accommodate learning diversity)
    Name of Accommodated Area:
    1. _____
    2. _____
    3. _____
    4. _____
    5. _____

X. Applicable Framework Standards: Kindergarten
    Standard _____
    _____
    _____
    _____
    _____

Standard _____

_____

_____

_____

_____

Standard _____

_____

_____

_____

_____

Standard _____

_____

_____

_____

_____

Standard _____

_____

_____

_____

_____

XI. **Evaluation and Comments** (i.e.: How well did the plan work? Great responses? What aspects are especially effective? Not effective? What improvements are needed? Ideas for follow up activities and other notes)

_____

_____

_____

_____

Multicultural Dances

There are myriad CDs available oriented toward younger children. One excellent CD is *World of Parachute Play*. The music on it is entirely not authentic, but it can be an opening to other, more authentic forms. There is no need to present watered down versions of authentic music. However, the responses we have seen to this particular CD have been quite positive from young children. If searching for music, remember that there are so many wonderful selections that the recommendation is to go to a store that allows customers an opportunity to preview CDs that seem interesting.

Children often feel freer if allowed to use props while dancing which is a good reason to consider using a parachute to music. It doesn't exactly seem like "dancing", but it is movement and music combined. Parachutes for children's activities can be quite costly from educational supply stores. However, the best source known to the authors is Discount School Supply. From that source at the time of publishing, the cost of a large parachute was in the $40 range

Be clear that even if the music and the props are absolutely authentic, the goal for this activity is not to produce performance quality dance, but to allow children to become accustomed to moving to music from cultural groups that are not their own. Building familiarity is key to acceptance.

When introducing a new music form, be aware that repetition in this case produces pleasure and excitement rather than negative responses of apathy and boredom. A teacher can work with a piece of music frequently. As the children remember and dance, their expression will broaden inside each piece of music as it becomes more familiar.

Dance is so basic to humans. Clear a space, pull out the props, put on the music, and let the children dance. In the case of dancing, particularly with young children, keep the structure to a minimum. When movement is presented in that way, the children will be freed to be self-expressed in movement and not preoccupied with trying to remember what to do next.

Materials
❖ An open space wherein children can move freely without concern for crashing into each other and without bumping into furniture and so forth
❖ Music CDs or tapes
❖ Props: fancy dress up hats, fans, scarves, parachute, rhythm sticks, cultural props (do not offer anything sharp or hard enough that a child might be injured by bumping into it)
❖ If a parachute is being used, the teacher can add a soft toy or small inflatable ball to the activity to add a dimension of the "keep the toy on the parachute" game

Method
❖ Teacher informs children that music will be played from another country
❖ Bring out props
❖ Play music and allow children to dance
❖ When dancing is complete, ask children to guess from what country the music came (try to identify the country of origin for the music)

Suggested Reading:

Ackerman, K. (1992). *Song and Dance Man.* ISBN: 0679819959.

Aliki. (2003). *Ah, Music!* ISBN: 0060287195.

Hamanaka, S. (1999). *All the Colors of the Earth.* ISBN: 0688170625.

Katz, K. (2002). *The Colors of Us.* ISBN: 0805071636.

Knowlton, J. & Barton, H. (1997). *Geography from A to Z: A Picture Glossary.* New York: HarperTrophy. ISBN: 0064460991.

Loomis, C. (2000). *Across America, I love you.* New York: Hyperion Books for Children. ISBN: 0786803665.

Medearis, A.S, & Byrd, S. (1993). *Dancing With the Indians.* (Beautifully illustrated story about an African American family that escapes slavery, finding a home among the Seminole Indians). ISBN: 0823410234

Smith, C., L, (2000). *Jingle Dancer.* ISBN: 068816241X. (About the Ojibway origins of jingle dancing, and the passing down of traditions through generations).

Spier, P, (1988) *People.* ISBN: 038524469X.

Sweeney, J. (1998). *Me on the Map.* New York: Dragonfly Books. ISBN: 0517885573

William, V.B (1988). *Music, Music for Everyone.* ISBN: 0688078117 (Music, life issues, friendship and community).

Suggested CDs:

Jenkins, E. (1992) *Adventures in Rhythm.* (Multicultural songs and activities with rhythm sticks). Ella Jenkins' CDs available from: amazon.com

Jenkins, E. (1995) *Multicultural Children's Songs.* (Greetings, thank yous, ABCs, counting, songs and dances in many languages).

Jenkins, E. (2003) *Sharing cultures.* (28 songs from around the world). Available from: amazon.com

Stewart, G. L. (1998) *Folk Dance Fun.* (Simplified dances from around the world) . ISBN: 1-56346-021-1. Available from: www.fitnessbeginnings.com.

Stewart, G. L. (1998) *Children's Folk Dances.* (21 simplified dances from around the world). ISBN :1-56346-090-4. Available from: amazon.com

Stewart, G.L. & Buck D. (1997). *A World of Parachute Play.* Georgiana Stewart's CDs are available from fitnessbeginnings.com.

Targeted Area of Learning

Physical Development

❖ **Gross Motor Skills:** using the large muscles of the arms, legs, and torso: balance, rhythm, walking, laterality; jumping; hopping; throwing; tumbling; running, dancing either as directed or as free expression of self

❖ **Fine Motor Skills:** using the small muscles of the hand and fingers: holding onto props, parachute, doing movement with hands and fingers as part of self expression

❖ **Eye-Hand Coordination:** coordinating visual acuity with hand and body movement: Keeping the soft toy on the parachute, using and spinning scarves, twirling and spinning movement props

❖ **Physical Principals:** learning physical weight; stability; equilibrium; balance in the context of moving with music

❖ **Sensory Discrimination including**
   • **Tactile Discrimination** (touch): identifying and differentiating textures with touch: touch parachute and other props
   • **Auditory Discrimination** (hearing): identifying sounds as related to various cultures and connecting those sounds to the distinctions loud/ soft; high/low pitch; fast/slow rhythms
   • **Visual Discrimination** (sight): recognizing various props visually

Cognitive Development

❖ **Language Arts**
   • **Verbal skills**
      o **Language development**: acquiring and using language while moving creatively and while describing/discussing movement activities in class and private discussions
      o **Vocabulary development**: adding words related to the movement activity to the body of words and phrases used in communication
   • **Emergent literacy**
      o **Creative writing**: expressing self in marks and pictures relating to the music and movement
      o **Story recall/sequencing** (temporal ordering): retelling the child's experience of the movement activity as it occurred in order

❖ **Math Skills**
   • **Mathematical literacy**
      o **1 to 1 correspondence**: counting number of dancers, counting beats
   • **Mathematical applications**
      o **Measurement**: comparing some aspect of size of one object to another as it relates to size of props or size of movements relative to one another
      o **Equivalency:** comparing one aspect of movement or rhythm pattern to other aspects of movement or rhythm patterns
      o **Seriation**: ordering sound or movement in a graduation of size from smallest to largest or vice versa, or in the context of time from earliest to latest
         – **Temporal ordering**: placing events in a particular predetermined
      o **Spatial relationships**: relating the aspects of movement to one another, thinking about objects in three dimensions
      o **Algebra**: sorting and matching movement or sound for one or more properties to discover a pattern

❖ **Science**
  • **Cause and effect**
    ○ **Relationships between actions and outcomes**: connecting musical patterns and movement responses
❖ **Social Studies**
  • **Understanding that being a good citizen involves certain behavior:** following rules, sharing, taking turns, individual responsibilities and consequences
  • **Recognizing diversity**: recognizing what makes people similar *and* different through musical and movement expression: knowing that superficial differences do not mean *bad*.
  • **Accepting human diversity**: types of families, cultures, races express themselves through music and movement in a variety of ways; learning to evaluate humankind based upon the impact of their choices and internal values on the rest of humanity rather than superficial differences of race or religious preferences, and so on
  • **Temporal ordering**: children put events in order in terms of selecting movements as related to music

Social Development

❖ **Self-respect:** valuing self as child learns to move and express self in motion, liking one's own body just as it is and isn't
❖ **Sharing:** allowing others fair use of space and props
❖ **Taking turns:** allowing others fair turns at choosing music selections, if creating group movement patterns, opportunities to act in a directorial role, letting others play with the parachute et cetera
❖ **Working cooperatively with others in a group:** working well with others in movement activities
❖ **Collaboration:** planning and creating movement activities as a small or large group
❖ **Following directions:** carrying out directions for movement activities
❖ **Social boundaries:** participating in movement activities with respect for other's physical space
❖ **Taking care of classroom environment:** participating in any cleanup of props, et cetera

Emotional Development

❖ **Self-esteem:** feeling good about oneself and one's body as one participates in movement activities
❖ **Self-confidence:** feeling safe and secure to express self in music and movement activities
❖ **Accomplishment:** developing a sense of self worth as related to movement expression, learning dances
❖ **Generosity:** allowing other's an opportunity to express themselves in movement and music activities

Creative Expression

❖ **Use of creative media and expression of imagination:**

❖ **Music**: expressing self through vocal and instrumental sounds
  • **Movement/dance**: expressing self through movement
  • **Dramatization/story telling**: expressing self through dramatic movement
  • **Developing aesthetic appreciation** for movement activities from many cultures
❖ **Creative risk**: being comfortable moving creatively
❖ **Creative Thinking**: inventing movements to fit music

Possible Accommodations for *Multicultural Dancing Activity*

ADHD
❖ Present activity in a small group situation so that child has plenty of room to be self-expressed without interfering with other children
❖ Make certain that there are sufficient "best" props to go around
❖ Select music with a cadence that will not over stimulate child
❖ Use positive reinforcement when child behaves appropriately with others by allowing others' personal space, not bumping into others intentionally or otherwise, sharing props and space fairly

Developmental Delays
❖ Using an appropriately adjusted vocabulary level, teach and re-teach any vocabulary words from the activity individually or in small groups including lyrics, music genres, names of props, names for movements and movement patterns such as jumping, spinning, skipping, walking, as well as names for body parts such as arms, legs, head and laterality
❖ Skipping, walking, as well as names for body parts such as arms, legs, head
❖ Use modeling to communicate vocabulary: e.g.: when jumping, say the word jump
❖ When appropriate, have children say the words for their movement as part of the activity
❖ Present movement activities in a small group

Autism Spectrum Disorder
❖ Using an appropriately adjusted vocabulary level, teach and re-teach any vocabulary words from the activity individually or in small groups including lyrics, music genres, names of props, names for movements and movement patterns such as jumping, spinning, skipping, walking, as well as names for body parts such as arms, legs, head and laterality
❖ When appropriate, have children say the words for their movement as part of the activity
❖ Have playing music and dancing part of the daily routine
❖ Offer fewer props, but be sure the child's favorites there
❖ If the child seems to respond to specific or a specific genre of music, use that music regularly
❖ Check to make sure volume, cadence is not disturbing to child
❖ Have child dance in small group settings in proximity to "buddy"

Visual Impairments
- ❖ Adjust lighting so child has optimal vision
- ❖ Set up environment so it is free of obstacles
- ❖ Present movement activities in a small groups
- ❖ Allow sufficient space such that the child is less likely to be startled by movements peripherally, outside of visual range, or from behind
- ❖ Have child work with a fully sighted "buddy"

Orthopedic Impairments
- ❖ Set up environment so it is free of obstacles
- ❖ Present activity in a small group setting
- ❖ Make sure there is sufficient room so child will not be bumped
- ❖ If child lacks mobility or strength to move independently, gently assist child in movement, being sensitive to child's movement cues
- ❖ Assist child in holding parachute
- ❖ Adjust tempo of music to accommodate child's movement range

Gifted and Talented Education (GATE)
- ❖ If appropriate, ask child to identify patterns in the music, reiterating the aphorism "A pattern repeats"
- ❖ Ask child to invent movement patterns to match musical patterns
- ❖ Ask child to invent movements that (for the child) fit the music
- ❖ Ask child to "draw" the music
- ❖ Offer music with more complex tempos and patterns

English Language Learners (ELL)
- ❖ Play music from child's home culture, if appropriate
- ❖ Teach and re-teach any vocabulary words from the activity individually or in small groups including lyrics, names of props, names for movements and movement patterns such as jumping, spinning, skipping, walking, as well as names for body parts such as arms, legs, head and laterality
- ❖ Use modeling to communicate vocabulary: e.g.: when jumping, say the word jump
- ❖ When appropriate, have children say the words for their movement as part of the activity
- ❖ Use positive reinforcement when child attempts using new vocabulary in speaking

Content Standards For Kindergarten Met By This Activity
English Language Arts
> Reading (1.0, 1.17, 1.18)
> Reading Comprehension (2.0, 2.3)
> Written and Oral Language (1.0, 1.1)
> Listening and Speaking (1.0, 1.1, 1.2, 2.0, 2.1, 2.2)

Mathematics
> Measurement and Geometry (2.0, 2.1)
> Statistics (1.0, 1.2)

Science
> Physical Science (1.a)
> Investigation and Experimentation (4.a, 4.b, 4.c, 4.d, 4.e)

History and Social Science
> Following Rules (K.1, K.1.1)
> Compare and describe people and places (K.4, K.4.1)
> Understanding that history relates to people and places in the past (K.6, K.6.3)

Theatre
> Creative Expression (2.0, 2.1, 2.3)
> History of Theatre (3.0, 3.1)
> Applications (5.0, 5.1)

Dance
> Artistic Perception (1.0, 1.1, 1.2, 1.3, 1.4)
> Creative Expression (2.0, 2.1, 2.2)
> Dance History (3.0, 3.1)
> Valuing Aesthetics (4.0, 4.1)
> Applications (5.0, 5.1)

Music
> Artistic Perception (1.0, 1.2)
> Music History (3.0, 3.1, 3.2, 3.3, 3.4)
> Valuing Aesthetics (4.0, 4.1)
> Applications (5.0)

Learning Plan

I. **Name of Activity:** Multicultural Dancing Activity

II. **Date of Presentation:**

III. **Age or Grade Level: Pre-K, Kindergarten**

IV. **Ratio of teachers to children needed for this activity:** 1:10

V. **Target Areas of Learning / Goals and Objectives** (target areas of learning directly relate to "VI. Evaluation Rubric")
    1. Physical: _____
    2. Cognitive: _____
    3. Social: _____
    4. Emotional: _____
    5. Creative: _____

VI. **Evaluation Rubric:** (if more than two learning areas are being evaluated, a spreadsheet form may be preferred)

Targeted Area of Learning

Targeted Area of Learning

_____
_____

4. Always _____
3. Usually _____
2. Sometimes _____
1. Rarely _____

4. Always _____
3. Usually _____
2. Sometimes _____
1. Rarely _____

VII. **Materials and Preparation**
1. An open space wherein children can move freely without concern for crashing into each other and without bumping into furniture and so forth
2. Music CDs or tapes
3. Props: fancy dress up hats, fans, scarves, parachute, rhythm sticks, cultural props (the teacher should not offer anything sharp or hard enough that a child might be injured by bumping into it)
4. If a parachute is being used, the teacher can add a soft toy or small inflatable ball to the activity to add a dimension of the "keep the toy on the parachute" game

VIII. **Procedure**
1. Teacher informs children that music will be played from another country,
2. Bring out props
3. Play music and allow children to dance

4. When dancing is complete, ask children to guess from what country the music came, (i.e. try to identify the country of origin of the music)

IX. **Accommodations** (changes to accommodate learning diversity)
Name of Accommodated Area:

1. _____
2. _____
3. _____
4. _____
5. _____

X. **Applicable Framework Standards: Kindergarten**

Standard _____
_____
_____
_____
_____

Standard _____
_____
_____
_____
_____

Standard _____
_____
_____
_____
_____

Standard _____
_____
_____
_____
_____

Standard _____
_____
_____
_____
_____

XI. Evaluation and Comments (i.e.: How well did the plan work? Great responses? What aspects are especially effective? Not effective? What improvements are needed? Ideas for follow up activities and other notes)

_____

_____

_____

_____

Chapter Thirteen

Cooking Activities and Learning Plans

"Bread deals with living things, with giving life, with growth, with the seed, the grain that nurtures. It is not coincidence that we say bread is the staff of life."

– Lionel Poilane (1945–2002)
The most famous bread baker in Paris, interviewed 10,000 bakers before taking over his father's boulangerie.
(www.quotegarden.com/food)

Basic Cooking

Cooking potentially employs all curricular areas. One must read the recipe (visual discrimination and language), measure the ingredients (physical and math), process the food with heat, cold, chopping, or blending (physical and science), present it in an appetizing manner (physical and social) with the outcome of accomplishment (emotional). If the food happens to have a cultural origin such as latkes or quesadillas, then social studies is also involved.

Food draws people's attention. People must eat, and generally enjoy eating. The skill of preparing food attractively and palatably is called culinary arts. This is because beautifully crafted food is an art. To be sure, culinary arts are ephemeral, and yet are still very, very much appreciated.

The teacher should consider the intended learning outcome when planning a cooking activity in the classroom, since within cooking there is so much potential learning. Is the emphasis change of physical state? That is science. Measuring? That is math. Is the emphasis upon foods representative of a culture? That is social science. What about creating an event for guests? That is socialization and creativity. It is all in there and it is upon the teacher to structure the presentation such that the intended learning is produced.

With younger children, start out with easy, no-fail recipes such as **Ants on a Log** or **Smoothies**. During holiday seasons, present traditional foods from a variety of cultural groups. Be certain to include foods from the cultures represented in your classroom population.

Before planning any cooking projects, find out if your students have particular dietary restrictions for health, cultural, or religious purposes. For example, children may be sensitive to nuts, wheat, or be lactose intolerant. Many people practicing Hinduism or Buddhism are vegetarians. Many Orthodox Jewish people eat no pork or shellfish, and have restrictions about combining meat and dairy at the same meal. Jehovah's Witnesses do not celebrate holidays. It is crucial for the teacher to be aware of these special needs and to plan accordingly when creating any activity for the class, and particularly for cooking activities.

Cooks, both men and women alike, are often depicted wearing aprons. That's because the nature of the cooking process tend to be on the messy side. In the classroom, smocks or old tee shirts may be worn to protect clothing. For convenience, the teacher might wish to use the child-sized disposable aprons available through discountschoolsupply.com. At less than five cents apiece, they might seem like quite a bargain at cleanup time for both cooking and other hands-on activities.

Suggested Reading:

Barrett, J. (1988). *Cloudy with a chance of meatballs.* ISBN: 0-689-70749-5. (Silly and fun).

Brown, M. (1987) *Stone Soup.* ISBN: 0689711034.

Bruchac, J. & Vojtech, A. (1998). *First Strawberries: A Cherokee Story.* ISBN: 0140564098.

Davis, A. (1997). *Bone Button Borscht.* ISBN: 1550742248.

De Paola, T. (1989). *Tony's bread: An Italian folktale.* ISBN: 0698113713.

De Regniers, B. S. (editor). (1988). *Sing a Song of Popcorn: Every Child's Book of poems.* ISBN: 0-590-43974-X.

Ehlert, L. (1990). *Growing Vegetable Soup.* ISBN: 0152325808.

Ehlert, L. (1993). *Eating the Alphabet: Fruits & Vegetables from A to Z.* ISBN: 0152244360.

Friedman, I. R. (1987). *How My Parents Learned to Eat.* ISBN: 039544235.

Galdone, P. (2006). *The Little Red Hen.* ISBN: 0618752501. (also in Spanish)

Gershator, D. & Gershator, P. (1998). *Bread is for Eating.* ISBN: 0805057986. (Bilingual English / Spanish. Vibrant illustrations and song about Mexican culture and the journey of bread from seed to flour to store to baking)

Gwynne, F. (2005). *A Chocolate Moose for Dinner.* ISBN: 068987827 (Ages 4-7; lots of funny puns and plays on words).

Harbison, E.M. (1999). *Loaves of Fun: A History of Bread with Activities and Recipes from around the world.* ISBN: 1556523114. (Lively history of bread from ancient times to present, with glossary and recipes).

Hoban, R. (1993). *Bread and Jam for Frances.* ISBN: 0064430960 (Ages 5-8; Frances learns the importance of trying new foods)

Jenness, A. (1993). *Come Home With Me: A Multicultural Treasure Hunt.* ISBN: 156584064X (a look at four different families and their homes and customs: Africa, Ireland, Cambodia, and Puerto Rico).

Johnson, A.A. (1997). *Smoothies: 22 Frosty Fruit Drinks.* ISBN: 1-57054-101-9.

Knight, B.T. (1997). *From Cow to Ice Cream.* ISBN: 0516260669.

McCloskey, R. (1976). *Blueberries for Sal.* ISBN: 014050169X.

Nadler, B. (1995). *The Magic School Bus Inside Ralphie: A Book About Germs.* ISBN: 0590400258 (Ages 4-8)

Numeroff, L. (1985). *If You Give a Mouse a Cookie.* ISBN:0060245867. (also in Spanish: (1995). *Si le das una galletita a un raton.* ISBN: 0060254386.

Pienkowski, J. (2000). *Dinner Time.* ISBN: 158117024.

Politi. L. (1994). *Three Stalks of Corn.* ISBN: 0689717822.

Selsam, M. E. (1976). *Popcorn.* ISBN: 0688220835.

Sendak, M. (1991). *Chicken Soup With Rice: A Book of Months.* ISBN: 006443253X.

Sendak, M. (1995). *In the Night Kitchen.* ISBN: 0060266686 (Caldecott Honor Book).

Suess, Dr. (1960). *Green Eggs and Ham.* ISBN: 0394800168. (Available in English and Spanish)

Vaughn, M.K. & Lofts, P. (2001). *Wombat Stew.* ISBN: 1865044482. (A lively take-off on the idea of "Stone Soup", Australian animals outwit the dingo and save their friend)

Ice Cream in Zip-Type Bags

This is a quick, easy, enjoyable activity that is especially good for warm days. Partner the children by putting them into teams of two. The children will find that the bag of ice and salt becomes quite cold. Even though the squeezing process only takes five to seven minutes, the children's fingers will become cold. Taking turns reduces the effect of painfully cold fingers, and the sharing of the work actually adds to the merriment of the activity.

As the salt water may possibly leak out of the bags, this is a good activity to present outside. A shady place with tables and no plants is preferable, as salt tends to kill plants.

The sugar content of this particular recipe is low, requiring only one tablespoon of sugar per cup of milk. The fat content of the milk does not change the procedure. The outcome, if using whole milk or half and half, of course is much creamier.

Materials (for each pair of children)
- ❖ 1 zipper style gallon-size freezer bag
- ❖ 2 zipper style quart-size freezer bags
- ❖ Measuring cups
- ❖ Measuring spoons
- ❖ Plastic spoons
- ❖ Ingredients for Ice Cream making (listed below)

Recipe for Ice Cream In Zip Bags
For Each Child
> 1 tablespoon sugar
> 1 cup milk
> 1/4 teaspoon vanilla or vanilla powder

For Each Team
> 6 cups of ice (enough to fill the gallon bags halfway)
> 6 tablespoons salt (rock salt is recommended, if available; if not, regular table salt that pours will work also)

Method
Teacher will
- ❖ Write the directions on the board
- ❖ Read directions aloud
- ❖ Demonstrate the steps of the activity (i.e., measuring out, squeezing air out of bags and sealing)
- ❖ Pair children up into teams
- ❖ Give **each** team **two** small (quart-size) bags and **one** large (gallon-size) freezer bag

Each team will

- ❖ Fill the large bag half full of ice. Measure and add the salt. Seal the bag.
- ❖ Measure milk, vanilla, & sugar to put into their small bags. (Children can take turns measuring ingredients and holding open the quart-sized bag)
- ❖ Air is squeezed out of small bags. Each bag is sealed and set aside.
- ❖ Open large bag, place small bags inside. Large bag is carefully resealed.
- ❖ Shake and squeeze until mixture becomes ice cream; (takes up to 5 minutes - Children should take turns squeezing as their hands will get cold)
- ❖ Wipe off top of small bag. Then open bags carefully & enjoy!

Notes

1. Activity is done when mixture firms up to the texture of soft serve ice cream
2. Salt water from the bags should be dumped down a drain and not into soil
3. Encourage children to document their observations in their journals; Journal entries can be dictated if writing is an emerging skill
4. This is a good activity to conduct outdoors, due to the possible enthusiasm of the children and possible subsequent mess

Suggested Reading:

Gibbons, G. (1987). *The Milk Makers.* (Reading Rainbow Book). ISBN: 0689711166.

Knight, B.T. (1997). *From Cow to Ice Cream.* ISBN: 0516260669.

Older, J. (2002). *Ice Cream: Including Great Moments in Ice Cream History.* ISBN: 0881061123. (The history of ice cream, illustrated by Lyn Severance, the designer of Ben & Jerry's ice cream carton).

Rey, H.A. (1989). *Curious George Goes to an Ice Cream Shop.* ISBN: 0395519373.

Suggested CD:

Greg & Steve. (1987). *We All Live Together. Vol.2.* (Includes: English / Spanish months of the year song, World is a Rainbow, Popcorn, **The Freeze**). CD Available from: amazon.com

Targeted Areas of Learning

Physical Development

- ❖ **Fine motor skills:** using the small muscles of the hand and fingers: scooping out, measuring, and pouring out ingredients
- ❖ **Eye-hand coordination:** coordinating visual acuity with the use of the small muscles of the hand and fingers; placing ingredients carefully into the bag
- ❖ **Sensory discrimination**
  - • **Tactile discrimination (touch):** experiencing the sensation of touching, squeezing and pressing the ingredients inside the zip bag; feeling the bag turning colder.
  - • **Visual discrimination (sight):** watching the ingredients change into ice cream

Cognitive Development
- ❖ **Language Arts**
  - • **Listening and speaking**
    - o **Verbal skills**
      - – **Language development:** understanding and following simple instructions; encourage use of complete sentences in discussing the observed changes in ingredients;
      - – **Vocabulary development:** comprehension; learning new words;
- ❖ **Math Skills**
  - • **Number recognition:** understanding the relationship between number symbols and specific quantities
  - • **Measurement**
    - o Understanding that objects have properties, such as length, weight and capacity
    - o Measuring ingredients of different quantities into zip bags
- ❖ **Science**
  - • **Physical sciences:** understanding that properties of materials can be measured and observed, and that the materials can change form.

Social Development
- ❖ **Working with others:** sharing materials, taking turns, following directions, working cooperatively
- ❖ **Taking care of the classroom environment:** participating in clean up

Emotional Development
- ❖ **Self-esteem:** building self-confidence: learning new letters and words;

Possible Accommodations for *Ice Cream In Zip-Type Bags Activity*

ADHD
- ❖ Use positive reinforcement (praise) when child works well with partner, and behaves appropriately
- ❖ Allow the activity to go on a little longer if child becomes engaged in it
- ❖ Cover zipper opening of bag with duct tape after bag is zipped in case of enthusiastic play
- ❖ Be sure to use freezer type bags (for strength) not sandwich type bags
- ❖ Place splat mats under tables of ingredients or have activity in an area where accidental spills are easily cleaned up
- ❖ Use an old tee shirt as a smock over child's clothes (for convenience, disposable children's aprons are available very inexpensively through discountschoolsupply.com)
- ❖ Have the child act as your helper, setting activity up
- ❖ Ask the child to repeat the instructions, to make sure that the child really understands what to do
- ❖ Check in on children frequently

Developmental Delays

- ❖ Go over steps of task more slowly to be sure child understands
- ❖ Use gallon-size freezer bags
- ❖ Use an old tee shirt as a smock over child's clothes (for convenience, disposable children's aprons are available very inexpensively through discountschoolsupply.com)
- ❖ Cover zipper opening of bag with duct tape after bag is zipped in case of enthusiastic play
- ❖ Place activity inside a large baking pan or aluminum roasting pan to contain spills
- ❖ Place splat mats under tables of ingredients or have activity in an area where accidental spills are easily cleaned up
- ❖ Check in on children frequently
- ❖ Have child work with a gentle peer with higher competency as a partner
- ❖ Offer more time to complete task
- ❖ Give authentic praise frequently for incremental achievements

Autism Spectrum Disorders

- ❖ Explain the activity using short simple phrases, emphasizing that the bag will get cold
- ❖ Present the activity as part of the centers routine, allowing the child to become accustomed to the activity
- ❖ Put an old tee shirt over child's clothing for less restricted play
- ❖ Use positive reinforcement when child participates; notice child's incremental achievements
- ❖ Allow child to warm up to the activity, perhaps offering sensory activities inside of zipper bags or balloons: gel, flour, cornstarch, oobleck before presenting this activity
- ❖ Have child work with a gentle peer who understands the task at hand

Visual Impairments

- ❖ Adjust the lighting to reduce glare
- ❖ Use gallon-size freezer bags
- ❖ Place splat mats under tables of ingredients or have activity in an area where accidental spills are easily cleaned up
- ❖ For less restricted play, use an old tee shirt as a smock over child's clothes (for convenience, disposable children's aprons are available very inexpensively through discountschoolsupply.com)
- ❖ Have child work with a gentle and more competent peer
- ❖ Place materials child has chosen on a tray
- ❖ Offer the child a magnifying glass on a stand (similar to the ones used for needlework, found in craft stores)
- ❖ Offer more time to complete task, and for clean up if necessary

Orthopedic Impairments

- ❖ Lower the adult to child ratio
- ❖ Be sure the height and angle of the table is adjusted for best access for the child

❖ If child is in a wheel chair, activity can occur on a tray, if that is a more effective presentation
❖ Be sure child is seated in a comfortable position; in the case of cerebral palsy, monitor child to ascertain that the child is in a comfortable position
❖ If necessary, either place your hand over child's or child's hand over teachers to guide the child's hand through the movement
❖ Place splat mats under tables of ingredients or have activity in an area where accidental spills are easily cleaned up
❖ Allow additional time, if needed

Gifted and Talented Education (GATE)
❖ Use more advanced words
❖ Child can act as an assistant to others in the class
❖ Children create a "personal recipe diary"
❖ Children copy recipe from a recipe card or from the board into their personal recipe diary
❖ Ask children to write/draw a story about children making and eating *Ice Cream in Zip Bags*
❖ Ask children to write or draw the steps taken to make *Ice Cream in Zip Bags*

English Language Learners (ELL)
❖ Offer more time
❖ Repeat activity frequently for additional practice, perhaps set it up as a centers activity
❖ Partner child with a peer who understands the task
❖ Explain the activity using short simple phrases
❖ Check with the child frequently to insure adequate comprehension

Content Standards For Kindergarten Met By This Activity
English Language Arts
>Listening and Speaking (1.0, 1.1, 1.2, 2.1)

Mathematics
>Numbers and Counting (1.0)
>Measurement and Geometry (1.0, 1.1)

Science:
>Physical Science (1.a, 1.b)
>Investigation and Experimentation (4.a, 4.b, 4.e)

History and Social Science
>Following Rules (K.1, K.1.1)
>Understanding that history relates to people and places in the past (K.6, K.6.3)

Learning Plan

I. **Name of Activity: Ice Cream in Zip-Type Bags**

II. **Date of Presentation:**

III. **Age or Grade Level: 3 years and up**

IV. **Ratio of teachers to children needed for this activity:** 1:6

V. **Target Areas of Learning / Goals and Objectives** (target areas of learning directly relate to "VI. Evaluation Rubric")

    1. Physical: _____

    2. Cognitive: _____

    3. Social: _____

    4. Emotional: _____

    5. Creative: _____

VI. **Evaluation Rubric:** (if more than two learning areas are being evaluated, a spreadsheet form may be preferred)

Targeted Area of Learning

_____

_____

    4. Always _____

    3. Usually _____

    2. Sometimes _____

    1. Rarely _____

Targeted Area of Learning

_____

_____

    4. Always _____

    3. Usually _____

    2. Sometimes _____

    1. Rarely _____

VII. **Materials and Preparation**

1. 2 quart-size zip-type freezer plastic bag (1 per child)
2. 1 gallon-size zip-type freezer plastic bag (1 per team)
3. Measuring cups
4. Measuring spoons
5. Plastic spoons
6. Ingredients for Ice Cream making (listed below)

Recipe for Ice Cream in Zip Bags
For Each Child

    1 tablespoon sugar

    1 cup milk

    1/4 teaspoon vanilla or vanilla powder

For Each Team

6 cups of ice - enough to fill the gallon bags halfway

6 tablespoon salt (Rock salt is recommended, if available; if not, regular, table salt that pours will also work)

VIII. Procedure

Teacher will

1. Write the directions on the board
2. Read directions aloud
3. Demonstrate the steps of the activity (i.e., measuring out, squeezing air out of bags and sealing)
4. Pair children up into teams
5. Give **each** team **two** small bags (quart-size) and **one** large freezer bag (gallon-size)

Each team will

1. Fill the large bag half full of ice. Measure and add the salt. Seal the bag.
2. Measure milk, vanilla, & sugar to put into each small bag.
3. Air is squeezed out of small bags. Each bag is sealed and set aside.
4. Open large bag, place small bags inside. Large bag carefully resealed.
   • Open large bag, place small bags inside. Large bag is carefully resealed.
   • Shake and squeeze until mixture becomes ice cream; (takes up to 5 minutes - Children should take turns squeezing as their hands will get cold)
5. Wipe off top of small bag. Then open carefully & enjoy!

Notes

• Activity is done when mixture firms up to the texture of soft serve ice cream
• Salt water from the bags should be dumped down a drain and not into soil
• Encourage children to document their observations in their journals; Journal entries can be dictated if writing is an emerging skill
• This is a good activity to conduct outdoors, due to the possible enthusiasm of the children and possible subsequent mess

IX. Accommodations (changes to accommodate learning diversity)

Name of Accommodated Area:

1. _____
2. _____
3. _____
4. _____
5. _____

X. Applicable Framework Standards: Kindergarten

Standard _____

_____

_____

_____

_____

Standard _____

_____

_____

_____

Standard _____

_____

_____

_____

Standard _____

_____

_____

_____

Standard _____

_____

_____

_____

XI. Evaluation and Comments (i.e.: How well did the plan work? Great responses? What aspects are especially effective? Not effective? What improvements are needed? Ideas for follow up activities and other notes)

_____

_____

_____

_____

Ants on a Log

Ants on a Log is a classic recipe to use with young children. It is easily prepared, and as easily eaten. Most children will gobble this healthy treat quickly.

Should there be a child or children sensitive to peanuts in the class, alternative nut butters, such as roasted soy nut butter, macadamia nut butter, cashew nut butter or almond butter can be substituted for the peanut butter. Firm tofu, well drained, sprinkled with a little salt and oil, and mashed into a smooth puree may also be substituted for the peanut butter. Unusual nut butters can be found at health food stores or Trader Joe's markets. Many grocery stores carry tofu, which also may be purchased at Asian stores or those indicated above.

Ingredients for spreads (for each group)
❖ Cards or recipes on full size sheets of paper (laminated so they remain clean) with recipes/ directions for assembling Ants *on a Log*
❖ Clip boards for recipes
❖ Plastic bowl
❖ Measuring cups and spoons
❖ Forks or appropriate tools for mashing/mixing
❖ 1/4 cup nut butter/soy butter/tofu/grate cheese or cheese spread to be used as the medium for the spread
❖ Honey, sea salt, or other seasonings such as garlic, curry, mild chilies (optional)
❖ Mild flavored vegetable oil to make topping easier to spread, if needed

Method for making spreads
❖ Have children work in groups of three or four
❖ Ask children to decide the type of spread they choose to make and to take a copy of the recipe (and a clip board) they choose to their work area
❖ Children tell teacher their decision, teacher gives children ingredients which they take back to their work area
❖ Children mash or mix ingredients thoroughly
❖ Mixture can be refrigerated to assemble *Ants on a Log* later or children may move on to assemble *Ants on a Log*

Ingredients for Ants on a Log
❖ Fresh celery stalks, washed and set on paper towels
❖ Paper bowls or other non-breakable containers with approximately 1/4 cup nut butter/ spread for each child or pair of children
❖ Plastic knives
❖ Small cups of raisins
❖ Paper plates
❖ Instructions for activity written on the board, or mounted on a sheet of paper set up on the table in clear view of all the children participating

Method for assembling Ants on a Log

- ❖ Have children wash their hands
- ❖ Go over the instructions with the group, asking them to restate the instructions back to the teacher or assistant
- ❖ Give each child a paper plate and a plastic knife
- ❖ Set out ingredients on trays easily accessible to children
- ❖ Children can measure a segment of celery in a predetermined measurement (three inches is good)
- ❖ Children count out the number of raisins for their *Ants on a Log* (each child makes one or more)
- ❖ With supervision, children cut their segments of celery
- ❖ Allow children to select their containers of nut butter/spread and raisins
- ❖ Model for children how to spread celery section with nut butter
- ❖ Children spread nut butter and place "ants" onto their "log"
- ❖ When process is complete, have children take their utensils to be washed, and straighten up the preparation mess
- ❖ Children will then eat their treat
- ❖ Children may write about the experience of preparing and eating *Ants on a Log*

Suggested Reading:

Cole, J., & Beech, L.W. (1996). *The Magic School Bus Gets Ants in its Pants: A Book About Ants.* ISBN: 059040024X (Ages 4-8)

Ehlert, L. (1993). *Eating the Alphabet: Fruits & Vegetables From A to Z.* ISBN: 0152244360

Nadler, B. (1995). *The Magic School Bus Inside Ralphie: A Book About Germs.* ISBN: 0590400258 (Ages 4-8)

Pallotta, J. & Thomson, B. (1992). *The Vegetable Alphabet Book.* ISBN: 0881064688.

Targeted Areas of Learning

Physical Development

- ❖ **Fine Motor Skills:** using the small muscles of the hand and fingers: taking nut butter from the individual containers and spreading nut butter, picking up and placing raisins on nut butter covered celery
- ❖ **Eye-hand coordination:** coordinating visual acuity with using the small muscles of the hand and fingers: picking up and placing raisins
- ❖ **Sensory discrimination**
  - **Tactile discrimination** (touch): identifying and differentiating textures with touch: sticky nut butter, shriveled texture of raisins
  - **Oral discrimination** (taste): identifying sweet/nutty flavors
  - **Olfactory discrimination** (smell): identifying different smells: identifying the smell of peanut or other nut butters

Cognitive Development

❖ **Language Arts**
- **Verbal skills**
  - o **Vocabulary development**: adding to the body of words and phrases understood and the body of words/phrases that can be used in speech: using the correct words for cooking and ingredients
- **Emergent literacy**
  - o **Symbol recognition**: recognizing that particular marks have meaning: reading the instructions for the activity
  - o **Word recognition**: recognizing words in the instructions for the activity
  - o **Story recall/sequencing (temporal ordering)**: retelling instructions for making *Ants on a Log* to the teacher/paraprofessional

❖ **Math Skills**
- **Conservation**
  - o **Conservation of quantity**: understanding that the number in a group of items remains constant no matter how the items are arranged: placing a predetermined number of raisins on the piece of celery
  - o **Conservation of mass**: equivalent masses are the same, no matter the shape the mass takes: spreading a pre designated quantity of nut butter/spread on the celery
- **Mathematical literacy**
  - o **1-to-1 correspondence**: counting items in an organized way: counting raisins
- **Mathematical applications**
  - o **Measurement**: using a standard measure to determine the size (height, length, weight, quantity, volume) of an object: measuring and cutting celery; measuring out nut butter/spread
  - o **Seriation**: ordering events in a pre designated sequence: order of preparation of *Ants on a Log*
  - o **Spatial relationships**: thinking about objects in three dimensions: thinking about the celery as a three dimensional object
  - o **Construction**: forming by putting together parts to create a three dimensional object: assembling *Ants on a Log*

❖ **Science**
- **Scientific processes**
  - o **Prediction**: relating an anticipated outcome: predicting what "Ants on a Log" will look like
  - o **Observation:** carefully watching and noting what is seen: observe outcome of *Ants on a Log*
  - o **Review**: comparing predictions and actual outcomes: compare prediction and observation of *Ants on a Log*
- **Life Science**:
  - o **Hygiene:** maintaining an appropriate level of personal cleanliness: washing hands correctly before handling food

Social Development

❖ **Sharing**: sharing cooking implements and ingredients
❖ **Taking turns:** everyone in the classroom deserves opportunities to participate in preparing *Ants on a Log*
❖ **Collaboration**: planning, creating, and presenting cooking activities in a group
❖ **Following directions**: carrying out instructions for preparing *Ants on a Log*
❖ **Impulse control**: managing an impulse to lick the spoon or fingers, "lick and dip" into spread
❖ **Taking care of classroom environment**: participating in cleanup of food preparation

Emotional Development

❖ **Self-esteem**: feeling good about participating in food preparation in which there is no "wrong" outcome
❖ **Accomplishment**: developing a sense of achievement by preparing food

Creative Expression

❖ **Use of creative media and expression of imagination**:
   • **Culinary arts**: expressing self through food preparation and presentation
❖ **Creative risk**: being comfortable playing creatively in the preparation of food

Possible Accommodations *for Ants on a Log Activity*

ADHD

❖ Lower the ratio; perhaps presenting the activity at the kidney-shaped table for best supervision
❖ Place small quantities of selection of spreads in soft plastic containers
❖ Allow children to taste the spreads before assembling *Ants on a Log*
❖ Use wooden ice cream spoons (such as are available with cuplets of ice cream) for spreading as they do not have anything like a sharp edge
❖ If children are cutting the celery with plastic knives, lower the ratio to one-to-one
❖ When child behaves appropriately, be sure to acknowledge that behavior

Developmental Delays

❖ Demonstrate the activity step-by-step, using simplified language, making sure eye contact is made
❖ Lower the ratio, particularly for cutting
❖ Pre-teach actions such as mixing the spread, spreading, and (possibly) cutting if needed
❖ Prior to activity offer multiple activities for practicing the pincer grasp and eye-hand coordination, such as stringing beads, placing progressively smaller pegs into puzzle with holes, et cetera.
❖ Use larger tools, with larger grips
❖ Use larger pieces of celery

❖ Break the spread making and *Ants on a Log* assembly into two separate activities during the day
❖ Allow more time

Autism Spectrum Disorders
❖ Lower the ratio
❖ Demonstrate the activity step-by-step, using simplified language, making sure eye contact is made
❖ Ask child to repeat instructions back to teacher or assistant to check for understanding
❖ Prior to activity present opportunities for the child to taste and smell the different spreads
❖ Keep variety of spreads within or close to the flavors familiar to the child
❖ Pair child with a buddy, preferable the same buddy for most activities
❖ Break the spread making and *Ants on a Log* assembly into two separate activities during the day
❖ Prior to activity offer multiple activities for practicing the pincer grasp and eye-hand coordination such as stringing beads, placing progressively smaller pegs in to puzzle with holes, et cetera. Allow more time

Visual Impairments
❖ Adjust lighting to reduce glare
❖ Use larger adapted tools and larger pieces of celery
❖ Use larger dried fruit such as cranberries
❖ Allow more time
❖ If necessary, guide child's hand for spreading, picking up raisins, placing raisins
❖ Use a magnifying lamp on a stand

Orthopedic Impairments
❖ Use adapted tools
❖ Use large pieces of celery, and dried fruit such as cranberries
❖ Assist child using the hand over hand method, if necessary
❖ Adjust height of table for easiest access
❖ Place activity on individual trays for easier access
❖ Offer more time
❖ Lower the ratio

Gifted and Talented and Talented Education (GATE)
❖ Allow children to make more than one kind of spread
❖ Allow them to extend the activity by doing a "spread tasting" event prior so the children can select their spread (see bread tasting in social studies chapter)
❖ Children create a "Personal Recipe Diary"
❖ Children copy recipe from a recipe card or from the board into their personal recipe diary
❖ Ask children to write/draw a story that includes the *Ants on a Log*
❖ Ask children to write or draw the steps taken to make *Ants on a Log*

English Language Learners (ELL)

- ❖ Pre-teach vocabulary words: celery, nut butter, tofu, bowl, fork, salt, spread mash, raisins, spreader, plate, food, knife, cut, taste, smell, sweet, salty, smooth, crunchy individually or in a small group setting
- ❖ Model activity for children, speaking slowly, combining words that child knows with new words so child can begin to decode contextually
- ❖ Use pictures or show activity
- ❖ Make sure eye contact is made
- ❖ Review vocabulary after food is prepared in small group setting or individually
- ❖ Acknowledge all attempts to use new vocabulary positively, whether the child has gotten the words "right" or not

Content Standards For Kindergarten Met By This Activity

English Language Arts

Reading (1.0, 1.2, 1.3, 1.4, 1.5, 1.17, 1.18)
Reading Comprehension (2.0, 2.3, 2.5)
Literary Analysis (3.0, 3.1, 3.2)
Writing (1.0, 1.1, 1.3, 1.4)
Written and Oral Language (1.0, 1.1, 1.2)
Listening and Speaking (1.0, 1.1, 1.2, 2.0, 2.1, 2.3

Mathematics

Numbers and Counting (1.0, 1.1, 1.2, 1.3, 2.0, 2.1)
Measurement and Geometry (1.0, 1.1)

Science

Physical Science (1.a)
Investigation and Experimentation (4.a, 4.b, 4.d, 4.e)

History and Social Science

Following Rules (K.1, K.1.1)
Matching work descriptions to related jobs in history and community (K.3)

Learning Plan

   I. **Name of Activity: Ants on a Log**

   II. **Date of Presentation:**

   III. **Age or Grade Level: 3 years and up**

   IV. **Ratio of teachers to children needed for this activity:** 1:4

   V. **Target Areas of Learning / Goals and Objectives** (target areas of learning directly relate to "VI. Evaluation Rubric")
   1. **Physical**: _____
   2. **Cognitive**: _____
   3. **Social**: _____
   4. **Emotional**: _____
   5. **Creative**: _____

   VI. **Evaluation Rubric:** (if more than two learning areas are being evaluated, a spreadsheet form may be preferred)

Targeted Area of Learning	Targeted Area of Learning
_____	_____
_____	_____
4. Always _____	**4.** Always _____
3. Usually _____	**3.** Usually _____
2. Sometimes _____	**2.** Sometimes _____
1. Rarely _____	**1.** Rarely _____

   VII. **Ingredients and Preparation Needed**
   1. Cards or recipes on full size sheets of paper (laminated so they remain clean) with recipes/directions for assembling ants on a log
   2. Clip boards for recipes
   3. Plastic bowl
   4. Measuring cups and spoons
   5. Forks or appropriate tools for mashing/mixing
   6. 1/4 cup of nut butter/soy butter/tofu/grate cheese or cheese spread to be used as the medium for the spread
   7. Honey, sea salt, or other seasonings such as garlic, curry, mild chilies (optional)
   8. Mild flavored vegetable oil to make topping easier to spread, if needed

For "Ants on a Log"
1. Fresh celery stalks, washed and set on paper towels
2. Paper bowls or other non breakable containers with approximately 1/4 cup nut butter/spread for each child or pair of children
3. Plastic knives
4. Small cups of raisins
5. Paper plates
6. Instructions for activity written on the board, or mounted on a sheet of paper set up on the table in clear view of all the children participating

VIII. Procedure

For Making Spreads
1. Have children wash their hands
2. Have children work in groups of three or four
3. Ask children to decide the type of spread they choose to make and to take a copy of the recipe (and a clip board) they choose to their work area
4. Children tell teacher their decision, teacher gives children ingredients which they take back to their work area
5. Children mash or mix ingredients thoroughly
6. Mixture can be refrigerated to assemble ants on a log later or children may move on to assemble **"Ants on a Log"**

For Assembling "Ants on a Log":
1. Have children wash their hands
2. Go over the instructions with the group, asking them to restate the instructions back to the teacher or assistant
3. Give each child a paper plate and a plastic knife
4. Set out ingredients on trays easily accessible to children
5. Children can measure a segment of celery in a predetermined measurement (three inches is good)
6. Children count out the number of raisins for their ants on a log (each child makes one or more)
7. With supervision, children cut their segments of celery
8. Allow children to select their containers of nut butter/spread and raisins
9. Model for children how to spread celery section with nut butter
10. Children spread nut butter and place "ants" onto their "log"
11. When process is complete, have children take their utensils to be washed, straighten up the preparation mess
12. Children may then eat their treat
13. Children may write about the experience of preparing and eating **"Ants on a Log"**

IX. Accommodations (changes to accommodate learning diversity)
Name of Accommodated Area:

1. _____
2. _____
3. _____
4. _____
5. _____

X. Applicable Framework Standards: Kindergarten
Standard _____

_____
_____
_____
_____

Standard _____

_____
_____
_____
_____

Standard _____

_____
_____
_____
_____

Standard _____

_____
_____
_____
_____

Standard _____

_____
_____
_____
_____

XI. Evaluation and Comments (i.e.: How well did the plan work? Great responses? What aspects are especially effective? Not effective? What improvements are needed? Ideas for follow up activities and other notes)

_____
_____
_____
_____

Smoothies

In essence smoothies are a fruit-based (milk) shake. Brainchild of the Sixties, the smoothie has become a universal favorite. A blender or a food processor is essential for making smoothies. This is a fabulous recipe for a basic "dump and pour" style of cook.

The ingredients vary widely, per the preferences of the people drinking them. Do you like and have bananas? Toss them in. Hate blueberries? Leave them out. Are your favorite strawberries out of season? Use the unsweetened frozen variety. It is possible to use frozen fruit, which will reduce the need to add as many ice cubes to the mix (the ice cubes lend a more "ice cream" like texture to the drink).

This can be an opportunity for the teacher to discuss the difference between a vegetable and a fruit in preparation for this activity.

This activity can be quite inexpensive if presented either early in the traditional school year, or in the spring when fruits are in season. Often local flea markets will have fruit and vegetable stalls where ripe fruit can be purchased quite inexpensively. If the school is in a suburban or agricultural area, it is possible that some of the children's parents might have a fruit tree or berry bush. The teacher may be able to prevail upon those parents to contribute from their harvest.

Ripe fruits make better smoothies. Under ripe fruits are generally unpalatable.

Be sure to wash all fruits thoroughly, peel if appropriate, cut off bruised or damaged parts, and cut into blendable-sized chunks.

If the children are not familiar with the flavors of raspberries, blueberries, boysenberries, mangoes, papayas, or even strawberries, the teacher may want to introduce the children to those flavors before presenting them to the children in the form of a smoothie.

Adding a little bit of unsweetened apple juice, orange juice, or milk thins the mixture to a drinkable consistency. It is advisable for the teacher to have some sort of sense regarding the flavor preferences of the students in the class as well as knowing the students' food sensitivities. A lactose intolerant child, for example, should not have a smoothie thinned with milk. Dairy products and certain citrus fruits, particularly grapefruit, interfere with the effectiveness of some medications. It is important to be aware of the medications the children are taking when preparing food for them.

Prepackaged "smoothie mixes" often contain sugar in some form or another as well as preservatives, artificial flavors, and colors. Each teacher needs to reflect upon the health message being sent by using such ingredients, and from there decide whether to use them in an activity.

Particularly if tropical fruits such as papayas, kiwis, or mangoes are used, show children the different kinds of seeds those fruits contain. Attempt to lead the conversation into the possibility of attempting to germinate those seeds using open-ended questions as an extension of this activity.

Note: If a large quantity of ice is used, or if the children drink the mixture too quickly the children may experience a "brain freeze".

Practice what you preach. Remember that much teaching occurs not within lectures and activities, but inside that which the teacher models. If the teacher speaks out loudly for a healthy diet and the children see the teacher drinking diet soda and eating sugary or greasy and salty foods, what message is really being sent to the children? The same would hold true for smoking. The teacher may play all the anti-smoking films available, but if the teacher or classroom paraprofessional slips outside at recess for a smoke, even outside of the view of the children, but smells of smoke when returning to class, the message is all too clear.

Materials

- ❖ One or more blenders or food processors with a motor strong enough to crush ice
- ❖ Fresh or frozen fruit, cleaned and cut into blendable size pieces
- ❖ Ice
- ❖ Milk or juice
- ❖ Plastic knives and plastic cutting boards
- ❖ Cards or laminated sheets of paper with the instructions
- ❖ Clipboards to hold the instructions
- ❖ Plastic measuring cups and spoons
- ❖ Plastic trays upon which the children can pour out their smoothies
- ❖ Paper cups (paper is biodegradable, which sends an ecological message)
- ❖ Plastic spoons
- ❖ Rubber scrapers for scraping out the last bits of smoothie
- ❖ Paper towels for clean up

Basic Recipe for Making "Smoothies"
For each child serving:

5 ice cubes

1/2 cup fruit (fresh or frozen)

1/4-1/2 cup milk or juice (teacher can choose for the texture to be thinner or thicker depending on amount of liquid added)

Optional: If children have additional nutritional or protein needs, 1 tablespoon of protein, soy or whey supplement powder can be added;

Method

- ❖ Before cooking, all children must wash hands thoroughly
- ❖ Have children work in groups
- ❖ Children select the flavors for their smoothie
- ❖ Children take a copy of the instructions to their work area, depending on the number of children, supervising adults, and number of blenders, several work stations could be created
- ❖ Children can cut soft fruits, such as bananas and strawberries into chunks
- ❖ Children measure ingredients and place in blender
- ❖ Make sure children do not start blender without an adult present, and with the lid firmly on top of the blender
- ❖ When children indicate they are ready, the supervising adult gives them permission to start the blender, often pulsing the blender works best initially (be sure lid is firmly on the blender)

❖ Children complete the blending process and pour out their smoothies.
❖ If various groups have used different fruits, perhaps small cups can be made available so the children have the opportunity to taste the other group's smoothies
❖ Children participate in clean up with teachers and adults
❖ Children can dictate, write, or draw about making smoothies

Suggested Reading:

Bruchac, J. & Vojtech, A. (1998). *First Strawberries: A Cherokee Story.* ISBN: 0140564098.
Ehlert, L. (1993). *Eating the Alphabet: Fruits & Vegetables From A to Z.* ISBN: 0152244360.
Johnson, A.A. (1997). *Smoothies: 22 Frosty Fruit Drinks.* ISBN: 1-57054-101-9.
McCloskey, R. (1976). *Blueberries for Sal.* ISBN: 014050169X.

Targeted Areas of Learning

Physical Development

❖ **Fine motor skills:** using the small muscles of the hand and fingers: cutting fruit, pick up fruits, placing fruits in a blender, pressing buttons on a blender
❖ **Eye-hand coordination:** coordinating visual acuity with using the small muscles of the hand and fingers: cutting fruits, pouring juice or milk into blender, pouring smoothie into cups
❖ **Physical principals:** learning physical weight change from the empty blender to the filled blender, from empty cups to filled cups
❖ **Sensory discrimination including:**
 • **Tactile discrimination** (touch): identifying and differentiating textures and sensations with touch: feeling the coldness of the ice, the textures of the fruits, the vibration of the blender, the smoothness of the pureed fruit
 • **Auditory discrimination** (hearing): identifying sounds: hearing the sound of the blender as it crushes the ices and the changes as the smoothie mixture is completed
 • **Visual discrimination** (sight): recognizing various objects visually: identifying shapes; colors; sizes of fruits and ingredients being prepared; visually comparing the appearance of the fruits and the smoothie mixture
 • **Oral discrimination** (taste): identifying sweet, salty, sour, and bitter tastes; identifying textures with tongue and mouth: identifying flavors of the fruits and combinations of fruits by taste
 • **Olfactory discrimination** (smell): identifying different smells of the fruits and combinations of fruits

Cognitive Development

❖ **Language Arts**
 • **Verbal skills**
  o **Language development**: acquiring and using language appropriately in interactions with others while preparing the smoothies

- o **Vocabulary development**: adding to the body of words and phrases related to fruits and the process of preparing a smoothie
- **Emergent literacy**
  - o **Word recognition**: recognizing the words used in the recipe/directions for the smoothie
  - o **Emergent writing**: beginning skills to document the experience of preparing a smoothie in writing
  - o **Journal writing:** observations and thoughts about making smoothies related through scribble writing, dictation, or emergent writing and drawings
  - o **Story recall/sequencing (temporal ordering)**: retelling and relating smoothie making event the child experienced
- ❖ **Math Skills**
  - **Conservation**
    - o **Conservation of volume**: equivalent quantities of smoothie remain constant no matter what size or shape container of the smoothie
  - **Mathematical literacy**
    - o **Associating number symbols with quantity**: understanding that a specific symbol is always associated with a specific quantity while following the recipe for making the smoothie
- ❖ **Mathematical applications**
  - **Measurement**: using a standard measure to measure out smoothie ingredients
  - **Common relatedness**: linking items that are not the same, but are associated with each other such as the various ingredients and processes involved in making smoothies
- ❖ **Science**
  - **Scientific processes**
    - o **Inquiry**: what will happen when these ingredients are blended, what will they look like, with the end result be palatable or unpalatable?
    - o **Prediction**: relating an anticipated outcome-based of making smoothies
    - o **Observation:** carefully watching and noting what is seen to respond to inquiry and predictions
    - o **Review**: comparing predictions and actual outcomes of making smoothies
  - **Cause and effect**
    - o **Relationships between actions and outcomes**: why did the smoothies turn out/ not turn out
  - **Life Science**
    - o Differentiating fruits from inorganic objects/substances
    - o **Hygiene:** maintaining an appropriate level of personal cleanliness before the preparation and consumption of food; cleaning up the cooking environment after food preparation
- ❖ **Social Studies**
  - **Recognizing diversity**: noting that certain fruits are from particular types of places, and that people from those places eat those fruits

- **Environmental responsibility**: developing a sense of stewardship for the planet: cleaning up and composting plant matter (if appropriate), using biodegradable cups, cleaning up workspace

Social Development

❖ **Sharing**: items intended for use by the community are to be shared: blenders, ingredients, tools

❖ **Taking turns:** allowing others a fair use of ingredients and cooking tools to make smoothies

❖ **Working cooperatively with others in a group**: working well as a member of a food preparation team

❖ **Collaboration**: taking responsibility for tasks associated with group food preparation including clean up

❖ **Following directions**: carrying out directions for making smoothies

❖ **Taking care of classroom environment**: participating in cleanup of food preparation

Emotional Development

❖ **Self-esteem**: building a sense of competence by participating in food preparation that has a little room for making errors

❖ **Accomplishment**: developing a sense of achievement by participating in food preparation

Creative Expression:

❖ **Use of creative media and expression of imagination**:
  - **Culinary arts**: expressing self through smoothie preparation and presentation

❖ **Aesthetic appreciation: developing appreciation** for the flavors of a variety of foods

❖ **Creative thinking**: brainstorming: considering a variety of possible combinations of fruits for preparing smoothies

Possible Accommodations for *Smoothies Activity*

ADHD

❖ Lower the ratio

❖ Reduce the selection of ingredients

❖ Be sure that top to blender fits snugly and is securely in place before it is used

❖ If child is pouring fluids, use a "spill proof" container

❖ Recognize all efforts to manage impulsivity and efforts to stay on task

❖ Be sure area for food preparation can be easily cleaned

Developmental Delays

❖ Pre-teach activity, using language easily understood by child, speaking slowly and clearly, making eye contact, possibly demonstrating or using pictures to clarify

❖ Lower the ratio
❖ Use adapted tools: larger tools, tools with hand grips
❖ Be sure that top to blender fits snugly and is securely in place before it is used
❖ Allow more time or break up the fruit preparation and blending into separate activities

Autism Spectrum Disorders

❖ Pre-teach activity, using language easily understood by child, speaking slowly and clearly, making eye contact, possibly demonstrating or using pictures to clarify
❖ Lower the ratio
❖ Bring in types fruits to be used in activity before hand so child is accustomed to their taste an smell
❖ Allow child time to be willing to try out the different types of fruits
❖ If child has sensitivity to loud noises, child may go to a quieter area for the blending part of the activity or use a blender occasionally before this activity, so that the noise is not entirely unfamiliar
❖ Place the activity on the calendar, preferably later in the week, so child can become used to the idea

Visual Impairments

❖ Adjust lighting to reduce glare
❖ Use a blender or food processor with a very wide mouth
❖ Offer adapted tools with adapted hand grips
❖ Guide child's hand if necessary when putting ingredients into blender or when using blender
❖ Allow children to smell fruits individually as well as taste them
❖ Use large measuring devices
❖ If child is pouring fluids, use a "spill proof" container
❖ Allow more time

Orthopedic Impairments

❖ Use a blender or food processor with a very wide mouth
❖ Offer adapted tools with adapted hand grips
❖ Guide child's hand if necessary when putting ingredients into blender or when using blender
❖ Adjust the height of work surfaces
❖ Place fruit preparation part of activity on a tray
❖ Allow more time

Gifted and Talented Education (GATE)

❖ Have the children invent funny or silly names for the smoothie concoctions
❖ Have children write their favorite smoothie combinations in their personal cookbook
❖ Ask children to invent new words for the colors of the smoothies, such as "panicking purple"

❖ If using tropical fruits, or fruits that are not locally grown, have children look up the kinds of places those types of fruits grow and something about the people who live in those environments

English Language Learners (ELL)

❖ Pre-teach vocabulary individually or in small groups: fruit names, blender, food processor, smoothie, ice, milk, juice, scraper, paper towel, pour, spill, sweet, tart, cold, smooth, wet, dry, puree, measure, cup, taste, flavor
❖ Acknowledge child's attempts to use new vocabulary
❖ Demonstrate activity step-by-step using vocabulary child knows, speaking slowly and clearly, repeating instructions as necessary, checking for understanding
❖ Have children who are learning English work with children who are native English speakers, or with children who have a good command of English
❖ Encourage conversation during the activity
❖ Review vocabulary in small groups or individually using realia, pictures, or photographs

Content Standards For Kindergarten Met By This Activity

English Language Arts
     Reading (1.0, 1.2, 1.3, 1.4, 1.5, 1.17, 1.18(
     Reading Comprehension (2.0, 2.3)
     Literary Analysis (3.0, 3.1, 3.2)
     Writing (1.0, 1.1, 1.3,
     Written and Oral Language (1.0, 1.1, 1.2)
     Listening and Speaking (1.0, 1.1, 1.2, 2.0, 2.1, 2.3)

Mathematics
     Numbers and Counting (1.0, 1.3, 2.0, 2.1)
     Algebra, Sets and Sorting (1.0, 1.1)
     Measurement and Geometry (1.0, 1.1)
     Statistics (1.0, 1.1)

Science
     Physical Science (1.a, 1.b)
     Life Science (2.a.2.c)
     Investigation and Experimentation (4.a, 4.b, 4.d, 4.e)

History and Social Science
     Following Rules (K.1)
     Compare and describe people and places (K.4, K.4.1)

Learning Plan

    I. **Name of Activity: Smoothies**

   II. **Date of Presentation:**

  III. **Age or Grade Level: Pre-K, Kindergarten**

  IV. **Ratio of teachers to children needed for this activity:** 1:6

   V. **Target Areas of Learning / Goals and Objectives** (target areas of learning directly relate to "VI. Evaluation Rubric")
      1. Physical: _____
      2. Cognitive: _____
      3. Social: _____
      4. Emotional: _____
      5. Creative: _____

  VI. **Evaluation Rubric:** (if more than two learning areas are being evaluated, a spreadsheet form may be preferred)

Targeted Area of Learning	**Targeted Area of Learning**
_____	_____
_____	_____
4. Always _____	**4.** Always _____
3. Usually _____	**3.** Usually _____
2. Sometimes _____	**2.** Sometimes _____
1. Rarely _____	**1.** Rarely _____

 VII. **Ingredients and Preparation Needed**
    1. One or more blenders or food processors with a motor strong enough to crush ice
    2. Fresh or frozen fruit, cleaned and cut into blendable size pieces
    3. Ice
    4. Milk or juice
    5. Plastic knives and plastic cutting boards
    6. Cards or laminated sheets of paper with the instructions
    7. Clipboards to hold the instructions
    8. Plastic measuring cups and spoons
    9. Plastic trays upon which the children can pour out their smoothies
   10. Paper cups (paper is biodegradable, which sends an ecological message)
   11. Plastic spoons
   12. Rubber scrapers for scraping out the last bits of smoothie
   13. Paper towels for clean up

Recipe for Making "Smoothies":
> 5 ice cubes
> 1/2 cup fruit (fresh or frozen)
> 1/4-1/2 cup milk or juice (teacher can choose for the texture to be thinner or thicker depending on amount of liquid added)
> **Optional:** if children have additional nutritional or protein needs, one tablespoon of protein, soy or whey supplement powder can be added;

VIII. Procedure
1. Before cooking, all children must wash hands thoroughly
2. Have children work in groups
3. Children select the flavors for their smoothie
4. Children take a copy of the instructions to their work area, depending on the number of children, supervising adults, and number of blenders, several work stations could be created
5. Children can cut soft fruits, such as bananas and strawberries into chunks
6. Children measure ingredients and place in blender
7. Make sure children do not start blender without an adult present, and with the lid firmly on top of the blender
8. When children indicate they are ready, the supervising adult gives them permission to start the blender, often pulsing the blender works best initially (be sure lid is firmly on the blender)
9. Children complete the blending process and pour out their smoothies.
10. If various groups have used different fruits, perhaps small cups can be made available so the children have the opportunity to taste the other group's smoothies
11. Children participate in clean up with teachers and adults
12. Children can dictate, write, or draw about making smoothies

IX. Accommodations (changes to accommodate learning diversity)
Name of Accommodated Area:
1. _____
2. _____
3. _____
4. _____
5. _____

X. Applicable Framework Standards: Kindergarten
Standard _____

_____
_____
_____
_____

Standard _____
_____
_____
_____
_____

Standard _____
_____
_____
_____
_____

Standard _____
_____
_____
_____
_____

Standard _____
_____
_____
_____
_____

XI. Evaluation and Comments (i.e.: How well did the plan work? Great responses? What aspects are especially effective? Not effective? What improvements are needed? Ideas for follow up activities and other notes)

_____
_____
_____
_____

Flat Bread: Tortillas

Many cultures have some sort of traditional flat bread. Flat breads are simple breads, prepared without leavening such as yeast, baking soda, or baking powder, and therefore do not "rise". In Mexico and Central America there are tortillas. In Scandinavia we find lefse and flatbrot, and in India, chapattis. The French are famous for their crepes. Matzoh is a traditional Jewish flat bread.

Before making tortillas, the teacher should talk about corn as a plant native to the Americas. A mortar and pestle can be shown so children can see how the corn was originally ground and prepared. Maps of countries where tortillas are a traditional food can be shown. Ask if they have ever eaten tortillas, and how they were served. Ask them if they have ever eaten corn chips, and with what the children ate the chips.

Ask the children what the masa feels like in their hands, how it smells, both cooked and uncooked. What do the uncooked tortillas feel like? How do the cooked tortillas feel? Ask the children to describe the tastes and textures of a homemade tortilla in their mouths. If the children have had commercial tortillas previously, how their homemade tortillas taste in comparison?

In many areas of the United States, ready-made masa is readily available in large grocery markets, found in the refrigerator section. Masa is the cornmeal dough from which tortillas are made. Prepared masa must be kept refrigerated until used.

Tortilla presses can be found in the foreign foods section of the market, however, sometimes the masa sticks to the presses, or if waxed paper is used, even with vegetable spray, the dough still sticks. For a young child, having the dough stick can be a very frustrating experience. For that reason, patting out the masa by hand is recommended.

Hand patting out the masa will produce a less beautiful product than the commercially made tortillas. This is fine. The hands on experience of patting out the tortillas can be a very satisfying one for the children.

Tortillas are cooked on a dry griddle. This part of the preparation is for adults only as the griddle is quite hot and a child may be burned while flipping the tortillas.

Homemade tortillas do not keep very well. Plan on serving them just a minute or two from the griddle with margarine, salsa, bits of chicken or other meat.

Variations
- **Gorditas**: make larger masa patties, stuff with a favorite filling, and grill
- **Quesadillas**: take two completed hand made tortillas, sprinkle on grated cheese (and bits of meat, if desired), regrill until the cheese is melted

Materials
- ❖ Commercially prepared masa
- ❖ A griddle, free standing electrical, if there is not stove available or a griddle which can be used on a stove top if there is a cook top available
- ❖ Waxed paper (upon which complete tortillas can be placed)
- ❖ A pan cake turner or two depending on the number of griddles
- ❖ Paper plates
- ❖ Plastic utensils

❖ Margarine, salsa, cheese, sour cream, guacamole or other toppings as desired
❖ Pictures of the tortilla making process
❖ Chart paper to document the children's opinions

Method

❖ Set out masa in bowls so several children can make tortillas at one time, with pieces of waxed paper where completed tortillas may be placed
❖ In separate area, place small containers or margarine, guacamole, salsa, sour cream and other toppings with spoons
❖ This can also be presented in small groups at the kidney-shaped table, if there are fewer adults available, although there will need to be one adult supervising the griddle at all times
❖ Children wash and rinse their hands thoroughly using liquid soap
❖ Demonstrate process of making tortillas by patting a ball of dough from hand to hand into flat round shape using words to describe shapes being made, weight of the dough, the size of the ball of dough relative to the size of the child's hands
❖ Ask the children to estimate the amount of masa needed to make the appropriate sized ball
❖ Children take turns patting out tortillas
❖ When tortillas are completed, child may bring the finished tortillas to the person grilling them. Have a designated place (away from the griddle) for the children to place the tortillas that are ready to be grilled.

Make sure children NEVER get within reaching distance of the griddle.

❖ Children wash their hands after they are done making tortillas
❖ Ask children to estimate how long they think it will take to cook the tortillas. Write the number down. Watch the clock and see how close the estimate is to the actual time it takes to cook a handmade tortilla.
❖ Children stay at a safe distance watching their personal tortillas cook.
❖ When tortillas are completed, place them on paper plates and allow children to "dress" their tortillas as desired.
❖ Children and adults clean up after everyone has had a chance to make and eat tortillas (do not force those children who do not want to eat the tortillas to do so)
❖ After clean up, gather the children in a large group and ask what they thought of the experience of making and eating tortillas
❖ Teacher can document the information using tally marks, charts, or graphs
❖ Children write about tortilla making in journals or writing activity

Suggested Reading:

Aliki. (1986). *Corn is Maize: The Gift of the Indians.* ISBN: 0064450260 (Ages 5-9)
Flood, N.B. (2006). *The Navajo Year Walk Through Many Seasons.* ISBN: 189335406. (April is the month for planting corn and other crops).

Galdone, P. (2006). *The Little Red Hen.* ISBN: 0618752501

Garza Lomas, C. (1998). *In My Family / En Mi Familia.* ISBN: 0-89239-138-3. (childhood memories of birthday pinatas and eating empanadas).

Hoban, R. (1993). *Bread and jam for Frances.* ISBN: 0064430960 (Ages 5-8)

Madrigal, A.H. (Tomie de Paola, illustrator). (1997*). Eagle and the Rainbow: Timeless Tales from Mexico.* ISBN: 155591-317-2.

Paulsen, G. (1998). The Tortilla Factory. ISBN: 0-15-201698-8. Spanish edition: La Tortilleria. (Process from the planting of the seeds to the making of tortillas)

Politi. L. (1994). *Three Stalks of Corn.* ISBN: 0689717822 (Ages 5-8)

Reiser, L. (Rebecca Hart, translator) (1998). *Tortillas and Lullabies / Tortillas y Cancioncitas.* ISBN: 0-688-14628-7. (Three generations make tortillas, sing songs, wash clothes and gather flowers; words and music for lullaby provided).

Targeted Areas of Learning

Physical Development
- ❖ **Fine motor skills:** using the small muscles of the hand and fingers: pulling off clumps of masa, patting out masa into a flat, round shape
- ❖ **Eye-hand coordination:** coordinating visual acuity with using the small muscles of the hand and fingers: pulling and patting out masa, pacing on waxed paper, taking cooked tortilla, topping it, and eating it
- ❖ **Physical principals:** learning physical weight: feeling and comparing the difference in the weight from the raw tortilla and the cooked tortilla
- ❖ **Sensory discrimination**
  - • **Tactile discrimination** (touch): identifying and differentiating textures and sensations with touch: soft raw dough, sticky raw dough, cold raw dough; firm, warm, dry cooked tortillas
  - • **Auditory discrimination** (hearing): identifying sounds: listening to the slapping sounds of patting out tortillas; the sizzling sounds of grilling tortillas
  - • **Visual discrimination** (sight): recognizing various objects visually: the ball of raw dough, the circle of the flattened tortilla (shapes), the color of the raw masa versus the color of a cooked tortilla, the differences in the sizes of the finished tortillas
  - • **Oral discrimination** (taste): identifying textures with tongue and mouth; identifying flavors by taste: salty, dry warm, soft but firm cooked tortilla, spicy if salsa is used as a topping, smooth or creamy if margarine or sour cream is used as a topping
  - • **Olfactory discrimination** (smell): identifying different smells: the smell of uncooked masa and the nutlike aroma of freshly grilled tortillas

Cognitive Development
- ❖ **Language Arts**
  - • **Verbal skills**
    - o **Language development:** acquiring and using language appropriately in interactions with other people: talking about experiences related to preparing and eating tortillas

- o **Vocabulary development**: adding to the body of words and phrases as related to preparing and eating tortillas
- **Emergent literacy**
  - o **Journal writing:** committing personal thoughts, ideas, reflections about preparation of and eating tortillas through scribble writing, dictation, or emergent writing and drawings
  - o **Matching spoken words to written words**: correctly associating the auditory expression with the written symbol grouping while writing about tortillas
  - o **Story recall/sequencing (temporal ordering)**: retelling and relating tortilla making in the order it occurred
- ❖ **Math Skills**
  - **Conservation**
    - o **Conservation of mass**: equivalent masses are the same, no matter the shape the mass takes: patting out the tortilla balls
  - **Mathematical applications**
    - o **Charting**: using an outcome to create various preliminary statistical diagrams to reflect outcomes of tortilla taste testing data
- ❖ **Science**
  - **Scientific processes**
    - o **Inquiry**: an organized search for knowledge regarding tortilla making
    - o **Prediction**: relating an anticipated outcome regarding tortilla making
    - o **Observation**: carefully watching and noting what is seen in tortilla making
    - o **Review**: comparing predictions and actual outcomes of tortilla making
  - **Life Science**:
    - o Differentiating organisms and plant matter such as corn from inorganic objects/ substances
    - o **Hygiene**: maintaining an appropriate level of personal cleanliness before, during, and after food preparation
- ❖ **Social Studies**
  - **Recognizing diversity**: recognizing what makes people similar *and* different: trying foods that are from Mexico, Central, and South America

Social Development

- ❖ **Self-respect:** valuing themselves as the children learn to prepare a variety of foods; particularly if the food is from another culture
- ❖ **Sharing**: that items intended for use by the community are available for the use by everyone in that community: tortilla making supplies
- ❖ **Taking turns:** everyone in the classroom deserves opportunities to participate in class activities: each person has an opportunity to make a tortilla before second turns are available
- ❖ **Patience**: managing a delay in gratification: waiting for tortilla to finish cooking
- ❖ **Working cooperatively with others in a group**: being patient, courteous, and supportive if another child is struggling in the tortilla making process

❖ **Collaboration**: planning, creating, and presenting group projects: working together to make tortillas; helping clean up
❖ **Following directions**: carrying out directions for tortilla making
❖ **Taking care of classroom environment**: participating in cleanup of tortilla making

Emotional Development:

❖ **Self-esteem**: feeling good about oneself when participating in tortilla making
❖ **Self-confidence**: feeling secure within one's self when participating in preparing foods, particularly foods one has not previously prepared
❖ **Stress relief**: finding acceptable vents for stress: pounding out stress on the tortilla dough
❖ **Accomplishment**: developing a sense of achievement from successfully making tortillas

Creative Expression

❖ **Use of creative media and expression of imagination**:
  • **Culinary arts**: expressing self through food preparation and presentation: making, serving, eating tortillas
❖ **Aesthetic appreciation: developing appreciation** for foods from a variety of cultures
❖ **Creative risk**: being willing to try making a food the child has previously not prepared

Possible Accommodations for *Tortilla Making Activity*

ADHD

❖ State reasons for the rules about staying away from the hot griddle very clearly, ask child to repeat rules to you
❖ Make sure the child's group is small
❖ Acknowledge child's efforts to stay on task and work cooperatively with others
❖ Lower the ratio

Developmental Delays

❖ Explain the rules about staying away from the hot griddle, using language the child knows, checking for understanding
❖ Model tortilla making, using language with which child is familiar, speaking slowly, making sure eye contact is made
❖ Demonstrate the activity to the children, checking for understanding
❖ Practice making "tortillas" with play dough in advance

Autism Spectrum Disorders

❖ Explain the rules about staying away from the hot griddle, using language the child knows, checking for understanding
❖ Model tortilla making, using language with which child is familiar, speaking slowly, making sure eye contact is made
❖ Demonstrate the activity to the children, checking for understanding

* Practice making "tortillas" with play dough in advance
* Bring in masa to touch and manipulate at an earlier time (instead of play dough), so child becomes used to the way it smells and feels
* Place "tortilla making" on the schedule so the child has a chance to become accustomed to the idea of making tortillas
* If the child and class become engaged by tortilla making, consider presenting the activity again

Visual Impairments
* Adjust the lighting
* Make sure the child's work area is away from the griddle, have someone accompany the child to where the tortillas to be grilled are place
* Practice making "tortillas" with play dough in advance
* Bring in masa to touch and manipulate at an earlier time (instead of play dough), so child becomes used to the way it smells and feels

Orthopedic Impairments
* Practice making "tortillas" with play dough in advance
* Bring in masa to touch and manipulate at an earlier time (instead of play dough)
* Allow more time
* If child's hands and fingers lack strength, hold their hands in yours, assisting them in patting out the masa

Gifted and Talented Education (GATE)
* Forewarn children about hot griddle, asking them to repeat the warning to you
* Instead of purchasing the masa, make the masa in class
* Have children experiment with grinding the corn with a mortar and pestle
* Have children look up other recipes that use masa
* Have children pat, roll, press tortillas and compare the different experiences

English Language Learners (ELL)
* Explain the rules about staying away from the hot griddle, using language the child knows, checking for understanding
* Pre-teach vocabulary individually or in small groups: griddle, corn, cornmeal, masa, pat, hot sticky, wet, dry, hot, crunchy, cheese, sour cream, guacamole, salsa, meat, cook, stove, plate, waxed paper, taste, smell
* Model activity for children using language children understand
* Acknowledge all attempts to use new vocabulary
* If child raises hand to share in the larger group, be sure to call on child to make sure someone else doesn't "share their share first"
* Review vocabulary individually or in small groups

Content Standards For Kindergarten Met By This Activity

English Language Arts

    Reading (1.0, 1.17, 1.18)

    Reading Comprehension (2.0, 2.2, 2.3)

    Writing (1.0, 1.1, 1.3)

    Written and Oral Language (1.0, 1.1, 1.2)

    Listening and Speaking (1.0, 1.1, 1.2, 2.0, 2.1, 2.3)

Mathematics

    Numbers and Counting (1.0, 1., 1.3, 2.0, 2.1, 3.0, 3.1)

    Algebra, Sets and Sorting (1.0, 1.1)

    Measurement and Geometry (1.0, 1.2, 2.0, 2.1)

    Statistics (1.0, 1.1)

Science

    Physical Sciences (1.a)

    Investigation and Experimentation (4.a, 4.b, 4.d, 4.e)

History and Social Science

    Following Rules (K.1, K.1.1)

    Compare and describe people and places (K.4)

    Understanding that history relates to people and places in the past (K.6, K.6.3)

Theatre

    Understanding Historical / Cultural Contributions of Theatre (3.0, 3.2)

Learning Plan

    I. **Name of Activity: Flat Bread: Tortillas**

    II. **Date of Presentation:**

    III. **Age or Grade Level: Pre-K, Kindergarten**

    IV. **Ratio of teachers to children needed for this activity:** 1:6

    V. **Target Areas of Learning / Goals and Objectives** (target areas of learning directly relate to "VI. Evaluation Rubric")

        1. Physical: _____

        2. Cognitive: _____

        3. Social: _____

        4. Emotional: _____

        5. Creative: _____

    VI. **Evaluation Rubric:** (if more than two learning areas are being evaluated, a spreadsheet form may be preferred)

Targeted Area of Learning	**Targeted Area of Learning**
_____	_____
_____	_____
4. Always _____	**4.** Always _____
3. Usually _____	**3.** Usually _____
2. Sometimes _____	**2.** Sometimes _____
1. Rarely _____	**1.** Rarely _____

    VII. **Ingredients and Preparation Needed**

        1. Commercially prepared masa
        2. A griddle, free standing electrical, if there is not stove available or a griddle which can be used on a stove top if there is a cook top available
        3. Waxed paper (upon which complete tortillas can be placed)
        4. A pancake turner or two depending on the number of griddles
        5. Paper plates
        6. Plastic utensils
        7. Margarine, salsa, cheese, sour cream, guacamole or other toppings as desired
        8. Pictures of the tortilla making process
        9. Chart paper to document the children's opinions

    VIII. **Procedure**

        1. Set out masa in bowls so several children can make tortillas at one time, with pieces of waxed paper where completed tortillas may be placed

2. In separate area, place small containers of margarine, guacamole, salsa, sour cream and other toppings with spoons

3. This activity can also be presented in small groups at the kidney-shaped table, if there are fewer adults available, although there will need to be one adult supervising the griddle **at all times**

4. Children wash and rinse their hands thoroughly using liquid soap

5. Demonstrate process of making tortillas by patting a ball of dough from hand to hand into a flat round shape using words to describe the shapes being made, the weight of the dough, the size of the ball of dough relative to the size of the child's hands

6. Ask the children to estimate the amount of masa needed to make the appropriate sized ball

7. Children take turns patting out tortillas

8. When tortillas are completed, child may bring the finished tortillas to the person grilling them. **Make sure children never get within reaching distance of the griddle.**

9. Children wash their hands after they are done making tortillas

10. Ask children to estimate how long they think it will take to cook the tortillas, write the number down, watch the clock and see how close their estimate is to the actual time it takes to cook a handmade tortilla

11. Children stay at a safe distance watching their personal tortillas cook.

12. When tortillas are completed, place them on paper plates and allow children to "dress" their tortillas as desired.

13. Children and adults clean up after everyone has had a chance to make and eat tortillas (do not force those children who do not want to eat the tortillas to do so)

14. After clean up, gather the children in a large group and ask what they thought of the experience of making and eating tortillas

15. Teacher can document the information using tally marks, charts, or graphs

16. Children write about tortilla making in journals or writing activity

IX. **Accommodations** (changes to accommodate learning diversity)
Name of Accommodated Area:

1. _____
2. _____
3. _____
4. _____
5. _____

X. Applicable Framework Standards: Kindergarten

Standard _____

_____
_____
_____
_____

Standard _____

_____
_____
_____
_____

Standard _____

_____
_____
_____
_____

Standard _____

_____
_____
_____
_____

Standard _____

_____
_____
_____
_____

XI. Evaluation and Comments (i.e.: How well did the plan work? Great responses? What aspects are especially effective? Not effective? What improvements are needed? Ideas for follow up activities and other notes)

_____
_____
_____
_____

Flavored Popcorn

Be aware that children under age three should not be served popcorn, as there is a choking hazard associated with popcorn. All food should be eaten sitting down. Please refer to the **Basic Cooking** introduction regarding choking.

There are as many recipes for flavored popcorn as a teacher can imagine. Children have more taste buds, and their taste buds are more sensitive than those of adults. For that reason, unless the population of the class is accustomed to spicy food, it would be prudent to select milder flavors for the popcorn.

Tomie de Paola has a wonderful book, *The Popcorn Book*, that talks about the tiny water droplets inside the unpopped popcorn that make it pop. When heated the water turns to steam, and the kernel of corn explodes, making popcorn. He cites the Aztec belief that within each kernel of popcorn lives a tiny little man (or demon) who becomes angry when heated up. *The Popcorn Book* briefly covers the history of popcorn. To preserve the water droplets in the popcorn, keeping popcorn in the freezer is suggested. To revive stale popcorn, sprinkle with water.

Popcorn, particularly when not drenched in butter and salt, is a very healthy, low calorie, high fiber food.

As a preparatory set, the teacher may decide to make plain popcorn with the children during an earlier class session. Some plain popcorn should be set aside in case the flavors of popcorn made turn out to be unpalatable to the children.

The air popcorn popping appliances are quite inexpensive and easy to use. This is the recommended method for popping popcorn in the classroom.

If several flavors of popcorn are made, when the class returns to the large group, the children can try the flavors that the other groups made. The children can write or draw reviews of the different flavors of popcorn. Each group could make up interesting or funny names for their particular popcorn flavor.

More ideas for possible flavors can be found in an on line web search for the key words, "flavored popcorn recipes".

Basic Recipe
- 3 quarts popped popcorn, with the unpopped kernels removed
- 1/4 cup melted butter or margarine
- Selected flavors

Place popped popcorn in a bowl. Melt butter in a microwave or on a stovetop. Add selected flavors, and mix well. Drizzle flavored butter over popcorn.

Optional: Oat rings, crispy wheat or rice cereal squares or other cereals, nuts, dried fruits, M & M candies, or pretzels can be added to the popcorn to make something more like a snack mix.

Suggestions for flavor combinations
- ❖ **Pizza popcorn**: 1/4 cup melted butter or margarine, add 1/2 teaspoon each crumbled basil, oregano, and garlic powder or granules, stir. Cook one minute. Drizzle flavored margarine over popcorn. Toss with hands. Serve.
- ❖ **Cheese popcorn**: 1/4 to 1/2 cup melted butter or margarine, 1 envelope dry cheese mix or 1/4 cup dry Parmesan cheese. At a very low heat, gently stir cheese into melted margarine. When mixed drizzle over popcorn, toss by hand to mix completely. Serve.

❖ **Soup or dressing mix popcorn**: 1/4 cup melted butter or margarine, one package soup or salad dressing/dip mix (such as onion, dill, spring vegetable, herb). Mix dressing mix into melted butter. When thoroughly mixed, pour over popcorn. Toss to cover popcorn. Serve.

❖ **Fruit-flavored drink mix popcorn**: 1/4 cup melted butter or margarine, 3 tablespoons fruit flavored powdered drink mix (the variety that includes the sugar). Add the drink mix into melted margarine. Stir to mix thoroughly. Drizzle over popcorn. Toss by hand. Serve.

❖ **Caramel corn**: Be advised that this recipe involves cooking sugar, which can cause painful burns. This should be prepared with close supervision, and a very low ratio. 1/2 cup butter or margarine, 10 large marshmallows, 1/2-cup brown sugar. Microwave for short periods or melt butter and marshmallows on a low heat on the stovetop. Add brown sugar. Bring to bubbling. Mix and pour over popcorn. Mix with a buttered spoon. This can be formed into ball shapes when it is cool enough to touch.

❖ **Chocolate popcorn**: Be advised that this recipe involves melting the chocolate, which can cause painful burns. This should be prepared with close supervision, and a very low ratio. 1/2 cup melted butter or margarine, 1/2 small package of chocolate (or white chocolate, peanut butter, butterscotch) chip pieces. Melt chips in butter. Stir well. Drizzle over the popcorn. Mix gently with a buttered spoon. Serve.

Materials

❖ Cards or laminated sheets of paper with the directions for making the flavored popcorn (one for each small group)
❖ Air popcorn popper
❖ Measuring cups
❖ Popcorn
❖ Large bowls for mixing in flavorings
❖ Small paper bowls for serving
❖ Sauce pan or glass bowl for melting butter
❖ Microwave (if stovetop is not used for making flavored butters)
❖ Butter or margarine
❖ Spoons
❖ Selected flavors

Method

❖ Read *The Popcorn Book* to the class.
❖ Tell the children about the different flavors for the popcorn.
❖ Have the children select the flavor or flavors of popcorn they are to make either as a class, or in small groups, depending on how many flavors the teacher wants to prepare and what will be most effective for that group of children.
❖ Have children wash their hands thoroughly, preferably with liquid soap.
❖ Have children measure out 1/4 cup of popcorn and place in air popper
❖ Turn on air popper, pop popcorn
❖ When popping is complete, turn off pop corn popper
❖ Place popcorn in large bowl

- ❖ Repeat until desired amount of popcorn is made
- ❖ Make flavored butters (see above)
- ❖ Mix into popcorn
- ❖ Serve
- ❖ Children can draw a picture of the angry little man inside the popcorn; write about the experience in their journals or as a writing exercise.

Suggested Reading:

Aliki. (1986). *Corn is Maize: The Gift of the Indians.* ISBN: 0064450260 (Ages 5-9)

De Paola, T. (1989). *The Popcorn Book.* ISBN: 082340533

De Regniers, B. S. (editor). (1988). *Sing a Song of Popcorn: Every Child's Book of Poems.* ISBN: 0-590-43974-X

Flood, N.B. (2006). *The Navajo Year Walk Through Many Seasons.* ISBN: 189335406. (April is the month for planting corn and other crops).

Nadler, B. (1995). *The Magic School Bus Inside Ralphie: A Book About Germs.* ISBN: 0590400258 (Ages 4-8)

Selsam, M. E. (1976). *Popcorn.* ISBN: 0688220835

Politi. L. (1994). *Three Stalks of Corn.* ISBN: 0689717822 (Ages 5-8)

Suggested CD:

Greg & Steve. (1987). *We All Live Together. Vol.2.* (includes: English / Spanish months of the year song, World is a Rainbow, **Popcorn,** The Freeze) CD Available from: amazon.com

Targeted Areas of Learning

Physical Development

- ❖ **Fine motor skills:** using the small muscles of the hand and fingers: measuring out popcorn and other ingredients, picking out the unpopped kernels from the popped corn, stirring the butter mixture, forming popcorn balls
- ❖ **Eye-hand coordination:** coordinating visual acuity with using the small muscles of the hand and fingers: pouring popcorn into popper, pouring popped popcorn into bowl, mixing in ingredients into melted butter, pouring butter mixture onto popcorn
- ❖ **Sensory discrimination**
  - **Tactile discrimination** (touch): identifying and differentiating textures and sensations with touch: soft, hard, rough, smooth, sticky: feeling the change in the state of the kernel from unpopped to popped, feeling the stickiness of the caramel and other sweet flavored popcorn, touching the various ingredients
  - **Auditory discrimination** (hearing): identifying sounds: listening to the sound of the popcorn popping
  - **Visual discrimination** (sight): identifying the change in the state of the popcorn visually
  - **Oral discrimination** (taste): identifying sweet, salty, sour, and bitter tastes; identifying textures with tongue and mouth; identifying flavors of the popcorn by taste

- **Olfactory discrimination** (smell): identifying different smells: noticing the changes in the smell of the unpopped corn and popped corn, tasting the flavored prepared: sweet, savory, spicy, pungent

Cognitive Development

❖ **Language Arts**
  - **Verbal skills**
    - ○ **Language development**: acquiring and using language appropriately in interactions with others; ability to carry on a conversation or discussion related to food preparation
    - ○ **Vocabulary development**: adding to the body of words and phrases understood and the body of words/phrases that can be used in speech as related to food preparation
  - **Emergent literacy**
    - ○ **Word recognition**: reading the recipe and instructions
    - ○ **Emergent writing**: writing about making popcorn, writing humorous names for popcorn, writing about tasting the popcorn, writing/drawing the "angry little man" in the popcorn
    - ○ **Journal writing:** writing about making popcorn, writing humorous names for popcorn, writing about tasting the popcorn, writing/drawing the "angry little man" in the popcorn
    - ○ **Creative writing**: writing original ideas about popcorn
    - ○ **Story recall/sequencing (temporal ordering)**: retelling and relating popcorn making, flavored popcorn making
❖ **Math Skills**
  - **Mathematical literacy**
    - ○ **Associating number symbols with quantity**: reading the recipes
    - ○ **Recognizing number words**: reading the recipes and instructions
  - **Mathematical applications**
    - ○ **Measurement**: using a standard measure to measure out the popcorn and other ingredients
    - ○ **Seriation**: ordering the cooking times correctly
      - **– Time**: cooking the popcorn flavorings for the designated amount of time
    - ○ **Common relatedness**: relating popcorn and steam, popcorn and popper, popcorn and butter
❖ **Science**
  - **Scientific processes**
    - ○ **Inquiry**: an organized search for knowledge regarding how popcorn works
    - ○ **Prediction**: relating an anticipated outcome regarding popcorn
    - ○ **Observation:** carefully watching and noting what happened
    - ○ **Documentation**: writing observations of popcorn popping which support/ disprove claims for outcomes of making flavored popcorn

- o **Review**: comparing predictions and actual outcomes, assessing value of any mistakes that occurred in making flavored popcorn
- o **Cause and effect**
  - – **Relationships between actions and outcomes**: why does the popcorn pop when heated? Will the popcorn become soggy if flavored butters are added? Why or why not? Will chocolate popcorn taste good? Why or why not?
- **Life Science**
  - o Differentiating popcorn and other foods from inorganic objects/substances
  - o **Hygiene:** maintaining an appropriate level of personal cleanliness during food preparation
- **Chemistry and Physics**
  - o Changes in the state of water: liquid to steam inside popcorn
  - o Popping popcorn
  - o Melting butter
- ❖ **Social Studies**
  - • **Recognizing diversity**: recognizing that even in the flavors preferred for popcorn, people are diverse; many people choose flavors for popcorn they are accustomed to from foods of their culture such as chilies, curries et cetera
  - • **Democratic process:** working out in the small or large group setting flavors to be prepared

Social Development

- ❖ **Self-respect:** valuing themselves, their opinions as their own in the classroom community
- ❖ **Sharing**: sharing the ingredients common to all recipes fairly with classmates
- ❖ **Taking turns:** allowing all the children in the small group to participate in cooking
- ❖ **Patience:** waiting until the food preparation is complete before eating
- ❖ **Working cooperatively with others in a group**: working well as a member of a cooking team
- ❖ **Collaboration**: planning, creating, and presenting flavored popcorn; taking responsibility for tasks associated with cooking including clean up
- ❖ **Negotiation**: learning to represent one's wishes related to flavoring popcorn in such a way that others in the group will consider those wishes favorably; respecting the ideas of others, even if they are not in agreement with the choices presented
- ❖ **Following directions**: carrying out directions for making flavored popcorn
- ❖ **Impulse control**: managing an impulse to nibble on ingredients (particularly chocolate chips) or eat popcorn before recipe is finished
- ❖ **Community building**: creating a sense of belonging in a group: working together on cooking projects
- ❖ **Taking care of classroom environment**: participating in cleanup of cooking projects
- ❖ **Safety practices**: being careful with warmed ingredients, using pot holders when appropriate

Emotional Development
❖ **Self-esteem**: feeling good about oneself as one learns to prepare foods
❖ **Self-confidence**: feeling secure about attempting to prepare foods
❖ **Accomplishment**: developing a sense of achievement as one learns to prepare foods

Creative Expression
❖ **Use of creative media and expression of imagination**
  • **Culinary arts**: expressing self through food preparation: making flavored popcorn
  • **2-dimensional visual arts**: drawing the "angry little man" inside the popcorn; making signs for the popcorn flavors
  • **Writing**: writing about popcorn making, about cooking, about observations

❖ **Aesthetic appreciation:** developing appreciation for different flavors, different foods
❖ **Creative risk**: being comfortable trying out recipes
❖ **Persuasion**: convincing others to make the flavor of popcorn preferred

Possible Accommodations for *Flavored Popcorn Activity*

ADHD
❖ Break the task into sessions: preparing the flavoring, making the popcorn
❖ Use large plastic bowls and utensils
❖ Make smaller batches of popcorn
❖ Model activity prior to presenting to class
❖ Set up directions using pictorial cues in a story board format
❖ Explain activity using language the child understands
❖ Use positive reinforcement for desired behavior
❖ Check on child regularly to ensure that the child remains on task

Developmental Delays
❖ Set up directions using pictorial cues in a story board format
❖ Model activity using language the child understands
❖ Model the activity step-by-step
❖ Present activity one or two steps at a time
❖ Check often for understanding of directions
❖ Use a recipe involving only a few steps or ingredients
❖ Offer adapted tools, such as: larger plastic bowls, spoons and other implements with chunky easy-grip handles
❖ Allow more time if necessary
❖ Lower the ratio of adults to children

Autism Spectrum Disorders

❖ Lower the ratio of adults to children
❖ Present activity one or two steps at a time
❖ Model the activity step-by-step
❖ Make smaller batches of popcorn
❖ Prepare plain popcorn a few times to increase familiarity with activity
❖ Use a recipe involving only a few steps or ingredients
❖ Select recipes using flavors familiar to the child
❖ Explain activity using language the child understands, including pictures or realia
❖ Have cooking occur in a place designated for cooking
❖ Use splat mat for easier cleanup

Visual Impairments

❖ Adjust lighting to reduce glare
❖ Offer adapted tools, such as: larger plastic bowls, spoons and other implements with chunky easy-grip handles
❖ Allow more time if necessary
❖ Lower the ratio of adults to children
❖ Story boards or written directions should be in a size easy to read for the child
❖ Allow child to work in an area where other people can not approach from behind
❖ Use splat mat for easier cleanup

Orthopedic Impairments

❖ Offer adapted tools, such as: larger plastic bowls with attached suction cup on the bottom for maximum stability, spoons and other implements with chunky easy-grip handles
❖ Allow more time if necessary
❖ Lower the ratio of adults to children
❖ Adjust the table height or place activity on a tray for maximum accessibility
❖ Use splat mat for easier cleanup
❖ Use hand-over-hand method if child's hands lack the strength or dexterity to manipulate utensils

Gifted and Talented Education (GATE)

❖ Encourage child to go online to select a recipe
❖ Allow child to invent own recipe for flavored popcorn (even if the recipe seems unworkable or silly, allow the child the freedom to experiment with the recipe)
❖ Allow the child to create similar snack mixes (i.e.: cereals)
❖ If the child is inventing a flavor or snack mix, ask the child to predict the outcome, including rationale for flavor or ingredient selection

English Language Learners (ELL)

- ❖ Model activity using words that the child understands, using realia and photographs
- ❖ Model the activity step-by-step
- ❖ Pre-teach vocabulary individually or in small groups (i.e.: flavor, popcorn, bowl, spoon, scrapper, air popper, pop, salt, taste, spicy, sour, sweet, salty, garlic, onion, butter, chocolate, cheese, stir, mix, measure, teaspoon, tablespoon, cup, quarter-cup, pepper, chilis, like, don't like, smell)
- ❖ Review the vocabulary after the activity in small groups or individually
- ❖ Use positive reinforcement whenever the child attempts to use any of the new vocabulary; whether correct or not, always reinforce the attempt
- ❖ Lower the adult to child ratio when appropriate

Content Standards For Kindergarten Met By This Activity

English Language Arts

Reading (1.0, 1.1, 1.2, 1.3, 1.4, 1.5, 1.17, 1.18)
Reading Comprehension (2.0, 2.1, 2.2, 2.3, 2.5)
Literary Analysis (3.0, 3.1, 3.2)
Writing (1.0, 1.1, 1.2, 1.3)
Written and Oral Language (1.0, 1.1, 1.2)
Listening and Speaking (1.0, 1.1, 1.2, 2.0, 2.1, 2.3)

Mathematics

Numbers and Counting (1.0, 1.2, 1.3)
Algebra, Sets and Sorting (1.0, 1.1)
Measurement and Geometry (1.0, 1.1, 1.2)

Science

Physical Sciences (1.a, 1.b)
Life Sciences (2.a, 2.c)
Investigation and Experimentation (4.a, 4.b, 4.c, 4.d, 4.e)

History and Social Science

Following Rules (K.1, K.1.1)
Compare and describe people and places (K.4)
Understanding that history relates to people and places in the past (K.6, K.6.3)

Visual Arts

Creative Expression (2.0, 2.5)
Valuing Aesthetics (4.0, 4.1, 4.2, 4.3)

Learning Plan

I. **Name of Activity: Making Flavored Popcorn**

II. **Date of Presentation:**

III. **Age or Grade Level: Pre-K to Primary**

IV. **Ratio of teachers to children needed for this activity:** 1:4

V. **Target Areas of Learning / Goals and Objectives** (target areas of learning directly relate to "VI. Evaluation Rubric")
   1. **Physical:** _____
   2. **Cognitive:** _____
   3. **Social:** _____
   4. **Emotional:** _____
   5. **Creative:** _____

VI. **Evaluation Rubric:** (if more than two learning areas are being evaluated, a spreadsheet form may be preferred)

Targeted Area of Learning	**Targeted Area of Learning**
_____	_____
_____	_____
4. Always _____	**4.** Always _____
3. Usually _____	**3.** Usually _____
2. Sometimes _____	**2.** Sometimes _____
1. Rarely _____	**1.** Rarely _____

VII. **Materials and Preparation Needed**
   1. Cards or laminated sheets of paper with the directions for making the flavored popcorn (one for each small group)
   2. Air popcorn popper
   3. Measuring cups
   4. Popcorn
   5. Large bowls for mixing in flavorings
   6. Small paper bowls for serving
   7. Sauce pan or glass bowl for melting butter
   8. Microwave (if stovetop is not used for making flavored butters)
   9. Butter or margarine
   10. Spoons
   11. Selected flavors

Basic Recipe

3 quarts popped popcorn, with the old maids or unpopped kernels removed

1/4 cup melted butter or margarine

Selected flavors (See **Flavored Popcorn** activity for complete listing of flavor suggestions)

VIII. Procedure

1. Read *The Popcorn Book* to the class.
2. Tell the children about the different flavors for the popcorn.
3. Have the children select the flavor or flavors of popcorn they are to make either as a class, or in small groups, depending on how many flavors the teacher wants to prepare and what will be most effective for that group of children.
4. Have children wash their hands thoroughly, preferably with liquid soap.
5. Have children measure out 1/4 cup of popcorn and place in air popper
6. Turn on air popper, pop popcorn
7. When popping is complete, turn off pop corn popper
8. Place popcorn in large bowl
9. Repeat until desired amount of popcorn is made
10. Make flavored butters (see above)
11. Mix into popcorn
12. Serve
13. Children can draw a picture of the angry little man inside the popcorn, and write about the experience in their journals or as a writing exercise.

IX. Accommodations (changes to accommodate learning diversity)

Name of Accommodated Area:

1. _____
2. _____
3. _____
4. _____
5. _____

X. Applicable Framework Standards: Kindergarten

Standard _____

_____

_____

_____

Standard _____

_____

_____

_____

Standard _____

_____

_____

_____

Standard _____

_____

_____

_____

Standard _____

_____

_____

_____

_____

XI. Evaluation and Comments (i.e.: How well did the plan work? Great responses? What aspects are especially effective? Not effective? What improvements are needed? Ideas for follow up activities and other notes)

_____

_____

_____

_____

Cookies in a Jar

Any of the "In a Jar" activities offer great opportunities for children to learn measuring and planning. The ingredients can get a bit expensive. A week or two before making a **"Cookies in a Jar"** type activity, ask parents to contribute the needed ingredients. The recipe for *Sand Art Brownies in a Jar* is recommended below. For further suggestions and ideas regarding other types of "In a Jar" activities, **All Recipes** @ www.cookie.allrecipes.com has helpful hints and a wide variety of recipes.

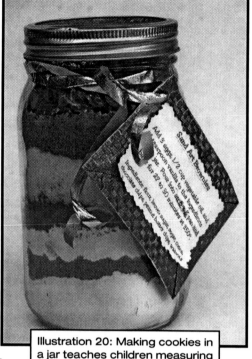

Illustration 20: Making cookies in a jar teaches children measuring and patterning.

The teacher will wish to separate the two recommended activities, and complete them on different days. One activity is involves actually making the jars that the children will take home as a gift, and the other activity involves the actual making and baking of the brownies themselves for the children to sample and taste. The children will have more of an appreciation of their *Sand Art Brownies in a Jar*, if they have the opportunity to create and taste this culinary delight in the classroom, before taking their jars home. This can be done, before the making of the jars, or possibly, the day after, but before the jars are sent home. The *Sand Art Brownies in a Jar* could also become gifts for Mother's Day, Father's Day, Grandparent's Day or some other holiday.

As creating the art jars is more complex than the making and baking, the full directions for completing the jars is given below. The set up for the making and baking portion of this two-step activity will be basically the same as for creating the jars. Children may wear smocks, old tee shirts or disposable aprons. A copy of the full recipe should be on the table, as a reference for the adults and children. As in making the jars, have one or more adults at the kidney-shaped table, and have the needed ingredients set out on the table in bigger bowls, with the appropriate measure (1/4 cup, 1/3 cup 1/2 cup, teaspoon). The recipe for one jar should be enough for a small group, so that each child has an opportunity to measure one or more of the ingredients into a large bowl. Let the children take turns measuring ingredients in the same order listed below for the jars. The additional ingredients may then be added. Three eggs, 1/2 cup of vegetable oil, and 1 teaspoon of vanilla will be needed for each group. When all ingredients have been added, give each child a turn to stir and let the children count to 20. A small spatula may be handy for pouring patter into the pan.

Small baking pans (8" x 8") can fit into a toaster oven to bake the brownies. Children should not handle the toaster oven, either putting the pan in or taking it out. Oven mitts will be needed for the adults. Parents may be willing to loan small baking pans, or small, disposable aluminum ones may be used. As each group's brownies go into the toaster oven, the children may help to clean the utensils and work space for the next group. A timer may be used to help children understand the baking time needed.

Ingredients for *Sand Art Brownies in a Jar*
(Note: The total amount of flour needed has been divided into two separate measurements, giving visual definition to the layering of ingredients!)

In order to maintain layered effect, place into jars, in specified order.
Each jar will require:
> 3/4 cup all-purpose flour (use 1/4 cup to measure)
> 3/4 teaspoon salt (use 1/4 teaspoon to measure)
> 1/3 cup unsweetened cocoa powder (use 1/3 cup to measure)
> 1/2 cup all-purpose flour (use 1/2 cup to measure)
> 2/3 cup brown sugar (use 1/3 cup to measure)
> 2/3 cup white sugar (use 1/3 cup to measure)
> 1/2 cup semi-sweet chocolate chips (use 1/2 cup to measure)
> 1/2 cup peanut butter (or vanilla) chips (use 1/2 cup to measure)
> 1/2 cup walnuts (optional) (use 1/2 cup to measure)

NOTE: If any child has a sensitivity to nuts or any other ingredient, other ingredients can and should be substituted.

Materials Needed

- ❖ A wide-mouth canning jar, ring and lid for each child (Wash in a hot dishwasher before use and let dry completely)
- ❖ Measuring cups, spoons, trays
- ❖ Table cloths to protect table surfaces, and for ease of clean-up
- ❖ Large bowls for ingredients and measuring utensils; should be placed on the table in the order that the ingredients will be put into jars (the number of bowls needed will depend on how many different types of ingredients are used)
  Optional: Labels may be made for each bowl of ingredients on card stock, placed on the table in front of the bowls, clearly designating to the children what each ingredient is and how much will be needed (i.e., "3/4 cup flour", "2/3 cup brown sugar") Bowls could even be numbered "1" to "9".
- ❖ Instructions for *Sand Art Brownies in a Jar* printed out on heavy paper
- ❖ **Recipe ingredients:** Calculate how much of each ingredient will be needed according to the size of the class. Estimate that this project will require the following ingredients for each child (or for each group of children when making and baking the brownies): 1 and 1/4 cup all-purpose flour, 3/4 teaspoon salt, 1/3 cup unsweetened cocoa powder, 2/3 cup brown sugar, 2/3 cup white sugar, 1/2 cup semi-sweet chocolate chips, 1/2 cup of another type of chips, either vanilla or peanut butter chips, and 1/2 cup walnuts; Be sure to add an extra measure of each ingredient so as to not run short. Also remember that adding nuts to any classroom recipe is optional.
- ❖ Recipe instruction cards (see the page following *Sand Art Brownies in a Jar* Learning Plan) photocopied onto card stock (cards will be cut out, and a hole will be punched into the upper left hand corner of the card)

The following may also be needed for decorating the jar:
- ❖ Pieces of fabric or foil type wrapping paper for decorating cover of jar
- ❖ Hole punch
- ❖ Ribbon (fabric ribbon or inexpensive curling gift wrap ribbon)
- ❖ Scissors for cutting ribbon and recipe instruction cards
   Optional: Decorative scissors such as Krazy Kut, zig zag or Fiskars decorative scissors may be used for cutting out the recipe instruction cards
- ❖ Pens, crayons, markers, or glitter glue pens or markers to decorate recipe instruction cards
- ❖ Glue sticks or Tacky glue or white glue or glitter glue in tubes
- ❖ Post-its for labeling jars with child's name when completed (or tape and paper)

Variation: For planning activity: drawing paper (perhaps with a simple outline of a jar copied onto it), pencils, crayons.

Note: This activity requires much supervision. Parent or high school volunteers can make a big difference in this activity.

Method
- ❖ Have children wash and dry their hands thoroughly
- ❖ On a clean work table top, set out ingredients with appropriately-sized measuring cups (at least two per bowl of ingredients)
- ❖ Have appropriate measuring cup (1/4, 1/3, 1/2) or spoon by each ingredient
- ❖ Explain the activity to the children. Remind them that "a pattern repeats"
- ❖ Give each child a clean, dry wide-mouthed quart size canning jar
- ❖ Working with no more than five children at a time: have children walk around the table, measuring the ingredients one at a time, in order, into their jars, creating the pattern of light and dark colors; While the children are working, talk with them, noticing how the pattern evolves

Note: Have adult volunteers supervise children as they measure out each ingredient, particularly if children are pre or emergent readers, making sure children do their own measuring and pouring for each ingredient

- ❖ Be sure to have enough chocolate chips so that the occasional nibble is okay
- ❖ As children complete their jars, allow them to choose a piece of foil type wrapping paper or fabric
- ❖ Over the opening of filled jar, children place the lid, then the fabric and then twist the metal ring over fabric (or foil wrapping paper may be used instead) to secure the contents
- ❖ Children choose and tie ribbon around neck of jar (Ribbons may be pre-cut, or children may cut the ribbon 18" to 24" long)

❖ Children may decorate instruction card (printed on white card stock); cards may be pre-punched with hole in corner, or children may do it themselves with supervision; drying time is needed if wet media or glue is used for decorations

❖ Children tie instruction card to jar with ribbon

❖ Label jars with a post-it (or tape and paper) with the child's name

Suggested Reading:

Barrett, J. (1988). *Cloudy with a chance of meatballs.* ISBN: 0-689-70749-5. (Silly and fun).

Hoban, R. (1993). *Bread and Jam for Frances.* ISBN: 0064430960 (Ages 5-8; Frances learns the importance of trying new foods)

Nadler, B. (1995). *The Magic School Bus Inside Ralphie: A Book About Germs.* ISBN: 0590400258.

Numeroff, L. (1985). *If You Give a Mouse a Cookie.* ISBN:0060245867. Also in Spanish: (1995). *Si Le Das una Galletita a un Raton.* ISBN: 0060254386.

Pluckrose, H. A. (1995). *Pattern. (Math Counts).* ISBN: 0516454552.

Pluckrose, H.A. & Choos, R.G. (1995). *Capacity (Math Counts).* ISBN: 051645451X.

Wood, A. J. (1993). *Egg!* ISBN: 0-316-8161607. (Twelve different eggs, twelve different creatures to guess!)

Target Areas of Learning

Physical Development

❖ **Fine motor skills:** using the small muscles of the hand and fingers: scooping out, measuring, and pouring out ingredients

❖ **Eye-hand coordination**: coordinating visual acuity with using the small muscles of the hand and fingers: pouring ingredients into jars

❖ **Sensory Discrimination**

• **Visual discrimination** (sight): using the eyes to identify ingredients visually, by sight; perhaps reading recipe

• **Oral discrimination** (taste): sampling the different ingredients and identifying the various tastes on the tongue

• **Olfactory discrimination** (smell)**:** using the nose to identify the different ingredients by their smell

Cognitive Development

❖ **Language Arts**

• **Verbal skills**

o **Language development**: conversation while assembling jar cookies

o **Vocabulary development**: learning new words such as words for measurement, ingredients, tastes, smells

• **Emergent literacy**

o **Symbol interpretation**: understanding that marks have meaning; reading or having the recipe instructions read to the children

- o **Matching spoken words to printed words:** realizing that the recipe is the same as the verbal instructions given by teacher
- o **Penmanship:** developing legible handwriting for labels and tags
- o **Spelling skills:** using correct letter symbol combinations to form words on labels and tags
- ❖ **Math Skills**
  - • **Mathematical literacy**
    - o **1 to 1 correspondence:** counting items in an organized way that shows understanding of the object's placement as a single entity in a group; understanding that each single count is associated with a specific item in a count
    - o **Number recognition:** recognizing that a specific symbol is associated with a specific quantity, and that symbol is constant in association with that symbol
    - o **Recognizing number words:** reading the recipes and instructions
    - o **Associating number symbols with quantity:** reading instructions for measuring out ingredients to assemble cookie jar
  - • **Mathematical applications**
    - o **Algebra:** categorization/grouping: making patterned layers of ingredients
    - o **Measurement**
      - – Understanding that objects have different properties, such as: weight and capacity
      - – Measuring out ingredients of different quantities
      - – Fractions: understanding
    - o **Time:** associating specific events with an appointed time in the day and identifying that appointed time on a clock
      - – Understanding that the banking of the brownies will take a specified amount of time;
      - – Using a timer, or clock to mark the length of baking time; noting the time of start and finish for the baking
    - o **Patterning:** placing layers into jar creating a recognizable pattern; "a pattern repeats"
- ❖ **Science**
  - • **Scientific processes**
    - o **Inquiry:** (informally) wondering how different materials behave when mixed, when poured, when wet, and so on
    - o **Prediction:** articulating an expectation of the manner in which materials will behave; "What do you think will happen if we add the . . . " or "What do you think made that happen?"
    - o **Observation:** playing with and noting (mentally) the manner in which materials behave in various circumstances
    - o **Cause and effect:** hands on experiences relating to "what happens if...?" or "What happens when...?"
    - o **Chemistry**

– **Properties of substances:** understanding that properties of materials can be measured and observed, and that the materials can change form.

⊙ Noting (mentally or in discussion) some of the properties of substances in their environment

⊙ Noting (mentally or in discussion) that the form of the ingredients may change as other ingredients are added and stirred

⊙ Noting (mentally or in discussion) "what happens when" different substances are subjected to different environments such as heat; (i.e., what changes do brownies undergo when cooked)

- **Life Science**
  o **Differentiating:** organic from inorganic objects;
  o **Discussing the different types of ingredients:** eggs, salt, flour, sugar, chocolate, nuts, oil and where they may come from
  o **Hygiene:** washing hands before working with food
- ❖ **Social Science**
  - **Diversity:** cultural/linguistic understanding: saying the names of the ingredients in languages other than English
  - **Diversity**: discussing from where some ingredients came such as sugar, and cocoa

Social Development

❖ **Working cooperatively with others in a group**: working well with others while assembling the cookie jar, and while measuring and stirring the ingredients when making and baking

❖ **Sharing**: using materials in turn with others, allowing others to complete layering, or stirring without upset

❖ **Taking turns**: being okay with waiting while other children fill their jars, add ingredients or stir

❖ **Responsibility**
- Building a sense of responsibility for classroom environment
- Being a willing participant in clean up

❖ **Community building**: appreciating the work of others as they fill and decorate the jars

❖ **Following directions**: carrying out directions for adding and measuring ingredients and when assembling cookie jar

❖ **Impulse control**: managing an impulse eat chocolate chips and other ingredients

❖ **Community building**: creating a sense of belonging in a group by making and baking together, and by creating cookie jars as a group project

❖ **Taking care of classroom environment**: participating in cleanup

Emotional Development

❖ **Self-esteem:** feeling good about creating something for someone else

❖ **Generosity**: creating something for another: experiencing the enjoyment of giving

❖ **Accomplishment**: developing a sense of achievement by baking the brownies and by assembling the cookie jar

Creative Expression

❖ **Use of creative media and expression of imagination**:
  - **2-dimensional visual arts**: painting/collage/drawing: label decorations
  - **3-dimensional visual arts**: layering ingredients in a decorative fashion
  - **Culinary arts**: expressing self through food preparation and presentation
❖ **Creative thinking**: creating interesting patterns with ingredients
  - **Art**: designing decorations for the label and jar

Possible Accommodations for *Sand Art Brownies In A Jar Activity*

ADHD

❖ Use positive reinforcement (praise) when child works well with others and behaves appropriately
❖ Lower the ratio: have fewer children in this child's group as they make and bake brownies and when they fill the jars
❖ Break the activity up into several sessions: baking the brownies, making the tags, filling the jars, decorating the jars
❖ Use cleaned plastic peanut butter jars instead of canning jars
❖ Place splat mats under tables of ingredients or have activity in an area where accidental spills are easily cleaned up
❖ Offer smock, old t-shirt or disposable apron to protect clothes
❖ For activities that require much clean up, there should be a longer clean up / transition time allowed.

Developmental Delays

❖ Break up activity into a 3 to 5 day project, over several sessions: baking the brownies, making the tags, filling the jars, decorating the jars, and offer more time to complete each task
❖ Explain each increment of the activity using simplified language to the child as the activity is being presented, making sure that eye contact is made
❖ Model the project from start to finish for the whole group, and again when child with developmental delays is at the kidney-shaped table.
❖ Repeat modeled instructions as needed, making sure eye contact is made when giving child directions
❖ Use simplified language when giving directions and praise
❖ Pair child with another child to work on their projects simultaneously
❖ Use positive reinforcement as the child succeeds completes the various tasks related to jar cookies (be sure praise is authentic)
❖ Lower the ratio to 1 teacher to 2 or 3 children
❖ Place splat mats under tables of ingredients or have activity in an area where accidental spills are easily cleaned up
❖ Offer smock, old t-shirt or disposable apron to protect clothes

❖ Provide easy to hold utensils, cleaned plastic quart jar, large size crayons to maximize independence

❖ Evaluate with attention on IEP / IFSP goals and accommodations

Autism Spectrum Disorders

❖ Break up activity into a 3 to 5 day project, over several sessions: baking the brownies, making the tags, filling the jars, decorating the jars, and offer more time to complete each task

❖ Explain each increment of the activity using simplified language to the child as the activity is being presented, making sure that eye contact is made

❖ Present activity later on in the week; have it on the weekly schedule so that child will have time to become used to the idea of the activity

❖ Show sample "jar cookies" early on in the week, so child will become used to the idea of the activity

❖ Use positive reinforcement when child participates

❖ Place splat mats under tables of ingredients or have activity in an area where accidental spills are easily cleaned up

❖ Offer smock, old t-shirt or disposable apron to protect clothes

Visual Impairments

❖ Break up activity into several sessions: baking the brownies, making the tags, filling the jars, decorating the jars

❖ Adjust the lighting to reduce glare

❖ Offer brighter, high contrast colors for recipe instruction tags in larger sizes with larger font size;

❖ Use larger writing tools, paint tubes

❖ Place splat mats under tables of ingredients or have activity in an area where accidental spills are easily cleaned up

❖ Offer smock, old t-shirt or disposable apron to protect clothes

❖ Have an adult work with child on any of the tasks that may be challenging for the child, encouraging and supporting the child in the activity, making certain child is working as independently as possible on the task

❖ Offer more time to complete the task, and for cleaning up the activity as well

Orthopedic Impairments

❖ Make sure child is seated comfortably

❖ Adjust furniture for accessibility and maximum independence for child

❖ Break activity down into several activities to prevent tiring child

❖ Make sure ingredients are presented in such a way that they are accessible to child, perhaps even having an adult hold bowls of ingredients for child to scoop

❖ If child lacks strength or dexterity to scoop assist child using the hand-over-hand method

❖ Use a plastic quart jar

❖ Stabilize jar while child fills it by holding or using suction cups

❖ Plan additional time for completing each activity
❖ Use adapted tools for decorating label and jar
❖ Use a larger label for the recipe instruction card
❖ Place splat mats under tables of ingredients or have activity in an area where accidental spills are easily cleaned up
❖ Offer smock, old t-shirt or disposable apron to protect clothes

Gifted and Talented Education (GATE)
❖ Allow child to make more elaborate patterns in the jars using non-exact measuring tools
❖ Instead of using exact measuring cups, let the child figure out which part of a 1 cup measure is 1/3 cup or how many 1/4 cup measures will make 3/4 cup; if the child is engaged in this measuring activity, allow the child repeat this with measuring spoons: how many teaspoons make one tablespoon, or how many tablespoons make 1/4 cup?
❖ Include decorative hole punches, weaving ribbons through labels, other decorative activities for labels
❖ Have children hand write out labels

English Language Learners (ELL)
❖ Break up activity into a 3 to 5 day project, over several sessions: baking the brownies, making the tags, filling the jars, decorating the jars
❖ Offer more time to complete each task, if needed
❖ Explain each increment of the activity using simplified language to the child as the activity is being presented, making sure that eye contact is made
❖ Using bold markers label the names of the ingredients on the table
❖ Repeat instructions frequently
❖ Lower the ratio, so child can have additional supervision
❖ Use positive reinforcement as child begins to use newly acquired vocabulary

Content Standards For Kindergarten Met By This Activity
English-Language Arts
     Reading (1.0, 1.2, 1.3)
     Written and Oral Language (1.0, 1.1)
     Listening and Speaking (1.0, 1.1, 1.2, 2.0, 2.1)

Mathematics
     Numbers and Counting (1.0, 1.1)
     Measurement and Geometry (1.0, 1.1)
     Statistics and Patterning (1.0, 1.2)

Science
     Physical Science (1.a)

History and Social Science

Following Rules (K.1, K.1.1)

Visual Arts

Artistic Perception (1.0, 1.1)

Creative Expression (2.0, 2.1)

Learning Plan

I. **Name of Activity:** Cookies in a Jar

II. **Date of Presentation:**

III. **Age or Grade Level: Pre-K to Kindergarten**

IV. **Ratio of teachers to children needed for this activity:** 1:6 *(Note: A low ratio/kidney-shaped table activity; Enlist assistance of as many parent volunteers to allow a 1-to-1 ratio when putting cookie ingredients into jars)*

V. **Target Areas of Learning / Goals and Objectives** (target areas of learning directly relate to "VI. Evaluation Rubric")
   1. **Physical:** _____
   2. **Cognitive:** _____
   3. **Social:** _____
   4. **Emotional:** _____
   5. **Creative:** _____

VI. **Evaluation Rubric:** (if more than two learning areas are being evaluated, a spreadsheet form may be preferred)

Targeted Area of Learning	**Targeted Area of Learning**
_____	_____
_____	_____
4. Always _____	**4.** Always _____
3. Usually _____	**3.** Usually _____
2. Sometimes _____	**2.** Sometimes _____
1. Rarely _____	**1.** Rarely _____

VII. **Materials and Preparation Needed For Making and Filling Jars**
   1. A wide-mouth canning jar, ring and lid for each student (Wash in a hot dishwasher before use and let dry completely)
   2. Measuring cups (1 cup, 1/2 cup, 1/3 cup, 1/4 cup), teaspoons, trays
   3. Table cloths to protect table surfaces, and for ease of clean-up
   4. Large bowls for ingredients and measuring utensils; should be placed on the table in the order that the ingredients will be put into jars (the number of bowls needed will depend on how many different types of ingredients are used)
      Optional: Labels may be made for each bowl of ingredients on card stock, and placed on the table in front of the bowls, clearly designating to the children what each ingredient is and how much will be needed (i.e., "3/4 cup flour", "2/3 cup brown sugar"). Bowls could even be numbered "1" to "9", and lined up.

5. Instructions for *Sand Art Brownies in a Jar* printed out on heavy paper
6. **Recipe ingredients:** Calculate how much of each ingredient will be needed according to the size of the class. Estimate that this project will require the following ingredients for each child (or for each group of children when making and baking the brownies): 1 and 1/4 cup all-purpose flour, 3/4 teaspoon salt, 1/3 cup unsweetened cocoa powder, 2/3 cup brown sugar, 2/3 cup white sugar, 1/2 cup semi-sweet chocolate chips, 1/2 cup of another type of chips, either vanilla or peanut butter chips, and 1/2 cup walnuts; Be sure to add an extra measure of each ingredient so as to not run short. Also remember that adding nuts to any classroom recipe is optional.
7. Recipe instruction cards (see the page following *Sand Art Brownies in a Jar* Learning Plan) photocopied onto card stock (cards will be cut out, and a hole will be punched into the upper left hand corner of the card)

The following may also be needed for decorating the jar:
- Pieces of fabric or foil type wrapping paper for decorating cover of jar
- Hole punch
- Ribbon
- Scissors for cutting ribbon and recipe instruction cards
- **Optional:** Art scissors such as Krazy Kut, zig zag or Fiskars decorative scissors may be used for cutting out the recipe instruction cards
- Pens, crayons, markers, or glitter glue pens or markers to decorate recipe instruction cards
- Glue sticks or Tacky glue or white glue or glitter glue in tubes
- Post-its for labeling jars with child's name when completed (or tape and paper)

Variation: For planning activity: drawing paper (perhaps with a simple outline of a jar copied onto it), pencils, crayons.

Ingredients for *Sand Art Brownies in a Jar*
(Note: The total amount of flour needed has been divided into two separate measurements, giving visual definition to the layering of ingredients!)
In order to maintain layered effect, place into jars, in specified order.
Each jar will require:
3/4 cup all-purpose flour (use 1/4 cup to measure)
3/4 teaspoon salt (use 1/4 teaspoon to measure)
1/3 cup unsweetened cocoa powder (use 1/3 cup to measure)
1/2 cup all-purpose flour (use 1/2 cup to measure)
2/3 cup brown sugar (use 1/3 cup to measure)
2/3 cup white sugar (use 1/3 cup to measure)
1/2 cup semi-sweet chocolate chips (use 1/2 cup to measure)

1/2 cup peanut butter (or vanilla) chips (use 1/2 cup to measure)
1/2 cup walnuts (optional) (use 1/2 cup to measure)
Note: This activity is best presented in small groups for optimal supervision. Parent or high school volunteers can make a big difference in this activity,

VIII. Procedures
1. Have children wash and dry their hands thoroughly
2. On a clean work table top, set out ingredients with appropriately-sized measuring cups (at least two per bowl of ingredients)
3. Have appropriate measuring cup (1/4, 1/3, 1/2) or spoon by each ingredient
4. Explain the activity to the children. Remind them that " a pattern repeats"
5. Give each child a clean, dry wide-mouthed quart size canning jar
6. Working with no more than five children at a time: have children walk around the table, measuring the ingredients one at a time, in order, into their jars, creating the pattern of light and dark colors; While the children are working, talk with the them, noticing how the pattern evolves
   Note: Have adult volunteers supervise children as they measure out each ingredient, particularly if children are pre or emergent readers, making sure children do their own measuring and pouring for each ingredient
7. Be sure to have enough chocolate chips so that the occasional nibble is okay
8. As children complete their jars, allow them to choose a piece of foil type wrapping paper or fabric
9. Over the opening of filled jar, children place the lid, then fabric and then twist the metal ring over fabric (or foil wrapping paper may be used instead) to secure the contents
10. Children choose and tie ribbon around the neck of jar (Ribbons may be pre-cut, or children may cut the ribbon 18" to 24" long)
11. Children may decorate instruction card (printed on white card stock); cards may be pre-punched with hole in corner, or children may do it themselves with supervision; drying time is needed if wet media or glue is used for decorations
12. Label jars with a post-it (or tape and paper) with the child's name

IX. Accommodations (changes to accommodate learning diversity)
Name of Accommodated Area:
1. _____
2. _____
3. _____
4. _____
5. _____

X. Applicable Framework Standards: Kindergarten

Standard _____
_____
_____
_____
_____

Standard _____
_____
_____
_____
_____

Standard _____
_____
_____
_____
_____

Standard _____
_____
_____
_____
_____

Standard _____
_____
_____
_____
_____

XI. Evaluation and Comments (i.e.: How well did the plan work? Great responses? What aspects are especially effective? Not effective? What improvements are needed? Ideas for follow up activities and other notes)

_____
_____
_____
_____

Sand Art Brownies

Add 3 eggs, 1/2 cup vegetable oil, and
1 teaspoon vanilla to the ingredients
in this jar. Pour into an 8x8 pan and bake
for 27 to 30 minutes at 350 degrees.

Ingredients: flour, brown sugar, sugar, cocoa,
chocolate chips peanut butter chips, walnuts

Sand Art Brownies

Add 3 eggs, 1/2 cup vegetable oil, and
1 teaspoon vanilla to the ingredients
in this jar. Pour into an 8x8 pan and bake
for 27 to 30 minutes at 350° degrees.

Ingredients: flour, brown sugar, sugar, cocoa,
chocolate chips peanut butter chips, walnuts

Sand Art Brownies

Add 3 eggs, 1/2 cup vegetable oil, and
1 teaspoon vanilla to the ingredients
in this jar. Pour into an 8x8 pan and bake
for 27 to 30 minutes at 350 degrees.

Ingredients: flour, brown sugar, sugar, cocoa,
chocolate chips peanut butter chips, walnuts

Sand Art Brownies

Add 3 eggs, 1/2 cup vegetable oil, and
1 teaspoon vanilla to the ingredients
in this jar. Pour into an 8x8 pan and bake
for 27 to 30 minutes at 350 degrees.

Ingredients: flour, brown sugar, sugar, cocoa,
chocolate chips peanut butter chips, walnuts

Sand Art Brownies

Add 3 eggs, 1/2 cup vegetable oil, and
1 teaspoon vanilla to the ingredients
in this jar. Pour into an 8x8 pan and bake
for 27 to 30 minutes at 350° degrees.

Ingredients: flour, brown sugar, sugar, cocoa,
chocolate chips peanut butter chips, walnuts

Sand Art Brownies

Add 3 eggs, 1/2 cup vegetable oil, and
1 teaspoon vanilla to the ingredients
in this jar. Pour into an 8x8 pan and bake
for 27 to 30 minutes at 350 degrees.

Ingredients: flour, brown sugar, sugar, cocoa,
chocolate chips peanut butter chips, walnuts

Sand Art Brownies

Add 3 eggs, 1/2 cup vegetable oil, and
1 teaspoon vanilla to the ingredients
in this jar. Pour into an 8x8 pan and
bake for 27 to 30 minutes at 350° degrees.

Ingredients: flour, brown sugar, sugar, cocoa,
chocolate chips peanut butter chips, walnuts

Sand Art Brownies

Add 3 eggs, 1/2 cup vegetable oil, and
1 teaspoon vanilla to the ingredients
in this jar. Pour into an 8x8 pan and bake
for 27 to 30 minutes at 350 degrees.

Ingredients: flour, brown sugar, sugar, cocoa,
chocolate chips peanut butter chips, walnuts

Veggies and Dips

Vegetables and fruits with a dip is a classic hors d'oeuvre for adults as well as children. Presenting vegetables with a mildly flavored dip is an easy introduction to a variety of vegetables. Keep in mind that the primary goal is to create dietary habits for a lifetime. If a child is reluctant to try a vegetable, or any food for that matter, forcing the child to eat it may prove counterproductive in the long term. It is always important for individuals working with children to have the long-range outcomes, the life long impact of interactions and presentation of curriculum, in mind. If an educator loses sight of the big picture, it may come at a measurable cost to the child.

With any food preparation activity, it is important to emphasize hygiene; that is thorough hand washing before food preparation and consumption, and after coughing, sneezing, toileting, or touching objects not used in food preparation.

This activity can be presented regularly. Initially use familiar vegetables and fruits including thin slices of carrots, broccoli florets, long slices of cucumber, sliced and peeled apples, bananas, celery with the strings removed, and various seasonal fruits such as strawberries and peaches. After presenting familiar vegetables and fruits, occasionally change the selection to include kiwis, mangoes, snow peas, jicama, cauliflower, bok choy, radishes, and other produce that looks attractive.

Light steaming might be appropriate for some of the vegetables from time to time. Steaming lightly generally makes the flavors milder, but at the same time makes the vegetables less crisp. Adding potatoes that have been steamed and cut into slices might be an interesting variation.

Before the children begin cooking, make sure all the produce is thoroughly washed, and all the bruised or unattractive parts removed. It is important to give appetizing produce to young children. Associating damaged parts of the fruit with the snack may make the child less willing to eat the produce.

The teacher must arrange to have very close supervision if children are to peel and slice vegetables. Adults should cut hard vegetables that are likely to roll around on the cutting surface such as carrots. Peeling and cutting should be demonstrated several times before allowing children to participate. Should the class have a high level of energy and impulsivity, do NOT allow the children to cut the produce.

Unless the children are culturally accustomed to spicy foods, it is recommended to start out with mildly flavored dips. Ranch flavor is often palatable to younger children. Depending upon the learning goals identified by the teacher, the children can pour out pre-made salad dressings. The children can use soup or dressing mixes available in envelopes at grocery stores, if preparation is part of the intended learning.

Other types of dips can be included as the school year progresses, including spring vegetable dip, spinach dip, creamy cucumber dip, mild guacamole, or mild cheesy dip. Sweeter dips such as honey flavored sour cream, tofu or cottage cheese blended with fruit juices can be used with fruits to be dipped. If children in the class are not sensitive to nuts, nut butters or sesame seed paste (tahini) can be used as a base for dips as well, particularly if some of the children are vegetarian. If children are extremely underweight or have exceptional nutritional needs, a small amount of protein, soy, whey, or nutritional supplement powder can be added if appropriate.

Children will need close supervision if a recipe for a dip requires the use of a blender or food processor.

For Vegetable Crudités
Materials

- ❖ Fresh vegetables such as carrots, celery, cucumber, broccoli florets, bell peppers
- ❖ A scrubbing brush
- ❖ A basin or sink in which vegetables can be washed
- ❖ Paper towels for draining vegetables
- ❖ Vegetable peelers (adult use / or children well-supervised)
- ❖ Plastic knives
- ❖ Plastic cutting surface mats
- ❖ Trays, platters, or plates onto which vegetables can be served

Method

- ❖ Before teacher, paraprofessional, or adult volunteer trims leaves, bruised or damaged areas from the vegetables and fruits
- ❖ Teacher cleans cooking areas with a 10% bleach solution
- ❖ Teacher, paraprofessional, or adult volunteer sets up an area appropriate for cleaning and peeling produce
- ❖ Teacher, paraprofessional, or adult volunteer sets up area suitable for preparing produce for serving. If cutting is part of the task, be absolutely sure area allows for very close supervision.
- ❖ Teacher, paraprofessional, or adult volunteer washes hands
- ❖ Teacher models scrubbing produce to the children, explaining that each type of produce needs to be cleaned in a different manner depending upon whether the item is hard, soft, needs peeling and so forth
- ❖ Children wash their hands
- ❖ Children scrub vegetables/fruits
- ❖ Adults or children, as appropriate, peel and cut produce into appropriately sized pieces for dipping and serving
- ❖ Children place vegetables onto serving dishes

For Dips
Materials

- ❖ Ingredients for dips (see recipes below)
- ❖ Recipe cards, using words or drawings as appropriate (laminate for durability)
- ❖ Plastic or other break resistant bowls (somewhat larger than quantities require)
- ❖ (Optional) Blender or food processor
- ❖ Large plastic, metal, or wooden spoons for mixing ingredients
- ❖ Rubber scrapers
- ❖ Serving dishes

Method

- ❖ Teacher and children decide upon dips to be prepared
- ❖ Teacher cleans cooking areas with a 10% bleach solution

❖ Teacher sets out ingredients for children buffet style
❖ Children and teachers wash hands
❖ Children mix ingredients in bowls per the dip recipe
❖ Children fill serving dishes with dip using rubber scrapers as necessary

Presentation
Materials

❖ Cleaned table upon which to serve food
❖ Completed foods to be served
❖ Paper plates, plastic ware, napkins
❖ Waste paper basket (for disposal of disposable eating ware)

Method

❖ Teacher cleans serving areas with a 10% bleach solution
❖ Children decorate serving table, if desired
❖ Children set out plates, plastic ware, crudités and dips attractively
❖ Call children to wash hands and eat

Suggested Reading:

Bruchac, J. & Vojtech, A. (1998). *First Strawberries: A Cherokee Story.* ISBN: 0140564098 (Ages 4-8)
Cheng, A. (2003). *Goldfish and Chrysanthemums.* ISBN: 1584300574. (Grandmother cuts carrots into flower shapes).
Ehlert, L. (1993). *Eating the Alphabet: Fruits & Vegetables From A to Z.* ISBN: 0152244360.
Krauss, R. (1989). *The Carrot Seed.* ISBN: 0064432106.
McCloskey, R. (1976). *Blueberries for Sal.* ISBN: 014050169X.
Pallotta, J. & Thomson, B. (1992). *The Vegetable Alphabet Book.* ISBN: 0881064688.

Target Areas of Learning

Physical Development

❖ **Gross Motor Skills:** using the large muscles of the arms, legs, and torso: carrying foods to the serving table, scrubbing produce
❖ **Fine Motor Skills:** using the small muscles of the hand and fingers: scrubbing, peeling, cutting, placing produce onto serving dishes; holding mixing bowls, stirring ingredients
❖ **Eye-Hand Coordination:** coordinating visual acuity with using the small muscles of the hand and fingers: peeling produce, cutting produce, placing produce intentionally onto serving platter; adding ingredients to a bowl, pouring out serving bowl quantities of dip from mixing bowl; decorating serving table
❖ **Physical Principals:** learning physical weight; stability; equilibrium: keeping produce stable while peeling and cutting, feeling the weight of the mixing bowl change as ingredients are added, carrying the finished food to the serving area without dumping the food onto the floor

❖ **Sensory Discrimination**
   • **Tactile Discrimination** (touch): identifying and differentiating textures and sensations with touch: differentiating between how peeled and unpeeled vegetables feel, cut and uncut produce, experiencing the sensory experience of mixing the dip ingredients together
   • **Visual Discrimination** (sight): recognizing various objects visually: identifying various types of produce, identifying various ingredients, measuring out and recognizing the appropriate measurement visually, seeing the procedures for preparation visually and replicating them
   • **Oral Discrimination** (taste): identifying the flavors of the produce and dips by taste
   • **Olfactory Discrimination** (smell): identifying ingredients and combinations of ingredients through the sense of smell

Cognitive Development
❖ **Language Arts**
   • **Verbal skills**
      ○ **Language development**: acquiring and using language appropriately as related to food preparation and presentation
      ○ **Vocabulary development**: adding to the body of words and phrases related to food preparation and presentation
   • **Emergent literacy**
      ○ **Symbol recognition**: recognizing pictorial and written directions for food preparation
      ○ **Symbol interpretation**: identifying the particular meaning associated with pictorial and written instructions for food preparation
      ○ **Matching spoken words to written words**: correctly associating the auditory expression with the written symbol grouping as related to food preparation activities
      ○ **Story recall/sequencing (temporal ordering)**: retelling and relating experience of food preparation in the order the preparation occurred
❖ **Math Skills**
   • **Conservation**
      ○ **Conservation of volume**: equivalent quantities of dip mixture are the same, no matter the size of the container; the number of pieces cut from a piece of produce are equivalent in size to the original produce item
   • **Mathematical literacy**
      ○ **1-to-1 correspondence**: counting prepared produce and ingredients in an organized way that shows a recognition of each items placement within the count of items
   • **Mathematical applications**
      ○ **Measurement**: using a standard measure to prepare produce in regular sizes and shapes

- o **Equivalency**: comparing food being prepared for consistency in terms of size or quantity
- o **Seriation**: ordering cooking activity as it occurred or should occur
  - **Time**: noting the sequential relationship from one event to another in the process of preparing and presenting food
  - **Temporal ordering**: placing cooking activity in a particular predetermined sequence
- **Spatial relationships**: placing the food onto a serving dish with attention to creating an attractive placement of the food items on the serving dish
- **Common relatedness**: linking items that are not the same but are associated with one another: in this case the dips, the ingredients in the dips and the produce being dipped

❖ **Science**
- **Cause and effect**
  - o **Relationships between actions and outcomes**: considering the process of food preparation and the culinary results achieved
- **Life Science**
  - o **Hygiene**: maintaining an appropriate level of personal cleanliness
    - **Washing hands thoroughly**: after toileting, before food preparation, before eating, after coughing or sneezing into hand
- **Chemistry:** foods served are described in terms of the ingredients from which they were prepared

❖ **Social Studies**
- **Recognizing diversity**: recognizing what makes people similar *and* different: preparing foods with ingredients from a variety of cultures

Social Development

❖ **Self-respect:** valuing themselves as people who are able to plan, prepare, and present foods successfully

❖ **Sharing**: allowing everyone to participate and have access to food preparation and serving materials

❖ **Patience**: managing a delay in gratification of a desire: waiting until the food is ready to be presented before stating to eat

❖ **Citizenship**: working cooperatively with others in a group in preparation and presentation of foods

❖ **Following directions**: preparing and presenting food according to the recipe and the instructions from adults in charge

❖ **Impulse control**: managing impulses to be rowdy during food preparation, pushing others around, eat discourteously, taking more than a fair share before everyone has had a first serving

❖ **Respecting others as individuals (behaving appropriately with others):** practicing the general rules of courtesy (manners) for preparing and enjoying food with others

❖ **Internalizing social values**: learning appropriate behavior for food preparation, presentation, and enjoyment as related to cultural values of the school community

❖ **Community building**: creating a sense of belonging in a group by the shared experience of preparing and enjoying food as a community activity

❖ **Taking responsibility**: practicing a willingness to take on tasks that support the individual and the group as a whole

❖ **Taking care of classroom environment**: assisting in decorating the serving area; participating in cleanup

Emotional Development

❖ **Self-esteem**: feeling good about oneself as a member of a community, recognizing personal uniqueness in a community of unique individuals: shared food preparation, presentation, and enjoyment as a community member

❖ **Self-confidence**: feeling secure within one's self in the process of learning about food preparation

❖ **Stress relief**: using food preparation and presentation as acceptable vents for stress and frustration (e.g.: mashing, stirring, blending); redirecting attention from areas of stress toward creative expression as related to food

❖ **Accomplishment**: developing a sense of achievement and self-worth from food preparation and presentation

❖ **Identifying and expressing emotions appropriately**
  • **Naming human feelings**: identifying pride and positive feelings of success as related to preparing and presenting foods; learning to shrug off mistakes as part of the cooking process: keeping perspective

❖ **Generosity**: sharing of time, prepared food, and effort as a community to create a gracious meal

Creative Expression

❖ **Use of creative media and expression of imagination**:
  • **3-dimensional visual arts:** setting up the table and serving area; arranging foods attractively in the serving dishes and on the table
    o **Culinary arts**: expressing self through food preparation and presentation
    o **Event presentation**: expressing self through planning, serving, and preparing meals

❖ **Aesthetic appreciation:** developing appreciation for appetizing food, the culinary experience, and attractively presented foods

❖ **Creative risk**: being comfortable learning to prepare and serve food

Possible Accommodations for *Veggies and Dips Activity*

ADHD

❖ Model instructions step by step, ask children to repeat instructions back to you to check for understanding

❖ Give instructions for only one or two steps at a time and check for understanding

❖ As children proceed successfully following directions, acknowledge incremental successes
❖ Allow additional time
❖ Break activity in two: veggie preparation and dip preparation
❖ Lower the ratio, particularly for peeling and slicing the vegetables
❖ Make sure environment is free of clutter
❖ Make dips that require fewer ingredients
❖ Place a plastic table cloth (perhaps the disposable variety) on the preparation surface easy clean ups
❖ Plan on spills and respond to spills and "OOPS's in a good humored, low stress manner

Developmental Delays
❖ Demonstrate the activity step-by-step, using simplified language, making sure eye contact is made using realia
❖ Allow additional time
❖ Break activity in two: veggie preparation and dip preparation
❖ Lower the ratio, particularly for cutting
❖ Pre-teach actions such as peeling, cutting, and slicing or using food processor
❖ Make certain child is appropriately supervised when peeling, cutting, and slicing or using food processor
❖ Offer adapted tools such as placing a no slip grip on the knife and vegetable peeler, bowls with a suction grip on the bottom, larger spoons, et cetera
❖ Make dips that require fewer ingredients
❖ Place a plastic table cloth (perhaps the disposable variety) on the preparation surface easy clean ups
❖ Make sure environment is free of clutter
❖ Plan on spills and respond to spills and "OOPS's in a good humored, low stress manner
❖ As children proceed successfully following directions, acknowledge incremental successes

Autism Spectrum Disorder
❖ Lower the ratio
❖ Allow additional time
❖ Break activity in two: veggie preparation and dip preparation
❖ Demonstrate the activity step-by-step, using language the child knows, making sure eye contact is made
❖ Ask child to repeat instructions back to teacher or assistant to check for understanding
❖ Prior to activity present opportunities for the child to taste and smell a variety of fruits, vegetables, and dips to develop familiarity
❖ Ask parents of child if there are particular produce items, flavors, and dips for which the child has strong preferences or dislikes prior to activity
❖ Have the child work with a familiar partner
❖ Make sure environment is free of clutter

❖ Designate places for cooking equipment and other materials and maintain that organization consistently

❖ Offer adapted tools such as placing a no slip grip on the knife and vegetable peeler, bowls with a suction grip on the bottom, larger spoons, et cetera

Visual Impairments

❖ Allow additional time

❖ Break activity in two: veggie preparation and dip preparation

❖ Make sure environment is free of clutter

❖ Designate places for cooking equipment and other materials and maintain that organization consistently

❖ Offer adapted tools such as placing a no slip grip on the knife and vegetable peeler, bowls with a suction grip on the bottom, larger spoons, et cetera

❖ Plan on spills and respond to spills and "OOPS's in a good humored, low stress manner

❖ Make sure that lighting, work areas are set up to maximize visibility: make sure there is no back lighting, adjust lighting to reduce glare, use tools in bright contrasting colors from work surface

❖ If appropriate, allow child to use a magnifying glass on a stand

Orthopedic Impairments

❖ Allow additional time

❖ Lower the ratio

❖ Break activity in two: veggie preparation and dip preparation

❖ Designate places for cooking equipment and other materials and maintain that organization consistently

❖ Offer adapted tools such as placing a no slip grip on the knife and vegetable peeler, bowls with a suction grip on the bottom, larger spoons, et cetera

❖ Make sure environment is free of clutter

❖ Make activity easily accessible by arranging tables for easy access, or placing cooking utensils on a tray for child

❖ If child's hands lack strength or flexibility, use hand-over-hand method to assist child, making sure that the child does as much of the activity independently as possible.

Gifted and Talented Education (GATE)

❖ Allow children to develop recipes or create variations of recipes for dips based upon recipes currently used in classroom

❖ Ask children to calculate quantities of ingredients for smaller and larger size batches of dips and crudités

❖ Have children use inexact measuring cups and calculate measures: e.g.: using 1/3 cup measures, how many 1/3 cup measures would equal one cup, et cetera

❖ Ask children to write or draw a story about serving hors d'oeuvres

English Language Learners (ELL)

- ❖ Pre-teach vocabulary words individually or in small groups:
    - Produce names: carrots, celery, cucumber, bell peppers, broccoli, potato, apples, strawberries, peaches, bananas, cauliflower (et cetera)
    - Dip ingredient names: sour cream, yoghurt, mayonnaise, tofu, milk, salt, pepper, garlic, honey, juice, avocado, cheese (et cetera)
    - Tools and process names: peeler, knife, rubber scraper, cutting board, bowl, spoon, plate, platter, tray, table, blender, food processor; mash, mix, stir, peel, add, blend, cut, slice, arrange, place, and so on
- ❖ Model activity for children, speaking slowly, combining words that child knows with new words so child can begin to decode contextually
- ❖ Use pictures or show activity
- ❖ Make sure eye contact is made
- ❖ Review vocabulary after food is prepared in small group setting or individually
- ❖ Acknowledge all attempts to use new vocabulary positively, whether the child has gotten the words "right" or not

Content Standards For Kindergarten Met By This Activity

English Language Arts

Reading (1.0, 1.2, 1.3, 1.5, 1.17, 1.18)
Reading Comprehension (2.0, 2.3, 2.4)
Literary Analysis (3.0, 3.1, 3.2)
Written and Oral Language (1.0, 1.1)
Listening and Speaking (1.0, 1.1, 1.2, 2.0, 2.1, 2.3)

Mathematics

Numbers and Counting (1.0, 1.2, 1.3, 2.0, 2.1)
Algebra, Sets and Sorting (1.0, 1.1)
Measurement and Geometry (1.0, 1.1, 1.2, 1.4)

Science

Physical Science (1.a, 1.b)
Investigation and Experimentation (4.a, 4.b, 4.c, 4.d, 4.e)

History and Social Science

Following Rules (K.1, K.1.1)
Compare and describe people and places (K.4, K.4.1)
Using a calendar to sequence events (K.5)

Visual Arts

Creative Expression (2.0, 2.2)
Understanding Historical / Cultural Contributions of Visual Arts (3.0, 3.1)
Valuing Aesthetics (4.0, 4.3)

Learning Plan

    I. **Name of Activity: Making Dips for Vegetable Snacks**

    II. **Date of Presentation:**

    III. **Age or Grade Level: Pre-K to Kindergarten**

    IV. **Ratio of teachers to children needed for this activity:** 1:4

    V. **Target Areas of Learning / Goals and Objectives** (target areas of learning directly relate to "VI. Evaluation Rubric")

        1. Physical: _____

        2. Cognitive: _____

        3. Social: _____

        4. Emotional: _____

        5. Creative: _____

    VI. **Evaluation Rubric:** (if more than two learning areas are being evaluated, a spreadsheet form may be preferred)

Targeted Area of Learning

_____

_____

        4. Always _____

        3. Usually _____

        2. Sometimes _____

        1. Rarely _____

Targeted Area of Learning

_____

_____

        4. Always _____

        3. Usually _____

        2. Sometimes _____

        1. Rarely _____

    VII. **Materials and Preparation Needed**

For Vegetable Crudités

Materials

1. Fresh vegetables such as carrots, celery, cucumber, broccoli florets, bell peppers
2. A scrubbing brush
3. A basin or sink in which vegetables can be washed
4. Paper towels for draining vegetables
5. Vegetable peelers (adult use / or children well-supervised)
6. Plastic knives
7. Plastic cutting surface mats
8. Trays, platters, or plates onto which vegetables can be served

Method

1. Beforehand, teacher (or paraprofessional, adult volunteer) trims leaves, bruised or damaged areas from the vegetables and fruits

2. Teacher cleans cooking areas with a 10% bleach solution
3. Teacher (or paraprofessional, adult volunteer) sets up an area appropriate for cleaning and peeling produce
4. Teacher (or paraprofessional, adult volunteer) sets up area suitable for preparing produce for serving. If cutting is part of the task, be absolutely sure area allows for very close supervision.
5. Teacher (and all adults participating in the activity) washes hands
6. Teacher models scrubbing produce to the children, explaining that each type of produce needs to be cleaned in a different manner, depending upon whether the item is hard, soft, needs peeling and so forth
7. Children wash their hands
8. Children scrub vegetables/fruits
9. Adults or children, as appropriate, peel and cut produce into appropriately sized pieces for dipping and serving
10. Children place vegetables onto serving dishes

For dips
Materials
1. Ingredients for dips (see recipes below)
2. Recipe cards, using words or drawings as appropriate (laminate for durability)
3. Plastic or other break resistant bowls (somewhat larger than quantities require)
4. (Optional) Blender or food processor
5. Large plastic, metal, or wooden spoons for mixing ingredients
6. Rubber scrapers
7. Serving dishes

Method
1. Teacher and children decide upon dips to be prepared
2. Teacher cleans cooking areas with a 10% bleach solution
3. Teacher sets out ingredients for children buffet style
4. Children and teachers wash hands
5. Children mix ingredients in bowls per the dip recipe
6. Children fill serving dishes with dip using rubber scrapers as necessary

VIII. Procedures
Presentation
Materials
1. Cleaned table upon which to serve food
2. Completed foods to be served
3. Paper plates, plastic ware, napkins
4. Waste paper basket (for disposal of disposable eating ware)

Method
1. Teacher cleans serving areas with a 10% bleach solution
2. Children decorate serving table, if desired
3. Children set out plates, plastic ware, crudités and dips attractively
4. Call children to wash hands and eat

IX. **Accommodations** (changes to accommodate learning diversity)
Name of Accommodated Area:
1. _____
2. _____
3. _____
4. _____
5. _____

X. **Applicable Framework Standards: Kindergarten**
Standard _____
_____
_____
_____
_____

Standard _____
_____
_____
_____
_____

Standard _____
_____
_____
_____
_____

Standard _____
_____
_____
_____
_____

Standard _____
_____
_____
_____
_____

XI. Evaluation and Comments (i.e.: How well did the plan work? Great responses? What aspects are especially effective? Not effective? What improvements are needed? Ideas for follow up activities and other notes)

_____

_____

_____

_____

Classroom Cookbook

Writing a classroom or community cookbook wonderfully creates a practical link between writing and cooking. In kindergarten, writing is an emerging skill. Associating writing with hands-on activities contextualizes this developing skill. The teacher should plan for this to be a long-range project. This make take from one month to all year to produce the class cookbook.

At this stage, taking the risk to write is more important than correct spelling, or even accurate recipes. It is a good idea to make a disclaimer about possible inaccuracies in the beginning of the book, in case the parents decide to try to prepare a recipe from the class cookbook. If accuracy is important for some reason, children can write, proof read, and correct several drafts before putting together the finished individual cookbook.

Although using a word processor to generate the cookbook is faster, and perhaps even produces work "cleaner" in appearance, it is better to have the children hand write their books. First of all, the children will gain crucial graphomotor practice to enhance these new writing skills. Secondly, completing a book with a minimum of assistance from surrounding adults will build the children's sense of esteem, competency, and self-worth. Thirdly, the handwriting and drawings of a child in kindergarten warms the heart of any adult who may see it. Finally, in creating a hand-written cookbook, the child has created a small piece of personal memorabilia to take into the future.

The recipes can be gathered in a variety of ways. Collecting recipes of foods prepared in class is excellent, as the children will make a connection between the written word and the food that they just prepared and enjoyed.

Other ideas for collecting recipes include having the children look in cookbooks and magazines (e.g.: Martha Stewart, Family Fun, Family Circle, et cetera), or use the Internet to find interesting dishes to include in their books. Not all of the children's cookbooks need necessarily contain the same recipes. The teacher can assign copying down a favorite family recipe as homework as a strategy to gather recipes, which will add a certain amount of relevance to homework.

A further enrichment to the homework assignment can be to have the children "interview the cook" to find out why and how this particular recipe was adopted by the family, how long the recipe has been prepared in the family, and any other anecdotal information related to the family recipe. The children can also draw a picture of the completed dish or the cook to include in the cookbook. The teacher can place file folders in a plastic project box into which children can safely store collected homework recipes and related drawings.

In the case of collecting the recipes made in class, children can also write recollections of events related to making the dishes in class. Did anything unusual occur while the food was prepared? How did it taste? Children again can draw pictures associated with either the anecdotal information or the actual food.

Please refer to the activities in *Journal Making* in the Language Arts Activities chapter for recommendations regarding creating covers and binding individual cookbooks.

Collecting recipes
Materials
❖ Cookbooks, magazines containing child friendly recipes (e.g.: Better Homes and Gardens, Sunset, Family Fun, Martha Stewart Kids)

- ❖ Recipes collected from families as homework assignments
- ❖ Recipes from foods prepared in class, perhaps printed out in large point in a simple font, and photocopied for the children to copy into their personal cookbooks
- ❖ Recipes collected from in class food preparation activities
- ❖ Scissors for cutting out magazine recipes
- ❖ Pencils, pens, markers for copying recipes
- ❖ Paper onto which selected recipes are copied as a first draft

Method

- ❖ Teacher collects magazines containing recipes which children may cut up
- ❖ Teacher gathers cookbooks with appropriate print from which children may copy
- ❖ Children take out any cookbook related homework assignments
- ❖ Children select magazines and cookbooks
- ❖ Children select recipes for their cookbooks
- ❖ Children write down a list of recipes chosen for their cookbooks

Assembling class cookbook

Materials (Find Appendix A @ www.cambriapress.com/kindergarten)

- ❖ Primary picture writing paper (see Appendix A for reproducible letter size paper)
- ❖ Children's list of selected recipes
- ❖ Recipes selected
- ❖ Writing and drawing tools

Method

- ❖ During a time designated for writing, children copy recipes they selected for their cookbooks
- ❖ Working in small groups, teacher gives direct instruction for proofreading if accuracy and spelling have been deemed important
- ❖ Children illustrate recipes
- ❖ Children create covers for books
- ❖ Refer to Language Arts Section: *Journal Making* for cover making and binding options

Suggested Reading:

Aliki. (1988). *How a Book Is Made* (Reading Rainbow book). ISBN: 0064460851. Spanish edition: *Como Se Hace un Libro/How a Book Is Made*. (1989). ISBN: 8426124003.

Barrett, J. (1988). *Cloudy With a Chance of Meatballs*. ISBN: 0-689-70749-5. (A just for fun book).

De Paola, T. (1989). *Tony's Bread: An Italian folktale*. ISBN: 0698113713.

Ehlert, L. (1993). *Eating the Alphabet: Fruits & Vegetables from A to Z*. ISBN: 0152244360.

Friedman, I. R. (1987). *How My Parents Learned to Eat*. ISBN: 039544235.

Gwynne, F. (2005). *A Chocolate Moose for Dinner*. ISBN: 068987827.

Hoban, R. (1993). *Bread and Jam for Frances*. ISBN: 0064430960. (Frances learns the importance of trying new foods).

Jenness, A. (1993). *Come Home With Me: A Multicultural Treasure Hunt.* ISBN: 156584064X (a look at four different families and their homes and customs: Africa, Ireland, Cambodia, and Puerto Rico).

Numeroff, L. (1985). *If You Give a Mouse a Cookie.* ISBN:0060245867. (also in Spanish)

Pienkowski, J. (2000). *Dinner Time.* ISBN: 158117024.

Politi. L. (1994). *Three Stalks of Corn.* ISBN: 0689717822.

Rowe, J.A, (1998). *The Gingerbread Man.* ISBN: 1-55858-906-6.

Sendak, M. (1995). *In the Night Kitchen.* ISBN: 0060266686 (Caldecott Honor Book)

Sendak, M. (1991). *Chicken Soup With Rice: A Book of Months.* ISBN: 006443253X

Targeted Areas of Learning

Physical Development
- ❖ **Fine motor skills:** using the small muscles of the hand and fingers: writing, holding paper in place to write, drawing, cutting out recipes from magazines, assembling book
- ❖ **Eye-hand coordination:** coordinating visual acuity with using the small muscles of the hand and fingers: writing, drawing, cutting, assembling book
- ❖ **Sensory discrimination**
  - **Tactile discrimination** (touch): identifying and differentiating textures and sensations with touch: holding the writing and drawing tools, feeling the texture of paper used, how the writing tools move across paper
  - **Visual discrimination** (sight): recognizing various objects visually: identifying recipes visually, looking at book to assess its progress visually, proof reading

Cognitive Development
- ❖ **Language Arts**
  - **Verbal skills**
    - o **Language development**: acquiring and using language appropriately as related to writing, creating cookbooks, food preparation and presentation
    - o **Vocabulary development**: adding to the body of words and phrases related to food preparation and presentation
    - o **Grammatical development**: learning rules of grammar and conventions of the use of language in the context of cookbooks and cooking
  - **Emergent literacy**
    - o **Symbol recognition**: recognizing pictorial and written directions for food preparation in recipes and cookbooks
    - o **Symbol interpretation**: identifying the particular meaning associated with pictorial and written instructions for food preparation in recipes and cookbooks
    - o **Emergent writing**: developing graphomotor skills while writing down recipes
    - o **Spelling skills**: using correct letter symbol combinations to form words in recipes
    - o **Penmanship:** developing legible handwriting for writing projects: words for recipes in a readable hand

- o **Matching spoken words to written words**: correctly associating the auditory expression with the written symbol grouping as related to recipes and cookbooks
  - o **Story recall/sequencing (temporal ordering)**: retelling and relating experience of food preparation in the recipe, the creation of a personal cookbook in the order it occurred
- ❖ **Math Skills**
  - • **Mathematical literacy**
    - o **1 to 1 correspondence**: counting recipes, creating page number for recipes for a table of contents
    - o **Associating number symbols with quantity**: understanding that a specific symbol is always associated with a specific quantity, in this case numbers of recipes and pages for the cookbook
  - • **Mathematical applications**
    - o **Measurement**: using a standard measure to prepare produce in regular sizes and shapes
    - o **Common relatedness**: linking items that are not the same but are associated with one another: in this case the recipes and the ingredients in the recipes, the illustrations created, perhaps stories collected about the recipes
- ❖ **Science**
  - • **Scientific processes**
    - o **Inquiry**: an organized search for recipes and possibly anecdotal stories related to recipes
    - o **Prediction**: relating an anticipated outcome of search-based on logic, experience, or research
    - o **Collection**: gathering recipes and information about the recipes in order to produce a personal cookbook
  - • **Chemistry:** foods in recipes served are described in terms of the ingredients from which they were prepared
- ❖ **Social Studies**
  - • **Recognizing diversity**: recognizing what makes people similar *and* different: collecting recipes from a variety of cultures

Social Development

- ❖ **Self-respect:** valuing themselves as people who are able to plan, collect, organize, and illustrate recipes into a personal cookbook
- ❖ **Sharing:** allowing everyone to participate and have access to writing and art materials, recipe resources
- ❖ **Patience:** diligence: staying with a project or activity until it is completed
- ❖ **Citizenship:** working cooperatively with others as a group while working on cookbooks
- ❖ **Collaboration:** sharing ideas/recipes to be included in cookbook
- ❖ **Following directions:** working on the writing project according to the instructions from adults in charge

- ❖ **Internalizing social values**: learning appropriate behavior academic collaboration
- ❖ **Community building**: creating a sense of belonging in a group by the shared experience of assembling and writing activity
- ❖ **Taking responsibility**: practicing a willingness to take on tasks that support the individual and the group as a whole
- ❖ **Taking care of classroom environment**: participating in cleanup

Emotional Development

- ❖ **Self-esteem**: feeling good about oneself as a creator of an original work of writing and art
- ❖ **Self-confidence**: feeling secure within one's self in the process of writing and illustrating a cookbook
- ❖ **Stress relief**: redirecting attention from areas of stress toward creative expression as related writing
- ❖ **Accomplishment**: developing a sense of achievement and self-worth from making a cookbook
- ❖ **Identifying and expressing emotions appropriately**
  - **Naming human feelings**: identifying pride and positive feelings of success as related to writing a cookbook
- ❖ **Generosity**: sharing ideas, recipes, collaboration while making a cookbook

Creative Expression

- ❖ **Use of creative media and expression of imagination**
  - **2-dimensional visual arts**: using artistic media to illustrate cookbook
  - **Culinary arts**: expressing self collecting recipes
  - **Writing and story telling**: expressing self through written and illustrated media of the cookbook
- ❖ **Aesthetic appreciation**: developing appreciation for art and writing as related to the cookbooks created by the child and others in the class
- ❖ **Creative risk**: being comfortable learning to assemble and illustrate a cookbook
- ❖ **Problem solving**: gathering data, interviewing family regarding food preparation, collaborating to create cookbooks

Possible Accommodations for *Class Cookbook Activities*

ADHD

- ❖ Model instructions step by step, ask children to repeat instructions back to check for understanding
- ❖ Give instructions for only one or two steps at a time and check for understanding
- ❖ As children proceed successfully following directions, acknowledge incremental successes
- ❖ Allow additional time to complete cookbook
- ❖ Offer a carrel to reduce unwanted stimuli

* ❖ Increase frequency and shorten length of writing sessions
* ❖ Reduce the number of recipes required for cookbook, or allow children to self select the number of recipes to be included

Developmental Delays

* ❖ Demonstrate the activity step-by-step, using simplified, familiar language, making sure eye contact is made using realia to show activity
* ❖ Allow additional time to complete cookbook
* ❖ As children proceed successfully following directions, acknowledge incremental successes
* ❖ Offer a carrel to reduce unwanted stimuli
* ❖ Increase frequency and shorten length of writing sessions
* ❖ Reduce the number of recipes required for cookbook, or allow children to self select the number of recipes to be included
* ❖ Offer adapted writing tools, scissors, larger size spaces for writing paper

Autism Spectrum Disorders

* ❖ Lower the ratio
* ❖ Allow additional time to complete cookbook
* ❖ Work on cookbooks at a regular time in the class schedule
* ❖ Offer adapted writing tools, scissors, larger size spaces for writing paper
* ❖ Demonstrate the activity step-by-step, using language the child knows, making sure eye contact is made
* ❖ Ask child to repeat instructions back to teacher or assistant to check for understanding
* ❖ Have the child work with a familiar partner
* ❖ Designate places for writing and drawing materials and maintain that organization consistently

Visual Impairments

* ❖ Allow additional time to complete cookbook
* ❖ Make sure environment is free of clutter
* ❖ Designate places for writing and drawing materials and maintain that organization consistently
* ❖ Offer adapted tools such as scissors, writing instruments, paper with larger spaces for writing
* ❖ Make sure that lighting, work areas are set up to maximize visibility: make sure there is no back lighting, adjust lighting to reduce glare, use writing and art materials in bright contrasting colors
* ❖ If appropriate, allow child to use a magnifying glass on a stand

Orthopedic Impairments

* ❖ Allow additional time
* ❖ Lower the ratio

❖ Designate places for writing and drawing materials and maintain that organization consistently

❖ Offer adapted tools such as scissors, writing instruments, paper with larger spaces for writing

❖ Make sure environment is free of clutter which may interfere with child's mobility and access to writing tools

❖ Make activity easily accessible by arranging tables for easy access, or placing cooking utensils on a tray for child

❖ If child's hands lack strength or flexibility, use hand-over-hand method to assist child, making sure that the child does as much of the activity independently as possible.

Gifted and Talented Education (GATE)

❖ Allow children to develop recipes or create variations of recipes class has used on prior occasions

❖ Ask children to calculate quantities of ingredients for smaller and larger size recipes (reduce by half, double recipes, et cetera)

❖ Have children sort their recipes by category (e.g.: main dishes, snacks, desserts)

❖ Ask children to write an original poem or rhyme about a food, cooking, cooks, or recipes

❖ Ask children to create a cookbook representative of their own culture, or from a culture in which the child has an interest

❖ Ask children to write or draw a story about cooking or cookbooks

English Language Learners (ELL)

❖ Pre-teach vocabulary words individually or in small groups:
  • Writing vocabulary: book, cookbook, front cover, back cover, binding, table of contents, page numbers, write, spell, illustrate, draw, pen, pencil, crayon, colored pencils, computer, recipe, ingredients, steps,
  • Ingredient names: depending upon the recipe, the ingredient names can vary widely
  • Tools and process names: peeler, knife, rubber scraper, cutting board, bowl, spoon, tablespoon, cups, pints, gallons, plate, platter, tray, table, blender, food processor; mash, mix, stir, peel, add, blend, cut, slice, arrange, place, and so on, bake, simmer, chop, toast, puree, add

❖ Model activity for children, speaking slowly, combining words that child knows with new words so child can begin to decode contextually

❖ Use pictures or show activity

❖ Make sure eye contact is made

❖ Review vocabulary after food is prepared in small group setting or individually

❖ Acknowledge all attempts to use new vocabulary positively, whether the child has gotten the words "right" or not

Content Standards For Kindergarten Met By This Activity

English Language Arts

Reading (1.0, 1.1, 1.2, 1.3, 1.4, 1.5, 1.11, 1.12, 1.13, 1.14, 1.15, 1.16, 1.17, 1.18)
Reading Comprehension (2.0, 2.1, 2.2, 2.3, 2.4, 2.5,)
Literary Analysis (3.0, 3.1, 3.2)
Writing (1.0, 1.1, 1.2, 1.3, 1.4)
Written and Oral Language (1.0, 1.1, 1.2)
Listening and Speaking (1.0, 1.1, 1.2, 2.0, 2.1, 2.3)

Mathematics

Numbers and Counting (1.0, 1.2, 1.3)
Algebra, Sets and Sorting (1.0, 1.1)
Measurement and Geometry (1.0, 1.1, 1.2, 1.4)
Statistics (1.0, 1.1)

Science

Physical Sciences (1.a)
Investigation and Experimentation (4.a, 4.b, 4.e)

History and Social Science

Following Rules (K.1, K.1.1)
Using a calendar to sequence events (K.5)

Visual Arts

Artistic Perception (1.0, 1.2)
Creative Expression (2.0, 2.2, 2.4)
Art History (3.0, 3.1)
Valuing Aesthetics (4.0, 4.1, 4.3)
Applications (5.0, 5.2)

Learning Plan

   I. **Name of Activity: Classroom Cookbook**

  II. **Date of Presentation:**

 III. **Age or Grade Level: Pre-K and up**

 IV. **Ratio of teachers to children needed for this activity:** 1:6 (This activity could be done at a kidney-shaped table)

  V. **Target Areas of Learning / Goals and Objectives** (target areas of learning directly relate to "VI. Evaluation Rubric")
      1. Physical: _____
      2. Cognitive: _____
      3. Social: _____
      4. Emotional: _____
      5. Creative: _____

 VI. **Evaluation Rubric:** (if more than two learning areas are being evaluated, a spreadsheet form may be preferred)

Targeted Area of Learning	**Targeted Area of Learning**
_____	_____
_____	_____
4. Always _____	**4.** Always _____
3. Usually _____	**3.** Usually _____
2. Sometimes _____	**2.** Sometimes _____
1. Rarely _____	**1.** Rarely _____

VII. **Materials and Preparation**
Collecting recipes
Materials
1. Cookbooks, magazines containing child friendly recipes (e.g.: Better Homes and Gardens, Sunset, Family Fun, Martha Stewart Kids)
2. Recipes collected from families as homework assignments
3. Recipes from foods prepared in class, perhaps printed out in large point in a simple font, and photocopied for the children to copy into their personal cookbooks
4. Recipes collected from in class food preparation activities
5. Scissors for cutting out magazine recipes
6. Pencils, pens, markers for copying recipes
7. Paper onto which selected recipes are copied as a first draft

Method
1. Teacher collects magazines containing recipes which children may cut up
2. Teacher gathers cookbooks with appropriate print from which children may copy
3. Children take out any cookbook related homework assignments
4. Children select magazines and cookbooks
5. Children select recipes for their cookbooks
6. Children write down a list of recipes chosen for their cookbooks

VIII. Procedures

Assembling class cookbook

Materials
1. Primary picture writing paper (see Appendix A for reproducible letter size paper)
2. Children's list of selected recipes
3. Recipes selected
4. Writing and drawing tools

Method
1. During a time designated for writing, children copy recipes they selected for their cookbooks
2. Working in small groups, teacher gives direct instruction for proofreading if accuracy and spelling have been deemed important
3. Children illustrate recipes
4. Children create covers for books
5. Refer to **Language Arts Section:** *Journal Making* for cover making and binding options

IX. Accommodations (changes to accommodate learning diversity)

Name of Accommodated Area:
1. _____
2. _____
3. _____
4. _____
5. _____

X. Applicable Framework Standards: Kindergarten

Standard _____

_____
_____
_____
_____

Standard _____

_____

_____

_____

Standard _____

_____

_____

_____

Standard _____

_____

_____

_____

Standard _____

_____

_____

_____

XI. **Evaluation and Comments** (i.e.: How well did the plan work? Great responses? What aspects are especially effective? Not effective? What improvements are needed? Ideas for follow up activities and other notes)

_____

_____

_____

_____

Glossary

1 to 1 correspondence: counting in such a way that each number in a count represents a single item in that count, with the final number of the count representing the total number of items counted

2-dimensional art: art media including: painting, collage, drawing with pens, pencils and other media (see also: **creative expression, creative media, collage, decoupage**)

3-dimensional art: art media including: sculptural: play dough, clay, papier mache, wood (see also: **creative expression, creative media**)

absorption: the process by which a material absorbs, or takes in, light or liquid

accommodation: a change in the presentation, environment, or physical materials used in an activity to include a child in that academic activity without changing the content of the activity; in contrast to modification (see also: **modification**)

active listening: the act of listening to a child, and then, without adding, or subtracting information and without giving advice or assessment, repeating what it is believed that the child has said, particularly if the child is upset

acuity: sharpness (of the senses or perceptions, such as visual acuity)

ADD: attention deficit disorder (without hyperactivity); children with this disorder are characterized by distractibility, inattention, a tendency towards day-dreaminess; may have better impulse control than ADHD; may exhibit tendency to over focus, creating difficult transitions from one activity to another (see also: **ADHD**)

ADHD: attention deficit hyperactivity disorder; children with this disorder are characterized by unusually high energy, restlessness, lack of impulse control, distractibility, inattention, lack of concentration, inability to filter out outside stimuli; such children are often highly verbal and respond well to positive reinforcement (see also: **ADD**)

appropriate risk: taking (perceived) risks, trying out ideas in an appropriate, emotionally safe, or non-judgmental environment; risks which do not endanger the child or classroom community, risks that foster the development of healthy self esteem and independence (see also: **inappropriate risk**)

articulation: creating correct word and letter sounds with mouth tongue and lips

ASD: autism spectrum disorders (see also: **autism, autism spectrum disorders, pervasive developmental disorder**)

attention: one of Dr. Mel Levine's eight neurodevelopmental constructs; the ability to focus, concentrate, and stay on task, which includes: planning, organization and management of behaviors in all environments; the other constructs include: higher order cognition, language, memory, neuromotor function, social cognition, spatial ordering, and temporal / sequential ordering (see also: **Levine, Mel, MD, PhD; neurodevelopmental construct, Neurodevelopmental Placemat, teaching by profile**)

attention deficit disorder: ADD (attention deficit without hyperactivity); children with this disorder are characterized by distractibility, inattention, a tendency towards day-dreaminess; may have better impulse control than ADHD; may exhibit tendency to over focus, creating difficult transitions from one activity to another (see also: **attention deficit hyperactivity disorder)**

attention deficit hyperactivity disorder: ADHD (attention deficit with hyperactivity); children with this disorder are characterized by unusually high energy, restlessness, lack of impulse control, distractibility, inattention, lack of concentration, inability to filter out outside stimuli; such children are often highly verbal and respond well to positive reinforcement (see also: **attention deficit disorder)**

auditory discrimination: identifying and differentiating different types & loudness of sounds: loud / soft; high / low pitch; fast / slow rhythms; comparing sounds using auditory receptors (see also: **sensory discrimination)**

authentic play: occurs whenever playfulness itself gives more pleasure than any goal associated with the activity (see also: **Brown, Stuart L., MD)**

autism: a neurobiological disorder characterized by impairment in the area of communication, social interaction, hypersensitivity to sensory stimuli, and internalized behavior controls; the most common of the autism spectrum disorders, 1 in 166 individuals are diagnosed with autism; (see also: **autism spectrum disorders, pervasive developmental disorders, PDD)**

autism spectrum disorders: ASD; characterized by delays in language and social skills, insistence on certain routines, avoidance of change; a reference to a group of several disorders including: autism, Pervasive Developmental Disorders (PDD), Asperger's Syndrome, Childhood Disintegration Disorder and Rett's Disorder (see also: **ASD, autism, obsessive compulsive disorder (OCD), pervasive developmental disorders, PDD)**

bar chart: a particular type of mathematical graph depicting relative variables in columns along the x (horizontal) axis (see example in Graphing activity in Mathematics Activities chapter)

bodily / kinesthetic: one of the nine intelligences of referenced in Dr. Gardner's theory of multiple intelligence relating to different ways people learn and how it impacts that learning; the ability to effectively control one's body and muscles; a control in handling objects; bodily / strengths in kinesthetic intelligence often exhibited by athletes, dancers, choreographers and artisans of all types (see also: **Gardner, Howard, PhD, multiple intelligences)**

bok choy: a long and narrow vegetable, with green leaves and stalks of white, sometimes referred to as "Chinese cabbage"; often used in Chinese cooking

Bos, Bev: an early childhood educator based in the Sacramento area of California, author of numerous books, and a proponent of interactive, child-centered, play-oriented curriculum (www.turnthepage.com)

Brown, Stuart L., MD: author, speaker, educator, founder of the Institute for Play; (www.instituteforplay.com); believes that authentic play is a state of being that adds a sense of vitality to one's life, regardless of one's age; Executive producer of PBS's *The Hero's Journey, The World of Joseph Campbell*, and National Geographic's *Play, the Nature of the Game* (see also: **authentic play)**

Bruner, Jerome, PhD: New York University Research Professor of Psychology, and Senior Research Fellow in Law; theorist and author (*The Process of Education*, 1960); developed constructivist approach to education, based upon the work of Piaget, influencing study of both education and psychology; In the 1960s, Bruner was the main architect for the Head Start early education program (see also: **constructivism; Piaget, Jean**)

carrell: a 3-sided structure placed on (or around) the desk to reduce distractions

charting: using an outcome to create various preliminary statistical diagrams; to reflect the outcomes of an activity presented in a diagram (i.e., diagramming the various outcomes of an activity to reflect patterns)

chemistry: science of the systematic study of composition and properties of substances, the transformations that they undergo, and activity of organic and inorganic substances and other elementary forms of matter

child-centered teaching: an educator observing which activities interest students; looking at subject areas of interest to children; taking their lead; giving them some power in the areas of their curriculum (see also: **emergent curriculum, teachable moment**)

cognitive development: intellectual development; refers to mental processes, including: judgment, reasoning, memory and perception in contrast to volitional emotional processes; in the educational environment cognitive often refers to the subject areas of language arts and literacy, math, science, social studies and cooking (see also: **domain, emergent literacy, phonemic awareness**)

collage: artwork created by assembling and adhering varying and sometimes dissimilar materials to a surface, may or may not be thematic (e.g.: gluing or pasting different types of cut or torn paper, pictures and photographs, cloth scraps, small objects like buttons and coins)

common relatedness: linking items that are not the same, but are associated with each other (e.g.: bat and ball, shoes and socks); can be considered in multiple categories

conservation of mass: (Piaget, as discussed by Berk, 2005) as a child moves into the concrete operational stage, developing a working understanding that the mass of a material does not change if the shape if the shape of that mass changes (see **Piaget, Jean**)

conservation of quantity: (Piaget, as discussed by Berk, 2005) as a child moves into the concrete operational stage, the child understands that the number in a group of items remains constant no matter how the items are arranged (see **Piaget, Jean**)

conservation of volume: (Piaget, as discussed by Berk, 2005) as a child moves into the concrete operational stage, the child understands that the volume of a liquid remains constant no matter the shape of the container within which it is kept (see **Piaget, Jean**)

constructivism: a way of teaching embracing the child as the active creator and constructor of the child's own working body of knowledge; often related to Piaget, Vygotsky, and Bruner; a manner of teaching that views mistakes as a natural part of the learning process (see also: **Bruner, Jerome, PhD; Piaget, Jean; Vygotsky, Lev S.**)

creative development: creativity and imagination, often, not always, related to emotional expression; independent thinking; using materials in individual ways, using a variety of materials; learning to risk creatively; experimentation though working with creative media; learning a sense of aesthetics and aesthetic appreciation for music, movement, visual, written, and dramatic arts (but not limited to those areas); process-oriented artistic endeavors (no wrong outcomes) foster initiative; (see also: **creative expression, creative media, creative risk, domain**)

creative expression: artistic expression; the expression of self through any media one might regard as being creative, and inspiring the imagination, including but not limited to music, painting, sculpture, drama, dance, movement, poetry, gardening, architecture, construction, social interaction and so on; (see also: **creative development)**

creative media: materials for creating artwork including but not limited to: various types of paints, inks, chalk, crayons, markers, pens, pencils, brushes, rubber stamps, stencils, many types of paper, clays, plaster, papier-mache, wood, metal, and so on; (see also: **2-dimensional art, 3-dimensional art, creative expression, collage, decoupage)**

creative risk: experimenting freely with creative media, without focus on outcome: developing a confidence to attempt new activities or experiences

critical thinking: assessing information and developing personal evaluations, and deriving meanings independently; not accepting information at face value

crudités: raw vegetables cut into pieces to be served with a dip as an appetizer

curriculum: refers to the courses of study offered by a school, and are generally specific to academic subject and grade or achievement level; any material planned by a teacher or paraprofessional and presented to students in a classroom

decoupage: a method of decorating a plain surface with designs or cut-out pictures; designs are arranged on the surface and then glued in place; when dry, has shellac or lacquer applied over the surface as protective sealer

delayed gratification: choosing to postpone immediate satisfaction of an impulse or desire (see also: **prosocial behavior)**

developmental delay: a disorder slowing a child's ability to acquire and become proficient at new skills; this may be due to exposure to lead in the environment or because of congenital challenges (see also: **Down Syndrome)**

developmentally appropriate: having activities and expectations designed for the age and the ability of the group of children

differential diagnosis: having the same symptoms for very different reasons; in education, some children will exhibit similar behaviors, but not for the same reason, and will probably not respond to the same intervention in the same or desired manner (see also: **Lavoie, Richard, MA, MEd)**

divergent thinking: independent thinking; problem solving using independently discovered solutions: thinking "out of the box", (see also: **critical thinking)**

domain: one of the five general types of learning: physical, cognitive, social, emotional and creative (see also: **cognitive development, creative development, emotional development, physical development, social development)**

Down Syndrome: a genetic disability (exhibiting three instead of the expected two of the 21st chromosome, trisome 21) resulting in delayed development in many areas, including lowered cognitive ability, possible heart defects, and some physical abnormalities (see also: **developmental delay)**

dramatic play: creative role playing depicting both real and imaginary people and situations; creates opportunities for the development of verbal skills, socialization and emotional relief

dysemia: an inability to pick up social cues

echolalic speech: speech characterized by repetition of phrases heard by child, often associated with autism spectrum disorders and developmental delays (see also: **perseveration)**

educafun: educational experiences, community and structures are set up for pleasure in the context of the learning experience (Reneé Berg)

educarer: a childcare provider that offers structured learning experiences

ELL: English language learners (sometimes also referred to as "ESL" - "English as a Second Language")

emergent curriculum: curriculum that is created from teachable moments, student interest, or events that draw student interest which create unexpected opportunities for learning (see also: **teachable moment, child centered teaching**)

emergent literacy: a child's active participation in constructing literacy skills from informal, process-based experiences

emergent writing: developing the fine motor skills for the pincer grasp, and creating marks to which they attach meaning (see also: **pincer grasp**)

emotional development: learning to recognize and identify different emotional states, managing them in socially acceptable ways, building self-esteem, developing willingness to take appropriate risks, differentiating between appropriate and inappropriate risks, learning to be caring toward others, empathy (see also: **domain, socialization**)

equivalency: comparing an object or a number of objects in terms of size or quantity

Erikson, Erik: German neo-Freudian theorist who developed the psychosocial theory that is significant in developmentally appropriate practices currently embraced by the NAEYC (see also **NAEYC, National Association for the Education of Young Children**)

ethnic: reference to societal group sharing common traits of language, religion, or culture, as opposed to a national, political or geographic distinction

evaluation rubric: a measurement instrument or standard for evaluating growth in learning (see also: **two-step evaluation, three-step evaluation, four-step evaluation, five-step evaluation, rubric**)

evaporation: to change a liquid into a vapor, to dry out

existential: the ability and natural tendency to reflect upon the meanings and realities of life, death and other questions of life; an ability reflected in philosophers; one of the nine intelligences referenced in Dr. Gardner's theory of multiple intelligences relating to different ways people learn and how it impacts that learning (see also: **Gardner, Howard, PhD; multiple intelligences**)

extensions: adding activities, music, stories and so on to an existing activity, due to the interest of students or as an opportunity for further learning (see also: **emergent curriculum**)

eye-hand coordination: coordinating visual acuity with fine motor skills

FAPE: "Free and Appropriate Public Education"; a part of the LRE provision of the IDEA 1997, whereby children with disabilities can receive "free and appropriate public education" designed to meet the child's specific needs, in a regular educational setting with peers without disabilities, to the maximum extent that is appropriate (see also **IDEA 1997, Individuals with Disabilities Education Act Amendments of 1997, Least Restrictive Environment, LRE**)

fine motor skills: movement & development of smaller muscles of hand, fingers, wrist

five-step evaluation: an evaluation rubric consisting of five levels of assessment: A, B, C, D, F (with "A" being the highest and "F" the lowest, may sometimes include I - incomplete); (see also: **evaluation rubric**)

four-step evaluation: an evaluation rubric consisting of four levels of assessment: 4 - Always, 3 - Usually, 2 - Sometimes, 1 - Rarely; (see also: **evaluation rubric**)

Free and Appropriate Public Education: FAPE; a provision of the IDEA 1997, part of the "Least Restrictive Environment" provision of this law (see also: **FAPE, IDEA 1997, Least Restrictive Environment, LRE**)

Froebel, Frederich: German scholar and educator; developed curricula for young children to encourage purposeful play; created the first kindergarten (garden for children) (see also: **Froebel's gifts; Wright, Frank Lloyd**)

Froebel's gifts: a set of precise geometric maple blocks and manipulatives, used with "occupations", the specific set of activities for the engagement of purposeful play (see also: **Froebel, Frederich; Wright, Frank Lloyd**)

Gardner, Howard, PhD: Harvard professor, author and theorist who developed the theory of multiple intelligences relating to different ways people learn and how it impacts that learning; references nine different kinds of intelligences (see also **multiple intelligences, bodily/ kinesthetic, existential, interpersonal, intrapersonal, linguistic, logical /mathematic, musicality, naturalistic, spatial**)

GATE: Gifted And Talented Education; designation for students identified with cognitive abilities of more than 10% above average; generally these children are offered additional academic challenges and enrichments to meet their abilities

genetic epistemology: referring to Piaget's theoretical framework and research on child development, the structure of cognition, and how human knowledge evolves. (see **Piaget, Jean**)

grammatical development: learning the rules of grammar and conventions of the use of language in various contexts

graphomotor skills: the perceptual-motor skills involved in handwriting

gross motor skills: movement & development of the large muscles of the arms, legs, torso (see also: **physical development**)

gustatory discrimination: identifying sweet, salty, sour, and bitter tastes; identifying textures with tongue and mouth; identifying flavors by taste (see also: **oral discrimination, sensory discrimination**)

higher order cognition: one of Dr. Mel Levine's eight neurodevelopmental constructs; being able to use all of the other constructs to reason abstractly; adds creativity and critical thinking to come up with solutions to unique problems; utilizes the other constructs which include: attention, language, memory, neuromotor function, social cognition, spatial ordering, and temporal / sequential ordering (see also: **Levine, Mel, MD, PhD; neurodevelopmental construct, Neurodevelopmental Placemat, teaching by profile**)

hors d'oeuvre: a small appetizer or bite-sized snack, often served before a meal

IDEA 1997: Individuals with Disabilities Education Act Amendments of 1997; changes wording of federal law from "handicapped" to "person with disabilities"; guarantees parental participation as a full partner in the IEP/ IFSP team and that all children will have a "Free and Appropriate Public Education" (FAPE) that meet the their learning needs; includes provision for "Least Restrictive Environment" (LRE); Text of the law, general information, articles http:// www.ed.gov/offices/OSERS/Policy/IDEA/index.html (see also: **FAPE, Least Restrictive Environment, LRE**)

IEP: Individualized Educational Plan (coordinated through the local school district, for children over the age of 3 whose special needs are not considered to be 'severe')

IFSP: Individualized Family Service Plan (managed through the county regional centers, for children under age three, and for individuals whose special needs are considered 'severe')

impulse control: choosing to behave in a socially acceptable manner, despite other thoughts

inappropriate risk: risks taken which endanger the well-being of the child, the class community, the classroom equipment or classroom environment (see also: **appropriate risk**)

Individualized Educational Plan: IEP; coordinated through the local school district, for children over the age of 3 whose special needs are not considered to be 'severe'

Individualized Family Service Plan: IFSP; managed through the county regional centers, for children under age three, and for individuals whose special needs are considered 'severe'

Individuals with Disabilities Education Act Amendments of 1997: IDEA 1997

internalization: refers to the process of learning, and taking in, a rich body of knowledge and tools of thought that first exist outside the child; occurs primarily through language and social interaction

internalized social values: appreciation and respect for self and others; learning appropriate behavior in the context of the particular culture in which a child is living (see also: **sociocultural theory, Vygotsky, L. S.**)

interpersonal: interactions between people; reference to our relationships with others; also one of the nine intelligences of referenced in Dr. Gardner's theory of multiple intelligences relating to different ways people learn and how it impacts that learning; strength in interpersonal intelligence may be exhibited by those who deal with other people in their vocation and are also good communicators, such as in sales, politics, and teaching (see also: **Gardner, Howard, PhD; multiple intelligences**)

intrapersonal: reflecting upon one's own personal thoughts and values; looking within oneself; also one of the nine intelligences of referenced in Dr. Gardner's theory of multiple intelligences relating to different ways people learn and how it impacts that learning; intrapersonal intelligence often exhibited by people who are shy and introspective (see also: **Gardner, Howard, PhD; multiple intelligences**)

jicama: root vegetable (pronounced "hic-ama")

kidney-shaped table: a table (actually curved in a kidney shape) that allows a teacher to sit across from a number of students and easily demonstrate, direct or supervise individual work or group projects

kinesthia: awareness of musculature; a feeling or awareness of the body in terms of the movement and position of the muscles, joints, limbs (see also: **bodily / kinesthetic, multiple intelligences, Gardner, Howard, PhD**)

lactose intolerance: an inability to easily digest foods containing milk proteins

language: one of Dr. Mel Levine's eight neurodevelopmental constructs, including both expressive and receptive language abilities; receptive language being the ability to understand words and word symbols; expressive language is the ability to communicate ideas and knowledge through speech and written word; Dr. Levine believes strength in language function is crucial to academic performance; other constructs include: attention, higher order cognition, memory, neuromotor function, social cognition, spatial ordering, and temporal /sequential ordering

(see also: **Levine, Mel, MD, PhD**; **neurodevelopmental construct, Neurodevelopmental Placemat, teaching by profile**)

laterality: understanding and distinguishing between right and left (e.g., distinguishing the left hand from the right hand, as well as orientation, moving to the left or to the right, or making a right or left turn)

Lavoie, Richard, MA, MEd: respected educator, lecturer and producer of several programs for Public Broadcasting Stations, such as *How Difficult Can This Be? Fat City* (FAT: Frustration, Anxiety and Tension) and *Learning Disabilities and Discipline: When the Chips are Down*, Mr. Lavoie deals with issues in education with a primary focus on learning disabilities and social interaction challenges

leading questions: in the context of child-centered education, asking questions in a manner that evokes a particular course of thought or a desired deductive process in contrast to closed questions which have but a single correct response, such as $1 + 1 = 2$ (see also: **child-centered teaching, open-ended questions, teachable moment**)

learned helplessness: unwillingness to take an independent learning risk, often occurs when teachers and parents in child's environment are more focused on producing pretty outcomes than allowing child to engage in the learning process; a situation in which a person has been conditioned to feel powerless regarding the circumstances and experiences of one's life; lacking confidence in one's own abilities to do things for oneself;

learning diversity: an term used by Renee Berg and Karen Petersen Wirth to reflect that each person has a learning style that is as unique to that person as DNA

learning plan: an inclusive document created by an educator in preparation for an academic experience with the intention of identifying desired learning; with particular attention placed on presenting the activity with said learning as a goal

Least Restrictive Environment: LRE; a provision of the IDEA 1997, emphasizes services as opposed to actual placement; regarding the educational environment whereby children with disabilities can and should receive "free and appropriate public education" (FAPE) designed to meet the child's specific needs, in a regular educational setting with peers without disabilities, to the maximum extent that is appropriate. (see also: **FAPE, IDEA 1997, Individuals with Disabilities Education Act Amendments of 1997, LRE**)

Levine, Mel, MD, PhD: an American pediatrician and author (*A Mind at a Time,* allkindsofminds.org.) famous for his work with learning disabled children, particularly in the area of neurodevelopmental constructs (see also the eight constructs which include: **attention, higher order cognition, language, memory, neuromotor function, social cognition, spatial ordering, temporal /sequential ordering, neurodevelopmental construct, Neurodevelopmental Placemat, teaching by profile**)

LRE: "Least Restrictive Environment" for learning for children with disabilities (see also: **FAPE, IDEA 1997, Individuals with Disabilities Education Act Amendments of 1997, Least Restrictive Environment**)

line chart: a particular type of graph depicting relative variables, shown by connecting a series of points (x, y) on the graph in a linear manner (see Graphing activity in Mathematics Activities chapter)

linguistic: an ability to use language to both express oneself and understand other people; lawyers, poets, authors, journalists, diplomats, orators may in fact exhibit strengths in linguistic intelligence; one of the nine intelligences referenced in Gardner's theory of multiple intelligences relating to different ways people learn and how it impacts that learning (see also: **Gardner, Howard, PhD; multiple intelligences**)

logical / mathematical: the ability to understand underlying principles or mathematical operations; strengths in logical / mathematical intelligence often exhibited by scientists and mathematicians; one of the nine intelligences referenced in Gardner's theory of multiple intelligences relating to different ways people learn and how it impacts that learning; (see also: **Gardner, Howard, PhD; multiple intelligences**)

manipulatives: a group of objects that can be handled, manipulated, constructed and arranged in the process of discovery (e.g.: blocks of all sizes and materials, Legos, Duplos, Tinker toys, K'Nex, wooden trains, Lincoln logs) (see also: **Froebel, Frederich; Froebel's gifts**)

Maslow, Abraham: American theorist, most famous for Maslow's Hierarchy of Human Needs; humans must meet certain basic needs before they can "actualize" inherent potentials of self, often represented in pyramid form, from basic physiological needs at the bottom, to opportunities for learning, creativity and "self-actualization" at the top when all lower needs are satisfied

memory: one of Dr. Mel Levine's eight neurodevelopmental constructs; the ability to register new information and to prioritize that piece of information so that it may be accessed for later use; Levine's other constructs include: attention, higher order cognition, language, neuromotor function, social cognition, spatial ordering, and temporal / sequential ordering (see also: **Levine, Mel, MD, PhD; neurodevelopmental construct, Neurodevelopmental Placemat, teaching by profile**)

modification: changing or adapting the actual curricular content for a learner as opposed to simply changing the presentation, materials or environment; in contrast to accommodation (see also: **accommodation**)

mortar and pestle: a two piece grinding device often made of stone, used from ancient times to today to grind grains and herbs, for use in cooking; consisting of a pestle (a small, rounded handle or rod) and a mortar upon which to grind or crush plant materials; a mortar may be anything from a bowl to a depression in a rock face, worn away from many years of grinding in the same place;

multiple intelligences: Dr. Howard Gardner's theory relating to the different ways in which people learn and how those abilities impact that learning; there are an infinite number of combinations of strengths and weakness related to each person's unique intelligence profile; each individual reflects a unique combination of intelligences and the expression of those intelligences; nine intelligences extend beyond the and to include bodily / kinesthetic (kinesthesia), existential, intrapersonal, interpersonal, linguistic, logical / mathematical, musicality (musical / rhythmic), naturalistic and spatial (see also: **Gardner, Howard, PhD**)

musicality: a musical rhythmic intelligence; an ability to recognize pitch, rhythm and timbre, to hear, recognize and possibly manipulate musical patterns; one of the nine intelligences referenced in Gardner's theory of multiple intelligences relating to different ways people learn and how it impacts that learning; musicians, composers, singers, ornithologists often exhibit strengths in musicality (see also: **Gardner, Howard, PhD; multiple intelligences**)

NACCRRA: National Association of Child Care Resource and Referral Agencies; Non-profit organization dedicated to providing child care information to parents, professionals, and advocates. @ www.naccrra.org

NAEYC: the National Association for the Education of Young Children - promoting excellence in early childhood education, based in Washington DC; a non-profit organization whose commitment is to continually monitor and develop best practices for children's development in all areas of life; there are local and state chapters across the United States; 1-800-424-2460; www.naeyc. org

Nancy bottles: plastic bottles with an easy, twist-to-open, narrow-tipped cap; good for dispensing different kinds of art media and glues; available inexpensively from Discount School Supply

National Association for the Education of Young Children: non-profit organization dedicated to "promoting excellence in early childhood education, whose commitment is to continually monitor and develop best practices for children's development in all areas of life; there are local and state chapters across the United States; 1-800-424-2460; www.naeyc.org

naturalistic: one of the nine intelligences referenced in Gardner's theory of multiple intelligences relating to different ways people learn and how it impacts that learning; an ability of great value in human evolutionary past; having a sensitivity to plants, animals and the natural world; farmers, botanists, geologists, gardeners, archaeologists and ecologists tend to exhibit strengths in naturalistic intelligence (see also: **Gardner, Howard, PhD; multiple intelligences**)

National Association of Child Care Resource and Referral Agencies:
Non-profit organization dedicated to providing child care information to parents, professionals, and advocates. @ www.naccrra.org

neurodevelopmental constructs: referring to the eight dimensions of learning identified, and articulated by Dr Mel Levine which include: attention, higher order cognition, language, memory, neuromotor function, social cognition, spatial ordering, and temporal / sequential ordering (see also: **Levine, Mel, MD, PhD, Neurodevelopmental Placemat, teaching by profile**)

Neurodevelopmental Placemat: Dr. Mel Levine's eight neurodevelopmental constructs, which include attention, higher order cognition, language, memory, neuromotor function, social cognition, spatial ordering, and temporal / sequential ordering (see also: **Levine, Mel, MD, PhD, teaching by profile**)

neuromotor functions: relating to a student's body awareness and movement in the gross motor, fine motor, and graphomotor senses; one of Dr. Mel Levine's eight neurodevelopmental constructs, which include: attention, higher order cognition, language, memory, social cognition, spatial ordering, temporal / sequential ordering (see **Levine, Mel, MD, PhD; Neurodevelopmental Placemat, teaching by profile**)

nonjudgmental atmosphere: in reference to the classroom, creating an environment where the behavior of the children is not evaluated in a moral sense; being able to view inappropriate behavior in an objective manner, such as viewing the behavior as "bad" and not the child

obsessive compulsive disorder: OCD; individuals with this anxiety disorder may often have the need for the security of a very consistent structure; exhibited behaviors may include continually recurring thoughts, excessive and repetitive mannerisms, a desire for sameness and inflexibility to change (e.g.: repeated and unnecessary washing of hands, an overwhelming desire to line objects, such as shoes, in a perfect row); inability to complete these tasks may increase anxiety; test taking may often result in unreliable outcomes, reflecting the special needs rather than the level of learning, as a person with these challenges may become fixated on one question and not be able move forward to complete the assessment (see also: **autism, autism spectrum disorders, pervasive developmental disorder**)

OCD: obsessive compulsive disorder (see also: **autism; autism spectrum disorder, obsessive compulsive disorder, pervasive developmental disorders**)

olfactory discrimination: identifying and differentiating different smells: sweet, spicy; pungent, floral, unpleasant odors, and so on (see also: **sensory discrimination**)

oobleck: not quite solid, and not quite liquid substance created by blending water and cornstarch (see *Oobleck Activity* in the Science Activities Chapter)

open-ended questions: a question that has no specific right answer, but guides child to the learning, and does not merely hand the information to the student; this teaching strategy (scaffolding) articulated by Lev Vygotsky; **(see also: scaffolding, Vygotsky)**

oral discrimination: identifying and differentiating different tastes (bitter, sweet, salty, sour tastes; identifying textures with tongue and mouth; identifying flavors by taste (see also: **gustatory discrimination, sensory discrimination**)

orientation: locating physical objects in space

orthopedic impairments: an impairment of the bones, muscles, and tissues including fractures, congenital abnormalities, and burns that impair a child's ability to actively participate in classroom activities and access the curriculum

osmosis: the diffusion of fluids or gases through porous membranes or partitions

outcome-based learning: learning experiences which focus primarily on the result, as opposed to the process of learning; mistakes are not generally welcomed; worksheets and testing are good examples of out-come based learning; in contrast to process-based learning **(see also: process-based learning)**

PDD: Pervasive Developmental Disorder: characterized by delays in language and social skills, insistence on certain routines, avoidance of change; one of the autism spectrum disorders, which also include: autism, Asperger's Syndrome, Childhood Disintegration Disorder and Rett's Disorder; **(see also: autism, autism spectrum disorders)**

pedagogy: the profession, art, and practices of teaching

penmanship: the art of handwriting

perception: the ability to use one's senses to glean information regarding one's physical or emotional well-being or the surrounding environment

perseveration: speech characterized by intensive repetition of patterns and words (see also: **autism, developmental delay**)

pervasive developmental disorder: PDD; characterized by delays in language and social skills, insistence on certain routines, avoidance of change; one of the autism spectrum disorders, which also include: autism, Asperger's Syndrome, Childhood Disintegration Disorder and Rett's Disorder; **(see also: autism, autism spectrum disorders, obsessive compulsive disorder)**

phonemic awareness: awareness of sounds associated with letters and letter combinations

physical development: motor learning dealing with the large and small muscle groups of the body; including: gross motor and fine motor activities, eye-hand coordination, balance, physical principals, sensory discrimination, and coordination between the use of one aspect of the physical and one or more of the other aspects of physical development. (see also: **articulation, domain, eye-hand coordination, fine motor skills, gross motor skills, physical principals, sensory discrimination**)

physical principals: learning physical weight; stability; equilibrium; balance; leverage (see also: **physical development**)

physics: a branch of science dealing with energy, matter, motion, and force; including the understanding of: surface tension of water, movement of light, movement of sound; the action of force on a moving or stationary object.

Piaget, Jean: A Swiss theorist, famous for the cognitive developmental theory and promotion of constructivist practices in education (see also: **conservation of matter, conservation of quantity, conservation of volume**)

pincer grasp: in context of curriculum, the use of the index finger and thumb to hold a pencil or other writing or drawing implement, in order to make meaningful marks, artwork and writing; term alludes to the pinching movement of lobster claw, or pliers to hold or grip something in a steady manner

polarity: positive and negative magnetic fields

process-based learning: learning experiences which focus on the process of the activity rather than the outcome; mistakes by learners are generally welcome in this approach; in contrast to out-come based learning (see also: **constructivism, out-come based learning**)

prosocial behavior: behavior which is appropriate in the context of a community

realia: using something that actually exists to model or demonstrate an activity to children

Rehabilitation Act of 1973: originally created for returning war veterans; allows for the creation of a 504 plan, which, though not funded, allows for a child whose special needs may not meet the criteria for an IEP; does create structures by which a child may be able to better access the curriculum voluntarily implemented by the classroom teacher

reversibility: as used in conservation theory: a substance can be returned to its original form without changing the original quantity of that substance

Rothko, Mark: American abstract expressionist painter, originally born in Dvinsk, Latvia in 1903, stated that "art is an adventure into an unknown world, which can be explored only by those willing to take risks."

rubric: (also evaluation rubric) measurement instrument or standard for evaluating growth in learning

scaffolding: a teaching strategy in which information is not merely handed to a student, but a process by which an older or more experienced person incrementally guides a learner to a higher level of understanding. Learner then implements the new understanding into a working body of knowledge, empowering learner to function more and more independently; this theory was developed and articulated by Lev Semonich Vygotsky; (see also: **open-ended questions, Vygotsky, L. S.**)

Schools Attuned: Dr Mel Levine is one of the major designers of this training, which is nationally available, and prepares teachers to identify a learner's particular strengths and weaknesses, and work with students using the **teaching by profile** technique (see also: **Levine, Mel, MD, PhD; neurodevelopmental constructs, Neurodevelopmental Placement; teaching by profile**)

self-esteem: self-respect: feeling good about oneself and accomplishments

sensory discrimination: identifying and differentiating physical sensations: auditory (hearing), gustatory or oral (tasting), olfactory (smelling), tactile (touching, feeling), visual (vision, seeing) (see also: **physical development**)

separation anxiety: experiencing anxiety, agitation and nervousness arising from being away from or distant from a significant other.

sequencing: recalling events in temporal order, as they occurred in time

seriation: ordering objects/events in graduation of size smallest to largest or vice versa

social cognition: understanding appropriate social behavior including verbal pragmatics; knowing how to behave in a way that fosters optimal relationships and development of political acumen; one of Dr. Mel Levine's eight neurodevelopmental constructs, which include: attention, higher order cognition, language, memory, neuromotor function, spatial ordering and temporal / sequential ordering (see **Levine, Mel, MD, PhD; neurodevelopmental construct, Neurodevelopmental Placemat, teaching by profile**)

social development: developing skills related to interacting with others in socially acceptable ways; including: following directions, socialization skills, sharing, taking turns, patience, being comfortable with delayed gratification, collaboration, working as a member of a team, cooperation, and internalized social values (**see also: collaboration, delayed gratification, internalized social values, socialization**)

socialization: process by which children become aware of societal expectations of behavior; learning how to get along with others in a community and learning appropriate behaviors for a group setting

sociocultural theory: the work of Lev Semenovich Vygotsky, the Russian theorist, who believed that culture is socially mediated; to succeed within a particular cultural group, the child must internalize an appreciation for the skills, behaviors, and interactions that are valued by that culture (Berk, 2005) (see also: **internalized social values, Vygotsky, L. S.**)

sociodramatic play: developmental play involving make-believe that assists children's understanding of social rules and roles

socioeconomic: an individual's or family's status in society as related to the amount of money earned, level of education achieved, and prestige of employment

spatial: one of the nine intelligences referenced in Dr. Gardner's theory of multiple intelligences relating to different ways people learn and how it impacts that learning ability; spatial intelligence being an ability to create the world and one's surroundings internally (i.e., creating a mental map); useful ability in the worlds of arts and sciences; often exhibited by sculptors, engineers and architects (see also: **Gardner, Howard, PhD, multiple intelligences**)

spatial ordering: one of Dr. Levine's eight neurodevelopmental constructs, referring to the ability to manage information through spatial arrangement; this is strongly related to the ability to visualize and create a mental picture of an outcome and then be able to produce that result (i.e., visualizing a word in order to spell it, or organizing physical materials for a project); the other constructs include: attention, higher order cognition, language, memory, neuromotor function, social cognition , temporal / sequential ordering (see also: **Levine, Mel, MD, PhD; Neurodevelopmental Placemat, teaching by profile**)

spatial relationships: relating the aspects of physical objects to one another, thinking about objects in three dimensions (i.e., height, width and depth)

spatial representation: representing something as it exists in a physical space

static electricity: an electrical charge, consisting of stationary ions (i.e., ions that do not move in a current), often caused by friction building up on an insulated object such as shoes on a carpet

structured classroom environment: defining appropriate limits, boundaries, and rules for behavior during activities and within the classroom community

suribachi: Japanese style mortar and pestle with grinding ridges in the bottom of the mortar

surface tension: an elastic property of liquids, that allows a minimizing and constricting of the surface area, enabling drops to form

tactile discrimination: identifying and differentiating textures and sensations with touch, such as: soft, hard, rough, smooth, sticky, slippery, and so on (see also: **sensory discrimination**)

tahini: sesame seed paste often available in Middle Eastern and Indo-European markets

teachable moment: a moment in which children are so fully engaged in an activity or project that they unselfconsciously want to explore it further

teaching by profile: developed by Dr. Mel Levine; a method of tailoring educational programs to match student's unique learning needs, using neurodevelopmental constructs; these eight constructs include: attention, higher order cognition, language, memory, neuromotor function, social cognition, spatial ordering and temporal / sequential ordering (see **Levine, Mel, MD, PhD; Neurodevelopmental Placemat)**

temporal ordering: placing events in a particular predetermined sequence; retelling a story or an event in a sequence, in a chronological manner; as it occurred in time

temporal / sequential ordering: the ability to understand time and time management, and sequential reasoning, as well as the ability to do tasks step-by-step; one of Dr. Mel Levine's eight neurodevelopmental constructs, which include: attention, higher order cognition, language, memory, neuromotor function, social cognition and spatial ordering (see **Levine, Mel, MD, PhD; neurodevelopmental constructs, Neurodevelopmental Placemat, teaching by profile**)

three-step evaluation: an evaluation rubric consisting of three levels of assessment: E- excellent, S - satisfactory, U – unsatisfactory (see also: **evaluation rubric**)

two-step evaluation: an evaluation rubric consisting of two levels of assessment: "Pass" or "Not Pass"; may also include commentary; (see also: **evaluation rubric**)

Venn diagram: a particular type of mathematical chart representing variables as circles; relationships are expressed as overlapping positions; in this way all possible interrelationships can be shown on one chart (see Graphing activity in Mathematics Activities chapter)

visual discrimination: identifying and differentiating different visual cues, such as: color, brightness; also identifying shapes, colors, sizes by sight (see also: **sensory discrimination**)

visual impairment: impairment in visual acuity such that the child cannot process or acquire information visually without intervention

Vygotsky, Lev Semenovich: a Russian born theorist, contemporary of Piaget and Maslow, best known for his sociocultural theory, that culture is socially mediated (see also: **open-ended questions, scaffolding, sociocultural theory**)

water absorbing polymer crystals: used in *Smelly Jelly* activity, water absorbing crystals which have an agricultural application in the facilitation of water conservation; enables soil to retain moisture more easily, and for longer periods of time (see *Smelly Jelly* activity in the Science Activities chapter)

References

American Psychiatric Association Task Force on DSM-IV. (1997) *Diagnostic and statistical manual of mental disorders: DSM-IV, fourth edition.* Washington, DC: American Psychiatric Association.

Barratta-Lorton, M. (1976). *Mathematics their way.* Menlo Park, CA: Addison-Wesley. ISBN#0-201-00494-1.

Barratta-Lorton, R. (1977). *Mathematics... A way of thinking.* Menlo Park, CA: Addison-Wesley. ISBN: 0-201-04322-x.

Berk, L. E. (2005). *Infants, children & adolescence, fifth edition.* (pages 28-29, 320, 330, 348, 428) Boston, MA: Allyn & Bacon. ISBN: 0-205-42061-3.

Berk, L. E., & Winsler, A. (1997). Scaffolding children's learning. Vol. 7 of the NAEYC Research into Practice Series. Second edition. Washington, DC: National Association for the Education of Young Children. ISBN: 0-935989-68-4.

Bos, B. *Children's books.* Turn the Page Press, Incorporated (para. 1, 5) (http://www.turnthepage.com/articles.php?pid=300)

Bos, B. *How do our children grow?* Turn the Page Press, Incorporated (para. 1) (http://www.turnthepage.com/articles.php)

Bos, B. *Separation anxiety.* Turn the Page Press, Incorporated (para. 2) (http://www.turnthepage.com/articles.php?pid=308)

Bos, B. (1990). *Together we're better: establishing a coactive learning environment.* Roseville, CA: Turn The Page Press. ISBN: 0-931793-01-7.

Bos, B. (1987). *Before the basics: creating conversations with children.* (page 1) Roseville, CA: Turn The Page Press. ISBN: 0-931540-01-1.

Bredekamp, S., Editor. (1986). *Childhood programs, serving children from birth through age eight, expanded edition.* Washington, DC: National Association For the Education of Young Children (NAEYC). ISBN: 0-935989-11-0.

Brosterman, (1997). *Inventing Kindergarten.* Rowayton, CT: Harry N. Abrams. ISBN: 0810935260.

Brown, S.L., M.D. *Play - Evolutionary, universal & essential.* Turn the Page Press, Incorporated *(para. 8)* (http://www.turnthepage.com/articles.php?pid=307).

Bruner, J., Ph.D. (1960). *The Process of Education: A Landmark in Educational Theory.* Cambridge, MA: Harvard University Press. ISBN: 0-674-71001-0.

Budworth, G. (2001). *The ultimate encyclopedia of knots and ropework.* (pp. 8-13, 246-247) London: Hermes House. ISBN: 1-84309-138-0

Covey, S. (1990). *The Seven Habits of Highly Effective People* (page 97), New York: Simon & Schuster Inc. ISBN: 0-671-66398-4.

Curriculum Development & Supplemental Materials Commission. (1999) *Reading/language arts framework for California public schools*. Adopted by the California State Board of Education. Sacramento, CA: California Department of Education, CDE Press. ISBN: 0-8011-1462-4.

Ehrlich, D. (2001). Frank Lloyd Wright Glass. (pp. 23-24, 53, 54 103) London: Courage Books ISBN: 0-7624-0881-

Gardner, H.E. (1993) *Multiple intelligences: The theory in practice*. New York: Basic Books. ISBN: 046501822X.

Gould, P., & Sullivan, J. (1999). *The inclusive early childhood classroom: easy ways to adapt learning centers for all children*. Beltsville, MD: Gryphon House. ISBN: 0-87659-203-5.

Gardner, H.E. (1993) *Multiple intelligences: The theory in practice*. New York: Basic Books. ISBN: 046501822X

Greg & Steve. (1987). *We All Live Together. Vol.2.* (includes: English / Spanish months of the year song, World is a Rainbow, Freeze) CD Available from: amazon.com

Hart, S., (1998) *Wright Rooms*. Rowayton, CT: Chartwell Books, Inc. (pp. 19-20) ISBN: 0-7858-0992-9.

History-Social Science Curriculum Framework and Criteria Committee. (2001). *History-social science framework for California public schools: kindergarten through grade twelve, 2001 updated edition with content standards*. Sacramento, CA: California Department of Education, CDE Press. ISBN #: 0-8011-1531-0.

The Individuals with Disabilities Education Act Amendments of 1997 (IDEA) (http://www.ed.gov/offices/OSERS/Policy/IDEA/index.html)

Jenkins, E. (1992) *Adventures in rhythm*. (Multicultural songs and activities with rhythm sticks). Smithsonian Folkways Recordings. Available from: amazon.com.

Jenkins, E. (1993) *Play your instruments (And make a pretty sound)*. Smithsonian Folkways Recordings. CD Available from: amazon.com.

Jenkins, E. (1994) *This is rhythm*. (Songs and rhythms for simple instruments). Smithsonian Folkways Recordings. CD Available from: amazon.com.

Jenkins, E. (1995) *Multi-cultural children's songs*. (Greetings, thank yous, ABCs, counting, songs and dances in many languages). Smithsonian Folkways Recordings. CD Available from: amazon.com

Jenkins, E. (2003) *Sharing cultures*. (28 songs from around the world). New Smithsonian Folkways Recordings. CD Available from: amazon.com

Johnson, L.T. (1976). *Simplified rhythm stick activities: Fun with rhythm sticks CD*. Long Branch, NJ: Kimbo Educational Audio. ISBN 1-56346-025-4. Available from: http://www.fitnessbeginnings.com/rhythm-stick-cd.html

Johnson, L.T. (1984). *Lummi Sticks for Kids CD*. Long Branch, NJ: Kimbo Educational Audio. ISBN 1-56346-049-1. Available from: http://www.fitnessbeginnings.com/lummi-sticks.html

Jones, E. (Editor). (1998). *Reading, writing and talking with four, five and six year olds*. Pasadena, CA: Pacific Oaks.

Kohl, M.A. (1994). *Preschool art: it's the process, not the art*. (page 11). Beltsville, MD: Gryphon House. ISBN: 0-87659-168-3.

Labinowicz, E. (1980). *The Piaget primer: thinking, learning, teaching*. Menlo Park, CA: Addison-Wesley Publishing Company. ISBN#0-201-04090-5

Lavoie, R., MA, MEd, (1989). *How difficult can this be? F.A.T. city.* (Frustration, Anxiety and Tension). United States: P.B.S Video. ISBN:0-7432-5463-5.

Lavoie, R., MA, MEd, (2005a.). *Beyond F.A.T. city: A look back, A look ahead.* (F.A.T.: Frustration, Anxiety and Tension). United States: P.B.S. Video. ISBN: 0-7936-9010-2.

Lavoie, R., MA, MEd. (2005b.) *Richard Lavoie: Learning disabilities and discipline: When the chips are down.* United States: PBS Video. ISBN: 0-7936-9046-3.

Levine, M., MD, PhD. *All kinds of minds* (AKOM) website, allkindsofminds.org,

Levine, M., MD, PhD. (2002). *A mind at a time.* New York: Simon and Schuster, Inc. ISBN #: 0-7432-0222-8.

Levine, M., MD, PhD. (2005). *Ready or not, here life comes.* New York: Simon and Schuster, Inc. (page 64) ISBN: 0-7432-6224-7.

McGrath, B.B. (1994). *The M & M's brand chocolate candies counting book.* Watertown, MA: Charlesbridge Publishing. ISBN 088106-853-5.

McGrath, B.B. (1998). *More M & M's brand chocolate candies math.* Watertown, MA: Charlesbridge Publishing. ISBN: 0881069949.

McGrath, B.B. (1999). *Pepperidge Farm goldfish counting book.* New York: Dancing Star Books. ISBN: 1893017516. (Counting 1 to 10; goldfish crackers now come in colors too).

McGrath, W. & McGrath, B.B. (1998). *The Cheerios counting book.* New York: Cartwheel Books. ISBN: 0590683578. (1 to 1 correspondence counting to 20)
Spanish language edition: McGrath, B.B. (2000). *A contar Cheerios / The Cheerios counting book.* Scholastic en Espanol. ISBN: 0439149797.

Merriam-Webster's collegiate dictionary, Tenth edition, pp. 292, 767, 856. (1996). Springfield, MA: Merriam-Webster, Inc. ISBN: 0-87779-707-2.

National Association of Child Care Resource and Referral Agencies: Non-profit organization dedicated to providing child care information to parents, professionals, and advocates. @ www.naccrra.org/

Oster, M. (1999). *Ortho's all about herbs.* Des Moines, IO: Meredith Books.
ISBN: 0-89721-420-x.

Palmer, H. (1969) Learning basic skills through music. Vol. 1. (songs about numbers, colors, rhythms, and body awareness). Pioneered concept of movement and music in early childhood education to teach language development, reading readiness, math concepts and self-awareness, Educational Activities. CD Available from: amazon.com.

Palmer, H. (1972). Getting to know myself. (songs about rhythms, laterality, feelings, and body awareness). Educational Activities. CD Available from: amazon.com

Perry, B. MD. (2000). *Safe from the start.* Sacramento, CA: Department of Justice, Attorney General's office. (Video of the May 2000, Safe From the Start symposium, Los Angeles, CA)

Rein, G., Ph.D., Atkinson, M., & McCraty, R., M.A. (1995). *The physiological and psychological effects of compassion and anger.* Journal of Advancement in Medicine, 8:2 p. 102.

Sandall, S., McLean, M.E., & Smith, B.J. (2000). *DEC recommended practices in early intervention/ early childhood special education.* Division for Early Childhood. Boulder, CO: Publisher? ISBN: 1-57035-353-0.

Stewart, G.L. (1992). *Multicultural rhythm stick fun.* Long Branch, NJ: Kimbo Educational Audio. ISBN1-56346-031-9. Available from: www.fitnessbeginnings.com/multicultural-rhythm-stick. html

Stewart, G.L. & Buck D. (1997). *A world of parachute play.* Long Branch, NJ: Kimbo Educational Audio. ISBN: 1563460580. Available from: www.fitnessbeginnings.com/world-parachute-play-cd.html

Stewart, G. L. (1998) *Folk dance fun.* (simplified dances from around the world) . Long Branch, NJ: Kimbo Educational Audio. ISBN :1-56346-021-1. Available from: www.fitnessbeginnings.com/folk-dance-fun-cd.html

Stewart, G. L. (1998) *Children's folk dances.* (21 simplified dances from around the world). Long Branch, NJ: Kimbo Educational Audio. ISBN :1-56346-090-4. Available from: amazon.com.

United States Department of Education, *Archived information IDEA '97: Individuals with Disabilities Education Act Amendments of 1997.* Text of the law, articles, general information @ www.ed.gov/offices/OSERS/Policy/IDEA/index/html

Visual and Performing Arts Curriculum Framework and Criteria Committee. (1989). *Visual performing arts framework for California public schools: kindergarten through grade twelve.* Adopted by the California State Board of Education. Sacramento, CA: California Department of Education. ISBN: 0-8011-0805-5

Vygotsky, L.S. (1978). *Mind in society: The development of higher psychological processes.* (page 57) Cambridge, MA: Harvard University Press. ISBN: 0674576292

Yeatts, K. L. (2000*). Cereal math.* New York, NY: Scholastic Inc. ISBN: 0-590-51208-0.

Discount School Supply
1 (800) 627-2829. http://www.discountschoolsupply.com
Adaptive Classroom Materials for Children with Learning Diversity
Note: While looking through this or any other catalog or website, please keep in mind the unique needs of students in your classroom. There is so much available, that a comprehensive list would be a challenge and may not even include what the children in a specific classroom might need.

Adaptive art / writing materials
Crayons:
Regular, Large, Extra Large, Jumbo, Chubby
Washable markers:
mini, fine, regular, chubby, big grip, & chubby-tipped, super washable chubby
Chalk:
Washable chalk
Chubby First chalk
Dustless chalk
Washable Sidewalk chalk
Window chalk (for temporary window art)
Easy grasp jumbo colored pencils
Scissors:
Blunt point
My First Scissors (large holed handles
     works with either hand)
Training scissors (double holes allows teachers to help child to cut)
Squizzers - Easy Squeeze one grip
Brawny Tough scissors
"Won't cut hair" scissors
Krazy Kut craft scissors
Chunky Zig-Zag craft scissors
Paint Brushes
Fingertip (bristles or foam tip)
Super Grip (natural grasp 2" knob handle)
 Shaving-style brushes (easy to grip)
Easy Grip (6" chubby handle)
No-Roll/No-Drip (stopper around bristles)
Chubby (natural or nylon bristles)
Jumbo Chubby Brushes
One Grip (3" wide-square handled)
Foam brushes of many styles and sizes
Art tools:
Nancy bottles (plastic bottles with a narrow easy twist open top for dispensing glues/paints)
Chunky dot bottles (as are used in marking bingo cards)

No-Mess Paint Cups
Disposable children's art aprons
Disposable plastic gloves
Art media:
Biocolor (washable, flexible watercolor; great with doughs, putties, oobleck)
Liquid watercolor
No-drip foam paint
Washable tempera
Jumbo washable watercolors/refills
Washable fingerpaint
Washable glitter paint
Washable school glue
No drip gel glue
Washable glue sticks
No mess adhesive rollers
Extra-Safe plastic glitter
Unscented & scented doughs
Manipulatives
An excellent resource for classic as well as distinctive manipulatives .
A myriad of different sizes and types, for construction and building, for design and patterning,
appropriate for a wide range of fine and gross motor skills, as well as creative storage possibilities.
For dramatic play: people and animal figures of many kinds and sizes.
Lego /Duplo "people" are available in diverse generations, occupations, and ethnic backgrounds.

Online Sources for Downloadable Large Squared Graph Paper

With http://www.Incompetech.com's free "Lite Graph Paper PDF Generator," choose document size,
orientation, square size, grid lines and color. *The Sourcebook for Teaching Science* (Norman Herr,
Ph.D. of California State University, Northridge) @ http://www.csun.edu/science/ref/measurement/
data/graph_paper.html offers free, downloadable graph paper and measurement tools. http://www.
Enchantedlearning.com allows members to download graph paper in six sizes.